Lexicon Thucydidæum

LEXICON THUCYDIDÆUM.

LEXICON THUCYDIDÆUM:

A DICTIONARY,

IN

GREEK AND ENGLISH,

OF THE

VORDS, PHRASES, AND PRINCIPAL IDIOMS,

CONTAINED IN THE

HISTORY OF THE PELOPONNESIAN WAR

OF

THUCYDIDES.

LONDON:

PRINTED FOR G. B. WHITTAKER, AVE-MARIA-LANE;

J. PARKER, OXFORD;

AND DEIGHTON AND SONS, CAMBRIDGE.

1824.

ρ

LONDON:

PRINTED BY R. GILBERT,

ST. JOHN'S SQUARE.

LEXICON THUCYDIDÆUM.

A.

'Αϐασανίστως, 1, 20. without examination, without applying to the touchstone, βάσανος.

ἀϐασίλευτοι, 2, 80. who have no king.

ἀϐλαϐὴς, 5, 18. σπονδὰς ἀδόλους καὶ ἀϐλαϐεῖς, sincere and inoffensive conditions of peace, 47.

ἀϐλαϐῶς, 5, 47. ἀ. καὶ ἀδόλως, without violence or fraud.

ἀϐουλία, 1, 32. folly; 5, 75. ἐς τὴν ἀϐουλίαν, on account of their unwise conduct.

ἄϐουλος, 1, 120. unwise, unskilful.

ἀϐροδίαιτον, 1, 6. διὰ τὸ ἀϐροδίαιτον, luxury of manners.

ἀγαθὸς, 1, 86. 120, 121. 2, 37. 44. 3, 43, 44. Ἧν τε καὶ ἔχοντές τι ξυγγνώμης εἶεν, εἰ τῇ πόλει μὴ ἀγαθὸν φαίνοιτο, and, although they had some pretensions to a pardon, [yet would I not grant it,] unless it were for the interest of the state: 1, 131. οὐκ ἐπ' ἀγαθῷ, not for any good purpose, 121. τὸ ἀγαθὸν, bravery, cou-

rage; 4, 87. 118. τύχῃ ἀγαθῇ τῇ Ἀθηναίων ποιεῖσθαι τὴν ἐκεχειρίαν, a solemn form in treaties, 5, 90. 6, 78. 7, 77. 8, 92.

ἀγάλλομαι, 2, 44. ἠγάλλεσθε, to exult, pride one's self, 63.: 3, 62. τούτῳ, 82. ἐπὶ τῷ (πανοῦργοι κεκλῆσθαι) ἀγάλλονται, they take a pride in being so called: 4, 95. ἀγάλλεται πατρίδα ἔχων πρώτην ἐν τοῖς Ἕλλησιν, to take a pride in having: 6, 41. to glory, exult, rejoice (in any thing.)

ἄγαλμα, 6, 28. a statue.

ἄγαν, 2, 49. 5, 71. 7, 63. 8, 46. too much.

ἀγανακτέω, 8, 43. ἀγανακτῶν, to be indignant.

ἀγανάκτησις, 2, 41. ἀγανάκτησιν ἔχειν, to cause indignation, to have (in one) a subject of indignation.

ἀγαπάω, 6, 36. to be content, to think one's self well off, 18. ἀγαπήσαντες τὴν ἡσυχίαν, to be contented with, to acquiesce in.

ἀγγελία, 1, 61. 2, 5. 3, 110. 6, 36. rumours, news, reports: 5, 44. a message: 8,

15. ἀγγελία τῆς Χίου, the relation concerning Chios, 39. ἀγγελίαν ἔπεμπον ἐπὶ τὰς ἐν τῇ Μιλήτῳ ναῦς τῦ ξυμπαρακομισθῆναι, concerning the conveying, in order to be conveyed by them, Matth. Gr. Gr. 457.

ἀγγέλλω, 6, 34. ἀγγελοίμεθα ἐπὶ τὸ πλεῖον, Tac. *In majus nuntiare*, to be exaggerated in report, to be reported with exaggeration, 36.: 8, 1. ἠγγέλθη, was told by messengers, 4, 93.: 4, 25. ἀγγελθείσης, to be reported, announced: 7, 17. ἤγγελλον, to announce, to bring word: 7, 8. οἱ ἀγγέλλοντες, messengers: 8, 26. ἀγγέλλεται: 5, 63. 7, 97.

ἄγγελμα, 7, 74. πρὸς τὸ ἄγγελμα, according or conformably to the intelligence.

ἄγγελος, 5, 82, πρεσβέων ἀπό τε τῶν ἐν τῇ πόλει ἀγγέλων καὶ τῶν ἔξω Ἀργείων, ambassadors having arrived (as) messengers, (i. e. to bring intelligence,) both from those in Argus, and from the fugitives from it: 2, 6. 3, 36. 7, 8.

ἀγείρω, 1, 9. to assemble collect, muster.

ἀγήρως, 2, 43. ἀγήρων ἔπαινον, immortal praise, that never decays.

ἄγκυρα, an anchor, ἐπ' ἀγκυρῶν ὁρμίζοντες (sc. πλοῖα,) to moor, station at anchor.

ἀγνοέω, 2, 49. ἠγνόησαν, not to know, i. e. recognize: 4, 96. ἠγνόησαν τε καὶ ἀπέ-

κτειναν ἀλλήλες: 5, 18. ἠγνοεῖτο: 7, 44. ἀγνοεῖσθαι: 3, 53. ἀγνῶτες ἀλλήλων, unacquainted with each other.

ἄγνοια, 3, 111. ignorance, doubt: 6, 89. (al. ἄνοια,) absurdity: 2, 47. ἀγνοία, from or through ignorance: 8, 92.

ἀγνῶς, unknown, inglorious, ignorant, 1, 137. 3, 53.

ἀγνωσία, ignorance, unacquaintedness with, 8, 66.

ἀγορά, a market, 6, 50. ἀγορὰν παρέξειν, to furnish or allow a market to any one, to allow any one to buy provisions, 44. οὐ δεχομένων αὐτοὺς ἀγορᾷ, 11. the market-place, forum.

ἀγοράζω, 6, 51. ἠγόραζον, to market, to walk up and down the market, to spend one's time, to loiter, ἐν ἀγορᾷ διέτριβον.

ἀγορεύομαι, 2, 35. to be spoken or pronounced (as an oration).

ἄγος, a pollution, 1, 126. ἄγος ἐλαύνειν τοῦ θεοῦ, 134, 135.

ἄγραφος, unenrolled, 1, 40: 2, 43. ἄγραφος μνήμη τῆς γνώμης, an unwritten record of the mind. The record, which every man's mind bears, in opposition to the record τοῦ ἔργου, of monumental inscription: ἄγραφοι νόμοι, unwritten, not enacted.

ἄγριος, 6, 60. ἀγριώτερον, more ferocious, savage, cruel.

ἀγρὸς, 2, 14. ἀγροῖς, the country: 2, 5. κατὰ τοὺς

ἀγρούς, in the fields, in the country: 1, 126. ἐκ τῶν ἀγρῶν, from the country: 2, 13. τοὺς ἀγροὺς, an estate, farms.

ἀγρυπνία, 2, 49. sleeplessness, want of sleep, inability to sleep.

ἀγχίστροφος, 2, 53. μεταβολὴν, a sudden change, a reverse, quick revolution, (of circumstances.)

ἀγχώμαλος, 3, 49, nearly equal: 7, 71. ἀγχώμαλα ἐναυμάχουν, to fight with like success, equally, indecisively: 4, 134.

ἄγω, 5, 6. ἄξοντα, leading, bringing: 5, 7. ἦγε, to lead on: 5, 12. ἦγον, to lead, to conduct: 8, 12. ἄξων, about to lead, raise: 8, 21. ἀγαγέσθαι, to take in marriage: 7, 46. ἄξων στρατιὰν, with intention to bring an army: 5, 48. εἰρήνην ἄγειν, to preserve peace: 5, 59. to live at peace, 7, 32. ἄξειν (τὸν στρατὸν,) to lead, to conduct: 7, 16. ἄγοντα εἴκοσι τάλαντα ἀργυρίου, to carry: 5, 54. ἄγοντες τὴν ἡμέραν, to keep or celebrate the day: 3, 86. ἄγομαι, to be imported.

ἀγωγὴ, 5, 85. Ἡ ἐς ὀλίγους ἀγωγὴ, this audience with the nobility: 4, 29, a transporting.

ἀγωγὸς, a guide, conductor, 2, 12. 4, 78.

ἀγὼν, a contest, conflict, an engagement, 5, 11. a task, trial, 2, 45. a dispute, question, 46. 4, 50. ἐν τῷ ἀγῶνι, in the place of contest, 3, 38. contention (of oratory:) 7, 71. ἀγῶνα τῆς γνώμης, agony, anxiety of mind, 49, ἀγῶνας ποιήσονται: to engage in battle, 66. 2, 42. μὴ περὶ ἴσου ἡμῖν εἶναι τὸν ἀγῶνα καὶ οἷς, that the contest is not about things of equal importance to us and them, 3, 49. ἦλθον ἐς ἀγῶνα τῆς δόξης, to come to a conflict of opinion, contend in support of different opinions.

ἀγωνίζω, 1, 6. ἠγωνίζοντο, to wrestle, to contend: 2, 63. ἀγωνίζεσθαι, to contend, strive: 3, 104. ἀγωνιούμενοι ἐφοίτων, to resort for the purpose of contending: 6, 16. ἀγωνίσασθαι περὶ τῶν ἀπάντων, to fight for their all, to stake their all: 29. ἀγωνίζηται, to be tried, contested: 8, 27. ἀγωνίσασθαι, to fight: 4, 87.

ἀγώνισις, 5, 50. a contesting.

ἀγώνισμα, 8, 12. an achievement: 7, 56. a prize-composition: 86. 1, 22. the prize of victory: 3, 82. a glory, distinction: 7, 85. καλὸν τὸ ἀγώνισμα ἐνόμιζέν οἱ εἶναι, he thought it would be a glorious distinction for him.

ἀγωνισμὸς, 7, 70. πρὸς ἀλλήλους, a contention, rivalry.

ἀγωνιστὴς, a prize-fighter, combatant, 3, 37.

ἀδεὴς, fearless, unalarmed, secure: 2, 20. ἀδεέστερον, with less fear, more boldly,

1, 36. less alarmingly, 4,92. 6, 91.

ἄδεια, 4, 92. security, tranquillity: 3, 58. fearlessness, absence of apprehension: 6, 60. immunity, indemnity: 4, 108. small risk: 7, 29. confidence: 8, 77. 81.

ἀδελφὴ, 2, 29. οὖ εἶχε τὴν ἀδελφὴν Σιτάλκης, whose sister Sitalces had in marriage.

ἀδελφιδοῦς, 4, 101. A nephew.

ἄδεσμος, 3, 34. ἐκεῖνον ἐν φυλακῇ ἀδέσμῳ εἶχεν, to put him in custody without chains, Lat. *Libera custodia*, 36.

ἀδεῶς, fearlessly, safely, securely, 4, 114. πολιτεύειν, to live in security, 118. 6, 27.

ἄδηλος, 1, 2. invisible, uncertain, 78. ἐν ἀδήλῳ, in the dark, as yet unknown : 2, 11. ἄδηλα τὰ τῶν πολεμίων, things fall out unexpectedly in war, war is uncertain: 7, 50. ἀδηλότατα ὡς ἠδύναντο, as securely as they could: 8, 108.

ἀδήλως, secretly, 6, 58.

ἀδικέω, 1, 6. ἠδικῆσθαι, to be aggrieved : 1, 34. ἠδίκουν, were the agressors: 3, 38. ἠδικηκότων, the culpable injurers: 6, 29. ἀδικεῖ, to be guilty of any breach of law: 1, 120. ἀδικεῖσθαι, to suffer injury: 5, 5. ἠδίκησεν, to do mischief, to injure : 5, 30. ἠδικοῦντο, to suffer injury, conceive one's self slighted: 3, 47. ἠδικηθῆναι ἑκόντας, to be willing to be injured, to connive or put up with an injury: 1, 53. ἀδικεῖτε, ὦ ἄνδρες Ἀθηναῖοι, πολέμου ἄρχοντες καὶ σπονδὰς λύοντες, with certain verbs, of which ἀδικεῖτε is one, the participle serves to express the action, with reference to which the finite verb determines any condition or quality, Matth. Gr. Gr. 844 : 1. 120. ἀνδρῶν γὰρ σωφρόνων μέν ἐστιν, εἰ μὴ ἀδικοῖντο, ἡσυχάζειν, ἀγαθῶν δὲ ἀδικούμενος ἐκ μὲν εἰρήνης πολεμεῖν, the part. is put here in the acc. because it belongs to the infin. but by an exception to the general rule, which requires it to be in the gen. because the subject of the infin. is the same as the object of the preceding sentence, Matth. 809 : 3, 56. Θηβαῖοι δὲ πολλὰ ἡμᾶς καὶ ἄλλα ἠδίκησαν, two accus. are taken by some verbs not only of the nearer and more immediate object of the action, but also of the more remote object, i.e. the person or thing to which the action with its immediate object passes. Matth. 579.

ἀδίκημα, 1, 37. πρὸς ἀδικήματα μάρτυρα ἔχειν, to have a witness of their evil actions, 35. ἀδικήματι θήσονται, to consider it an injustice, 4, 23.

ἀδικία, 3, 66. wrong, injustice, 8, 40.

ἄδικος, 4, 85. ἐλευθερίαν, freedom, not justly so called, a false pretext of freedom, 3, 9. 66, 67. 4, 61: 6, 39. ἀδικώτατος.

ἀδίκως, unjustly, 2, 71.

ἀδόκητος, 7, 29. ἀπὸ τοῦ ἀδοκήτου, unexpectedly, through

some unforeseen contingency, 6, 34. τὸ ἀδόκητον, an unexpected, unlooked for circumstance, 4, 36. 47. ἀδοκήτως, 4, 17, unexpectedly.

ἄδολος, sincere, without guile, 5, 18.

ἀδόλως, sincerely, without treachery, 4, 118. ἀδόλως, καὶ ἀδεῶς, without fraud or fear, a formula in treaties : 5, 23.

ἀδοξία, 1, 76. disgrace.

ἀδυνασία, 8, 8. weakness : 7, 8. τοῦ λέγειν, incapacity, inability.

ἀδύνατος, 1, 1. 25. 2, 11. 3, 42. ; 88. ἀδύνατα ἦν, impossible, Matth. Gr. Gr. 644.: 4, 86. 129. 7, 1. *Ων οὐκ ἀδύνατος, to be powerful, have great power. 15, 28. ἀδύνατοι ἐγένοντο τοῖς χρήμασι, to be weak in money, in want of treasure. 8, 56. 68, 100. Μηθυμναίων γὰρ οὐχ οἱ ἀδυνατώτατοι φυγάδες, Matth. 669.: 1, 5. ἀδυνατώτατος.

ᾄδω, 2, 54. ᾄδεσθαι, to be chanted, repeated.

ἄδωρος, 2, 65. ἀδωρότατος χρημάτων, most incorruptible in respect of money, Matth. Gr. Gr. 454.

ἀεί, 1, 11. 22. ἐς ἀεί, for ever, 4, 36. 7, 71. incessantly, every moment.: 4, 68. ὁ ἀεὶ ἐντὸς γιγνόμενος, as fast as they came severally in from time to time : 7, 61. ξυστρατευόμενοι ἀεί, from time to time, on each occasion, 57. ἐπὶ τοὺς ἀεὶ πολεμίους σφίσιν ἀποδεικνυμένους, enemies for the time pointed out, who happen to

be proposed : 3, 23. ὁ δὲ διακομιζόμενος ἀεὶ ἵστατο, and ever as a man got over, he drew up : 2, 36. ἀεὶ οἱ αὐτοὶ οἰκοῦντες, the same people inhabiting a country from age to age : 3, 37. τῶν ἀεὶ λεγομένων ἐς τὸ κοινόν, advice given on each successive debate for (the good of) the public. i. e. wise but ordinary advice : 2, 14. διὰ τὸ ἀεὶ τοὺς πολλοὺς ἐν τοῖς ἀγροῖς διαιτᾶσθαι, by reason of most of them being used to live in the country.

ἀείδω, 2, 8. see ᾄδω.

ἀείμνηστος, 1, 33. Not to be forgotten, that which is to be perpetually (for ever) commemorated.

ἀζήμιος, 2, 37. harmless, inflicting no real injury.

ἀηδών, 2, 29. ἐν μνήμῃ ἀηδόνος, in the mention of the nightingale.

ἀήθεια, 4, 55. ἐκ τῆς πρὶν ἀηθείας τοῦ κακοπραγεῖν, from being formerly unaccustomed to reverses.

ἀήθης, unwonted, extraordinary, 4, 34.

ἀήσσητος, 6, 70. 7, 44. unbroken, unvanquished.

Ἀθήναζε, 5, 47. towards Athens.

Ἀθηναῖος, an Athenian, 1, 52. ὁρῶντες προσγεγενημένας ναῦς ἐκ τῶν Ἀθηναίων ἀκραιφνεῖς, for ἐξ Ἀθηνῶν, an instance of the interchange of subst. amongst one another, as also in 1, 107. 110. "words which signify the inhabitants of a country, are sometimes put for the the name of the country," Matth. Gr. Gr. 617: 1, 89. Ἀθηναίων δὲ τὸ κοινὸν διεκομίζοντο, a plur. after a verb of number in the singular, because the idea of several subjects is always included in such noun, Matth. 437.

ἀθλητὴς, 4, 121. a wrestler, combatant, victor in the Olympic games.

ἄθλιος, woeful, wretched, miserable.

ἄθλον, 2, 46. ἄθλα ἀρετῆς prizes for virtue, 87. ἄθλοις τοῖς προσήκουσιν τῆς ἀρετῆς, the rewards which belong to good conduct: 1, 6. 3, 82.

ἀθρέω, 5, 26. to view, contemplate.

ἀθροίζω, to collect, assemble, crowd together: 6, 44. ἠθροίζοντο, to muster: 5, 64. προεῖπον ξυμμάχοις ἀθροισθεῖσιν ἰέναι, to be assembled: 1. 50. 5, 6. : 7, 85. τὸ ἀθροισθὲν τοῦ στρατεύματος, the part of the army which was crowded into one common mass.

ἄθροισις, 6, 26. an accumulation, a collectd store.

ἀθρόος, 4, 34. collected, united, embodied : 6, 34. Τῷ ταχυναυτοῦντι ἀθροωτέρῳ, sailing quicker and closer together: 2, 39. ἀθρόᾳ τῇ δυνάμει, the whole assembled forces (of a state,) 4, 55. ἀθρόᾳ μὲν οὐδαμοῦ τῇ δυνάμει, with nowhere a collected force: 1, 141. ἀθρόον φθειρόμενον, to perish unperceived:

1, 3. 11. 2, 31. 3, 78. 6, 56. 80.

ἀθυμέω, 8, 11. ἀθυμήσαντες, losing heart: 7, 75. ἠθύμουν, to be out of heart, to be depressed, 21. to be alarmed: 5, 91.

ἀθυμία, 7, 55. ἐν παντὶ δὴ ἀθυμίας, in absolute, total dejection of spirit, 24. : 2, 51. 4, 26. 7, 24.

αἰγιαλὸς, 6, 52. σχόντες ἐς τὸν αἰγιαλὸν, to touch on a coast, to come close up to a shore: 1, 7. ἐπ' αὐτοῖς τοῖς αἰγιαλοῖς, on the very shores.

ἀΐδιος, 2, 41. perpetual, everlasting, 64. ἐς ἀΐδιον, for ever : 4, 87. δόξαν, 20. 7, 21.

αἰδοῖα, τὰ, the privy members.

αἰδὼς, 1, 84. αἰδὼς σωφροσύνης πλεῖστον μετέχει, modesty, largely partakers of prudence : 5, 29. Matth. Gr. Gr. 890.

αἰκία, 7, 75. ἡ ἄλλη αἰκία, the calamitous disgrace of the rest.

αἱμασιὰ, 4, 43. a hedge of thorns, a quickset-hedge.

αἱματόω, 7, 85. ᾑματωμένον τὸ ὕδωρ, to be stained with blood.

αἱματώδης, 2, 49. bloody in appearance.

αἵρεσις, 5, 3. a choice (being given between war and security :) 2, 75. a capture, a taking of a town: 3, 97. a choice, an option, 2, 58. 61. 8, 89.

αἱρέω, 3, 52. βίᾳ, to take

by storm, to catch, seize, surprise, take by seige : 4, 66. ἐλεῖν (τὰ μακρὰ τείχη,) to take, to seize, 68. ἑαλωκότων (τῶν τειχῶν,) being taken : 8, 1. ἑλέσθαι, to choose : 6, 44. ἑλομένη, to choose, elect : 2, 19. ἑλεῖν, to take (by siege :) 6, 8. ᾑρημένος, appointed to command, 1, 62. ᾕρηντο, to appoint (as a general :) 3, 49. ᾑροῦντο ὕπνον, to sleep, to enjoy sleep : 2, 75. αἱρεῖσθαι ὕπνον καὶ σῖτον, to take rest and food : 7, 43. ᾕρουν, to take possession of : 1, 90. ἑλομένους, chosen : 1, 11. 55. εἷλον, to take (as a town :) 5, 3. ἑαλωκυῖαν, having been taken : 8, 23. ἑάλωκεν, had been captured : 5, 3. ἑλόντες, having taken, having made one's self master of : 8, 31. 3, 29. Ἡμέραι δὲ μάλιστα ἦσαν τῇ Μυτιλήνῃ ἑαλωκυίᾳ ἑπτὰ, to be nearly seven days after Mytilene was taken : 4, 29. 7, 31. ᾑρέθη, to be chosen, elected, made choice of : 1, 103. ᾑρηκότες, which they had just taken : 4, 20. ἑλώμεθα εἰρήνην ἀντὶ τοῦ πολέμου, to prefer : 3, 63. εἵλεσθε, to choose for one's self : 4, 60. to take for one's self : 2, 68. 78. 4, 20. 130. 8, 82.

αἴρω, 1, 90. 118. ἤρετο, to arise : 6, 18. Ἤιραν ἐς τάδε, to raise, exalt any thing (to a certain pitch :) 5, 10. ἄραντες, having lifted, taken away, 4, 11. having weighed anchor, 45. 1, 52. τὰς ναῦς, to put

off from the land, 3, 32. ἄρας, to weigh anchor, 7, 26. to strike tents, move camp, 8, 28. to decamp : 1, 49. ᾔρθη, to be raised (as a signal,) 63. 7, 34. ἀρθέντος, having been raised, hoisted : 4, 111. ὁπότε τὸ σημεῖον ἀρθείη, when the signal was raised, elevated : 3, 39. ἤραντο, to raise war : 7, 41. ᾐρμέναι, suspended, hung up : 1, 80. ἄρασθαι πόλεμον, to raise war, to undertake, commence a war : 2, 23. ἄραντες ἐκ τῶν Ἀχαρνῶν, to raise their camp and depart from Acharnæ : 1, 130. πολλῷ μᾶλλον ἤρτο, to be raised, elevated, intoxicated, buoyed up : 6, 59. οὐκ ἤρτο νοῦν ἐς ἀτασθαλίην, (poetic phrase).

αἰσθάνομαι, 1, 47. 4, 89. 7, 4. 48. 8, 7. 9. to perceive, learn, hear, observe : 4, 81. πείρα αἰσθομένων, knowing by experience : 6, 59. αἰσθανόμενος αὐτοὺς μέγα παρὰ βασιλεῖ Δαρίῳ δύνασθαι, an instance of the infin. after αἰσθάνομαι instead of the participle, Matth. Gr. Gr. 8, 36. : 5, 83. ᾔσθοντο τειχιζόντων, they perceived them walling : 1, 72. ὡς ᾔσθοντο τῶν λόγων, as they had heard of the speeches : 1, 50. ᾐσθημένοι, to be aware : 7, 65. παρῆν αἰσθάνεσθαι Γυλίππῳ, to be able to discern : 7, 30. αἰσθόμενος ἐκ λογισμοῦ, to perceive by calculation, to compute, perceive by intelligence, to hear : 5, 3. :

2, 51. αἴσθοιτο κάμνων, to feel one's self falling ill : 1, 26. Κερκυραῖοι ἐπειδὴ ᾔσθηντο τοὺς οἰκήτορας ἥκοντας, perf. formed from αἰσθέομαι, Matth. 313. : 8, 24. ᾐσθόμην, I am acquainted with, 9.

αἴσθησις, 2, 50. αἴσθησιν παρεῖχον, to afford means of observation, 3, 22. to occasion a discovery : 2, 4. a discovery : 2, 6. αἴσθησιν ἔχει, to have (in one) an occasion or cause of feeling or perceiving to another, (as in Latin habere invidiam, i. e. causam invidiæ).

αἰσχρὸς, disgraceful, dishonourable, base, 3, 58. 5, 111. 6, 11. 8, 27. 2, 40. αἴσχιον, 6, 10. ἐκ τοῦ αἰσχίονος, from a more dishonourable cause, on more dishonourable grounds, 2, 62. αἴσχιον δὲ ἔχοντας ἀφαιρεθῆναι ἢ κτωμένους ἀτυχῆσαι, it is ·more dishonourable, when one has aught, to be deprived of it, than .to fail in making an acquisition : 3, 59. αἰσχίστῳ τῷ ὀλέθρῳ λιμῷ τελευτῆσαι : αἴσχιον, 1, 82. 2, 62. 4, 86. : 6, 21. αἰσχρὸν δὲ βιασθέντας ἀπελθεῖν ἢ ὕστερον ἐπιμεταπέμπεσθαι, τὸ πρῶτον ἀσκέπτως βουλευσαμένους, an instance of the positive employed for the comparative, Matth. Gr. Gr. 662.

αἰσχρῶς, 6, 80. disgracefully.

αἰσχύνη, 1, 84. 2, 27. shame, disgrace, modesty, a feeling of honour : 5, 101. αἰσχύνην ὄφλειν, to incur disgrace : 104, 111. . 2, 37. αἰσχύνην ὁμολογουμένην φέρουσι, to bring (certain) confessed shame, disgrace, upon any transgressors : 8, 73. : 4, 19. ἑτοιμότερός ἐστιν αἰσχύνῃ ἐμμένειν οἷς ξυνέθετο, the use of the dat. for the Lat. abl. answering to the question, from what, whence, Matth. Gr. Gr. 567.

αἰσχύνω, 4, 92. τὰς προσηκούσας ἀρετὰς, to shame, disgrace : 2, 43. αἰσχυνόμενοι ἐν τοῖς ἔργοις, to have a sense of shame in action : 3, 44. αἰσχυνθέντες τὰς τῶν Ἑλλήνων ἐς ὑμᾶς, to respect, have regard to the hopes, which the Greeks repose in you : 1, 84. 3, 14. 36.

αἰτέω, 1, 40. δίκας, to seek, ask, demand a trial, satisfaction, 5, 30. ᾐτιῶντο, to blame, accuse : 3, 61. οὐδὲ ᾐτιαμένων, not even a charge being made : 6, 46. αἰτέομαι, to ask for, require the loan of any thing to borrow : 2, 97. 3, 59. 113.

αἴτησις, 75. a request, petition.

αἰτία, a blame, fault, reproach, cause, motive, an occasion, expostualation, a reprehension, 1, 35. ἐν πλείονι αἰτίᾳ ἕξομεν, to hold a thing in great reprobation, 5, 60. ἐν αἰτίᾳ εἶχον πολλῇ, to blame severely : 6, 46. πολλὴν τὴν αἰτίαν εἶχον ὑπὸ τῶν στρατιώτων, to be severely censured by, 75. ἐπιφερομένην αἰτίαν ἐς τὴν μαλακίαν, a reproach for cowardice cast upon them : 6, 14. αἰτίαν σχεῖν, to carry blame (with it :) 3, 13. αἰτίαν εἴχετε μὴ βοηθεῖν, to be blamed for not assisting, 53. ὁ μὴ ῥηθεὶς λόγος τοῖς ὧδ᾽ ἔχουσιν αἰτίαν ἂν παράσχοι ὡς, εἰ ἐλέχθη, σωτήριος ἂν ἦν, a speech, not being spoken by men circumstanced as we are are, would give occasion for saying that, had it been spoken, it would have saved : 1, 69. αἰτία μὲν γὰρ φίλων ἀνδρῶν ἐστὶν ἁμαρτανόντων, κατηγορία δὲ ἐχθρῶν ἀδικησάντων.

αἰτιάζω, 1, 120. αἰτιάω, 1, 82. αἰτιάομαι, to blame, censure, find fault with, expostulate with, 140. αἰτιᾶσθαι τὴν τύχην, to accuse fortune : 3, 61. ᾐτιασμένων, an instance of the perf. pass. of verbs, which are used as active, occurring in a pass. sense, Matth. Gr. Gr. 716.

αἰτίαμα, 5, 72. διὰ τοῦτο, a fault.

αἴτιος, culpable, obnoxious, guilty, instrumental, causing, promoting, 7, 56. αἴτιοι αὐτῶν, the author of them, i. e. of the benefits to redound to Greece, 3, 38. ὑμεῖς, you are to blame : 2, 21. αἴτιον σφίσιν ἐνόμιζον, they thought them to blame for, 65. αἴτιον δὲ ἦν, and the reason was : 3, 50. αἰτιωτάτους τῆς ἀποστάσεως, most instru-

mental in causing, principal authors : 4, 20. αἰτιώτερος : 4, 26. αἴτιον δὲ ἦν οἱ Λακεδαιμόνιοι προειπόντες, for αἴτιοι ἦσαν, 3, 93. 8, 9. see Matth. Gr. Gr. 445.

αἰφνίδιος, 8, 14. sudden, unexpected, 20. , αἰφνίδιον, suddenly : 4, 125. φυγὴν, sudden, 75. 5, 65. 8, 20.

αἰφνιδίως, 7, 23. suddenly, at once.

αἰχμαλωτὸς, 1, 52. a prisoner of war : 3, 70. 6, 5.

αἰών, an age, the life of man, 1, 70. δι᾽ ὅλου τοῦ αἰῶνος, through all their lives.

αἰωρέω, 7, 77. αἰωροῦμαι, to be suspended, ἐν τῷ αὐτῷ κινδύνῳ τοῖς φαυλοτάτοις, in the same danger with the meanest among you, Matth. Gr. Gr. 539

ἄκαιρος, unreasonable, illtimed, unprofitable, 5, 65.

ἀκάτιον, a small boat, a skiff, 4, 67.

ἀκέραιος, pure, unmixed, entire, unbroken, un-injured, fresh, sound, untouched, 2, 61. δύναμιν, 3, 33. : 2, 18. 3, 3.

ἀκηρυκτὶ, 2, 1. without a herald, without the intervention of a herald.

ἀκηρύκτως, 1, 145. without the formality of a herald.

ἀκίνδυνος, without danger, risk, secure, 4, 18. 5, 16. : 4, 72. ἀκινδυνότερος.

ἀκινδύνως, 6, 80. τὴν αὐτίκα ἀκινδύνως δουλείαν, servitude without danger for the present: 7, 68. τὸ ἀκινδύνως ἀπελθεῖν αὐτοὺς, their departing safe, unhurt, without risk, danger to us, *sine nostro periculo.*

ἀκίνητος, immoveable, stationary, unvarying, 3, 37. νόμοις: 1, 71.

ἄκλητος, unbidden, un-invited, 1, 118. 6, 87.

ἀκμάζω, 1, 1. ἀκμάζοντες ἦσαν, i. e. ἤκμαζον, to flourish, to be at the highest point of prosperity: 7, 12. ἤκμαζε, to be complete, perfect, in a flourishing condition, (of a fleet:) 7, 63. ἤκμαζε, to be in one's prime, to flourish: 2, 20. ἀκμάζοντας πολλῇ νεότητι, to abound in young men: 3, 3. ἀκμάζοντος τοῦ πολέμου, to be at its height, to be vigorously prosecuted: 2, 19. ἀκμάζοντος θέρους καὶ τοῦ σίτου, midsummer, and the harvest ripe. 31. to be in its prime, (of a city:) 6, 17. ἀκμάζω μετ' αὐτῆς (νεότητος,) to flourish in youthful ardour: 2, 49. ἀκμάζοι, Matth. Gr. Gr. 774.

ἀκμὴ, the height, highest point of perfection, the flower, the moment of greatest elevation, the turning point, 7, 14. ἀκμὴ πληρώματος, the most perfect state, height of vigour in a ship's crew: 2, 42. ἅμα ἀκμῇ τῆς δόξης μᾶλλον ἢ τοῦ δέους, at the very height of their hopes rather than (at the lowest point) of their fears: 8, 46. the flower.

ἀκοὴ, report, hearsay, fame, 4, 8. ἀκοῇ νομισάντων, to judge by report: 1, 4. 20. 3, 38. 4, 126. 6, 53.

ἀκολασία, licentiousness, intemperance, arrogance.

ἀκολουθέω, 7, 57. ἠκολούθουν, to follow: 4, 42. To follow, to be in train, 4, 94. ἀκολουθῆσαι τῇ γνώμῃ, to follow an opinion: 2, 98. 3, 38.

ἀκόλουθος, a servant, serving man, an attendant, 4, 118.

ἀκονιτὶ, without trouble.

ἀκοντίζω, 3, 23. ἠκόντιζον, to throw a javelin: 7, 40. ἐς τὰς ναύτας.

ἀκόντιον, a dart, javelin.

ἀκοντιστὴς, 7, 6. A darter, javelin-man.

ἀκούσιος, 3, 40. τὸ ἀκούσιον, what is involuntary: 4, 98. ἁμαρτημάτων, involuntary.

ἀκουσίως, with reluctance.

ἀκούω, 1, 22. ἤκουσα, to hear: 5, 28. κακῶς ἤκουσε, to labour under a bad reputation, to suffer in the opinion of: 7, 71. ἀκοῦσαι πάντα ὁμοῦ (ἦν,) all were to be heard at once: 1, 125. ἐπειδὴ ἀφ' ἀπάντων ἤκουσαν γνώμην, after they had heard an opinion from all, i. e. the opinion of all: 3, 38. τὸ ἀκουσθὲν, any thing heard: 2, 35. 6, 93. 8, 106.

ἄκρα, a promontory, cape, headland, high ground, a height: 7, 4. ἀντιπέρας τῆς πόλεως, a headland over-against the city: 4, 112.

κατ' ἄκρας καὶ βεβαίως, situated on an eminence and securely: 4, 3. 25. 100. 7, 34. 8, 33.

'Ακράγας, 7, 45. 50. Matth. Gr. Gr. 118.

ἀκραιφνὴς, pure, entire, whole, fresh, untouched, 1, 19.

ἄκρατος, intemperate, immoderate, 2, 49. διαρροίας ἅμα ἀκράτου ἐπιπτούσης, immoderate diarrhœa.

ἀκρίβεια, accuracy, exactness, the very truth, accuracy of discipline, 7, 13. τοῦ ναυτικοῦ, completeness of the navy: 1, 22.

ἀκριβὴς, accurate, exact, precise, strict: 6, 55. τὸ ἀκριβὲς, diligence, exactness, 54. ἀκριβὲς οὐδὲν λέγοντας, certain, accurate: 5, 90. καί τι καὶ ἐντὸς τοῦ ἀκριβοῦς, although a little within or on this side of an exact or complete defence: 2, 18. τὸ πάνυ ἀκριβὲς, consummate or mature wisdom: 5, 26. 6, 18.: 6, 55. ἀκριβέστερος.

ἀκριβῶς, exactly, accurately, precisely, 1, 97. 7, 49.

ἄκριτος, 2, 67. without trial, a hearing: 4, 20. undecided, unsettled : 8, 48. untried.

ἀκρίτως, dubiously, so that only a doubtful or confused judgment can be formed, 7, 71.

ἀκροάομαι, 2, 21. ἠκροᾶτο, to hear: 6, 10. ἐνδοιάστως,

ἀκροῶνται, to yield, a doubtful, precarious obedience: 3, 27. ἠκροῶντο, to obey: 6, 17. ἀκροᾶσθαι λόγου μιᾷ γνώμῃ, to listen to advice with unanimity, to adopt unanimously a measure proposed, 89.

ἀκρόασις, 2, 37. a hearing, obedience: 1, 21. ἐπὶ τὸ προσαγωγότερον τῇ ἀκροάσει, more seducing to the ear: 22. ἐς ἀκρόασιν, to the ear, for gratification: 3, 43.

ἀκροατὴς, a hearer, listener, 2, 35. 3, 38.

ἀκροβολίζω, 3, 73. ἠκροβολίσαντο, to fight with missiles: 4, 34. to throw darts upon.

ἀκροβολισμὸς, 7, 25. a skirmishing with missile weapons.

ἀκροθίνιον, 1, 132. the first fruits, prime spoil.

ἀκρόπολις, 3, 72. the fortress: 4, 130, 131.

ἄκρος, 6, 57. extreme, at the end: 4, 100. ἄκραν κεραίαν, the extreme mast, i. e. at the end of the mast, 57. ἄκροις τοῖς κρημνοῖς, the summit of the precipice: 6, 97.

ἀκροτελεύτιον, 2, 9. 17. last, fag-end.

ἀκροφύσιον, 4, 100. the spout of a pair of bellows.

ἀκρωτήριον, 2, 49. 4, 24. 6, 44. the promontory, headland.

ἄκυρος, 3, 37. νόμοις, not binding, without authority, ineffective.

ἄκων, 8, 3. reluctant: 2, 90. in spite of one: 6, 34, ἄκοντος ἡγουμένου, to be appointed commander against one's will: 3, 40. ἄκοντες ἔβλαψαν, to do an involuntary injury: 4, 37. ἄκοντα προσαναγκάζειν, to press any one against his wish: 3, 37. 63.

ἀλάομαι, 2, 102. to wander, Matth. Gr. Gr. 811.

ἀλγεινὸς, wretched, painful, woeful, 7, 75. ἀλγεινὰ αἴσθεσθαι, wretched to behold, dreadful to see: 2, 39. τοῖς μέλλουσιν ἀλγεινοῖς μὴ προκάμνειν, not to sink under calamities only in prospect.

ἀλγέω, to grieve, to endure grief, 2, 65.

ἄλγιστος, 7, 68. most grievous.

ἀλείφω, 1, 6. ἠλείψαντο, to anoint themselves: 4, 68. ἀληλιμμένων, to be anointed.

ἀλέξω, 5, 77. ἀλεξέμεναι, to ward off, drive away, (Dor. for ἀλέξειν.)

ἀλέω, 4, 26. ἀληλεσμένον, to be pounded, Matth. Gr. Gr. 207.

ἀλήθεια, truth, 2, 41. βλάψει, the truth will destroy, confute, 35. 4, 120.

ἀληθὴς, 6, 34. τῇ ἀπὸ τοῦ ἀληθοῦς δυνάμει, i. e. τῇ ἀληθεῖ δυνάμει: 7, 67. τὸ ἀληθέστατον γνῶτε, know for certain: 3, 53. 4, 126. 6, 89.

ἀληθῶς, truly, in fact, 8, 87.

ἄληπτος, difficult to be laid hold of, impracticable, im-

pregnable, unarraignable, not to be convicted, 1, 27. 143. ἀληπτότερος.

ἀλίμενος, without port, harbour, 2, 25.

ἀλίσκω, 7, 23. ἡλίσκετο, to be captured: 2, 31. ἑάλω, ἁλῷ, have a passive signif. from the root ἀλόω, see Matth. Gr. Gr. s. 222. to be taken prisoner, captured as a town, 1, 102.: 4, 46. ἄν τις ἁλῷ, if any one be caught running: 1, 121. μιᾷ νίκῃ ἀλίσκονται, to be undone, ruined by one victory or other, 8, 34.: 7, 40. κόπῳ ἀλίσκεσθαι ὑπὸ σφῶν αὐτῶν, to be seized or overcome with fatigue by themselves, their own means.

ἀλιτήριος, sacrilegious, 1, 126. τῆς θεοῦ, founded on the sense of the gen. with respect to, this adj. derived from a verb active (ἀλιτέω τινὰ,) expressing an idea of relation not complete without the addition of another word, takes it in the gen. Matth. Gr. Gr. 460.

ἀλκὴ, strength, 1, 80. 2, 84. 3, 108. 6, 34.: 2, 87. τέχνη δὲ ἄνευ ἀλκῆς οὐδὲν ὠφελεῖ, unless it be backed by energy, unless it be enforced.

ἀλλὰ, 5, 43. Οὐ μέντοι ἀλλὰ καὶ φρονήματι φιλονεικῶν ἠναντιοῦτο, to give opposition not through love of contempt indeed, but through mortification and wounded pride;

not to oppose for opposition-
sake, (or from pure love of
the sport,) but from a feeling of wounded pride: 5,60.
ἀλλ' ἤ, except, but only, further than, 7, 50. οὐδὲ ὁ Νικίας
ἠναντιοῦντο, ἀλλ' ἤ μὴ φανερῶς
γε ἀξιῶν ψηφίζεσθαι, Nicias did
not oppose them further than
requiring that it should not
openly at least be put to the
vote, 77. 2, 44.

ἀλλήλων, ἀλλήλοις, ἀλλή-
λους, one another, 1, 24. ἐν
ἀλλήλοις, with one another,
66. ἐς ἀλλήλους, reciprocally,
1, 1. πρὸς ἀλλήλους, against
one another: 4, 19. 61. 66.
7, 34. 40. : 3, 81. οἱ πολλοὶ
τῶν ἱκετῶν—διέφθειραν αὐτοῦ ἐν
τῷ ἱερῷ ἀλλήλους, where the
reciprocal is for the re-
flexive, Matth. Gr. Gr. 710.

ἄλλοθεν, from elsewhere,
1, 22. πόθεν, some from one
quarter, some from another,
35. from any other quarter
whatever.

ἄλλοθι, elsewhere, 1, 77.
ἄλλοθί που, anywhere else,
16. from other quarters.

ἀλλοῖος, different, changed,
varied, 4, 106. οἱ δὲ πολλοὶ
ἀκούσαντες ἀλλοιότεροι ἐγένοντο
τὰς γνώμας, the majority were
becoming inclined to change
in their sentiments, their
sentiments were beginning
to be somewhat changed.

ἀλλοιόω, 2, 59. ἠλλοίωντο
τὰς γνώμας, changed their
minds, sentiments.

ἀλλόκοτος, 3, 49. monstrous.

ἄλλομαι, 7, 45. ἄλλεσθαι κατὰ
τῶν κρημνῶν, to leap.

ἄλλος, 6, 70. Τὰ μὲν ἄλλοις—
τὰ δὲ αὐτοὺς, on the one hand,
side : 7, 27. τὸν ἄλλον χρόνον,
for the rest of the time, the
remainder of the year : 4,
120. οὐδὲν ἄλλο ἤ νησιῶται,
nothing else but islanders :
1, 15. τὸ ἄλλο Ἑλληνικὸν, the
rest of Greece : 7, 58. ἄλλος
ὅμιλος, a multitude besides,
50. στρατιὰν ἄλλην—καὶ τοὺς
ἐκ τῆς Πελοποννήσου ὁπλίτας,
besides an army from—
troops also from Pelopon-
nesus, (ἄλλην refers to καὶ
τοὺς, etc. and not to any previous army from Sicily :) 3,
19. ἄλλης στρατιᾶς πολλοὶ,
many others of his soldiers :
8, 92. : 1, 77. ἡ ἄλλη Ἑλλὰς,
the rest of Greece, where
the art. prefixed to the
adjective substantives it,
Matth. Gr. Gr. 393.

ἄλλοσε, to elsewhere, to
any other place, 7, 30. ἄλ-
λοσέ ποι τῆς Σικελίας καθεζομέ-
νους, to go to another port of
Sicily, to settle, anywhither,
51.

ἀλλότριος, alien, foreign,
another's, strange, 4, 95. ὡς
ἐν τῇ ἀλλοτρίᾳ (γῇ) οὐ προσῆκον κίνδυνον ἀναρριπτοῦμεν, un-
necessarily to volunteer danger in the enemy's country,
92. ἀλλοτρίοις ἱεροῖς τὸ πρῶτον
ἐπελθόντας οἰκεῖα νῦν κεκτῆσθαι,
to gain possession of the
temples of other countries,
and afterwards possess them

as their own: 3, 82. καὶ μὴν καὶ τὸ ξυγγενὲς τοῦ ἑταιρικοῦ ἀλλοτριώτερον ἐγένετο, relationship was not so near a tie as fraternity, association in parties, clubs, and conspiracies: 6, 21. ἐς ἀλλοτρίαν πᾶσαν (γῆν,) an entirely foreign land: 1, 78. ἀλλοτρίαις γνώμαις πεισθέντες, to be persuaded by foreign sentiments, the opinions of foreigners, 70. τοῖς σώμασιν ἀλλοτριωτάτοις ὑπὲρ τῆς πόλεως χρῶνται, to use their bodies for the service of the State as much as possible, as if they did not belong to them, i. e. in the most unselfish manner, with an utter disregard of labour and danger: 3, 82. ἀλλοτριώτερον: 3, 13. 4, 98.

ἀλλοτριόω, 3, 65. 8, 73. to alienate.

ἀλλόφυλος, of another tribe, race, foreign, a stranger, 6, 9. ἀνδράσιν: 4, 64. 86.

ἄλλως, 6, 47. otherwise, in vain, uselessly, to no end. 1, 10. 70. 7, 1. ἄλλως τε καὶ, especially, more especially as, 7, 75. ἄλλως τε καὶ ἀπὸ οἵας λαμπρότητος—ἐς οἵαν τελευτὴν ἀφῖκτο, especially (when they reflected) from what a splendid condition to what a miserable end they had come: 2, 3. 4, 36.

ἁλμυρὸς, 4, 26. brackish, briny.

ἀλογία, 5, 111. absurdity.

ἀλόγιστος,. irrational, in-

considerate, 5, 99. τῷ ἀλογίστῳ, by rashness.

ἀλογίστως, 1, 37. without good reason, rashly: 3, 45. absurdly, without reason.

ἄλογος, irrational, absurd, without reason, rash, unaccountable, inexcusable, 1, 32. ἐπιτήδευμα πρὸς ὑμᾶς ἐς τὴν χρείαν ἡμῖν ἄλογον, a custom, which is irrational, when viewed with reference to our interests as now connected with you: 6, 46. ἀλογώτερα, what one less calculates upon: 3, 82. 6, 59. τόλμα ἀλόγιστος, inconsiderate, rash, foolhardy courage: 6, 85.

ἀλόγως, 6, 79. without good reason, good grounds, inexcusably, 84. absurdly: 5, 104. 8, 27. rashly.

ἄλοχος, 3, 104. a wife.

ἅλυσις, 2, 76. 4, 100. a chain.

ἄλφιτον, barley, bran, 3, 49: ἄλφιτα, bread (generally for means of sustenance:) 4, 10. ἀλφίτων, 16.

ἁλώσιμος, easy to be captured, 4, 10. τὸ χωρίον.

ἅλωσις, 2, 2. a capture, taking, seizure, the reduction of a town, 5, 15. capture, surrender: 4, 70. 113. 7, 24.

ἁλωτὸς, 6, 77. conquerable.

ἅμα, at the same time with, besides, 7, 72. ἅμα ἕῳ, at dawn, as soon as it was morning, 23, τῇ ἕῳ: 5, 80. ἀλλ' ἢ

ἅμα, otherwise than in conjunction with : 1, 25 : ἅμα δὲ
καὶ, as well as, 70, καὶ ἅμα,
moreover, besides, 48 : 4, 79.
τελευτῶντος τοῦ χειμῶνος ἅμα
ἦρι, as soon as the winter
broke up and the spring began, 5, 20. : 4, 93. ὅπως φύλα-
κές τε ἅμα εἶεν, as well together :
3, 11. ἅμα μὲν—ἐν τῷ αὐτῷ δὲ,
they (at once) and at the same
time : 2, 5. τῆς ἀγγελίας ἅμα
ῥηθείσης προσεβοήθουν, as soon
as, 20. 4, 27. 100. 6, 47.

ἀμαθὴς, 3, 82. untaught, ignorant, simple, 37, ἀμαθέστεροι, less wise, 1, 119. : 6,
39. ἀμαθέστατοι, most stupid,
blind.

ἀμαθία, 2, 40. ignorance,
want of skill, information, 1,
142. awkwardness, 68. ἀμαθίᾳ
χρῆσθε, to be ignorant : 3, 37,
dulness, meanness of intellect, want of parts : 2, 62.
ἀπὸ ἀμαθίας εὐτυχοῦς, from
lucky ignorance, ignorant
luck.

ἀμαθῶς, 1. 140. uncertainly,
darkly, on no certain grounds,
by no fixed laws, unexpectedly.

ἅμαξα, 2, 34. 5, 72. a waggon, wain, cart, baggage-
waggon : 1, 93. δύο ἅμαξαι
ἐναντίαι ἀλλήλαις, two carts
meeting each other : 2, 3.
ἁμάξας ἐς τὰς ὁδοὺς καθίστασαν,
ἵν' ἀντὶ τείχους ᾖ, this is a rare
deviation from proper construction; with the plur. fem.
the verb is singular, as with

neuters ; in this instance the
author had ἅρματα in his head.
Matth. Gr. Gr. 439.

ἁμαρτάνω, 1, 38. to err : 3,
62. ἥμαρτεν, to err, μὴ μετὰ
νόμων, not with the conni-
vance of the laws : 7, 18.
ἡμάρτητο, to sin, fail in duty :
2, 65. Ἄλλα τε πολλὰ ἡμαρ-
τήθη, many other errors were
committed : 1, 92. ἁμαρτάνον-
τες τῆς βουλήσεως, to fail in
one's design : 3, 47. ὅσον ἂν
καὶ τοῦτο ἁμαρτάνοιτε, how
much you will err in this
respect, 53. μὴ ἀμφοτέρων ἅμα
ἡμαρτήκαμεν, lest we have
missed of both at once, 40.
ὡς ξυγγνώμην ἁμαρτεῖν ἀνθρωπείως λήψονται, to receive
pardon for erring, 98. τῶν
ὁδῶν ἁμαρτάνοντας, to miss
the way : 3, 20. ἔμελλον
ἁμαρτήσεσθαι, to be likely to
err (in computing :) 4, 56.
καὶ πᾶν ὅ,τι κινήσειαν ᾤοντο
ἁμαρτήσεσθαι, they expected
to fail in whatever they undertake : 7, 54. ἁμαρτὼν τοῦ
Ἀκράγαντος, to fail (in his
designs) upon Agrigentum :
1, 32. γνώμης ἁμαρτάνει, he is
not correct in his opinion.

ἁμάρτημα, an error, a fault,
slip, mistake, transgression,
2, 65. γνώμης, an error of
judgment, 53. τῶν ἁμαρτημάτων τὴν τιμωρίαν ἀντιδοῦναι, to
be punished for offences, to
pay the penalty of offences,
(literally, to give satisfaction, the punishment being

considered as the price,) ἀντὶ ἁμαρτημάτων: 5, 26. ἁμαρτήματα, trespasses, transgressions : 4, 30. 98. 7, 5.

ἁμαρτία, an error, a mistake, fault : 3, 46. ἁμαρτίαν καταλῦσαι,, to cancel a fault : 1, 32. δόξης μᾶλλον ἁμαρτίᾳ, through error of opinion, 78. : 4, 29.

ἁμάρτυρος, untestified, unwitnessed, 2, 41. οὐ δή τοι ἁμάρτυρόν γε, surely not untestified.

ἁμαχητὶ, without contest, a blow, 4, 73.

ἁμαχὶ, without contest, a blow, 5, 7. 7, 14.

ἀμβλύνω, 2, 87. ἀμβλύνεσθαι, to have one's courage blunted, spirits damped.

ἀμβλὺς, 2, 40. blunt, languid, remiss, insensible, hardened, 65. insensible, hardened, ἀμβλύτερα ποιεῖν, to enfeeble, impede : 3, 38. τῇ ὀργῇ ἀμβλυτέρᾳ, duller resentment, resentment having its edge blunted.

ἄμεινον, 1, 140. Ὡς ἔμοιγε ἄμεινον δοκεῖ εἶναι; as I for my part think the better way : 6, 33. ἄμεινον πρὸς τοὺς ἄλλους, better as regards the rest : 1, 138. 5, 47. 115.

ἀμέλεια, carelessness, indifference, negligence, 1, 141. παρὰ τὴν ἑαυτοῦ ἀμέλειαν, on account of, or by means of his own neglect : 5, 38.

ἀμελέω, 5, 44. not to think of, not to heed, to disregard : 6, 33. τοῦ ξύμπαντος ἀμελήσετε,

to be guilty of a total neglect : 3, 40. ἀμελήσαντες τῶν πολεμίων : 1, 68. ἀμελούμενοι ὑπὸ ὑμῶν, to be neglected, Matth. Gr. Gr. 711.

ἀμελὴς, negligent, careless, 5, 30. ἀμελέστερον, somewhat carelessly, with too much negligence : 2, 11. ἀμελέστερόν τι παρεσκευασμένους, prepared at all less carefully.

ἀμελῶς, 6,'100. negligently.

ἀμέτοχος, 1, 39. not partaking.

ἀμηχανέω, 7, 48. to be without resource, not to know what to do, to be in great difficulties.

ἄμικτος, not to be mixed up with others, incommunicable, separate and different, incompatible, 1, 77. ἄμικτα γὰρ τά τε καθ' ὑμᾶς αὐτοὺς νόμιμα τοῖς ἄλλοις ἔχετε, your institutions have nothing in common with those of the rest of Greece.

ἄμιλλα, 7, 71. a contention, striving to be first, a race, contest, fight, 6, 32. ἄμιλλαν ἐποιοῦντο, to make haste, crowd all sail.

ἀμιλλάομαι, to strive, contend with, 6, 31. ἀμιλληθὲν πρὸς ἀλλήλους, to strive, contend with, rival one another.

ἀμιξία, 1, 3. ἀλλήλων, want of intercourse, correspondence.

ἄμιππος, along with a horse, 5, 57. a foot-soldier appointed to accompany a horse-soldier.

ἀμνημονέω, 3, 54. to be forgetful, to lose the remembrance of: 5, 18.

ἀμνηστέω, 1, 20. χρόνῳ ἀμνηστούμενα, to be erased from the memory, obliterated by time.

ἀμόθι, 5, 77. somewhere.

ἄμπελος, 4, 100. a vine-stalk.

ἄμυδρος, 6, 54. γράμμασι, half or nearly worn out, hardly legible, almost erased by time.

ἀμύνω, 5, 3. ἠμύνοντο, to resist, defend, 10. to defend one's self, to offer resistance: 4, 11. 68. to encounter, oppose: 4, 56. ἠμύνατο: 2, 36. Ἠμυνάμεθα βάρβαρον καὶ Ἕλληνα πόλεμον ἐπιόντα, to repel a war coming on, whether Greek or barbarian, waged against us by Greeks or barbarians: to ward or hold off any thing or person, either τί τινος, or τί τινι, any thing from any one or any thing for any one, (with a dat.) to assist, succour, defend, support, 5, 38. τῷ δεομένῳ, 2, 60. αὐτῇ, 1, 105. Αἰγινήταις: 1, 69. οὐ τῇ δυνάμει, ἀλλὰ τῇ μελλήσει ἀμυνόμενοι, to repel not by an exertion of force, but by delay: 3, 38. ἀμύνεσθαι δὲ τῷ παθεῖν ὅτι ἐγγυτάτω κείμενον, ἀντίπαλον ἂν, revenge or vengeance following as close as possible upon the injury, being equivalent or proportion-

able: 2, 67. ἀμύνεσθαι τοῖς αὐτοῖς—οἷσπερ, to inflict the same punishment which—to retaliate in the same way that: 1, 42. ἀμύνεσθαι τοῖς ὁμοίοις, to requite with similar benefits: 4, 92. ἡσυχάζοντα καὶ ἐν τῇ ἑαυτοῦ μόνον ἀμυνόμενον, only acting upon the defensive.

ἀμφηρικὸς, 4, 67. ἀκάτιον, having two oars.

ἀμφὶ, about, 7, 40. τὰ ἀμφὶ τὸ ἄριστον, preparations for breakfast.

ἀμφίβολος, ambiguous, equivocal, (literally, shot at on both sides, in Thuc. shot at on every side, 4, 32.: 2, 76.) ἐν ἀμφιβόλῳ γίγνεσθαι, to be exposed to weapons on every side: 2, 15. 4, 36.

ἀμφιδήριτος, 4, 134. νίκη ἐγένετο, disputed, undecided.

ἀμφίλογος, 5, 79. dubious, 4, 118. disputed.

ἀμφισβητέω, 6, 10. τὰ ἀμφισβητούμενα, controverted points, 7, 18.

ἀμφισβήτητος, 6, 6. περὶ γῆς ἀμφισβητήτου, concerning the debateable land.

ἀμφορεὺς, 4, 115. ὕδατος, a vessel, pitcher.

ἀμφότερος, 7, 48. ἐπ' ἀμφοτέρων ἔχων, to be dubious, to hesitate between two things, 47. κατ' ἀμφότερα, on two accounts, in two ways: 1, 13. ἀμφότερα, both ways, (viz. by sea and land:) 7, 44. ἀμφοτέρων οὐκ ὀλίγοι, numerous on

both sides: 1, 83. 4, 73. 6,
78. 8, 18.

ἀμφοτέρωθεν, 4, 1. 11. 5, 73.
from both sides.

ἄν, 6, 38. ἄν γενόμενα, which
will happen, likely to happen, Schol. οὐκ οἷά τε γενέσθαι;
7, 62. διὰ τὸ βλάπτειν ἄν, because it would injure: with
a participle for εἰ with the
finite verb νομίσατε, 6, 18. τό
τε φαῦλον καὶ τὸ μέσον καὶ τὰ
πάνυ ἀκριβὲς ἂν ξυγκραθὲν μάλιστ' ἂν ἰσχύειν, for ὅτι μάλιστ'
ἂν ἰσχύοι, εἰ ξυγκραθείη, see
Matth. Gr. Gr. 5, 97.: 1,
136. ἐκεῖνον δ' ἄν, εἰ ἐκδοίη αὐτὸν, σωτηρίας ἂν τῆς ψυχῆς
ἀποστερῆσαι, here ἄν is redundant, where the principal proposition, to which ἄν
belongs, is divided by a parenthesis, Matth. Gr. Gr.
927. see too Hermann, ad.
Viger. 781.: 3, 37. ὡς οὐκ ἂν
δηλώσαντες τὴν γνώμην, as if
they could not display their
judgment: 2, 18. Καὶ ἐδόκουν οἱ
Πελοποννήσιοι ἐπελθόντες ἂν διὰ
τάχους πάντα ἔτι ἔξω καταλαβεῖν, on the infin. with ἄν see
also 3, 11. 89. ἄνευ σεισμοῦ οὐκ
ἄν μοι δοκεῖ τὸ τοιοῦτο ξυμβῆναι
γενέσθαι, the same as οὐκ ἂν
ξυνέβη, where the conditional
limitation is contained in
ἄνευ σεισμοῦ, i. e. εἰ μὴ σεισμὸς
ἦν, 2, 49. τὰ ἐντὸς οὕτως ἐκαί-
ετο, ὥστε—ἥδιστα ἂν ἐς ὕδωρ
ψυχρὸν σφᾶς αὐτοὺς ῥιπτεῖν, i. e.
ὥστε ἔρριπτον ἄν, they would
gladly have thrown them-
selves, 2, 20. (see ἐπεξέρχο-

μαι,) 2, 80. 93. 6, 18. 7, 62.
"It is joined with infinitives
and participles, and gives to
these moods (not the sense of
the future, although in Latin
it can only be expressed by
this sense, but) the same
signif. as the opt. conj. or
infin. with ἄν would have, in
the resolution by means of
the finite verb." Matth. 922.:
2, 34. μία δὲ κλίνη κενὴ φέρεται
ἐστρωμένη τῶν ἀφανῶν οἱ ἂν μὴ
εὑρεθῶσιν, (Si qui non inveni-
untur,) εἰς ἀναίρεσιν,—ἀνὴρ
ᾑρημένος ὑπὸ τῆς πόλεως, ὃς ἂν
γνώμῃ τε δοκῇ μὴ ἀξύνετος εἶναι
καὶ ἀξιώματι προήκῃ, λέγει ἐπ'
αὐτοῖς ἔπαινον τὸν πρέποντα,
where the proposition is general; the conj. with ἄν is
used after the relative, (and
not the opt.) when the
proposition is of something
present or future, (not the
indic.) and when the relative does not refer to a definite thing, Matth. 787.

ἀνά, along, 4, 72. ἀνὰ τὰ
πεδίον: 3, 22. ἀνὰ τὸ σκοτεινὸν,
through or in the dark.

ἀναβαίνω, 7, 2. ἀναβὰς, having ascended: 3, 22. to go
up, to ascend (a ladder:) 4,
44. ἀναβάντες ἐπὶ ναῦς, to embark, go on board, 5, 6. 7,
67. ἀναβήσεσθαι, 7, 4. ἀναβε-
βήκεσαν, 5, 9. ἀναβῆναι: 5, 6.
ὥστε οὐκ ἂν ἔλαθεν αὐτόθεν ὁρμώμενος. ὁ Κλέων τῷ στρατῷ,
ᾄπερ—ἀναβήσεσθαι, the relative explained by an infin.
Matth. Gr. Gr. 687.

ἀναβάλλω, to throw or cast up, 4, 90. ἐκ τοῦ ὀρύγματος ἀνέβαλλον αὐτὶ τοῦ τείχους τὸν χοῦν, 63. τὰς ἰδίας διαφορὰς ἐς αὖθις ἀναβαλώμεθα, let us defer our private quarrels to a future time: 5, 82. ἀναβαλόμενοι τὰς γυμνοπαιδίας, to defer the celebration of the games, 46. ἀναβάλλεσθαι τὸν πόλεμον, to put off the war, 45. ἡ ἐκκλησία αὕτη ἀνεβλήθη, this assembly was adjourned.

ἀναβιβάζω, 7, 33. ἀκοντιστάς τινας ἐπὶ τὰς ναῦς, to put or take on board, 35. ἀναβιβάζομαι, to embark, go on board.

ἀναβοάω, 1, 53. to shout out.

ἀναβολή, 2, 42. ἀναβολὴν τοῦ δεινοῦ ἐποιήσατο, to put off, decline, get out of the way of the danger: 7, 15.

ἀναγγέλλω, 4, 122. to announce.

ἀναγιγνώσκω, 3, 49. 4, 50. 7, 10. to read, peruse.

ἀναγκάζω, 2, 15. ἠνάγκασε, to compel: 7, 38. ἠνάγκαζεν, 58. ἐς τὸν πόλεμον, to compel to go to war: 8, 3. : 4, 125. ἠνάγκασαν, to be forced of necessity: 7, 57. ἠναγκάζοντο, to be forced (to fight:) 7, 62. ἠναγκάσμεθα ἐς τοῦτο, to be reduced to any thing: 6, 22. ἠναγκασμένος, to be constrained, obliged: 1, 71. 136. 3, 2. 5, 84.

ἀναγκαῖος, 7, 6. necessary, absolutely expedient: 6, 37. ἀναγκαίας παρασκευῆς, hasty,

insufficient, v. Schol. et Bav.: 5, 99. τῆς ἀρχῆς τὸ ἀναγκαῖον, necessity, compulsion : 4, 87. δόκησιν, a necessary inference : 7, 69. οὐχ ἱκανὰ μᾶλλον ἢ ἀναγκαῖα, not so much what was enough, adequate, as what he could, what the time would allow, necessarily brief : 4, 60. διαλλακτὰς πολὺ τῶν ἐμῶν λόγων ἀναγκαιοτέρους Ἀθηναίους, the Athenians much more urgent reconcilers than any speech of mine: 5, 8. ὁπλίτῃ, sorry armour, just such as could be got : 1, 84. ἐν τοῖς ἀναγκαιοτάτοις, in great difficulties : 4, 60. ἀναγκαιότερος, 1, 84. 90. 7, 82. ἀναγκαιότατός : 1, 2. ἀναγκαῖος τροφῆ, see Matth. Gr. Gr. 150.

ἀναγκαίως φέρειν, 2, 64. to bear with resignation what cannot be helped.

ἀναγκαστὸς, compelled, constrained, pressed, on compulsion, 7, 13. οἱ ἀναγκαστοὶ ἐσβάντες, who were pressed into the service, 58. : 8, 24. compelled to serve, involuntary.

ἀνάγκη, necessity, 4, 87. κατὰ δύο ἀνάγκας, on two urgent accounts : 3, 40. σὺν ἀνάγκῃ τι παθὼν, to suffer any thing of necessity : 4, 98. ἐν τῇ ἀνάγκῃ, on a pressing emergency : 4, 120. οὐκ ἀνέμειναν ἀνάγκην σφίσι προσγενέσθαι, not to wait until necessity forced them.

ἀνάγραπτος, 1, 129. engraven in one's memory.

ἀναγράφω, 3, 57. ἐς τὸν τρίποδα, to inscribe upon a tripod: 5, 47. to write out, inscribe from one end to the other.

ἀνάγω, 1, 137. ἀναγομένης, a vessel bound for Ionia, ἐπ' Ἰονίας: 6, 65. ἀνῆκται, to be gone, set out, to sail, : 8, 10. ἀνήγοντο, to set out from, 11. ἀνηγμέναι, had set out, 12. ἀνήγετο, ἀναγαγόμεναι, 19. sailing out: 23.; 31. ἀνάγεται, sails forth: 3, 104. χορούς ἀνῆγον, to get up dances in honour of Apollo: 4, 31. to put out to sea: 7, 69. ἀνάγεσθαι ὅσον οὐκ ἔμελλον, to be on the point of putting out to sea.

ἀναγωγὴ, 6, 32. εὐχὰς τὰς νομιζομένας πρὸ τῆς ἀναγωγῆς, the solemn prayers before putting out to sea, 29.

ἀναγώνιστος, see ἀνανταγώνιστος.

ἀναδάζομαι, to parcel out, make a division of, 5, 4. ὁ δῆμος τὴν γῆν ἐπενόει ἀναδάσασθαι, to make a division of the lands.

ἀναδέω, 7, 25. ἀναδούμενοι, to fasten, bind with a rope, cable, 74. 4, 121. χρυσῷ στεφάνῳ, to crown with: 2, 90.

ἀναδιδάσκω, 3, 97. to teach, prove, shew (by a detail of particulars,) 8, 86.

ἀναδίδωμι, 3, 88. to send up, give out as fire does smoke, 58. ἡ γῆ ἀνεδίδου, to yield fruit as the earth.

ἀνάδοτος, restored, returned.

ἀναζητέω, 2, 8. to weigh, sift, examine thoroughly.

ἀναθαρσέω, 6, 31. 7, 71. to take courage, heart, recall one's courage, Matth. Gr. Gr. 925.

ἀνάθημα, 1, 132. an offering: 2, 13. a votive building, depository of offerings, perhaps merely an offering: 6, 46. ἀναθήματα, things dedicated in a temple.

ἀναθρέω, to look up, 4, 87. τὰ ἔργα ἐκ τῶν λόγων ἀναθρούμενα, actions examined by or with a view to speeches.

ἀναίρεσις, 2, 34. carrying off the field for burial, 3, 107.: 7. 72. leave, liberty to fetch away the dead: 3, 113.

ἀναιρέω, 4, 97. ἀνελόμενοι τοὺς νεκρούς, to pick up, 114. 2, 22. : 4, 44. ἀνείλοντο, to receive back: 8, 24. ἀνεῖλον, to pull down, destroy : 4, 12. ἀνελόμενοι, to take : 6, 38. ἀναιρεῖται ἀγῶνας πρὸς τοὺς πολεμίους, to take up, undergo, sustain a conflict, contest with any one : 1, 126. to take up (the bones of the dead:) 5, 33. to destroy, raze : 5, 1. to remove, carry away: 1, 118. 2, 54. ἀνεῖλε αὐτοῖς, to answer as an oracle: 6, 1. ἀνῃροῦντο πόλεμον, to undertake.

ἀναίσθητος, 2, 43. 6, 86.
dull, unobservant, without
sense, feeling, perception :
1, 69. διὰ τὸ ἀναίσθητον, on
account of your insensibility,
stupidity.

ἀναισθήτως, blindly, stu-
pidly.

ἀναισχυντέω, 1, 37. to be
shameless, to brazen it out.

ἀναίσχυντος, 2, 47. 52. ἐς
ἀναισχύντους θήκας ἐτράποντο,
to have recourse without
shame to the sepulchres of
others, for the burial of the
dead : 8, 45.

ἀνακαλέω, 1, 3. 7, 69. 73.
to call upon, to address,
name: 1, 131. to recal (a general from his command :)
7, 70. to call out aloud upon any one, 73. to call out
for any one.

ἀνάκειμαι, 3, 114. to be deposited in : 7, 71. ἀνακειμένων
ἐς τὰς ναῦς, to be laid up in,
to centre in, to depend upon, (equivalent to ἐν ταῖς
ναυσίν.)

ἀνακηρύσσομαι, 5, 50. to be
proclaimed.

ἀνακλάω, 7, 25. τοὺς σταυ-
ροὺς, to crane up, pull up:
2, 76. to pull (a thing) out
of its direction, to draw
aside.

ἀνάκλησις, 7, 7. θεῶν, a calling out upon, an invocation
to, the gods, 71. Matth. Gr.
Gr. 925.

ἀνακομίζω, 8, 13. to bring
back : 6, 7. ἀνεκόμισαν σῖτον,

to carry off, convey back :
2, 31. ἀνακομίζομαι, to return,
(of a fleet.)

ἀνακόπτω, 4, 12. ἀνεκόπη, to
be cut down.

ἀνακρίνω, to examine, in-
terrogate, 1, 95. 7, 62.

ἀνάκρουσις, a tacking about,
a retreat performed by back-
ing water, a rowing back
stern-foremost keeping the
prow still opposed to the
enemy, which was done by
striking the oar the contrary
way, i. e. pushing it towards
the stern or from the rower
instead of pulling towards
the prow and the rower, 7,
36. 70. : 7, 62. αἱ σχήσουσι
πάλιν ἀνάκρουσιν, to prevent
a falling back.

ἀνακρούω, 7, 38. ἀνακρουό-
μενοι, to be mutually driven
back, 40. ἀνακρούσασθαι πρὸς
τὴν πόλιν. to retreat, fall back,
62. τὸ μήτε αὐτοὺς ἀνακρούεσθαι,
μήτ᾽ ἐκείνους ἐᾷν, neither to retreat ourselves, nor to suffer
them to do so.

ἀνακτάομαι, to re-gain, re-
acquire, 6, 92. ἀνακτᾶσθαι.

ἀνακῶς, sedulously, dili-
gently, 8, 102. ὅπως αὐτῶν
ἀνακῶς ἕξουσιν, Matth. Gr. Gr.
465.

ἀνακωχὴ, a truce, cessation
from hostilities, an absence
of them, a suspension of hostilities, an armistice, 1, 40.
66. 3, 4. 4, 117.

ἀναλαμβάνω, ἀναλαμβάνομαι,
to recover, regain possession

of, to resume, take along or
associate with one, take on
board again, under one's
command (as an army,) put
one's self at the head of, (in
order to lead to an enter-
prize or to march,) take revenge, recover one's self
(from disease,) take into
one's own ranks, 7, 83. *ἀνα-
λαμβάνουσι τὰ ὅπλα*, (where the
present tense is put for the
aorist, Matth. Gr. Gr. 737.)
7, 1. *ἀναλαβὼν τοὺς ὡπλισμένους*, to put one's self at the
head of: 6, 26. *ἀνειλήφει
ἑαυτὴν ἀπὸ τῆς νόσου*, to recover from disorder: 7. 74.
ἀναλαβόντας αὐτὰ ὅσα, to take
along with them only or
merely the things, which—:
3, 38. *ἀναλαμβάνει μάλιστα τὴν
τιμωρίαν*, to take especial
vengeance: 2, 62. *ἀναληφο-
μένην*, 16. *ἀνειληφότες*: 8, 27.
ἀναλαβόντας, to take up.

ἀνάλγητος, not aggrieved,
3, 40. *ἀναλγητότερος*.

ἀνάληψις, 5, 65. *βουλομένην*,
an intended reparation.

ἀναλίσκω, 1, 117. 2, 41. 8,
4. *ἀναλίσκεσθαι*, to be spent:
7, 48. *ἀναλίσκοντας ἐν περιπο-
λίοις*, to expend upon works
around the city: 6, 31. *ἀνα-
λίσκει περὶ τὸ σῶμα καὶ ἐς τὴν
ναῦν*, to expend or lay out
on his person and ship: 2,
70. *ἀναλωκυίας ἐς τὴν πολιορ-
κίαν*, to expend upon the
siege: 1, 117. *χρήματα ἀνα-
λωθέντα*, expences, 109. *ἀνα-
λοῦτο*, to be expended: 2,

14. 3, 81. 8, 45. *ἀνάλουν*,
Matth. Gr. Gr. 814. *ἀναλω-
κέναι*, Matth. 725. : 8, 31.
ἀνάλωσαν.

ἀναλογίζομαι, 5, 7. to weigh,
reflect upon, 3, 32. 8, 83.

ἀναλογισμὸς, 3, 36. reflection, re-consideration, 8, 84.

ἀνάλωμα, 1, 99. *ἱκνούμενον*,
incidental expences, as
much as they might amount
to: 7, 28. *ἀναλωμάτων προσ-
τιππόντων*.

ἀνάλωσις, 7, 31. expence.

ἀνάλωτος, not taken, captured, 4, 70. *οἰόμενος τὴν Νί-
σαιαν ἔτι καταλήψεσθαι ἀνάλω-
τον*.

ἀναμάχομαι, 7, 61. to fight
again, engage the enemy
over again.

ἀναμένω, 2, 84. to wait for,
4, 120. to procrastinate, delay, 135. : 1, 90. *ἀναμένειν
τοὺς ξυμπρέσβεις*, to wait for
his fellow ambassadors.

ἀναμιμνήσκω, to remind a
person of (any thing,) 6, 6.
*ξυμμαχίαν ἀναμιμνήσκοντες τοὺς
Ἀθηναίους*, an instance, where
the active of a verb of recol-
lecting, (which usually takes
the gen.) is constructed with
a double accus., Matth. Gr.
Gr. 464.

ἀναμίξ, promiscuously, 3,
107.

ἀναμνάομαι, 2, 54. *ἀνεμνή-
σθησαν τοῦδε τοῦ ἔπους*, to bethink themselves of, call to
mind.

ἀναμφισβήτητος, 1, 132. in-
dubitable, unquestionable.

ἀνανδρία, 1, 83. pusillanimity.

ἄνανδρος, effeminate, 3, 82. a coward.

ἀνανεόω, to renew, 5, 18. 43. 80. ἀνανεωσάμενοι τὰς σπονδὰς τοῖς Ἐπιδαυρίοις, to renew the truce with the Epidaurians, 49. ἀνανεοῦσθαι τοὺς ὅρκους.

ἀνανέωσις, a renewal, 6, 82.

ἀνανταγώνιστος, without an antagonist, unmatched, without rivalry, 4, 92. ἀνανταγώνιστοι ἀπ' αὐτῶν οὐκ ἀπίασι, not to go away without having met with their match, without a severe struggle : 2, 45. εὐνοίᾳ, goodwill unmixed with feelings of rivalry, without any thing to detract from it, pure, unmixed.

ἀναξίως, 3, 59. undeservedly.

ἀνάπαυλα, cessation, rest, 2, 38. τῶν πόνων ἀναπαύλας τῇ γνώμῃ ἐπορισάμεθα, to provide rest, recreations for the mind from labour, 75.

ἀνάπαυσις, 4, 20. cessation.

ἀναπαύω, 4, 11. to cease : 7, 73. ἀναπαύομαι ἀπὸ ναυμαχίας, to rest from or after battle.

ἀναπείθω, 8, 5. to persuade, 1, 126. to persuade, prevail upon, 140. 5, 80. to seduce : 1, 84. ἀναπείθομαι, to be persuaded, 3, 94. to change one's opinion, 6, 87. 89. 2, 65. ἀνεπείθοντο δημοσίᾳ, to be won over, to comply in matters of state.

ἀναπειράομαι, to try, exercise, practise, 7, 7. οἵ τε Συρακόσιοι ναυτικὸν ἐπλήρουν καὶ ἀνεπειρῶντο, the Syracusans went on board and practised with the fleet, manœuvered for exercise, 53. ἀνεπειρῶντο ἡμέρας ὅσαι, as many days as, 12. ἀναπειρώμεναι.

ἀναπέμπω, 2, 67. to convey up, give a convoy up (the country.)

ἀναπίμπλαμαι, 2, 51. ἀναπιμπλάμενοι, (τῆς νόσου understood,) to be filled with infection.

ἀναπίπτω, to fall back, to yield, 1, 76, ἀναπίπτουσιν ἐπ' ἐλάχιστον, as little as possible, 70.

ἀναπληρόω, 2, 28. ἀνεπληρώθη, to become full again, to have its orb renewed (of the sun after an eclipse.)

ἀναπράσσω, 8, 107. καὶ χρήματα ἀνέπραξαν, to exact.

ἄναρκτος, 5, 99. unsubdued.

ἀνάρμοστος, 7, 67. unprepared.

ἀναρπάζω, 6, 104. a false lection for ἁρπάζω.

ἀναρρήγνυμι, to cleave up, break to pieces, 7, 36. ἀναρρήξειν τὰ πρώραθεν (ταῖς ἐμβολαῖς χρώμενοι,) 40. ἀνερρήγνυσαν τὰς ναῦς ἐπὶ πολὺ τῆς παρεξειρεσίας, to shatter the vessels very much on the forecastle, the part betwixt the beak and oars, 34.

ἀναρριπτέω, ἀναρρίπτω, to cast up, throw, 5, 103. ἐς ἅπαν τὸ ὑπάρχον ἀναρριπτοῦσι, (sc. κύβον,) to toss up for all, that belongs, i. e. to run the risk of one's all to cast (the die) for one's all (the stake,) to venture one's all; hence ἀναρρίπτειν comes to mean, to venture, run the risk : 4, 85. τοσόνδε κίνδυνον ἀναρριπτοῦμεν, to venture so great a danger, incur so great a risk as this, 95. 6, 13.

ἀναρρώννυμι, 7, 46. πάλιν ἂν ἀναρρωσθέντες, to take heart, to be re-animated, to re-gain courage once more.

ἀναρχία, 6, 72. anarchy, misrule, confusion, disobedience.

ἀνασείω, to wave aloft, 4, 38. ἀνέσεισαν τὰς χεῖρας, to wave the hands.

ἀνασκευάζω, to rebuild, refit, 4, 116. τὴν Λήκυθον καθελὼν καὶ κατασκευάσας τέμενος ἀνῆκεν ἅπαν, to pull down and then rebuild in a different form and for a different purpose: ἀνασκευάζομαι, to gather together one's furniture, stores, baggage, 1, 18. ἀνασκευασάμενοι, ἐς τὰς ναῦς ἐμβάντες, ναυτικοὶ ἐγένοντο.

ἀνασκοπέω, 1, 132.. 7, 42. to revolve in one's mind, to reflect upon.

ἀνασπάω, to draw up, draw (vessels on shore,) 4, 9. τὰς τριήρεις ἀνασπάσας ὑπὸ τὸ τείχισμα, to draw up the triremes under the fortification, 97. τὸ ὕδωρ ἀνασπάσαντας ὑδρεύεσθαι, to draw up and use the water for common purposes.

ἀνάσσω, to rule over, 1, 10. πόλλῃσι νήσοισι καὶ Ἄργει παντὶ ἀνάσσειν.

ἀνάστασις, 2, 14. a removal, 7, 75. a breaking up (of a camp,) dislodging, removal: a raising up from a posture of supplication, a departure from a temple, where sanctuary had been taken, 1, 133. πίστιν ἐκ τοῦ ἱεροῦ διδόντος τῆς ἀναστάσεως, he pledged his word that no danger should attend his removal from the altar.

ἀνάστατος, overturned, displaced, transplanted, 6, 76. ποιεῖν ἀναστάτους, to subvert, 8, 24. ἀνάστατα ἐποίησαν, subverted, laid in ruins: 6, 5. ἀναστάτων γενομένων πολέμῳ ὑπὸ Συρακουσίων, to be expelled.

ἀνασταυρόω, to crucify, 1, 110. προδοσίᾳ ληφθεὶς ἀνεσταυρώθη.

ἀναστέλλω, to send for back, check (a pursuing army,) 7, 70. ἀνέστελλον τοὺς ὁπλίτας: 3, 98 ἀναστέλλομαι, to retreat.

ἀναστρέφω, 2, 49. to turn upside down, to disturb (the stomach,) occasion vomitings : 4, 43. πάλιν δὲ ἀπὸ τῶν νεῶν ἀνέστρεψαν οἱ Ἀθηναῖοι, the Athenians drove them back again from the ships: ἀναστρέφομαι, to turn one's self about, move about backwards and forwards, 4, 35. ἐν τῷ αὐτῷ, in the same spot: 7, 44. ἐν στενοχωρίᾳ ἀνεστρέφοντο, to be engaged in a small space, (of two armies:) 8, 94.

ἀναστροφὴ, 2, 89. a turning round, putting the ship about.

ἀνασχετὸς, endurable, tolerable, 2, 21. ἀνασχετὸν ποιεῖσθαι, to be able to forbear, to think it endurable: 1, 118.

ἀνατίθημι, to dedicate, consecrate, offer up (to a deity,) 1, 131. 3, 104. 6, 54. : 2, 64. ἀναθήσετε, to ascribe, impute: 2, 57. ἀνατεθῆναι πρὸς ἱεροῖς τοῖς κοινοῖς, to be offered up on the common altars (of the country :) 8, 51. ἀνατιθέναι, 82.

ἀνατρέχω, to run up, 3, 89. ἀναδραμόντες, to run up (the hills.)

ἀναφαίνω, 4, 36. ἐπὶ τοῦ μετεώρου ἐξαπίνης ἀναφανεὶς κατὰ νώτου αὐτῶν, to appear above, to be seen over.

ἀναφέρω, 4, 115. ἀνεφόρησαν, to carry up (to the housetop:) 5, 28. ἀνήνεγκαν, to bring before, to propose : 3, 38. τοὺς κινδύνους, to sustain: 5, 16. ἐκ τῆς ἀλλοτρίας εἰς τὴν ἑαυτῶν ἀναφέρειν, 28. : 2, 84. 8, 97.

ἀναχωρέω, 8, 15. ἀνακεχωρήκεσαν, had returned, 10. ἀνεχώρησαν, 20. ἀναχωρήσαντες, having withdrawn from : 1, 102. οἱ Ἀθηναῖοι—εὐθὺς ἐπειδὴ ἀνεχώρησαν—ξύμμαχοι ἐγένοντο, the use of the aor. for the plusq. perf. where it was not necessary to express defi-

nitively the continuance of the one action during the passing of the other, Matth. Gr. Gr. 727. : 8, 28.

ἀναχώρησις, 5, 5. a return, retiring : 1, 128. ἐκ Κύπρου, a return : 5, 65. a retreat : 1, 93. μετὰ τὴν Μήδων ἀναχώρησιν, after the departure or retreat, of the Medes, 12. : 7, 49. ἀναχωρήσεις καὶ ἐπίπλους, a retiring and then renewing the onset, manœuvres in a naval engagement, 85 : 3, 109. 4, 31. 128.

ἀναψηφίζω, to put again to the vote, collect the suffrages a second time, 6, 14.

ἀνδραγαθία, 3, 57. virtue, honour, 64. bravery, 2, 42. τὴν ἐς τοὺς πολέμους ὑπὲρ τῆς πατρίδος, valour in war for or in defence of one's own country.

ἀνδραγαθίζομαι, 3, 40. to be a good, upright man, 2, 63. to act the good sort of man, the upright and conscientious man.

ἀνδραποδίζω, 1, 98. to sell for slaves: 2, 68. ἠνδραπόδισαν, to reduce to slavery, make slaves of, 5, 3. 32. : 3, 28. 5, 116. : 4, 48. ἠνδραποδίσαντο, to use as slaves.

ἀνδραποδισμὸς, 2, 68. 5, 9. a receiving of fetters, a reduction to slavery.

ἀνδράποδον, a slave, prisoner of war sold for a slave, 1, 139. ἀνδραπόδων ἀφισταμένων, runaway slaves: 8, 28. ἀνδράποδα πάντα, καὶ δοῦλα καὶ

E

ἐλεύθερα, all the prisoners, both slaves and freemen : 7, 13.

ἀνδρείως, 2, 39. τὸ ἀνδρεῖον μετέρχονται, to pursue, endeavour after manliness, hardiness, fortitude, 87. 4, 126.

ἀνδρείως, manfully, 4, 120. 5, 9.

ἀνδρία, bravery, manly courage, 3, 39. 82.

ἀνδριὰς, a statue of a man, 1, 134. οἱ δὲ ποιησάμενοι χαλκοῦς ἀνδριάντας δύο ὡς ἀντὶ Παυσανίου ἀνέθεσαν, having cast two statues of brass, they dedicated them as equivalent to Pausanias.

ἀνειλέω, to crowd together, 7, 81. ἀνειληθέντες ἰς τι χωρίον, Matth. Gr. Gr. 334.

ἀνειμένως διαιτώμενοι, 2, 39. to live in a free, liberal manner, without strictness, with a relaxed discipline.

ἀνειπεῖν, 2, 2. to proclaim aloud, 4, 105. 8, 67.

ἀνέκβατος, 8, 98. impassable, 96.

ἀνεκτὸς, what ought to be borne, tolerable, 7, 5. τῇ γνώμῃ οὐκ ἀνεκτὸν, intolerable in thought, in idea, a thought not to be endured, 77. ἀνεκτὰ ἔπαθον, to meet with punishments, that can be tolerated : 2, 35. 8, 90.

ἀνέλεγκτος, unquestioned, 6, 53. ἀνέλεγκτον διαφυγεῖν, to pass, escape unobserved : 5, 85. ἀνέλεγκτα, arguments not to be refuted.

ἀνελκύσαι, 8, 11. to draw

upon shore : 7, 1. 12. : 8, 44. ἀνελκύσαντες.

ἀνέλπιστος, 4, 55. 6, 17. 34. unlooked for : 7, 47. Τά τε ἄλλα ὅτι ἀνέλπιστα αὐτοῖς ἐφαίνετο, the connection seems to be, Τοῖς τε γὰρ ἐπιχειρήμασιν—καὶ τοὺς στρατιώτας—τά τε ἄλλα ὅτι, for καὶ ὅτι τὰ ἄλλα, all which circumstances are reasons to make it necessary they should deliberate on the present posture of affairs : 8, 1. ἀνέλπιστοι, they despaired : 2, 51. πρὸς τὸ ἀνέλπιστον τραπόμενοι, to be reduced to despair : 3, 46. ἀνέλπιστον καταστῆσαι τοὺς ἀποστᾶσιν, to reduce the revolters to despair. In an active sense, not expecting, without expectation, 3, 30. ἀνέλπιστοι ἐπιγενέσθαι ἄν τινα, not expecting, 6, 17. ἀνέλπιστοι ἰς ἡμᾶς, hopeless with respect to us, 7, 4. ἀνελπιστότερα.

ἄνεμος, 6, 2. κατιόντος ἀνέμου, to come on, to begin to flow, ventus spirans et crebrescens, et quidem a tergo euntes prosequens : 2, 25. 4, 23. 7, 53.

ἀνεξέλεγκτος, 1, 21. not possible to be convicted of falsehood : 4, 126.

ἀνεξεύρετος, 3, 87. unascertainable, undiscoverable.

ἀνεπαχθῶς, 2, 37. easily, without irksomeness, offence given or taken.

ἀνεπιβούλευτος, 3, 37. security from treason, unexposed to treachery.

ἀνεπιεικὴς, unjust, iniqui-
tous, 3, 66. ἀνεπιεικέστερος.

ἀνεπικλήτως, 1, 92. un-
charged with, uncensured
for.

ἀνεπίληπτος, not to be taken hold of, furnishing no
handle of reproach, 5, 17.
τοῖς ἐχθροῖς ἀνεπίληπτος εἶναι,
to present no mark to the
enemy.

ἀνεπιστημοσύνη, 5, 7. inexperience, ignorance, incapacity.

ἀνεπιστήμων, 2, 89. without
skill in arrangement: 4, 100.
7, 67. 69. unskilful, inexpert.

ἀνεπίτακτος, unprescribed,
not laid down, ordained, 7,
69. ἀνεπίτακτον πᾶσιν ἐς τὴν
δίαιταν, with uncontrolled
power, as regards the way
of life, the power of living at
one's pleasure.

ἀνεπιτήδειος, injurious to
the interests of the city, 3,
71.

ἀνεπίφθονος, 6, 83. irrepre-
hensible, not subject to
blame: 1, 75. not to be car-
ped at: 7, 77.: 8, 50, not
productive of envy: 1, 73.

ἀνεπιφθόνως, 6, 54. κατεστήσατο, to conduct one's self ir-
reproachably, without odium,
without being invidiously
looked upon.

ἀνερεθίζω, 2, 21. ἀνηρέθιστο,
to be in a commotion : 1,
132. 4, 78.

ἄνευ, 7, 45. ψιλοὶ ἄνευ τῶν
ἀσπίδων, unarmed with re-
spect to their shields, i. e.

without their shields: 5, 28.
ἄνευ τοῦ δήμου, without the
concurrence of the people,
53. τῆς αἰτίας, apart from, or
independent of, the cause:
1, 39. ὑμῶν, without you: 6,
31. ἄνευ τοῦ ἐκ δημοσίου μισθοῦ,
without, independent or ex-
clusive of: 1, 132. 4, 78.

ἀνεύθυνος, 3, 43. not ac-
countable, responsible.

ἀνευρίσκω, 1, 128. ἀνευρέθη,
to be discovered.

ἀνεχέγγυος, unwarranted,
not to be depended or relied
upon, 4, 55. διὰ τὸ τὴν γνώμην ἀνεχέγγυον γεγενῆσθαι, on
account of want of confi-
dence in their opinion, of
their opinion having become
not to be relied upon.

ἀνέχω, 1, 46. to rise up,
141. τοὺς πολέμους, to support, maintain wars: 5, 69.
ἀνέχεσθαι, to submit: 6, 86.
ἀνέχοντας τὴν Σικελίαν μὴ ὑπὸ
αὑτοὺς εἶναι, to keep Sicily
from being in subjection to
them: 4, 53. ἀνέχει, to lie
along, to stretch along: 7,
34. ἀνεχούσας, to protrude,
project, jut out: 2, 74.
ἀνέχεσθαι ὁρῶντας, to bear,
endure to see: 1, 122. ἀνέχεσθαι, to bear any thing, to
endure: 2, 19. πρὸς ἥλιον ἀνί-
σχοντα, to the rising sun, to
the East: 7, 48. ἀνεῖχε διασκοπῶν, to keep deliberating, to
be unable to make up one's
mind: 5, 45. ἠνειχόμην, an instance of a verb, which
receives a double augm.

Matth. Gr. Gr. 210.: 6, 16.
ὥσπερ δυστυχοῦντες οὐ προσαγορευόμεθα, ἐν τῷ ὁμοίῳ τις ἀνεχέσθω καὶ ὑπὸ τῶν εὐπραγούντων
ὑπερφρονούμενος, an example
of a participle nomin. after
a verb, whose subject it has.

ἀνεψιὸς, 1, 132. a cousin-
german.

ἀνήκεστος, 1, 132. ἀνήκεστόν
τι, any thing, which cannot
be remedied or recalled : 4,
20. incurable : 3, 39. μηδὲν
παθεῖν, very severe, 45. in-
superable, invincible (passion :) 5, 111.

ἀνηκουστέω, 1, 84. not to
listen to, to disobey.

ἀνήκω, 3, 45. ἐς τὸν θάνατον,
to be extended or to reach
to the loss of life, to become
capital.

ἀνὴρ, 1, 74. στρατηγὸς, a
general, a kind of circumlocution, a personal denomination, which expresses an
office or business, accompanied by the subst. ἀνὴρ,
which indicates respect,
Matth. Gr. Gr. 621.: 6, 10.
ἔνθενδε ἄνδρες, persons from
hence, some of our own
men : 8, 39. 90.

ἀνθαιρέω, 6, 103. ἀνθείλοντο,
to be chosen in place of.

ἀνθάπτομαι, 8, 50. ἀνθήπτετο,
conducted himself, 97.

ἀνθεκτέος, 1, 93. τῆς θαλάσσης ὡς ἀνθεκτέα ἐστὶ, that ma-
rine affairs ought to be applied to (rather than any
thing else,) Matth. Gr. Gr.
512. 645.

ἀνθέλκω, 4, 14. ἀνθεῖλκον,
to pull back, to drag on the
other end.

ἀνθέω, 1, 19. ἤνθησαν, to
flourish.

ἀνθησσάομαι, 4, 19. to be
worsted or give way in turn.

ἀνθίστημι, 6, 70. 7, 13. ἀνθεστῶτα, to oppose, to be in
array against, standing out,
resisting : 2, 87. ἀνθίστασθαι,
to engage with in battle, to
meet or stand against, 3, 39.
to withstand, resist, 1, 93.
πρὸς ἅπαντας, 5, 101. πρὸς τοὺς
κρείσσονας : 7, 21. ἀντιστῆναι
πρὸς τὸ Ἀθ. ναυτικὸν, to stand
up against, to encounter, to
meet the Athenian fleet : 7,
45. ἀντέστησαν, to stop any
one's progress, 4, 115. πύργον ξύλινον, to set up against,
to rear in opposition, 1, 54.:
5, 38. to take a wrong turn,
to contradict expectation, to
furnish opposition, to belie
expectation, ὡς δὲ ἀντέστη τὸ
πρᾶγμα, as the affair did not
succeed : 1, 41. ἀντιστάντα, to
resist, 43. ἀντιστὰς, 5, 4. ἀν-
τιστάντος, giving trouble, resisting, furnishing obstacles :
4, 85. ἀνθίστασθε : 7, 63. ἀντιστῆναι ἡμῖν, to resist, to
meet in battle.

ἀνθορμέω, 7, 31. ἀνθορμοῦσαι,
moored or anchored over
against each other, 19. ἀνθώρ-
μουν ταῖς ναυσὶν, to take up
an opposition-station, to be
opposed to, in front of, 2,
86. to keep their stations,
to lie at anchor in sight of

one another, 7, 34. πρὸς τὰς ναῦς, to have one's station over against another, to face.

ἄνθος, a flower, 4, 133.

ἄνθραξ, 4, 100. ἄνθρακας, coals.

ἀνθρώπειος, 3, 45. φύσεως, human nature : 5, 89. ἐν ἀνθρ. λόγῳ, in human computation : 1, 22. κατὰ τὸ ἀνθρ. according to the nature of man : 1, 76. χρησάμενοι τῇ ἀνθρ. φύσει, to follow the dictates of human nature : 5, 105. ἀνθρωπείας τῶν ἐς τὸ θεῖον νομίσεως, human belief in respect of divine affairs, religion, 68. διὰ τὸ ἀνθρώπειον κομπῶδες, because of the boasting, exaggeration natural to men in such cases, ἐς τὰ οἰκεῖα πλήθη, as regards their own numbers : 2, 50. 4, 61. 116.

ἀνθρωπείως, 5, 103. after the usual manner of men, in a human manner.

ἀνθρωπίνως, 3, 40. humanly, incidentally to humanity.

ἄνθρωπος, a man or woman, 1, 77. 140. 4, 19. 130. 8, 73.

ἀνθυπάγω, 3, 70. to cite to trial in return or revenge.

ἀνθυποπτεύω, 3, 43. to suspect in return.

ἀνίημι, 7, 18. τὸν πόλεμον, to remit, to relax : 6, 18. to let slip, to release our hold of, to keep a strict watch over, to carry it with a high head : 7, 51. τὰ τῶν Ἀθ. i. e. τοὺς Ἀθ., to let go, to let the Athenians slip through their

hands : 2, 77. ἀνῆκε, to send, to cast up, 4, 116. to dedicate : 6, 86. ἀνιᾶσιν, i. q. ἀφιᾶσιν, to let slip, Matth. Gr. Gr. 279. : 4, 27. ἀνέντων, giving up, 123. putting off, 7, 43. ἀνέντων σφῶν τῆς ἐφόδου, to give up, let go, neglect: ἀνήσουσι, 5, 46. τὴν συμμαχίαν, to relinquish, 31. ἀνέντες τὴν ἐπιτροπὴν, to neglect or refuse the arbitration, 32. ἀνεῖσαν τῆς φιλονεικίας, to relax from, in their eagerness : 1, 6. ἀνειμένῃ διαίτῃ, through a relaxation of manners : 5, 9. ἐν τῷ ἀνειμένῳ τῆς γνώμης, in the present state of carelessness of mind (before their resolution is strung for a contest :) 1, 76. εἰ ταύτην (sc. ἀρχὴν) μὴ ἀνεῖμεν, 5, 32. ἀνεῖσαν, the plur. aor. 2. Attic idiom similar to ἀφεῖμεν, ἀφεῖτε, ἀφεῖσαν, Matth. Gr. Gr. 282.

ἀνίστημι, 1, 87. ἀναστήτω, let him rise and go ἐς ἐκεῖνο χωρίον, on that side : 1, 12. ἀνισταμένη, to be unsettled and shifting: 1, 87. ἀναστάντες, having risen up, 2, 49. τοὺς παραυτίκα, directly upon their rising up, upon their recovery : 4, 112. ἀναστήσας (τὸν στρατὸν,) having set in motion, 93. ἀναστήσας ἦγε τὸν στρατὸν, to set the army in motion and march, to break up: 2, 68. ἀναστήσαντες, to stir up, raise (any one in order to accompany you :) 3, 7. ἀναστήσας Ἀκαρνᾶνας πανδημεί, to raise the Acarna-

nians *en masse*, to call out
the whole force of the Acarnanians, 4, 90. Ἀθηναίους,
πανδημεί, having set in motion, having marched off, (in
an active sense:) 4, 77. τὸ
ξυμμαχικὸν, having set in motion: 5, 1. to remove, to
expatriate, to disturb: 1, 136.
ἀνίστημι, to raise from a posture of supplication: 6, 4.
ἀναστάντες ἐκ τῆς Θάψου, to remove from, or to be expelled
from, 1, 12. to be expelled,
6, 2. ὑπὸ Αἰγύων, 2, 27.: 1,
105. ἀναστήσεσθαι, to recall
(troops) ἀπ' Αἰγίνης: 7, 50.
ἀναστάντες, removing, (they
repented) they had not removed: 1, 8. to be expelled,
to change one's abode, οἱ
κακοῦργοι ἀνέστησαν ὑπ' αὐτοῦ,
the malefactors were com-
pelled by him to change
their abode: 8, 45.

ἀνίσωσις, 8, 87. equalizing,
making equal.

ἀνόητος, 6, 11. mad, foolish.

ἄνοια, 3, 42. madness, folly:
3, 48. indiscretion, rashness,
unadvisedness : 6, 17. folly,
extravagance, ἡ ἐμὴ δοκοῦσα
εἶναι, my seeming folly, this
which seemed to be folly in
me : 2, 61.

ἀνοίγω, 4, 68. τὰς πύλας, to
open : 2, 2. ἀνέῳξαν, to open
(doors, gates:) 5, 10. : 7, 29.
ἀνεῳγμένων, being open: 2, 4,
ἀνεῳγμέναι εἶναι, to be open:
4, 111. αἱ πύλαι ἀνεῴγοντο : 3,
65. 4, 130.

ἀνοικίζω, 1, 58. ἀνοικίσασθαι

ἐς Ὄλονθον, to migrate, to
transfer their habitation to
Olynthus : 1, 7. ἀνῳκισμένοι,
to be settled or planted at a
distance from up the coast:
8, 31. καὶ ἐκέλευσεν αὐτῶν τοὺς
τὰ Ἀθηναίων φρονοῦντας ἀνοικί-
ζεσθαι ἐς τὸν Δαφνοῦντα καὶ
προσχωρεῖν σφίσι, Matth. Gr.
Gr. 412.

ἄνοιξις, 4, 67. τῶν πυλῶν, the
act of opening (gates,) 68.

ἀνοικοδομέω, 1, 89. to rebuild : 8, 16. ἀνῳκοδόμησαν,
had built.

ἀνολκὴ, support, rearing,
propping, 4, 112. πρὸς λίθων
ἀνολκὴν, for the purpose of
drawing up stones.

ἀνολοφύρομαι, 8, 81. to lament, bewail.

ἀνομία, 2, 53. Πρῶτόν τι
ἤρξε—ἐπὶ πλέον ἀνομίας, to be
the first beginning of licentiousness, lawlessness, to a
greater extent.

ἀνομοίως, 1, 84. dissimilarly.

ἄνομος, 3, 67. ἄνομα, out-
rages.

ἀνόμως, 4, 92. sacrilegi-
ously, in contempt of privilege.

ἀνορθόω, 6, 88. ἀνορθώσαν-
τες, to re-erect.

ἄνοσος, 2, 49. Ἄνοσον ἐς τὰς
ἄλλας ἀσθενείας, free in respect
of all other diseases, com-
plaints, healthy.

ἀνταγωνίζω, 6, 72. ἀνταγω-
νισαμένους, to contend against,
to strive with: 3, 38. ἀντα-
γωνιζόμενοι τοῖς τοιαῦτα λέγουσι,
to resist, to contradict.

ἀνταίρω, 3, 32. ἀνταιρομένους χεῖρας, to lift up (their) hands against, to carry arms: 1, 53. ἀνταιρόμενοι ὅπλα, to take up arms against us.

ἀνταιτέω, 4, 19. ἀνταιτοῦντες τοὺς ἐκ τῆς νήσου ἄνδρας, claiming in return, asking as a price.

ἀνταλλάσσω, 3, 82. ἀντήλλαξεν, to change (a name) for another: 4, 14. ἀντηλλαγμένος, having been interchanged: 8, 80.

ἀνταμύνω, 4, 19. ἀνταμυνόμενος, holding out, resisting.

ἀντανάγω, 1, 29. ἀντανα- γόμενοι, to put out to sea for action, 1, 117. ἀνταναγομένας, to be drawn up against : 7, 52. ἀντανῆγον, to put out, to launch out, to sail out, 40. ἀντανήγοντα, to advance against, 4, 13. to put out to sea in opposition : 8, 38. ἀν- ταναγαγειν, 80.

ἀντεναμένω, 3, 12. to wait in turn.

ἀντάνειμι, 2, 75. ἀντανῄει, to ascend, to be raised over against.

ἀνταξιόω, 6, 16. to claim or to require in return.

ἀνταπαιτέω, 3, 58. to claim a return : 5, 17. ἀνταπαιτούν- των, to demand in exchange.

ἀνταποδίδωμι, 4, 19. ἀρετὴν, to contend in generosity, to make a return of generosity: 1, 43. ἀνταπόδοτε τὸ ἴσον, to make a requital, 3, 40. to retaliate, 63. to return a kindness.

ἀνταπόδοσις, 4, 81. χωρίων, exchange.

ἀνταποφαίνω, 3, 38. ἀνταπο- φῆναι, to shew on the other hand, to prove on one's own side, 67. ἀνταποφαίνομεν, to make a counter-disclosure.

ἀντειπεῖν, 2, 65. ἔχων, being enabled to contradict, gain- say, oppose: 1, 40. ἀντείπομεν, to maintain a contradiction: 5, 43. ἀντεῖπεν, to speak against: 1, 136. to deny: 1, 86. ἀντεῖπον, to reply to: 4, 22. ἀντεῖπον, to say again, to answer; 3, 61. ἀντεῖπειν, to contradict, 8, 9. ἀνταπόντος, opposing.

ἀντεκπλέω, 4, 13. to sail out opposite.

ἀντελπίζω, 1, 70. to hope something in compensation of a loss.

αντεμβιβάζω, 7, 13. ἀντεμβι- βάσαι, to take on board in- stead of another.

ἀντεπανάγω, 4, 25. ἀντεπα- ναγόμενοι, having been led out to sea against.

ἀντέπειμι, 4, 96. ἀντεπῄεσαν, to assault again or in turn, to answer the attack, 33. to make a corresponding move- ment forward, 7, 4. to go to meet, to march against an advancing army, 7, 6. to proceed against from the opposite side.

ἀντεπεξάγω, 8, 104. ἀντεπε- ξῆγον, to advance against in turn.

ἀντεπέξειμι, 7, 37. to go out against on their side.

ἀντεπεξελαύνω, 4, 72. ἀντεπεξελάσαντες, having ridden out up against.

ἀντεπεξέρχομαι, 4, 130. ἀντεπεξελθόντες, to advance against in turn.

ἀντεπιβουλεύω, 1, 33. to counterplot, 3, 12.

ἀντεπιμελλῆσαι, 3, 12. to defer in return, to delay on our part.

ἀντεπιτάσσω, 1, 135. ἀντεπέταξαν, to require in return or in answer.

ἀντεπιτειχίζω, 1, 142. ἀντεπιτετειχισμένων, to erect counter-works.

ἀντεπιτίθημι, 1, 129. ἐπιστολὴν, to write a letter in answer.

ἀντερῶ, 3, 38. 44. to gainsay: 1, 73. ἀντεροῦντες τοῖς ἐγκλήμασι, to contradict, to reply to, to rebut.

ἀντέχω, 6, 69. ἐς ὅσον ἡ ἐπιστήμη ἀντέχοι, to extend, reach: 2, 49. ἀντεῖχε, to bear up against, to resist (a malady:) 7, 34. ἀντεῖχον, to hold out against, to maintain a contest, 1, 11. to strive against, to contend with, 4, 35. 7, 22.: 4, 68. ἀντίσχοντες, maintaining opposition, holding out against: 2, 64. ἀντέσχομεν πολέμοις μεγίστοις: 1, 14. ἀντίσχειν πρὸς ἅπαντας, to withstand, to stand out against all: 2, 70. ἀντέχειν, to hold out against a siege: 3, 102. ἀντίσχωσιν: 7, 43. ἀντίσχον, to make a stand against, to check: 2, 64.

ἀντέχει ἐπὶ πολὺ, to last long, ἀντέχουσιν ἔργῳ μάλιστα, to resist most steadily indeed: 6, 22. ἀντέχωσι πρὸς τὸ ἱππικὸν, to withstand, to make head against.

ἀντηρὶς, 7, 36. prop, raft planted against any thing to support it.

ἀντὶ, 5, 36. ἀντ' αὐτοῦ, in exchange for it, instead of it, in lieu of it: 7, 28. ἀντὶ τοῦ φόρου, in the place of, instead of: 7, 68. ἀνθ' ὧν, wherefore, 86. ingratitude for which: 1, 62. ἀνθ' αὐτοῦ, instead of himself as his deputy.

ἀντιβάλλω, 7, 25. to shoot, to throw darts in return.

ἀντιβοηθέω, 7, 58. ἀντεβοήθησαν, to bring aid on the contrary side.

ἀντιβολία, 7, 75. a supplication, beseeching.

ἀντιγράφω, 1, 129. ἀντεγέγραπτο, to be written in reply.

ἀντιδίδωμι, 1, 41. ἀντιδοθῆναι, to be returned: 3, 40. ἀντιδίδοσθαι, to be repaid, to be given in turn: 3, 66. ἀντιδοῦναι δίκην, to submit to punishment, 63. ἀντιδιδόναι, to return a favour.

ἀντικαθέζομαι, 1, 30. to be stationed over against one another: 5, 6. ἀντεκάθητο, to take up a station opposite, to occupy a corresponding post.

ἀντικαθίστημι, 1, 71. ἀντικαθεστηκυίας, to be an adversary, to be set up in opposi-

ation, the perfect is used in all moods, when the writer wishes to shew that the condition mentioned is to be continued on, Matth. Gr. Gr. 730: 1, 62. ἀντικαθίσταντο, to take a station over against: 3, 47. ἀντικαθισταμένης, to be adverse, hostile: 2, 65. ἀντικαθίστη ἐπὶ τὸ θαρσεῖν, to re-instate in confidence: 2, 13. ἀντικαταστῆσαι, to put in the place of, to restore: 7, 39. ἀντικαταστάντες, to oppose mutually, to face one another.

ἀντικελεύω, 1, 128. to counter-desire, 139. to direct any thing to be performed in return.

ἀντικρούω, 6, 46. ἀντεκέκρουκει, to happen, turn out contrary to one's hopes, to disappoint, blast, cross one's hopes.

ἀντικρυς, 1, 122. plainly, absolutely: 5, 30. openly: 6. 10. πολεμοῦσιν, downright, 49. straightforward, directly: 1, 132. 8, 64.

ἀντιλαβὴ, 7, 65. a means of laying hold of, something to catch hold of.

ἀντιλαμβάνω, 3, 22. ἀντιλάβοιντο τοῦ ἀσφαλοῦς, to gain a place of safety: 2, 8. ἀντιλαμβάνονται, to take in hand, to undertake, set about a thing: 2, 62. ἀντιλαμβανόμενοι, to keep fast hold of: 7, 77. Ἢν ἀντιλαβώμεθά του φιλίου χωρίον, if we reach a friendly territory: 3, 40.

ἀντιλήψονται ἐκ τοῦ εὖ εἰπεῖν, to receive in return in consequence of, 7, 60. ἀντιλήψεσθαι, to reach (a place,) to arrive at: 7, 66. ἀντιλάβεσθε αὐτῶν, to lay hold of, i. e. to embrace, to take in hand, to undertake (προθύμως:) 3, 58. ἀντιλαβεῖν, to get in return, 1, 143. to possess one's self instead of.

ἀντιλέγω, 3, 41. 5, 45, to argue against: 7, 49. ἀντιλέγοντος, to object, 8, 24. to deny: 4, 3. ἀντιλεγόντων, refusing: 5, 49. ἀντέλεγον μὴ δικαίως καταδεδικάσθαι, to deny that they were justly fined: 1, 77. ἀντέλεγον, to alledge against any one, 5, 30. to deny, to contradict, to give an answer to, 6, 15. to oppose, 1, 28. to reply: 8, 45.

ἀντίλεκτος, 4, 92. dubious, subject to discussion.

ἀντίληψις, 2, 49. τῶν ἀκρωτηρίων, a seizure of the extremities of the body (by the plague:) 1, 120. a return.

ἀντιλογία, 4, 49. 59. δι' ἀντιλογιῶν, by debates, by offering [their] respective opinions: 5, 78. debate, wordy contention: 1, 73. ἐς ἀντιλογίαν τοῖς ὑμετέροις ξυμμάχοις ἐγένετο, for disputing with, for the purpose of debating with, the dat. often accompanies a subst. which is derived from a verb governing the dat. Matth. Gr. Gr. 558.: 1, 31. a debate, dispute: 2, 87. an excuse, something to alledge in one's defence.

ἀντιμάχομαι, 4, 68. to fight on the other side.

ἀντιμηχανάομαι, 7, 53. ἀντεμηχανήσαντο, to contrive, devise in opposition to.

ἀντιμίμησις, 7, 67. imitation in return, on the part of.

ἀντιναυπηγνύω, 7, 36. 62. to counteract the enemy in the construction of ships, to provide against the enemy's expedients, Matth. Gr. Gr. 637. ἀντινεναυπηγμένας ὁμοίως, to be similarly constructed on their part, to have their ships on their side built in like manner.

ἀντίπαλος, 1, 142. equal in strength, of equal power: 7, 13. opposite, fronting: 5, 8. a match, an equivalent: 7, 38. 4, 10.: 4, 92. 117. πρός τε γὰρ τοὺς ἀστυγείτονας πᾶσι τὸ ἀντίπαλον καὶ ἐλεύθερον, the balance of power is the secret of liberty, 1, 91. μὴ ἀπὸ ἀντιπάλου παρασκευῆς, unless there is a balance of power, in the use of the dat. for the Latin abl. answering to the question, wherewith? whereby? it is observed that instead of the dat. sometimes a gen. with a prep. is used, Matth. Gr. Gr. 566.: 3, 11. δέος, mutual fear, equal awe, each of the other: 7, 12. ἀντιπάλους τῷ πλήθει, equal in number, force: 2, 45. φθόνος πρὸς τὸ ἀντίπαλον, envy, a spirit of contention towards

rivals, competitors, towards that, which rivals (any one:) 3, 49. ἀντιπάλων μάλιστα πρὸς ἀλλήλας, diametrically opposite to each other.

ἀντιπάλως, 8, 87. equally.

ἀντιπαρακαλέω, 6, 86. to exhort, invite on our part, 88.

ἀντιπαρακέλευομαι, 6, 13. τοῖς πρεσβυτέροις, to counter-exhort, to exhort on my side in turn.

ἀντιπαραλυπῶ, 4, 80. to harass in opposition, to make reprisals.

ἀντιπαραπλέω, 2, 83. to sail against.

ἀντιπαρασκευάζω, 1, 80. ἀντιπαρασκευασόμεθα, to make counter-preparations: 7, 3. ἀντιπαρεσκευάζοντο ἀλλήλοις ὡς ἐς μάχην, to make ready against each other for battle: 5, 59. ἀντιπαρεσκευάζοντο, to prepare themselves in opposition, 7, 3.

ἀντιπαράσχωσιν, 6, 21. to furnish, afford on our side in opposition to.

ἀντιπαρατάσσω, 1, 63. ἀντιπαρετάξαντο, to draw themselves up in opposite array: 1, 48. 7, 5. 37. ἀντιπαρετάσσοντο: 5, 9. ἀντιπαραταχθέντος, in battle array.

ἀντιπάσχω, 3, 61. ἀντέπασχον, to suffer retaliation: 6, 35. ἀντιπάθοιεν, to be made to suffer in turn: 4, 35.

ἀντιπαταγέω, 3, 22. ἀντιπαταγοῦντος ψόφῳ, to drown, over-power a noise, to make a noise in opposition to.

ἀντιπέμπω, 6, 99. to send in turn.

ἀντιπέρας, 1, 10. opposite, over against, 2, 66. 86. opposite to, on the opposite coast: 4, 92. Εὐβοίας, 2, 66.

ἀντιπληρόω, 7, 22. ἀντιπληρώσαντες, having manned in opposition, (against the enemy:) 7, 69. ἀντιπλήρουν, to man on their side : 8, 17.

ἀντιποιέω, 1, 28. ἀντιποιοῦνται, to justify one's self, to persist in thinking one's self right in opposition to another, to alledge in one's own behalf: 4, 122. ἀντεποιοῦντο (τῆς πόλεως,) to lay claim to.

ἀντιπολεμέω, 1, 23. ἀντιπολεμούντων, to attack one's fellow citizens in a sedition: 3, 39. ἀντεπολέμησαν, to make or wage war against.

ἀντιπολέμιος, 3, 90. an antagonist in war.

ἀντιπολιορκέω, 7, 28. to besiege on the other hand.

ἀντιπρεσβεύω, 6, 75. to send an opposition-embassy.

ἀντιπρόσειμι, 6, 66. ἀντιπρόσῇσαν, to march out to meet an enemy, to draw out.

ἀντίπρωρος, 2, 91. with prow facing the enemy, or towards the open sea: 7, 34. 36. 40. with prows opposed : 4, 14. 8, 85.

ἀντισόω, 3, 11. ἀντισουμένου, to be equal to, on a level with, on equal terms.

ἀντιστράτηγος, 7, 86. the commander on the enemy's side.

ἀντιστρατοπεδεύω, 4, 124. to encamp over against : 1,30. ἀντεστρατοπεδεύοντο, to make an hostile encampment over against some one.

ἀντισχυρίζω, 3, 44. ἀντισχυριζόμενος, to assist, maintain in return, on the contrary.

ἀντίσχω, 1, 7. 65. 4, 68. see ἀντέχω.

ἀντίταξις, an opposite drawing up, a corresponding disposition : 7, 17. πρὸς τὴν σφετέραν ἀντίταξιν τὴν φυλακὴν ποιούμενοι, to keep guard over against, to watch, face their (i. e. the Corinthian) line of battle drawn up in front of them.

ἀντιτάσσω, 2, 87. ἀντιτάξασθε, to match against, to array against : 4, 55. ἀντετάξαντο, to draw out again : 3, 83. ἀντιτετάχθαι ἀλλήλοις τῇ γνώμῃ ἀπίστως, to match their wits one against the other without any mutual confidence, 5, 55. : 3, 56. 4, 55.

ἀντιτείχισμα, 2, 77. a counter-work.

ἀντιτέχνησις, 7, 70. reciprocal, mutual contrivance, counter-manœuvring.

ἀντιτίθημι, 3, 56. to set off against the balance : 6, 18. to object, to urge against, on the contrary, in opposition : 2, 85. ἀντιτιθέντες, to set off against, to compare with.

ἀντιτιμωρήσασθαι, 3, 82. to make a revenge.

ἀντιτολμάω, 7, 21. to be daring, adventurous, enterprising against an enemy, who is equally so : 2, 89. to dare to meet (in fight.)

ἀντιτυγχάνω, ἀντετυχεῖν, ἐπικουρίας, 6, 87. to obtain in return (for something else.)

ἀντιφυλακή, 2, 84. πρὸς ἀλλήλους, caution towards each other (to prevent collision.)

ἀντιχειροτονέω, 6, 13. 24. to hold up hands against, to vote against any thing.

ἀντοικτιοῦντας, 3, 40. to pity in return, the Doric form of the fut. for ἱσω, Matth. Gr. Gr. 221.

ἀντονομάζω, 6, 5. ἀντωνόμασι, to change the name (of a place,) to call by another name instead of the old one.

ἀντοφείλων, 2, 40. one, who owes a good turn to another, who has to return an obligation.

ἀνυδρία, 8, 88. deficiency of water, the shallowness of the water about the island.

ἀνυποπτότερος, 3, 43. more unsuspected.

ἀνύειν, 2, 75. to expedite the work, to complete, to fill up, 76.

ἄνω, 1, 187. 3, 34. τῆς ἄνω πόλεως, the upper city, i. e. farther from the sea : 3, 22. ἐγένοντο, to be up (upon a wall :) 7, 54. 64.

ἄνωθεν, 7, 63. τῶν ἄνωθεν τὸ ἔργον, the business, duty of those above, i. e. on deck : 4, 74. ὕδατος ἄνωθεν γενομένου, from above : 3, 21.

ἀνωθέω, 8, 93. ἀνῶσαι, ob-

jectare, to thrust, dash, cast with violence.

ἀνώμαλος, 7, 71. unequal.

ἀνώτατος, 4, 110. φυλακτήριον, the heights, higher place.

ἀνωφελής, 2, 47. to no purpose : 4, 122. ἰσχύι, useless, unavailing : 6, 33. hurtful, dangerous, Cic. Multis modis inutile, i. e. noxium.

ἀξία, 6, 68. Τῆς ὑμετέρας αὐτῶν ἀξίας μνησθέντες, mindful of your worth, value : 7, 77. παρὰ τὴν ἀξίαν, οὐ κατ' ἀξίαν, unmerited.

ἀξιόλογος, 1, 14. 4, 23. 48. worth mention : 1, 1. ἀξιολογώτατον, 6, 60. ἄνθρωποι, reputable, respectable : 6, 74. ἀξιολογωτάτων, most considerable, ὥστε καὶ ἀξιόλογόν τι ἀπογενέσθαι, so as to be of any material consequence : 2, 10. ἀξιολογωτάτους παρεῖναι, most deserving, fit to be present : 1, 17. ἀξιόλογον, of consequence.

ἀξιόμαχος, 4, 57. 5, 2. in fighting condition, trim : 5, 60. ἀξιόμαχοι δοκοῦντες, having the reputation of being a match : 8, 38, 80.

ἄξιος, 1, 70. entitled, 86. 73. λόγου, worthy of consideration, 6, 21. τῆς διανοίας, worthy of the plan, design : 4, 81. πλεῖστον, of the greatest service, consequence : 7, 30. ὀλοφύρασθαι, deserving that one should deplore it, worthy one's lamentation : 7, 56. deserving of notice, praise,

4, 120. ἀξιωτάτους ἐπαίνου, most worthy of applause: 3, 63. ἀξιώτεροι πάσης ζημίας, more worthy of all punishment: ἄξιος θαυμάσαι, from the principle of the infin. after an adj. expressing fitness and ability, by which adj. a verb following is affected, in this instance, but this partic. adj. has here as sometimes the verb act. infin. for the pass., Matth. Gr. Gr. 799. : 2, 40. ἀξίαν εἶναι τὴν πόλιν θαυμάζεσθαι, *Dignam esse quæ in admiratione sit*, Matth. *l. c.* : 8, 88.

ἀξιοχρέως, 6, 34. εἴ τι ἀξιόχρεων ἀφ' ἡμῶν ὀφθείη, weighty, important (measure) on our part: 5, 13. competent to, fully qualified for, equal to: 6, 10. considerable, important: 1, 10. worthy of notice, of consequence: 4, 80. 6, 21. 31.

ἀξιόω, 1, 43. to claim: 2, 81. ἀξιούμενοι, accounted: 5, 89. Ἀξιοῦμεν ὑμᾶς οἴεσθαι πείσειν, to demand of you, to think of persuading: 4, 80. to arrogate to one's self (the merit :) 4, 78. to think fair: 6, 47. to call upon, to require: 2, 42. 3, 40. 7, 5. 63. to resolve: 1, 132. to think proper: 7, 75. to entreat: 3, 43. ἐν τῷ τοιῷδε ἀξιοῦντι, amid such thoughts, imaginations: 3, 88. to presume: 7, 25. ἀξιώσοντας ξυμβοηθεῖν, to call upon any one to assist, to claim succour, 4,

72. to claim (a victory,) 3, 64. 7, 34. : 1, 138. to desire : 5, 36. ἀξιώσει, to deem right : 4, 65. ἠξίουν, to claim, to require, 4, 40. to think, to hold an opinion : 3, 42. ἀξιοῦσθαι ἔτι μειζόνων, to deserve : 7, 38. ἀξιοῦσθαι, to be thought to deserve, to be judged worthy : 3, 37. ἀξιοῦσιν ἀμαθέστεροι εἶναι, not to pretend to be wise : 3, 14. ἄνδρες οἷουσπερ ὑμᾶς ἀξιοῦσι, men, such as they think, judge you (to be :) 3, 44. ἀξιῶ ὑμᾶς ἀπώσασθαι, to ask of you, to entreat, to demand that you reject : 7, 15. ἀξιῶ δ' ὑμῶν ξυγγνώμης τυγχάνειν, to think one has a claim to expect leave of any one, that any one ought to give leave.

ἀξίωμα, 2, 34. dignity, estimation : 5, 8. worth, efficiency, 43. estimation, nobility : 2, 65. δυνατὸς ὢν τῷ ἀξιώματι καὶ τῇ γνώμῃ, being powerful from his rank and abilities, having very great authority and abilities : 2, 37. ἀξιώματος ἀφάνεια, obscurity of rank, condition : 6, 15. ὧν γὰρ ἐν ἀξιώματι ὑπὸ τῶν ἀστῶν, for being held in repute by the citizens, where the neuter is taken for a pass., Matth. Gr. Gr. 720. : 4, 18. estimation, consideration : 1, 130. 4, 18. 7, 15.

ἀξίως, 6, 16. τῆς νίκης. i. e. ἱκανῶς πρὸς τὴν νίκην : 3, 39. τῆς ἀδικίας, adequately, proportionably to the guilt, Matth. Gr. Gr. 485.: 1, 69. consistently with one's dignity, 86. 2, 58.

ἀξίωσις, a good opinion entertained of one's self either by one's self or by others, 6, 54. ὡς ἀπὸ τῆς ὑπαρχούσης ἀξιώσεως, i. e. ὡς κατὰ τὴν ὑπάρχουσαν αὐτῷ δύναμιν, as well as his weight, influence, authority, rank would enable him, allow: 3, 82. εἰωθυῖαν ἀξίωσιν τῶν ὀνομάτων ἐς τὰ ἔργα, the customary acceptation of names for deeds: 1, 37. a claim, 41. χάριτος, a claim of favour : 2, 61. τὴν ἀξίωσιν ἀφανίζειν, to eclipse one's glory, to sully one's reputation, to injure one's estimation: 1, 69. τῆς ἀρετῆς, a reputation for superior virtue, a high claim to consideration on account of merit in freeing Greece: 2, 37. rank, dignity (of a magistrate or principal officer:) 3, 9. an opinion, estimation: 8, 43. will, desire: 2, 88.

ἀξυγκρότητος, 8, 95. Ἀθηναῖοι δὲ κατὰ τάχος καὶ ἀξυγκροτήτοις πληρώμασιν ἀναγκασθέντες χρήσασθαι, Schol. ἤγουν ἑτοίμοις ναυσίν, such as could in the hurry of the moment be got together.

ἀξύμβατος, 3, 46. τὸ ἀ., non-capitulation, impossibility of capitulation, inability of coming to a composition.

ἀξύμφορος, 1, 37. unfortunate, inconvenient : 3, 40.

ἀξυμφορωτάτους τῇ ἀρχῇ, most disadvantageous, prejudicial to an empire : 8, 50.

ἀξυνεσία, 6, 36. simplicity, folly, 1, 122.: 3, 42. μετὰ ἀξυνεσίας καὶ ἄδικος (γίγνεται,) corrupt as well as foolish, knave as well as blockhead.

ἀξύνετος, 3, 42. 4, 17. wanting, defective in understanding, dull of comprehension: 2, 34. Ὃς ἂν γνώμῃ τε δοκῇ μὴ ἀξύνετος εἶναι καὶ ἀξιώματι προήκῃ, to be not of a wise understanding, distinguished for wisdom: 1, 142. ἀξυνετώτεροι, more unskilled, inexpert : 6, 89. ἀξυνετώτατοι, most unwise, foolish, inconsiderate: 8, 27. imprudent, without understanding.

ἀξύντακτος ἀναρχία, 6, 72. a disorderly anarchy.

ἄοκνος, 1, 70. active, 74. ἀοκνοτάτην, most vigorous, active.

ἄοπλος, 4, 9. unarmed, unequipped.

ἀόριστος, 1, 139. τῆς γῆς, the debateable ground.

ἀπαγγελία, 3, 67. announcement, relation (of news.)

ἀπαγγέλλω, 1, 29. ἀπήγγειλεν, to report, to bring back news : 5, 37. ἀπήγγειλαν, to relate at returning, to deliver in one's message, charge : 8, 6. ἀπαγγείλαντος : 1, 91. 2, 73. 3, 24. 4, 38. 5, 46. 7, 8. : 8, 6. οἱ Λακεδαιμόνιοι—πέμψαντες Φρῦνιν—ἀπαγγείλαντος αὐτοῖς (τοῦ Φρύνιος) ἐποιήσαντο, (see Matth. Gr. Gr. 862 :) 8,

86. ἀπήγγελον, (" it is very seldom that a verb has the two tenses aor. 1. and aor. 2. act. ἀπήγγειλα and ἀπήγγελον," Math. 244.)

ἀπάγχομαι, 3, 81. ἀπήγχοντο, to hang one's self : 4, 48. ἀπαγχόμενοι, suspending, hanging.

ἀπάγω, 5, 35. ἀπαγαγών (τοὺς στρατιώτας,) to recall, withdraw : 2, 59. ἀπαγαγὼν τὸ ὀργιζόμενον τῆς γνώμης, to withdraw, divert the irritation of mind, i. e. to put an end to it, 2, 65. ἀπάγειν τὴν γνώμην, to divert, withdraw the mind, thoughts : ἀπήγαγον, 4, 48. to lead out, 83. to draw out, 7, 3. 8, 15. ἀπαγαγόντες : 5, 53. ἀπαγαγεῖν, to pay (what is due :) 5, 63. ἀπάγειν ἐκ τῆς πόλεως, to lead away out of the city : 1, 126. ἀπαγαγόντες, to take aside : 5, 10. ἀπῆγε, to lead back.

ἀπαθὴς, 1, 26. without hurt, safe : 5, 16. being free from the stain of a single miscarriage : 8, 24. unhurt, uninjured.

ἀπαιδευσία, 3, 84. ὀργῆς, ungovernable passion, unruliness of anger, 42. inexperience, imperitia.

ἀπαίρω, 7, 17. to weigh anchor from, to depart, 19. ἀπῆραν, to pass over, to cross, 4, 46. to sail off, 4, 26. ἀπαίροντες : 6, 34. ἀπᾶραι ἀπὸ Κερκύρας, to put out to sea from a place : 5, 83. ἀπάραντος, having gone away : 8, 55. 103.

ἀπαιτέω, 5, 35. asking for back, reclaiming, claiming the restoration, 44. ἀπαιτήσοντες, about to ask back, requesting back : 4, 99. ἀπαιτοῦσιν, to ask (at any body's hands,) to solicit, 23. ἀπῄτουν, to demand, claim back.

ἀπαλγέω, 2, 61. ἀπαλγήσαντες τὰ ἴδια, to have done or to cease grieving for private disasters, on a private account.

ἀπαλλαγὴ, 7, 2. τοῦ πολέμου, a cessation, riddance, an end, termination, conclusion : 1, 51. a separation : 4, 61.

ἀπαλλάσσω, 1, 90. to get rid of, to dismiss, 95. ἀπαλλαξείοντας, 4, 64. 87. 7, 100. ἀπαλλαγῆναι : 8, 2. ἀπηλλάχθαι, they would be freed, 1, 143. 2, 42. ἀπηλλάγησαν, to depart this life : 7, 53. τοῦ κινδύνου, to be freed, delivered from (any thing :) 1, 138. ἀπήλλακτο, to be rid of, to be removed from, κρῖναι ἱκανῶς οὐκ ἀπήλλακτο, to be unable to form a complete judgment : 6, 40. ἀπαλλαγῆτε τῶν ἀγγελιῶν, to abstain from, to desist from (any thing :) 1, 122. ἀπήλλακται, to be rid of, to avoid : 4, 28. ἀπαλλαγήσεσθαι, to be rid of : 6, 82. ἀπηλλάγημεν τῆς ἀρχῆς, to be freed from : 1, 129. ἀπαλλάξαντα, to dismiss from government : 7, 42. εἰ πέρας μηδὲν ἔσται σφίσι τοῦ ἀπαλλαγῆναι τοῦ κινδύνου, an end of danger, (literally) an end with respect to delivery from danger : 8, 106.

12

ἀπαναλίσκω, 7, 14. to consume: ἀπανηλώθη, 7, 30. to be
destroyed, 11. ἀπαναλωκυίας,
deducting: 2, 13. ἀπανηλώθη,
to be disbursed.

ἀπανίστημι, 7, 48. ἀπανίστα-
σθαι, to rise up from before a
town, to raise a siege : 1, 2.
ἀπανίσταντο, to change one's
habitation; to remove: 1, 61.
ἀπανίστανται, to depart from :
2, 70. ἀπανίστασαν, to make
to rise up from before a place,
to force to raise the siege, to
remove from, 1, 140. ἀπανί-
στασθαι.

ἀπαντάω, 4, 91. κήρυκι, to
meet, 70. 78. ἀπαντήσαντες,
having come to oppose : 4,
89. ταῖς ναυσὶν, to meet (by
appointment:) 7, 2. ὡς ἀπαν-
τησόμενα ἐξῆλθον, to go out to
meet any one: 7, 1. ἐς τι
χωρίον, to meet at an ap-
pointed place, 35. ἐς τὸ αὐτὸ,
31. αὐτῷ, to meet, encounter
(amicably :) 6, 34. ἀπαντῆσαι,
to go to meet, to confront: 7,
2. ἀπαντησόμενοι, having intention to meet: 5, 38. to meet,
fall in with : 7, 22. ἀπήντων
ἐπὶ τὰς—, to go against (an
enemy,) to go to meet: 4,
127.

ἀπαξιόω, 1, 5. to disdain,
scorn (a thing.)

ἀπαραιτήτως, 3, 84. incura-
bly.

ἀπαράκλητος, 2, 98. unin-
vited, voluntary, Schol. ἑκού-
σιοι.

ἀπαράσκευος, 6, 84. un
armed, Apparatu belli carens:

1, 69. 80. unprepared, 3, 4.
18. 5, 9.

ἀπαράσσω, 7, 63. ἀπαράξητε,
to dash, beat, drive, sweep
from.

ἀπαρίθμησις, 5, 20. a reck-
oning, computation, sum-
mary.

ἀπαρνοῦμαι, 6, 56. ἀπαρνηθέντα τὴν πείρασιν, to decline.

ἀπαρτάω, 6, 21. ἐς ἀλλοτρίαν
πᾶσαν (γῆν sc.) ἀπαρτήσαντες,
to depart from, to set out.

ἀπαρχὴ, 3, 58. 6, 20. tithes,
first-fruits, tribute.

ἄπας, 7, 69. ὑπὲρ ἁπάντων
παραπλήσια, alike for all, 58.
ἅπαντας, altogether: 5, 9. 38. :
4, 100. ἅπασαν κεραίαν ἐκοίλαναν, to hollow throughout:
2, 13. 4, 68.

ἀπατάω, 3, 38. ἀπατᾶσθαι, to
be deceived, gulled : 5, 9.
ἀπατήσας, having deceived,
out-manœuvred, 85. ἀπατη-
θῶσι, to be led astray, 16.
ἠπατημένων, being over-
reached, deceived : 2, 39.
ἀπατηθέντες ἐξ ὁμολογίας, to be
deceived through a composition, a feigned agreement:
5, 46.

ἀπάτη, 4, 46. 86. ἢ βίᾳ ἢ
ἀπάτῃ, by force or fraud : 1,
55. deceit, manœuvre, 34. :
7, 74. à cheat, deception.

ἄπαυστος, 2, 49. δίψῃ ξυνεχόμενοι, to be seized, possessed
with unconquerable, insati-
able thirst.

ἀπαυτομολέω, 7, 75. ἀπηυτο-
μόλησαν, to have deserted.

ἀπάχθομαι, 1, 75. ἀπηχθημένους, to be regarded with hostility: 2, 53. Καὶ κινδύνου ὧν ἐν τῇ ἀρχῇ ἀπήχθεσθε, ob offensas in imperia contractas.

ἄπεδος, 7, 78. plain, even.

ἀπείδω, 7, 71. ἀπιδόντες, i. q. σκοποῦντες, βλέψαντες, to look from one place to another, 4, 18. looking upon, beholding.

ἀπιθής, disobedient, 2, 84. ἀπιθεστέρας τὰς ναῦς παρεῖχον, more unmanageable.

ἀπεικότως, 1, 73. unreasonably, improperly: 2, 8. οὐκ, not without reason, as was natural, to be expected: 6, 55. Abs re, Immerito, without reason.

ἀπειλέω, 8, 33. ἀπειλήσας, to menace.

ἀπειλή, a threat, 4, 126. 8, 40.

ἄπειμι, 5, 44. ἀπόντες, being away, 1, 141. ἀπὸ τῶν ἰδίων, to be absent from their domestic, private business, concerns, labours: 6, 24. ἀπούσης, far off, remote: 5, 37. ἀπιόντες, returning, coming away: 6, 10. ἀπιοῦσιν, turning away, 36. ἀνῄεσαν, to be on the way back: 2, 46. 8, 87.

ἀπεῖπον, 5, 32. to reject, refuse, 43. ἀπειπόντος, to renounce: 7, 60. ἀπειπεῖν, to forbid, 5, 23. ἀπειπεῖν, to annul, deny, negative, 6, 99. ἀπειπεῖν, to renounce.

ἀπείργω, 4, 89. ἀπείρξαντες, to keep off: 2, 30. ἀπείργειν τινα ἢ μαθήματος ἢ θεσμῶν, to debar, exclude any one from

schools, spectacles, or simply, from learning or getting sight of any thing, from any thing to be learned or seen: 2, 53. ἀπείργει, to restrain, withhold: 3, 45. ἀπείρξει, to prevent: 4, 37.

ἀπειρία, 1, 80. ὥστε μήτε ἀπειρίᾳ ἐπιθυμῆσαί τινα τοῦ ἔργου, μήτε ἀγαθὸν καὶ ἀσφαλὲς νομίσαντα, neither from inexperience nor from conjecture; the dat. put in the sense of the Latin abl. answering to the question, from what? whence? Matth. Gr. Gr. 567. the part. stands for various conjunctions with the finite verb, here in assigning a reason, because, 865. : 2, 8. ὑπὸ ἀπειρίας, from inexperience, 89. want of skill: 4, 114. ἀπειρίᾳ (πεφοβῆσθαι) 7, 21. want of skill, inexperience.

ἀπειρόκακος, 5, 105. τὸ ἀ. simplicity.

ἄπειρος, 1, 141. χρονίων πολέμων, inexperienced in wars long-protracted, of long continuance: 2, 4. ignorant of, unable to find: 6, 1. uninformed, ignorant: 4, 29. τῆς χώρας, unacquainted with: 1, 49. ἀπειρότεροι, rather unskilfully: 2, 35. one unacquainted with any thing, opposed to ξυνειδώς: 1, 72. ὧν ἄπειροι ἦσαν, of what they were ignorant: 8, 61. ἀπειρότατος.

ἀπελαύνω, 6, 56. ἀπήλασαν, to reject, spurn, 8, 45. ἀπήλασεν, drove away.

ἀπεοικότως, 6, 55. see ἀπεικότως, Matth. Gr. Gr. 352.

ἀπέραντος, 4, 36. Ἐπειδὴ δὲ ἀπέραντον ἦν, interminable.

ἀπερέω, 1, 121. ἀπεροῦσιν, to refuse, to deny to pay: 1, 29. ἀπεροῦντο μὴ πλεῖν, to forbid from sailing: 5, 48. ἀπείρηντο.

ἀπερίοπτος, 1, 41. ἀπάντων παρὰ τὸ νικᾶν, regardless or careless of every thing in comparison of victory.

ἀπερίσκεπτος, 6, 65. ἀπερισκεπτότερον, too incautiously, rashly: 4, 108. ἐλπίδι.

ἀπερισκέπτως, 4, 10. thoughtlessly, recklessly, carelessly: 6, 57. without regard to any thing, without consideration.

ἀπέρχομαι, 2, 34. 7, 13. : 5, 13. ἀπεληλυθότων, having departed: 6, 18. ἀπελθεῖν, 5, 8. 7, 48. : 5, 10. ἀπελθών, having made one's departure, 1, 24. 5, 4. : 1, 134. ἀπῆλθον, 5, 3. 27. 33. 37. 54. 56. 7, 48. : 8, 63. πυθόμενος τὸν Στρομβιχίδην καὶ τὰς ναῦς ἀπεληλυθότα, (here the participle is governed in gender and number by one only of the substantives, which rule sometimes obtains, Matth. Gr. Gr. 641. :) 1, 89. Ἀθηναίων τὸ κοινὸν, ἐπειδὴ αὐτοῖς οἱ βάρβαροι ἐκ τῆς χώρας ἀπῆλθον, διεκομίζοντο—παῖδας, the dat. is put for the accus. in reference to the verb ἀπῆλθον instead of the noun χώρας, Matth. Gr. Gr. 548. : 6, 86.

ἀπέφθος, 2, 13. refined.

ἀπέχθομαι, 1, 75. καὶ οὐκ ἀσφαλὲς ἔτι ἐδόκει εἶναι, τοῖς

πολλοῖς ἀπηχθημένους—ἀνιέναι κινδυνεύειν, the tenses of the defective verb ἀπεχθάνομαι, to hate, are from ἀπέχθομαι, whence the perf. ἀπήχθημαι, Matth. Gr. Gr. 315.

ἀπέχω, 3, 20. οὐ πολὺ, to be not far distant off, 2, 21. 5, 2. 6. 7, 34. 4, 35. 67. ἀπεῖχεν, 103. 8, 11. 5, 3. ἀποσχών, being distant: 1, 49. ἀπεχομένῳ, to hold off: 4, 37. Ἱερῶν τῶν ἐνόντων ἀπέχεσθαι, to refrain from, to abstain: 1, 20. 5, 25. ἀπέσχοντο, to refrain, avoid, hold off: 8, 92.

ἀπηλιώτης, 3, 23. an easterly wind.

ἀπιάλλω, 5, 77. the Doric form for ἐπιπέμπω, στέλλω, Schol.

ἀπιστέω, 7, 44. to distrust, doubt: 1, 10. ἀπιστοίη, to be incredulous, to disbelieve: 6, 33. ἀπιστήσαντες, to disbelieve: 1, 91. ἀπιστῆσαι: 3, 37. ἀπιστοῦντες τῇ ἑαυτῶν ξυνέσει, to be diffident of, to distrust one's own abilities, wisdom, 40. ἀπιστοῦντες μὴ εἶναι τοὺς παραδόντας τοῖς τεθνεῶσιν ὁμοίους, the infin. is put after verbs ' to say' and ' to deny,' and μὴ is sometimes inserted before the infin., Matth. Gr. Gr. 802. : 5, 88. ἠπιστεῖτο : 6, 49. ἀπιστεῖν σφᾶς μὴ ἕξειν : 7, 28. ἠπίστησεν, to be ignorant of, inexperienced in : 8, 83.

ἀπιστία, 3, 75. want of confidence : 7, 75. distrust : 1, 10. incredulity : 8, 66.

ἄπιστος, 1, 23. 6, 31. in-

credible : 1, 120. θράσει, a
groundless confidence: 5,16.
ἀπιστότερος, less likely to be
believed : 1, 68. ἀπιστοτέρους,
more incredulous : 5, 89.
ἄπιστον μῆκος λόγων, a monstrous length of speech: 3,
113. 8, 66. : 4, 18. ἀπιστότατος.

ἀπισχυρίζω, 1, 140. ἀπισχυ-
ρισάμενοι, to give a decided,
firm refusal, stiff denial.

ἄπλοια, 2, 85. 6, 22. in-
ability to proceed on a voyage from being weather-
bound, being laid up in
port, difficulty of navigation: 4, 4.

ἀπλόος, 3, 18. τείχει, a
single wall, 7, 4. 11.

ἄπλοος, 7, 34. ἐποίησαν, to
disable : 7, 60. Ὅσαι ἦσαν καὶ
δυναταὶ καὶ ἀπλοώτεραι, less
serviceable, fit for sailing,
fit for service, either from
being damaged or wanting
hands to man them.

ἀπλῶς, 3, 38. 45. plainly,
frankly, simply, in a word :
7, 34. absolutely.

ἀπὸ, 3, 36. ἀπὸ βραχείας
διανοίας, from or in pursu-
ance of a brief, hasty deliberation, plan, design : 3,
10. ἀπὸ τοῦ ἴσου ἡγοῦντο, to
lead in fairness, to conduct
(matters) fairly, on equal
terms, on an equal footing :
3, 38. ἀπὸ τῶν λόγῳ καλῶς
ἐπιτιμησάντων (τὸ ἀκουσθὲν,)
from (the mouth of) those,
who censure with : elo-
quence : 3, 48. ἀπὸ τῶν παραι-
νουμένων, from or upon con-

sideration of the advice : 6,
19. ἀπὸ μὲν τῶν αὐτῶν λόγων
οὐκ ἂν ἔτι ἀποτρέψειε, by,
through, by means of : 3, 11.
ἀφ' ἡμῶν ἤρξαντο, to begin
from or with any one : 7, 23,
ἀπὸ πρώτου ὕπνου, (beginning)
with the first watch : 7, 29.
ἀφ' ἑσπέρας, (beginning) with
the evening, at the close,
shutting in of evening : 3,
36. ἄλλαι γνῶμαι ἀφ' ἑκάστων
ἐλέγοντο, to be spoken, delivered by each, (this use is
rare, it is generally ὑπὸ,
Matth. Gr. Gr. 710. 880. :)
5, 17. : 3, 5. ἀπὸ τῶν Μυτιληναίων, on the side of, on the
part of, 7, 13. ἀπὸ πολεμίων :
1, 76. ἀπὸ τοῦ ἀνθρωπείου τρόπου, beside or unlike the
usual manner of men : 1, 71.
ἀπὸ τῆς πολυπειρίας, from,
owing to, much experience :
6, 27. μηνύεται ἀπὸ μετοίκων,
information is given by : 3,
43. ἀπὸ τοῦ εὐθέος λεγόμενα, to
be spoken readily, straightforward, sine ambagibus : 3,
46. φυλακὴν ἀπὸ τῶν νόμων τῆς
δεινότητος ποιεῖσθαι, to watch
over, to keep in allegiance
by the terror of laws : 1, 3.
ἀφ' ἑαυτῶν, from themselves,
out of themselves : 6, 61. ἀπὸ
ξυνθήματος ἥκειν, to be come
in consequence of, upon an
appointment : 1, 144. Οὐκ
ἀπὸ τοσῶνδε ὁρμώμενοι, not
commencing with such great
advantages : 1, 124. ἀφ' ἡσυ-
χίας, out of a love of ease;
126. ἀπὸ τούτου, from or

owing to this circumstance:
7, 48. ἀπὸ τοῦ τείχους, (to
fight) on or from the wall:
4, 68. ἀφ' ἑαυτοῦ γνώμης, of
his own head: 1, 103. ἀπὸ
τοῦδε, from this time: 7, 29.
ἀπ' αὐτῶν βλάψαι, through, by
means of: 1, 74. from, as, to
set off from a place: 7, 63.
ἀπὸ τῶν καταστρωμάτων (παρα-
σκευήν,) i. e. ἐπὶ τῶν κ,: 1, 17.
ἀπ' αὐτῶν, by them: 1, 110.
ἀπὸ πολλῶν, (a few) out of
many: 7, 10. ἀπὸ γλώττης
ἔφητο αὐτοῖς, to give orders to
any one by word of mouth,
verbally: 7, 44. ἀπ' ἀμφοτέρων,
from or on both sides: 7, 22.
ἀπὸ ξυνθήματος, from or by or
according to agreement: 1,
77. ἀπὸ τοῦ ἴσου ὁμιλεῖν, to
associate with us upon an
equality: 5, 60. ἀφ' ἑαυτῶν,
καὶ οὐ τοῦ πλήθους κελεύσαντος,
of their own authority, out
of their own heads, an instance of the use of a prep.
which with the gen. gives
this phrase the meaning,
from one's own inclination,
of one's self, Matth. 879.: 7,
56. ἀπὸ τῶν παρόντων, through,
on account of present circumstances, from the pre-
sent posture of things: 1, 11,
ἀφ' ὧν, in consequence of
which: 7, 70. ἀπὸ τῶν ναυτῶν
προθυμία, ardour from, i. e.
on the part of, the sailors,
60. ἀπὸ τοῦ ἄλλου, from, out
of the number of, with the
rest of, 57. ἀπὸ ξυμμαχίας
αὐτόνομοι, (independent) ac-

cording to the alliance, i. e.
from the provisions of the
alliance, 62. ἀπὸ τῶν νεῶν πε-
ζομαχίᾳ, a land-fight from,
i. e. on ship-board, as μάχεσθαι ἀφ' ἵππων, 41, ἀπὸ τῶν
καταστρωμάτων, from i. e. on
the decks, 21. ἀπ' αὐτοῦ τι ἐς
τὸν πόλεμον κατεργάσασθαι,
through or by means of it
to effect something, strike
a blow conducive to the war,
promote the success of the
war, 30. ἀπὸ τριακοσίων, out
of (a number) 2. ἀπὸ τῆς
ἱπποτροφίας ὅπως θαυμασθῇ, on
account of breeding horses,
of a breed of horses, 78. ἀπὸ
τῶν ἱππέων, owing to, in consequence of (the attacks of)
cavalry: 1, 46. ἀπὸ θαλάσσης,
away from the sea, 63. ἀπὸ
τῆς διώξεως, from the pursuit
(to return from,) 24. ἀπὸ πολέμου τινὸς, in consequence
of a certain war: 3, 24. ἄνδρες
διακόσιοι ἀπὸ πλειόνων, two
hundred men out of a greater
number: 5, 20. ἀπὸ τιμῆς, by
the office of any one, post of
dignity and trust: 4, 105.
ἀπ' αὐτοῦ δύνασθαι, to derive
an influence from that circumstance: 2, 93. 8, 82. ἀπὸ
τοῦ προφανοῦς, openly, Palam,
it is here used with an adj.
in the gen. for an adverb,
although the proper reference does not take place to
the meaning of ἀπὸ, Matth.
879.: 3, 88. ἀπὸ τῶν εὖ εἰπόν-
των σκοπαύντες, to judge from
(the words of) according to

good speakers : 5, 26. ἀπὸ χρησμῶν τι ἰσχυρισάμενοι, putting any faith in oracles, relying in any degree on oracles : 3, 64. μὴ προφέρετε τὴν τότε γενομένην ξυμμοσίαν ὡς χρὴ ἀπ᾽ αὐτῆς νῦν σώζεσθαι, the use of the prep. with the gen. is here instead of the dat. alone, to signify the mean or instrument, Matth. 566.; 7, 10. : cum gen. " 2, 77. 3, 11. 64. ἀπὸ μικρᾶς δαπάνης, with little expense, 1, 91. 8, 87." Matth. 566. : 1, 125. ἐπειδὴ ἀφ᾽ ἁπάντων ἤκουσαν γνώμην, the sense of the gen. here expresses the person, from whom any thing proceeds, particularly with the verbs to hear, founded on the principle that it expresses the person, to whom any thing belongs, Matth. 521. : 2, 62. 3, 64. 5, 17. 6, 12. on account of, Matth. 879. : 4, 14. οἱ Ἀθηναῖοι—ἀπὸ νεῶν ἐπεζομάχουν, whereas ἀπὸ with the gen. signifies a removal, it arises that from the idiom of ἀπὸ placed with the measures of the distance, it is also used where the direction of the action is from one place to another, Matth. 878.

ἀπόβαθρον, 4, 12. gangway.

ἀποβαίνω, 2, 25. ἀποβάντες ἐς Μεθώνην, having sailed to Methone and disembarked : 4, 31. ἀπέβαινον, to debark, 1, 50. 45. 4, 9. 12. 29. 8, 10. : 4, 39. ἀπέβη, to be accom-

plished : 2, 87. τῷ ἀποβάντι τῆς ξυμφορᾶς, the event happening of a misfortune, a misfortune happening : 3, 38. ἀποβησόμενα ἐξ αὐτῶν, the consequence of any thing, which will result from, 1, 39. τὰ ἀποβαίνοντα, the consequences, 5, 14. ἀποβαίνοντος, resulting, 2, 50. τοῦ ἀποβαίνοντος, a thing, that has taken place, a circumstance, effect : 3, 93. ἀπέβη, to turn out, 53. μὴ οὐ κοινοὶ ἀποβῆτε, lest you may not turn out impartial, depart with clean hands : 1, 100. ἀπέβησαν ἐς τὴν γῆν, to disembark and go on land.

ἀποβάλλω, 4, 7. ἀπέβαλε πολλοὺς (τῶν στρατιωτῶν,) to lose : 1, 63. ἀποβαλὼν, to lose (as the killed in an engagement :) 2, 33. ἀποβάλλουσι ἄνδρας σφῶν αὐτῶν, to lose certain of their own men.

ἀπόβασις, 2, 26. ποιεῖσθαι, to make a descent upon a country, 33. ἐς τὴν γῆν : 3, 7. ἀπόβασιν ἐς Νηρίκην ποιησάμενος, to make a descent upon, 4, 54 : 6, 75. a landing, 4, 10. 13. a debarking : 4, 108. ἐν ἀποβάσει τῆς γῆς, in the departure from the country, from the idiom, the gen. put objectively, arises that in certain passages substantives derived from verbs which, or corresponding to such as take the obj. in the dat. are constructed with the gen. Matth. Gr. Gr. 450.

ἀποϐιϐάζω, 7, 29. ἀπεϐίϐασεν ἐς τὴν Τάναγραν, to land men at a place, to debark.

ἀποϐλέπω, 3, 58. ἀποϐλέψατε ἐς θήκας, to cast your eyes upon the sepulchres.

ἀπογίγνομαι, 2, 34. ἀπογινομένων, the departed (from life:) 1, 39. ἀπογενόμενοι, to be apart from ἁμαρτημάτων, from injustice, to have been free from it: 2, 98. 5, 74.

ἀπόγνοια, 3, 85. despair.

ἀπόγονος, 1, 101. a descendant of.

ἀποδασμὸς, 1, 12. a portion, division.

ἀποδείκνυμι, 1, 26. ἀποδεικνύντες, to point out: 7, 57. ἀποδεικνυμένους, πολεμίους σφίσιν, being shown: 1, 35. ἀποδείκνυμεν, to prove, shew: 7, 48. ἀποδεικνύναι τῷ λόγῳ, to confess by word of mouth, declare, make known in so many words: 4, 85. ἀποδεικνύναι, to shew, offer, exhibit: 1, 129. ἀποδεῖξαι, to shew, point out, 2, 72. ἀποδείξατε: 1, 87. ἀποδεικνυμένους, to display publicly: 5, 27. ἀποδεῖξαι, to open one's mind, explain one's views: 7, 64. ἀποδειξάμενος, to display, manifest: 2, 15. ἀποδείξας, to appoint: 1, 6. ἀποδείξεις, to demonstrate: 8, 89.

ἀπόδειξις, a narration of a history, 1, 97. ἅμα δὲ καὶ τῆς ἀρχῆς ἀπόδειξιν ἔχει τῆς τῶν Ἀθηναίων, ἐν οἵῳ τρόπῳ κατέστη, an instance of the constr. of the nomin. "the subject is also constructed with the preceding verb in other cases besides the accus." Matth. Gr. Gr. 429.: 2, 13. ἐς ἀπόδειξιν τοῦ περιέσεσθαι, for a demonstration, in order to shew that they were likely to be superior.

ἀποδέχομαι, 7, 48. ἀποδέξονται, to be well received: 3, 57. ἀποδέξωνται, to approve: 3, 3. ἀπεδέχοντο τὰς κατηγορίας, to entertain, listen to: 5, 83. ἀπεδέχοντο, to receive, take a fugitive: 3, 4. ἀπεδέξαντο, to hearken to, consult, accept (a proposition,) 1, 44. to listen to and be somewhat persuaded by a speech, 5, 26. 6, 53. ἀποδεχόμενοι πάντας, to admit, listen to: 6, 29. ἀποδέχεσθαι διαϐολὰς, to receive, listen to, admit; 41.

ἀποδέω, 2, 13. ἀποδέοντα τριακοσίων, all but three hundred, 4, 38. ὀκτὼ, wanting eight, Matth. Gr. Gr. 174.

ἀποδημητὴς, 1, 70. a roamer, rambler.

ἀποδιδράσκω, 5, 65. ἀποδιδράσκοντας, to be running away: 4, 46. ἀποδιδράναι, to get away, make off: 7, 86. ἀποδρᾷ, to make our excuse, run away: 1, 128. ἀπέδρασαν αὐτὸν, to escape, flee from him, run away from, this verb takes an accus. of the object, to which the action has only generally an immediate reference, Matth. Gr. Gr. 578.: 4, 46. 5, 65.

ἀποδίδωμι, 4, 14. ἀπέδοσαν, 23. to restore: 5, 17. ἀποδιδόντας, 35. ἀποδεδώκεσαν, 42.:

3, 52. ἀποδίδοσθαι, to restore: 4, 16. ἀποδοῦναι, to render back, make restitution: 3, 63. ἀποδιδομένας ἐς ἀδικίαν, to return (a just debt) in an unjust manner, at the expence of justice: 4, 65. ἀποδοῦσιν, disbursing, paying: 7, 83. Μέχρις οὗ δ' ἂν τὰ χρήματα ἀποδοθῇ, until the money were paid: 5, 21. ἀποδιδόναι, to release, set free: 3, 36. Τινὰς σφίσιν ἀποδοῦναι βουλεύσασθαι, to give a (second) opportunity of deliberating to restore, recall: 5, 35. ἀποδεδωκότες, having restored, dismissed: 1, 63. ἀπέδοσαν, to sell, 29. ἀποδόσθαι, to sell for slaves, 55. ἀπέδοντο, 5, 14. to release: 4, 116. ἀπέδωκεν ἐς τὸ ἱερὸν, to award: 2, 71. Πλαταιεῦσι γῆν καὶ πόλιν τὴν σφετέραν ἔχοντας αὐτονόμους οἰκεῖν, to resign, restore to the Platæans their land and city to have and to hold in freedom, that they might have and hold: 7, 10. ἀπέδοσαν, to deliver, give up: 2, 5. ἀποδώσειν, to restore, 5, 39.: 5, 14. ἀποδώσει, to trust to, commit one's self to: 2, 40. ἀποδώσων, to return, repay: 5, 18. ἀποδιδόντων, of verbs in μι the 3rd pers. plur. of the imper. pass. and aor. 2. is as in verbs in ω frequently —ντων for —τωσαν, Matth. Gr. Gr. 281.: 8, 106.

ἀποδιώκω, 3, 108. ἀπεδίωξαν, to pursue off the field.

ἀπόδοσις, 5, 35. the surrender, delivery, restoration.

ἀποδοχὴ, 4, 81. χωρίων, restitution.

ἀποδύντες, 1, 6. to strip.

ἀποζῆν, 1, 2. to live from, get subsistence from, ὅσον ἀποζῆν, as much as would suffice for subsistence.

ἄποθεν, 4, 125. apart at a distance, 92. at a distance, remote: 8, 69.

ἀποθήκη, 6, 57. a military chest.

ἀποθνήσκω, 5, 10. to die, to be killed: 1, 20. ἀποθανεῖν, to be slain, 9. ὑπὸ Ἡρακλειδῶν ἀποθανόντος, to be slain by the Heraclidæ: 1, 63. 4, 68. ἄπέθανον, to perish, 7, 30.: 5, 51. ἀπέθανε, to be slain (in battle).

ἀποικία, 1, 12. a colony, 4, 7. 5, 11.

ἀποικίζω, 1, 24. ἀπῴκισαν, to colonize.

ἀποικοδομέω, 1, 134. ἀπῳκοδόμησαν, to build up, wall in: 7, 73. ἀποικοδομῆσαι τὰς ὁδοὺς, to block up, build up.

ἄποικος, 7, 57. a colonist.

ἀποκάθαρσις, 2, 49. χολῆς, a purging, evacuation, throwing up.

ἀποκαλέω, 5, 34. ἀπεκαλοῦντο, to send for.

ἀποκαυλίζω, 2, 76. ἀπεκαύλιζε, properly to break the stem of any thing, to break off.

ἀποκινδυνεύω, 3, 39. ἀποκεκινδυνεύσεται, to be hazarded, endangered: 7, 67. ἀποκινδυνεύσαι, 81.

ἀποκλείω, 5, 80. ἀπέκλῃσε τὰς πύλας, to shut the gates against them, ἀποκεκλεισμένων,

enclosed, shut up : 4, 34.
ἀποκεκλημένοι τοῦ ὁρᾶν, hindered, prohibited : 3, 109.
ἀποκεκλεισμένος, blocked out,
shut out : 6, 64. ἀποκλείσαν,
to cut off, intercept, 34.
ἀποκλειομένους, to be excluded, i. e. prevented, deterred,
101. ἀποκλῦσασθαι τῆς διαβά-
σεως, to cut off, intercept
their passage : 8, 42. ἀπε-
κλείοντο, were cut off from,
shut out from : 2, 176.

ἀπόκλεισις, 4, 85. μοῦ τῶν
πυλῶν, exclusion, Matth. Gr.
Gr. 569. : 6, 99. an intercep-
tion, exclusion.

ἀποκληρόω, 4, 8. ἀποκληρώ-
σαντες, having selected them
by lot : 8, 70.

ἀπόκλῃσις, 7, 60. a barring
up, closing up the mouth of
the harbour.

ἀποκνέω, 4, 11. to make a
difficulty, have a fear : 6, 18,
ἀποκνοῖμεν, to shrink from
(any thing pusillanimously,)
to refuse to undertake (any
thing:) 3, 20. ἀπόκνησαν, to
shrink from (an attempt,) desist from (any thing through
fear,) to give up, 55. ἀποκνεῖτε,
to hang back, loiter behind :
8, 12. ἀποκνῆσαι, to give up :
7, 21. ἀποκνεῖν, to be deterred
by fear, to keep aloof from
fear, 6, 92. : 3, 30. ἀποκνή-
σωμεν τὸν κίνδυνον, to shrink
from the danger.

ἀπόκνησις, 1, 99. a hanging
back, reluctance to engage.

ἀποκολυμβάω, 4, 25. ἀποκο-
λυμβησάντων, having swum.

ἀποκομιδή, 1, 137. a retreat,
a getting conveyed away.

ἀποκομίζω, 7, 26. ἀπεκομίζετο,
to betake one's self home :
5, 10. 8, 19. ἀπεκομίσθησαν,
to return, 6, 52. to return,
betake one's self back, 4,
109. to be carried to, conveyed, 96. κατὰ θάλασσαν ἐπ'
οἴκου : 3, 81. ἀποκομίζονται, to
make off, get away : 8, 23.
ἀπεκομίσθη, returned.

ἀπόκρημνος, 4, 36. abrupt,
precipitous, 6, 96.

ἀποκρίνω, 5, 32. 85. ἀπεκρίνατο, to answer, 1, 28. 54.
7, 10. ἀπεκρίνοντο, 44. ἀπο-
κρίναιντο, 5, 42. ἀποκρινάμενοι,
112. 1, 90. to send an answer
back. : 1, 3. ἀποκεκρίσθαι, to
be separated, distinguished
by being apart : 8, 61. τοὺς
μὲν λόγους οὐκ ἂν ἡγησάμεθα
εἰπεῖν, εἰ καὶ αὐτοὶ βραχέως τὸ
ἐρωτηθὲν ἀπεκρίναντο, whereas
in the use of a double
accus. after a verb active,
the 2nd. accus. is often to be
explained by a prep. so in
the phrase ἀποκρίνεσθαί τι, to
answer to any thing for πρός
τι, Matth. Gr. Gr. 588.

ἀπόκροτος, 7, 27. ἐν γῇ,
rough, rugged, rocky.

ἀποκρούω, 7, 43. ἀπεκρούοντο,
to be beaten off : 2, 4, 4, 115.
ἀπεκρούσαντο, to drive off, repel, repulse, 107. ἀπεκρούσθη,
to be repelled : 8, 100.

ἀποκρύπτω, 5, 65. ἀπέκρυψαν,
(the Lacedæmonians) hid
(the Argians) i. e. vanished
from their sight, Virg. Æn.

3, 291. *Phaeacum abscondimus arces :* 2, 53. Ἁ πρότερον ἀπεκρύπτετο μὴ καθ' ἡδονὴν ποιεῖν, to conceal one's doing a thing for pleasure's sake, to dissemble one's pleasure in doing any thing : 7, 85. ὅσους μὴ ἀπεκρύψαντο, (as many prisoners,) as they did not conceal (for their own slaves.)

ἀποκτείνω, 1, 20. 30. 126. 4, 25. 5, 32. ἀπέκτειναν, to slay, kill, 2, 5. : 1, 53. ἀποκτεῖναι : 7, 30. 8, 10. ἀποκτείνουσιν : 7, 41. ἀποκτείναντες : 2, 5. ἀποκτενεῖν : 3, 41. 68.

ἀποκωλύω, 3, 28. ἀποκωλύσειν, to prevent, hinder : 1, 72. ἀποκωλύοι, to hinder, to be an obstacle.

ἀπολαμβάνω, 5, 8. ἀπολαβεῖν, to find, catch, 39. ἀπολάβοιεν Πάνακτον, to get back, recover, 35. : 5, 36. 6, 2. ἀπολαβόντες, to seize, take possession of, occupy, get back : 7, 60. ἀπολαβόντες διατειχίσματι, to take in, surround with a wall : 4, 45. ἀπολαβόντες, having cut across, 7, 51. ἀπολαμβάνουσι, to intercept, cut off, 1, 134. ἀπολαβόντες εἴσω, to cut off from egress, fasten up within : 4, 113. ἀπειλημμένον ἐν στενῷ ἰσθμῷ, having been cut off, intercepted : 6, 87. ἀπολαβόντες, *excerpere,* to pick out : 4, 14. ἀπειλημμένων, to be cut off, separated, 120. : 2, 4. ἀπειλημμένους, to be caught, intercepted : 4, 102. ἀπολαβὼν

τείχει μακρῷ, to build, part off : 1, 7. ἀπελάμβανον, to occupy, take up : 8, 13. ἀποληφθεῖσαι, intercepted, 5, 54. ἀπειληφέναι, to be intercepted : 6, 22. ἀπολαμβανώμεθα ὑπὸ ἀπλοίας, to be overtaken, caught, stopped, detained : 2, 90. ἀπολήψεσθαι, to intercept.

ἀπόλαυσις, 2, 42. τὴν ἔτι ἀ., the further enjoyment, 38.

ἀπολαύω, 7, 27. τῆς γῆς, to enjoy the fruits of, to possess : 1, 70. ἀπολαύουσιν : 2, 53.

ἀπολέγω, 4, 9. ἀπολεξάμενος, having selected, chosen, 5, 8. : 4, 70. ἀπολέξας.

ἀπολείπω, 1, 2. 2, 16. 3, 9. ἀπολείποντας, to forsake, desert : 4, 100. ἀπολιπόντας, getting off (the wall,) quitting : 3, 64. ἀπελίπετε, to forsake (a thing :) 8, 15. ἀπολιπούσαι, having left : 7, 70. βραχὺ γὰρ ἀπέλιπον γενέσθαι, to want little to be, to be very nearly, Matth. Gr. Gr. 431. : 5, 3. ἀπολιπὼν, quitting, getting away from, abandoning : 3, 10. ἡμῖν δὲ καὶ Ἀθηναίοις ξυμμαχία ἐγένετο πρῶτον, ἀπολιπόντων μὲν ὑμῶν ἐκ τοῦ Μηδικοῦ πολέμου, παραμεινάντων δὲ ἐκείνων πρὸς τὰ ὑπόλοιπα τῶν ἔργων, an instance of the confounding of verbs, here a transitive for a neuter, in the sense to depart, Matth. 719. : 8, 22. ἀπολείποντες, remitting.

ἀπόλειψις, 4, 126. a desertion.

H

ἀπόλεκτος, 6, 68. picked, choice.

ἀπόληψις, 7, 54. intercepting, cutting off from, Matth. Gr. Gr. 401.

ἀπολισθαίνω, 7, 65. to slip, glide off, not to stick, cleave.

ἀπόλλυμι, 7, 48. Ἐπ᾽ αἰσχρᾷ τε αἰτίᾳ καὶ ἀδίκως ὑπ᾽ Ἀθηναίων ἀπολέσθαι μᾶλλον ἢ ὑπὸ τῶν πολεμίων, εἰ δεῖ, κινδυνεύσας τοῦτο παθεῖν ἰδίᾳ, to perish, to be put to death, to suffer any thing by means of, from: 4, 25. ἀπολλύουσι, to lose, 2, 75. ἀπόλλυσι (τὰς ναῦς,) 25. ἀπολέσας: 7, 28. ἀπώλλυντο αἱ πρόσοδοι, to decay, decrease, 44. 45. 2, 4. ἀπώλλυτο, 7, 28. to be lost: 4, 25. ἀπώλεσαν, to lose: 7, 30. ἀπώλετο, to be killed: 1, 123. ἀπολέσθαι, to lose, to be lost: 4, 71. ἀπόληται, to be ruined: 7, 13. ἀπολλυμένων, to be cut off, killed, 2, 53. ἐν ἴσῳ, equally, alike: 7, 27. ἀπολώλει, to be lost: 2, 65. 7, 75. ἀπολωλεκότες: 8, 42. ἀπολλύασι, they lost, 55.

Ἀπολλώνιον, the temple of Apollo, 2, 91. in such gentiles ιον is often interchanged with ειον in the same word, Matth. Gr. Gr. 137.

ἀπολογέομαι, 1, 72. ἀπολογησομένους, to make a defence, to apologize: 5, 21. 44. ἀπολογησόμενον, about to explain away, to apologize for: 3, 62. ἀπολογούμεθα, to say in defence: 8, 109.

ἀπολογία, 3, 61. a defence:

6, 53. an answer to an accusation.

ἀπολοφύρομαι, 2, 46. ἀπολοφυράμενοι, to have done lamenting, to make an end of it.

ἀπολύω, 4, 69. ἀπολυθῆναι, to be set free, to be dismissed, to be released, delivered: 5, 75. ἀπελύσαντο, to wipe away: 7 44. ἀπελύοντο, to be parted from: 1, 70. ἀπολυθήσεσθαι τῶν δεινῶν, to be delivered, freed from dangers: 6, 29. ἀπολυθείη, to be acquitted, absolved: 1, 49. ἀπελύοντο, to be separated: 7, 56. ἀπολύεσθαι φόβου, to be released from fear: 3, 39. ἀπολύσητε, to acquit, 1, 95. ἀπολύεται, to be acquitted (of guilt,) 1, 128. ἀπελύθη: 8, 87.

ἀπομάχομαι, 1, 90. ὥστε ἀπομάχεσθαι, (high enough) to fight from (it.)

ἀπομισθόω, 3, 68. ἀπεμίσθωσαν ἐπὶ δέκα ἔτη, to let out (to him) for ten years.

ἀπομνάομαι, 1, 137. ἀπομνήσεσθαι, to remember, bear in mind (a favour.)

ἀπομονόω, 3, 28. ἀπομονωθήσονται τῆς ξυμβάσεως, to be excluded from the composition.

ἀπομόσαι, 5, 50. to swear.

ἀπόνοια, 1, 82. despair: 7, 67. ἐς ἀπόνοιαν καθεστήκασιν, to be reduced to mad folly, desperation.

ἀπονοέω, 7, 81. τὸ ἀποκινδυνεύειν πρὸς ἀνθρώπους ἀπονενοημένους, to run risk against men reduced to despair.

ἄπονος, 1, 11. ἀπονώτερον, with less difficulty, labour.

ἀπονοστέω, 7, 87. ἐπ᾿ οἴκου, to return home.

ἀπόνως, 5, 91. without trouble, labour : 2, 36.

ἀποξηραίνω, 7, 12. ἀποξηρᾶναι, i. q. διαψύξαι, to dry.

ἀπόπειρα, 7, 21. Καὶ ναυμαχίας ἀπόπειραν λαμβάνειν, a trial, attempt.

ἀποπειράω, 7, 36. ἀποπειράσαι, to try, make an essay, 43. : 4, 24. 107. ἀποπειράσας, having ventured an attack, made an attempt, 121. ἀποπειράσαι τῆς Μένδης, to make an attempt upon : 7, 12. ἀποπειρώμεναι, 17. ὅπως ναυμαχίας ἀποπειράσωσι πρὸς τὴν φυλακὴν, to try, make experiment of, venture, hazard a sea-fight with, (i. e. against) the guard-ship, squadron of observation.

ἀποπέμπω, 4, 41. ἀπέπεμπον, to send away, 5, 53. : 37. ἀπέπεμψαν, 7, 3. : 5, 22. 64. ἀποπέμψαντες : 7, 31. ἀπεπέμφθη : ἀποπέμψωμεν : 3, 75. ἀποπεμφθῶσι : 4, 53. ἀποπέμπωμεν : 3, 4. ἀποπέμψασθαι, to send off, get rid of : 7, 27. ἀποπέμπειν πάλιν, to send away back : 7, 18. ὡς ἀποπέμψοντες ἐπόριζον, to prepare to send, with a view to sending.

ἀποπίπτω, 4, 4. ἀποπίπτοι, to fall off.

ἀποπλέω, 1, 55. ἀποπλέοντες, to sail away, 7, 31. ἀποπλέων, to sail off, away : 2, 33. ἀπέπλεον, to sail away (from a place,) 66. ἀπέπλευσαν ἐπ᾿

οἴκου : 5, 4. ἀπέπλει, to sail away, 6, 50. back : 7, 34. ἀποπλευσάντων, having sailed away : 4, 65. 5, 11. 8, 19. ἀπέπλευσαν : 6, 53. ἀποπλεῖν, to sail off home, back : 3, 75. ἀποπλεύσεσθαι.

ἀποπλήθω, 7, 68. ἀποπλῆσαι τῆς γνώμης τὸ θυμούμενον, to satiate the anger of the mind, to wreak one's vengeance, Matth. Gr. Gr. 947.

ἀπορέω, 1, 63. ἠπόρησε, to be at a loss, in doubt : 7. 40. ἀπορεῖν, to be in want, 1, 107. to be at a loss : 6, 55. ἠπόρησεν, to be at a loss what to do, how to act : 5, 40. ἀποροῦντες ταῦτα, being at a loss, perplexed : 8, 11. ἠπόρουν, 7, 55. 4, 24. : 4, 13. ἀπορήσαντες.

ἀπορία, 7, 29. 48. τῶν χρημάτων, scarcity, want, 75. ἐς ἀπορίαν καθίστασαν, to reduce to perplexity, to a standstill, to perplex : 7, 44. ἀπορίαν παρεῖχεν, to occasion perplexity : 1, 123. ἀπορίᾳ, difficulty : 7, 75. irresolution, perplexity of mind : 1, 126. ἀπορίᾳ σίτου τε καὶ ὕδατος, through want both of provisions and water: 4, 4. lack, absence, want, 69. σίτου : 6, 68. a critical situation, perplexity, straight : 2, 49. τοῦ μὴ ἡσυχάζειν, inability to rest, impossiblity of resting : 4, 32. distress, incommodiousness, 29. τοῦ χωρίου : 6, 86. φυλακῆς πόλεων, want of means to guard : 7, 48.

ἄπορος, 7, 73. impracticable : 4, 34. ἄπορον ἦν, there was no means : 3, 16. ἄπορα νομίζοντες, to be at a loss what to do, to be perplexed in thought, to be in an embarrassing situation : 4, 32. ἀπορώτατοι, (men) most unprovided, defectively accoutred, appointed : 7, 14. ἀπορώτατον, the most dispiriting circumstance : 1, 52. τὰ ἄπορα, difficulties : 1, 9. poor in want, distressed : 1, 135. κατὰ τὸ ἄπορον, at a moment of difficulty: 4, 65. ἀπορώτερα, more impossible, impracticable, 1, 82. 5, 110. more difficult, τῶν κρατούντων ἀπορώτερος ἡ λῆψις, a compar. as well as a superl. is sometimes put with a noun fem. in the masc. gender, where the radical adj. is common or used as common, Matth. Gr. Gr. 633.

ἀπορρήγνυμι, 4, 69. ἀπορρήξαντες, having razed, broken down, battered down : 5, 10. ἀπορραγεὶς, having been penetrated, broken.

ἀποσαλεύω, 1, 137. to ride at anchor, out at sea.

ἀποσημαίνω, 4, 27. ἀπεσήμαινεν, to point out.

ἀποσιμόω, 4, 25. ἀποσιμωσάντων, having struck off to the deep.

ἀποσκίδνασθαι, 6, 98. to ramble to a distance from, Matth. Gr. Gr. 362.

ἀποσπάω, 3, 81. ἀπεσπῶντο ἀπὸ τῶν ἱερῶν, to drag from the altars : 7, 80. 'πεσπάσθη,

to be torn asunder, to be separated.

ἀποσπεύδω, 6, 29. ἀπέσπευδον ῥήτορας, to dissuade, to be remiss, to slacken, abate one's diligence (in any pursuit.)

ἀπόστασις, 1, 99. 3, 5. 4, 122. a revolt : 4, 80. ἐπὶ ἀποστάσει σφᾶς ἐπικαλουμένων, inviting them to assist in the revolt : 8, 5. 23.

ἀποστατέον, 8, 2. that they ought not to stand back.

ἀποσταυρόω, 4, 69. ἀπέσταυρουν, to form a palisado : 7, 80. to block up the way by driving in piles.

ἀποστέλλω, 1, 57. ἀποστέλλοντες ἔτυχον, to happen to be sending off : 1, 45. ἀπέστειλαν, to despatch : 7, 20. ἀπεστέλλοντο, to send : 2, 12. ἀποστέλλει, to despatch, send off: 5, 37. ἀποστελεῖν, to commission, send off : 7, 8. ἀποστέλλωσιν, to send out : 3, 13. βοήθειαν : 7, 17. ἀποστελοῦντες, 2. ἀποστειλάντων, 2, 85. ἀποστεῖλαι : 4, 16. ἀπεστάλησαν : 7, 50. ἀποσταλέντες : 7, 2. ἀποστειλάντων, to send out (of a mission :) 6, 30. ὅσον πλοῦν ἐκ τῆς σφετέρας ἀπεστέλλοντο, what a long voyage, what a distance they were going to be sent : 3, 89.

ἀποστερέω, 1, 69. ἀποστεροῦντες ἐλευθερίας, to deprive of freedom : 3, 42. ἀποστερεῖται τῶν ξυμβούλων, to be deprived of counsellors : 7, 6. ἀποστερηκέναι, to take away, shut away from.

ἀποστέρησις, a depriving. 8, 70.

ἀποστολὴ, 8, 9. a sending away, a departure, sailing.

ἀποστρέφω, 4, 97. ἀποστρέψας (αὐτὸν,) having turned back, 80. to divert, effect a diversion, to distract, turn off their attention, to give a new direction or turn to the war: 5, 75. ἀπέστρειψαν, to turn back: 6, 18.

ἀποστροφὴ, 4, 76. a rendezvous, retreat.

ἀποσύρω, 7, 43. ἀπέσυρον ἐπάλξεις, to throw, pull down the battlements, parapet (of a wall.)

ἀποσφάζω, 7, 85. ἀπέσφαξε, to slay, put to death.

ἀποτειχίζω, 3, 94. to blockade (a city,) 51. to wall off, separate by a wall: 6, 96. ἀποτειχισθῆναι, to be cut off by a wall of circumvallation, to have one's communication with the country cut off: 7, 1. ἀποτετειχισμέναι, to be invested, enclosed with lines of circumvallation, blocked up: 1, 65. ἀποτειχίσαντες, to wall off, build a wall of partition, ἀπυτειχισθείσης, to be cut off by lines of circumvallation, 8, 26. circumvallated: 7, 6. ἀποτειχίσαι, to hem in, surround.

ἀποτείχισις, 1, 63. a blockade.

ἀποτείχισμα, 7, 43. see παρατείχισμα.

ἀποτελέω, 4, 69. ἀπετετέλεστο, to be completed, perfected, 90. to be finished, accomplished (of a building.)

ἀποτίθημι, 1, 77. ἀποθέμενοι τὸν νόμον, to lay aside.

ἀποτολμάω, 7, 67. ἀπετολμήσαμεν, to dare, venture.

ἀποτρέπω, 3, 63. ἡμᾶς ὑμῶν, to turn aside, 89. ἀπετράποντο, to turn back, 5, 13. to return, fall back, 8, 10.: 7, 31. ἀποτραπόμενος, to turn aside from one's course, change one's route, tack about, to return back, 1, 51.: 1, 76. ἀπετράπετο τοῦ μὴ πλέον ἔχειν, to be turned away, aside from: 3, 68. ἀποτετραμμένος, to be turned against, set against (a person,) 11. ἀποτρέπεται, to be diverted from (any thing,) 39. ἀποτρέπειν ὦν, to divert from, 6, 38. τῆς κακουργίας, from mischief, 6, 8. ἀποστρέψαι, to divert from (his purpose,) dissuade, 2, 40. ἀποτρεπόμενοι, to be diverted, deterred: 6, 29. ἀπέτρεπον, to divert, put off, suspend, delay: 8, 108.

ἀποτροπὴ, 3, 39. 45. a preventive, means of prevention, 82. tergiversation.

ἀποφαίνω, 3, 38. to demonstrate, prove, 94. ἀπέφαινον, to shew, prove, 63. to shew, demonstrate, 2, 13.: 3, 83. ἀποφαίνῃ, to point out, indicate, prescribe: 4, 3. ἀπέφαινε πολλὴν εὐπορίαν ξύλων, to point to, direct another's attention to: 1, 133. ἀποφαίνοντος, to disclose plainly: 4, 59. ἀποφαινόμενος, displaying, expressing, explaining, unfolding: 8, 45. ἀπέφαινε, to declare.

ἀποφέρω, 5, 31. to pay, 10. ἀπήνεγκαν, to bear away, carry off : 7, 50. ἀπενεχθέντες, to be driven out of (one's country :) 4, 97.

ἀποφεύγω, 7, 25. ἀποφεύγουσιν, to make their escape : 7, 31. ἀποφυγόντες, having made escape, got off, 3, 70. ἀποφυγὼν, to escape, 13. ἀποφεύξεσθε αἰτίαν, to avoid blame, clear one's self of blame.

ἀποφράσσω, 8, 104. ᾗ μὲν ἐβούλοντο ἀποφράξασθαι αὐτοὺς οἱ ἐναντίοι, intercludo, to blockade, intercept, cut off their retreat.

ἀποφυγὴ, 8, 106. escape, retreat.

ἀποχράομαι, 6, 17. ἀποχρήσασθε, to make free use of, to make every use of : 7, 42. ἀποχρήσασθαι for χρήσασθαι.

ἀποχρώντως, 1, 21. sufficiently, 7, 77. sufficiently, enough.

ἀποχωλόω, 7, 27. ἀπεχωλοῦντο, to be lamed.

ἀποχωρέω, 7, 52. ἀπεχώρησεν, to withdraw, retreat, draw off, depart, 1, 87. ἐπ' οἴκου, to return home, 7, 2. : 3, 42. ἀπεχώρει, to depart, come off, go off : 4, 65. ἀποχωρήσειαν, to depart : 3, 13. ἀποχωρήσονται, to retreat from, withdraw : 7, 69. ἀποχωρήσας, to withdraw, 60. ἀποχωρεῖν πεζῇ, to retreat on foot, by land, 13. ἀποχωροῦσιν, to withdraw, 70. to sneak, steal off, withdraw.

ἀποχώρησις, 5, 73. a retreat : 8, 76.

ἀπόψύχειν, 1, 134. to die, expire.

ἀπραγμόνως, 4, 61. without trouble, 6, 87.

ἀπραγμοσύνη, 6, 18. τῶν λόγων, quiet, tranquillity, (laziness, sloth,) freedom from cares, business, 2, 63. indolent leisure, love of ease, dislike of business : 1, 32. avoidance of negotiation and intercourse.

ἀπράγμων, 2, 63. τὸ ἄπραγμον, freedom from cares, carelessness of business, leisure, quiet : 1, 70. inactive, idle, 2, 40. one, who takes no part in public affairs, consults his ease, has nothing to do : 6, 18.

ἄπρακτος, 1, 24. 4, 22. 46. 61. 99. without one's errand, unsuccessful : 6, 52. *qui nihil efficit*, who does not accomplish his purpose, fails of his end, object, loses his labour, *re infecta*, 33. ἀπράκτους ὧν ἐφίενται, not accomplishing, obtaining what one desires, 5, 56. unsuccessful, 38. unsuccessful in one's suit, unrecompensed for one's toil, disappointed in one's views, baulked of one's purpose.

ἀπράκτως, 6, 48. *re infecta*, without effecting any thing, to no purpose.

ἀπρεπὴς, 3, 57. disgraceful, unbecoming, 7, 111. : 2, 36. ἐπὶ τῷ παρόντι, unsuitable, improper on the occasion : 5, 46. τῷ ἐκείνων ἀπρεπεῖ : 7, 68. ἀπρεπέστατα, indecent, dishonouring, dishonest (insults:) 4, 30.

ἀπρόθυμος, 4, 86. heartless, slow, backward, dispirited, downhearted : 8, 32.

ἀπροσδόκητος, 2, 5. 91. 6, 69. not looking for, expecting, without expectation, 103. all of a sudden, unawares : 7, 29. (act.) not expecting : 3, 39. unexpected, unlooked for : 7, 46.

ἀπροσδοκήτως, 4, 29. unexpectedly, unawares : 7, 21.

ἀπροφάσιστος, 6, 83. προθυμία, the sincerest, honestest, downright zeal, promptitude.

ἀπροφασίστως, 1, 49. openly : 6, 72. without tergiversation, fairly, promptly, without double dealing : 8, 2. without excuses : 3, 82. unhesitatingly, without scruple.

ἀπροφύλακτος, 4, 55. πολέμου, impossible to guard against.

ἅπτω, 4, 100. ἦψε τοῦ τείχους, to set on fire : 2, 77. ἦψαν, to kindle.

ἅπτομαι, 8, 2. ἅπτεσθαι, 11. ἁπτόμενοι, applying themselves to, engaging in : 2, 48. ἥψατο τῶν ἀνθρώπων, to seize, attack (of the plague :) 8, 15. ἅψασθαι, to touch : 1, 78. τῶν λόγων, to lay hold of : 2, 50. ἅπτεται, to prey upon, 17. ἥπτοντο τῶν πρὸς τὸν πόλεμον, to apply to the business of war : 1, 118. ἥπτοντο, to lay hold of, seize upon : 4, 100. ἡμμένους ἄνθρακας, glowing, live, burning : 1, 97. ἥψατο,

to touch upon (as a writer :) 5, 61. ἅπτεσθαι τοῦ πολέμου, to prosecute the war, cling to it : 2, 49. τὸ μὲν ἔξωθεν ἁπτομένῳ σῶμα, if you touched the body externally, the body externally to the touch, here the partic. in the dat. expresses the action, with respect to which this definition of a property is applied, Matth. Gr. Gr. 545. : 5, 14. ἅψασθαι, to meddle with, move in (a business :) 8, 15. 92.

ἀπωθέω, 3, 23. ἀπώσαντες, to throw down : 5, 22. ἀπεώσαντο, to keep off, refuse, excuse one's self : 5, 45. ἀπωσθῇ, to be rejected : 3, 44. ἀπώσασθαι, to reject, 39. ἀπωθοῦνται, to repel : 1, 144. ἀπιώσαντο, to drive back (an enemy :) 1, 32. ἀπεωσάμεθα, to repulse in battle, to defeat : 2, 39. ἀπεῶσθαι, to be overthrown, beaten in battle : 2, 4. ἀπεωθοῦντο, to repel : 1, 37. ἀπώσησθε, to reject : 6, 33. ἀπώσωμεν, 87. : 1, 18. ἀπωσάμενοι, to drive away, to repel.

ἄπωσις, 7, 34. a carrying, driving or forcing along.

ἄρα, 1, 68. 4, 8. 8, 100.

ἄρα, 1, 75. ἆρ' ἄξιοι ἐσμέν, ὦ Λακεδαιμόνιοι, sometimes ἄρα is put for ἆρ' οὐ, as the Latin ne enclit. for nonne, Matth. Gr. Gr. 941.

ἀργὸς, 2, 7. empty : 3, 82. lazy, inactive : 7, 67. ἀργότεραι, slow, less expeditious, quick.

ἀργυρεῖον, 2, 55. a silver-mine.

ἀργύρεος, 5, 16. ἀργυρέᾳ εὐλάκᾳ εὐλάξει, to plough with a silver plough.

ἀργύριον, 4, 26. 65. a sum of money, 69. : 5, 49. the money : 3, 50. ταξάμενοι ἀργύριον τοῦ κλήρου ἑκάστου δύο μνᾶς φέρειν, to agree, covenant to pay money, rent for each division, lot : 2, 7.

ἀργυρολογέω, 2, 69. ἀργυρολογῶσι, to collect tribute : 8, 3. ἠργυρολόγησεν, collected contributions : 3, 19. ἠργυρολόγει ἄλλα, to levy money elsewhere, in divers places.

ἀργυρολόγος, 2, 69. 3, 19. ναῦς, money-levying, collecting : 4, 50. 75. tax-gathering.

ἀρέσκω, 4, 113. οἷς ταῦτα ἤρεσκε, to whom these things gave satisfaction, 8, 43. 48. : 1, 129. ἀρέσκομαι, to be pleased : 5, 17. ἤρεσκε, to satisfy, please, 37. Τοῖς δὲ τῶν Βοιωτῶν πρέσβεσιν ἀκούουσιν ἤρεσκε, to please, delight, give peculiar satisfaction : 1, 35. ἀρέσκηται, to be pleasing, agreeable : 7, 49. ἀρέσκειν : 5, 41. ἀρέσκοντα, satisfactory, giving general satisfaction : 2, 68. 8, 84. οὔτε ἠρέσκετο αὐτοῖς, to be pleased with, take delight in, delectari aliqui re, Matth. Gr. Gr. 534.

ἀρετὴ, 1, 2. the goodness, fertility, 69. excellence, merit, virtue : 6, 11. δόξαν ἀρετῆς μελετῶσιν, to study (to acquire) the reputation of valour : 1, 33. confidence, valour, the result of confi-

dence : 2, 45. ἧς ἂν ἐπ᾿ ἐλαχίστου ἀρετῆς πέρι ἢ ψόγου κλέος ᾖ, about whom there is least said, least talk, conversation, either concerning (her) virtues or faults, either by way of commendation or blame, (the word here denotes not virtue, but the commendation, which properly belongs to virtue, Plut. in the beginning of his dissertation de Virt. Mul. quotes the passage and has, ψόγου πέρι ἢ ἐπαίνου :) 4, 81. virtue, generous nature, liberality : 8, 68.

ἀριθμέω, 6, 17. ἠρίθμουν, to number, count : 5, 20. ἀριθμῶν, computing, calculating : 3, 20. ἠριθμοῦντο.

ἀριθμός, 2, 7. ἐς τὸν πάντα, altogether, with regard to the sum total : 4, 101. πολὺς, a great number : 5, 66. γράψαι, to record the number : 1, 74. 3, 87.

ἀριστερὸς, 6, 62. παραπλέοντες δ᾿ ἐν ἀριστερᾷ τὴν Σικελίαν, to coast along having Sicily on the left hand, to sail along the coast of Sicily having it on the left hand : 2, 100.

ἀριστοποιέω, 4, 30. ἀριστοποιεῖσθαι, to take breakfast, 7, 39. ἀριστοποιήσονται, to dine : 8, 108.

ἄριστον, 4, 90. dinner : 7, 40. τὰ ἀμφὶ τὸ ἄριστον, dinner : 81. τὸ περὶ ἀρίστου ὥραν, about the hour of breakfast : 8, 95.

ἄριστος, 6, 26. αὐτοῖς δοκῇ εἶναι Ἀθηναίοις, to seem to be best for the Athenians : 1, 2.

ἀρίστη, the most fertile: 3, 38. ἄριστοι ἀπατᾶσθαι, excellent at being deceived, most easy to be deceived: 4, 74. βουλεύειν τὰ ἄριστα, to consult the city's best interests : 7, 81. τὰς ἄριστα σφίσι πλεούσας, those, which sailed best to them, i. e. the best sailors out of the whole number: 4, 80. γεγενῆσθαι σφίσιν ἄριστοι, to have evinced the greatest courage in their cause : 1, 2. μάλιστα δὲ τῆς γῆς ἡ ἀρίστη ἀεὶ τὰς μεταβολὰς τῶν οἰκητόρων εἶχεν, the best of countries, here, (which is common in Greek,) the adjective is not considered as the epith. of the subst., but as the part, of which the subst. is the whole, whose gender it takes, Matth. Gr. Gr. 643.: 8, 39.

ἀρκέω, 5, 48. σφίσι, to be sufficient for them : 5, 9. ἀρκείτω, to suffice, to serve the turn, to do, 62. to suffice, 6, 2.: 2, 35. ἀρκοῦν εἶναι, to be sufficient : 1, 93. ἀρκέσειν, to suffice : 3, 67. ἀρκεῖ : 6, 84. ἀρκοῦμεν πρὸς τοὺς πολεμίους, to be a match for: 4, 17. οὐ μὲν βραχεῖς ἀρκῶσι : 1, 71. to be supplied, to accrue.

ἀρκούντως, 1, 22. ἕξει, it will be sufficient: 6, 101. ἔχειν, to be sufficient: 8, 36. in sufficient quantity.

ἄρκτουρος, 2, 78. arcturus.

ἅρμα, 5, 50. a chariot.

ἁρμοστὴς, 8, 5. a Lacedæmonian magistrate.

ἀρνέομαι, 8, 9. ἀρνουμένου, denying : 6, 60.

ἁρπαγὴ, 4, 104. ἐς ἁρπαγὴν τραπέσθαι, to turn to plunder: 7, 13. 26. 29. 30. booty : 8, 62. σκεύη καὶ ἀνδράποδα ἁρπαγὴν ποιησαμένους, for ἁρπάζοντας, Matth. Gr. Gr. 590.: 2, 98.

ἁρπάζω, 1, 5. ἥρπαζον, to plunder.

ἀρρωστία, 3, 15. τοῦ στρατεύειν, fatigue in consequence of disinclination for, weariness of military service, Suid. ἀπροθυμία : 7, 47. κατὰ πάντα, weakness, infirm condition, depression, i. e. general weakness (of spirits.)

ἀρρώστερος, 8, 83. ἀρρωστότερον γενόμενον, more languid, less disposed.

ἀρσὴν, 2, 45. a male, a man.

ἀρτάω, 4, 100. ἤρτησαν, to fasten: 2, 76. ἀρτήσαντες ἀπὸ τῆς τομῆς ἑκατέρωθεν, to suspend by each end, extremity of the beam.

ἄρτι, 1, 71. lately, just now : 7, 78. recently : 4, 96. in fact, 106. truly : 6, 91.

ἄρτος, 1, 138. bread.

ἀρτύνης, 5, 47. an Argive magistrate.

ἀρχαιολογέω, 7, 69. to speak tritely, say antiquated, hackneyed, common-place things.

ἀρχαῖος, 4, 3. τὸ ἀρχαῖον, in former time, 5, 80. anciently, originally : 2, 16. ἐκ τῆς κατὰ τὸ ἀρχαῖον πολιτείας, from the ancient form of government: 6, 2. τὸ ἀρχαῖον, in ancient

I

31

times, anciently: 1, 21. τὰ ἀρχαῖα, antiquity : 2, 15. ἀπὸ τοῦ πάνυ ἀρχαίου, from a very remote period : 2, 15. ἀρχαιότερα, more ancient.

ἀρχαιότροπος, 1, 71. obsolete, old-fashioned.

ἀρχὴ, 5, 28. ἀρχὰς, the authorities: 6, 4. τὴν ἀρχὴν, originally, 56. omnino, at all. : 8, 5. ἀρχῆς, province : 1,128. ἀρχὴν ἐποιήσατο, to make a beginning of the whole affair: 5, 37. command, authority, influence: 4, 98. τὴν ἀρχὴν ἐσελθεῖν ἐπὶ τούτῳ, at first, in the first instance, to begin with: 5, 27. government, 28. dominion, 1, 9. 67. 77. the government, 3, 45. ἄλλων, empire over others, 5, 54. post of honor, place of power : 2, 65. ἀρχὴ ὑπὸ τοῦ πρώτου ἀνδρὸς, a government under the leading man: 7, 16. a military command, government : 6, 54. εἶναι ἐν ἀρχαῖς, to be in office, in the magistracy, 5 84. ἐν ταῖς ἀρχαῖς καὶ τοῖς ὀλίγοις, before or among the magistrates and chief people, 47. αἱ ἔνδημοι ἀρχαὶ, the city-magistrates, 2, 15. : 5, 69. ὑπὲρ ἀρχῆς, for government : 5, 20. beginning, outset : 1, 75. ἆρ' ἄξιοι ἐσμὲν, ὦ Λακεδαιμόνιοι, ἀρχῆς γε, ἧς ἔχομεν, τοῖς Ἕλλησι μὴ οὕτως ἄγαν ἐπιφθόνως διακεῖσθαι, the gen. expresses the cause, in which case it is to be rendered on account of, Matth. Gr. Gr. 489. : 8, 64.

ἀρχικὸς, 2, 80. γένος, a family qualified for, eligible to magistracy.

ἄρχω, 1, 1, ἀρξάμενος, having begun for myself, commenced, 103. ἤρξατο, began : 2, 12. ἄρξει, to be the beginning : 7, 14. ἄρξαι, to govern, manage : 7, 70. ἦρχον, to command (the fleet:) 5, 66. ἄρχεται ὑπ' ἐκείνου, he is ruled by him, 2, 41. : 5, 34. ἄρχειν, to hold a command, 29. to rule, 19. ἄρχει, to be president : 7, 4. ἀρξάμενοι, having commanded, begun : 6, 10. καλῶς ἄρξαι, to be a good magistrate, 18. ἀρχθῆναι, to be ruled over, to be subject: 1, 69. ἀρχομένην αὔξησιν, incipient increase : 3, 37. ἀρχομένους ἄκοντας, to be subject against one's will, on compulsion : 6, 54. ἦρξαν τὴν ἐνιαύσιον ἀρχὴν, to discharge: 5, 18. ἄρχουσιν, to govern : 7, 2. ἄρχων, commanding (as general :) 1, 93. ἦρξε, to rule, command : 5, 26. 95. ἀρχομένοις : 2, 8. ἀρχθῶσι, to be subject to, fall under the government of: 7, 7. ἦρχε, to command, 34. 1, 19. 1, 4. ἦρξε : 1, 5. ἦρξαντο, to begin, 5, 60. : 5, 52. θέρους εὐθὺς ἀρχομένου, immediately on the commencement of summer, 7, 19. : 1, 25. ἤρχοντο, to begin (a war,) 23. ἤρξαντο, 5, 20. ἀρχομένοις, entering on one's office : 4, 69. ἀρξάμενος ἀπὸ τοῦ τείχους, commencing, beginning : 1, 49. μάχης δὲ οὐκ

ἦρχον (αἱ ʼΑττικαὶ νῆες, or οἱ
ʼΑθηναῖοι,) δεδιότες οἱ στρατηγοὶ
τὴν πρόῤῥησιν τῶν ʼΑθηναίων,
here the subject of the part.
(δεδιότες,) οἱ στρατηγοὶ, being
contained in part in the main
subject αἱ ʼΑττ. is put in the
nomin. thus constituting no
deviation from the rule of
the gen. absolute, Matth. Gr.
Gr. 860. : 4, 64. ἄπερ καὶ ἀρ-
χόμενος εἶπον, this verb in the
participle, being put with
another verb, (whether) alone
as here, (or with the gen.)
obtains in such position a
different expression, In the
beginning, Matth. Gr. Gr.
852. : 8, 67.

ἄρχων, 8, 5. principal man:
1, 78. πολέμου ἄρχοντας, to
commence a war : 5, 20.
being Archon : 1, 57. the
commander (of a ship :) 4,
74. τῶν πόλεων, generals,
commanders : 5, 3. 9. a
leader : 1, 74. admiral, commander : 7, 39.

ἀρωγὸς, 7, 62. useful, advantageous.

ἀσαφὴς, 4, 86. τὴν ἐλευθερίαν,
uncertain, unstable, tran-
sient, not permanent, 108.
βουλήσει, unstable fancy : 3,
22. ἀσαφῆ, uncertain, obscure,
misunderstood.

ἀσαφῶς, 4, 125. vaguely.

ἀσεβέω, 6, 53. ἀσεβούντων,
to be guilty of impiety, pro-
faneness, to be profane.

ἀσέβημα, 6, 27. a deed of
impiety, piece of profana-
tion.

ἀσέληνος, 3, 22. νύκτα, a
moonless night.

ἄσημος, 2, 13. uncoined :
6, 8. ἀργυρίου, unstamped,
uncoined.

ἀσθένεια, 2, 49. 7, 50. sickness, ill-health, 16. ἐν ἀσθενείᾳ, through, from, by ill-
health, in his weak state of
health : 1, 3. 5, 95. weakness, 61. weakness (of the
walls :) 1, 32. feebleness,
imbecility : 4, 36. οἱ Λακεδαιμόνιοι ἀσθενείᾳ σωμάτων διὰ τὴν
σιτόδειαν ὑπεχώρουν, an instance of the use of the dat.
for the Latin abl. answering
to the question, from what ?
whence ? when the cause
proceeding from an affec-
tion or disposition of the
mind, or a subjective quality,
is assigned as the motive of
an action, in this instance the
dat. expresses the nearer, διὰ
with the accus. the remoter
motive, Matth. Gr. Gr. 567.:
8, 45.

ἀσθενέω, 7, 47. μάλιστα ἀσθε-
νοῦσιν, to be most liable to
sickness, to be usually ill.

ἀσθενὴς, 7, 36. weak, 48.
τὰ πράγματα, to be in a feeble
condition, 29. weak, defenceless : 2, 61. ἐν τῷ ὑμετέρῳ
ἀσθενεῖ τῆς γνώμης, in the
weakness of your mind,
judgment, resolution, i. e.
by reason of : 3, 52. 4, 9.
ἀσθενεστάτου τείχους, least of
all tenable, 7, 4. ἀσθενές τι
τείχους, weak : 1, 35. feeble,
without strength : 7, 4. 1, 5.

weak, helpless, imbecile : 7, 75. sick : 6, 9. λόγος, a weak argument, ineffectual, having little weight : 1, 141. ἀσθενέστερα ἕξομεν, to possess weaker, meaner, feebler (resources than another.) 7, 56. Matth. Gr. Gr. 657.

ἄσιτος, 7, 40. without dinner, fasting, without refreshment.

ἀσκέπτως, 6, 21. inconsiderately, rashly.

ἄσκησις, 5, 67. τῶν ἐς τὸν πόλεμον, instruction, education, military discipline : 2, 39. ἐπιπόνῳ, laborious exercises, hard labour.

ἄσκος, 4, 26. a vessel.

ἄσμενος, 4, 28. pleased, 5, 29. pleased, acting with alacrity : 7, 73. joyful, full of joy, rejoicing : 1, 26. πέμπειν ἄσμενοι, to send with pleasure : 6, 34. ἄσμενον πρόφασιν λαβόντας, glad to find a pretext, gladly to lay hold of, embrace a pretext : 3, 83. ἀσμένη, with pleasure, willingly : 6, 12. ἄρχειν ἄσμενος αἱρεθείς, delighted or glad at being chosen to command.

ἀσμένως, 4, 21. gladly, joyfully.

ἀσπίς, 3, 22. 4, 9. 93. 5, 71. a shield : 7, 45. 79.

ἄσπονδος, 5, 22. ἀναιρεῖσθαι αὐτοὺς ἀσπόνδους, without (having solicited) a truce, 32. being without solemn ratification : 1, 57. τὸ εὐπρεπὲς ἄσπονδον, a plausible scheme of non-alliance : 2, 22.

ἀστάθμητος, 4, 62. unstable, uncertain : 3, 59. ὡς ἀστάθμητον τὸ τῆς ξυμφορᾶς, how uncertain calamity is.

ἀστασίαστος, 1, 2. free from sedition.

ἀστέγαστος, 7, 87. διὰ τὸ ἀ., on account of the uncovered state of the place.

ἀστήρ, 2, 28, ἀστέρων τινῶν ἐκφανέντων, to appear, to be visible.

ἀστικός, 5, 20. ἀστικῶν, city-festival (times.)

ἀστὸς, 2, 34. ὁ βουλόμενος καὶ ἀστῶν καὶ ξένων, whoever chose, whether citizen or stranger : 6, 17. τὸν βουλόμενον ἀστῶν, any citizen, who pleased, 54. ἀνὴρ τῶν ἀστῶν, one of the townsmen.

ἄστυ, 1, 122. a city, (Athens,) 2, 13. πρὸς τὸν κύκλον τοῦ ἄστεως, to the circuit, circumference of the city-(wall:) 8, 92. ἄστεως, Matth. Gr. Gr. 1, 81, 107.

ἀστυγείτων, 1, 80. a confine, frontier neighbour : 4, 41. neighbouring, 44. 92. 6, 33.

ἀσφάλεια, 1, 17. δι' ἀσφαλείας, with safety, safely : 4, 68. security, safety : 1, 120. μετὰ ἀσφαλείας, in security : 2, 11. 8, 1. : 6, 24. ἀσφάλεια νῦν δὴ καὶ πολλή, now certainly there would be security even-yet much, i. e. very great.

ἀσφαλὴς, 1, 6. 75. 4, 61. 108. 5, 7. 7, 24. 38. 8, 88. safe, secure : 1, 39. ἐπὶ τοῦ ἀσφαλοῦς, in safety, security :

1, 69. steady, firm, to be depended upon: 7, 14. ἀσφαλέστερα, safer, more for security, 2, 17. 3, 14.: 1, 34. ἀσφαλέστατος, 39. 2, 11. 7, 86.

ἀσφαλῶς, 2, 63. 4, 107. to be in security, 18. ἴθεντο: 8, 89.

ἀσχολία, 1, 70. occupation, 90. business: 8, 72.

ἄτακτος, 8, 10. confused: 7, 80. ἀτακτότερον, rather out of order, 6, 97.: 8, 25. in a somewhat irregular manner.

ἀτάκτως, 3, 108. in disorder, 7, 53.: 5, 9. without exact discipline, out of regular order.

ἀταλαίπωρος, 1, 20. careless, impatient of labour.

ἀταξία, 5, 10. want of order, disarray: 7, 43. disorder.

ἀτασθαλία, 6, 59. οὐκ ἤρθη νοῦν ἐς ἀτασθαλίην, her mind was not buoyed up into insolent pride.

ἄταφος, 2, 50. unburied.

ἅτε, 7, 24. ἅτε ταμιείῳ χρωμίνων, as they used (it) for a magazine, store-house: 4, 130. 8, 52.

ἀτείχιστος, 1, 2. unwalled, 5. unrivalled, without walls, unfortified: 3, 33, unfortified: 8, 62.

ἀτέκμαρτος, 4, 63. obscure.

ἀτελὴς, 5, 46. unaccomplished: 8, 27. unfinished, imperfect, 40.

ἀτερπὴς, 1, 22. ἀτερπέστερον, less pleasant.

ἀτιμία, 5, 34. a state of infamy or ineligibility.

ἄτιμος, 5, 34. infamous, ineligible to places of honour: 3, 58.

ἀτιμώρητος, 3, 57. ἔρημοι καὶ ἀτιμώρητοι, unassisted.

ἄτμητος, 1, 82. undevastated.

ἀτολμία, 4, 120. cowardice: 5, 9. a want of confidence, abatement of determination: 2, 89: : 1, 17. ἀτολμότερα, more unenterprising, timid.

ἄτολμος, 2, 43. 4, 55. ἀτολμότερος, less alert, daring: 2, 39. περιγίγνεται ἡμῖν τοῖς τε μέλλουσιν ἀλγεινοῖς μὴ προκάμνειν καὶ ἐς αὐτὰ ἐλθοῦσι μὴ ἀτολμοτέρους τῶν ἀεὶ μοχθούντων φαίνεσθαι, the accus. is here put with the infin. for the dat. by exception, Matth. Gr. Gr. 809.: 8, 96.

ἀτοπία, 3, 82. strangeness, extravagance: 2, 51. peculiarity, strangeness, deviation from what is usual.

ἄτοπος, 3, 38. extraordinary, strange, new: 2, 49. noisome.

ἀτόπως, 7, 30. disorderly, in confusion, ἀκόσμως, unsuccessfully.

ἄτρακτος, 4, 40. a spindle or distaff.

ἀτραπὸς, 4, 36. way, path, 129.

ἀτριβὴς, 4, 8. pathless, trackless, 10, 29. impassable.

ἄττα, 1, 113. certain, quædam.

Ἀττικὴ, Attica, a province of Greece, the country, of which Athens was the capital, 2, 18. ὁ δὲ στρατὸς τοῦ Πελοποννησίων προιὼν ἀφίκετο τῆς Ἀττικῆς ἐς Οἰνόην, the name of a city accompanied by the name of the country, in which it lies, has the latter in the gen. from the sense of the gen. put *partitivé*, Matth. Gr. Gr. 499. : 2, 21.

Ἀττικίζω, 3, 62. to Atticise, to join heart and soul on the Athenian side of the question : 8, 87.

ἀτυράννευτος, 1, 18. free from tyrants.

ἀτυχέω, 1, 32. ἀτυχῶσι, to fail of a purpose : 2, 62. ἀτυχῆσαι, to be unsuccessful, to miscarry.

αὖ, 1, 81. εἰ δ᾽ αὖ, but if on the contrary : 6, 16. denotes proceeding to a new subject, as to proceed, again, further on : 7, 47. again, besides, moreover, on the other hand, in another point of view, to give an additional reason, 56. again, moreover : 1, 10. 3, 62. 4, 87. 5, 43.

αὐθάδης, 8, 84. ὁ δὲ αὐθαδέστερόν τε τι ἀπεκρίνατο, somewhat too boldly, audaciously, insolently, Matth. Gr. Gr. 661.

αὐθαίρετος, 1, 144. voluntary, 78. at the option, eligible, capable of being chosen : 7, 40. voluntary, self-chosen : 8, 27. voluntarily sought for.

αὐθέντης, 3, 58. the author of the death, the slayer.

αὐθημερὸν, 2, 12. 22. the same day, 67. 7, 39.

αὖθις, 6, 52. *posthac, postea:* 7, 70. εἴποτε καὶ αὖθις, at any other time, 58. : 4, 60. ἐς αὖθις, unto another occasion, opportunity, time, 63. 5, 76.

αὐλητὴς, 5, 70. a flute-player.

αὐλίζομαι, 6, 7. ἄπωθεν αὐλισαμένου, to encamp (for the night) at a distance : 7, 4. αὐλιζόμενοι, being in act of passing the night : 7, 29. λαθὼν ηὐλίσατο, to pass the night unobserved, undetected, 3, 29. 35. : 8. 26. ηὐλίσαντο, they had taken up their station : 6, 64. *pernocto:* 3, 96. αὐλισάμενος, to take up their quarters for the night, Matth. Gr. Gr. 563.

αὐλὸς, 4, 100. a pipe, reed.

αὔξειν, 1, 17. εἰς τὸ τὸν ἴδιον οἶκον αὔξειν, to the aggrandizement of their private families : 1, 2. αὐξηθῆναι, to be increased, enlarged, 12. to increase, 16. to grow : 1, 89. ηὐξήθησαν, to be aggrandized (in power and wealth), 6, 33. τῷ ὀνόματι, to be increased in reputation : 6, 12. ηὐξῆσθαι χρήμασι καὶ σώμασι, to be improved in one's finances, increased in wealth, number, 6, 40. : 1, 99. ηὔξετο, to increase.

αὔξησις, 1, 69. increase, strength.

αὐτάγγελος, 3, 33. voluntary messenger.

αὐταρκέω, 7, 15. sufficing,

being equal to, sufficient of one's self, able by one's self.

αὐτάρκης, 1, 37. independent, sufficient in itself: 2, 51. σῶμά τε αὔταρκες ὂν οὐδὲν διεφάνη πρὸς αὐτὸ ἰσχύος πέρι ἢ ἀσθενείας, there was no constitution with regard to strength or weakness, i. e. (whether weak or strong,) able to support it, 41. sufficient of one's self, able, fit (for any thing,) 36. αὐταρκεστάτην, one, that is most sufficient to himself, most capable of depending upon his own resources.

αὐτεπάγγελτος, 4, 100. of one's own accord, voluntary: T, 33. spontaneous, of its own accord.

αὐτερέται, 1, 10. soldiers, who navigated themselves: 6, 90. who work their own passage: 3, 18.

αὐτήκοος, 1, 133. one, who himself hears a fact, an ear-witness.

αὐτίκα, 1, 38. τὸ αὐτίκα, the present state of affairs, 124. τὸ αὐτίκα δεινὸν, the present danger: 6, 57. τὸ αὐτίκα, for the moment, present, 69.: 1, 42. τῷ αὐτίκα φανερῷ, by an immediate and apparent advantage.

αὐτοβοεὶ, 3, 74. by sudden impulse: 5, 3. with one impulse, simultaneously: 2, 81. by their very clamour, shout, by their clamour alone: 8, 23. at the first onset, on raising the first shout, 72.

αὐτοδεκαέτης, 5, 20. αὐτοδεκαετῶν διελθόντων, decennio exacto, Schol. ὁλοκλήρων.

αὐτόδικος, 5, 18. governed by one's own jurisprudence.

αὐτόθεν, 1, 11. from the place itself, 3, 7, οἱ αὐτόθεν, the people of that country, the natives of that part: 7, 71. ὁ αὐτόθεν, he of the place, country: 6, 4. ὕστερον αὐτόθεν, afterwards (removing) from them: 1, 141. 2, 69.

αὐτόθι, 4, 97. there, 8, 31.

αὐτοκράτωρ, 4, 108. λογισμῷ, overbearing reasoning, argument, 63. 64. lord, master: 6, 72. having absolute command, 6, 8. στρατηγοὺς, with full powers, absolute authority: 1, 126. governor with absolute authority: 5, 27. 45. 46.: 3, 62. οὐκ αὐτοκράτωρ οὖσα ἑαυτῆς, the city not being its own master: 8, 67.

αὐτόματος, 2, 77. ἀπὸ αὐτομάτου, accidentally: 6, 91.

αὐτομολέω, 7, 13. to desert, go over, 26.: 3, 77. ηὐτομόλησαν, 4, 41. 5, 14. αὐτομολούντων, 5, 35. 7, 27. ηὐτομολήκεσαν: 7, 13. τὰ δὲ πληρώματα διὰ τόδε ἐφθάρη τε ἡμῖν καὶ ἔτι νῦν φθείρεται, τῶν ναυτῶν τῶν μὲν διὰ φρυγανισμὸν καὶ ἁρπαγὴν μακρὰν καὶ ὑδρείαν ὑπὸ τῶν ἱππέων ἀπολλυμένων, οἱ δὲ θεραπεύοντες—αὐτομολοῦσι, " the construction of a participle both with the genitive absolute, and referring to a subject preceding, expresses

several relations of propositions to each other, and
stands for various conjunctions with the finite verb;"
here " in assigning a reason,
BECAUSE." Matth. Gr. Gr.
2, 865.

αὐτομολία, 7, 13. desertion:
1, 142. 8, 40.

αὐτόμολος, 5, 2. a deserter,
2, 57. ἐπυνθάνοντο τῶν αὐτομό-
λων, to hear from the de-
serters : 4, 118.

αὐτονομέω, 1, 144. αὐτονο-
μεῖσθαι, to regulate one's own
laws : 2, 72. αὐτονομεῖσθε, be
ye free.

αὐτονομία, 3, 46. πρὸς αὐτονομίαν ἀποστάντα, to revolt to
independence : 4, 87. : 8, 65.
αἱ πόλεις τὴν ὑπὸ τῶν Ἀθηναίων
ὕπουλον αὐτονομίαν οὐ προτιμή-
σαντες, Matth. Gr. Gr. 847. :
8, 21.

αὐτόνομος, 1, 139. 2, 63. independent, under one's own
laws : 3, 10. subject to or
governed by their own laws :
5, 18. 27. 31. 33. independent : 7, 57. 1, 67. 113.

αὐτός, 7, 69. καὶ αὐτοί, on
their side, 1, 22. ἐν αὐτῷ ἤδη
ὄντες, being actually now engaged in it (the war :) 7, 1.
αὐτούς τε ἐκείνους, those themselves, i. e. the forces of that
state itself, 48. αὐτός γε οὔκουν βούλεσθαι, that he for his
part at least did not wish,
the oratio obliqua : 3, 13. ἐν
τῷ αὐτῷ, at the same time, by
the same stroke : 5, 45. ὧν
καὶ αὐτὸς ἦν, of whom he was

one : 7, 6. ταὐτὸν (sc. τεῖχος)
this same, single, 1, 78. ταύτῃ,
in the same way : 7, 63. καὶ
ἐν τῷ αὐτῷ, and withal : 7, 30.
οὗ αὐτοῖς τὰ πλοῖα ὥρμει, when
the vessels were at anchor
for them, i. e. when their
vessels rode, lay at anchor :
7, 57. αὐτοῖς τῇ αὐτῇ φωνῇ, the
same dialect as they (used)
for them : 7, 25. μίαν ναῦν
λαμβάνουσιν αὐτοῖς ἀνδράσι, to
take a ship with its crew,
34. ὡς αὐτοὺς ἑκατέρους ἀξιοῦν
νικᾶν, so as to claim each of
them the victory, so that
they each claimed, might
each claim the victory : 6,
87. τὸ αὐτό, idem simul, 1, 36.
ἐς τὸ αὐτὸ ἐλθεῖν, to join in
one, to be united : 4, 101.
ταὐτὰ ἀπεκρίναντο, they made
the same answer, 5, 45. : 7,
28. αὐτὴν καθ' αὑτὴν, it by itself, i. e. considered independently of subject states :
5, 38. τὸ γὰρ αὐτὸ ἐποίουν, to
act in concert : 3, 47. τὸ αὐτὸ
δίκαιον καὶ ξύμφορον, the union,
identity of justice and interest, that measure at once
just and advantageous : 7,
16. αὐτῷ δύο προσείλοντο, to
select, depute two besides,
in addition to him, to join
two others in command with
him, for him, on his behalf :
7, 4. αὐτῷ ἐφαίνετο ἔσεσθαι : 3,
13. νῆες αὐτοῖς εἰσὶν, for αὐτῶν,
their ships are, 43. τὰς ὑμετέρας αὐτῶν, i. e. τῶν ὑμῶν αὐτῶν :
2, 29. αὐτῷ ἔπεισεν ἀποδοῦναι,
he persuaded (them) to re-

store to him : 1, 69. ἀντὶ τοῦ
ἐπελθεῖν αὐτοὶ ἀμύνεσθαι βούλεσθε μᾶλλον ἐπιόντας, the nom.
is here used with the infin.
as its subject, because this
subject is the subject also of
the preceding finite verb
βούλεσθε, and it would be
omitted but for emphasis,
Matth. Gr. Gr. 807. : 1, 46.
Κορινθίων στρατηγὸς ἦν Ξενο-
κλείδης ὁ Εὐθυκλέους πέμπτος
αὐτὸς, where αὐτὸς is used
after an ordinal number to
shew that one person with
several others, whose number is less by one than the
number mentioned, has done
something, Matth. 681. : 1,
82. τὰ αὐτῶν ἅμα ἐκποριζώμεθα,
for ἡμῶν αὐτῶν, the use of the
reflexive pronoun, " which
is put for the other personal
pronouns compounded with
αὐτὸς," Matth. 709. : 2, 37. οὐ
παρανομοῦμεν ἀκροάσει τῶν νόμων καὶ μάλιστα αὐτῶν, ὅσοι ἐπ᾽
ὠφελείᾳ τῶν ἀδικουμένων κεῖνται,
where αὐτὸς is used for οὗτος
or ἐκεῖνος, taking the relative
after it. Here the demonstr.
pronoun is omitted, and αὐτῶν, (ex iis,) governed of μάλιστα, et ex iis maxime earum.
Matth. 681.

αὐτόσε, 7, 26. αὐτομολῶσι,
thither, to that place.

αὐτοσχεδιάζω, 1, 138. τὰ δέοντα, to despatch readily,
without consideration the
needful.

αὐτοτελὴς 5, 18. self-suffi-
cient, independent.

αὐτοῦ, 4, 68. on the spot,
there.

αὐτουργὸς, 1, 141. one, who
lives by his own labour, cul-
tivates the soil himself.

αὐτοφυὴς, 1, 93. natural.

αὐτόφωρος, 6, 38. a person
caught in the act (of doing
any thing,) taken in the act,
caught in the fact.

αὐτόχθων, 6, 2. indigenous,
aboriginal.

αὐχέω, 2, 39. to boast.

αὔχημα, 2, 62. i. q. φρόνημα,
elevated spirits, confidence :
7, 66. an arrogant hope,
75. pride, elation (of mind,)
glory : 8, 75.

αὔχησις, 6, 16. a boasting,
room or occasion to boast,
glory.

αὐχμὸς, 1, 23. a draught.

ἀφαιρέω, 1, 81, ἀφαιρήσομεν,
to take away : 7, 13. ἀφαιρή-
σομέν τι καὶ βραχὺ τῆς τηρήσεως,
to take off the least portion
of attention, to abate, though
only in a small degree, but
a little, to remit but a small
part of the vigilance : 1, 2.
ἀφαιρήσεται, to take off, to
plunder, 3, 43. ἀφαιρούμεθα
ὠφελίαν τῆς πόλεως, to deprive
the state of an advantage : 7,
13. ἀφῄρηνται, to destroy : 1,
120. ἀφαιρεθείη, to be deprived :
2, 41, ἀφαιρεθῆναι, to be deprived of (any thing :) 6, 39.
ξύμπαν ἀφελομένη ἔχει, to seize,
abstract, monopolize the
whole : 6, 40. ἀφαιρεθήσεται
τὴν ὑπάρχουσαν ἐλευθερίαν οὐχὶ
ἐκ τοῦ ἀκούειν, not to be strip-

K

ped, deprived of the existing freedom by, for, in conse-quence of a rumour: 8, 76. ἡ Σάμος παρ ἰλάχιστον ἦλθε τὸ Ἀθηναίων κράτος ἀφελέσθαι, Matth. Gr. Gr. 797.: 8, 46. ἀφείλετο, to destroy, steal away.

ἀφάνεια, 2, 37. ἀξιώματος, obscurity of rank, condition.

ἀφανής, 4, 63. unseen, not clear: 1, 134. secret: 3, 23. ἐν τῷ ἀφανεῖ ὄντες, to be in the shade: 2, 34. φέρεται ἀφανῶν, to be carried for, on the be-half of those, who have dis-appeared, are missing: 6, 9. ἑτοίμοις περὶ τῶν ἀφανῶν κινδυ-νεύειν, to risk, hazard what you have for something you have not, an uncertainty, 'a bird in hand for two in a bush :' 4, 96. ἐκ τοῦ ἀφανοῦς, secretly, unobservedly, 1, 51. out of sight : 3, 45. invisible : 4, 67. εἴη ἡ φυλακή, put off guard, unregardful, deprived of seeing, unable to discover: 1, 23. ἀφανεστάτην, obscure, not conspicuous: 7, 75. 8, 69.

ἀφανίζω, 2, 42. ἀφανίσαντες, to obliterate, expunge: 4. 80. ἀφάνισαν, to take off, make to disappear : 6, 54. ἠφάνισε τοὐ-πίγραμμα, to obliterate, de-face: 5, 11. ἀφανίσαντες, having put out of sight, concealed : 7, 69. to obscure, cast a shade upon, obliterate : 3, 58. to wipe out, efface, cover, 83. ἠφανίσθη, to banish, 7, 8. ἀφα-νισθεῖσαν ἐν τῷ ἀγγέλῳ, to be concealed, suppressed by,

by means of the messenger: 8, 38. ἀφανίζεται, to disappear, withdraw himself.

ἀφειδέω, 2, 43. ἀφειδοῖεν, to be unsparing, prodigal of.

ἀφειδής, 4, 26. unsparing, unceasing.

ἄφθονος, 7, 58. large, great, 78, abundant (water :) 6. 90. ξύλα, abundant, in abun-dance.

ἀφθόνως, 7, 70. in abun-dance.

ἀφίημι, 5, 18. ἀφιέναι, to let go, suffer to pass, let out, 1, 91. : 2, 78. ἀφέντες, to dismiss, 5, 75. to dismiss, 78. to give up, 1, 101. : 1, 144. ἀφήσομεν, to let go: 4, 28. 5, 49. ἀφιέναι, to remit, give up: 4, 122. ἠφίει τὴν πόλιν, to let go, part with, 2, 49. πνεῦμα, to breathe, the imperf., because ι admits of no increase, Matth. Gr. Gr. 210.; "the compound ἀφίημι has frequently the aug-ment at the beginning," Matth. 282.: 5, 81. ἀφεῖσαν, in the plur. of aor. 2. the Attics for ἀφεῖμεν, ἄφετε, ἄφεσαν more frequently say ἀφεῖμεν,—εῖτε, —εισαν, Matth. 282. : 3, 32. ἀφῆκε, to release : 7, 80. ἀφεθῆ-ναι, to let go: 8, 41. 1, 140. ἀφιέναι Αἴγιναν αὐτόνομον ἀφεῖναι, to restore Ægina to liberty, leave Ægina to its own laws, suffer any one to be inde-pendent: 4, 106. ἀφιέμενοι κιν-δύνου παρὰ δόξαν, being rid, freed from : 2, 13. ἀφίησιν, to yield up, give up, the indic. is here put for the dat., because the words are quoted as if the person himself spoke, Matth. Gr. Gr. 744. see too 774. 791. 812.: 5, 21. ἀφίεσαν, to let go, set at liberty, dismiss, 2, 76. to let fall, 4, 48. to let fly, to shoot: 7, 19. ἀφῆκαν, to get off from, push off: 2, 60. ἀφίεσθε τοῦ κοινοῦ τῆς σωτηρίας, to neglect the common safety: 7, 19. ἀφῆκαν ἐς τὸ πέλαγος, to put off to sea, set sail, i. q. ἄφῶσαν: 3, 70. ἀφεθέντες, to be dismissed, sent home (as a prisoner:) 5, 91. ἀφείσθω κινδυνεύεσθαι, to permit to run the risk: 5, 65. ἀφεθῆναι, to let go, to be permitted to escape: 8, 41. ἀφεὶς τὸ ἐς τὴν Χίον (sc. πλεῖν) ἔπλει ἐς τὴν Βαῦνον, (when a noun, which has just preceded, is to be repeated once again, the article belonging to it stands alone, Matth. 406.:) 8, 87. ἵνα τοὺς Φοίνικας προαγαγὼν ἐς τὸν Ἀστυνδον, ἐν χρηματίσαιτο ἀφείς, " where consistently with the words, it must signify ἐκχρηματισάμενος ἀφείς, but ἀφείη, ἀφεὶς might be omitted," Matth. 848.: 8. 39. ἀφειμένοι, dismissed from, 41. ἀφείς, dismissing.

ἀφικνέομαι, 8, 6. ἀφικνοῦνται, to come: 5, 2. ἀφικνεῖται, to come up to, to arrive (before a place,) 16. ἀφικνουμένοις, coming to: 2, 12. ἀφίκετο ἐς τὸ στρατόπεδον, to come into the camp: 5, 4. ἀφικόμενοι, having made good his arrival, 7, 48. having arrived, 5, 12.

37. reaching home: 1, 124. ἐπ' ἀνάγκαν ἀφίχθαι, to become a matter of necessity, 3, 31. οὐδενὶ ἀκουσίως, to come acceptably to every one, to be welcome to every one: 4, 18. ἀφιγμένοι, being arrived: 8, 82.

ἀφίστημι, 1, 38. ἀφεστῶσι, to hold off, to be in a state of revolt, 5, 38. to fall off from, to refuse to co-operate with: 7, 7. ἀφεστήκει, to abstain from, keep clear of: 8, 2. 12. ἀφίστασθαι, to revolt: 1, 89. ἀφεστηκότες, to be in a state of revolt, 98. ἀποστῶσι: 5, 64. ἀφίστημι πρὸς Ἀργείους, to revolt to the Argives: 1, 56. ἀποστῶσιν, to revolt, 60. ἀφεστηκυίας, 10. ἀπέστησεν, to cause to revolt, 99. ἀποσταίεν, to revolt, 93. ἀφιστάνει τὰς τῶν πολεμίων ἐπιβουλάς, to avert the enemy's designs, 8, 22. ἀποστῆσαι, to cause to revolt: 5, 31. ἀφεστηκυῖαν, having revolted, 4, 79.: 4, 118. ἀποστήσονται οὐδενός, to be rejected: 8, 5. ἀφεστῶτα, having revolted, 8. ἀποστήσαις, to cause to revolt, 14. ἀφίστανται, to revolt, 17. ἀποστήσας, 19. ἀπέστησαν, to make to revolt, 4. ἀποστήσωνται, 3, 13. διπλῆν ἀπόστασιν ἀποστήσεσθαι, to make a double revolt, 4, 81. ἐπέστησε τὰ πολλά, to shake the faith, sap the allegiance, turn from (their) allegiance, occasion the revolt: 2, 65. ἀφεστηκόσι τῶν ξυμμάχων ἐπὶ ταῖς πλείοσιν, the greater part of their allies besides, who had revolted,

5, 64. ἀφέστηκεν, to be in a state of revolt: 6, 88. ἀφειστή-κεσαν, to keep aloof, 7, 7. ἀφειστήκει, to hold off from: 1, 62. ἀπέστη, to desert: 5, 82. ἀπέστησαν Ἀθηναίων πρὸς Χαλ-κιδέας: 2, 47. ἀπέστησαν, to desist from, give up any thing: 7, 58. ἀφέστασαν, to revolt from: 8, 6. ἀποστήσειε, instead of the form αιμι in the optat. aor. 1. the Attics chiefly use the primitive Æolic form εια, ειας, ειε, after the example of the Ionians and Dorians, but only in the second and third pers. sing. and the third plur., Matth. Gr. Gr. 254. : 1, 61. ἀφεστᾶσι, instead of ἕστηκα the form ἕστα by syncope is more used, Matth. 280. : 8. 22. ἀφιστᾶσιν, to instigate to revolt, 35. ἀφειστή-κει, had revolted, 61.

ἀφνειὸς, 1, 13. wealthy.

ἄφνω, 4, 103. unexpected, sudden.

ἀφόρητος, 4, 126. βοῆς μεγέ-θει ἀφόρητοι, intolerable.

ἀφορμάω, 7, 75. πάλιν τούτων τοῖς ἐναντίοις ἀφορμᾶσθαι, to return back, the reverse of these, on the contrary : 8, 10. ἀφορμηθεῖσαι: 4, 78. ἀφώρ-μησεν, to set off from.

ἀφορμὴ, 1, 90. a place to sally forth from : 6, 90. opportunity, al. ἐφορμὴ, an attack, assault.

ἄφρακτος, 3, 39. ἦσαν ἄφρα-κτοι πρὸς αὐτοὺς, to be unfortified, unarmed against any one, 82. unprotected, 1, 6. 117. un-

fortified: 6, 33. ἄφρακτον ληφ-θήσεσθε, to be taken unawares, unprepared for defence.

ἀφροσύνη, 1, 122. folly.

ἄφρων, 5, 105, τὸ ἄφρον, folly : 6, 33. foolish, destitute of common sense.

ἀφύλακτος, 2, 13. 3, 30. unguarded : 7, 29. without guards, 32. off one's guard, unprepared.

ἀχείρωτος, 6, 10. unsubdued, not reduced.

ἀχθηδὼν, 4, 40. δι' ἀχθηδόνα, with sarcasm, malice : 2, 37. pain, sadness, moroseness, censure.

ἄχθομαι, 1, 92. to be incensed, 95. ἤχθοντο, to take any thing ill : 7, 47. ἀχθομέ-νους, to be oppressed, weary, worn out, vexed, chagrined, 5, 7. bearing hardly, grumbling, shewing signs of discontent, 17. vexed, angered, chagrined : 1, 84. ἀχθεσθέντες, to smart with pain, 6, 15. τοῖς ἐπιτηδεύμασιν αὐτοῦ, to be angry at, displeased with : 8, 48. ἤχθετο, grieved.

ἄχθος, 4, 115. μείζόνι, too great a weight, charge.

ἀχρεῖος, 8, 4. unprofitable, 1, 74. 84. τὰ ἀχρεῖα, useless : 2, 6. ἀχρειοτάτους, most unfit for service : 2, 40. ἀχρείους, good for nothing, 44. ἐν τῷ ἀχρείῳ τῆς ἡλικίας, in the unseasonable period of life, the age incapable of service : 1, 93. ἀχρειοτάτων, the most useless, insufficient, disabled from service.

ἀχρηματία, 1, 11. the want of wealth, poverty.

ἄχρηστος, 6, 16. unprofitable, without use : 2, 78, πλῆθος, the useless multitude, who are of no service.

ἄψαυστος, improper to touch, unconscious of a touch, set apart, inapplicable, inappropriable, privileged from, 4, 97.

B.

Βάθος, 5, 68. ἐπὶ βάθος, in depth.

βακτηρία, 8, 84. καὶ ἐπανήρατο τὴν βακτηρίαν, lifted up his staff, (ὡς πλήξων, Schol. as with an intention to strike.)

βάλανος, 2, 4. an iron peg, or pin, (which fastened the bar of the gates.)

βάλλω, 1, 63. 2, 62. βαλλομένους, to be shot at, darted at, 75. : 7. 70. ἐμβεβληκέναι, to run foul of, charge with the beak : 4, 33.

βαρβαρικὸς, 7, 29. ὅμοια τοῖς μάλιστα, like most people of barbaric descent, equally with the most genuine barbarians, i. e. those, who are more peculiarly of barbarian descent, equally with the most barbarous.

βάρβαρος, 1, 1. 7, 90. a barbarian, one who is not a Greek : 1, 73. φαμὲν Μαραθῶνι μόνοι προκινδυνεῦσαι τῷ βαρβάρῳ, against the barbarian, this construction arises out of the use of the Greek dat. for the Latin abl., in which situation it is used with verbs of contending,

answering to the question wherewith? Matth. Gr. Gr. 562. : 8, 98. βαρβαρώτατος.

βαρύνω, 2, 64. βαρυνόμενοι, to be hard pressed : 8, 1. ἐβαρύνοντο, they were heavily grieved : 5, 7. βαρύνεσθαι, to be distressed, afflicted, annoyed ; 2, 16. ἐβαρύνοντο καταλιπόντες, to be grieved to forsake.

βαρὺς, 1, 77. heavy, harsh.

βαρύτης, 7, 62. τῶν νεῶν, heaviness.

βασανίζω, 6, 53. βασανίσαι τὸ πρᾶγμα, to sift the transaction (as by torture,) to examine, investigate closely, strictly : 7, 86. βασανίζομαι διὰ τὸ τοιοῦτον, to be examined on this account.

βασιλεία, 1, 9. the empire over, 13. a kingdom.

βασιλεὺς, 5, 16. a king, monarch : 8, 5. ὑπὸ βασιλέως πεπραγμένος τοὺς φόρους, (with verbs, which govern a double accusative in the active, the thing is put in the accusative, in the passive also, Matth. Gr. Gr. 603. :) 2, 100.

βασιλεύω, 1, 14. 2, 15. ἐβασίλευσε, to be king, to reign

over, 4, 101, Ὀδρυσῶν : 7, 1.
βασιλεύων Σικελῶν, to be king
of, to reign over.

βέβαιος, 1, 141. τὸ μὲν πιστὸν
ἔχοντες, τὸ δὲ οὐ βέβαιον, to be
confident, but not sure : 6,
34. καὶ τὰ τῶν πόλεων οὐκ ἂν
βέβαια ἔχοντες, to have the
cities sure, to be sure of the
cities : 4, 3. constant, continual, unremitting, 67. τὰς
πύλας, firm, safe, 81. ἐλπίδα,
62. stable, firm : 3, 10. εἰδότες φιλίαν ἰδιώταις γιγνομένην,
to know that there is lasting
friendship for, among individuals, 43. δοκήσεως, a firm
suspicion, fixed idea : 1, 2.
stable, little liable to change,
revolution : 5, 43. trustwor-
thy, sincere, to be depended
on : 2, 33. βεβαιότερον ἀναγα-
γόμενοι, to be forced to put
out to sea, 6, 72. πόλεμον,
more decided, regular, positive, 1, 8. with more stabi-
lity, 3, 39. κίνδυνον, a safer
risk, hazard : 3, 11. βεβαιότε-
ροι ἂν ἡμῖν ἦσαν μηδὲν νεωτερεῖν,
to be secure of their attempt-
ing no innovation : 8, 56.

βεβαιότης, 4, 51. 66. security, protection, 132.

βεβαιόω, 1, 124. ἐκ πολέμου
εἰρήνη μᾶλλον βεβαιοῦται, a
peace is confirmed, strengthened by following a war : 4,
70. βεβαιώσεσθαι, to confirm,
to give assurance to, 1, 33.
to strengthen, re-inforce : 1,
122. βεβαιοῦμεν ἡμῖν αὐτοῖς, to
secure for ourselves : 2, 35.
βεβαιοῦται, to be established
(of an opinion :) 6, 34.

βεβαίως, 1, 2. constantly,
in a settled manner : 6, 38.
καταλελυμένους, surely, posi-
tively : 1, 134. εἰδότες, having
certain information : 2, 7. 4,
114. 6, 28,

βεβαίωσις, 1, 140. a con-
firmation, proof : 4, 87. πρὸς
τοῖς ὅρκοις, confirmation.

βέβηλος, 4, 96. profane,
unsanctified.

βέλος, 7, 67. τὸ βέλος ἀφιέναι, to discharge a missile.

βελτίων, 1, 102. 2, 94. 7,
17. better, more prosperous.
Βέλτιστος, 2, 24. 3, 56. 4, 59.
7, 39. ἄρχειν ἄριστα, most apt,
fit to govern well, most capable of governing well, 4,
68. 6, 39. βουλεύεται ἂν βέλτι-
στα, to advise most sagacious-
ly : 4, 78. τῷ βελτίστῳ τοῦ ὁπ-
λιτικοῦ, the flower, 7, 19.

βὴξ, βηχός, 2, 49, ἰσχυρόν,
a violent, bad cough. The
adj. is here common, as βὴξ
is feminine.

βία, 1, 68, ἡμῶν, in defiance
of us, 43. in spite of us : 5,
7. βίᾳ, by storm, assault, 56 :
1, 11. by force, 4, 92. βίᾳ τὰ
ἡμέτερα ἕξουσι, to possess by
force, a strong or high hand,
5, 50. : 4, 62. might, 19. βίᾳ
διαφυγεῖν, the dat. in its sense
of the Latin abl. expresses
the kind and manner of an
action, Matth. Gr. Gr. 571.

βιάζομαι, 1, 28. βιαζομένων,
to force against their will :
7, 36. βιάζονται, to be forced
to give way : 4, 15. 19. 6,
21. 7, 11. 43. 45. βιασθέντος,
the perf. pass. of verbs, which

are used as actives, frequently occur in a pass. sense,
Matth. Gr. Gr. 716. : 3, 35.
ἐδιάπαντο, to oppress any one:
1, 95. βιάζεται: 1, 75. βιασάμε-
νος, to use violence, 4, 103. :
7, 36. βιάζονται, to suffer violence, a repulse, 1, 37. to
commit violence, to oppress:
3, 47. βιασθῇ: 7, 38. βιάζοιτο:
4, 44. ἐβιάσθη; to suffer repulse: 7, 69. βιάσασθαι ἐς τὸ
ἔξω, to force a way out, to
open a way out vi: 1, 93.
βιασθῆναι; to be oppressed,
put to straits: 7, 22. βιάσασθαι τὸν ἔσπλουν, to force an
entrance : 8, 27. βιαζομένη,
compelled.

βίαιος, 6, 54. οὐδὲν βίαιον
δρᾶν, to commit no violence:
1, 141. ἐσφοραί, contributions
exacted by force : 5, 73.
ἀποχώρησις, a precipitate,
headlong flight : 6, 20. hard,
oppressive, violent : 1, 95.
violent, haughty : 6, 85.
βιαιότερον, more arbitrarily,
8, 48. more cruelly : 3, 36.
βιαιότατος, most violent.

βιαίως, 3, 23. by main force,
after struggling hard.

βιοῦς, from an obsolete
root βιόημι, 2, 53. οὐδεὶς ἐλπίζων
μέχρι τοῦ δίκην γενέσθαι βιοὺς
ἂν, no one expecting that he
should live till law could
take effect, till he could be
brought to trial, till judgment.

βίος, 3, 83. ξυνταραχθέντος
τοῦ βίου, the discipline, or
manner of living being put

into confusion : 6, 16. τῷ καθ'
αὑτοὺς βίῳ, one's own age,
generation : 1, 5. τὸν πλεῖστον
τοῦ βίου ἐντεῦθεν ἐποιοῦντο, to
derive thence the greatest
part of their livelihood : 2,
57. 8, 24.

βιοτεύω, 1, 130. ἐν τῷ καθεστηκότι τρόπῳ βιοτεύειν, to live
in the ordinary mode, 11. to
procure food, find support,
(in a neutral sense.)

βλάβη, 3, 38. injury, detriment, blow, danger : 5, 52. :
1, 90. ἐπὶ βλάβῃ, to the injury :
2, 65. καθίστατε, to be rui-
nous, 40. an injury, impediment, obstruction : 6, 41.
οὐδεμία βλάβη τοῦ κοσμηθῆναι,
no loss on account of : 3, 14.
injury, detriment : 8, 72.

βλάπτω, 1, 33. ἑτέρους, to
commit injustice against, 35.
βλάψαι, to inflict punishment
upon, 41. βλάπτειν, to injure :
7, 26. βλάπτουσιν, to injure,
27. ἔβλαπτε: 4, 61. βλάπτοντας,
injuring : 7, 21. βλάψοντας, to
do injury, damage : 4, 64.
βλαπτόμενοι, to be ill-used :
1, 69. βλάπτεσθαι, to be injured: 7, 62. ἐλαττόμεθα πρὸς
τὴν ἐκείνων, against : 1, 140.
βλαβῆναί τι, to suffer or sustain any loss, injury : 3, 46.
βλάπτεσθαι, to injure one's
self : 7, 27. ἐβλάπτοντο, to
damage, injure seriously.

βλαστάνω, 3, 26. ἐβεβλαστή-
κει, to grow up again, sprout
out, put forth.

βλέπω, 7, 71. βλέψαντες ἐπὶ
τὸ—, to have the eyes fixed

upon, look to or upon (any thing:) 5, 98. 7, 71.

βῆμα, 2, 34. a pulpit.

βοάω, 7, 48. βοῶσιν, to make a clamour, to exclaim: 7, 48. βοήσεσθαι τὰ ἐναντία, to bawl out: 6, 28. βοῶν, to vociferate, exclaim.

βοεικὸς, 4, 128. ζεύγεσιν, *plaustris boum*, waggons drawn by oxen.

βοὴ, 1, 87. 4, 34. 7, 44. clamour: 1, 87. acclamation: 7, 71. a shriek: 3, 22. a cry, an alarm: 8, 92.

βοήθεια, 3, 24. a pursuit (of an enemy:) 7, 41. succour, re-inforcement: 5, 53. βραχυτέρα, a shorter road, by which to send a re-inforcement: 8, 11. assistance, 5, 64. ὀξεῖα καὶ οἴα οὔπω πρότερον, succour is sent with greater quickness and in greater force than ever before: 4, 8. 105. τῶν νεῶν, a re-inforcement: 7, 18. an expedition, succour, i. e. intended succour: 8, 15.

βοηθέω, 1, 126. ἐβοήθησαν, to attack: 4, 96. ἄρτι βεβοηθηκότες, to do splendid service, 14. to bring succour, to come up to relieve: 1, 74. 2, 25. ἐβοήθει, to succour: 3, 22. βοηθεῖν ἐκ τῆς ἑαυτῶν φυλακῆς, to run or march from their own posts: 2, 73. βοηθήσειν κατὰ δύναμιν, to succour with one's own might: 1, 62. βοηθῦντες, to re-inforce: 7, 2. ἐβοήθουν, to carry effective assistance to: 5, 3.

ἐβοηθήσαντες, 1, 71. 74. βοηθήσατε, 41. ἡ εὐεργεσία αὕτη τε καὶ ἡ ἐς Σαμίους τὸ δι' ἡμᾶς Πελοποννησίους αὐτοῖς μὴ βοηθῆσαι παρέσχεν ὑμῖν. Αἰγινητῶν μὲν κράτησιν, Σαμίων δὲ κόλασιν, the infin. joined with the neuter article stands as a subst., Matth. Gr. Gr. 814.: 8, 40.

βοηθὸς, 6, 8. Ἐγεσταίοις πρὸς Σελινουντίους, succours to the Egesteieans against the Selinuntians: 1, 45. an auxiliary: 3, 3. τριήρεις, auxiliary ships: 5, 10. a succour.

Βοιωτάρχης, 5, 38. a Bœotian ruler.

βολὴ, 5, 65. μέχρι λίθου βολῆς, within stone's throw.

βορέας, 6, 104. the northwind.

βορρᾶς, 6, 2. τὰ πρὸς βορρᾶν, the parts to the north.

βόσκω, 7, 48. βόσκοντες ἐνιαυτὸν ἤδη, to have maintained now a whole year, to have had in one's pay a year already.

βοτάμιον, 5, 53. a pasture.

βούλευμα, 3, 36. a determination.

βουλευτέος, 7, 60. τοῖς 'Αθ. βουλευτέα ἐδόκει, the Athenians judged they ought to deliberate, hold a council: 1, 72. ἔδοξεν αὐτοῖς παριτητέα ἐς τοὺς Λακεδαιμονίας εἶναι δηλῶσαι περὶ τοῦ παντὸς ὡς οὐ ταχέως αὐτοῖς βουλευτέον εἴη, the opt. is employed particulary after the particles ὅτι, ὡς, in *oratione obliqua*, Matth. Gr. Gr. 791.

βουλευτήριον, 1, 141. a council: 2, 15. ἐν, one general council: 8, 93. οἱ τετρακόσιοι ἐς τὸ βουλευτήριον ὅμως καὶ τεθορυβημένοι ξυνελέγοντο, Matth. Gr. Gr. 866.

βουλευτής, 3, 70. a senator: 8, 69.

βουλεύω, 5, 30. βουλευσάμενοι, to conspire, come to a resolution: 7, 14. βουλεύσασθαι, to advise, debate, deliberate: 6, 47. πρὸς τὰ παρόντα, conformably to, as the present posture of affairs required: 8, 8. ἐβουλεύοντο, consulted together: 3, 38. βουλευομένοις περὶ πόλεως, to deliberate on state-subjects: 3, 28. βουλεύσαι περὶ Μυτιληναίων ὁποῖον ἄν τι βούλωνται, to take what measures they please regarding the Mytileneans: 1, 120. ἃ καλῶς δοκοῦντα βουλευθῆναι, things, which appear wisely designed: 1, 69. βεβουλευμένοι, to plan: 1, 43. βουλεύσεσθε, to counsel.

βουλή, 1, 138. δι' ἐλαχίστης βουλῆς, with the least deliberation: 5, 38. 45. a council, 47. ἡ β., the senate: 3, 70. 6, 9.

βούλησις, 6, 78. οὐκ ἀνθρωπείας δυνάμεως βούλησιν ἐλπίζει, to conceive a hope beyond the power of man (to fulfil:) 5, 105. wish, desire: 3, 68. τῇ ἑαυτῶν δικαίᾳ βουλήσει, with perfectly just intentions on their part, 39. ἐλάσσω τῆς βουλήσεως, less than or infe-

rior to the intention: 1, 92. a design: 2, 35. βουλήσεώς τε καὶ δόξης τυχεῖν, to meet, satisfy the wishes and opinions of: 7, 57. good-will, inclination: 4, 108.

βούλομαι, 7. 48. βούλοιντο, to wish: 6, 50. βουλόμενοι τὰ Συρακοσίων, to be on the side of the Syracusans, to favour their side: 5, 35, βούλονται, to want, desire: 7, 49. τὸ βουλόμενον, a party, that wished: 6, 54. ἐβούλετο, to mean, purpose, intend, 38. ὧν βούλονται, for what they desire, (but are unable) to do: 7, 35. οὐκ ἂν σφίσι βουλομένοις εἶναι τὸν στρατὸν ἰέναι, that it would not be with their will, consent that the army should go, that they would not consent to the army's march, to let the army go: 5, 7. βούληται, to chuse, think proper: 3, 2. βουληθέντες, to wish, intend, design: 1, 90. τὸ βουλόμενον τῆς γνώμης, their real thoughts, their meaning: 6, 57. ὅ, τι βούλονται, εἰπεῖν, to speak their minds: 7, 73. βουλήσεται, to please: 1, 34. ἐβουλήθησαν, wished: 8, 56.

βράγχος, 2, 49. hoarseness.

βραδέως, 1, 78. deliberately, 5, 70. slowly.

βραδὺς, 1, 84. 7, 43. tardy, slack: 3, 38. προνοῆσαι, slow: 4, 34. βραδυτέρους, slacker, slower, less alert, 8. βραδυτέρα, slower.

βραδύτης, 1. 71. slowness, tardiness, 5, 75.

βραχέως, 1, 97. briefly: 3, 61. 5, 9.

βραχὺς, 1, 130. ἔργοις προύδήλου, to discover (one's designs) by trifling circumstances before the time: 1, 140. περὶ βραχέος πολεμεῖν, to go to war for a trifle: 6, 8. προφάσει, upon, from a slight, light, inconsiderable, and specious, i. e. hollow, unsound, reason, motive, pretext, ground: 7, 2. πλὴν κατὰ βραχύ τι, except by a very little, all but a small part: 1, 78. ὡς οὐ περὶ βραχέων, (to deliberate) as if not about trifles: 4, 14. διὰ βραχέος, through the little intervening space, 4,

76. at a short distance: 7, 29. βραχέος ᾠκοδομημένου, low, built low, short: 4, 6. βραχυτάτην, of shortest continuance, 3, 46. Matth. Gr. Gr. 161.: 4, 102. φυλακὴ δέ τις βραχεῖα, some little guard: 8, 106.

βραχύτες, 3, 42. γνώμης, meanness, want of judgment, sense.

βροντὴ, 2, 77. thunder: 7, 79.

βρόχος, 2, 76. a rope.

βρῶμα, 4, 26. food, 59. βρώματα, food, articles of food.

βρῶσις, 2, 70. περὶ ἀναγκαίας, for the sake of, in the place of necessary food.

βύζην, 4, 8. tightly, closely, thoroughly, 10.

βωμός, 5, 50. an altar, 60.

Γ.

Γαλήνη, 4. 26. a calm.

γαμέω, 1, 126. γεγαμηκέναι, to marry, espouse, 128. γῆμαι, 6, 55.

γαμικὸς, 2, 15. γαμικῶν, nuptials: 6, 6. nuptial, connubial, relating to marriage.

γὰρ, 7, 67. ὑπερβαλλόντων γὰρ, nempe, to wit, (declaratory, explanatory:) 66. Ἀθηναίους γὰρ ἐλθόντας, (explanatory,) seeing that, to wit, for example, 50. for, because, moreover, besides, 28. τὸ γὰρ αὐτοὺς, the construction, (ἠπίστησεν ἄν τις, repeated from the preceding sentence, or something like that under-

stood,) τὸ αὐτοὺς πολιορκουμένους ὑπὸ Π. μηδ᾽ ὡς ἀποστῆναι—ἀλλ᾽—ἀντιπολιορκεῖν—καὶ τὸν παράλογον τοσοῦτον ποιῆται—ὥστε—ἦλθον ἐς Σ., no one would have believed that they would have acted in such a way, or their acting in such a way would have appeared incredible, (an anacoluthon:) 8, 96.: 5, 66. γάρτοι.

γε, 1, 32. at least, 70. ἡμῖν γε, to us at least, 80. ἑνί γε, one at least: 6, 10. εἴ γε, for ὅτι, 68. ἦλθόν γε, in fact, 56. ἔχοντάς γε ὅπλα, particularly as they had arms: 7, 14. οὐ μέντοι γε, not however, in fact, atleast, 6, 3. particularly, 40. ὡς τῆς γε ἡμέρας, surely, certainly, for certain : 6, 34. ᾗ τοῖς γε ἐπιχειροῦσι, or to give at least previous intimation to the invaders, 8, 97.

γεγωνίσκω, 7, 76. καὶ βουλόμενος ὡς ἐπὶ πλεῖστον γεγωνίσκων ὠφελεῖν, to speak aloud audibly.

γείτων, 4, 64. a neighbour.

γέλως, 4. 28. laughter : 6, 35. ἐς γέλωτα ἔτρεπον τὸ πρᾶγμα, to turn the office into laughter, ridicule, to laugh at the whole affair.

γεμίζω, 7, 53. γεμίσαντες ὁλκάδα κληματίδων, to fill full, to laden.

γέμω, 7, 25. γέμοντα χρημάτων, to laden with goods, stores.

γενεά, 1, 14. a generation.

γενναῖος, 4, 92. noble, daring : 3, 83. τὸ γ., nobleness, generosity : 1, 136.

γενναιότης, 3, 82. nobleness, candour.

γενναίως, 2, 41. nobly, bravely.

γένος, 7, 57. Ἀργεῖοι, Argives by birth.

γεραιός, 6, 18. γεραιτέροις, seniors, elders.

γέρας, 1, 25. an honour, a mark of respect : 3, 58. ἀτίμους γερῶν, despoiled of their honours : 1, 13. γέρασι, privileges, 50.

γεύω, 2, 50. γευσάμενος, to taste.

γέφυρα, 1, 137. 4, 103. a bridge.

γεωμόροι, 8, 21. landed proprietors, colonists, men of property, see Duker.

γεωργέω, 3, 88. to cultivate, farm, till.

γεωργία, 1, 11. tillage, agriculture.

γεωργὸς, 1, 142. an agriculturist, a husbandman.

γῆ, 5, 14. 23. a territory : 7, 28. κατὰ γῆς, by land : 3, 7. : 1, 2. κατὰ γῆν, by land : 7, 4. τὰ ἐκ τῆς γῆς, affairs on shore : 5, 4. territory, country : 8, 24, 40.

γηραιός, 6, 54. in old age.

γίγνομαι, 4, 106. ἐγένετο λαβεῖν, to be going to take : 5, 45. γενομένου, occurring : 3, 40. γενόμενοι ὅτι ἐγγύτατα τῇ γνώμῃ τοῦ πάσχειν, to come as near as possible to the suffering in idea, in one's mind : 4, 68. οὐκ ἐγένετο, to be impossible, impracticable 5, 20. ἐγένοντο, to take place, to happen : 7, 18. τοῖς Λακ. ἐγένετό τις ῥώμη, the Lacedæmonians conceived a kind of confidence, resolution, 5, 14. ἐγεγένητο, an instance of the omission of the 2d. augm. in the plusq. perf., Matth. Gr. Gr. 203. : 6, 54. τῶν γιγνομένων εἰκοστὴν (sc. μοίραν,) a twentieth of the produce, proventuum, quæ proveniunt, fructus, περὶ τοῦ γενομένου, about the fact, event, de re egesta : 4, 44. τὸ γεγενημένον, the fact, state of the case : 5, 45. ἐγένετο οὕτως, it fell out in this manner, 25. γενομένῳ, being present, attending at: 6, 58. τὸ γενόμενον, the occurrence, spot, where the occurrence took place: 5, 49. ὃ τῷ θεῷ γίγνεται, that, which belonged to the god : 2, 19. τὰ ἐν Πλαταιᾷ τῶν ἐσελθόντων Θηβαίων γενόμενα, the gen. expresses the cause from its sense of 'with respect to,' and hence is rendered 'on account of,' (with the passive, though rarely, it is used for ὑπὸ, as here, but the participle stands for a subst., Matth. Gr. Gr. 493.)

γιγνώσκω, 1, 86. to understand, 124. to decree : 5, 36. ταῦτα, to take cognizance of: 6, 9. to judge, to be of opinion : 1, 8. γνωσθέντες, to be known, recognized : 8, 1. ἔγνωσαν, to ascertain, 4, 44. to know, understand : 3, 37. γνωσόμεθα, to be aware of: 4, 60. γνῶναι, to understand: 7, 47. ἐγίγνωσκεν τοιαῦτα, to be of opinion, to judge, such was the opinion: 3, 16. ἐγνώκασιν, to judge, think, 38. ἔγνωσται, to be decreed, restored : 1, 36. γνώτω, let him understand : 1, 25. 4, 14. 5, 15. γνόντες, to be aware, have a notion, 3, 46. ἄλλως, to decree otherwise, 3, 48. ἀμείνω τάδε ταῦτα, to be convinced : 3, 44. γιγνώσκω τἀναντία, to be of quite a contrary opinion, *longe aliter sentire*: 2, 48. ὡς ἕκαστος γιγνώσκει, every one according to his knowledge :

3, 36. ἐγνῶσθαι τὸ βούλευμα, to be decreed, passed : 1, 70. γνῶσι, to decree, decide : 6, 15. γνοὺς, to perceive, 7, 4. to have knowledge, 8, 12. to learn : 3, 46. γνῷ, to be assured : 1, 77. γνώσεσθε, to command, direct to be done: 7, 3. ἔγνω, to perceive, find : 7, 48. ἐπιτιμήσει γνώσεσθαι, to learn from, by the invectives, *i. q.* ἐξ ἐπιτιμήσίων, as below, ἐκ τούτων : 1, 120. γνωσθέντα : 1, 102. οἱ δ' Ἀθηναῖοι ἔγνωσαν —ἀποπεμπόμενοι, they perceived that they were sent away, the second verb ἀποπεμπόμενοι is put in the part., because it marks merely the object of the former imperfect verb, Matth. Gr. Gr. 794.: 1, 102. οἱ δ' Ἀθηναῖοι ἔγνωσαν οὐκ ἐπὶ τῷ βελτίονι λόγῳ ἀποπεμπόμενοι, the verbs of perceiving, of which is ἔγνωσαν here, take the participle; when the object of such verbs is to be expressed by a verb, it is in the nomin., because its subject is the same as that of the principal action, Matth. 829.: 7, 77. γνῶτε ἀναγκαῖόν τε ὂν ὑμῖν ἀνδράσιν ἀγαθοῖς γίγνεσθαι, Matth. 829.

γλίχομαι, 8, 15. ἐγλίχοντο, had desired.

γλῶσσα, 1, 138. τῆς Περσίδος, the Persian language: 3, 112. Δωρίδα γλῶσσαν ἱέντας, speaking the Ionian dialect: 2, 68. 7, 10.

γνήσιος, 6, 55. legitimate.

γνώμη, 4, 56. opinion, view:

5, 26. attention, mind : 1, 32. τῇ τοῦ πέλας γνώμῃ, at the will or opinion of one's neighbour : 7, 68. τὸ θυμούμενον τῆς γνώμης, the indignation of the mind : 7, 64. an intention, a design, 3, 40. τῇ γνώμῃ, in (their) intention : 3, 50. Κλέωνος γνώμῃ διέφθειραν, at the motion, *ex sententia* : 1, 54. γνώμᾳ τοιᾷδε, by reasoning of this nature : 5, 13. mind, inclination : 7, 72. εἶχον τὴν γνώμην, to be intent upon, to resolve, 4, 125. γνώμην εἶχεν, to have intention, 7, 15. to entertain an opinion, to think : 3. 91. ἀπὸ τοιᾶσδε γνώμης, with some such design as this, 9. ἴσοι γνώμῃ, like-minded, ὁμοιότροποι ταῖς γνώμαις : 5, 75. γνώμῃ, at heart, 38. ὁ αὐτός εἰμι τῇ γνώμῃ, to be of the same opinion, to persist in the same opinion : 1, 70. γνώμῃ οἰκειοτάτῃ, a spirit of mind most at home, within call, ready for service : 6, 9. παρὰ γνώμην εἶπον, to say, speak against one's own judgment, opinion : 1. 62. a design, plan, purpose, 71. spirit, temper : 4, 85. γνώμῃ ξυμμάχους, friends at heart, allies in intention and disposition : 5, 48. εἶχον τὴν γνώμην πρὸς Λ., to look towards : 6, 45. πάσῃ τῇ γνώμῃ, with the utmost attention, with all their mind and soul : 5, 38. concurrence, assent : 1, 22. τῆς ξυμπάσης γνώμης τῶν ἀληθῶς λεχθέντων, the general sense of what was really

spoken, the drift of the arguments : 8, 87. 90.

γνώμων, 1, 138. κράτιστος, a judge, Schol. κριτής.

γνωρίζω, 7, 44. γνωρίσαι, to recognize, distinguish : 5, 103. γνωρισθεῖσαν, being discovered, found out.

γνῶσις, 7, 44. a distinguishing, discerning, (as of a friend from an enemy in the dark,) τοῦ οἰκείου, the recognition of a friend.

γοῦν, 1, 10. however, 20. for instance, 74. forsooth : 5, 40, at worst : 7, 47. ταῖς γοῦν ἐπελθούσαις ναυσὶ, certainly, nevertheless, surely with the reinforcement of ships.

γράμμα, 7, 8. 1, 133. γράμματα, a letter : 4, 50. 5, 29. an expression, a sentence.

γραμματεὺς, 7, 10. τῆς πόλεως, a clerk, scribe.

γραμματεύω, 4, 118. ἐγραμμάτευε, to act as clerk.

γραφὴ, 1, 29. the writing letter, 134. an inscription.

γράφω, 1, 133. 5, 26. γέγραφε, to write, 29. γεγράφθαι, to be written, worded, expressed, 20. γέγραπται, to be written, 24. to be compiled : 7, 8. ἔγραψεν ἐπιστολὴν, to write, compose : 5, 29. ἐγέγραπτο, to be said : 7, 14.

γυμνάζω, 1, 6. γυμνάζεσθαι, to exercise one's self.

γυμνητία, 7, 37. the light-armed, (abstract for concrete,) Liv. *levis armatura*.

γυμνικὸς, 3, 104. 5, 80. gymnastic.

γυμνοπαιδία, 5, 82. the festival of the naked games at Lacedæmon.

γυμνός, 5, 10. τὰ γυμνὰ πρὸς τοὺς πολεμίους δοὺς, leaving exposed to the enemy that part unprotected by the shield : 2, 49. μηδ᾽ ἄλλο τι ἢ γυμνοὶ ἀνέχεσθαι, nor bear to be any thing else but naked: 2, 4.

γυναικεῖος, 2, 45. ἀρετῆς, i. e. τῶν γυναικῶν, female virtue, the virtue or duty of woman.

γυνή, 5, 32. a woman.

γωνιώδης, 8, 104. ὀξεῖαν καὶ γωνιώδη τὴν περιβολὴν, angular.

Δ.

Δαιμόνιος, 2, 64. τὰ δ., divine infliction, evils from above.

δαίμων, 4, 97. a demi-god, a deity.

δαὶς, 7, 53. δᾳδὸς, a firebrand, brand, combustible.

δάκρυ, 7, 75. δάκρυσι πλησθὲν, to be filled with tears.

δάνεισμα, 1, 121. ποιησάμενοι, to make a loan.

δαπανάω, 3, 46. to expend (one's) funds, income : 7, 29. to expend money, to be at an expence : 4, 3. τὴν πόλιν, to plunge the city in expence: 1, 141. δαπανῶντες ἀπὸ τῶν αὑτῶν, to lay out from their own, to take out of their own pocket, 8, 45. to live a life of luxury or expence.

δαπάνη, 6, 31. μεγάλαις δαπάναις τῶν τριηράρχων, at great expence to the trierarchs: 3, 46. δαπάνην ἀποδοῦναι, to reimburse or pay expences; 7, 28. δαπάναι, expences : 3, 13. χρημάτων, the expenditure, laying out, consump-

tion of money : 3, 31. 6, 15.: 1, 83. 99. ἀπὸ τῆς δαπάνης, by means of or out of the expence : 2, 77. 8. 46.

δάπανος, ὁ, ἡ, lavish, expensive, 5, 103.

δασὺς, 4, 29. thick.

δεῖ, 5, 26. δέοι, to follow of necessity: 6, 56. ἔδει ἄρξαι μὲν αὐτοὺς, compositum erat, convenerat, they were to begin: 7, 27. οὓς ἔδει ξυμπλεῖν, who were to have sailed with: 1, 81. δεήσει, there will be required : 7, 48. εἰ δεῖ, ' if needs must': 1, 71. δεῖ, there is need, cum gen.: 5, 15. ἰδεῖ, to happen of necessity : 3, 44. δεῖν, to need, require ; 3, 2. ὅσα ἔδει, (to wait till) what they wanted, (had arrived;) 8, 33. δέωνται, should want: 6, 13. δεηθέντες ὠφελείας : 1, 27. ἐδεήθησαν, to request : 1, 75. δεηθέντων : 3, 55. αὐτὸς δεόμενος, at his own request: 5, 32. ἐδέοντο, to entreat : 1, 32. δεησομένους, to request petition for : 1, 70. τὰ δέοντα πράξαι, to do what is necessary to be done : 5, 66. τὸ δέον, what is wanted : 8, 7. νῆες μιᾶς δέουσαι τεσσαράκοντα, nine and thirty ships, 25. νευσὶ δυοῖν δεούσαις πεντήκοντα, 8, 6. ἑνὸς δέον εἰκοστὸν ἔτος, the nineteenth year, 4, 102. Matth. Gr. Gr. 174. : 2, 77. τοὺς Πλαταιέας τἄλλα διαφυγόντας ἐλαχίστου ἐδέησε διαφθεῖραι, perparum aberat quin ignis deleret, here the verb impers., followed by a proposition dependent on it, does not, as usually is the case, take the chief word of the following prop. as a subject, Matth. 431. 476. 796.

δείδω, 1, 56. δείσαντες, to be apprehensive, 7, 53. δείσαντες περί, to have an anxiety about, 5, 34. 44. : 5, 40. ἔδεισαν, to fear: 7, 73. δεδιὼς, afraid, 5, 8. 38. 50. 8, 7. : 5, 14. ἐδεδίεσαν, to fear: 2, 11, δεδιότας τῷ ἔργῳ παρασκευάζεσθαι, to prepare for action with fear, fearful care, (i. e. with a proper sense of danger :) 1, 136. δεδιέναι, to be afraid : 6, 38. δέδοικα μέντοι, μήποτε, I fear indeed but sometime or other : 1, 36. γνώτω τὸ μὲν δεδιὸς αὐτῶν ἰσχὺν ἔχον τοὺς ἐναντίους μᾶλλον φοβῆσον, τὸ δὲ θαρσοῦν μὴ δεξαμένου ἀσθενὲς ὂν πρὸς ἰσχύοντας τοὺς ἐχθροὺς ἀδεέστερον ἐσόμενον, where τὸ δεδιὸς—θαρσοῦν is used for τὸ δέος—θάρσος, i. e. participles used as substantives, Matth. Gr. Gr. 376.

δείκνυμι, 4, 78. ἔδειξαν ἕτοιμοι ὄντες, to shew, prove one's self: 5, 8. δείξειεν, to expose, betray to view : 6, 34. δείκνυσθαι, to be shewn, displayed : 1, 74. ἐδείξαμεν, to display, 76. δεῖξαι, to prove, 5, 41. to lay open, to make a disclosure of, to shew, 9. δείξω, to demonstrate, prove, 72. ἔδειξαν, to shew one's self, (in a middle sense.)

δείλη, 4, 69. περὶ δείλην, about dusk, evening : 3, 74. 8, 26. twilight.

δειλία, 3, 82. pusillanimity : 1, 122. διὰ δειλίαν, through pusillanimity : 5, 100. cowardice, pusillanimity.

δειλὸς, 2, 62. τινὶ, a coward.

δεῖμα, 2, 102. 7, 80. δείματα, terrors, apprehensions.

δεινὸς, 7, 48. ἐν δεινοῖς ὄντες, to be in danger, in a critical state, 3, 9. in dangers, difficulties, extremities : 7, 29. δεινὴ, dreadful, 77. ἐκ δεινοτέρων, out of or in more dangerous circumstances: 6, 60. ποιούμενοι δεινὸν, to be vexed, incensed, 1, 102. ποιησάμενοι, to consider it a henious affront: 5, 91. 8, 5. formidable: 6, 36. able, clever, skilful : 6, 30. δεινὰ, dangers, perils, 77, τὸ δεινὸν, danger, calamity : 5, 22. dreadful, worth apprehension, 42. δεινὰ ἐποίουν, to be highly offended: 7, 73. νομίσας δεινὸν εἶναι, a sad, dangerous thing: 8, 45. ἦλθεν ἐς τὸ δεινὸν, to incur danger : 2, 21. δεινὸν φαίνεσθαι, to shew himself worthy of indignation : 7. 12. strange, surprising : 5, 9. δεινότερος, more dreadful, 4, 10. more dangerous: 3, 37. δεινότατος, most dangerous, mischievous, 6, 49. formidable: 8, 46.: 6, 60. δεινὸν ποιούμενοι εἰ τοὺς ἐπιβουλεύοντας σφῶν τῷ πλήθει μὴ εἴσονται, where εἰ is used to express the object of wonder, and does not mean if, as usual, Matth. Gr. Gr. 939.

δεινότης, 3, 46. terror: 4, 10. the formidable appearance : 8, 68.

δεινόω, 8, 74. ἐπὶ τὸ μεῖζον πάντα δεινώσας, to exaggerate, to paint in dreadful colours.

δειπνοποιέω, 4, 103. δειπνοποιησάμενος, cænatus, having taken supper, refreshment.

δέκα, ten, 8, 77. οἱ δὲ ἀπὸ τῶν τετρακοσίων πεμφθέντες ἐς τὴν Σάμον οἱ δέκα πρεσβευταὶ, Matth. Gr. Gr. 401. : 1, 57. μετ᾽ ἄλλων δέκα, a phrase equivalent to δέκατος αὐτὸς, where is to be remarked the use of αὐτὸς, which put after an ordinal number shews that one person with several others, whose number is less by one than the number implied in that ordinal, has done something, Matth. Gr. Gr. 681. : 6, 50.

δεκαετὴς, 5, 25. of ten years' continuance.

δεκάπλεθρον, 6, 102. προτείχισμα, of the extent of ten plethra.

δέκατος, 1, 18. tenth : 7,

18. δέκατον ἔτος τῷ πολέμῳ ἐτελεύτα, the tenth year ended to the war, i. e. the tenth year of the war.

δελφινοφόρος, 7, 41. κεραῖαι, bearing dolphins, i. e. masts of lead formed in that shape.

δένδρον, 4, 69. fruit-tree: 2, 75.

δενδροτομέω, 1, 108. to cut down trees.

δεξιὸς, 1, 24. ἐν δεξιᾷ, on the right hand: 3, 82. dexterous, able: 5, 10.

δεξιότης, 3, 37. quickness of wit, shrewdness, cleverness.

δέος, 1, 26. δέει, through fear: 4, 125. διὰ τὸ δέος αὐτῶν, through fear of them : 5, 30. μέγα, a great fear, 3, 45. δεινότερον, a greater terror, more alarming fear: 1, 75. fear, apprehension: 4, 84. τοῦ καρποῦ, fear for (their) fruit: 3, 14. 5, 50.

δέῤῥεις, 2, 75. hides.

δεσμὸς, 4, 41. δεσμοῖς φυλάσσειν, to keep in chains.

δεσμώτης, 5, 35. a prisoner bound.

δεσμωτήριον, 6, 60. a prison.

δεσπότης, 6, 80. a master.

δεῦρο, 3, 64. μέχρι τοῦ δεῦρο, up to this moment.

δεύτερος, 2, 97. 6, 78. second.

δεχήμερος, 5, 32. of ten days' continuance, 26. δεχήμερον.

δέχομαι, 1, 143. δέξαιτο, to concert, undertake : 5, 28. ἐδέξαντο, to receive well: 1, 9. δεδεγμένοι, to receive as a tradition, 35. δεχόμενοι, to reosive into alliance : 5, 31. δέξασθαι, to take hold of, 37. δεχομένους τὸν λόγον, lending a favourable ear to, 1, 95. : 7, 77. ἂν ἐπιόντας δέξαιτο, to resist your onset : 1, 33. δεξάμενοι, to receive into one's protection, 3, 13. ξυμμάχους ἡμᾶς, to receive us into alliance, 4, 43. δεξαμένων ἐν χερσὶν, engaging hand to hand, 5, 25. δεξαμένοις, acknowledging, accepting, 4, 56. : 4, 21. 6, 50. δέξασθαι, to receive : 1, 24. ἐδέξαντο, to admit, consent to, 76. ἐδεξάμεθα, to accept : 1, 40. δέχοισθε, to receive into alliance : 8, 20. δέχεσθαι, 25. δεξομένους, who would receive or sustain (their thack.)

δέω, 4, 47. δεδεμένους, to be bound : 1, 30. δήσαντες εἶχον, to keep in chains, 93. : 3, 28. δῆσαι, to put in chains.

δὴ, 1, 8. 4, 78. 6, 50. φίλους δὴ, hîc acerbissimæ ironiæ inservit, 37. εἰ δὴ ἔλθοιεν, but suppose they were really to come : 8, 52.

δῆθεν, 1, 92. in truth.

Δήλια, τὰ, a festival celebrated at the island of Delos, 3, 104. καὶ τὴν πεντετηρίδα, τότε πρῶτον μετὰ τὴν κάθαρσιν ἐποίησαν οἱ Ἀθηναῖοι, τὰ Δήλια: " with subst., which have a generic signif., a more precise definition of them or the name is put in the nomin.," Matth. Gr. Gr. 446. Here, however, the obs. applies to an accus.

δῆλος, 1, 93. ἡ οἰκοδομία δήλη ἐστὶν, the building shews (that,) an instance of the use of the nomin., where a verb used impersonally in other languages being followed by a proposition dependent on it, takes the chief word of that proposition for a nomin., Matth. Gr. Gr. 429. : 1, 140. δῆλοι ἦσαν ἐπιβουλεύοντες, to be plainly, clearly, manifestly designing to attack us, conspiring against us, 71. δῆλοι ὦσι μὴ ἐπιτρέψοντες, to be manifestly men, who will not permit : 3, 64. δῆλον ἐποιήσατε οὐδὲ τότε τῶν Ἑλλήνων ἕνεκα μόνοι οὐ μηδίσαντες, after verbs ' to shew' the object is put in the participle, and here is the nomin., because the subject of it is the same, as the finite verbs, Matth. Gr. Gr. 831.

δηλόω, 1, 10. δηλῶν, to shew, 90. δηλοῦντες, to disclose, 82. to declare, 67. to lay open, 11. δηλοῦται, 13. δεδήλωται, 74. δηλωθέντος, to be made manifest, cum apparuisset, the gen. of the participle here stands alone without a subject, as often when the subject is indefinite, Matth. Gr. Gr. 862. : 7, 25. δηλώσαντες, to explain : 8, 14. δηλωσάντων, to communicate : 2, 50. μάλιστα ἄλλο τι ὂν ἢ ἐδήλωσε, to shew particularly that it was something else than : 1, 2b. δηλῶσαι, to shew (itself,) appear :

3, 37. ὡς ἐν ἄλλοις μείζοσιν οὐκ ἂν δηλώσαντες τὴν γνώμην, the participle here with the use of ἂν has the same signif., as the opt., ὡς εἰ οὐκ ἂν δηλώσειαν, quasi non possint ostendere, Matth. 924. : 83, 84. ἡ ἀνθρωπεία φύσις—ἀσμένη ἐδήλωσεν ἀκρατὴς μὲν ὀργῆς οὖσα, κρείσσων δὲ τοῦ δικαίου, πολεμία δὲ τοῦ προύχοντος, verbs of shewing take the participle, (not the infin.) to express their object, Matth. 830.

δήλωσις, 1, 73. a declaration, disclosure : 2, 61. a manifestation, an evidence : 4, 40. δήλωσιν ποιούμενοι, implying, intending, intimating, 126.

δημαγωγὸς, a leader of the people, a demagogue, 4, 21.

δημεύω, 5, 60. ἐδήμευσαν, to confiscate.

δημιουργὸς, 5, 47. a magistrate of the people.

δημοκρατέω, 5, 29. δημοκρατουμένην, to be governed by a democrasy : 7, 55. to have a popular government : 8, 73.

δημοκρατία, a democrasy, popular government, 2, 65. 8, 90.

δῆμος, 5, 4. the commons, the people, the plebeians, 27. : 1, 24. the populace, democratical part of a state, 6, 27. δήμου καταλύσεως, a putting down, a subversion of the democrasy : 2, 85. the generality, populace : 5, 81. πρὸς τὸν δῆμον προσῆγον, to conduct any one to an audience with the popular assembly : 2, 65. 8, 64. 70. δημόσιον, 5, 18. a state-prison.

δημόσιος, 1, 90. : 2, 13. δημόσια, public property, 37. (κατὰ τὰ,) in public affairs, 6, 12. τὰ δ., the public state, common-wealth : 1, 128. δημοσίᾳ, by the public authority, 67. at the public expence, 5, 11. : 5, 50. 6, 31 : 1, 80. πλούτῳ, public wealth : 4, 121. δημοσίᾳ, by public decree, 2, 34. ταφὰς ἐποιήσαντο, to inter publicly, with public honours.

δημοτικὸς, 6, 28. suitable, becoming to, proper to, consistent with democrasy.

δῃόω, 1, 81. 96. 2, 11. 4, 56. to lay waste, to devastate, ravage : 7, 18. 19. 26. ἐδῄωσαν : 4, 2. 5, 33. ἐδῄουν : 4, 1. 5, 23. δῃώσαντες, 8, 36. δῄπου, 8, 87.

διὰ, 6, 11. διὰ πολλοῦ γε ὄντων, to be at a great distance, to be a long way off : 3, 21. δι' ὀλίγου ὄντων, to be at a little distance : 1, 77. διὰ τὴν ἀρχὴν, by means of our dominion, 2. 68. δι' αὐτὸ, on this account, 7, 34. δὶ ὅπερ, 5, 60. διὰ τὸν νόμον, on account of the law, as by law enacted : 3, 23. διὰ τοῦ μεταπυργίου, through or by the intermediate space : 3, 21. διὰ δέκα ἐπάλξεων, every ten battlements : 6, 34. διὰ φόβου εἰσὶ, to be afraid, 90. διὰ μακροῦ, shortly, 7, 71. 5,

14. δι' ὀλίγου, within a little
of it, soon after, 7, 4. δι'
ἐλάσσονος, at a less distance :
5, 61. διὰ βραχείας μελλήσεως,
after the interval of a short
delay : 1, 63. διὰ τάχυυς,
quickly, 1, 80. 3, 13. διὰ
ταχέων : 1, 11. διὰ τοὺς ποιητὰς,
through the poets, by means
of the poets : 7, 40. διὰ πολλοῦ θορύβου ἀντανήγοντο, in
great disorder, much con-
fusion, in a hurry : διὰ παντὸς, 4, 61. by all means, 1,
76. throughout, 14. διὰ πάσης
(sc. ναὸς,) throughout the
whole length of the ship : 7,
1. διὰ τοῦ πορθμοῦ, through
the multitude : 5, 29. δι'
ὀργῆς ἔχοντες, to be angry
with, 46. : 6, 60. διὰ δίκης
ἐλθεῖν, to stand trial : 1, 73.
εἰ καὶ δι' ὄχλου ἔσται, although
it shall be with some dis-
gust and weariness to you :
6, 59. διὰ φόβου μᾶλλον ὢν, to
be in fear, to stand in fear :
1, 63. διὰ τῆς θαλάσσης, close
by the side of the sea : 6, 57,
ὡς ἂν μάλιστα δι' ὀργῆς, with
all possible anger, all the
anger in the world, in the
greatest rage imaginable :
1, 70. διὰ ὅλου τοῦ αἰῶνος,
throughout (their) lives . 2,
18. ἐδόκουν οἱ Πελοποννήσιοι
ἐπελθόντες ἂν διὰ τάχους πάντα
ἔτι ἔξω καταλαβεῖν, εἰ μὴ διὰ τὴν
ἐκείνου μέλλησιν, this prep.
with the accus. signifies 'on
account of,' hence in the
Latin sense of *propter*, 'with
respect to,' or 'in considera-

tion of,' especially in the
phrase εἰ μὴ διὰ τοῦτο, unless
this prevent ; διὰ τάχους for
ταχέως, with the adj. in the
gen. for an adverb. Matth. Gr.
Gr. 890. 891. : 5, 29. δι' αἰδοῦς
ὄμμ' ἔχειν, to look ashamed,
an instance of the prep. διὰ,
which with this verb con-
stitutes a phrase, Matth. 890.

διαβαίνω, 7, 31. 4, 103. διέβη
τὴν γέφυραν, to cross, 1, 115.
διέβησαν, to pass over, 4, 38.
3, 22. : 2, 5. διαβάντες, to
pass, cross, 67. 8, 25. 1, 64. :
1, 114. 7, 71. διαβεβηκότες, to
cross over : 1, 109. διαβὰς,
to cross over, 3, 3.

διαβάλλω, 5, 16. to calumniate, slander, 6, 83. to cri-
minate : 3, 109. διαβαλεῖν, to
cast (disgrace) on : 4, 22.
διαβληθῶσιν, to be calumniated, slandered : 2, 18. διέ-
βαλεν, to expose to suspicion, occasion calumny : 5,
46. διαβληθῇ, to suffer reproach : 3, 42. 5, 45. διαβα-
λὼν, to calumniate: διαβαλλό-
μενός, to be calumniated,
slandered : 6, 30. διαβαλοῦσιν
ἐπὶ τὴν ἄκραν, to cross over to.

διάβασις, 3, 23 a passage
across, a passing over : 4,
103. 8, 5. : 7, 4. a ford, 74.

διαβατήριος, 5, 54. τὰ δ.,
the sacrifices celebrated on
crossing the borders with an
army, 116.

διαβατὸς, 2, 5. to be passed, passable, which can be
forded.

διαβιβάζω, 1, 105. διεβίβαεαι, to send over, transport (troops) into, 4, 8. to convey, ferry over.

διαβοάω, 8, 63. διαβοώντων, to raise a thorough clamour, to clamour vehemently.

διαβολή, 1, 131. a charge: 5, 17. calumny, slander, scandal: 6, 29. περὶ αὑτοῦ, a charge, accusation against any one: 2, 13. ἐπὶ τῇ ἑαυτοῦ διαβολῇ, with a view to render himself suspected: 6, 41. calumnies, slanders, 29. ἐκ μείζονος, with a heavier accusation, more matter of accusation: 1, 127. reproach, reflection: 8, 91.

διαβόλως, 6, 15. ἐμνήσθη αὐτοῦ, to make dishonourable, invidious mention, calumniate, speak ill of.

διαβουλεύομαι, 2, 5. διαβουλευομένων, to deliberate: 7, 34. διαβουλευσαμένους, to deliberate, spend time in deliberation.

διάβροχος, 7, 12. soaked, rotten, leaky.

διαγγέλλω, 7, 73. διήγγειλαν, to report, make a report, Matth. Gr. Gr. 418.

διάγγελοι, 7, 73. τῶν ἔνδοθεν, informers, who give secret information, intelligence.

διαγίγνομαι, 5, 16. διεγένετο, to pass through life, to persevere.

διαγιγνώσκω, 1, 87. to distinguish, 6, 29. διαγνῶσι, to try (a cause,) decide, give verdict: 1, 91. διαγιγνώσκονται τά τε σφίσιν αὐτοῖς καὶ

τὰ κοινά, to discern what was for their own peculiar advantage and what was for the common interest of Greece: 7, 44. διαγνῶναι, to distinguish, discern, make out, hear distinctly, 4, 46. to decide, decree: 1, 118. διέγνωστο, to be discerned: 4, 40. διεγίγνωσκε, to distinguish: 1, 69. διεγνωκότας, to decide, settle: 8, 53. διαγνωσμένην κρίσιν, a sentence, trial already decided: 1, 126. ᾗ ἂν ἄριστα διαγιγνώσκωσι, in what way they should decide to be best.

διαγνώμη, 1, 87. a decree: 3, 42. a deliberation, consultation, 67.

διάγνωσις, 1, 50. a distinction, discovery, perception.

διάγω, 4, 47. διῆγον, to lead through, 78. 108. διαγόντων: 1, 90. δῆγε, to loiter, lose time: 4, 78. διάξειν, to be about to traverse: 7, 39. ἐπὶ πολὺ διῆγον τῆς ἡμέρας, to spend, draw out much of the day: 7, 71. ἐν τοῖς χαλεπώτατα διῆγον, Matth. Gr. Gr. 421.

διαγωνίζομαι, 1, 39. to contend in a cause or trial: 5, 10. διαγωνίσασθαι, to contend 8, 46.

διάδηλος, 4, 68. to be distinguishable, notable.

διαδιδράσκω, 7, 85. διαδιδράσκοντες, to run away and escape.

διαδίδωμι, 1, 76. 4, 36. διαδιδόναι, to give in parts, to

divide: 8, 29. διέδωκε, distributed.

διαδικαιόω, 4, 106. διαδικαιούντων, shewing their fairness, equity.

διαδοχή, 2, 36. τῶν ἐπιγιγνομένων, successive generations: 7, 28. κατὰ διαδοχήν, by relief, turns, in succession.

διάδοχος, 1, 110. one who relieves another, being a further supply: 3, 115. a successor: 8, 85.

διάδυμι, 4, 110, διαδύντες, getting through, under.

διάζωμα, 1, 6. a broad belt hanging from the waist like the Scotch kelt.

διαζώννυμι, 1, 6. διεζωσμένοι, to be bound with a girdle.

διαθορυβέω, 5, 29. διαθορύβει, to alarm, throw into a tumult, to provoke, disturb.

διαθροέω, 6, 46. διεθρόησαν, to publish, divulge: 8, 91.

διαιρετός, to be discerned.

διαιρέω, 5, 2. διελὼν, having thrown down, demolished: 6, 51. ἔλαθον διελόντες, to break open, cleave in two: 4, 110. διήρουν τυλίδα, to burst open, break through: 5, 3. διῃρημένον, what has been thrown down, demolished: 2, 75. διῃρημένοι κατ᾽ ἀναπαύλας, to be distributed so as to relieve one another, divided into companies for relieving one another: 5, 26. διῄρηται, to be divided, marked, distinguished: 7, 19. διελόμενοι, to divide into portions, to distribute, 5,

76. to divide into shares, 4, 11. κατ᾽ ὀλίγας ναῦς, to be divided, 69. taking in shares, having apportioned: 2, 76. τὸ διῃρημένον, the cleft chasm: 3, 114. διείλοντο, to be divided among, (κατά:) 2, 78. κατὰ πόλεις, to distribute among the several cities, (i. e. the troops of,) to assign a portion of circumvallation to each city.

δίαιτα, 1, 185. ἔχειν δίαιταν, to reside in a place: 7, 82. τῆς ἀναγκαιοτάτης ἐνδείᾳ διαίτης, through want of necessary sustenance: 1, 6. daily life, mode of living, habits, ξυνήθη δίαιταν μεθ᾽ ὅπλων ἐποιήσαντο, they went about their ordinary business in armour: 6, 15. extravagance in diet, (food, and clothing:) 2, 16. way of life: 7, 74. ὅσα περὶ τὸ σῶμα ἐς δίαιταν ὑπῆρχεν ἐπιτήδεια ἀφῃρημάσθαι, to be necessary with regard to the body for food (and clothing.)

διαιτάομαι, 7, 77. πολλὰ ἐς θεοὺς νόμιμα δεδιῄτημαι, in my course of life I have paid my numerous duties to the gods, 87. διῃτήθησαν, to live: 1, 6. διαιτώμενοι, to be disciplined, mannered.

διαίτημα, 1, 6. custom, mode of life.

διάκειμαι, 1, 75. ἐπιφθόνως, to be envied: 7, 77. to be affected (by disease:) 4, 92. ὡς αὐτοῖς διάκειται, how it is with them: 8, 38. affected.

διακελεύομαι, 7, 71. a cheering.

διακελεύω, 8, 97, διεκελεύοντ-
ται, to order, command.

διάκενος, 5, 71. τὸ διάκενον,
the void space.

διακηρευκεύομαι, 4, 38ι διακη=
ρευκεύσασθαι, to dismiss a
herald.

διακινδυνεύω, 4, 19. 27. διακινδυνεῦσαι, to try an experiment, run a risk, 5, 46. to
put all to hazard: 7, 1. δια-
κινδυνεύσωσιν, to venture, try
at all hazards: 1, 142, διακιν-
δυνεύσειαν, to make an attempt,
put any thing to the hazard :
7, 60. to decide by a battle,
try one's fortune in engagement, 47. ἀλλ' ἅπερ καὶ διανοηθεὶς ἐς τὰς Ἐπιπολὰς διακινδυνεῦσαι, ἐπειδὴ ἔσφαλτο,but which
also having intended he had
made an attempt upon Epi-
polæ, since he had failed ;
but according to the intention, with which he ventured
the attack upon Epipolæ,
since he had failed; but as
he intended when he made
&c. (the infinitive διακινδυνεῦσαι is better than the vulgar
reading διεκινδύνευσεν, since
the sentence is in the *oratio
obliqua.*) 6, 99.

διακινέω, 5, 25. διεκίνουν, to
disturb, counteract.

διακλέπτω, 7, 85. τὸ διακλαπὲν,
the part privately secreted.

διακληρόω, 8, 30, διακληρω-
σάμενοι, to cast lots.

διακομιδὴ, 3, 76. transpor-
tation, carriage over.

διακομίζω, 1, 136. to convey,
3, 23 : 1, 89. διεκομίζοντο, to

convey, transport : 8, 8. 4,
46. διεκόμισαν, to convey, 38.
διεκομίσαντο, to convey away:
7, 4. διακομίσας : 8, 23. διεκόμισαν, to transport.

διακονία, 1, 133. an agency,
a commission.

διάκονος, 1, 133. an agent.

διακόπτω, 4, 111. διακοπέντος
μοχλοῦ, having been cut in
two, broken asunder : 2, 4.
διακόψαντες, to cut, cleave
through, split.

διακοσία, 1, 62. two hun-
dred.

διακοσμέω, 1, 20. to arrange,
set in order: 6. 54. διεκόσμη-
σαν καλῶς τὴν πόλιν, to adorn,
beautify : 2, 15. διεκόσμησε,
to put in order, to settle : 6,
57. διεκόσμει, to arrange, set
in order.

διάκοσμος, 4, 93. παρασκευὴ
καὶ διάκοσμος, the preparation
and arrangement.

διακρίνω, 3, 9. διακρίνοιντο,
to separate, secede, revolt
from : διεκρίθησαν, 7, 34. to be
separated, to part, 38. 1, 18.
to separate into parties, to
join in different leagues for
peaceful purposes, 105. to
part asunder (as comba-
tants:) 5, 79. διακριθῆμεν, Dor.
for διακριθῆναι, to decide by
arbitration, Matth. Gr. Gr.
267.: 8, 11. διακριθέντες, separated from : 1, 49. διεκί-
κριτο, to make a difference.

διακριτέος, 1, 86. to be
settled, decided.

διακωλύω, 7, 2. διεκώλυσέ, to
prevent : 1, 138. to impede :

5, 52. διεκώλυσᾰν, 7, 2. to hinder: 2, 17. διεκώλυε, to forbid : 3, 49. διεκώλυσε μὴ διαφθεῖραι, to hinder (him) from putting to death, to prevent the execution : 7, 18. διεκωλύθη, to be hindered, diverted, prevented : 8, 82.

διακωχὴ, 3, 87. an intermission.

διαλαμβάνω, 7, 73. διαλαβόντας, to beset, intercept (with a guard.)

διαλανθάνω, 3, 25. διαλαθὼν ἐσέρχεται, to get through undiscovered : 2, 68.

διαλέγω, 5, 59. διελεγέσθην μὴ ποιεῖν μάχην, entered into a compact (with Agis) to induce him not to engage, to withdraw his army : 6, 57. 8, 93.

διαλείπω, 3. 74. διαλιπούσης ἡμέρας, a day intervening : 1, 112. διαλιπόντων τριῶν ἐτῶν, three years having expired : 7, 38. διαλιπούσας, to be apart, distant : 5, 10. διαλιπὼν, to faint, swoon away.

διαλλακτὴς, 4, 60. a peacemaker.

διαλλάσσω, 3, 10. τῷ διαλλάσσοντι τῆς γνώμης, a difference, diversity, dissonancy of mind, judgment, thought, 4, 20. διαλλαγῶμεν, to agree, make up, where the article communicates to the participle the power of a subst, Matth. Gr. Gr. 394. : 3, 82. διηλλαγμένα τοῖς εἴδεσι, varying in external form : 6, 47. διαλλάξοι Σελινουντίοις αὐτοῖς, to

reconcile the S. to them, to settle the differences between the two people : 6, 47.

διάλυσις, 4, 19. dissolution: 1, 51. διάλυσιν ἐποιήσαντο, to make a dismissal, to dismiss (one's fleet :) 5, 36. dissolution, rupture : 1, 137. destruction.

διαλυτὴς, 3, 82. a dissolver.

διαλύω, 3, 83. διαλύσων, one about to break an engagement : 4, 118. διαλύοντος ἀμφίλογα, to settle, compose : 2, 12. διαλύσας, to dissolve, break up (the council ;) 7, 34. διαλυθέντος, to disband, to be dispersed : 1, 140. διαλύεσθαι τὰ ἐγκλήματα, to decide their differences, quarrel, to end, determine their allegations : 4, 74. διαλυθέντων, to be disbanded, dismissed : 5, 50. διελύθησαν, to separate, 2, 23. κατὰ πόλεις ἕκαστοι, they dispersed, departed severally to their own cities, home, 3, 26. to be disbanded, 2, 78. : 4, 19. διαλύεσθαι βεβαίως, to be completely eradicated, effectively abolished : 5, 55. διαλῦσαι τὰ στρατόπεδα, to break up the encampments, disband the army, 8, 46. to finish : 5, 113. διαλυόμενοι, to separate one's self from : 1, 131. διαλύσειν τὴν διαβολὴν, to disperse the calumny, rid one's self of the charge : 5, 36. διαλῦσαι τὰς σπονδὰς, to break off, to dissolve : 5, 1. διελύοντο, to be dissolved, to be at an end.

διαμαρτάνω, 1, 106. διαμαρτὼν τῆς ὁδοῦ, to miss the way, 7, 44. διεμαρτόντες τῶν ὁδῶν, to miss one's way: 2, 78. διήμαρτον τούτου, to fail in an attempt.

διαμαρτία, 4, 89. τῶν ἡμερῶν, mistake of the day.

διαμάχομαι, 7, 63. to fight it out strenuously: 3, 42. to contend (in argument:) 5, 41. to fight it out, to settle a dispute by battle: 1, 143. to fight: 3, 40. μὴ μεταγνῶναι ὑμᾶς, to contend against your changing your opinion.

διαμάω, 4, 26. διαμώμενοι, digging up.

διαμέλλησις, 5, 99. ὅσοι ἠπειρῶταί που ὄντες τῷ ἐλευθέρῳ πολλὴν τὴν διαμέλλησιν τῆς πρὸς ἡμᾶς φυλακῆς ποιήσονται, will have a good deal of indifference in respect to keeping guard against us owing to their freedom.

διαμέλλω, 1, 71. διαμέλλετε, to delay, go on delaying: 7, 49. διεμέλλησαν, to delay: 1, 112. διαμέλλωσι, to be dilatory, to delay: 7, 40. διαμέλλοντας, to loiter, dally, protract, 8, 40. to delay: 6, 75.

διαμέμφομαι, 8, 89. διεμέμφοντο τὰ πράγματα, to complain about the state of affairs.

διαμνημονεύω, 1, 22. διαμνημονεῦσαι, to remember.

διαναυμαχέω, 7, 60. διαναυμαχήσαντες, to fight it out, to decide by an engagement: 8, 27. διαναυμαχεῖν, to engage in a naval fight.

διανέμω, 3, 27. ἅπασιν, to distribute to all.

διανίστημι, 4, 128. διαναστάς, to be alienated, ἀποστάς, Schol.

διανοέω, 1, 18. διανοηθέντες, to determine upon: 8, 2. διενοοῦντο, determined: 5, 10. διενοεῖτα, to have intention, 43. to intend, have in view, 8, 33. to decide: 1, 140. διανοήθητε αὐτόθεν, to resolve thenceforward, from this point, moment, 124. to design (to do any thing:) 3, 2. πρότερον ἢ διενοοῦντο, before or sooner than they intended: 4, 13. διενοήθησαν, to expect, lay one's account for: 7, 12. διανοοῦνται, to scheme, resolve, plan: 4, 72. διανενοημένοι, to decide, design, 46. διανοηθείς, to design: 1, 143. διανοηθέντας, to conceive, imagine: 8, 40.

διάνοια, 6, 11. counsels, designs, plans: 4, 52. intention, design, plan: 2, 87. μέγα τι τῆς διανοίας τὸ βέβαιον, very great confidence of mind, 20. τοιαύτῃ διανοίᾳ, with such reflections: 6, 15. mind, idea, conception, 65. εἶναι ἐν διανοίᾳ, to intend, purpose: 1, 144. a design (of the enemy:) 5, 9. a design, an intention: 1, 138.

διαπαντός, 7, 6. thoroughly, decidedly: 1, 37. ever, always.

διαπειράομαι, 6, 91. διαπειρᾶσθαι, to experience.

διαπέμπω, 1, 129. διαπέμψαι,

to convey : 4, 123. διέπεμψε, to send along with, to appoint an escort, to dismiss with : 2, 14. διεπέμψαντο, to transport : 4, 55. διέπεμψαν, to dismiss into divisions, to appoint variously to different spots.

διαπεραιόω, 3, 23. διεπεπεραίωντο, to cross over : 8, 32. διαπεραιοῦται, passes over.

διαπλέω, 4, 24. διαπλεῦσαι, to sail through : 7, 29. διέπλευσε, to sail across : 1, 111, διαπλεύσαντες πέραν, to sail to parts beyond, 8, 24. to depart : 6, 44. διέπλει, to sail over : 4, 38. διαπλεύσας, having sailed, being despatched, having sailed as a despatch, 6, 50. to sail, cross over.

διάπλοος, 4, 8. the transverse sailing : 3, 93. the passage over : 6, 31. μέγιστος, a very long voyage.

διαπολεμέω, 6, 37. διαπολεμῆσαι, to fight it out, to go through with a war, to bear or support a war : 7, 14. διαπεπολεμήσεται ὁ πόλεμος, to be ended, brought to an end, decided, 25. διαπολεμησόμενον, Matth. Gr. Gr. 871. : 5, 56. ὡς διαπολεμησόμενον, an instance of a participle in the nomin. absolute, Matth. 864.

διαπολέμησις, 7, 42. an end of war, a conclusion of war.

διαπολιορκέω, 3, 17. διεπολιόρκησαν, to continue at a

siege to the end of it, to remain during a whole siege.

διαπόμπιμος, circular messenger, διαπομπή, circular message, 6, 41. τὴν δ' ἐπιμέλειαν καὶ ἐξέτασιν αὐτῶν ἡμεῖς ἕξομεν, καὶ τῶν πρὸς τὰς πόλεις διαπομπῶν ἅμα, ἔς τε κατασκοπὴν καὶ ἤν τι ἄλλο φαίνηται ἐπιτήδειον.

διαπόντιος, 1, 141. πόλεμος, maritime.

διαπορεύομαι, 1, 107. διαπορεύσονται, to make a passage through : 5, 52. διαπορευόμενος, to traverse.

διαπορθέω, 8, 24. διεπόρθησαν, ravaged.

διαπράσσω, 5, 89. διαπράσσεσθαι τὰ δυνατὰ, to discuss the probabilities (of a question :) 1, 131. διαπραξάμενος, to use management, to take effectual means, 87, to transact : 7, 40. διεπράσσοντο, to set about business : 3, 82. διαπράξασθαι, to manage, negociate : 4, 28.

διαπρεπής, 2, 34. τὴν ἀρετὴν, signal, pre-eminent virtue : 6, 16. τῷ ἐμῷ διαπρετεῖ, splendour.

διαρκὴς, 6, 90. sufficient : 1, 15. sufficient (for maintenance.)

διαρπάζω, 1, 49. 8, 31. διήρπασεν, to plunder, ravage, 36. διαρπασθέντα, to ravage.

διάρροια, 2, 49. ἀκράτου, violent flux, diarrhœa, excessive looseness.

διασκεδάζω, 1, 54. διασκεδάσειν, to scatter, spread about:

3, 98. διεσκεδάσθησαν, to be dispersed.

διασκευάζω, 4, 38. διεσκευάζοντο, to fit, equip.

διασκοπέω, 8, 4. διασκοπούντες, to pay attention : 1, 52. τοῦ δὲ οἴκαδε πλοῦ μᾶλλον διεσκόπουν ὅπη κομισθήσονται, to look out for, the gen. after the verb in its first especial sense of ' with regard to,' where otherwise περὶ with the gen. is used, Matth. Gr. Gr. 457.: 7, 48. διασκοπῶν, to weigh, consider, deliberate upon, 71. διεσκόπουν περὶ σφᾶς αὐτούς, to be thinking, deliberating about themselves : 6, 59. διεσκοπεῖτο πρὸς τὰ ἔξω, to look, cast one's eye abroad.

διασπάω, 7, 77. διεσπασμένος, separated from, straggling, 44. 5, 70. διασπασθείη, to be separated, disordered, unlinked, Matth. Gr. Gr. 548.

διασπείρω, 3, 30. διεσπάρθαι κατ' οἰκίας, to be dispersed among, up and down the houses : 1, 11. διεσπαρμένων, scattered about, separated from one another.

διάστασις, 6, 18. τοῖς νέοις ἐς τοὺς πρεσβυτέρους, a division, dissension, difference between the young and old, of the young towards the old.

διασταυρόω, 7, 97. διασταυρωσάμενος τὸν ἰσθμὸν, to run a palisado across.

διασώζω, 7, 63. ὡς ἀξία ἐστὶ διασώσασθαι, how it deserves that you should preserve it: 5, 16. διασώσασθαι, to pre-

serve, 46. : 7, 53. διέσωσαν, to preserve, save, 5, 10. διασώσαντες : 2, 62. διασώσωμεν, to preserve: 5, 4. διασώσειαν, 33. διασῶσαι, 4, 60. 6, 23. : 4, 113. διασώζονται, to escape to: 7, 34. διεσώζοντο, to save one's self, to get away safe: 1, 82. διασωθῆναι, to be preserved : 3, 39. : 7, 53. τὰς ναῦς διέσωσαν δυοῖν δεούσας εἴκοσιν, Matth. Gr. Gr. 171.

διατάσσω, 7, 4. τοὺς ἄλλους ξυμμάχους κατὰ τὸ ἄλλο τείχισμα διέταξαν, to dispose the other troops among, along the rest of the works, (or, as we say,) to distribute the rest of the works among the other troops : 4, 31. 130.

διατείχισμα, 3, 34. a fortification, wall (running across, and separating one part of a town from the other.)

διατελέω, 7, 38. διετέλεσαν, to accomplish, finish : 1, 34. διατελοίη, to continue to the end : 6, 89.

διατίθημι, 1, 126. διαθεῖναι, to order, arrange, manage: 6, 15. διαθέντα τὰ τοῦ πολέμου, to administer, conduct, 57. οὐ ῥᾳδίως διετέθη, apparently for διεχρήθη, confectus est, despatched, Schol. οὐδὲ εὐκόλως ἀνῃρέθη.

διατρέφω, 4, 39. διετρέφοντο, to be supported, kept alive.

διατρέχω, 2, 7. 35. διαδραμὼν, to run through (the middle of:) 4, 39.

διατριβὴ, 5, 82. delay, want (of time:) 3, 38. χρόνου, a

waste, loss of time : 5, 38. procrastination : 8, 9. delay.

διατρίβω, 7, 43. to linger, delay, remain, 47. : 8, 9. διέτριβον, to wait, delay : 1, 125. 7, 43.

διαφαίνω, 1, 18. 2, 57. διεφάνη, to appear : 6, 17. διεφάνησαν, to turn out upon inspection.

διαφερόντως, 1, 38. considerably, especially, remarkably, 138. particularly, remarkably : 2, 60. 8, 68.

διαφέρω, 6, 54. τοὺς πολέμους διέφερον, to support, maintain, bring to an end : 4, 58. διαφερομένων, to state one's differences, shew one's grounds of quarrel : 3, 83. ἐπὶ πολὺ διήνεγκεν, was of most avail : 5, 102. κατὰ τὸ διαφέρον ἑκατέρων πλῆθος, according to the different numbers on each side : 3, 39. διαφέροντας τῶν ἄλλων τετιμῆσθαι, to be distinguished in a peculiar manner, to be honoured above, more than the others : 4, 74. διενεγκεῖν ψῆφον, to pass : 8, 8. διαφέρειν, to transport : 5, 86. τὰ τοῦ πολέμου διαφέροντα αὐτοῦ φαίνεται, these warlike preparations appear at variance with it : 6, 92. διαφερόντων μεγίστων, concerns, interests : 1, 11. διέφερον, to carry through : 1, 70. τὰ διαφέροντα, differences, discrepancies :~ 5, 31. διαφερόμενοι τῶν ἐναντίων, to surpass, excel the enemy, our antago-

nists : 1, 18. διενεχθέντες, to quarrel, differ.

διαφεύγω, 4, 19. διαφύγοιεν, to effect an escape, to fly : 7, 44. διέφυγον οἱ πολέμιοι, to escape, evade, elude : 8, 1. διαπεφευγόσι, who had escaped, 5, 82. τῶν διαπεφευγότων, the fugitives : 8, 13. διαφυγοῦσαι, having escaped : 7, 43. διαφυγόντες : 3, 40. διαφεύγοντες, to escape from danger : 7, 71. παρ' ὀλίγον ἢ διέφευγον, to be within a little of, to want but little to, to be all but escaping : 7, 32. διαφυγόντας : 2, 60. 3, 22. 6, 78.

διάφευξις, 3, 23. an escape.

διαφθείρω, 2, 2. διαφθεῖραι, to destroy : 1, 25. διαφθειρομένους, to perish totally, 8, 25. διαφθείρονται, to sustain a loss of : 4, 57. διεφθάρησαν, to slay, massacre, sacrifice, 5, 10. 7, 23. 41. to be destroyed : 7, 30. 44. διέφθειραν, to cut off, 71. διαφθαρεισῶν τοῖς Λ., to be lost to the Lacedæmonians : 2, 77. διαφθεῖραι ἐλαχίστου ἐδέησε, to want very little of destroying : 7, 25. φθάσωσι διαφθείραντες, to be beforehand with in destroying, to destroy (an army) before the expected succours arrive : 2, 49. διεφθείροντο ὑπὸ τοῦ ἐντὸς καύματος, to die of the internal heat, the fever : 8, 1. διεφθάρθαι : 6, 27. μόλις οὐκ ἂν παντάπασιν διεφθάρησαν, with difficulty, hardly to escape utter destruction : 3, 13. διαφθαρῆναι, to be ruined, undone, destroyed, 57. λιμῷ, to perish by hunger : 1, 74. διαφθαρεῖναι, to be ruined : 4, 37. διαφθαρησομένους, about to be destroyed.

διαφθορά, 8, 86. οἱ δ᾽ ἀπήγγελλον ὡς οὔτε ἐπὶ διαφθορᾷ τῆς πόλεως ἡ μετάστασις γένοιτο, ἀλλ᾽ ἐπὶ σωτηρίᾳ, for the destruction, 98.

διαφίημι, 7, 32. διαφήσουσι τοὺς πολεμίους, to permit to pass through, to yield a free passage.

διαφορά, 3, 10. τῶν ἔργων, a diversity of deeds, conduct : 7, 57. dispute, quarrel, 1, 23. 81. ἄρξαι τῆς δ., to begin the quarrel : 1, 112. 2, 37. 62. 4, 83. 5, 26. 42.

διάφορος, 1, 38. 8, 2. ὄντες αὐτοῖς, to be at variance, enmity with, to have a difference with : 1, 78. τὰ δὲ διάφορα δίκῃ λύεσθαι, for ἡ διαφορὰ, the difference, the art. put with an adj., to which it gives the sense of a subst., Matth. Gr. Gr. 391. : 7, 75. τὸ διάφορον, a reverse, a change of circumstances : 2, 37. πρὸς τὰ ἴδια διάφορα, with respect to private suits, between man and man : 6, 62. τὰ διάφορα πρὸς Ἐγεσταίους, variance, quarrel with the Egestæans, 16. at variance with, in opposition to : 1, 56. διάφορα ἐς τὸ πολεμεῖν, difference leading to war : 8, 75.

διαφόρως, 6, 18. ἥκιστα δια-

φόρως πολιτεύωσιν, with the least discord : 7, 71.

διάφραγμα, 1, 133. a partition.

διαφυγγάνω, 7, 44. διαφύγγανον, to escape.

διαφυγή, 8, 11. an escape.

διαφυλάσσω, 2, 65. διαφύλαξει, to guard, preserve in safety.

διαχειμάζω, 6, 72. διαχειμάσοντες, to pass the winter, to winter : 7, 42. διεχείμαζεν, to winter, spend the winter.

διαχείρισις, 1, 97. τῶν πραγμάτων, the management of affairs.

διαχέω, 2, 75. διαχέοιτο, to be scattered, diffused, to slip, fall away, spread abroad : 2, 76. διαχεόμενον, to slip, slide down (with loose earth.)

διαχράομαι, 1, 126. to slay : 3, 36. διαχρήσασθαι, to put to death, to slay.

διαψύχω, 7, 12. διαψύξαι, to dry, air, repair (a ship.)

δίγλωσσος, 4, 109. speaking two tongues : 8, 85.

διδασκαλεῖον, 7, 29. a school.

διδασκαλία, 2, 42. ποιούμενοι διδασκαλίαν, to teach, instruct, shew, 87. παρέξει, to teach a lesson.

διδάσκαλος, 3, 82. βίαιος, a stern task-master : 5, 30. fomenter, author, prime mover, instigator : 3, 42. τοὺς λόγους διδασκάλους τῶν πραγμάτων, instructors, directors.

διδάσκω, 1, 76. 6, 39. to admonish, advise : 4, 88. ἐδίδασκον αὐτὸν, to warn, admonish, suggest, instil into : 5, 27. διδάξαντες, to hint, insinuate, 86. : 2, 60. σαφῶς διδάξας, to state clearly, 93.

διδαχή, 4, 126. a lesson, piece of advice : 1, 120. instruction.

δίδραχμος, 3, 17. ὁπλῖται, heavy-armed soldiers having two drachms per day.

δίδωμι, 5, 47. διδότω, to supply : 2, 27. ἔδοσαν Θυρέαν οἰκεῖν καὶ τὴν γῆν νέμεσθαι, gave them Thyrea to inhabit and the territory to possess, for a possession : 3, 109. ἐδέδοτο, to be granted, 43. διδοὺς φανερῶς τι ἀγαθὸν, to confer a benefit openly : 5, 77. δόμεν for δοῦναι : 1, 28. δοῦναι δίκας, to submit to trial : 4, 56. ἴδοσαν, to grant : 2, 68. διδόασιν ἑαυτοὺς Ἀκαρνᾶσι, to put one's self under, 1, 42. an Attic form of the third person plural pres. indic., Matth. Gr. Gr. 279. : 2, 36. οὐκ ἀπόνως δίδοσθαι, with great labour, pains, 5, 11. διδώκασιν, to institute : 4, 21. διδορένης, offering : 6, 47. διδόναι τροφὴν, to give pay.

διηγυάομαι, 3, 70. διηγγυημένοι τοῖς προξένοις, to be bailed by their foreign connexions, to be ransomed, their friends giving their words for the payment of the money.

διείργω, 3, 107. διεῖργε, to

divide, separate (two hostile armies :) 6, 1. διείργεται, to be severed, separated, divided from : 8, 33. διείργοντε, to be divided from.

διεκπλέω, 1, 50. διεκπλέοντες, to perform the manœuvre of the διέκπλους.

διέκπλους, 2, 89. breaking through the enemy's lines : 2, 83. 7, 36. 69. 70. : 1, 49. a naval manœuvre, the object of which was to dash away the oars of the enemy's vessel by sailing along side of him.

διέξειμι, 2, 49. διέξει, to pass through, to pervade.

διεξέρχομαι, 7, 85. τὴν φυλακὴν διεξῆλθον, to make their way through the guard : 3, 45.

διέξοδος, 3, 98. a way out through (the wood.)

διεορτάζω, 8, 9. διεορτάσωσιν, they had celebrated.

διέρχομαι, 1, 82. διελθόντων, to pass, transpire, (as time :) 5, 50. διῆλθεν, to pass, 1, 21. to run through, take a cursory view of, 6, 46. to go abroad, to spread (of a rumour :) 4, 115. διελθουσῶν τῶν σπονδῶν, being out of date, expired : 7, 73. προφθάσωσι διελθόντες, to get through, pass through before, to have the start and get through before : 7, 32. διελθεῖν, to pass through, 43. to go through with, to have done with : 2, 47. διελθόντος, to be ended, (of time :) 4, 62. διέλθοι, to go through : 5, 13. διῆλθον, to proceed, to continue one's march.

διετήσιος, 2, 38. anniversary, all the year round.

διέχω, 2, 86. διείχετον, to be distant :˙3, 21. διείχον ἀπ' ἀλλήλων, to be distant from each other, to have a space between them, 22. διέχοντες ᾔεσαν, to go with an interval, space between each man : 8, 95.

διηγέομαι, 6, 54. διηγησάμενος ἐπὶ πλέον, to relate, unfold at length, state, detail, narrate.

διήκω, 3, 21. διήκοντες ἐς τὸ ἔσω μέτωπον, to reach to, to extend.

διιέναι, 4, 78. to traverse : 5, 47. διὰ τῆς γῆς, to pass through a country, to march through their territory : 3, 21. διῄεσαν δι' αὐτῶν μέσων, to pass through the middle of them.

διικνέομαι, 7, 79. to pass through, make its way, (as a weapon)

διίστημι, 1, 15. διέστη, to divide into two parties, side with one or other of two, 18. διασταῖεν, to differ, to be at variance, the opt. pres. and aor. 2. as in the aor. pass. of verbs in ω have in the plural, in the poets as well as prose-writers, more commonly the contracted form, Matth. Gr. Gr. 281. : 1, 87. διέστησαν, to divide : 6, 77. διιστάναι, to separate, dissever : 4, 61. διέσταμεν, to be at variance : 6, 79. διαστῶμεν

τἀναντία, to be disunited, broken into opposite factions.

δικάζω, 5, 31. ἐδίκασαν, to pass, pronounce judgment: 3, 44. δικαζόμεθα, to go to law, to try judicially, (opposed to βουλευόμεθα :) 1, 77. δικάζεσθαι, to go to law, 28. to be litigating, 1, 28. δικασθῇ, to be decided, adjudged.

δίκαιος, 4, 106. κήρυγμα, fair, just, kind : 2, 71. οὐ δίκαια ποιεῖτε, to act unjustly : 5, 35. just, fair, equitable, 30. just, right: 3, 10. περὶ τοῦ δικαίε τοὺς λόγους ποιησόμεθα, to speak on the head of justice, equity, fairness : 5, 18. 29. : 5, 22. δικαιοτέρας, more equitable, advantageous : 3, 54. δίκαια πρὸς τὰ Θηβαίων διάφορα, satisfactions as regards the differences with the Thebans : 4, 61. τῷ δικαίῳ, right, (in opposition to βίᾳ,) the dat. for the Latin abl. expresses the kind and manner of an action, Matth. Gr. Gr. 572.

δικαιοσύνη, 3, 63. μετὰ δικαιοσύνης, justly.

δικαιόω, 1, 140. to think just, fair, equitable, to require : 4, 64. to think just, to demand, to require : 2, 61. 5. 105. : 7, 68. δικαιώσωσιν, to excuse, justify, use a justification : 3, 40. δικαιώσεσθε, to condemn : 2, 71. δικαιῶσε, to ordain : 4, 122. ἐδικαίουν, to shew cause, to make appear.

δικαίωμα, 5, 97. δικαιώματι, in right and justification : 6, 80. a justification, an allegation, a defence, an excuse: 1, 41. justification: 6, 79. τὸ ἔργον τοῦ καλοῦ δικαιώματος.

δικαίως, 5, 23. with uprightness, integrity: 6, 34. κατεγνωκότες, to think meanly, to disparage, hold in contempt: 4, 62. 118.

δικαίωσις, 3, 82. δικαιώσει, for the purpose of justification: 1, 141. a demand, claim, injunction: 5, 17. a justification, apology, explaining away: 1, 141. 8, 66.

δικαστήριον, 3, 105, κοινῷ, a common place of meeting for matters of justice: 6, 51. a court of justice.

δικαστὴς, 1, 37. he, who gives the verdict in a cause: 3, 52. an arbitrator, 46. ἀκριβῶς, strict judges: 1, 73. a judge, an umpire: 4, 83.

δίκη, 5, 80. τὰς ἀπὸ στρατιᾶς δίκας, military trials: 1, 28. a trial, 140. : 7, 18. διδόναι δίκας, to abide a trial, decision, judgment, to give satisfaction in a judicial way, to stand a trial, to submit: 1, 78. τὰ διάφορα δίκῃ λύεσθαι, to settle the differences by arbitration: 5, 49. a fine imposed by a verdict, 31, judgment, arbitration, decision, 27. δίκας ἴσας καὶ ὁμοίας δίδωσι, to enjoy the advantage of a fair and equal judicature: 6, 29. δίκην δοῦναι, to suffer punishment, the penalty of the law: 1, 77. ἐν ταῖς ξυμβολαίαις δίκαις, in actions relating to compacts.

δίοδος, 7, 32. road, passage, 78. pass, 2, 4. a way through, 5, 47.

διοικέω, 8, 21. διῴκουν, managed.

διοικοδομέω, 4, 69. διοικοδομήσαντες, building transversely: 8, 90.

διόλλυμαι, 3, 59. διολέσαι, to destroy, 40. διόλλυνται, to destroy for one's own sake: 8, 26.

διόπερ, 1, 71. wherefore.

διόρυγμα, 4, 109. an excavation, a digging through.

διορύσσω, 2, 3. διορύσσοντες, to dig through, to break through.

διότι, 1, 52. because, 23. why, wherefore, 77. wherefore, why it is that: 3, 81. 4, 62.

διπλάσιος, 1, 10. twofold, double, 86. : 3, 67. 7, 67.

διπλασιόω, 1, 69. διπλασιουμένην, doubled, twofold.

διπλασίως, 8, 1. doubly.

δὶς, 2, 51. ; 6, 37. τοσαύτη, twice as great.

διφθέρα, 2, 75. tarpauling.

δίχα, 4, 99. κεραίαν πρίσαντες, to saw in two, asunder: 7, 81. ὄντας, being parted: 1, 64. γιγνομένοις, to be separated, divided, 122. separately: 4, 61. οὐ γὰρ τοῖς ἔθνεσιν, ὅτι δίχα πέφυκε, τοῦ ἑτέρου ἔχθει προσίασιν, the use of the nomin. of an adverb in the predicate, Matth. Gr. Gr. 445. : 8, 46.

διχόθεν, 2, 44. in two ways.

δίψα, 2, 49. thirst.

διωθέω, 2, 84. διωθοῦντο, to keep asunder, push off : 4, 87. διωθεῖσθαι, to repel, keep off, 108.

διώκω, 2, 4. διώκοντας, to pursue, 4, 83. : 1, 62. to pursue (a flying enemy :) 2, 91. διώκοντες ἀτάκτως : 5, 41. 8, 24. διώκοντας τὴν ἐπ᾽ Ἀθηνῶν φέρουσαν, to pursue along a road: 2, 4. διωκόμενοι, to be pursued, chased, 8, 44.

δίωξις, 1, 49. 63. 3, 33. 97. 5, 10. pursuit, 73. 7, 34. 8, 16. 1, 134. : 4, 44. οὐ κατὰ δίωξιν πολλὴν, through there being no such pursuit.

διῶρυξ, 1, 109, foss.

δοκέω, 1, 22. ἐδόκουν, to seem : 7, 1. 11. δοκοῦντας : 5, 41. ἐδόκει, to appear : 5, 38. ἐδόκει, to please, seem right, judge expedient : 7, 43. ἐδόκει διατρίβειν, to resolve, see fit, determine: 5, 18. δοκῇ, to seem right, 47. ἢν μὴ ἀπάσαις δοκῇ, unless it be agreed by all: 1, 31. ἔδοξεν αὐτοῖς, it appeared good to them, 7, 1. to resolve, determine: 4, 104. δοκεῖν ἂν ἑλεῖν, to be likely : 5, 66. δοκοῦντας, to think, fancy, 14. imagining, thinking, 3, 36. δεδογμένων, decree: 5, 72. δόξαντας, to be esteemed : 1, 79. ξυνετὸς δοκῶν εἶναι καὶ σώφρων, to have the reputation of ability and prudence 3, 38. τὸ πάνυ δοκοῦν, an absolute decree, what is plainly decreed, 28. μέχρι οὗ ταῖς Ἀθηναίοις τὶ δόξῃ, till the Athenians had come to some

resolution : 7, 12 : δόξῃ, to deem or appear : 1, 81. δόξομεν, to have the reputation of : 5, 65. Αὐτῷ ἄλλο τι ἢ κατὰ τὸ αὐτὸ δόξαν ἐξαίφνης, on account of some other plan having occurred to him than after the manner of the same: 8, 79. ἀπὸ ξυνόδου δοκεῖν, see 81. 7, 57. Matth. Gr. Gr. 879. the council was the origin of the determination : 1, 125. δεδογμένον, cum visum esset, an example of an impersonal verb in its construction as a participle, which is the nomin. and not the gen. absolute, Matth. 863. : 4, 3. ἐδόκει, videbatur, the accus. with the infin. is used after δοκέω, Matth. 811. : 5, 65. ὁ δὲ εἴτε καὶ διὰ τὸ ἐπιθύμει εἴτε καὶ αὐτῷ ἄλλο τι ἢ κατὰ τὸ αὐτὸ δόξαν ἐξαίφνης πάλιν τὸ στράτευμα—ἀπῆγε, an instance of the use of the participle, where a verb, which is commonly used impersonally, though it receives a subject in its construction as a participle, is put in the nomin. absolute, so long as it is commonly used impersonally, with which class of verbs the rule obtains, Matth. 863. : 8, 90.

δόκησις, 6, 64. an opinion, estimation : 4, 87. ἀναγκαίαν, an inference, 18. a reputation: 3, 45. ἧσσον τῇ δοκήσει, too little in the estimation, opinion : 2, 84. a reputation, 35. ἀληθείας, an opinion of the truth, (entertained by a person speaking, as his idea of what is true, or entertained by the audience, i. e. their belief of the truth of what the speaker says :) 4, 55, expectation : 7, 67. an estimation, opinion : 4, 126.

δοκιμάζω, 6, 53. δοκιμάζοντες τοὺς μηνυτὰς : to try, examine, inquire into the persons of the informers : 3, 38. δεδοκιμασμένου, to be proved, tried, experienced : 2, 35. ἐδοκιμάσθη, to be the opinion of, to be judged.

δοκός, 2, 76. a beam : 4, 112, a rafter, beam, plank.

δόξα, 4, 81. 5, 9. reputation, estimation : 4, 12. opinion, 5, 9, opinion, thought : 3, 61. glory, 4, 17. : 6, 11. πεῖραν τῆς δόξης, a proof, trial of reputation : 1, 5. fame, glory, 32, 2. 42. 4, 12. 126. 7, 66.

δοξάζω, 1, 120. δοξάζομεν, to speculate : 3, 45. ἐπὶ πλέον τι αὐτὸν ἐδόξασεν, to conceive too high an idea of one's self, to magnify one's self, to think more of one's self than is fit.

δόξασμα, 1, 141. idea, opinion.

δοράτιον, 4, 34. spear : 3, 22. javelin.

δόρυ, 5, 10. δοράτων, a spear : 4, 99.

δορυφορέω, i. e. δορυφόρος εἰμί τινος, 1, 130. ἐδορυφόρουν αὐτὸν, to attend, as a guard, a person of consequence, one of the verbs, which has an

accus., which does not mark the passive object of the action, but the object, to which it has only generally an immediate reference, Matth. Gr. Gr. 576.

δορυφόρος, 6, 55. a guard.

δόσις, 1, 137. : 143. δόσεως, a gift.

δουλεία, 1, 8. 5, 9. 23. 69. 86. slavery : 2, 63. ἀντ᾽ ἐλευθερίας, servitude instead of freedom : 2, 71. ἐπὶ δουλείᾳ, with a view to subjecting them : 4, 114, 6, 40.

δουλεύω, 1. 81. δουλεῦσαι τῇ γῇ, to submit to slavery for the sake of the territory : 3, 13. οἱ πρὶν δουλεύοντες, the former dependents, subjects : 1, 74. δουλευόντων, to submit to slavery : 2, 63. ἀσφαλῶς δουλεύειν, to be safe, secure in servitude.

δοῦλος, 5, 9. a slave : 1, 34. ἐπὶ τῷ δοῦλοι εἶναι, (to be sent out) for the purpose of being slaves.

δουλόω, 7, 68. δουλωσόμενοι, with an intention to subjugate, 75. : 1, 98. ἐδουλώθη, to be reduced to slavery, 69. δουλωσαμένου, to enslave : 5, 29. δουλώσασθαι : 1, 16. ἐδούλωσε, to subjugate, subdue : 7, 71. ἐδουλοῦντο γνώμην, to be reduced in spirit, dejected, cast down : 1, 68. δεδουλωμένους, to be enslaved, 124. to enslave, 4, 34. 6, 77.

δούλωσις, 3, 10. ἐπαγομένους δ᾽ ἐλωσιν τῶν ξυμμάχων, to bring

o

slavery, servitude upon the allies, (for τοῖς ξυμμάχοις.)

δοῦπος, 3, 22. δοῦπον ἐποίησε, a clatter (of a falling tile,) a noise.

δραστήριον, τὸ, 2, 63. readiness for action, activity, promptitude: 4, 81. δραστήριον ἐς τὰ πάντα, up to every thing, capable, efficient.

δραχμή, 3, 17. δραχμὴν ἐλάμβανε τῆς ἡμέρας, to receive a drachma a day: 5, 47. Αἰγιναίαν, about a shilling English.

δράω, 7, 67. ἀργότεραι ἐς τὸ δρᾶν, slower in executing, to execute: 1, 142. ἄξιόν τι δρῷεν, to perform any exploit, 131. τὸν βασιλέα δρᾶσαι τοῦτο, to do this to the king: 1, 71. δρῶμεν δ' ἂν ἄδικον οὐδὲν, instance of the use of the opt. and conjunct., where the antecedent with εἰ is wanting, Matth. Gr. Gr. 786. (N.B. it appears by Matth. that οὕτω should be in this instance here in the premises:) 3, 84. ἐν δ' οὖν τῇ Κερκύρᾳ τὰ πολλὰ αὐτῶν προετολμώθη, καὶ ὁπόσα ὕβρει μὲν ἀρχόμενοι τὸ πλέον ἢ σωφροσύνῃ ὑπὸ τῶν τὴν τιμωρίαν παρασχόντων οἱ ἀνταμυνόμενοι δράσειαν, where ἂν usually accompanying the dat. in abstract propositions is omitted, Matth. 758.; an instance of the use of the opt. in abstract propositions, which is used thus, where the indic. is put in other languages, with the expression of indeterminate-

12

ness, although the thing is intended to be determined, ' which they, as is to be expected, may do, are wont to do,' Matth. 757. : 2, 64. ὁ βουλόμενος δρᾶν τι, the active man, the man ready for action : 3, 10. τοὺς βουλομένους δρᾶσαι τοῦτο, to do any thing to any one : 1, 71. δρῶμεν, to do, 43. δράσετε, to perform; 8, 40. ἔδρασαν, effected : 3, 38. τῷ δράσαντι, the injurer, defendant, criminal, 6, 27. δράσαντας, to perpetrate, commit, 1, 20. to accomplish : 1, 69. δρῶντες, to be in action: 1, 5. δρᾶν, to do, perform, accomplish, 5, 13. : 3, 68. δεδρακότες εἰσὶν, to perform, do : 5, 102. τοῦ δρωμένου, by means of acting resolutely, 107. δρᾶσθαι, to be done : 3, 49. δράσειν τὰ δεδογμένα, to execute, 38. τὸ δρασθὲν, a deed, 54. τῶν εὖ δεδρασμένων ὑπόμνησιν, a memorial of service, from δέδρακα, κα being changed into μαι, δέδραμαι, here, however, δεδραμένων, Matth. 231. : 6, 16. ἐκ τοῦ δρωμένου, from the deed, fact, thing done, 71. ἀπὸ τῶν δρωμένων τῆς ὄψεως, from or through the sight of, beholding what was done, the deeds.

δρεπανοειδής, 6, 4. scythelike, shaped like a scythe, resembling a scythe.

δρέπανον, 6, 4. a scythe.

δρόμος, 1, 63. δρόμῳ, by a sally, an impetuous rush : 5,

10. a rapid rate: 5, 3. δρόμῳ ἐχώρει, to retire with speed: 5, 9. δρόμῳ, with rapidity: 4, 31. 112.

δύναμαι, 3, 83. ἢ πιστεῦσαι ἐδύναντο, than bring themselves to believe: 7, 4. δύναιντο, to be able: 5, 9. δύνωμαι, to be able, 5, 4. δύνωνται, 23.: 7, 21. ὡς δύνανται πλείστας, as many as they could: 5, 72. δυνηθῆναι, to be able, 68. οὐκ ἂν ἐδυνάμην, I could not: 3, 46. τὸ αὐτὸ δύναται, to be the same thing, not to matter, to make no difference: 7, 11. δυναίμεθα χρήσασθαι, to be able to employ, make use of: 3, 11. οὐ μέντοι γ᾽ ἂν ἐδοκοῦμεν δυνηθῆναι, we did not, however, think we should be able : 1, 69. δυνάμενος παῦσαι, able to make an end of, 88. μὴ ἐπὶ μεῖζον δυνηθῶσιν, lest they were going on becoming more and more powerful: 6, 36. ἀγγελίαι τοῦτο δύνανται, to mean, to be designed for (any purpose,) to effect, produce an effect, 38. ἐκ τοῦ μὴ δύνασθαι ὑμᾶς, in consequence of your incapacity: 8, 23.

δύναμις, 2, 41. αὐτὴ ἡ δ., the very power itself: 5, 4. dominion, power: 1, 45. κατὰ δύναμιν, as far as their power would admit, 70. power, means: 5, 95.: 1, 18. 65. δυνάμει, by force, power: 1, 2. δυνάμεις, influence, power: 5, 9. ability, 14.: 3, 93. 4, 108. 6, 92. 7, 77. 8, 2.

δυναστεία, 3, 62. power, influence : 4, 78. the exertion of power, violence : 6, 38. ἀδίκους, illegal dynasties, dominations.

δυναστεύω, 6, 89. τῷ δυναστεύοντι, a prince: 2, 102.

δυνάστης, 7, 33. a chief, ruler.

δυνατὸς, 4, 51. powerful, a man in power : 5, 4. a nobleman, a patrician, 21. powerful, able, 89. τὰ δυνατὰ, those things, which are possible: 1, 8. δυνατώτεροι, more powerful : 1, 22. παρὰ τῶν ἄλλων ὅσον δυνατὸν ἀκριβείᾳ περὶ ἑκάστου ἐπεξελθὼν, whereas words signifying ability, possibility, are often added to the superlative, in order to strengthen the signification, these particles are also used without the superlative, ὅσον δ. ἀκρ. for ἀκριβέστατα, Matth. Gr. Gr. 666.: 1, 139. λέγειν τε καὶ πράσσειν δυνατώτατος, after an adj. expressing ability the infin. is usual, Matth. 798.: 3, 11. δυνατώτεροι αὐτοὶ αὐτῶν ἐγίγνοντο, an instance where the compar. is followed by the gen. of the reciprocal pronouns, and the same subject is compared to itself with regard to its different circumstances at different times, Matth. 656.: 5, 47. τρόπῳ ὁποίῳ ἂν δύνωνται ἰσχυροτάτῳ κατὰ τὸ δυνατὸν, an instance of pleonasm, Matth. 949.: 7, 36. κατὰ τὸ δυνατὸν, to the best of their power, as much as they could, 5, 47. to the extent of their power: 5, 35. τὰ δυνατὰ πεποιηκέναι, to do what one can, to act or do to the best of one's ability: 1, 2. δυνατώτατοι, potent, wealthy: 3, 27. τοὺς δυνατοὺς, the rich, the men of property, 2, 65. οἱ δ., sc. τῷ πλούτῳ, the wealthy, 3, 47. τοῖς δ. τῶν ἀνθρώπων, the powerful, the aristocracy, the men of substance: 8, 63. Τῶν Σαμίων προτρεψάντων τοὺς δυνατοὺς ὥστε πειρᾶσθαι μετὰ σφῶν ὀλιγαρχηθῆναι, Matth. 798.

δύο, 3, 15. τοῖς δύο μέρεσιν, two thirds, 3, 89. 1, 74. τῶν δύο μοιρῶν: 1, 20. 22. δνεῖν, two, *dat. sed raro*, δνεῖν is here in the dative, whereas elsewhere in the same author δύο is indeclinable, Matth. Gr. Gr. 171. but we have 8, 101. δνσὶν ἡμέραις, see, however, Lobeck, *ad* Phryn. 211.: 8, 63.

δυσανασχετέω, 7, 71. δυσανασχετοῦντες τὰ γιγνόμενα, to be inflamed, indignant, unable to bear any thing.

δύσβατος, 4, 129. λόφῳ, a false lection for δυσπρόσβατος.

δυσέμβατος, 4, 10. difficult to land.

δύσερως, 6, 13. τῶν ἀπόντων, to dote upon any thing extravagantly, to be bent upon any thing.

δυσεσβολώτατος ἡ Λοκρὶς, 3, 101. most difficult of access, an instance of a masc. adj. with a noun fem., when it is so put from no reference to any word implied in that noun, but a superl. from an adj. common (δυσέσβολος) is sometimes put in the masc. for the fem., Matth. Gr. Gr. 632.

δύσις, 5, 97. πρὸς ἡλίου δύσιν, towards or to the west.

δύσκλεια, 3, 58. infamy,

δύσνους, 2, 60. τῇ πόλει, disaffected to the state.

δύσοδος, 1, 107. difficult of access, hard to pass.

δυσπρόσβατος, 4, 129. λόφῳ, inaccessible, difficult of ascent.

δυσπρόσοδος, 1, 130. αὐτὸν παρεῖχε δυσπρόσοδον, he made himself difficult of access: 5, 65.

δυστυχέω, 6, 16. δυστυχοῦντες, unfortunate, *i. q.* κακῶς πράσσοντες: 5, 46. δυστυχοῦσιν, suffering under misfortune: 7, 18. to be unfortunate, to miscarry.

δυστυχία, 7, 86. ἐς τοῦτο δυστυχίας ἀφικέσθαι, to arrive at this pitch of misfortune: 6, 55.

δυσχερὴς, 4, 85. ποιούμενοι δυσχερὲς, a difficulty.

δυσώδης, 2, 49. fetid.

δύω, 7, 25. δυόμενοι, to go under (water,) to dive.

δωρεὰ, 3, 58. a boon, gift.

δῶρον, 5, 16. a gift, bribe.

E.

Ἐὰν, *Si*, if, 4, 23.

ἔαρ, 3, 116. the spring, 5, 17.: 7, 17. ἦρι : 5, 81. πρὸς ἔαρ, towards near spring : 8, 61. ἅμα τῷ ἦρι εὐθὺς ἀρχομένῳ, Matth. Gr. Gr. 2, 850.

ἑαυτοῦ, 7, 69. τὸ καθ᾽ ἑαυτὸν, what belongs to one as his own : 1, 90. πρὸς ἑαυτῷ, in addition to himself : 1, 8. πλουσιώτεροι ἑαυτῶν γιγνόμενοι, grown richer than themselves, i. e. than they were before: 4, 68. 7, 36.

ἑάω, 2, 21. οὐκ ἐῶντες, forbidding: 2, 36. ἑάτω, to let alone, to pass over (in speaking:) 1, 144. ἑάσομεν, to suffer, permit : 6, 72. οὐκ εἴα, to forbid, 1, 28. οὐκ εἴων, to be unwilling : 1, 70. 5, 47. ἑᾷν, to let, permit, 142. ἑασόμενοι, to be suffered, permitted, 67. 68. ἑάσαντες, to permit: 5, 41. ἑώντων, to suffer, endure, allow : 8, 46.

ἑβδομαῖος, 2, 49. *see* ἐνναταῖος.

ἐγγηράσκω, 6, 18. ἐγγηράσεσθαι, to grow or wax old, to run to decay.

ἐγγίγνομαι, 7, 49. ἐνεγένετο, to ensue, 68. ἐγγενησόμενον, to be in one's power, to have an opportunity : 1, 2. ἐγγινόμεναι, to be coming : 2, 49. 8, 9.

ἐγγράφω, 1, 128. ἐνεγέγραπτο, to be written in a letter: 1, 132. Ἀργίλιος λύει τὰς ἐπιστολὰς, ἐν αἷς, ὑπονοήσας τι

τοιοῦτον προσεπεστάλθαι, καὶ αὑτὸν εὖρεν ἐγγεγραμμένον κτείνειν, a rare constr., which is this, Ἀργίλιος ἐνεγέγραπτο κτείνειν for ἐνεγεγρ. Ἀργίλιον κτείνειν, it was in the letter that Artabazus should put to death Arg., and it flows from this that many verbs used impersonally in other languages, particularly where the accus. is constructed with the infin., usually take the chief word of the following proposition as a subject, Matth. Gr. Gr. 431.

ἐγγύθεν, 3, 13. *ex propinquo*.

ἐγγὺς, near, 2, 44. 71. 7, 69.

ἐγγύτατος, 6, 4. ἐγγύτατα, very nearly, about, *propemodum*, 1, 20. 3, 62. 4, 67. 8, 96. : 2, 21. ἐγγύτερος.

ἐγγώνιος, 1, 93. angular, cornered.

ἐγείρω, 1, 121. 129. ἐγείρομεν τὸν πόλεμον, to raise a war : 7, 51. ἐγηγερμένοι, to be intent, alert, encouraged, stimulated, Matth. Gr. Gr. 207.

ἐγκαθίζω, 4, 2. ἐγκαθεζόμενοι, fixing their camp, pitching their tents, taking up a military station, 3, 1. to encamp.

ἐγκαθίστημι, 5, 70. ἐγκαθεστώτων ὑπὸ νόμῳ, to be arranged as an army, to stand in rank, to walk in step : 1, 4. ἐγκαταστήσας, to appoint, establish: 1, 122. ἐγκαθεστάναι,

ἐγκαθορμίζω, 4, 1. ἐγκαθορμισάμενοι, to take their station, to come to anchor.

ἐγκαλέω, 6, 53. ἐνεκάλει, 4, 123. τοῖς Ἀθηναίοις, to recriminate upon : 6, 53. to lay to the charge of, to impeach, accuse : 5, 46. ἐνεκάλουν, to ask satisfaction for : 1, 72. ὧν αἱ πόλεις ἐνεκάλουν, of which the cities had accused them.

ἐγκαλλώπισμα, 2, 62. πλούτου, an embellishment, the bravery or finery of wealth.

ἐγκάρσιος, 7, 7. oblique, transverse, 7, 4. τεῖχος, 6, 99.

ἐγκαρσίως, 2, 76. transversely.

ἐγκαρτερέω, 2, 61. ταπεινὴ ὑμῶν ἡ διάνοια ἐγκαρτερεῖν ἃ ἔγνωτε, your mind is (too) abject, you are (too) dispirited, (too) much troubled to adhere to or persist in your resolution, ταπεινοτέρα ἢ ὥστε ἐγκ., or ταπεινὴ πρὸς τὸ ἐγκ.

ἐγκαταλαμβάνω, 7, 30. ἐγκαταληφθὲν, to be caught, found : 5, 3. ἐγκαταληφθῇ : 3, 33. ἐγκαταληφθεῖσαι : 4, 35. ἐγκατελαμβάνοντο, to be seized.

ἐγκαταλέγω, 1, 93. ἐγκατελέγησαν, to be collected and put in, piled in.

ἐγκαταλείπω, 2, 102. καὶ ἀπὸ Ἀκαρνᾶνος παιδὸς ἑαυτοῦ τῆς χώρας τὴν ἐπωνυμίαν ἐγκατέλιπε, to leave behind : 4, 44. ἐγκατέλιπον, to leave behind, among : 1, 115. ἐγκαταλιπόντες, 3, 51.: 2, 78. ἐγκαταλελειμμένοι, to be left behind in a place : 4, 19.

ἐγκατάληψις, 5, 72. a seizure, being laid hold of.

ἐγκατασκήπτω, 2, 47. ἐγκατασκῆψαι, to attack (of the plague.)

ἐγκατοικοδομέω, 3, 18. ἐγκατῳκοδόμηται, to build, erect in a place.

ἔγκειμαι, 5, 43. ἐνέκειντο, to push on, to press, promote the business, to use vigorous measures, 2, 59. to inveigh against : 2, 81. ἐνέκειντο, to fall back upon with precipitation : 5, 73. ἐγκεῖσθαι, to press upon an enemy in pursuit : 4, 80. ἐγκειμένων τῇ Πελοποννήσῳ, to hang over, to threaten : 1, 69. ἐγκείσονται ἰσχυρῶς, to lay on, to press to the attack vigorously, 144. ἐγκεισομένους, to press upon, to harass : 4, 22.

ἔγκλημα, 1, 26. 42. 72. 4, 80. charge, accusation, ground of dispute : 1, 67. ἐγκλήματα ἐποιοῦντο, to make charges : 3, 53. 4, 23.

ἐγκρατής, 1, 118. ἐγκρατεστέραν : 5, 35. καὶ εἴ του ἄλλου ἐγκρατεῖς ἦσαν, and as to whatever else they exercised unshackled authority over, and as to whatever else they were absolute masters of.

ἐγκρατῶς, 1, 76. with a strong hand : 6, 92.

ἐγκύπτω, 4, 4. ἐγκεκυφότες, to stoop down.

ἐγχειρέω, 4, 47. ἐγχειρῆσαι, to take in hand : 4, 4. ἐγχειρήσαντες, to undertake, take in hand : 8, 24. ἐνεχείρησαν, undertook : 1, 84.

ἐγχείρησις, 6, 83. in act, performance.

ἐγχειρίδιον, 3, 70. 4, 110. 6, 57. a dagger.

ἐγχειρίζω, 2, 67. ἐγχειρίσαι τοὺς ἄνδρας σφίσιν, to put the men in their hands, to deliver up the men to them : 5, 108. ἐγχειρίσασθαι, to take in hand, to undertake.

ἐγχρονίζω, 3, 27. ἐνεχρόνιζον, to loiter, lose time.

ἐγχώριος, 2, 71. θεοὺς, the gods of a country, peculiar to it, indigenous : 4, 78.

ἐγώ, 6, 33. ἔμοιγε, to me at least, 89.

ἔδαφος, 4, 109. ἐς ἔδαφος, to the ground : 3, 68. to level with the earth : 1, 10. ἐδάφη, a floor, foundation.

ἕδρα, 5, 7. inaction.

ἐδώδιμος, 7, 39. ἐδώδιμα, eatables, provisions, 78. τὶ ἐδώδιμον, some provision.

ἐθὰς, 2, 44. γενόμενος, to become accustomed to, to be used, accustomed to.

ἐθελοντηδὸν, 8, 98. voluntarily.

ἐθελοντὴς, 1, 60. a volunteer : 3, 20.

ἐθελοντὶ, 8, 2. voluntarily.

ἐθελοπρόξενος, 3, 70. a voluntary public friend, the friend of a state, of his own accord, and not expressly appointed by his own state as a guardian of the interests or hospitalities due to another.

ἐθέλω, 5, 21. ἤθελον, to will,

14. to be minded, willing: 1, 75. ἐθελησάντων, to be willing : 7, 18. θέλωσι, to consent to, to be willing, 5, 35. to do willingly, act voluntarily : 5, 72. μὴ θελῆσαι, to refuse, 9. ἐθέλειν, to bear a willing mind.

ἔθνος, 1, 24. 5, 51. 7, 33. a race, nation : 6, 2. a nation, tribe : 2, 9. ἐν ἔθνεσι τοσοῖσδε, in so many nations, in all those nations.

ἐθίζω, 1, 77. εἰθισμένοι, to be accustomed, habituated.

ἔθος, 4, 32. κατὰ τὸ ἔθος, according to custom, as usual : 2, 64. ἐν ἔθει ἦν, to be the way, according to the practice, maxims.

ἔθω, 1, 67. εἰωθότα, 99. εἰωθόσιν, accustomed, 140. εἰώθαμεν : 4, 55. 7, 75. παρὰ τὸ εἰωθὸς, contrary to custom, 4, 67. κατὰ τὸ εἰωθὸς, according to custom : 6, 18. τῷ εἰωθότι κόσμῳ, in the usual decency, decorum.

εἰ, 1, 27. lest : 6, 63. whether, πότερον, num : 3, 43. quamvis, although : 1, 35. εἰ δὲ μὴ, but if that is impossible, 28. but if not, why then : 1, 17. εἰ μὴ εἴ τι, unless perhaps something or other : 1, 58. Ποτιδαιᾶται δὲ πέμψαντες μὲν καὶ παρ' Ἀθηναίους πρέσβεις, εἴ πως πείσειαν μὴ σφῶν πέρι νεωτερίζειν μηδὲν, instance of the use of the optative, (compare 2, 12. 64. 3, 45. 7, 79.) " where εἰ, signifying whether, takes the opt. without ἂν, in a past

action," Matth. Gr. Gr. 786. :
2, 5. τὰ ἔξω ἔλεγον αὐτοῖς μὴ
ἀδικεῖν, εἰ δὲ μὴ, καὶ αὐτοὶ ἔφασαν
αὐτῶν τοὺς ἄνδρας ἀποκτενεῖν,
where εἰ δὲ μὴ is for εἰ δὲ ἀδι-
κοῖεν. In the constr. of conjunctions negative propositions are usually followed in
the antithesis by a negative
condition instead of an af-
firmative, Matth. 939. : 2, 7.
Ἀθηναῖοι δὲ ἐπρεσβεύοντο—ὁρῶντες εἰ σφίσι φίλια ταῦτ' εἴη, where
we see the use of the opt.
after a particle in *oratio obliqua*, Matth. 790. : 2, 39. εἰ
ῥαθυμίᾳ μᾶλλον ἢ πόνων μελέτῃ,
καὶ μὴ μετὰ νόμων τὸ πλεῖόν ἢ
τρόπων ἀνδρείας ἐθέλοιμεν κινδυνεύειν, περιγίγνεται ἡμῖν τοῖς
μέλλουσιν ἀλγεινοῖς μὴ προκάμνειν, where we have εἰ with
the opt. and the indic. in
the conclusion, because the
thing in the conclusion is
determinately asserted, while
the premises convey only a
possible case, Matth. 783. :
2, 60. whereas, when ἂν is
employed with the opt. in
conclusion, εἰ with the opt.
is usual in the premises, here
εἰ is with the indic., where a
circumstance in past time is
represented as a condition
in its relation to a consequence, which is still present, Matth. 783.

εἶδος, 2, 41. ἐπὶ πλεῖστ' εἴδη,
for most kinds of things, the
greatest diversity of pursuits,
actions, circumstances, 50.
8, 56. 90.

εἴδω, εἰδέω, 7, 14. εἰδότας, to
know, 2, 36. 4, 59. εἰδόσι, 74.
1, 78. 5, 13. 39. : 6, 12. εἰδέναι
χάριν μὴ ἀξίαν, not to know
gratitude, not to know how
to be grateful, 7, 21. to be
assured, certain, 1, 5. to learn,
know, 5, 21. 46. to know,
ascertain : 7, 44. οἶδεν, to
know : 2, 21. εἶδον, to see, 5,
8. 10. εἶδε : 6, 6. εἰσομένους, to
learn, know : 6, 60. εἴσονται,
to know, discover : 5, 26.
εἴσομαι, to discern, know : 7,
44. εἰδείη, to know, 1, 51. 5,
9. ἰδὼν, to observe, see, 4, 55.
7, 42. : 7, 29. ἴδοιεν, to see :
1, 72. ᾔδεσαν, to know, to be
aware of, 2, 6. : 8, 87. : 6, 64.
εἰδότες οὐκ ἂν ὁμοίως δυνηθέντες,
that they would not have
been equally able, Matth.
Gr. Gr. 828.

εἰκάζω, 1, 10. 2, 54. ᾔκαζον,
to imagine, suppose : 6, 60.
εἰκάζεται ἐπ' ἀμφότερα, to be
guessed, conjectured both
ways : 4, 126. 5, 9. : 6, 31.
εἰκασθῆναι, to be conjectured,
supposed, imagined : 5, 65.
οὐκ εἶχον ὅ,τι εἰκάσωσιν, were
unable to conjecture, did not
know what to think : 3, 20.
4, 126. 8, 46.

εἰκαστὴς, 1, 138. a conjec-
turer.

εἰκοστὴ, 7, 28. τὴν εἰκοστὴν
τοῖς ὑπηκόοις ἐποίησαν, to impose a twentieth upon the
subject states, i. e. a tax of
a twentieth : 6, 54. : 5, 16.
εἰκοστῶ.

εἰκότως, 3, 2. naturally, as

might be expected : 1, 37.
with justice, with reason :
7, 18. reasonably, justly : 1,
77. likely enough, with good
reason : 4, 24. likely, probably, 73. : 3, 46. fairly, with
reason : 2, 93. probably.

εἴκω, 5, 102. τὸ μὲν εἶξαι, to
yield : 1, 140. εἴκειν Πελοπον-
νησίοις, to submit, make concessions : 2, 61. εἰ δ᾽ ἀναγκαῖον
ἦν ἢ εἴξαντας εὐθὺς τοῖς πέλας
ὑπακοῦσαι ἢ κινδυνεύσαντας περιγενέσθαι, if it were a matter
of necessity, if there was no
other alternative but, either
instantly to submit and be
subject to others, another
state, or to fight it out and
conquer : 2, 64. διὰ τὸ ταῖς
ξυμφοραῖς μὴ εἴκειν, from not
yielding to the pressure of
calamity : 8, 27. εἴξας, to
yield, give way.

εἴκω, to be like, 6, 23. ἀπὸ
τῶν εἰκότων ἀσφαλὴς, reasonably secure, *quantum (per
apparatum) conjici possit :* 3,
40. παρὰ τὸ εἰκὸς, contrary to
or otherwise than what is
fair, just : 7, 66. ἐκ τοῦ εἰκότος,
in all likelihood, most likely,
65. οἷον εἰκὸς, as is natural,
to be expected : 5, 86. κατὰ
τὸ εἰκὸς, as is likely : 3, 40.
εἰκὸς ἦν, to be probable, 6,
55. : 6, 18. τῷ εἰκότι, in all
probability, in reason, reasonably to be expected : 4,
92. εἰκὸς, *consentaneum rationi,*
expedient, free from objection, proper, 98. πᾶν δ᾽ εἰκὸς
εἶναι τῷ πολέμῳ, all is fair to

war : 6, 2. ὡς εἰκὸς, probable,
likely : 6, 17. οὐκ εἰκὸς, it is
not likely to be expected,
nequit fieri : 3, 38. ἐοικότες, to
be like, to resemble : 7, 71.
οὐδενὶ ἐοικὼς, like to none, i. e.
beyond or exceeding any
other, 75. ἐῴκεσαν, to resemble : 5, 77. εἴκωντι the third
pers. plur. in —σι, in the
Doric ends in —τι, Matth.
Gr. Gr. 255.

εἰμὶ, to be, 4, 68. τῷ ὄντι,
in reality, 108. οὐ τὰ ὄντα,
lies, 3, 22. τὸ ὂν, the fact,
truth : 1, 25. ἔστιν ὅτι, sometimes : 6, 96. εἶεν, εἴησαν, Matth.
Gr. Gr. 292. : 2, 2. προϊδόντες
οἱ Θηβαῖοι ὅτι ἔσοιτο ὁ πόλεμος,
the opt. is put particularly
after ὅτι, ὡς, whether the
action be the present, past,
or future tense in *oratio obliqua;* Matth. 791. : 2, 80. : 5,
77. ἤμεν for εἶναι, an instance
where in the Doric η, in the
permutation of letters, is
put for ει, Matth. 29. 294. :
5, 79. ἐσοῦνται, the Doric
form of the fut. ἔσομαι, Matth.
294. : 2, 54. ὁμοῖα εἶναι, to
agree, accord (with some
prediction,) to be the fulfil-
ment of : 7, 61. ἔστι τῳ, many
will be able, it will be for
many a one, (τις in a collective sense :) 7, 70. ἔστιν ᾗ,
somewhere, in some places,
3, 18. ἔστιν οἷ, somewhere, in
some places : 2, 26. Κλεώνυμ-
πος τῆς παραθαλασσίου ἔστιν ἃ
ἐδῄωσε, ἔστιν οἳ does not accord with the constr. of the

P.

proposition, but stands by itself in an adj. sense, ἔνιοι, ἔνιαι, ἔνια, Matth. 698. : 3, 92. 7, 11. 6, 82. ξυγγενεῖς ὄντας δεδουλῶσθαι, to have reduced to servitude though our kinsmen, *quamvis essent* : 1, 130. ὁ Παυσανίας ὢν καὶ πρότερον ἐν μεγάλῳ ἀξιώματι ὑπὸ τῶν Ἑλλήνων, an example of verbs confounded, here a verb neuter, (at least a noun derived from one,) for a passive, Matth. 720.

εἶμι, to go, 1, 82. ἴμεν ἐπ᾿ αὐτοὺς, we will go against them, we will make war upon them : 3, 64. 4, 72. : 5, 65. ἐστρατοπεδεύσαντο ὡς ἰόντες ἐπὶ τοὺς πολεμίους, this verb in the pres. has regularly the signif. of the fut., Matth. Gr. Gr. 738.

εἰπεῖν, to speak, 3, 38. 4, 118. 6, 82. 7, 5. : 6, 82. ἐνὶ δὲ ἔπει πάντα συλλαβόντα εἰπεῖν, the infin. put absolutely, Matth. Gr. Gr. 823.

εἴπως, 1, 58. if any how : 3, 4. πέμπουσι εἴπως πείσειαν, to send (persons) to endeavour to prevail upon, to try if they could persuade.

εἴργω, εἴργω, 4, 9. εἴρξων, to oppose (their landing:) 3, 23. εἴργον βάλλοντες, to check or keep off with missiles : 2, 85. εἴργεσθαι, to be excluded : 1, 62. εἴργωσι, to prevent, hinder : 3, 1. εἴργον τὸ μὴ κακουργεῖν, to prevent the wasting, plundering, ravaging of a territory : 8, 40. εἰργομένην, shut out from : 5, 49. εἴρχθησαν, to be excluded : 1, 141. εἰργόμενοι θαλάσσης, to be excluded from the sea : 8, 24. εἰργομένοις αὐτοῖς τῆς θαλάσσης καὶ κατὰ γῆν πορθουμένοις, ἐνεχείρησάν τινες πρὸς Ἀθηναίους ἀγαγεῖν τὴν πόλιν, Matth. Gr. Gr. 861. : 3, 6. τῆς μὲν θαλάσσης, εἶργον, μὴ χρῆσθαι, Μιτυληναίους, a use of the infin. as epexegesis, the infin. is often put where the preceding verb or the phrase gives a complete and independent sense ; thus, where ὥστε ought to be put in order to express a consequence, Matth. 806.

εἰρεσία, 7, 14. the bench of rowers.

εἴρηκα, 1, 140. 2, 54. 4, 28. 7, 10. 18.

εἰρηναῖος, 1, 29. pacific.

εἰρήνη, 1, 40. 124. 2, 65. 4, 20. 61. 5, 26. peace.

εἱρκτὴ, 1, 131. ἐσπίπτειν ἐς εἱρκτὴν, to be put into prison.

εἰς, 1, 69. ἐς τόδε ἀεὶ, ever since, up to this time, 73. ἐς τὰς ναῦς, into : 3, 34. ἔσχε ἐς Νότιον, to touch at, 20. ἐς ὁ ἐβούλοντο, as far as they wanted : 5, 29. ἐς θροῦν καθίστατο, to be moved to tumult, to undergo commotion : 3, 22. ἐς αὐτὸ τοῦτο παρεσκευασμένους, for this very purpose, 11. ἐς ξυμμαχίαν (πιστὸν,) a security or basis for, with regard to an alliance, *quod attinet ad :* 3, 37. ἐς τὴν τῶν ξυμμάχων χάριν, in order to (winning) the thanks, gratitude of the allies, for the gratitude of the allies : 7, 1. ἐς χιλίους τοὺς πάντας, about 1000 in all, amounting altogether to 1000, 3, 20. 7, 30. 6, 67. : 6, 54. ἐς τὰ ἱερὰ ἔθυον, for ἐν τοῖς ἱεροῖς : 3, 46. ἐς τὸν ἔπειτα χρόνον, for the future : 1, 14. ἐς πλῆθος, to a considerable number : 2, 56. ἐς ἐλπίδα ἦλθον τοῦ ἑλεῖν, to entertain hopes : 7, 44. φίλοι τε φίλοις οὐ μόνον ἐς φόβον κατέστησαν, 36. ἐς ὀλίγον, into a small space, a confined situation, 18. ἐς δίκας προκαλουμένων, to challenge, invite to a legal arbitration, a judicial determination : 3, 27. φέρειν ἐς τὸ φανερὸν, to produce, bring out, expose, 39. ἐς τὰ πρῶτα τιμώμενοι, to be had in the highest honour : 7, 21. ἰέναι ἐς τὴν πεῖραν, to proceed to an experiment, a trial, to venture, make a trial, 28. ἐς φιλονεικίαν καθέστασαν τοιαύτην, to get to such a pitch, 69. ἐς γυναῖκας, touching or with respect to : 3, 22. ἐς τὰς Θήβας ἤροντο, to lift up, towards, on the side of Thebes : 7, 53. ἐς μάχην κατέστησαν πρὸς αὐτοὺς, to come to battle with them, 13. ἐς ἀντίπαλα καθεστήκαμεν, to be reduced to equal terms, to come to close contest, 15. μὴ πράσσετε ἐς ἀναβολὰς, do it without (proceeding to) delay : 3, 10. ἐς οὐδὲν, in no respect, nulla in re, not at all : 7, 56. ἐς τοὺς Ἕλληνας καλὸν

σφίσιν, honourable, glorious towards, before, in the eyes of, the Greeks : 5, 3. βοηθήσαντες δὲ ἐς αὐτὸ, to introduce a succour : 1, 74. ναῦς ἐς τὰς τετρακοσίας, with numerals this prep. signifies sometimes about, 'about 400 ships,' it takes only the accus. case, Matth. Gr. Gr. 887. : 2, 19. into, as ἀφίκοντο ἐς Ἀχαρνὰς —καὶ καθεζόμενοι ἐς αὐτὸ, an instance of a verb, which of itself not implying motion, receives this sense by the constr. with the prep. εἰς, Matth. 885.

εἰς, 3, 39. μάλιστα μίαν πόλιν ἠδικηκότας, to injure (your) above all other cities : 7, 75. καθ' ἓν μόνον τῶν πραγμάτων, with respect to one circumstance alone, in one respect only : 8, 68. τοὺς ἀγωνιζομένους πλεῖστα εἰς ἀνὴρ δυνάμενος ὠφελεῖν; so Lat. unus omnium maxime, Matth. Gr. Gr. 2, 667.

εἰσαγγέλλω, 1, 131, ἐσηγγέλλετο, to be informed of, 6, 51. ἐκ Καμαρίνης, to receive intelligence from Camarina, 41. εἰσαγγελλόμενα, to be announced, reported : 3, 3. ἐσηγγέλθη αὐτοῖς, to be informed, to have word brought : 1, 116. Περικλῆς ᾤχετο κατὰ τάχος ἐπὶ Καύνου καὶ Καρίας, ἐσαγγελθόντων, ὅτι Φοίνισσαι νῆες ἐπ' αὐτοὺς πλέουσιν, the gen. absolute here stands alone, because its subject can be easily sup-

plied from the preceding
words, Matth. Gr. Gr. 869.

εἰσάγω, 4, 26. to introduce :
2, 6. εἰσήγαγον, to lead, convey into : 8, 16. εἰσηγάγοντο,
to bring in, to introduce : 3,
34. εἰσαγαγὼν, to conduct in,
4, 71. : 5, 35. εἰσαγαγεῖν ἐς τὰς
σπονδὰς, to draw in, lead to,
inveigle into, to engage : 4,
67. εἰσῆγον κατὰ τὰς πύλας, to
introduce, bring in.

εἰσακοντίζω, 2, 79. εἰσηκόντι-
ζον, to shoot at with javelins,
3, 23. ἐς τὰ γυμνὰ, to shoot at
the unarmed parts (of the
body :) 5, 10. εἰσακοντίζοντες,
to cast darts : 7, 78.

εἰσακούω, 4, 34. εἰσακούοντας,
to hear, 3, 4. εἰσακηνυόντων, to
hearken to, to obey : 5, 45.
εἰσήκουον, to give heed to : 1,
126. ἢν μή τι εἰσακούωσι, if they
would not hearken at all : 5,
40. εἰσήκουον, to agree, 22. to
listen, obey, 17. εἰσακούοιεν,
to apply one's attention, to
listen : 8, 32. εἰσήκουον, to
comply with.

εἰσάπαξ, once.

εἰσβαίνω, 1, 73. 3, 16. εἰσβάν-
τες, to embark, 1, 74. 7, 13.
εἰσβῆναι, 91.

εἰσβάλλω, 1, 46. εἰσβάλλει,
discharges itself, 6, 17. : 2,
21. εἰσβαλὼν, 13. 5, 71. to fall
into (a position, as soldiers
into the ranks :) 4, 2. εἰσέβαλον
ἐς τὴν Ἀττικὴν, to make an
irruption into, to invade, 7,
19. 4, 41. εἰσβάλωσιν, 2, 13,
ὁπότε οἱ πολέμιοι εἰσβάλοιεν,
whenever the enemy were
about to invade them : 2, 10.

ὡς εἰσβαλοῦντες, intending to
invade : 3, 96. εἰσβεβλήκει, to
invade, 2, 48. εἰσβεβλήκοιεν, to
throw into, 4, 1. εἰσεβεβλήκεσαν
ἐς τὴν Ῥηγίνων, to make an
aggression upon, to cast
one's self into, to invade : 1,
58. εἰσβαλεῖν, βάλλω is conju-
gated regularly here with the
fut. βαλῶ, Matth. Gr. Gr.
319, : 8, 31. εἰσβαλλόμενοι, putting on board their own ships.

εἴσβασις, 7, 30. an embarka-
tion.

εἰσβατὸς, 2, 41. accessible,
which can be entered, open.

εἰσβολὴ, 7, 27. an incursion:
2, 13. 20. 3, 89. 5, 20. 7, 18.

εἰσδέχομαι, 8, 16. to expect:
4, 111. εἰσεδέχοντο, to receive
into, to admit.

εἰσδρομὴ, 2, 25. rushing in.

εἰσέρχομαι, 5, 8. εἰσέρχεται,
to enter : 2, 2. εἰσῆλθον, to enter into (a place,) 5, 36. εἰσελ-
θεῖν ἐς τὰς σπονδὰς, to become
a party to, to accede to, 48.
4, 110. 7, 1. : 3, 102. εἰσεληλυ-
θυῖαν, to enter, 7, 29. εἰσεληλυ-
θότες ἄρτι ἔτυχον, to be lately
entered in : 2, 54. 3, 25.

εἰσηγέομαι, 4, 76. εἰσηγουμένου,
to be at the head : 6, 99. εἰση-
γησαμένου, to advise, 3, 20.
εἰσηγησαμένων πεῖραν, to be the
author of the attempt, to propose the attempt.

εἰσήγησις, 5, 30. the head,
prime cause, source.

εἰσηγητὴς, 8, 48. an intro-
ducer, author.

εἰσιέναι, 5, 35. εἰσιόντας, to
become accessory, declare
assent, 30. : 4, 30. εἰσῄει αὐτὸν,

Matth. Gr. Gr. 610. to occur
(to one's mind,) enter (one's
mind :) 5, 40. ἐσιέναι ἐς τὰς
σπονδάς : 6, 31. μᾶλλον αὐτοὺς
ἐσῄει τὰ δεινὰ, where the prep.
governs the same case, as it
does out of composition,
Matth. l. c.

εἴσκειμαι, 6, 32. ἐσέκειτο, to
be got on board, to be put in.

εἰσκομιδὴ, 7, 4. 24. entrance,
importation.

εἰσκομίζο, 6, 22. 49. ἐσκομι-
ζομένων, to get in, to be conveyed in : 2, 18. ἐσεκομίζοντο :
5, 10. ἐσεκόμισαν, to take into:
4, 110. ἐσκομίζουσι, to conduct into : 2, 13. ἐσκομίζεσθαι,
to convey into : 1, 117. ἐσε-
κομίσαντο, to import, 2, 5. to
convey into (a place.)

εἰσνέω, 4, 26. ἐσένεον, to swim
to.

εἴσοδος, 2, 6. ἅμα τῇ ἐσόδῳ
γιγνομένῃ, at the time entrance
took place.

εἰσοικοδομέω, 2, 75. ἐσῳκοδό-
μουν ἐς αὐτὸ πλίνθους, to line
with bricks, to build it up
within with bricks.

εἰσπέμπω, 4, 26. 30. to send
in : 1, 137. to send (letters)
into the interior : 4, 16. to
import, send into : 5, 18. ἐσί-
πεμψε, to send to, to throw
into, 31. 49. 56.

εἰσπίπτω, 2, 4. to rush into
(a place :) 1, 131. ἐς εἰρκτὴν
ὑπὸ τῶν Ἐφόρων, to be put
into prison by the Ephori :
5, 65. ἐσπίπτῃ, to fall in (as a
stream of water on a plain :)
5, 72. ἐσπεσόντες κατὰ τὸ διάκι-

νον, to fall upon by the void
space, 7, 29. ἐς τὴν Μ., to
break into : 1, 106. ἐσέπεσαν,
to fall in by chance.

εἰσπλέω, 1, 24. 3, 51. to sail
in : 7, 23. ἐσέπλεον, to sail
into, to enter : 2, 89. ἐσπλεύ-
σομαι, to sail into : 2, 69. φυλακὴν εἶχε μήτ' ἐκπλεῖν μηδένα
μήτ' ἐσπλεῖν, to guard against
any one's sailing out or in,
to keep guard to prevent,
that no one may : 7, 7. ἐσέ-
πλευσαν : 4, 75.

εἴσπλους, 4. 8. the entrance,
7, 22. 41.

εἰσπραξις, 5, 53. an exac-
tion of payment.

εἰστίθημι, 7, 100. ἐσθέντες, to
put into.

εἰσφέρω, 6, 21. ἐσφέρεται : 3,
19. εἰσενεγκόντες ἐσφορὰν, to
pay a tax, make a contribution: 5, 38. ἐσήνεγκαν, to urge,
promote, press, push on, to
forward : 3, 98. ἐσφερομένους
ἐς τὴν ὕλην, to be driven into
the wood : 6, 46. ἐσέφερον, to
introduce, bring in : 5, 115.
ἐσενεγκάμενοι : 8, 45. ἐσφέρειν,
to contribute.

εἶτα, 5, 65. afterwards.

εἴωθα, to be wont, 2, 45. 4,
108. 8, 68. : 6, 58. εἰώθησαν,
a form of the perf. middle
varied from ἔωθα, Matth. Gr.
Gr. 242.

ἐκ, 1, 23. ἐκ τοῦ πρὶν χρόνου,
of former times, 123. ἐκ τῶν
πόνων τὰς ἀρετὰς κτᾶσθαι, to
acquire virtues in struggling
with difficulties, in consequence of, 64, τὸ ἐκ τοῦ ἰσ-

θμοῦ τείχος, the wall from thence to the isthmus, the idea of a distance is contained in this phrase: ἐκ frequently signifies a removal, generally from the inside of a place or thing, hence it is sometimes put for ἔξω, Matth. Gr. Gr. 880.: 6, 50. ἐξήκοντα ναῦς ἐκ πασῶν, out of, out of the whole number: 7, 37. ἐκ τοῦ ἐπὶ θάτερα, from the opposite side, on the other side, from the (part) on the other side: 1, 141. ἐξ ὧν, by which means, whereby: 7, 67. γνῶτε ἐξ ὧν, know from what, i. e. by, through: 4, 108. ἐξ ὀλίγου, from the short notice, at the brief warning, 5, 64.: 7, 31. τὴν ἐκ τῆς Λακωνικῆς, the fortifying in Laconia, (literally out of Laconia, or from Laconia,) i. e. considering the spot as selected or taken out of the Laconian territory, or with reference to the particular spot itself, ἰσθμῶδές τι χωρίον, supra 26. a neck of land, which the fortification detached, cut off from the rest of the territory. At all events I see not how it can possibly be, ἀποπλέον ἐκ τῆς Λ. μετὰ τὴν χείρισιν, (sc. ἐν αὐτῇ,) which, besides dilating the passage, is objectionable on the score of grammar, 7, 9. ἐκ τοῦ ποταμοῦ ἐπολιόρκει, to block up (a town) from the river, on the side of the river, 3, 22. ἐκ τοὖμπαλιν ἢ ὑπερέβαινον, on the opposite side, to

where they were mounting, on the side opposite to that, which they were ascending, 40. ἐκ τοῦ ἀκινδύνου, safely, without risk, 45. ἐκ τῶν ὑποδεεστέρων κινδυνεύειν προάγειν, to impel (men) to encounter dangers with unequal, too few resources: 7. 48. ἐκ τούτων πείσεσθαι, to be persuaded by, to give credit to, to form an opinion from: 3, 91. ἐκ βραχέος, within a short distance: 7, 71. ἐκ τῆς γῆς πεζὸς, the land-force on shore, from: 5, 104. ἐκ τοῦ θείου, by some divine aid, 89. ἐξ ὧν, according to which (we judge:) 6, 72. ἐκ τοῦ προφανοῦς, openly, 1, 143. ἐκ τοῦ ὁμοίου, on an equality, the same thing: 7, 77. καὶ ἐκ τῶν παρόντων, even under present circumstances.: 3, 22. οἱ ἐκ τῆς πόλεως Πλαταιῆς, the Platæans in the city: 7, 13, ἐκ πολλῆς περιουσίας, through or in consequence of a large, abundant force, a plentiful supply, 27. ἐκ παρέργου τὸν πόλεμον ἐποιεῖτο, to prosecute the war negligently, slackly: 5, 20. ἐκ Διονυσίων εὐθὺς τῶν ἀστικῶν, immediately succeeding the Bacchanalian festival: 4, 100. ἐκ πολλοῦ, from a distance: 7, 6. ἐκ πλαγίου τάξας, to post on the flank: 3, 29. ἐκ τῶν παρόντων ἐβουλεύοντο, to deliberate on the present posture, exigency of affairs, 18. ἐκ γῆς καὶ ἐκ θαλάσσης, by sea and land, 10. ἐκ τοῦ πολέμου, after the war, (for μετά :) 7, 79. ἐκ τοῦ ὄπισθεν, in the rear, *a tergo* : 1, 61. ἐκ τῶν λόγων πείσαντες, by their speech to persuade, 6, 17. : 7, 62. ἐκ τῶν παρόντων ἡτοίμασται, as well as circumstances would allow, as circumstances required : 1, 141. ἐκ τῶν κινδύνων περιγενέσθαι, to escape, survive dangers : 6, 34. ἐξ ἑνός γέ του τρόπου, in some one way, in one way or other at least : 7, 74. ὡς ἐκ τῶν δυνατῶν, as well as they could, as circumstances would admit, permit : 1, 120. ἐκ μὲν εἰρήνης πολεμεῖν, to give up peace and go to war, ἐκ πολέμου ξυμβῆναι, to come to terms and give up war, ἐκ expresses the relation of two things, by which it appears that one proceeded from the other, Matth. 881. : 7, 40. ἐκ παρακελεύσεως ἐπιφερομένου, to charge, fall on with a cheer, an animating sound : 2, 62. τὴν τόλμαν ἀπὸ τῆς ὁμοίας τύχης ἡ ξύνεσις ἐκ τοῦ ὑπερφρονος ἐχυρωτέραν παρέχεται, by, on account of, Matth. 881. : 3, 67. ἐκ προσηκόντων, 7, 57. ἐκ τοῦ εὐπρεποῦς, it is put with words, which import an affection of the mind, an internal or external impulse, Matth. 881. : 6, 7. ὑπὸ δὲ νύκτα—ἐκδιδράσκουσιν οἱ ἐκ τῶν Ὀρνέων, here ἐκ, a prep. marking removal from a place, is substituted for one implying rest as ἐν, Matth. 920. ; 7, 31.

ἑκάς, 1, 80. afar off, at a distance, 69.

ἑκασταχόθεν, 7, 20. ὅσοις ἑκασταχόθεν οἷόν τ' ἦν πλείστοις χρήσασθαι, as many as it was possible to get, (obtain by way of loan, borrow,) from every quarter.

ἑκασταχόσε, 4, 54. 8, 5.

ἕκαστος, 5, 68. καθ' ἑκάστους ἑκατέρων, severally on either side : 7, 4. ᾗπερ ἕκαστοι ἔμελλον φρουρεῖν, where or as in the order they were intended to keep guard, where each were to have their station in guarding, 67. ἑκάστου ἡ ἐλπίς, the hope of each individual, the hope (arising) from each of these mentioned things, ἐξ ἑκάστου, 57. τῆς παραυτίκα ἕκαστοι ἰδίας ὠφελίας, each for their present, individual advantage : 8, 1.

ἑκάτερος, 7, 57. on each side, respectively, 4, 14. 5, 15.

ἑκατέρωθεν, 3, 6. τῆς πόλεως, on both sides of the city, on each side : 7, 34. on either side, flank, 78.

ἑκατόμποδος, 3, 68. νεὼν, having a hundred feet.

ἑκατὸν, 2, 56. a hundred.

ἐκβαίνω, 6, 65. ἐξέβαινον ἐς τὸν κατὰ τὸ Ὀλυμπίειον, to disembark on a place near : 7, 14. μὴ ὁμοῖον ἐκβῇ, to happen differently, not according to what we are led to expect : 1, 137. to disembark : 5, 77. ἐκβῶντας, to evacuate, (Dor. from βάω, Matth. Gr. Gr.

318.:) 7, 53. ἐκβαίνοντας ἀφέλ-
κειν τὰς ναῦς, to draw off.

ἐκβάλλω, 2, 68. to eject, 5,
4.: 4, 71. ἐκβάλῃ: 1, 126. ἐξέ-
βαλον.

ἐκβιβάζω, 7, 39. ἐκβιβάσαντας,
to disembark, land: 8, 41.
ἐκβιβάσαι, to set ashore: 5, 98.

ἐκβοήθεια, 3, 18. a sally out
(of a town) upon (an enemy.)

ἐκβοηθέω, 1, 105. ἐκβοηθήσαν-
τες, to make a sally out, (vulgo
ἐκβοήσαντες, which the Schol.
interprets μετὰ βοῆς ἐξελθόντες.)

ἐκβολή, 1, 97. τοῦ λόγου, a
discussion in a history: 4, 1.
σίτου, the shooting, budding,
2, 102.

ἔκγονος, 1, 9. a descendant.

ἔκδεια, 1, 99. an arrear of
payment.

ἔκδημος, 1, 15. forensic, distant from home: 2, 10. ἐπὶ
ἔκδημον ἔξοδον, in order to, for
an expedition abroad.

ἐκδιαιτάω, 1, 132. ἐξεδεδιήτη-
το τῶν καθεστώτων νομίμων, to
depart from the usual custom
of the country, a verb with a
double augment, Matth. Gr.
Gr. 210.

ἐκδιδράσκω, 1, 126. to make
one's escape out: 6, 7. Matth.
Gr. Gr. 920.

ἐκδίδωμι, 1, 137. ἐκδίδωσιν,
to deliver up a fugitive, 136.
ἐκδοίη, to give up, surrender:
8, 21. ἐκδοῦναι, to betroth.

ἐκδιδάσκω, 6, 80. to teach
plainly.

ἐκδιώκω, 1, 24. ἐξεδίωξε, 1, 24.
to drive out, to expel.

ἔκδρομος, 4, 125. a man ap-

pointed to run out, an out-
runner (from the phalanx.)

ἐκδρομή, 4, 127. a guerilla
party, excursores, i. q. ἔκ-
δρομοι.

ἐκεῖ, 1, 36. πρὸς τἀκεῖ, to the
parts there.

ἐκεῖθεν, 1, 36. thence.

ἐκεῖνος, 3, 88. 4, 124.; 6,
29. δι' ἐκεῖνον, on his account:
8, 48. τὸ ἐπ' ἐκείνοις εἶναι, as
far as regards them, Matth.
Gr. Gr. 409.: 8, 82.

ἐκείνως, 6, 11. in that case,
on that supposition: 3, 46.:
1, 77. then, in that case.

ἐκεχειρία, 5, 1. 2, 26. 32.
interval of repose, suspension
of arms: 4, 58. 117.: 5, 26.
49. a truce, 6, 26.

ἐκκάμνω, 2, 51. ἐξέκαμνον τὰς
ὀλοφύρσεις, to be wearied out,
spent, to sink under.

ἐκκαρπόω, 5, 26. ἐκκαρπωσά-
μενοι, to gather in their har-
vests, to flourish in peace.

ἐκκλησία, 1, 44. an assembly
of the people: 6, 8. ἐκκλησία
ἐγίγνετο, καθότι χρὴ, there
was an assembly to consider
how they must: 1, 87. 2, 22.
5, 46.

ἐκκλησιάζω, 7, 2. ἐκκλησιά-
σειν, to be on the point of assembling, to hold an assembly (about:) 8, 93. ἐξεκλησία-
σαν, not ἐξεκκλησίασαν, Matth.
Gr. Gr. 209.: 8, 77.

ἐκκλίνω, 5, 73. ἐξέκλινεν, to
turn aside from.

ἐκκολάπτω, 1, 132. ἐξεκά-
λαψαν, to erase, obliterate,
scratch out.

ἐκκομίζω, 2, 6. ἐξεκόμισαν, to bring, conduct away; 78; οἱ ἐκκομιζόμενοι, to convey out of a place : 7, 23. ἐξεκόμιζοντο, to get away from.

ἐκκρεμάννυμι, 7, 75: ἐκκρεμάννύμενοι τῶν ξυσκήνων, to hang from about the neck.

ἐκκρίνω, 6, 31. καταλόγοις ἐκκριθὲν, to be selected, picked from the two levies, (the dat. for ἐκ, ἀπό, as οἱ ἐδέξατο.)

ἐκκρούω, 6, 100. ἐξεκρούσθησαν, to be driven, forced out: 4, 128.

ἐκλέγω, 4, 59. to deliver a speech; 74: ἐξελέξαντο, to select, pick out : 8, 44. ἐξλέξαν, to collect from, to exact, levy.

ἐκλείπω, 5, 42. ἐξελελοίπεσαν τῆς ξυνθήκης; to come short of : 3, 87. to cease (as a decree) for an interval: 2, 28. ἐξέλιπε, to be eclipsed : 4, 91. ἐκλιπόντες τὰ ὅπλα; to relinquish : 6, 48. τῆς νῦν παρασκευῆς ἐκλίπωσι, to retrench their present expenditure, to fall short of, to diminish : 1, 114. to evacuate : 4, 114. ἐκλείπειν; to quit.

ἔκλειψις; 1, 23. ἡλίου, an eclipse of the sun.

ἐκλιπὴς, 1, 97. ὅτι τοῖς πρὸ ἐμοῦ ἅπασιν ἐκλιπὲς τοῦτο ἦν τὸ χωρίον, because this spot of history has been overlooked by all writers before me : 4, 51.

ἐκλογίζομαι, 4, 10. ἐκλογιζόμενος, to reckon up, to compute : 1, 70. ἐκλογίζεσθαι, to discover by consideration : 2, 40. ἐκλογίζεσθαι περὶ, to weigh, consider : 1, 80. ἐκλογίζοιτο, to come to a conclusion by reasoning.

ἐκνέω, 2, 90. ἐξένευσαν, to swim out.

ἐκνικάω, 1, 3. ἐκνικῆσαι ἅπασιν, to prevail among all; 21. ἐκνενικηκότα ἐπὶ τὸ μυθῶδες; to encroach upon the fabulous, the regions of fiction.

ἐκούσιος, 7, 8. κινδύνων ἐπιμελεῖτο, to concern one's self about, to provide against dangers, which happen of their own accord, spontaneously, which one cannot prevent. (Ἐκουσίων, applied to a person, would mean, voluntarily undertaken, voluntary, intentional, i. e. by keeping on the defensive he guarded against dangers, that might arise from the enemy, and provided only for those, which he might intentionally undergo. But even in this way the latter hardly agrees with the sense of the passage, which intimates ' that he kept on the defensive.') 1, 32: 138. ἐκούσιον, voluntarily : 7, 8. : 8, 27. καθ' ἑκουσίαν, voluntarily.

ἑκουσίως, 4, 19. willingly.

ἐκπέμπω, 5, 52. ἐξέπεμψαν, to send away, to discharge, 1, 2. 12. to send out : 2, 26. περὶ τὴν Λοκρίδα, to send about to different parts of : 4, 56. 5, 5. ἐξεπέμφθησαν, to be sent out : 3, 54. ἐξεπέμφθην, to despatch (troops) from (the city:) 1, 59. ἐξεπέμποντο, to be sent out (on a commission,) 38. ἐκπεμφθείησαν, to be sent out (as a colony,) 95. : 4, 108.

ἔκπεμψις, 4, 85. a mission, commission.

ἐκπίπτω, 1, 2. ἐκπίπτοντες, to be expelled, banished, 8, 34. ἐκπίπτουσιν, to escape : 7, 33. ἐκπεπτωκότας στάσει, i. q. κατὰ στάσιν, to be banished, exiled on account of, through, in consequence of an insurrection : 7, 71. ἐξέπεσον ἐς τὸ στρατόπεδον, to rush into, to jump out of (a ship,) to take shelter in : 1, 127. ἐκπεσόντος, to be banished : 7, 74. ἐκπεπτωκυίαν, to be run aground, to be stranded : 1, 123. 8, 81.

ἐκπλέω, 4, 13. ἐκπλεούσας, to sail out, 67. : 1, 65. ἐκπλεῦσαι, to sail out of harbour : 7, 56. ἐκπλεύσαντες, to sail out : 1, 57. ἐκπλέοντας ἐπὶ τοὺς πέλας, to sail abroad to their neighbours : 2, 89. οὔτε γὰρ ἂν ἐκπλεύσειέ τις ὡς χρὴ εἰς ἐμβολὴν οὔτε ἂν ἀναχωρήσειεν ἐν δέοντι, the opt. in connexion with ἂν in an abstract or independent proposition may be rendered, 'to be able,' Matth. Gr. Gr. 756. : 6, 23. 8, 102.

ἐκπληκτικὸς, 8, 92. θόρυβος, terrific, calculated to alarm.

ἔκπληξις, 4, 112. ἔκπληξιν παρασχόντας, to cause or spread dismay, alarm : 7, 71. consternation : 4, 14. panic,

55. : 6, 46. wonder, amazement, surprize : 6, 36. ἐς ἔκπληξιν καθιστάναι, to throw into alarm : 4, 126. ἔχειν ἔκπληξιν, to entertain a terror : 7, 69. ἐπὶ τῇ ἐκπλήξει, on account of, upon the present consternation : 2, 94. 4, 34. 7, 42.

ἐκπλήγνυμι, ἐκπλήσσω, 4, 125. ἐκπλήγνυσθαι, to be panic-struck, 63. to be struck : 5, 10. ἐκπεπληγμένοις, to be struck with consternation, 6, 11. to stand in awe of any one, to be afraid of, to dread, 7, 69. ὑπὸ τῶν παρόντων, to be roused, alarmed, exceedingly agitated by the critical state of affairs : 7, 63. ἐκπεπλῆχθαι, to be daunted, dismayed, in consternation : 5, 66. ἐξεπλάγησαν : 3, 42. ἐκπλῆξαι, to intimidate : 2, 87. ἐκπλήσσει, to drive away (recollection,) to force out, to expel.

ἔκπλους, 3, 51. a sallying out, 1, 117. : 7, 70. κατὰ τὸν ἔκπλουν, at the outlet : 3, 4. ἔκπλουν τινὰ ἐποιήσαντο τῶν νεῶν, to draw out (a certain number of) ships, to advance out on board some of their ships.

ἐκπνεῦσαι, to blow from out : 6, 104.

ἐκποδὼν στῆναι ἀμφοτέροις, to stand out of the way of, 1, 40.

ἐκπολεμέω, 6, 77. to excite to war.

ἐκπολιορκέω, 7, 14. ἐκπολιορκηθέντων, to be besieged, 4, 19. 1, 131. ἐκπολιορκηθεὶς, to be forced out of a place by siege, 134. ἐξεπολιόρκησαν λιμῷ, to reduce by starvation, 94. : 7, 75. ἐκπεπολιορκημένῃ, to be taken by siege or storm, to be conquered, Matth. Gr. Gr. 948.

ἐκπομπὴ, 3, 51. an expedition.

ἐκπονέω, 6, 31. ἐκπονηθὲν, to be wrought, elegantly prepared : 3, 38.

ἐκπορθέω, 4, 57. ἐξεπόρθησαν, to plunder : 8, 41. ἐκπορθεῖ, to destroy.

ἐκπορίζω, 1, 82. ἐκπορίζωμεθα, to provide resources, 125. ἐκπορίζεσθαι, to furnish oneself : 6, 83.

ἐκπρεπὴς, 3, 55. ἐκπρεπέστερον, dishonourable, unbecoming.

ἐκπρίω, 7, 25. ἐξέπριον μισθοῦ, to saw away, off, in two, for hire, reward.

ἔκπυστος, 4, 70. being in people's mouths, noised about, renowned: 3, 30. ἐκπύστους γενέσθαι, to be heard of, to be informed of : 8, 42. heard of.

ἔκπωμα, 6, 32. a cup.

ἐκστρατεύω, 5, 55. ἐκστρατεύεσθαι, to march away, 58. ἐξεστράτευσαν, to take the field : 2, 12. ἐξεστρατευμένων, to be upon their march out, to be in the field.

ἐκτειχίζω, 4, 45. ἐξετείχισαν, to complete the fortification:

7, 4. φρούρια, to build forts, raise redoubts, 26.

ἐκτίνω, 5, 49. ἐκτίνοντες, to pay, discharge a fine.

ἕκτος, 5, 64. a sixth, 8, 33. ἐκτὸς, without, 2, 7. 4, 25.

ἐκτρέπω, 5, 65. ἐξέτρεπε, to divert a water-course.

ἐκτροπὴ, 5, 65. turning a stream of water out of its course.

ἐκτρυχόω, 3, 93. ἐξετρύχωσαν, to wear out : 7, 48. ἐκτρυχώσειν, to exhaust, reduce to great straights.

ἐκφέρω, 1, 54. ἐξενεχθέντα, borne out to sea, 4, 12. brought up, picked up : 4, 105. ἐκφερόμενον τὰ ἑαυτοῦ, carrying away, bearing off : 3, 84.

ἐκφεύγω, 2, 4. τοῦ μὴ ἐκφεύγειν, an instance of the use of the infin., where the prefix of ἕνεκα is omitted, and the infin. is used as a subst. in the gen. case, the subst. power being given to it by the neuter article, Matth. Gr. Gr. 816.

ἐκφοβέω, 2, 87. 6, 49. ἐκφοβῆσαι, to terrify, 11. ἐκφοβοῦσι, 3, 42. ἐκφοβοῦντα.

ἐκφορὰ, 2, 34. a carrying out to burial.

ἐκφροντίζω, 3, 45. to plan, devise.

ἐκχρηματίζομαι, 8, 87. ἐκχρηματίσαιτο, to raise money.

ἑκὼν, 4, 92. τινὶ ἐπέρχεται, of one's own motion, voluntary : 1, 52. 7, 57. : 3, 39.

τοῖς ἐκρύσιν ἀποσπάσι, volunteers
in a revolt, 47. ταρίδωτι, to
deliver up voluntarily, spontaneously ; 2, 89, τὸν δὲ ἀγῶνα οὐκ ἐν τῷ κόλπῳ ἑκὼν εἶναι
ποιήσομαι, an instance of the
use of the infin. put absolute
and redundant, where the
discourse is with certain li-
mitations. Matth. Gr. Gr.
826. : 4, 98. 7, 81.

ἐλαία, 7, 81. an olive-tree :
6, 99.

ἔλασις, 1, 139. a banish-
ment, driving out.

ἐλασσόω, 4, 58. ἐλασσοῦσθαι,
to be deteriorated, impaired :
5, 72. ἐλασσωθέντες, to be ex-
celled, cut out : 3, 42. τὴν
ὑπαρχούσης σφ. τιμῆς, to detract from, abridge : 1, 77.
ἐλασσωθῶσιν, to be injured,
deteriorated : 5, 30. ἐλασσοῦσθαι, to be slighted, ill-treat-
ed, 43. : 5, 104. ἐλασσώσεσθαι,
to be worsted : 4, 59. : 5, 34.
ἐλασσωθήσεσθαι, to be about to
be degraded, to suffer in reputation : 2, 64. πάντα πέφυκε
καὶ ἐλασσοῦσθαι, the infin. is
put after verbs, which imply any object whatever,
and require the addition of
this object or its effect, by
means of another verb, here
after πέφυκε, ita, natura com-
paratum est ut, Matth. Gr.
Gr. 797.

ἐλάσσων, 3, 5. ἔλασσον ἔχειν,
to be worsted, to have the
worse : 1, 125. 2, 22. 65, 4,
60. 7, 4. 8, 87. : 6, 95, ἡ λεία
ἐπράθη ταλάντων οὐκ ἔλαττον

ποτὲ καὶ εἴκοσι, where ἤ is
omitted, Matth. Gr. Gr. 660.

ἐλαύνω, 1, 126. 135, to
banish ; 3, 49. ὑσθῶσί τε ἅμα
ἐλαύνοντες, to eat and row at
the same time, to ply the
oar : 8, 118.

ἐλάχιστος, 1, 10. 4, 74. 5,
16. 7, 50. the least, 70. πλεῖσται γὰρ δὴ αὗται ἐν ἐλαχίστῳ
ἐναυμάχησαν, for being in fact
very many in number they
engaged in a very small
space, for the numbers, that
engaged, were very nume-
rous in fact, and the space
they fought in, very small :
2, 18. 77. 7, 68.

ἐλεγεῖον, 1, 132. an elegiac
distich.

ἔλεγχος, 1, 135. περὶ Παυσανίου, a charge against Pausanias : 3, 53.

ἐλέγχω, to prove, convict,
1, 131. 6, 86.

ἕλος, 1, 110. a marshite.

ἐλευθερία, 5, 9. freedom : 2,
63. εἰκὸς — μὴ νομίσαι περὶ ἑνὸς
μόνον, δουλείας ἀντ᾽ ἐλευθερίας
ἀγωνίζεσθαι, the adj. is in the
neuter, because it designates
the thing generally, which
is in the sequel further explained by nouns, whether
masc. or fem., Matth. Gr.
Gr. 638. : 4, 86. 7, 86. 8, 64.

ἐλευθέριος, 2, 71. ἱερὰ Διῒ
Ἐλευθερίῳ, (to sacrifice) victims to Jupiter the Deliverer.

ἐλεύθερος, 5, 9. free, independent, 34. enfranchised :
7, 69. ἐλευθερωτάτης. : 2, 43.

ἐλευθερόω, 3, 51. ἐλευθερώσας

τὴν ἔπηλυσιν, to clear a passage : 8, 15. ἐλευθέρωσεν, made
free : 1, 95. ἠλευθέρωντο ἀπὸ
βασιλέως, to be freed from the
King, 8, 46. ἀπὸ δ' ἐκείνων μὴ
ἐλευθερῶσαι, 2, 71. Παυσανίας
ἐλευθερώσας τὴν Ἑλλάδα ἀπὸ τῶν
Μήδων, Matth. Gr. Gr. 473. :
2, 8. ἡ δὲ εὔνοια παρὰ πολὺ ἐποίει
τῶν ἀνθρώπων μᾶλλον ἐς τοὺς Λα
κεδαιμονίους, ἄλλως τε καὶ προει
πόντων ὅτι τὴν Ἑλλάδα ἐλευθε
ροῦσιν, here the indic. is used
as in the *oratio obliqua* with
ὅτι, as quoting the words of
any one, because the thing
exists independently of the
ideas of the speaker, and
need not be considered as
uttered in the person of another, Matth. 743. : ἐλευθεροῦ
σιν is the fut. in ώσω. contracted, Matth. 221. : 4, 85.
ἐλευθεροῦντες τὴν Ἑλλάδα : 4,
52. 7, 56.

ἐλευθέρως, 2, 65. freely.

ἐλευθέρωσις, 5, 9. enfranchisement, liberty : 1, 132.
manumission : 3, 10 ἀπὸ τοῦ
Μήδου τοῖς Ἕλλησι, freeing or
liberating the Greeks from
the (power of the) Mede,
freedom to the Greeks from
the Mede, 39. liberation :
2, 72.

ἕλκος, 2, 49. an ulcer.

ἕλκω, 1, 50. 4, 14. εἷλκον, to
drag, tow.

ἕλκωσις, 2, 49. an ulceration.

ἐλλείπω, 2, 61. τῆς ὑπαρχού
σης δόξης, to be wanting to
one's reputation, glory : 1,

120. ἐλλείπωμεν, to come short
of (a desire :) 5, 103. to be
left, to remain : 6, 69. τῷ
ἐλλείποντι, defect, deficiency.

Ἑλληνίζω, 2, 68. ἑλληνίσθαι
σαν, to Hellenize.

Ἑλληνικός, of or belonging
to the Greeks, 1, 1. τὸ Ἑλλη
νικὸν, an adjective of those
ending in κος, put in the
neuter singular with the
prefix of the corresponding
article, is employed as a
substantive in the sense of a
whole : the example signifies *the whole of Greece,
Greece universal*. See Matth.
Gr. Gr. 392.

Ἑλληνοταμίας, a treasurer
of the Greeks, a receivergeneral, 1, 96. καὶ Ἑλληνοτα
μίαι τότε πρῶτον Ἀθηναίοις κα
τέστη ἀρχή, οἳ ἐδέχοντο τὸν
φόρον ——, ἦν δὲ ὁ πρῶτος
φόρος ταχθεὶς τετρακόσια τάλαν
τα καὶ ἑξήκοντα, two examples,
where subst. which have a
generic signification, have
the name in the first, and
the more precise definition
in the second in the nomin.,
Matth. Gr. Gr. 429.

ἐλλιπής, 5, 1. left undone,
remaining to do : 7, 8. τῆς
μνήμης, failing, losing, failing
in memory, to recollect : 4,
55. τῆς δοκήσεως, coming short
of, 63. 6, 69.

ἕλος, 1, 110. a marsh.

ἐλπίζω, 3, 39. ἐλπίσαντες μα
κρότερα τῆς δυνάμεως, to hope
things beyond their power :
7, 36. to expect : 5, 7. ἠλπι

σεν, to expect : 5, 9. τοὺς ἐναντίους εἰκάζω—οὐκ ἂν ἐλπίσαντας
ὡς ἂν ἐπεξέλθοι τις αὐτοῖς ἐς
μάχην ἀναβῆναι, an instance,
where, (which is rare,) a
verb of hoping is not followed by an infin., but by
ὡς, Matth. Gr. Gr. 800.

ἐλπὶς, 4, 81. βέβαιον, a persuasion, presumption : 1, 69.
ὑμέτεραι, confidence in you,
74. ἐν βραχείᾳ, almost despaired of : 7, 6. τοῦ φόβου,
the expectation of fear, τὴν
φοβερὰν ἐλπίδα, expectation of
evil : 4, 70. ἐν ἐλπίδι εἶναι, 96.
ὡς ἕκαστοί τινα εἶχον ἐλπίδα σωτηρίας, chance, hope : 2, 64.
κρεῖσσον ἐλπίδος, beyond expectation, unexpected, worse
than one could expect,
Matth. Gr. Gr. 656. : 8, 48.
81.

ἐλώδης, 7, 47. swampy,
marshy, full of swamps.

ἐμβαίνω, 1, 18. ἐμβάντες, to
embark : 4, 100. ἐμβὰν, to
get on board.

ἐμβάλλω, 7, 25. ἐμβάλλοντες,
to assault, to strike with a
shock, to bear down upon :
4, 25. ἐνέβαλον, to attack : 7,
34. ἐμβαλλόμεναι, to receive a
shock, to be violently struck,
53. ἐμβαλόντες πῦρ, to throw
fire into (a ship,) to set on
fire, 70. ἐμβεβλῆσθαι, to be
run foul of : 4, 14. ἐνέβαλλον,
to rush or break in upon :
7, 34.

ἐμβιβάζω, 2, 90. ἐμβιβάσας,
to embark (one's men,) to
get (one's men) on board : 1,

53. ἐμβιβάσαντες, to embark,
put on board.

ἐμβοάω, 4, 34. ἐμβοήσαντες,
to raise a shout, utter a cry,
112. vociferating, shouting.

ἐμβολὴ, 2, 76. 89. a shock,
an onset, a charge with the
beak of a ship : 7, 36. 40. 70.

ἔμβολον, 7, 36. a beak of a
vessel, a prow.

ἐμμένω, 2, 2. ἐνέμειναν, to
last, continue : 3, 20. τῇ ἐξό-
δῳ, to persist in marching
out : 4, 118. ἐμμενεῖν, to
abide, 4, 19. to stand to, to
abide by, 8, 23. to remain
steady in : 1, 5. ἐμμεμένηκε, to
last, continue : 2, 19. ἐμμεί-
ναντες, to stay, remain in or
at (a place,) 72. ἐμμείνατε τοῖς
ὅρκοις, to abide by one's oath,
5, 56.

ἔμμισθος, 6, 22. hired, receiving wages.

ἐμός, mine, 6, 78. τοῖς ἐμοῖς
ἀγαθοῖς : 7, 86.

ἐμπαλάσσω, 7, 84. ἐμπαλάσ-
σομαι, to be entangled together.

ἐμπαρέχω, 7, 56. ἐμπαρα-
σχόντας, to put forward, to
expose, offer, present : 6, 12.
ἐμπαράσχητε τούτῳ, to permit,
allow, afford.

ἐμπειρία, 4, 10. experience :
5, 7. skill, invention : 7, 44.
μᾶλλον τῆς χώρας, more knowledge of, a better acquaintance with : 1, 121. πολεμικῇ,
in military discipline : 7, 49.
τὰ τῆς ἐμπειρίας, i. q. τὴν ἐμπει-
ρίαν, skill, Matth. Gr. Gr.
412. : 7, 56. : 2, 85. ἐκ πολλοῦ,

skill derived from long practice : 2, 3. τῆς κατὰ τὴν πόλιν
ἐμπειρίας, knowledge of the
city.

ἔμπειρος, 2, 4, acquainted
with : 7, 61. : 6, 36. πολλῶν,
of great experience : 1, 80.
πολλῶν πολέμων, of many
wars, 18. ἐμπειρότεροι, more
skilful, experienced, 2, 77.

ἐμπίμπλημι, 3, 82. ἐμπιμπλά-
ναι τὴν φιλονεικίαν, to satiate
the lust of contention.

ἐμπίπρημι, 1, 8. 3, 74. ἐμπι-
πρᾶσι, to set on fire : 1, 30.
ἐνέπρησαν, 49. 108. to burn :
7, 53. ἐμπρῆσαι : 2, 4. ἐμπρήσαντες, 3, 85. 4, 30. : 4, 29.
ἐμπρησθεῖσα, to be burnt : 6,
75,

ἐμπίπτω, 2, 91. φόβος, to
fall upon : 4, 28. ἐνέπεσε, 2,
48. to fall into, upon, (of the
plague,) 4, 34. ἀνθρώποις, 6,
24. ἔρως, to invade, take po-
session of : 2, 53. πρὶν ἐμπεσεῖν,
before it fell, 76.

ἐμπλήκτως, 3, 82. madly,
wildly.

ἔμπνους, 1, 134. still alive :
5, 10. breathing, warm.

ἐμπόδιον, 1, 31. a hindrance,
an impediment.

ἐμποδὼν, 6, 28. ὄντι σφίσιν
αὐτοῖς, to be in the way of
any one, to be a hindrance,
an obstacle to any one : 1,
53. ἵστασθε ἐμποδὼν, to stand
in the way of, to hinder, impede : 2, 45.

ἐμποιέω, 1, 2. ἐνεποίουν, to
give birth to, to cause, 2,
51. to create, occasion : 3,

38. ἐμποιησάντων, to create,
occasion : 4, 81.

ἐμπολιτεύομαι, 4, 103. to be
enrolled among the citizens,
to be admitted to citizenship,
106.

ἐμπορεύομαι, 7, 3. to barter,
traffic, make purchases, 13.
ἐμπορευόμενοι.

ἐμπορία, 1, 7. 6, 2. 44. traffic,
commerce.

ἐμπόριον, 7, 50. an empo-
rium, 1, 13. a place of traffic,
an emporium, a depôt, 100. :
4, 103.

ἔμπορος, 3, 74. 7, 24. a merchant, trader, 31.

ἐμφανὴς, 2, 21. ἐν τῷ ἐμφανεῖ,
openly, before their eyes : 7,
48. τῷ ἐμφανεῖ λόγῳ, avowedly
in words, opposed to τῷ ἔργῳ :
4, 86. βίᾳ, undisguised.

ἐμφανῶς, 7, 48. openly, un-
equivocally.

ἐμφράσσω, 7, 34. ἐμφράξασαι,
to block up, keep in blockade : 4, 8. ἐμφράξαι, to bar or
block up.

ἐμφρουρέω, 4, 110. ἐμφρου-
ροῦντας, garrisoning, protect-
ing.

ἔμφρων, 1, 84. σωφροσύνη,
rational.

ἔμψυχος, 7, 29. a living
thing, any thing that has life.

ἐν, 1, 77. ἐν τοῖς ὁμοίοις νόμοις, by, with, or according
to impartial laws : 7, 73. τοῖς
ἐν τέλει οὖσιν, the magistrates,
6, 88. : 4, 119. ἐν αὐτῇ sc. ἐκε-
χειρίᾳ, in, during : 3, 28. ἐν ὅσῳ,
until, during : 1, 82. ἐν τούτῳ,
in the mean time, 7, 23. ἐν.

τούτῳ δὲ, in the mean while, 33. ἐν τούτῳ τύχης, in this condition, these circumstances, i. q. ταύτῃ τύχῃ: 1, 81. κἀν τούτῳ, in this juncture: 5, 68. ἐν τῷ παρόντι, on the present occasion, 7, 42. at this present, very moment: 4, 80. ἐν τοῖς πολεμίοις, against the enemies, during hostilities, 43. ἐν χερσὶ, hand to hand, 5, 10. off hand, at the moment, 5, 3.: 6, 52. ἐν ὑμῖν ἐστὶν, it rests with you: 8, 36. ἐν τῷ τότε, at that time, 39. ᾧ, where, on which side, 6, 55. ἐν ᾧ οὐ πρότερον ὡμιλήκει, because, from not having, 1, 79. ἐν τάχει, with speed, without delay, 3, 29. speedily, quickly: 6, 18. ἐν τῷδε καθέσταμεν, to be in this situation, to be thus situated, 16. ἐν τῷ ὁμοίῳ, in like manner, i. q. ὁμοίως, 54. ἐν Πυθίου, in the temple of Apollo: 3, 9. ἐν ἡδονῇ ἔχειν (τινὰ,) to like, caress (any one,) to be in good humour with, to be pleased with: 5, 52. οἷς ἦν ἐν βλάβῃ ταιχισθὲν, to whom this fort was an injury: 1, 74. ἐν ταῖς ναυσὶ τῶν Ἑλλήνων τὰ πράγματα ἐγένετο, the affairs of the Greeks were in or depended upon the fleet: 6, 35. ἐν πολλῇ πρὸς ἀλλήλους ἔριδι ἦσαν, to have much altercation with one another, 34. ἐν πόνῳ εἶναι, to be in difficulty, trouble, danger: 5, 3. ἐν μεθορίοις, upon the frontier, 46. ἐν μὲν τῷ σφετέρῳ καλῷ, ἐν δὲ τῷ ἐκείνων ἀπρεπεῖ, re-

dounding to our credit and to their dishonour: 7, 11. ἐν ἄλλαις ἐπιστολαῖς ἐστι, through or by other letters, Matth. Gr. Gr. 884.: 7, 5. ἐν χερσὶ γενόμενα, to come to close fight, to close: 3, 18. ἐν ὑστέρῳ, i. q. ὕστερον, in future, hereafter: 7, 2. ἐν ᾧ, when, 11. in, what situation, condition, 7, 8. ἐν δεινοῖς εἶναι, to be in danger, a critical situation, 7, 1. ἐν τῷ Ῥηγίῳ παρούσων, to be at or to come to Rhegium: 5, 47. ἀναγράψαι ἐν στήλῃ λιθίνῃ, to engrave upon a pillar: 3, 22. ἐν ἀπόρῳ ἦσαν εἰκάσαι τὸ γιγνόμενον, to be at a loss to conjecture what had happened: 7, 29. τὸ γὰρ γένος τὸ τῶν Θρᾳκῶν ὅμοια, τοῖς μάλιστα τοῦ βαρβαρικοῦ, ἐν ᾧ ἂν θαρσήσῃ, φονικώτατόν ἐστι, when, Matth. 863.

ἐναγὴς, 1, 139. under excommunication, 126. polluted.

ἐνάγω, 2, 21. 6, 61. ἐναγόντων, to mitigate, 7, 18. at the instance of: 8, 26. ἐνάγοντος, instigating, 1, 67. ἐνῆγον, to bring on, to accelerate, 4, 21. to urge, impel, 24. 6, 15. τὴν στρατιὰν, to advise, urge on.

ἐναγωνίζω, 2, 74. ἐναγωνίσασθαι, to contend, fight in.

ἐναλλάσσω, 1, 120. ἐνηλλάγησαν, to have intercourse with.

ἐναντίος, 1, 39. τοὐναντίον, on the contrary: 7, 44. τὸ τὸ ἐξ ἐναντίας, all before, opposite, facing (one,) all that one meets, encounters, 11.

an enemy : 5, 36. averse, 38. disagreeable, 50. ἐναντίον τῶν Ἑλλήνων, in the presence of the Grecians, 66, 67. 6, 25.: 7, 21.: 3, 42. ἐναντιώτατα, the most adverse, 43. ὧν ἐναντία, the reverse of what : 8, 90.

ἐναντιόω, 2, 40. ἠναντιώμεθα, to be opposite to, to differ toto cœlo : 1, 136. ἐναντιωθῆναι, to oppose, 5, 32.: 3, 49. ἐναντιωθέντος: 1, 127. ἠναντιοῦτο πάντα τοῖς Λ., to oppose the L. in every respect : 4, 21.

ἐναντίωμα, opposition, 4, 69.

ἐναντίωσις, 8, 50. πρὸς τὴν ἐναντίωσιν τῶν λεχθέντων ὑφ' αὐτοῦ, on account of the opposite sentiments, which he had delivered.

ἐναποθνήσκω, 2, 52. ἐναποθνησκόντων, to die in (a place :) 3, 104.

ἐναποκλάω, 4, 54. ἐναποκέκλαστο, to be broken open.

ἐναυλίζομαι, 4, 54. to take up a temporary post: 8, 33. ἐνηυλίσατο, to station himself.

ἐνδεεστέρως, more frugally, sparingly, 2, 35.

ἐνδεής, 3, 83. τὸ αὐτῶν ἐνδεὲς their own infirmity: 2, 11. 4. 65. ἐνδεέστερος: 7, 69 ἐνδεᾶ ἔργῳ, defective in deed, preparation : 1, 102. τούτου ἐνδεᾶ ἐφαίνετο, affairs seemed to stand in need of this: 8, 36. defective : 1, 77. 2, 87. 5, 9.

ἔνδεια, 4, 18. failure, lack : 7, 82.

ἐνδείκνυμι, 4, 126. τὸ εὔψυχον ἐνδείκνυνται, to demonstrate, give a proof of.

ἐνδεκαταῖος, 2, 97. τελεῖ, on the eleventh day, see ἐνναταῖος.

ἐνδέχομαι, 7, 49. ἐνεδέχετο, to approve : 4, 92. ἐνδέχεται λογισμὸν, to admit of, to be susceptible of : 1, 124. ἐνδέχεται, to be right, fit : 5, 15. ἐνδεξομένους, to receive, admit, listen to, 3, 31. ἐνεδέχετο ταῦτα, to listen to, approve of, adopt : 2, 87. ἐνδέχεσθαι, to be wont, to be liable, 8, 27. to undertake, 50. ἐνδέξονται, would receive, admit : 3, 87. 4, 18. 7, 49.

ἐνδεῶς, 2, 40. μὴ ἐνδεῶς γνῶναι, to understand as well as others, sufficiently well : 4, 39. ὁ γὰρ ἄρχων Ἐπιτάδας ἐνδεεστέρως ἑκάστῳ παρεῖχεν ἢ πρὸς τὴν ἐξουσίαν, when a subst. is not compared with another, but the quality of a thing, in its proportion to another, is considered and compared in degree with this proportion, where in Latin quam pro is used, then ἢ κατὰ or ἢ πρὸς is put after the compar., Matth. Gr. Gr. 654.

ἔνδηλος, 2, 64. ἐστε, to be seen, perceived, to let it be known: 6, 36. seen through, manifest, detected: 1, 139. ἐνδηλότατα, most plainly : 4, 41. exposed, betrayed, open.

ἔνδημος, 5, 47. ἀρχαὶ, the magistrates of the people, the city-magistrates: 1, 70. ἐνδημοτάτους, one, who stays at home.

ἐνδιαιτάομαι, 2, 43. ἐνδιαιτά-

R

ται, to live in, abide in the minds of men.

ἐνδιατρίϐω, 7, 81. to lose time in : 2, 18. ἐνδιέτριψαν χρόνον, to spend much time in, 85. 3, 29. : 5, 12. ἐνδιατρι-ϐόντων, to linger about.

ἐνδίδωμι, 7, 48. ἐνδοῦναι τὰ πράγματα, to surrender the state-affairs, 4, 66. τὴν πόλιν, to surrender, betray, give up, 4, 35. ἐνέδοσαν, to give ground : 3, 37. ἐνδῶτε οἴκτῳ, to yield, relent from compassion : 4, 103. ἡ πόλις ἐνδοθήσεται; to be given up: 2, 12. οὐδέν πω ἐνδώ-σουσιν, will still make no con-cession, εἴτι ἄρα μᾶλλον ἐνδοῖεν οἱ Ἀθηναῖοι, the opt. pres. and aor. 2. of verbs in μι have the contraction οἶμεν, οἶτε, οἶεν, for εἴημεν, Matth. Gr. Gr. 281.: 5, 62. ἐνεδίδοσαν, to betray : 7, 66. ἐνδιδόασιν, to yield, give up : 8, 54.

ἔνδοθεν, 8, 71. καὶ οἱ Ἀθη-ναῖοι τὰ μὲν ἔνδοθεν οὐδ᾽ ὁπωσ-τιοῦν ἐκίνησαν, made no move-ment whatever within the city.

ἐνδοιάζω, 1, 36. ἐνδοιάζῃ, to doubt, hesitate, 122. ἐνδοια-σθῆναι καὶ λόγῳ, to doubt about even in word : 6, 91.

ἐνδοιαστῶς, 6, 10. suspici-ously, doubtfully, without firmness.

ἔνδον, 3, 30. μετὰ τῶν ἔνδον, along with, with the aid of, the inhabitants, of those with-in : 4, 104.

ἐνέδρα, 7, 3. an ambush, ambuscade : 3, 90. 4, 67. 5, 56.

ἐνεδρεύω, 4, 67. ἐνήδρευσαν ἐς

τὸν Ἐννάλιον, to (go to) the temple of Mars, to lie in am-buscade.

ἐνείδω, 7, 62. ἐνείδομεν, to perceive, discern: 1, 95. ἐνεῖ-δον, 7, 36. 58.

ἐνείλλω, 2, 76. ἐνείλλοντες, to involve, invest, inclose, wrap or fold.

ἔνειμι, 5, 21. ἔνεισιν, to be within: 7, 24. ἐνῆν, to be in, to be contained in: 1, 104. ἐνῆσαν, to be in: 4, 17. ἐνόντα, the contents: 5, 2. 4, 48. ἐνοῦσαι : 2, 20. ἐνέσεσθαι στάσιν, there would be a division, disunion of sentiments: 8, 66.

ἕνεκα, 1, 57. for the sake of: 4, 73. ὧν ἕνεκα, for what, the wherefore : 1, 73. παραι-τήσεως ἕνεκα, for the sake of a deprecation, or for a de-precation, 45. προεῖπον δὲ ταῦ-τα τοῦ μὴ λύειν ἕνεκα τὰς σπον-δὰς, the infinite with the neuter article and here in the genitive with ἕνεκα must be rendered by a suitable cau-sal proposition, ne fœdera frangerent, Matth. Gr. Gr. 432.: 1, 23. τοῦ μή τινας ζητῆ-σαί ποτε, where ἕνεκα is under-stood, compare 2, 4. 22. 24. Matth. 815.: 8, 87.

ἐνεργὸς 3, 17. ἥης, fit for service, well-manned, in ac-tion, at service.

ἔνερσις, 1, 6. a lacing or binding to serve as a kind of comb in the hair.

ἐνευδαιμονέω, 2, 44. ἐνευδαιμο-νῆσαι, to live happily in, to be fortunate in.

ἐνθάδε, hic, 7, 62.

ἔνθεν, hinc, 7, 81.

ἐνθένδε, 1, 36. τὸ, that proceeding from thence: 6, 38. ἐνθένδε ἄνδρες, (some) men (of our own city) in this place: 2, 1.

ἐνθυμέομαι, 1, 122. ἐνθυμώμεθα, to reflect: 5, 32. ἐνθυμούμενοι τὰς ἐν ταῖς μάχαις ξυμφοράς: 1, 120. ὁ ἐν πολέμῳ εὐτυχίᾳ πλεονάζων οὐκ ἐντεθύμηται θράσει ἀπίστῳ ἐπαιρόμενος, a verb of perceiving takes its object in the participle and nomin. because the subject of that part. is here the same as that of the finite verb, Matth. Gr. Gr. 829.: 1, 42, ἐνθυμηθέντες, to reflect upon (cum gen.:) 2, 60. ἐν ἴσῳ (sc. ἐστὶ) καὶ εἰ μὴ ἐνεθυμήθη, he is just as if he had not thought at all, might as well not have thought: 7, 18. ἐνεθυμοῦντο, to bear in mind, reflect upon, bethink oneself, 8, 68.

ἐνθύμησις, 1, 132. a reflection, consideration,

ἐνθυμία, 5, 16. ἐς ἐνθυμίαν τοῖς Λ. ἀεὶ προβαλλόμενος ὑπ' αὐτῶν, being continually subject to reflections.

ἐνθύμιος, 7, 50. ἐνθύμιον ποιούμενοι, to hold, esteem any thing ominous, to scruple any thing (from superstition, religion,) trahere in religionem aliquid.

ἐνιαύσιος, 4, 117. of a year's continuance, 5, 1.

ἐνιαυτὸς, 1, 31. a year, 93. κατ' ἐνιαυτὸν, during the year: 4, 118.

ἐνίημι, 2, 29. ἐνιέντες, to set on, suborn: 4. 115. ἐνῆσαν πῦρ, to inject.

ἐνίστημι, 3, 23. ἐνιστάντες, to take part in, post oneself in: 8, 69.

ἐνναταῖος, 2, 49. on the ninth day, a numeral in αιος, which answers to the question, on what day? Matth. Gr. Gr. 177.

ἐννέα, nine, 5, 26.

ἐννικάω, 3, 36. ἐνενικήκει, to carry the (motion).

ἔννομος, 4, 60. ὀνόματι, legitimate, not obnoxious to law, legal: 6, 38. legal, according to law: 3, 67. πείσονται ἔννομα, to suffer legal punishment.

ἐνοικέω, 4, 56. to live in, tenant: 1, 18. ἐνοικούντων, to inhabit, 6, 1. 33. πλείους, in greater numbers, force: 1, 91. 3, 68.

ἐνοίκησις, 2, 17. inhabiting a place.

ἐνοικίζω, 6, 2. ἐνοικισάμενοι, to settle in a place.

ἐνοικοδομέω, 3, 85. 4, 92. ἐνοικοδομησάμενοι, to build within: 6, 51. ἐνῳκοδομημένην κακῶς, badly, unskilfully, clumsily, ill-built, constructed: 8, 4. ἐνῳκοδόμησαν.

ἔνοικος, 4, 61. an inhabitant.

ἐνοράω, 3, 30. to discern, espy.

ἔνορκος, 2, 72. to be under oath, bound by oath.

ἔνσπονδος, 1. 31. 35. 40. 3, 10. bound by treaty, confederate: 5, 28.

ἐνστρατοπεδεύω, 2, 20. ἐνστρατοπεδεῦσαι, to encamp in (a place.)

ἐνταῦθα, 1, 11. then, (as *ibi* for *tum*.)

ἐντειχίζω, 6, 90. ἐντειχισάμε- νοι, to blockade.

ἐντελὴς, 6, 45. in good, complete, absolute condition: 8, 29.: 50. finished, full: 78.

ἐντελευτάω, 2, 44. ἐντελευτῆ- σαι, to die in.

ἐντέμνω, 5, 11. to sacrifice to, worship with sacrifice.

ἐντεῦθεν, 1, 5. thence, by those means.

ἐντίκτω, 3, 104. to bring forth a child.

ἐντόνως, 5, 70. eagerly.

ἐντὸς, 5. 90. within, 4, 67. τῶν πυλῶν: 2, 9. 4, 28.

ἐντυγχάνω, 5, 5. ἐντυχὼν, to encounter, 7, 43. to light on, meet by chance: 2, 39. ἐνέ- τυχε, to meet with, encounter: 7, 29. ὅτῳ ἐντύχοιεν, whomsoever they met, whoever fell in their way: 4, 40.

ἐνωμοτάρχες, 5, 66. a subaltern officer.

ἐνωμοτία, 5, 66. a small company of private soldiers.

ἐξάγγελος, 8. 51. one, who tells out, abroad, a discoverer.

ἐξάγγελτος, 8, 14. discovered.

ἐξάγω, 6, 31. τὰ πάντα ἐξαγό- μενα, to be exported, exported upon the whole, the sum or amount of things carried out: 4, 80. ἐξήγαγεν, to lead out: 6, 89. ἐξῆγον, to stimulate, instigate: 1, 93. ἐξήχθη,

to be extended, sketched out, (of boundaries:) 5, 80. ἐξά- ξοντα: 5, 21. 35. ἐξαγαγεῖν, to cause to evacuate, to withdraw: 3, 45. ἐξάγουσιν ἐς τοὺς κινδύνους: to impel into dangers: 7, 5. ἐξάγων ἀεί, to lead out from every day.

ἐξαίρετος, 2, 24. ἐξαίρετα ποιή- σασθαι, to take out from amongst a number of others: 3, 68. excepted.

ἐξαιρέω, 3, 50. ἐξεῖλον, to select, set apart as sacred to the gods, 114. ἐξῃρέθησαν, to be picked out: 4, 69. ἐξέλοιεν, to take, 122. ἐξελεῖν, to subdue by force: 8, 28. ἐξείλοντο, had removed from: 6, 24. τὸ μὲν ἐπιθυμοῦν τοῦ πλοῦ οὐκ ἐξῃρέ- θησαν, an instance of the thing in the pass. put in the accus. with a verb, which governs in the act. two accus., Matth. Gr. Gr. 604.

ἐξαίρω, to take, raise out, 7, 24.

ἐξαίφνης, 3, 4. on a sudden, without warning: 7, 32. suddenly, 40.

ἐξακόσιοι, 1, 64. 3, 85. six hundred, Matth. Gr. Gr.

ἐξαλείφω, 3, 57. ἐξαλεῖψαι, to erase, wipe out, 20. ἐξαληλιμ- μένον, (sc. τεῖχος,) to be plaistered over.

ἐξαλλάσσω, 5, 71. τῶν ἐναν- τίων τὴν ἑαυτοῦ γύμνωσιν, to turn off, to shift from.

ἐξαμαρτάνω, 3, 46. to offend: 2, 22. τοῦ μὴ ὀργῇ τι μᾶλλον ἢ γνώμῃ ξυνελθόντας ἐξαμαρτεῖν, that they might not by coming together with more heat than judgment, make some mistake.

ἐξαναγκάζω, 8, 95. ἐξαναγκάσειαν, Matth. Gr. Gr. 254. but Bekker reads ἀναγκάσειαν more correctly, see ἀφίστημι (at the end of the article.)

ἐξανάγω, 2, 25. καὶ ἐξανάγονται ἐκλιπόντες Φειὰν, to sail thence.

ἐξαναχωρέω, 4, 28. καὶ ἐξανεχώρει τὰ εἰρημένα, to recede from, to evade.

ἐξανθέω, 2, 49. ἐξηνθηκὸς, to be thickly set, to abound, to be full of.

ἐξανίστημι, 7, 77.: 7, 49. ἐξανίστασθαι, to move out (of camp:) 3, 107. ἐξαναστάντες, to rise up out of (an ambush.)

ἐξαπαλλαγὴ, 4, 28. to be rid off.

ἐξαπαλλάσσω, 4, 28. ἐξαπαλλαγῇ τῶν εἰρημένων, to be released from, to evade the execution of his promises.

ἐξαπατάω, 3, 4. ἐξαπατήσαντα, to deceive: 2, 4. ἐξηπατημένοι. deceived, circumvented, 5, 46.: 5, 42. ἐξηπατῆσθαι, to be deceived, trifled with.

ἐξαπιναίως, 3, 3. suddenly: 1, 117. 2, 3. 48. 93. 4, 25.

ἐξαπίνης, 1, 50. 4, 36. 115. suddenly, 5, 10.

ἐξαργυρίζω, ἐξαργυρόω, 8, 81. to convert into money, to sell for money.

ἐξαρτάομαι, 6, 96. ἐξήρτηται γὰρ τὸ ἄλλο χωρίον, for the rest of the place rises (to a great height.)

ἐξαρτύω, 1. 13. ἐξηρτύετο, to attend to, to be addicted to,

4, 107: to consolidate, put in an attitude of vigour : 1, 14. ἐξηρτυμένα, to be provided or furnished with : 2, 13. ἐξαρτύεσθαι, to equip: 1, 121. ἐξαρτυσόμεθα, to fit out (a navy :) 7, 65. ἐξηρτύσαντο πρὸς τἆλλα ὡς ἔκαστα, to prepare against, for the rest, one by one : 2, 17. ἐξαρτύοντες ἐπίπλουν, to fit out an expedition, a fleet : 6, 31. ἐξαρτυθείς, to be equipped : 1, 80. ἐξήρτυντο ἅπασιν, 6, 17. ἐξήρτυται ὅπλοις, to be furnished or provided with.

ἐξεγείρω, to stir, rouse up, 7, 51.

ἔξειμι, 5, 22. ἐξῆν, to be lawful, 47. ἐξέστω, let it be lawful, 18.: 1, 35. ἐξεῖναι: 4, 65. ἐξὸν αὐτοῖς, the game being in their hands, when they might : 3, 39. οἷς γ' ἐξῆν, to have it in one's power.

ἔξειμι, 1, 46. ἔξεισι, to disembogue (of a river,) 77. ἐξιὼν, to go out (to a foreign command.)

ἐξείργω, 1, 118. τὸ δέ τι καὶ πολέμοις οἰκείοις ἐξειργόμενοι, the circumstance of their being straitened by wars near at home had some influence : 2, 13.

ἐξελαύνω, 3, 61. ἐξελάσαντες, to drive out, to banish, 4, 102.: 4, 35. ἐξελάσασθαι, to drive off: 7, 27.: 5, 82. ἐξέλασειν: 5, 43. ἐξέλωσι, to exclude: 7, 27. ἐξελαυνόντων, to ride, gallop out, forth.

ἐξελέγχω, 3, 64. ἐξηλέγχθη, to be proved true.

ἐξεργάζομαι, 7, 2. ἐξειργα-
σμένα, to be completed, finished: 1, 82. ἐξείργασται, to be
cultivated (of land:) 3, 51.
ἐξειργάσαντο, to accomplish:
2, 78. ἐξείργαστο, to be completed (of a building:) 1, 142.
ἐξείργασθε, completely to at-
tain to, to acquire perfection:
4, 4. 6, 101.

ἐξέρχομαι, 4, 100. ἐξεληλυθό-
των, to evacuate, come out
from : 1, 70. ἐξέρχονται ἐπὶ
πλεῖστον, to push success as
far as it will go : 4, 5. ἐξέλθωσιν, to come out, proceed
forth : 3, 108. τὸ πολὺ τοῦ ἔργου ἐξῆλθον, to despatch the
greater part of the business,
1, 103. 4, 69. 81. 5, 8. 7, 2. 11.

ἐξετάζω, 2, 7. ἐξήταζον, to
survey, review : 7, 33. ἐξετά-
σαι, to examine, review, 35.
ἐξετάσαντες : 6, 27. 8, 35.

ἐξέτασις, 6, 41. a muster,
review, survey, 45. an inspection, 97.: 4, 74.

ἐξευρίσκω, 4, 118. ἐξευρήσωμεν,
to find out.

ἐξηγέομαι, 1, 76. to take the
lead out: 5, 26. ἐξηγήσομαι,
to relate, tell, 66. ἐξηγουμένου,
to give out orders : 6, 85.
ἐξηγούμεθα τοὺς ἐκεῖ ξυμμάχους :
1, 138, ἐξηγήσασθαι, to make a
statement of, to explain : 1,
71. 9, 5. 3, 55. 93.: 6, 85. τοὺς
ξυμμάχους ἐξηγούμεθα, Matth.
Gr. Gr. 482.

ἐξήγησις, 1, 72. instruction,
information.

ἐξήκοντα, 1, 63. sixty.
ἐξηκοστὸς, 1, 12. sixtieth.

ἐξῆς, 5, 25. in order, regular
series, 67. 1, 125. in order,
by rotation: 7, 29. succes-
sively, one after another, i. e.
indiscriminately : 2, 1.

ἐξιέναι, 7, 47. to depart,
move out (of camp,) 4, 114.
ἐκ τῆς Ληκύθου, to go out from,
to quit, 2, 75. τοῦ μηδένα ἐπι
ἐξιέναι, in order that no one
might have egress, to prevent
any one from, 7, 3. ἐκ τῆς Σικελίας, to quit, go out of : 4,
103. ἐξίησιν, to disembogue,
discharge itself, or empty:
2. 6. ἔξῃει, to go out, set off,
5, 7. to go out at, 80. ἐξίωσι,
to depart, 5, 13. ἐξῄεσαν, to
come away, set out, 1, 15.
to go out upon, 3, 22.: 5, 10.
ἐξιόντων, about to come out.

ἐξικνέομαι, 1, 70. ἔργῳ ἐξικί-
σθαι τὰ ἀναγκαῖα, to accomplish
what is necessary.

ἐξισόω, 6, 87. ἐξισώσαντι
(sc. ἑαυτοὺς) τοῖς ἄλλοις, to render themselves equal with, to
be as others are : 5, 71. ἐξισῶ-
σαι, to equal in length.

ἐξίστημι, 4, 28. ἐξίστατο τῆς
ἀρχῆς, to relinquish: 2, 63.
ἐκστῆναι, to recede from, relinquish, yield up: 2, 61. ἐξί-
σταμαι, to depart, flinch from
(an opinion.)

ἔξοδος, 5, 10. a sally : 2, 4.
a passage out, an escape.

ἐξοικέω, 2, 17. ἐξῳκήθη, to
be filled with inhabitants.

ἐξοικίζω, 6, 76. ἐξοικίσαι, to
eject, unsettle, expel : 1, 114.
ἐξοικίσαντες, to transplant out
of (a place into another.)

ἐξορκίω, 5. 47. ἰξορκούντων, to administer an oath.

ἐξορμάω, 6, 80. ἐξώρμησε, to stimulate, move, 6, 6. to impel, instigate : 7, 14. ἐξορμῶντες ναῦν, to move out, to clear a vessel out of harbour, to steer, to row, impel a vessel with oars.

ἐξοτρύνω, 1, 90. ἐξοτρυνόντων, to urge or spur on.

ἐξουσία, 1, 38, ὕβρει καὶ ἐξουσίᾳ πλούτου, through arrogance and wealth : 5, 50. κατὰ τὴν οὐκ ἐξουσίαν τῆς ἀγωνίσεως, on account of their not being entitled to enter into the contest : 6, 31. opulence : 7, 12. ability, opportunity, means, 4, 39. means, ability : 3, 45. wealth, large possessions.

ἐξυβρίζω, 3, 39. ἐξύβρισαν ἐς τόδε, to come to this pitch of insolence : 1, 84. ἐξυβρίζομεν.

ἔξω, 5, 105, different from, inconsistent with, 26. τούτων, besides all this, in addition, moreover : 1, 10. besides, 68. τὰ ἔξω πράγματα, foreign transactions : 5, 97. ἔξω καὶ τοῦ πλεόνων ἄρξαι, besides an extension of dominion, 80. φρουρίου, outside of the garrison : 7, 69.

ἔξωθεν, 1, 65. τὰ, the affairs without : 2, 49.

ἐξωθέω, 2, 90. ἐξέωσαν, to drive from : 7, 36. ἐξωθουμένοις, to be driven back, to be forced or thrust (towards or on shore, a naval phrase :) 5, 71. ἐξωθεῖται, to be pushed away towards : 6, 34. ἐξωσθῆναι ἐς χειμῶνα, to be driven into the winter season, to be driven late, protracted, put off : 7, 52. ἐξεώθουν, to drive (an enemy's ship to shore.)

ἑορτάζω, 3, 3. πανδημεί, to celebrate a festival *en masse*, with the whole body of the people.

ἑορτὴ, 5, 50. a festival : 1, 70. a festival, holiday, 126. : 7, 73. 8, 10. : 2, 15. δημοτελῆ, a public festival.

ἱὸς, 6, 54. ἧς for ἧς, his.

ἐπαγγέλλω, 5, 49. to proclaim (a truce :) 6, 88. ἐπαγγελλομένων, to promise : 7, 17. στρατιὰν ἐπαγγέλλων, to proclaim or give notice of an expedition : 8, 10. ἐπηγγέλθησαν, had been told : 6, 56. ἐπαγγείλαντες, to summon : 5, 47. καθ᾽ ὅτι ἐπαγγέλλωσιν, in conformity to the information they may send, 49. ἐπηγγέλθαι ἐς Λακεδαίμονα, to be proclaimed in Lacedæmon : 8, 10.

ἐπάγω, 5, 4. ἐπάγονται, to introduce, let in, invite : 6, 86. ἐπηγάγεσθε, to call in, *arcessere* : 3, 34. ἐπαχθέντων, to be called, introduced : 5, 41. ἐπηγάγοντο, to obtain, insist upon, impel, urge : 1, 81. ἐπάξονται, to import : 4, 1. ἐπαγογομένων, to invite, make the first advances : 7, 5. ἐπάξειν, to lead on, conduct to : ἐπῆγον, 1, 107. to solicit, tamper with, 93. to carry, 8, 10. to retreat, 7, 3. 6. to

lead on, forward : 1, 87. ἐπαγαγεῖν ψῆφον, to put the question, to take the votes : 5, 5,
ἐπαγαγόμενον, to introduce :
8, 82. ἐπάγεσθαι, to introduce
(into the state for party-
purposes:) 6, 10. ἐπαγαγέσθαι,
to draw, bring over : 3, 63.
ἐπηγάγεσθε, to associate (any
one) into one's alliance : 6,
6. ἐπαγόμενοι ξυμμάχους, to
call in, fetch (to one's assistance,) 1, 104. ἐπηγάγετο : 3,
62. ἐπηγάγοντο, to introduce,
let in (a conqueror into a
city :) 5, 45. ἐπαγάγωνται, to
lead away, seduce : 4, 64.
ἐπαξόμεθα, to call in, associate : 8, 46. ἐπάγειν, to instigate against.

ἐπαγωγή, 7, 4. an attack,
3, 100. an invasion, attack :
5, 82. an importation, 7, 24.
τῶν ἐπιτηδείων, the importation of necessaries, supplies :
3, 82. an introduction (of
foreign troops.)

ἐπαγωγός, 6, 8. calculated
to persuade : 5, 85. persua-
sive : 4, 88. seductive, en-
ticing, engaging, attractive :
5, 111. ὀνόματος ἐπαγωγοῦ δυνάμει, by the power of a seducing word.

ἐπαινέτης, 2, 41. a panegy-
rist.

ἐπαινέω, 3, 82. ἐπῄνειτο, to
be commended : 1, 76. ἄξιοι
ἐπαινεῖσθαι, entitled to praise :
4, 65. ἐπαινεσάντων, to be ap-
plauded, approved, 1, 86. to
praise, 5, 37. τοὺς λόγους, to
approve, commend, testify

one's approbation : 2, 25.
ἐπῃνέθη, to be praised, commended : 3, 42. to commend,
8, 28. ἐπῃνέθησαν, to obtain
glory.

ἔπαινος, 1, 76. praise, honour : 2, 34. λέγειν ἐπ᾽ αὐτοῖς τὸν
πρέποντα ἔπαινον, to pronounce
upon, over them a suitable
panegyric : 3, 61. an eulogy :
2, 35. ἔπαινοι περὶ ἑτέρων λεγό-
μενοι, what is said in praise
of others, 44. 4, 120.

ἐπαίρω, 1, 120. ἐπαιρόμενος
θράσει ἀπίστῳ, to elevate by a
groundless confidence : 7, 13.
ἐπαρθέντες, to be discussed, 1,
42. to be excited, moved : 1,
25. ἐπαιρόμενοι, to be puffed
up, elevated : 8, 2. ἐπηρμένοι:
3, 38. ἐπαιρόμενος κέρδει, to be
instigated by gain, 5, 14. to
be buoyed up, elevated upon, 3, 37. to be elated, carried away, 7, 41. τῇ νίκῃ, to
be elated by, with the victory : 6, 11. ἐπαίρεσθαι πρὸς
τὰς τύχας, to be elevated,
puffed up on account of the
disasters, misfortune, 1, 120.
81. ἐπαιρώμεθα ἐκείνῃ γε τῇ ἐλπίδι, to be elevated, buoyed
up with that hope at least,
84. ἐπαιρόμεθα ἡδονῇ, to be
elevated with pleasure, fas-
cinated with flattery : 4, 108.
ἐπήρθησαν ἐς τὸ νεωτερίζειν, to
be inclined, 121. τοῖς λόγοις,
to be put on one's mettle :
2, 11. τῇδε τῇ ὁρμῇ ἐπῆρται, is
aroused, erect, on tiptoe at
this movement, is full of expectation : 8, 2.

ἐπαιτιάομαι, 8, 9. ἐπῃτιῶντο, to accuse, 5, 16. to charge, accuse, stigmatize, reproach, 6, 28. ὤν, to accuse any one of any thing: 2, 70. ἐπῃτιάσαντο τοὺς στρατηγοὺς, to blame, call to account.

ἐπαίτιος, 5, 65. censured, blamed: 6, 61. ἦν, to be accused.

ἐπακολουθέω, 8, 10. ἐπηκολούθησαν, followed: 7, 75. ἐπακολουθοῦντες, to follow after: 4, 96. ἐπηκολούθουν, to follow up, 5, 65. to pursue a retreating enemy: 4, 128.

ἐπακούω, 2, 36. ξύμφορον εἶναι τὸν πάντα ὅμιλον ἐπακούσαι, to be expedient or profitable that the whole assembly should hear: 1, 82. ἐπακούσωσι, to attend, give ear to.

ἐπακτὸς, 6, 20. imported, foreign: 7, 28.

ἐπαληθεύω, 4, 85. to verify: 8, 52.

ἔπαλξις, 4, 69. 115. ἀπ’ οἰκιῶν ἔπαλξεις ἐχουσῶν, battlements: 3, 21. 7, 27. : 2, 13. παρ’ ἔπαλξιν, at the battlement.

ἐπαμύνω, 1, 101. to render assistance in repelling an attack: 6, 6, ἐπαμῦναι σφίσι, to succour: 1, 33. ἐπαμυνεῖτε, to assist, succour: 3, 14. ἐπαμύνατε Μυτιληναίοις, to protect, succour.

ἐπαμφοτερίζω, 8, 85. ἐπαμφοτερίζοντα, to be of vacillating fidelity, to lean towards both parties.

ἐπαναβαίνω, 7, 29. ἐπαναβάντα, to land.

ἐπαναβιβάζω, 3, 23. ἐπαναβιβάσαντες, to cause to ascend.

ἐπαναγκάζω, 5, 31. ἐπηνάγκαζον, to enforce (payment.)

ἐπανάγω, 7, 3. ἐπανῆγε τὸ στρατόπεδον, to cause this army to fall back, to draw off: 8, 42. ἐπανάγονται, to go out against.

ἐπαναγωγὴ, 7, 34. drawing out (a fleet) against (an enemy,) an advance against.

ἐπαναίρω, 8, 84. see βακτηρία.

ἐπανάσεισις, 4, 126. ἥ τε διὰ κενῆς ἐπανάσεισις τῶν ὅπλων, "clashing on their sounding shields the din of war, hurling defiance," Milton.

ἐπανάστασις, 2, 27. a rising up against, an insurrection: 4, 56. an insurrection, a rebellion: 8, 21.

ἐπαναχωρέω, 1, 131. ἐπανεχώρει, to return back again, 3, 33. : 4, 44. ἐπαναχωρήσασα τὰ μετέωρα, to regain: 5, 55. ἐπανεχώρησαν, to retreat back upon (their own country,) 8, 10. : 1, 63. ἐπανεχώρουν, 5, 41. ἐπαναχωρήσαντας, 6, 49.

ἐπαναχώρησις, 3, 89. a rising or encroachment of the sea.

ἐπανεῖπον, 6, 60. ἀργύριον, to advertise a reward.

ἐπανέρχομαι, 4, 74. ἐπανελθὼν ἐς τὴν Κόρινθον, to return back to, 16.

ἐπανιέναι, 6, 102. ἐπανῄει, to return.

ἐπανισόω, 8, 57. ὥσπερ ἐβούλετο ἐπανισοῦν τοὺς Ἕλληνας

πρὸς ἀλλήλους, to make equal, put on an equal footing.

ἐπανίστημι, 2, 28. ἐπανίστηται, to rise up, rebel : 3, 39. ἐπανέστησαν.

ἐπανορθόω, 7, 77. to restore to prosperity, to set to rights again.

ἐπάντης, 7, 79. precipitous.

ἐπάρατος, 2, 17. ὃ καὶ ἐπάρατον ἦν μὴ οἰκεῖν, which it was forbidden by a curse to inhabit : 8, 97.

ἐπαυλίζομαι, 3, 5, ἐπηυλίσαντο, to pass the night in the field, to continue in the field all night : 4, 134.

ἐπαύξω, 2, 36. ἐπηυξήσαμεν, to enlarge, extend : 7, 70. ἐπαυξῆσαι, to add to (the renown,) increase (the glory of.)

ἐπαύρεσις, 2, 53. ταχείας τὰς ἐπαυρέσεις ποιεῖσθαι, to take quick enjoyment, to hasten to enjoy.

ἐπαχθής, 6, 54. τὴν ἄλλην ἀρχὴν, oppressive, burdensome.

ἐπεὶ, 1, 5. 41. καὶ, when even, 4, 67. 6, 51.

ἐπείγω, 1, 93. ἐπείγοντο, to hurry, hasten one's work, 3, 2. ἐπείγονται τὴν παρασκευὴν ἅπασαν, to hasten on all kinds of preparation, 4, 5. πλοῦν : 1, 82. 85. 3, 3. ἐπειχθέντας, to be hurried, the aor. pass. used as the middle, Matth. Gr. Gr. 716. : 1, 80. ἐπειχθῆναι : 3, 45. ἐπείγεσθαι, to hasten, 81.

ἐπειδὰν, 2, 34. ἐπειδὰν δὲ κρατήσωσι γῆ, when or after, Matth. Gr. Gr. 774.

ἐπειδὴ, 5, 50. since : 7, 55. ἐπειδή γε, particularly since : 2, 10. ἐπειδὴ δὲ ἑκάστοις ἕτοιμα γίγνοιτο κατὰ τὸν χρόνον τὸν εἰρημένον, ξυνῄεσαν τὰ δύο μέρη ἀπὸ πόλεως ἑκάστης ἐς τὸν ἰσθμὸν, the opt. is used after a particle of time, when the discourse is of a past action; in this instance, because the discourse is concerning several parts, and the action is considered as repeated with each. Matth. Gr. Gr. 774. : 2, 70. Matth. 865.

ἐπειδέω, 4, 132. ἐπιδεῖν τὰ πράγματα, to inspect : 7, 61. Matth. Gr. Gr. 703.

ἔπειμι, 6, 18. ἀλλὰ καὶ μὴ ὅπως ἔπεισι, in order that he may not invade : 4, 38. 5, 10. 7, 27.

ἔπειπον, 1, 67. to address after another.

ἐπεισαγωγὴ, 8, 92. τεῖχος πυλίδας ἔχον, καὶ ἐσόδους, καὶ ἐπεισαγωγὰς τῶν πολεμίων, a receptacle, lodgment, an opening, a place, by which entrance can be made.

ἐπεισβαίνοντες, 2, 90. to enter in, rush, dash in against : 4, 14.

ἐπεισβάλλω, 3, 13. ἐπεισβάλητε τὸ δεύτερον, to invade or make an irruption into (a country) a second time.

ἐπεισέρχομαι, 2, 38. to be imported, to flow in upon.

ἐπεισπλέω, 4, 13. ἐπεισπλευσούμενοι, about to make their way in by sailing : 6, 2.

ἐπεισφέρω, 3, 53. ἐπεισενέγκαμενοι, to produce (a witness upon a trial.)

ἔπειτα, 1, 108. ἐς τὸν ἔπειτα χρόνον, for the future: 6, 65. ἐς τὰ ἔπειτα, for (ever) after: 1, 10. τοῖς ἔπειτα, posterity: 7, 31. ·

ἐπεκβαίνω, 1, 49. ἐπεκβάντες, to disembark: 8, 105.

ἐπεκβοηθέω, 7, 53. ἐπεκβοηθήσαντες, to march out against (an enemy) in support (of one's own side.)

ἐπεκδρομὴ, 4, 25. a sally.

ἐπέκεινα, 6, 63. τὰ ἐπέκεινα τῆς Σικελίας, the other parts, other side of, illic: 7, 58. ἐν τῷ ἐπέκεινα (sc. μέρει,) in the part beyond: 8, 104.

ἐπεκθέω, to run out, 5, 9. σὺ δὲ Κλεαρίδα ὅταν ἐμὲ ὁρᾷς ἤδη προσκείμενον—αἰφνιδίως τὰς πύλας ἀνοίξας ἐπεκθεῖν καὶ ἐπείγεσθαι ὡς τάχιστα ξυμμῖξαι, an instance of the use of the infin. for imper., Matth. Gr. Gr. 824.: 4, 34.

ἐπέκπλους, 8, 20. a sally.

ἐπελπίζω, 8, 1. ἐπήλπισεν, had inspired hope.

ἐπεξάγω, 7, 52. ἐπεξαγαγόντα, to draw out (a line of battle,) to extend (his line,) 5, 71. to march out of (one position into another:) 2, 21. ἐπεξάγοι, to lead out against.

ἐπεξαγωγὴ, 8, 105. ναυσάμενοι τῆς ἐπεξαγωγῆς ἤδη τοῦ κέρως, omissa jam contentione circumagandi cornu.

ἐπέξειμι, 1, 64. ἐπέξῃσι, to turn out (for battle:) 2, 13. ἐπεξίεναι, to go out against,

4, 68. ἐς μάχην, 1, 84. to undertake, 5, 7. 2, 55. : 3, 17. ἐπεξιὼν τοῖς Ά., to march out upon: 5, 10. ἐπεξίωμεν, to rush out: 3, 82. ἐπεξῄεσαν τὰς τιμωρίας, to prosecute, 8, 24. to go out against: 2, 20. εἰ ἐπεξίασιν, whether they will come out against him.

ἐπεξέρχομαι, 3, 38. τῷ δράσαντι, to prosecute, pursue: 2, 20. ἐπεξελθεῖν, to march, come out against, 5, 9. to follow up, to execute: 3, 67. ἐπεξήλθομεν ταῦτα, to dwell or enlarge upon: 5, 89. ἐπεξερχόμεθα, to invade, attack: 5, 9. ἐπεξέλθοι, to come out against: 3, 26. ἐπεξῆλθον, to make incursions upon (a country,) 1, 62. to advance in pursuit: 6, 38. ἐπεξελθεῖν, obviam ire, to oppose (the machinations of any one,) to proceed against: 1, 22. ἐπεξελθών, to examine, investigate.

ἐπεξέτασις, 6, 42. a second review, a review.

ἐπέρομαι, 3, 92. ἐπήροντο τὸν θεὸν, they consulted the God: 8, 29. ἐπέρεσθαι, to consult, send a message to.

ἐπέρχομαι, 3, 11. ἐπῆλθον, to invade, make an aggression upon: 1, 69. ἀντὶ τοῦ ἐπελθεῖν, instead of invading them: 1, 2. ἐπελθών, to invade, 7, 71. οἱ ἐπελθόντες, the invaders, 47. ἐπελθούσης, to come in addition to, as a reinforcement, accession: 5, 10. ἐπέλθε, to go up to, 4, 93.: 4, 92. ἐπέρχεται τινι; to encroach upon, to aggress : 4, 1. ἐπέλθωσιν, to invade, advance against: 3, 47. ἐπέρχεσθε ἐς πόλεμον, to go to war : 7, 64. οἷς ἐπῆλθετε, to come to, 42. ἐπεληλυθότα, to be arrived : 4, 120. ἐπήρχοντο, to go to, to have free passage to, to visit : 7, 56. μόναις ἤδη ὁμοιοτρόποις ἐπελθόντες, the only ones similar in institutions, i. e. the only ones of all they had invaded : 2, 20. τοὺς Ἀθηναίους ἤλπιζεν ἴσως ἂν ἐπεξελθεῖν καὶ τὴν γῆν οὐκ ἂν περιιδεῖν τμηθῆναι, i. e. ὅτι ἐπεξέλθοιεν ἂν—περιίδοιεν ἂν, more indefinite than περιόψεσθαι, ἂν is used with the infin., to which it gives the same signification, as the opt., Matth. Gr. Gr. 923.

ἐπερωτάω, 1, 25. ἐπηρώτων, to ask a question of, 118. τὸν θεὸν, to enquire of the god : 2, 54. ἐπερωτῶσιν, to enquire : 5, 45. ἐπερωτώμενοι, to undergo, interrogate : 3, 92. 8, 29.

ἐπερώτημα, 3, 53. a question.

ἐπερώτησις, 4, 38. questioning, examination.

ἐπέχω, 7, 62. ἐπέχῃ, to occupy, 1, 50. ἐπεχουσῶν : 4, 124. δύο μὲν ἢ τρεῖς ἡμέρας ἐπέσχον, to put off, to delay, 31. 5, 63. to defer, stay an intended act, 7, 74. to abide, stay, stop (sc. ἑαυτοὺς,) 8, 16. 31. to refrain from : 7, 50. ἐπισχεῖν, to stay, stop, tarry, 8, 5. to pause, 1, 90. to detain, 5, 32. to come into, to join : 1, 137. ἐπισχὼν ἐνιαυτὸν,

11

to wait, stay behind, 4, 78. to press one's march, mend one's pace : 7, 33. ἐπέσχοντο, to abstain from, to defer : 1, 48. ἐπεῖχον, to occupy : 5, 46. ἐπισχόντας, deferring, 4, 73. χρόνον, putting on, extending.

ἐπηλυγάζομαι, to throw a shade over, to screen, hide, 7, 36.

ἔπηλυς, 1, 29. a stranger, foreigner.

ἐπηλύτης, 1, 9. a stranger, foreigner.

ἐπήρεια, 1, 26. κατ' ἐπήρειαν, with insult, insultingly.

ἐπὶ, 1, 141. ἐφ' ἑαυτὸν σπεύδειν, to pursue his own interests : 7, 11. ἐφ' οὓς, against whom (in particular,) 48. ἐπὶ πλέον, far and wide, more extensively, completely, decidedly : 1, 118. οἱ Ἀθηναῖοι ἐπὶ μέγα ἐχώρησαν δυνάμεως, here ἐπὶ μέγα is put adverbially and the gen. is employed in its signification, with regard to, Matth. Gr. Gr. 456.: 6, 61. ἐπὶ πλοῖον ἐπεραιώθη, on board a vessel : 5, 31. ἐπὶ τῇ ἡμισείᾳ τῆς γῆς, on consideration of receiving one half of the territory : 7, 68. ἐφ' ὅπλοις ποιούμενοι, to be under arms, to be drawn up in arms, (i. e. in readiness in case of an attack,) distinguished from the soldiers, who were ἐπὶ τοῦ τείχους : 5, 45. οὐκ ἐπὶ κακῷ, not with a view to injure, 18. : 5, 6. ἐπὶ μετεώρου, on a rising ground, a high hill, an eminence: 5, 27. ἐπὶ ἀγαθῷ, for the advantage : 7, 57. ἐπὶ Συρακούσας ἐπολέμησαν, at or before Syracuse, (ἐπολ. refers to both sides, the besiegers and defenders,) 56. : 5, 67. οἱ ἐπὶ Θρᾴκης, who had (served) in Thrace : 5, 4. ἐπὶ πολιτείᾳ, on terms of free citizenship, with an equality of political privilege, 36. ἐφ' ὧν αἱ σπονδαὶ ἐγένοντο, by whose instrumentality the truce was concluded : 5, 68. ἐπὶ ὀκτώ, eight deep, 2, 90. ἐπὶ τεσσάρων ταξάμενοι τὰς ναῦς, to stand four deep, Matth. 899. : 7, 36. ὡς ἐπὶ ἓξ πήχεις, about six cubits: 1, 103. ἐφ' ᾧ τε ἐξίασιν, on the condition that they should depart from, 1, 74. ὑμῖν ἐπὶ τῷ τὸ λοιπὸν νέμεσθαι ἐβοηθήσατε, with the prospect, in order to, Matth. 900. : 1, 116. Ἀθηναῖοι πλεύσαντες ναυσὶν ἐξήκοντα ἐπὶ Σάμου, this prep. has the gen. in definitions of place answering to the question whither ? Matth. 897. : 5, 68. ἐπὶ πᾶν, generally : 3, 28. ἐπὶ τοὺς βωμοὺς καθίζουσι, to go to and sit down at the altars : 7, 4. ἐπὶ φρυγανισμὸν ἐξελθεῖν, to go out for or to fetch wood, fuel, firing, fire-wood : 6, 89. ἐπὶ τῶν πάλαι καὶ νῦν, et majorum et nostra memoria, 38. ἐφ' ἡμῶν, in our time, 6. : 7, 11. ἐπὶ πολὺ τῆς χώρας, far into the country, to a distance in the country : 2, 101. ὑπο-

σχόμενος ἀδελφὴν ἑαυτοῦ δώσειν καὶ χρήματα ἐπ' αὐτῇ, with her, the use of the prep. with the dat. is "at,' and hence this, Matth. 902. : 7, 4. ἐπὶ θαλάσσῃ, at, or near, or close by the sea : 7, 7. ἐπὶ στρατιὰν ᾤχετο, to depart, go for, in order to procure an army : 4, 69. ἐφ' ἡμέραν, day by day : 7, 59. ἐπὶ τῇ γεγενημένῃ νίκῃ, besides or following upon the present victory, 79. οὐκ ἐπ' ὀλίγων ἀσπίδων, many ranks deep, 36. ἐπ' αὐτὸ τοῦτο, for this very purpose : 7, 66. ἐπὶ ὅσον, as far, to the extent, degree : 1, 73. ἐπ' ὠφελείᾳ, for the purpose of obtaining, advantage, 7, 46. ἐπὶ ἀπροσδοκήτῳ εὐπραγίᾳ, upon or on account of unexpected success, ἐπ' αὐτομολίας προφάσει, upon a pretext for desertion, 3, 56. ἐπὶ τοῖς αὐτοῖς : 1, 17. τὸ ἐφ' ἑαυτῶν, their own interest : 6, 46. ὡς ἐπὶ τὸ πολύ, for the most part, generally : 1, 69. ἐπ' ἔχθρᾳ, out of a hostile feeling, through hatred, 70. τοῖς δεινοῖς, in extremities, dangerous circumstances : 5, 73. ἐφ' ἑκάτερα, at either end, 67. ἐπὶ σφῶν αὐτῶν, by themselves, unmixed with others, Matth. 899. : 3, 12. ἐπ' ἐκείνοις, in their power, reach : 4, 28. τὸ ἐπὶ σφᾶς εἶναι, as far as regarded him : 1, 76. ἐπὶ τὸ ὑμῖν ὠφέλιμον, with a view to your own advantage : 2, 34. λέγει ἐπ' αὐτοῖς ἔπαινον τὸν πρέποντα, here the signif. of ἐπὶ

is similar to what it would
be with a gen., ' to utter a
panegyric upon any one,' a
definition of place appears
to have been understood, at
or over the grave of any
one, Matth. Gr. Gr. 902. : 2,
35. ἐπὶ δύο ἡμέρας, for two
days, Matth. 904.: 2, 63. ἐφ'
ἑαυτῶν οἰκεῖν, a phrase from
the use of ἐπὶ with the gen.,
here of states, ' to live by
themselves, not dependent
upon others,' ' to have a
peculiar constitution,'Matth.
899. : 2, 80. ἐπ' ἐπησίῳ προστα-
σίᾳ ἠγεῖσθαι, with the prospect, in order, it here signifies a condition, Matth. 900.

ἐπιβαίνω, 7, 70. to board :
1, 103. ἐπιβήσονται αὐτῆς, to
put foot upon a territory,
137. ἐπιβὰς, to embark, 2, 90.
to go on board, 1, 111. ἐπὶ
τὰς ναῦς : 4, 116. ἐπιβάντι,
mounting, scaling : 2, 25.
ἐπέβησαν, to embark.

ἐπιβάλλω, 2, 52. ἐπιβαλόντες
ἀπρόσω, to throw upon, 76.:
4, 25. ἐπιβληθείσῃ : 6, 40. ἐπι-
βαλεῖται, to throw upon (one's
own shoulders.)

ἐπιβάτης. 3, 95. a mariner,
soldier on board a ship : 7,
1. a heavy-armed soldier on
board a vessel. (distiguished
from ναῦται, the unarmed
crew, who navigated the
ship :) 6, 43. 7, 62. 70. 8, 24.

ἐπιβιβάζω, 4, 31. ἐπιβιβάσαν-
τες, to put on board.

ἐπιβιόω, 2, 65. ἐπιβίω, to
survive, live after (a period :)

5, 26. ἐπιβίων, to live, Matth.
Gr. Gr. 18. : 3, 51.

ἐπιβοάω, 3, 59. 6, 16. ἐπιβοώ-
μενος, i. q. ἐπιβόητος, to be
pursued with detraction,
abuse, to be defamed : 4, 28.
ἐπιβοῶν, clamorously to name,
direct : 7, 69. ἐπιβοῶνται, to
exclaim aloud, ring in the
ears (of men,) 75. ἐπιβοώμεναι,
to call out upon, cry out to:
5, 65. ἐπιβοήσειν Ἄγιδι, to call
out : 7, 70.

ἐπιβοήθεια, 3, 51. the means
of assistance, a power of
throwing in succour.

ἐπιβοηθέω, 4, 7. ἐπιβοηθησάν-
των, to come up and attack,
7, 53. to bring additional
aid : 2, 90. ἐπιβοηθῶν : 3, 26.
ἐπιβοηθήσουσιν ταῖς ναυσίν, to
pursue, sail against the
ships : 1, 73. ἐπιβοηθεῖν, to
succour : 2, 5. ἐπιβοήθουν, to
advance or march to the aid
of : 4, 66. ἐπιβοηθήσωσιν ἐκ τῆς
Νισαίας, to bring up rein-
forcements : 4, 29. 7, 3. 14. :
6, 99. : 8, 33. ἐπιβοηθήσειν.

ἐπιβόημα, 5, 65. διὰ τὸ, on
account of the cry, shout,
Matth. Gr. Gr. 863.

ἐπιβόητος, 6, 16. ὧν γὰρ
πέρι ἐπιβόητός εἰμι, about
which a clamour has been
raised against me.

ἐπιβολή, 2, 49. laying or
putting on (clothes :) 3, 20.
πλίνθων, a layer of bricks:
7, 62. throwing or casting
upon (any thing :) 3, 45. an
enterprise, aggression.

ἐπιβούλευμα, 3, 45. a criminal project, conspiracy: 4, 68. a plot.

ἐπιβουλεύω, 3, 40. ἐπιβουλευσάντων, to conspire against, 20. ἐπιβουλεύουσιν ἐξελθεῖν, to project, resolve upon a consultation: 6, 33. ἐπιβουλευθεῖσιν, to be conspired against: 3, 82. ἐπιβουλεύσας, 40. ἐπιβούλευσαν: 2, 5. ἐπεβούλευον, to form or have designs upon or against: 1, 2. ἐπεβουλεύοντο, to be conspired or plotted against, 82. ἀνεπίφθονον, ὅσοι ὥσπερ καὶ ἡμεῖς ὑπ᾽ Ἀθηναίων ἐπιβουλευόμεθα διασωθῆναι, in Greek the object, which was in the gen. or dat. with the act. may become the object of the pass., Matth. Gr. Gr. 711.: 4, 64. 6, 60.: 6, 29. πέμπεινπ νὰ ἐπὶ στρατεύματι, as commander of an army, an instance of ἐπὶ with the dat. to express occupation, Matth. 903.

ἐπιβουλή, 1, 93. a hostile design: 7, 65. 70. a plotting, designing against: 4, 76. 8, 24.

ἐπιγίγνομαι, 7, 32. ἐπιγενόμενοι, falling upon, coming upon: 6, 26. ἐπιγεγενημένης, to succeed, spring up in place of those, who are dead: 2, 64. τοῖς ἐπιγιγνομένοις, posterity: 4, 93. ἐπιγένοιντο τοὺς Βοιωτοῖς, to take in rear: 3, 80. ἐπιγενέσθαι, to approach, arrive: 5, 51. ἐπιγιγνομένου, ensuing, 7, 10. coming on, approaching, 1, 71. τὰ ἐπιγιγνόμενα, those things, which happened after others, 126.: 2,

64. ἐπιγεγένηται, to ensue, happen subsequently: 8, 96.

ἐπιγιγνώσκω, 1, 132. ἐπιγνῷ, to discover: 3, 57. ἐπιγνῶναι, to decree, sentence, 1, 70. to devise any thing new: 2, 65.

ἐπίγραμμα, 6, 59. inscription, epitaph.

ἐπιγραφή, 2, 43. σνηλῶν, inscription.

ἐπιγράφω, 1, 132. ἐπιγράψασθαι ἐπὶ τὸν τρίποδα, to inscribe upon a tripod, 31. ἐπεγράψαντο ἑαυτοὺς, to enrol themselves, 5, 4.

ἐπιδείκνυμι, 5, 17. ἐπιδείξαντες, to declare, 6, 47. to make a display.

ἐπίδειξις, 8, 16. 42. a display, parade, a specimen (of one's cleverness,) 16. ἐπίδειξιν ἐποιοῦντο, to make a show, display: 6, 31. a display, manifestation.

ἐπιδημέω, 1, 180. to be at home.

ἐπιδημιουργὸς, 1, 56. a prefect, an overseer, annual magistrate (sent by a parent state to preside over a colony.)

ἐπιδιαβαίνω, 6, 101. ἐπιδιαβὰς, to cross.

ἐπιδίδωμι, 6, 72. ἐπιδώσειν ἀμφότερα αὐτὰ, to increase: 7, 8. ἐπιδιδοῦσαν, to grow, increase: 4, 2. ἐπιδοῦναι, to present, bestow: 6, 60. ἐπεδίδοσαν ἐς τὸ ἀγριώτερον, to grow more savage: 8, 24. ἐπεδίδου ἐπὶ τὸ μεῖζον, increased, grew in strength and opulence, 83.

ἐπιδιώκω, 1, 14. to follow the pursuit, give chase, 7, 23. ἐπεδιώκοντο : 3, 33. ἐπεδιώ-ξιν. μέχρι Πάτμου, to pursue or follow the chase as far as Patmos : 3, 69. ἐπιδιωχθεῖσαι ἐκ τῶν 'A., to be pursued by the Athenians : 7, 53. ἐπεδίω-ξαν, to pursue, 4, 43. 7, 41.

ἐπιδοχὴ, 6, 17. a succession, an accession, admission, a reception (of new-comers, foreigners.)

ἐπιδρομὴ, 4, 34. a running or rushing at, an attack at full speed, 56. a charge, an assault.

ἐπιείκεια, 3, 48. lenity, for-bearance, 40. clemency, in-dulgence : 5, 86. moderation, justice.

ἐπιεικὴς, 1, 76. ἐκ τοῦ ἐπιεικοῦς, from or on account of your moderation : 3, 9. just, fair, reasonable : 3, 4. ὁμολογία τινὶ ἐπιεικεῖ, fair, reasonable, not very vigorous, specious, plausible : 4, 19. 8, 93.

ἐπιέναι, 4, 73. to come up to oppose : 2, 49. 6, 31. πρὸς οὓς ἐπῄεσαν : 7, 4. ἐπῄει, to ad-vance to attack, to march against, 27. ἐπιόντων, to make an attack : 7, 27. ἐπιούσαις, to come after, to succeed, 74. 4, 38. : 1, 86. ἐπίωμεν πρὸς τοὺς ἀδικοῦντας, to attack, go against: 4, 6. ἐπίεσε τὸ στράτευ-μα, to drive back : 1, 72. ἐπιέ-ναι, to come forward, (to ad-dress an audience,) 2, 11. πρὸς τὸ ἐπιέναι, for the ad-vance : 7, 79. εἰ μὲν ἐπίοιεν οἱ Ἀθηναῖοι, ὑπεχώρουν, εἰ δ' ἀνα-

χωροῖεν, ἐπεκεῖντο, Matth. Gr. Gr. 775.

ἐπιζήμιος, 1, 32. injurious, prejudicial.

ἐπιθαλασσίδιος, 4, 76. one, who lives on the coast.

ἐπιθαλάσσιος, 3, 7. χωρία, maritime places on the sea-coast, 91.: 2, 56. 4, 102.

ἐπιθειάζω, 2, 75. ἐπιθειάσας τοσαῦτα, to invoke or call the gods to witness. : 8, 53.

ἐπιθειασμὸς, 7, 75, an impre-cation, a curse, calling on the gods to witness.

ἐπιθεραπεύω, 8, 47. to take measures for, 84.

ἐπιθυμέω, 6, 10. to be de-sirous, eager, 24. τὸ ἐπιθυμοῦν τοῦ πλοῦ ἐξῃρέθησαν, to be deprived, divested of (any thing, for ἡ ἐπιθυμία ἐξῃρέθη αὐ-τοῖς: 1, 80. ἐπιθυμῆσαι τοῦ ἔργου, eagerly to deserve the busi-ness : 5, 36. ἐπιθυμοῦντος, par-ticularly desirous, 41.

ἐπιθυμία, 6, 13. eager desire, passionate or sanguine hopes, wishes, 15. ἐπιθυμίαις ἐχρῆτο, to entertain or have desires : 4, 81. ἐς τοὺς Λ., a powerful impulse or bias towards : 5, 15. ἐπιθυμίᾳ τῶν ἀνδρῶν τῶν ἐκ τῆς νήσου κομίσασθαι, an in-stance of pleonasm, where two kinds of constr. are united, Matth. Gr. Gr. 949.

ἐπικαθαιρέω, 8, 20. ἐπικαθε-λὼν, to destroy the remnant of.

ἐπικάθημαι, 7, 27. ἐπικαθημέ-νων, to encamp, settle, take up (a post in an enemy's country,) to be in garrison.

ἐπίκαιρος, 6, 34. politic, expedient: 1, 68. ἐπικαιρότατος, most opportune, suitable: 6, 85. convenient.

ἐπικαλέω, 6, 6. 18. ἐπικαλούμενοι, to implore aid, call upon, conjure: 1, 139. 5, 59. 83. to accuse, charge: 2, 27. ἐπικαλέσαντες, to charge, lay blame upon, accuse: 5, 56. ἐπεκάλουν, to remonstrate: 3, 52. ἐπικαλεσάμενοι, to call upon by name.

ἐπικαταβαίνω, 4, 11. ἐπικαταβάντες, to descend to, 7, 35. to go down to (the beach, 23.) πρὸς τὴν θάλασσαν, 84. to descend, make an attack, 6, 97. to disembark against.

ἐπικατάγω, 3, 49. ἐπικατάγεται ὑστέρα αὐτῆς, to come to port after it: 8, 28. ἐπικατάγονται, to go against.

ἐπικαταδαρθάνω, 4, 133. ἐπικαταδαρθούσης, to fall into a deep sleep.

ἐπικαταλαμβάνω, 2, 90. ἐπικαταλαβόντες, to intercept.

ἐπικαταψεύδομαι, 8, 74. καὶ ἄλλα πολλὰ ἐπικαταψευδόμενος ἔλεγεν, uttering many other falsehoods besides.

ἐπικατιόντος, 2, 49. to settle upon, descend into.

ἐπίκειμαι, 2, 49. ἐπέκειτο, to press upon, oppress: 2, 14. 4, 44. ἐπικειμένας, adjacent, 8, 15. imposed, 7, 71. to press hard upon: 3, 70. ἐπέκειτο, to be set (as a fine:) 8, 31. ἐπικειμένας, adjacent to.

ἐπικέλευσις, 4, 95. καὶ ὑπόμνησιν μᾶλλον ἔχει ἢ ἐπικέλευσιν,

it is more with a view to remind than to command.

ἐπικελεύω, 4, 28. ἐπεκελεύοντο, to bid, call to: 3, 82. ἐπικελεύσας, to bid (any one) to do (any thing.)

ἐπικηρυκεύω, 3, 101. 7, 48. ἐπεκηρυκεύετο, to send a message to, to correspond with, 2, 19. ἐπεκηρυκεύοντο, to send a herald to (to solicit peace, 6, 52.: 6, 48. ἐπικηρυκεύεσθαι, to send heralds, ambassadors to a place: 4, 44. ἐπικηρυκευσάμενοι, to ask by a herald, 27.: 8, 44. ἐπικηρυκευομένων, to be summoned by a herald.

ἐπικίνδυνος, 3, 54. enterprising, hazardous: 4, 92. ἐπικινδυνοτέραν, more formidable, threatening: 2, 63. hazardous, perilous.

ἐπικινδύνως, 3, 37. ἐς ὑμᾶς, hazardously for you, with hazard to you, at your peril.

ἐπικλάω, 4, 37. ἐπικλασθεῖεν, to be abated: 3, 67. ἐπικλασθῆτε, to be softened, to relent, 59. ἐπικλασθῆναι τῇ γνώμῃ, to give way.

ἐπίκλησις, 1, 3. a name, denomination: 7, 68. αἰσχίστην, a most ignominious appellation, surname.

ἐπίκλητος, 4, 61. called upon, summoned.

ἐπικλινὴς, 6, 96. sloping.

ἐπικλύζω, 3, 89. ἐπέκλυσε, to break in upon the land (as the sea.)

ἐπίκλυσις, 3, 89. an inundation.

ἐπικομπέω, 4, 126. τὸ ἀνδρεῖον ἐπικομποῦσιν, *ostento*, to make a vain boast of: 8, 81.

ἐπικουρέω, 1, 49. ἐπεκούρων, to aid, assist: 7, 57. ἐπεκούρησαν, to bear a hand, give aid, Matth. Gr. Gr. 450.: 5, 23.

ἐπικουρία, 1, 32. succour, aid: 3, 54. ἐς ἐπικουρίαν, for succour: 1, 33. ἐπικουρίαν ποιήσεσθε, to render succour: 7, 18. 59.

ἐπικουρικὸς, 4, 51. auxiliary: 7. 48. ἐπικουρικὰ μᾶλλον ἢ δι' ἀνάγκης, auxiliary, i. e. mercenary kind of troops, (in opposition to those, who served of necessity, ἠναγκασμένοι, i. e. citizens, who took their necessary turn of duty:) 8, 25.

ἐπίκουρος, 4, 46. an ally: 1, 40. a succourer, 115, 2, 33.

ἐπικρατέω, 5, 82. ἐπεκράτησεν, to be conqueror: 1, 49. 6. 74. 7, 42. ἐπεκράτουν, to prevail, 30. to bear sway over: 4, 19. ἐπικρατήσας τοῦ πολέμου, to have the upper hand, the superiority, 4, 74.: 5, 46. 7. 71.

ἐπικρατής, 6, 88. ἐπικρατέστεροι τῇ μάχῃ, superior.

ἐπικράτησις, 1, 41. conquest, subjugation.

ἐπικρέμαμαι, 3, 40. ἐπικρεμασθέντος, to be suspended, 1, 18. to be suspended, imminent: 2, 53. ἐπικρεμασθῆναι πολὺ μεῖζω, that a much worse sentence (δίκην, τιμωρίαν) impended: 7, 75. ἐπικρεμαμένου.

ἐπικτάομαι, 2. 65. ἐπικτωμένους ἀρχὴν, to acquire further dominion, enlarge one's dominions by fresh acquisitions, 4, 61. coveting, aiming to possess: 1, 144. ἐπικτᾶσθαι, to acquire any thing additional.

ἐπικυρόω, 3, 71. ἐπικυρῶσαι, to confirm, sanction: 5, 45. ἐπικυρωθῆναι, to be formally concluded.

ἐπικωλύω, 6, 17. i. q. κωλύω.

ἐπιλαμβάνω, 4, 27. ἐπιλάβοι, to surprise, 96.

ἐπιλέγω, 6, 28, ἐπιλέγοντες τεκμήρια, to state besides, in addition, to add, subjoin: 7, 19. ἐπιλεξάμενοι, to select.

ἐπιλείπω, 3, 26. ἐπελελοίπη, to fail, to be wanting. 2, 70. to fall short, to fail: 5, 103. ἐπιλίπωσιν, to desert: 3, 20. ἐπιλιπόντι τῷ σίτῳ, by the failure of provisions.

ἐπίλειψις, 2, 50. a scarcity.

ἐπιμανθάνω, 1. 138. ἐπιμαθὼν, to gain an addition of intelligence after deliberation.

ἐπιμαρτυρία, an attestation, a calling to witness, 2, 74.

ἐπιμαρτύρομαι, 6, 29. ἐπεμαρτύρετο, to conjure, protest against.

ἐπιμαχέω, 5, 27. to fight for, to defend.

ἐπιμαχία, 1, 44. a defensive alliance, 5, 48.

ἐπίμαχος, 4, 31. pregnable, 4. ἐπιμαχώτατα, in the best posture of defence, 35, 115. vulnerable, assailable.

ἐπιμέλεια, 7, 16. a care, regard, attention: 3, 46. ἔργων, precaution, caution, looking after: 4, 53. πολλὴν ἐπιμέλειαν ἐποιοῦντο, to make much of, to be chary of, 7, 56. to be solicitous for, to be studious of : 2, 39. attention, application : 6, 41.

ἐπιμελὴς, 1, 5. ἐπιμελὲς εἶναι, to be a care to, a desire to : 5, 66. τὸ ἐπιμελὲς τοῦ δρωμένου, the care : 4, 67. οἷς ἦν ἐπιμελὲς, whose concern it was.

ἐπιμέλομαι, 3, 25. ἐπιμελησόμενος τῶν ἄλλων, to take care of, look after : 4, 118. ἐπιμελεῖσθαι, to take care : 6, 54. ἐπεμέλοντο, to take care, to mind, 41. : 4, 2. ἐπιμεληθῆναι τῇ πόλει, to take care that the town received no detriment : 7, 39. ἐπιμελομένους τούτου, the magistrates, those whose business it was : 8, 68.

ἐπιμένω, 3, 2. νεῶν ποίησιν ἐπέμενον τελεσθῆναι, they were waiting till the building of the ships was completed, 1, 109. : 4, 4. ἐπιμένειν, to keep on, to remain : 3, 26. ἀεὶ ἐπιμένοντες, still waiting, constantly expecting.

ἐπιμεταπέμπω, 6, 21. ἐπιμεταπέμπεσθαι, to send for any thing additional, over and above (what there was before :) 7, 7. ἐπιμεταπεμπόμενον, to send for an additional (reinforcement.)

ἐπιμίγνυμι, 2, 1. ἐπεμίγνυντο, to have intercourse with, 1, 145. ἐπεμίγνυντο : 1, 2. ἐπιμιγνύντες, to keep up intercourse, mix together : 4, 118.

ἐπιμιξία, 5, 35. an interview, commerce, intercourse, 78.

ἐπιμίσγω, 1, 13. ἐπιμισγόντων

παρ᾿ ἀλλήλους, to mix or have intercourse with one another : 4, 118. ἐπιμισγομένους ἐς τὴν ξυμμαχίαν, to have intercourse, hold communication.

ἐπιμνάομαι, 1, 97. ἐπεμνήσθη, to be commemorated, 3, 104. ἑαυτοῦ, to make mention of.

ἐπιμονὴ, 2, 18. a delay.

ἐπίνειον, 2, 8. a post, dock, arsenal.

ἐπινέμω, 2, 54. ἐπενείματο, to prey upon, ravage, depopulate.

ἐπινοέω, 7, 37. ἐπινοήσαντες, to invent, devise, 1, 70. to scheme, design : 8, 11. ἐπενόησαν, to think of : 4, 32. 5, 4. 13. 7, 43. ἐπενόει, to plan, intend, 59. ἐπενόουν ὀλίγον οὐδὲν ἐς οὐδὲν, to meditate, design great things in every respect, 72. ἐπενόουν, to think of, entertain a thought of : 2, 75. ἐπινοοῦσι, to devise : 2, 11. ἐπινοοῦμεν, to meditate against : 1, 70. οἱ μέν γε νεωτεροποιοὶ καὶ ἐπινοῆσαι ὀξεῖς καὶ ἐπιτελέσαι ἔργῳ ὃ ἂν γνῶσιν, the infin. after the adj. which requires the addition of its object by means of a verb, or by which a verb following is affected, Matth. Gr. Gr. 799.

ἐπίνοια, 5, 8. plan, intention, design : 4, 92. ἐς ἐπίνοιαν ἐλθεῖν, to come into (one's) mind, to enter (one's) thoughts : 3, 46. ἐς ἐπίνοιαν τούτου ἴωσι, to entertain a thought or idea, to fall into a train of thought.

ἐπιπαιωνίζω, 1, 50. ἐπιπαιώηστο, the pœan was raised (as a signal for onset.)

ἐπιπαρανέω, 2, 77. ἐπιπαρένη-σαν, to pile up against, to raise piles.

ἐπιπάρειμι, 7, 76. ἐπιπαριών, 5, 10. to advance, to attack, 4, 94. τὸ στρατόπεδον, to move along up to, 6, 67. ἕκαστα, to ride up to: 4, 108. ἐπιπαριέναι, to come in person: 1, 61. ἐπιπαρόντας, to arrive in addition (to others.)

ἐπιπάσχω, 6, 88. ἐπεπόνθεσαν, to be affected, disposed.

ἐπιπαύω, 4, 13. ἐπεπαύοντο, to cease, desist.

ἐπιπέμπω, 7, 15. to despatch, send in addition.

ἐπίπεμψις, 2, 39. ἐπὶ πολλά, despatching, sending to various places.

ἐπιπήγνυμι, 7, 38. ἐπεπήγει, were fixed, driven down, 3, 23. to be frozen, to be of a consistence, to be congealed.

ἐπιπίπτω, 7, 29. ἐπιπεσών, to fall upon, 1, 110. to fall upon, to attack, 117. 4, 4. ἐπέπεσε, to fall upon, occur to, 3, 82. to befall: 3, 3. ἐπιπεσεῖν, to fall upon any one suddenly, unexpectedly, to surprise: 2, 48. ἐπιπέσοι, to make an attack: 7, 84. ἐπέπιπτον ἀλλήλοις, to fall upon one another.

ἕπιπλα, τὰ, 3, 68. moveable materials,

ἐπίπλευσις, 7, 36. a sailing against, advance upon.

ἐπιπλέω, 8, 16. ἐπέπλει, to sail to: 7, 22. ἐπέπλεον, 1, 30. ἀλλήλοις, to sail against one another: 7, 70. προθυμία ἐς

τὸ ἐπιπλεῖν, ardour as to or for, 12. ἐπιπλεύσονται, to sail against, 34. ἐπέπλευσαν, to sail up with hostile intent, 3, 16. ἐπιπλεύσεσθαι, to sail to (a place:) 1, 15. ἐπιπλέοντες, to sail to attack, to invade by sea: 8, 99. ἐπιπλεύκισαν, Matth. Gr. Gr. 254.: 2, 93. ἦν προσδοκία οὐδεμία μὴ ἄν ποτε οἱ πολέμιοι ἐξαπιναίως οὕτως ἐπιπλεύσειαν, an instance of ἄν being used with the opt. after μὴ, Matth. 772.

ἐπιπληρόω, 1, 29. ἐπεπλήρωντο, to be manned: 7, 14. ἐπιπληρωσόμεθα, to make up a complement, to repair the loss (in a ship's crew,) to recruit the (ship's) companies.

ἐπίπλους, 2, 17. 8, 30. an incursion upon, 86.

ἐπιπολεμόω, 1, 57. ἐπιπολέμωτο, to become an enemy, to be rendered hostile.

ἐπιπολῆς, 6, 96. τοῦ ἄλλου, above.

ἐπιπολὺ, 5, 16. often, frequently: 1, 62. a considerable distance: 1, 12. 4, 12. 6, 46.

ἐπιπονέω, 7, 38. ἐπεπονώμεθα, to suffer, to be damaged.

ἐπίπονος, 4, 26. troublesome, laborious, 1, 70.: 8, 11. full of difficulty: 3, 58.

ἐπιπόνως, 1, 22. laboriously.

ἐπιπορίζω, 6, 29. ἐπεπόριστο, were ready, provided against.

ἐπικράσσω, 7, 24. ἐπεπράγωσαν, to fare, succeed.

ἐπιρρώννυμι, 7. 7. ἐπιρρώσαντο, to exert oneself vigorously, (to be encouraged, *Hobbes*,) to pluck up courage, take heart : 7, 2. ἐπιρρώθησαν, to be fortified (in one's mind,) invigorated, inspirited : 4, 36. ἐπίρρωσε, to confirm, give, impart vigour : 3, 6. ἐπιρρωσθέντες, to be encouraged, inspirited, confirmed : 8, 89.

ἐπισημαίνω, 2, 49. ἐπεσήμαινε, to indicate by marks, to mark.

ἐπίσημος, 2, 13. ἀργύριον, coined silver, 43. ἐπισημότατος. most illustrious, signal.

ἐπισιτίζω, 6, 94. ἐπισιτισάμενοι, to take provisions on board, *assumptis cibariis* : 8, 95.

ἐπισκεπτέον, 6, 18. to be considered, consulted, regarded, studied, ἐπιτηδευτέον, 34.

ἐπισκευάζω, 7, 38. τὰς ναῦς, to repair, refit, 7, 1. ἐπεσκεύασαν, 24. ἐπισκευάσαντες : 1, 29. ἐπισκευάσαντες, to prepare for action, to fit up : 7, 36. ἐπισκευασάμενοι πρώραθεν, to prepare at the prow, i. e. strengthen or fortify the prows.

ἐπισκευή, 1, 52. materials for refitting.

ἐπισκήπτω, 2, 73. to enjoin (specially :) 3, 59. to supplicate.

ἐπισπάω, 5, 111. to seduce : 4, 9. ἐπισπάσασθαι, to be drawn on or to, to be allured, enticed, induced : 3, 43. ἐπισπώμενος, to follow advice, (opposed to κωλύεις,) 4, 35. to follow up : 3, 44. ἐπισπάσαιτο, to draw, win to, over.

ἐπισπένδω, 5, 22. ἐπισπένδεσθαι, to make a peace, embark in a treaty.

ἐπισπέρχω, 4, 12. ἐπίσπερχε, to incite, one of the verbs, which take an accus. of the pronoun neuter, besides an accus. of the subst., Matth. Gr. Gr. 588.

ἐπισπονδή, 5, 32. a truce.

ἐπίσταμαι, 4, 126. to come to know, get at the knowledge of : 4, 10. 7, 31. ἐπιστάμενοι, to understand, know, 4, 73. 5, 89. 7, 48. 8, 40. : 1, 69. ἐπιστάμεθα, to be aware (from experience :) 5, 36. ἠπίσταντο, to know, to be assured, 7, 44. : 2, 44. ἐν πολυτρόποις ξυμφοραῖς ἐπίστανται γραφέντες, *sciunt se educatos esse*, verbs of 'knowing' take the object in the participle, Matth. Gr. Gr. 828. : 8, 48. : 7, 14. ἐπισταμένοις ὑμῖν γράφω, Matth. 848.

ἐπιστατέω, 4, 118. ἐπιστάτει, to act as president, to be in the chair.

ἐπιστέλλω, 2, 6. ἐπέστελλον, to give orders to, to enjoin : 1, 57. ἐπιστέλλουσι, to give orders, directions (to a general :) 5, 37. ἐπεστάλκεσαν, to charge with, to commission about : 7, 14. ἐπιστέλλειν, to write word : 1, 91. ἐπεστάλη, to be directed : 4, 48. ἐπεσταλμένα, orders, commands, injunctions, instructions, 5, 37. to receive (as despatches,) to be charged with (as commissions :) 5, 46. ἐπιστείλαντες, to subjoin instructions, to give a person his message, 37. οἱ Κορίνθιοι ταῦτα ἐπεσταλμένοι, the object which was in the gen. or dat. with the active may become the subject of the pass. and the pass. of verbs take an accus., whose actives take two accus., Matth. Gr. Gr. 712.

ἐπιστήμη, 7, 21. skill, science, knowledge, 37. experience, knowledge, 62. 63. τῆς φωνῆς, proficiency or knowledge of the dialect, 64. 6, 18. 1, 49. 72. 121. 2, 87. 7, 21.

ἐπιστήμων, 1, 142. τῆς θαλάσσης, expert at sea: 8, 45. skilled in.

ἐπιστολὴ, 1, 129. 132. 7, 8. 16. a letter.

ἐπιστρατεία, 2, 79. ἡ τῶν Πλαταιέων, the march against the Platæans, Matth. Gr. Gr. 450.

ἐπιστρατεύω, 1, 16. ἐπεστράτευσε, to attack, make war upon: 5, 4. ἐπιστρατεῦσαι, to make war against: 4, 92.

ἐπιστρέφω, 5, 10. ἐπιστρέψας, to cause to face about, to turn, 1, 61. ἐκεῖθεν, to turn back from thence.

ἐπιστροφὴ, 3, 71. a revolution, turning upside down.

ἐπίσχεσις, 2, 18. a stay, stopping.

ἐπίσχω, 3, 45. to restrain: 5, 46. ἐπίσχοντας: 6, 33. ἐπισχήσω (sc. ἑαυτὸν,) to refrain: 1, 129. ἐπισχέτω, to stop, hinder, stay: 7, 50.

ἐπίτακτος, 6, 67. τῶν, a reserve of troops appointed to support those parts of the advanced line, which were giving way.

ἐπιταλαιπωρέω, 1, 123. τοῖς παροῦσι βοηθοῦντας χρὴ ἐπιταλαιπωρεῖν, it is fit (for the sake of the future) to take trouble in attending to the present.

ἐπιτάσσω, 6, 19. ἐπιτάξειε, to require, demand, enjoin: 5, 72. ἐπιτεταγμένων, to be drawn up, to guard: 8, 11. ἐπέταξεν, to appoint, 1, 139. to urge the performance of any thing: 2, 7. ἐπετάχθησαν, to give orders to: 1, 140. ἐπιτάσσοντες, to lay a command upon, to order, 141. ἐπιτασσομένη, to be imposed upon: 1, 140. ἐπιταχθήσεσθε, to have an order, command imposed upon.

ἐπιταχύνω, 4, 47. ἐπετάχυνον, to quicken, accelerate.

ἐπιτειχίζω, 7, 47. ἐπιτειχίζοντας, to fortify a post against.

ἐπιτείχισις, 6, 91. raising a hostile fort.

ἐπιτειχισμὸς, 7, 18. a fort: 1, 142. a fortification (raised against any one,) 122. a building, fortification.

ἐπιτελέω, 7, 4. ἐπιτελέσαντες, to complete, finish: 1, 138. ἐπιτελέσαι, to perform, accomplish: 4, 90. to push to completion, 1, 70. ἔργῳ, to accomplish, carry into execution, 5, 60.: 1, 108. ἐπετέλεσαν, to complete, finish:

2, 87. ἐπιτελεῖν, to execute: 7, 2. ἐπετετέλεστο διπλοῦν τεῖχος, to be perfected, completed.

ἐπιτελὴς, 1, 141. ἐπιτελὲς γίγνεσθαι, to be accomplished, completed, fully executed.

ἐπιτέχνησις, 1, 71. contrivance, new invention, device in art.

ἐπιτήδειος, 2, 52. 3, 75. τὰ ἐπιτήδεια, necessaries, necessary materials, 10. οἷα εἰκὸς ἔχειν ἐπιτήδεια, necessaries, provisions such as it would be necessary to have, 7, 4. 13. 24. 77. : 1, 60. friendly, serviceable, 5, 64. 76. 81. 6, 64. friendly, well-disposed, 4, 113. σφίσιν, favourable to their cause, 1, 58. serviceable, 5, 82. 7, 86. τὸν δὲ διὰ τὰ αὐτὰ ἐπιτηδειότατον, the other as most friendly on account of the same business, 3, 40. πρὸς τοὺς ἐπιτηδείους διδόναι, i. q. τοῖς ἐπιτηδείοις, 2, 18. favourable, disposed to befriend, 6, 46. : 8, 11. opportune : 5, 21. advantageous, satisfactory, 44. suitable, 2, 20. ἐπιτήδειος φαίνεσθαι, to be convenient, after an adj. expressing fitness the infin. is usual, Matth. Gr. Gr. 798., see δυνατὸς, 4, 73. convenient, suitable: 8, 46. ἐπιτηδειοτέρους, more convenient, desirable : 4, 41. ἐπιτηδειοτάτους, most adapted, fittest, best qualified : 8, 63.

ἐπιτηδείως, 1, 19. : 4, 54. ἐπιτηδειόστερον, more expediently, commodiously : 5, 82.

ἐπίτηδες, 3, 112. on purpose. ἐπιτήδευμα, 1, 71. a custom, 138. τῆς χώρας : 2, 37. τῶν καθ' ἡμέραν ἐπιτηδευμάτων, the habits and pursuits of everyday life, the daily course, way of life: 6, 15. ἐπιτηδεύματα, a pursuit, manner, habits, course of life, 18. 28.

ἐπιτήδευσις, 2, 36. 7, 87. διὰ τὴν νενομισμένην ἐς τὸ θεῖον ἐπιτήδευσιν, on account of his exact and religious performance of his duty towards the deity.

ἐπιτηδεύω, 6, 54. ἐπιτήδευσαν ἀρετὴν, to cultivate, observe, practise, 1, 37. to practise a custom.

ἐπιτίθημι, 2, 3. 33. 3, 19. ἐπιθεμένων, to make an attack upon, 5, 91. 3, 66.: 7, 36. ἐπέθεσαν, to affix, put on, attack : 5, 82. ἐπέθεντο τοὺς ὀλίγους, to attack the noble, 3, 39. : 4, 80. ἐπιθέσθαι σφίσιν, to set oneself against : 1, 64. ἐπιτίθωνται, to attack, assault, the conj. of this verb in μι in the pres. pass. and aor. 2. in Attic has the form of a barytone verb in ω, the distinction, however, is only in the accentuation, Matth. Gr. Gr. 287.: 7, 50. ἐπιθησόμενοι, to be about to attack, 5, 8. 7, 41. with a view to attack: 4, 71. ἐπίθηται σφίσι, to inflict: 7, 42. ἐπιθέσθαι τῇ πείρᾳ, i. q. ἐγχειρῆσαι, to undertake, set about the attempt, to execute the attempt, to attempt : 6, 61. ὑπωπτεύθησαν ἐπιτίθεσθαι τῷ δήμψ, to be suspected of designs against, 3, 72. ἐπιτίθενται τῷ δήμῳ : 8, 51. ἐπιθήσεσθαι : 6, 34. ἐπιθοίμεθα, the opt. pres. pass. and aor. 2. middle have frequently the form of the opt. of a barytone verb in ω, Matth. 287.

ἐπιτηρέω, 4, 42. ἐπιτήρουν, to keep a sharp look out for, to keep a vigilant eye on, 5, 37. to watch, wait for : 1, 62. to watch, attend to diligently.

ἐπιτιμάω, 3, 38. ἐπιτιμησάντων, to censure, blame, criticize severely.

ἐπιτίμησις, 7, 48. an accusing, invective, harangue.

ἐπίτιμος, 5, 34. eligible to posts of dignity, offices of trust, public honors.

ἐπιτολή, 2, 11. 78. περὶ ἀρκτούρου ἐπιτολὰς, at the rising of Arcturus, about the beginning of September.

ἐπιτρέπω, 4, 54. ἐπιτρέψαι Ἀθηναίοις περὶ σφῶν αὐτῶν, to refer, shift to the shoulders of : 2, 90. ἐπιτρέψας, to turn against, towards, 6, 15. to commit (to any one,) 1, 126. 2, 42. ἐλπίδι, to commit (the event) to hope, (as we say, to Providence,) to trust to their good fortune, to hope for the best : 2, 65. ἐπέτρεψαν, to commit to, to entrust, 1, 9. : 5, 99. ἐπιτρέφοντες, 6, 40. to suffer, allow : 1, 82. ἐπιτρέφομεν, to look over, to be careless : 1, 95. to yield,

give up : 1, 28. 4, 83. to refer, commit to arbitration, 7, 18. : 2, 72. ἐπιτρέπωσιν σφίσιν, to permit, leave to the disposal of another, to take out of the hands of its possessor : 5, 31. ἐπιτραπείσης : 1, 126. ἐπιτετραμμένοι τὴν φυλακὴν, relied upon with respect to the guard, to whose charge the guard was committed : 1, 72. κελεύω—πέμπειν καὶ αἰτιᾶσθαι μήτε πόλεμον ἄγαν δηλοῦντας, μήθ' ὡς ἐπιτρέψομεν, i. e. καὶ (τε in μήτε) μὴ δηλοῦντας ὡς ἐπιτρέψομεν, or καὶ δ. ὡς οὐκ ἐπιτρ., where for ὡς ἐπιτρ. some such word as ἀμέλειαν should stand, an instance of anacoluthon, Matth. Gr. Gr. 944. (where, however, there is a mistake in the reference :) 8, 27. ἐπιτρέψειν, would permit.

ἐπιτροπεύω, 1, 132. ἐπιτρόπευειν, to educate, to be a tutor or guardian to any one, a verb, which has an accus., that does not mark the passive object of the action, but the object, to which it has an immediate reference, Matth. Gr. Gr. 577.

ἐπιτροπὴ, 5, 41. ἠξίουν δίκης ἐπιτροπὴν, to require or call for an award of justice, a reference for trial, arbitration.

ἐπιτυγχάνω, 6, 38. to catch, take : 7, 25. ἐπιτυχοῦσαι τῶν πλοίων, to fall in with, light upon, meet with : 8, 14. ἐπιτύχοιεν, to chance to meet : 3, 3. ἐπιτυχὼν ὁλκάδος, to meet

with a merchant vessel on
the point of sailing.

ἐπιφανής, 6, 72. ἀνδρείᾳ, distinguished by, 2, 43. : illustrious, 7, 69. 7, 3. 19.
manifest, visible, 5, 10. discernible, exposed to view :
7, 19. to afford a prospect,
(active :) 1, 21. ἐπιφανέστατος,
the clearest, 5, 105.

ἐπιφανῶς, 1, 91. ὡς ἥκιστα
ἐπιφανῶς, with as little appearance (of the fact) as
possible.

ἐπιφέρω, 3, 82. ἐπέφερε, to
urge on : 4, 78. ὅπλα, to bear
arms against, 5, 17. 7, 18. :
2, 34. to bring offerings,
funeral offerings (to the
corpse :) 4, 87. to take a
thing. to : 3, 58. ἐπιφέροντες,
to offer up : 3, 46. τὴν αἰτίαν,
to lay blame upon : 3, 56. to
bring on : 7, 55. ἐπενεγκεῖν, to
bring upon, to occasion, 1,
70. ψόγον, to cast reproach,
censure : 5, 75. ἐπιφερομένης,
to be cast upon, laid to the
charge, 7, 37. bearing down
upon, 40, 70. : 7, 56. ἐπενε-
χθησόμενον πόλεμον, to be carried against, made upon : 3,
23. ἐπεφέροντο αὐτοῖς, to set
upon, to attack : 4, 67. ἐπι-
φερομένοις, coming up to rein-
force : 3, 42. ἐπιφερομένης ἀδικίας, to be urged against,
imputed to, corruption or
criminality being imputed :
8, 83.

ἐπιφήμισμα, 7, 75. an omen,
οἰώνισμα, Hesych.

ἐπίφθονος, 1, 64. τὸ ἐπίφθονον

λαμβάνειν, to get ill, evil : 7,
77. εἰ τῳ θεῶν ἐπίφθονοι ἐστρα-
τεύσαμεν, if by this expedition
we caused the envy and dis-
pleasure of any of the gods.

ἐπιφθόνως, 1, 75. enviously :
3, 82. gloriously, attractively
of emulation.

ἐπιφλέγω, 2, 77. ἐπιφλέξαι, to
set on fire.

ἐπιφοβέω, 5, 50. ἐπεφοβήντο,
to be afraid.

ἐπιφοιτάω, 1, 81. ἐπιφοιτῶν-
τες, to make an incursion,
135. to go about visiting.

ἐπιφορά, 6, 31. additional
pay (over and above the
stated allowance,) a gratuity.

ἐπίφορος, 2, 77. πνεῦμα, a
favourable wind : 3, 74.
ἄνεμος.

ἐπίχαρτος, 3, 67. rejoiced
(at the punishment or calamity of another.)

ἐπιχειμάζω, 1, 89. ἐπιχειμά-
σαντες, to abide by all winter.

ἐπιχειρέω, 1, 126. ἐπεχείρησε
τῷ ἔργῳ, to commence the
execution of an undertaking,
7, 21. to undertake, essay,
take in hand, 3, 45. τούτῳ :
7, 7. ἐπιχειρήσοντες τούτῳ, to
undertake or attempt any
thing : 7, 38. ἐπιχειρήσειν, to
attack : 6, 11. ἐν τῷ ὁμοίῳ καὶ
πρὶν ἐπιχειρῆσαι ἔσται, to be in
the same condition as one
was previous to doing any
thing : 7, 40. ἐπιχειρεῖν, to go
to business, 1, 125. 4, 29. 73.
to undertake, take in hand,
7, 33. τοῖς Ἀθηναίοις, to contend with, 3, 12. 94. : 2, 84.

υ

to commence (the action:) 8, 27. to undertake: 7, 21. ἐπιχειροῦντες, to essay, enterprise: 4, 73. ἐπεχειρεῖτο, to be entered upon: 3, 30. ἐπιχειροίη, to attack: 7, 39. ἐπιχειρῶσι, to undertake, 37. ἐπεχείρουν, to make an attack upon, to begin the attack: 6, 31. ἐπεχειρήθη, to be undertaken, 54. τὸ Ἀριστογείτονος καὶ Ἁρμοδίου τόλμημα δι' ἐρωτικὴν ξυντυχίαν ἐπεχειρήθη, an instance of the object, which was in the gen. or dat. in the act. becoming the subject of the pass., Matth. Gr. Gr. 711.

ἐπιχείρημα, 7, 47. an attempt, undertaking, enterprise.

ἐπιχείρησις, 1, 70. 2, 11. ἐξ ὀλίγου καὶ δι' ὀργῆς, attacks (made) suddenly and in heat, without warning, 4, 29. 5, 9. 19.: 1, 33. a subjugation, mastering, 70. taking in hand to execute: 7, 43. τῶν Ἐπιπολῶν, an attempt against Epipolæ: 2, 87. ἐπιχείρησιν παρασκευάσομεν, to prepare the onset, for action: 7, 12. choice of attack, the management: 3, 82. an enterprise: 4, 130.

ἐπιχειρητέος, 2, 3. ἐπιχειρητέα εἶναι (αὐτοῖς sc.) that the attempt should be made, 1, 118. to be taken in hand, to be dealt with.

ἐπιχειρητὴς, a man of enterprise, 8, 96. οἱ μὲν ἐπιχειρηταί, οἱ δὲ ἄτολμοι.

ἐπιχθόνιος, 3, 104. ἀνθρώπων, terrestrial, mortal.

ἐπιχράομαι, 1, 41. φίλοι, ὥστ' ἐπιχρῆσθαι, so as to exchange good offices, 68.

ἐπιχώριος, indigenous, peculiar to the country, national, 1, 20. 126. 4, 17. 5, 18. 47. ὅρκον, 7, 30. τάξει: 5, 105. ἐπιχώρια, the laws of one's country: 6, 30. ἐπιχώριοι, people of the country, countrymen: 8, 30.

ἐπιψηφίζω, to put the question, take the poll, 1, 87. ἐπεψήφιζε αὐτὸς ἐς τὴν ἐκκλησίαν τῶν Λακεδαιμονίων, whereas verbs, (expressing a direction,) compounded with ἐπί, which signifies a more precise direction, (though the prep. by itself require an accus.,) take the dat., and ἐπιψηφίζειν is not one of that order, which means to permit one to vote, in suffragia mitto, the constr. seems to arise from this, that ἐπιψηφίζειν is the same as ψῆφον προθεῖναι, ἐπαγαγεῖν τινι, Matth. Gr. Gr. 557.: 2, 24. εἴπῃ ἢ ἐπιψηφίσῃ, to express an opinion or to move: 8, 15. ἐπιψηφίσαντι, to put the question to the vote: 6, 14.

ἐποικέω, 6, 86. ἐποικοῦντες, imminentes: 7, 27. ἐπῴκειτο, to be garrisoned.

ἐποικοδομέω, 7, 4. ἐποικοδομήσαντες, to build upon, to raise a building.

ἔποικος, 5, 5. a settler, 6, 4. ἐποκέλλω, 4, 26. ἐπώκελλον, to shelter: 8, 102.

ἔπομαι, 1, 42. ἕπεται, to follow as a consequence: 5, 60.

εἵποντο, to follow a leader, 7, 57. : 7, 1. ἕπεσθαι, to follow, accompany : 6, 83. οὐκ ἄλλῳ ἑπόμεθα, alterius auspicia sequi, hoc unum sequi, tenere, amplecti, nulli alii rei inniti : 2, 35. ἑπόμενος τῷ νόμῳ, to follow or comply with the law, 3, 22. : 2, 87. ἕπεσθε ἕκαστος τὸ καθ᾽ ἑαυτὸν, to follow each his own business : 6, 33. ἕπεσθαι, to follow, comply with (advice.)

ἐπόμνυμι, 2, 5. ἐπομόσαι, to swear to the observance of any thing, to add an oath.

ἐπονομάζω, 1, 13. ἐπωνόμασαν, to name : 7, 69. ἐπονομάζων πατρόθεν, to call by his father's name : 2, 29. ἐπωνόμασται, to be surnamed, called in addition to its usual name: 6, 2. ἐπωνομάσθη, to be surnamed, called after.

ἔπος, 3, 104. verse : 1, 3. τὰ ἔπη, poems, verses.

ἐποτρύνω, 6, 69. ξύνοδον ἐπώτρυνον τοῖς ὁπλίταις, to excite, rouse the soldiers to the conflict, to sound a charge : 7, 25. ἐπωτρύνωσι, to goad on, incite, give a spur and motive : 1, 84. ἐποτρυνόντων, to urge on.

ἐποφείλω, 8, 5. ἐπωφείλησε, to owe.

ἔποψις, 7, 71. a view, survey.

ἑπτά, seven, 7, 34. 8, 10.

ἔπω, 5, 37. εἰπὼν, saying, promising, 5, 36. adducing in conversation, 46. declaring, 7, 29. bidding, ordering:

5, 38. εἴπωσιν, to confer : 1, 1. ὡς εἰπεῖν, so to speak, as may be said, 7, 58. to speak generally, on a rough calculation, with a few grains of allowance, almost, nearly, 67. to speak generally, generally speaking, 1, 22. : 5, 30. εἶπον, to say, declare, 7, 10. : 5, 85. εἴπατε, to say.

ἐπωνυμία, 1, 9. the naming of, the power of giving a name to : 1, 3. a name, denomination, 46. an appellation : 2, 102.

ἐπωτίδες, 7, 34. 36. the stays, ears, (because projecting from the other side of the prow of a ship,) 62.

ἔρανος, a contribution, 2, 43.

ἐραστὴς, 2, 43. γιγνομένους, to contract an affection, to grow enamoured : 6, 54.

ἐργάζομαι, 3, 50. εἰργάζοντο, to cultivate, till, 4, 8. to labour hard, 69. 90. to ply one's task : 3, 66. εἴργασθε δεινὰ, to perpetrate : 1, 3. ἐργασαμένη, to be done, performed, 3, 39. εἰργάσαντο, to perpetrate : 6, 29. εἴργαστο, to commit, perpetrate, (in a bad sense:) 1, 93. εἰργασμένοι, carved, worked, (as a stone,) 4, 8. constructed, manufactured : 2, 71. ἐργαζόμενοι, to cultivate (the ground :) 1, 137. κακὰ πλεῖστα Ἑλλήνων εἴργασμαι τὸν ὑμέτερον οἶκον, I have worked your house much evil.

ἐργαλεῖα, 7, 18. tools, instruments : 6, 44.

ἐργασία, 4, 105. working (a mine:) 7, 6. a work, building, an operation: 1, 139. cultivation, tilling: 6, 26. workmanship.

ἔργον, 3, 26. τὶ πεύσεσθαι τῶν νεῶν, to hear some news of the ships: 5, 67. τὸ, the action, fight, ὅτι ἐν τῇ (sc. γῇ) ἐκείνων τὸ ἔργον ἐγίγνετο, because the action was taking place in their country: 1, 5. the matter, deed, business, 17. a deed, exploit, 6, 33. κάλλιστον, a most glorious, honourable action: 6, 80. οὐδὲν ἔργον, i. q. οὐδὲν χάλεπον: 1, 75. ἐξ αὐτοῦ τοῦ ἔργου, from the nature of the thing itself: 7, 40. τῷ ἔργῳ, in reality, 71. τῶν ἐν τῷ ἔργῳ, the men in action : 1, 69. ὁ λόγος τοῦ ἔργου ἐκράτει, the report was greater than the fact: 3, 3. μέγα ἔργον ἡγοῦντο, to think it a work of great difficulty, a great blow, misfortune, hardship : 1, 73. ἧς τοῦ μὲν ἔργου μέρος μετέσχετε, to share in the actual advantage derived from which: 1, 68. ἐν τῷ ἔργῳ ἐσμὲν we are in the act of suffering.

ἐρέτης, 1, 31. a rower.

ἐρημία, 3, 67. 4, 8. a desert state, 29. 33. : 1, 71. desertion : 6, 102. 8, 71.

ἔρημος, 1, 49. deserted, 5, 3. defenceless, deserted : 2, 90. φοβηθεὶς περὶ τῷ χωρίῳ ἐρήμῳ ὄντι, to fear for the place, which was without guard, 57. unattended : 5, 7. in a

desolate condition : 2, 4. neglected, unguarded : 1, 32. alone, solitary : 2, 17. τὰ ἔρημα τῆς πόλεως, the uninhabited, vacant places of the city : 3, 11. ἐρημότεροι αὐτοὶ αὐτῶν ἐγίγνοντο, to be more desolate than heretofore: 4, 26. ἐν νήσῳ τῇ ἐρήμῃ, many of the adj. of the third termination occur as common, and ἔρημος γῆ was peculiar to the Attics, Matth. Gr. Gr. 150. yet here ἐρήμη νῆσος, but see the note of Duker: 8, 96.

ἐρημόω, 1, 10. ἐρημωθείη, to become desolate, 23. ἠρημώθησαν, to become desert : 5, 4. ἐρημώσαντες, to render desolate: 3, 58. ἐρημοῦντε, the Doric fut. contracted, Matth Gr. Gr. 221. : 2, 44.

ἐρίζω, 5, 79. ἐρίζοι, to contend against.

ἔρις, 2, 21. εἶναι ἐν πολλῇ ἔριδι, to have great altercation, 54. 6, 34.

ἔρμα, 7, 25. ὥσπερ περὶ ἔρμα περιβάλῃ τὴν ναῦν, to strike or bulge a ship against (any thing) as it were against a rock, upon a rock.

ἑρμηνεύω, 2, 60. ἑρμηνεῦσαι, to explain, unfold, develope (in a speech, i. q. σαφῶς διδάσκειν.)

ἔρομαι, 4, 40. ἐρομένου, inquiring.

ἐρύθημα, 2, 49. ὀφθαλμῶν, a redness, Lucr. 1, 1144. oculos suffusa luce rubentes.

ἔρυμα, 1, 11. a rampart,

defence: 4, 35. 6, 94. a fort:
4, 69. 5, 4. a bulwark, entrenchment: 4,31. a fortress:
6, 66. 8. 40.

ἐρυμνός, 5, 65. naturally
strong, impregnable.

ἔρχομαι, 5, 36. ἐλθουσῶν, to
arrive, 8. 21. to make one's
appearance, 7, 2. : 7, 15. ἐφ'
ἃ μὲν ἤλθομεν, in the matters,
for which we are come: 7,
11. ἤλθε, to come: 1, 9. ἤλθεν
ἔχων, he brought with him,
the participle is put, because every action, which
admits of being considered
as only accompanying ano-
ther, which is the main
action, and may thus be represented as an accessary
circumstance of another, the
Greeks are fond of expressing by the part., Matth. Gr.
Gr. 853. : 8, 72.

ἔρως, 6, 24. desire, passion,
infatuation : 3, 45. desire,
love : 2. 86.

ἐρωτάω, 1, 5. ἐρωτῶντες, to
ask, put questions : 3, 61.
τὸ ἐρωτηθὲν, the question, 54.
ἐρωτᾶτε, to inquire : 7, 10.
ἠρώτα, to make inquiries,
44. : 4, 40. : 7, 70. ἠρώτων,
Matth. Gr. Gr. 868.

ἐρώτημα, 3, 60. 7, 44. a
question, an enquiry.

ἐρωτικὸς, 6, 54. ξυντυχίαν,
an accident of, belonging to,
connected with love, a love-
affair.

ἐρωτικῶς, 6, 54. after the
manner of lovers, in consequence of his passion, lover-

like, as lovers use, ἐπὶ τῷ
ἔρωτι.

ἔσθημα, 3, 58. a garment
used in funeral ceremonials.

ἐσθὴς, 1, 6. a garment.

ἐσπέρα, 7, 29. evening.

ἑστία, 1, 36. a hearth.

Ἑστιαιεὺς, 1, 114. Ἑστιαιᾶς
ἐξοικίσαντες αὐτοὶ τὴν γῆν ἔσχον,
the accus. plur. of words de-
clined like βασιλεὺς, should
be in ἑας, but when a vowel
precedes, the Attics con-
tract into ᾶς, Matth. Gr. Gr.
103.

ἑστίασις, 6, 46. a banquet,
an entertainment.

ἔσχατος, 4, 92. ἐπὶ τὸ ἔσχατον
ἀγῶνος, to the last extremity
of resistance, (to fight) to
the last drop of blood: 2, 96.

ἑταιρία, 3, 82. good fellowship.

ἑταιρικὸς, 3, 82. τὸ ἑταιρικὸν,
the tie of fellowship.

ἑταῖρος, 6, 30. a companion,
an associate : 7, 73. a friend,
confidant, 75. ἑταίρων ἢ οἰκεί-
ων, companions, friends, intimates, familiars.

ἕτερος, 7, 59. μηδὲ καθ' ἕτερα,
neither one way nor the
other, neither way, 34. οὐδ'
οἱ ἕτεροι νικᾶν, the others, i. e.
the enemy : 5, 36. ἕτεροι,
other, different : 1, 85. ἔξεστι
δ' ἡμῖν μᾶλλον ἑτέρων (καθ' ἡσυχίαν βουλεύειν,) an extraordinary case, where the gen.
is used instead of ἢ with the
dat., Matth. Gr. Gr. 658.

ἔτης, 5, 79. a friend, an
ally.

ἐτήσιος; 5, 11. yearly.

ἔτι, 6, 31. ξύμμαχοι ἔτι. πολ-λοὶ, besides, moreover: 7, 7. ὅπως στρατιὰ ἔτι περαιωθῇ, that a further reinforcement, an additional force might be sent over, transported : 1, 74. yet, still: 4, 123. πολλῷ ἔτι μᾶλλον, more than ever: 8, 2. 45.

ἑτοιμάζω, 1, 57. ἑτοιμάσαιντο, to make ready, to procure so as to be at hand: 4, 77. ἡτοιμάζετο, 7, 31. ἡτοιμάζοντο: 7, 18. ἡτοίμαζον, to get in readiness : 6, 17. ἑτοιμάζεται, to procure, get, acquire : 2, 7. ἑτοιμάζων ἀργύριον ῥητὸν, to provide, furnish a stated, (assessed,) sum of money.

ἕτοιμος, 6, 8. ready, in rea-diness : 1, 70. τὰ ἕτοιμα, one's own, possessions, 4, 61. what is in hand, present posses-sions : 7, 1. ready, freely disposed, 3. ready, alert, well-disposed : 2, 3. εἶναι, to be in readiness, to be pre-pared : 5, 41. ready, full of alacrity, 1, 28. ready, pre-pared, willing : 4, 19. ἑτοιμό-τερος, more disposed, ready.

ἑτοίμως, 1, 80. at hand : 4, 92. with levity, ready will, keenly.

ἔτος, 1, 11. ἔτει, a year, 5, 14. ἐτῶν, 18. ἔτη, 6, 3. τοῦ ἐχομένου ἔτους, the next, fol-lowing year : 7, 28. τριῶν γε ἐτῶν, for three years at most: 5, 25.

εὖ, 3, 40. 5, 15. φερόμενος, fortunate, carried away by

their good fortune : 6, 34. εὖ οἶδ᾽ ὅτι, I am aware, I am sure, certainly, beyond doubt : 7, 48. τὶς εὖ λέγων, any plausible speaker, 23. τριήρους εὖ πλεούσης, a fast-sailing ship, a good sailer : 8, 82.

εὐαπόβατος, 4, 30. εὐαποβα-τωτέραν, more accessible.

εὐαποτείχιστος, 6, 75. easy to be circumvallated.

εὐβουλία, 3, 42. sound or mature or sage counsel, 44. τῆς ἡμετέρας, counsel advan-tageous, best for ourselves: 1, 78. wise counsel.

εὔβουλος, 1, 84. wise.

εὐδαιμονέω, 8, 24. εὐδαιμονή-σαντες, to enjoy good fortune.

εὐδαιμονία, 2, 97. prosperity.

εὐδαιμονίζω, 8, 24. Χῖοι γὰρ μόνοι μετὰ Λακεδαιμονίους, ὧν ἐγὼ ᾐσθόμην, εὐδαιμονήσαντες ἅμα καὶ ἐσωφρόνησαν, were equally prosperous and mo-derate, united moderation with their good fortune.

εὐδαίμων, 1, 6. wealthy : 2, 43. καὶ τὸ εὔδαιμον τὸ ἐλεύθερον, τὸ δὲ ἐλεύθερον τὸ εὔψυχον κρί-ναντες, to think that prospe-rity consists in freedom, and freedom in valour : 2, 53. the rich, (opposed to,) οἱ οὐδὲν κεκτημένοι, men worth nothing.

εὐδοκιμέω, 2, 37. ὡς ἕκαστος εὐδοκιμεῖ ἔν τῳ, according as each is in esteem for any thing, excels in any thing.

εὐδοξότατος, 1, 84. πόλιν, most glorious, distinguished.

εὔελπις, 1, 70. sanguine : 4,

II

10. keeping a stout heart, entertaining a good hope: 6, 24. confident, full of hope, Matth. Gr. Gr. 859.: 8, 2. in good hope: 4, 62. full of promise, affording ground for hope, redolent of hope.

εὐεπίθετος, 6, 34. (παρασκευὴ sc.) easy or liable to be attacked.

εὐεργεσία, 1, 41. a kindness, good office: 4, 11. 56. good office, benefit: 1, 32. 137.: 1, 128. εὐεργεσίαν ἐς βασιλέα κατέθετο, to lay up a benefit with.

εὐεργέτης, 1, 136. a benefactor: 3, 47. who deserves well of any one, a benefactor, 57. 63. 2, 27. 6, 50.

εὐέφοδος, 6, 66. εὐεφοδώτατος, most accessible.

εὐήθεια, 3, 45. egregious folly.

εὐήθης, 3, 83. simple, honest-hearted.

εὔζωνος, 2, 97. ἀνδρὶ, well-girt, expeditious.

εὐθύνω, 1, 95. τῶν μὲν ἰδίᾳ πρός τινα ἀδικημάτων εὐθύνθη, τὰ δὲ μέγιστα ἀπολύεται μὴ ἀδικεῖν, to be found guilty, an example of an interchange of tenses, the pres. for the aor., Matth. Gr. Gr. 737.

εὐθὺς, 3, 1. μετὰ τὴν ἐσβολὴν, immediately after: 1, 1. 34. 2, 100. 5, 3. 7, 77.

εὐθὺς, 5, 10. direct, straight: 1, 34. ἐκ τοῦ εὐθέος, immediately, without delay, precipitately.

εὐκαθαίρετος, 7, 18. εὐκαθαι-

ρετωτέρους, more easy to be reduced.

εὐκατηγόρητος, 6, 77. obnoxious to accusations.

εὔκοσμος, 6, 42. εὐκοσμότεροι, in better order: 1, 84.

εὐλὰξ, 5, 16. a plough; εὐλάξειν, to plough.

εὐληπτος, 6, 85. facilis subigi.

εὐλογία, 2, 42. an eulogy, a praise.

εὔλογος, 6, 67. agreeable to reason, 84. meet, reasonable, 87.: 6, 79. προφάσει, reasonable, probable, plausible, colourable, quam improbare nemo possit.

εὐλόγως, 4, 61. with good words.

εὐμένεια, 5, 105. benevolence.

εὐμενὴς, 2, 74. benignant, friendly.

εὐμεταχείριστος, 6, 85. facilis expugnari, easily managed, disposed of.

εὐνὴ, 3, 112. ἔτι ἐν ταῖς εὐναῖς, still in their beds: 6, 67.

εὔνοια, honesty, good intention, 1, 22. οὐ ταυτὰ περὶ τῶν αὐτῶν ἔλεγον, ἀλλ' ὡς ἑκατέρων τις εὐνοίας ἢ μνήμης ἔχοι, to the verb here (in the phrase ὡς ἔχει) genitives are added, which shew the respect, in which the sense of the verb must be taken, whose proper signification is with regard to, Matth. Gr. Gr. 451.: 2, 11. εὔνοιαν ἔχειν to be zealous for, to wish

well : 1, 77. 3, 12. 4, 46. 7,
57. : 2, 8. good will, affection : 3, 37. τῇ ἐκείνων εὐνοίᾳ,
from or through their good
will.

εὐνομέω, 1, 18. εὐνομήθη, to
have a good constitution.

εὐνομία, 8, 64. a false lection for αὐτονομία.

εὔνους, 4, 78. in one's favour, well-affected, 114. 87.
τῷ ὑμετέρῳ εὔνῳ, benevolence;
favourable disposition, 71.
οἷς τις εἴη εὔνους, to be favourable, 36. οὐκ εὔνους τῇ πόλει,
disaffected to the state, 29. :
6, 64. εὔνων, Matth. Gr. Gr.
150.

εὐξύνετος, 4, 18. εὐξυνετώτε-
ρον, more skilfully, in a more
ready manner.

εὐοργήτως, 1, 122. with
good temper.

εὐορκέω, 5, 30. to act religiously and consistently with
one's oath.

εὔορκος, 5, 18. valid, 231
valid, not vitiating the contract : 6, 88. agreeable to the
oath, what ought to be religiously observed.

εὐπορέω, 6, 34. to be easily
managed, conducted, 44. ὡς
ἕκαστοι εὐπόρησαν, prout cuique
facultas data est.

εὔπορος, 4, 10. of easy passage : 6, 17. εὐπορώτερος, more
commodious, convenient, affording greater facilities,
90. cujus copia nobis est : 2,
64. εὐπορωτάτη πᾶσιν, most
abundant in all things, rich
in every thing : 8, 48.

εὐπόρως, 8, 36. in abundance.

εὐπραγέω, 2, 60. εὐπραγού-
σαν, prosperous : 6, 16. εὐπραγούντων.

εὐπραγία, prosperity : 4, 65.
fortunate issue, happy result, successful event, 7, 46. :
5, 46. : 1, 89. μόνοι δέ αὐτό εὐ-
πραγίαις τε οὐκ ἐξυβρίζομεν καὶ
ξυμφοραῖς ἧσσον ἑτέρων εἴκομεν,
the dative, when it supplies
the place of the Latin ablative, expresses among other
relations that of an external
cause, here the datives must
be rendered, ' on account
of,' Matth. Gr. Gr. 569.

εὐπραξία, prosperity, 3, 39.
αἱ——εὐπραξία ἔλθῃ.

εὐπρέπεια, 3, 11. λόγου,
speciousness, plausibility,
specious words, 38. : 6, 31.
ornament, splendour.

εὐπρεπής, 3, 44. τῷ εὐπρεπεῖ,
speciousness, plausibility :
2, 38. εὐπρεπέσιν, handsome,
magnificent : 3, 38. τὸ εὐπρεπὲς τοῦ λόγου, plausibility of
speech, 82. specious : 6, 31.
εὐπρεπεστάτη, 2, 44. 8, 109.

εὐπρεπῶς, 1, 38. justly,
honourably : 6, 6. speci-
ously, plausibly.

εὐπρόσοδος, 6, 57. easy of
access, affable.

εὐπροφάσιστος, 6, 105. most
fair, plausible.

εὑρετέον ἐστι, is to be, must
be found out.

εὕρημα, 5, 46. ὅτι τάχιστα
εὕρημα εἶναι διακινδυνεῦσαι, a
piece of unexpected luck,
a gain.

εὑρίσκω, 1, 20. 2, 6. 5, 42. εὗρον, to find, 1, 1. 4, 44. εὑρεῖν : εὑρίσκεσθαι, to discover for oneself: 5, 32. εὕροντο, to obtain, get : 6, 2. ὡς ἀλήθεια εὑρίσκεται, as is clearly ascertained, is evident, found to be true : εὑρήσει, 5, 20. 26.: 7, 67. εὑρήσουσι, to see, understand : 1, 71. εὕροιμεν, to find, discover : 1, 21. εὑρῆσθαι, to be investigated : 7, 62. εὕρηται, to find out, invent, discover.

εὕρημα, 5, 46. a profitable speculation, an object of solicitude, a gain.

εὐρυχωρία, 2, 83. 7, 6. 36. wide extent of space, open space : 8, 3.

εὐσκέπαστος, 5, 71. εὐσκεπαστότατον, most impenetrable (to the shock of an enemy.)

εὐσέβεια, 3, 82. piety, religion.

εὐσταλὴς, 3, 22. τῇ ὁπλίσει, lightly equipped, armed compactly.

εὐτακτέω, 8, 1. rightly to arrange.

εὔτακτος, 7, 77. in good order : 2, 89. in good order, orderly.

εὐταξία, 6, 72. discipline, (opposed to ἀταξία.)

εὐτέλεια, 2, 40. frugality, moderation in expenditure : 8, 1. ἐς εὐτέλειαν σωφρονίσαι, frugally.

εὐτελέστερος, 8, 46. cheaper.

εὐτραπέλως, 2, 41. elegantly, with elegance, in a becom-

ing manner, with facility, easy motion.

εὐτρεπίζω, 2, 18. ηὐτρεπίζοντο, to prepare, 4, 123. to set in order, get in good order.

εὐτυχέω, to be prosperous, 4, 79. εὐτύχει, in the augment ευ is often changed into ηυ in this instance it is not, Matth. Gr. Gr. 206. : 6, 69. διὰ τὸ εὐτυχῆσαι, through success : 2, 61.: 5, 7. εὐτυχήσας, to have luck, to be fortunate, 6, 15. to succeed : 2, 60. 3, 39. : 7, 77. Matth. 432.

εὐτυχὴς, 2, 44. τὸ δ᾽ εὐτυχὲς, an adj. with the article for a subst., the same as ἡ εὐτυχία, Matth. Gr. Gr. 391.

εὐτυχία, 1, 120. good fortune, 5, 14. 16. : 2, 44. εὐτυχίαις, prosperity.

εὐφύλακτος, 3, 92. well-fortified : 8, 55. εὐφυλακτοτέρα.

εὐχὴ, 7, 75. a vow, prayer (for success in an expedition :) 8, 70.

εὔχομαι, 2, 43. to pray, wish for : 3, 58.

εὐψυχία, 1, 84. magnanimity, 121. courage, blood : 2, 89. εὐψυχίᾳ, in natural courage : 7, 64.

εὔψυχος, 5, 9. spirited, valorous : 2, 39. τῷ ἀφ᾽ ἡμῶν αὐτῶν εὐψύχῳ, the gen. marks that, to which any thing belongs, therefore the quality is considered as something, that proceeds from any one, the prep. is here employed in addition. Matth.

Gr. Gr. 519. : 4, 126. : 2, 11. εὐψυχότατος.

εὐώνυμος, 1, 48. 7, 6. κέρα, the left wing : 5, 10. 67.

ἐφαιρέω, 4, 38. ἐφῃρημένου, to be chosen, elected.

ἐφεδρεύω, 4, 71. to plot against.

ἐφέλκω, 4, 26. to drag : 1, 42. ἐφέλκεσθε, to be induced, drawn on.

ἐφέπομαι, 4, 96. 120. to follow, 3, 45. 6, 58. : 5, 3. ἐπισπόμενοι, to follow, press after, 11. to follow, attend, 7, 52. μετ' αὐτοῦ, to follow, accompany.

ἐφηγέομαι, 7, 73. ἐφηγεῖται, to give counsel, to advise, move.

ἐφήμερος, 2, 53. ephemeral, lasting but a day, a very short time, fleeting.

ἐφιέναι, 6, 6. ἐφιέμενοι, to long for, to desire, covet : 1, 95. ἐφίεσαν τὴν ἡγεμονίαν, to give in, to yield : 1, 128. ἐφιέμενος τῆς Ἑλληνικῆς ἀρχῆς, to be ambitious of, 1, 8. τῶν κερδῶν, desirous of, 4, 108. ἐς Λακεδαίμονα, to be sent : 2, 42. ἐφίεσθαι, to seek, achieve, purchase, win, 8, 46. to desire : 4, 61.

ἐφίστημι, 4, 63. ἐφεστῶτας, to hover about : 2, 75. ἐπιστήσαντες, to place upon, plant, fix upon : 3, 82. ἐφιστῶνται, to be circumstanced : 8, 69.

ἐφόδιον, 6, 34. provision for a voyage, 31. necessaries for a voyage : 2, 70.

ἐφόδιος, 2, 70. καὶ ἀργύριόν τι ῥητὸν ἔχοντας ἐφόδιον, by way of provision for the expences of the journey.

ἔφοδος, 3, 11. γνώμης, an aggression, invasion of policy, cunning, adroit intrigues : 7, 43. ἀνιέναι τῆς ἐφόδου, to slacken in one's approach, Matth. Gr. Gr. 388. : 4, 8. advance : 7, 544. τῇ πρώτῃ ἐφόδῳ, onset, attack : 4, 36. an approach, a pass : 1, 6. a passage, journey, 7, 43. the entrance, advance, approach (of an hostile army,) 51. the entrance (to the camp :) 1, 93. τὴν κατὰ θάλασσαν ἔφοδον, an invasion by sea : 5, 35. ἔφοδοι πρὸς ἀλλήλους, mutual intercourse, excursions into each other's territory, visits to each other.

ἐφολκὸς, 4, 108. seductive, attractive, engaging.

ἐφοράω, 3, 104. ἐφεωρᾶτο, to be seen, beheld.

ἐφορεύω, 8, 6. Ἐνδίῳ ἐφορεύοντι, to perform the office of ephorus.

ἐφορμέω, 7, 12. ἐφορμοῦσιν ἄλλοις, to lie opposite to others, to have one's station in front of an enemy : 7, 24. ἐφορμοῦντες, to be in station against, to lie in wait for, 4, 24. 1, 64. ἐφορμούσαις, to ride or to be moored at anchor, 116. 142. 8, 20. ἐφορμούμεναι, watched over, 30. ἐφορμεῖν, to form a naval blockade against, 17. ἐφώρμουν, to station (their ships,) 3, 107. ἐκ θαλάσσης, to lay on shore out of the sea, 31. ἐφορμῶσιν αὐτοὺς, to watch with a stationary fleet, to keep a fleet stationed: 1, 142. ἐφορμεῖσθαι, to be watched: 6, 49. ἐφορμηθέντας, to put into port, to take up a station: 7, 4. ἐφορμήσειν πρὸς τῷ λιμένι, to ride at anchor at or off the harbour: 1, 116. Περικλῆς λαβὼν ἑξήκοντα ναῦς ἀπὸ τῶν ἐφορμουσῶν, an example of the gen. put *partitivé* and accompanied by the prep. ἀπὸ, Matth. Gr. Gr. 501.

ἐφόρμησις, 3, 33. a guard of ships stationed (to watch an enemy :) 2, 89. the (enemy's) station: 6, 48.

ἐφορμίζω, 4, 8. ἐφορμίσασθαι, to harbour, lie in moorings or at anchor.

ἐφόρμος, 3, 6. ἐφόρμους ἐπὶ τοῖς λιμέσιν ἐποιοῦντο, a station of ships over against a port (to watch or blockade it :) 4, 27. moorage, 32. 3, 76. moored, stationary.

ἐφυβρίζω, 6, 63. to taunt, *probra ingerere.*

ἐφυστερίζω, 3, 82. to happen after; to be subsequent.

ἐχέγγυος, 3, 46. affording a guarantee, pledge, security.

ἐχθίονα, 4, 86. more hateful: 5, 27. ἔχθιστος, most hostile, 1, 71. οἱ ἔχθιστοι, the greatest enemies, 7, 68.

ἔχθος, 1, 95. τῷ ἐκείνου ἔχθει, out of hatred to him: 4, 1. aversion, hatred: 7, 57. Matth. Gr. Gr. 450.; 2, 11.

Ἀθηναίων, hatred for the Athenians.

ἔχθρα, 1, 56. enmity, hatred, 69. ἐπ' ἔχθρᾳ, through hatred: 2, 68. ἔχθραν ἐποιή-σαντο, to conceive enmity, to be at enmity: 3, 10. τοῦ Μή-δου ἔχθραν ἀνιέντα, to relax (in) their hostility to the Mede, remit their enmity against: 5, 36. 6, 80.

ἐχθρὸς, 1, 44. 5, 16. 17. an enemy.

ἐχυρὸς, 1, 90. ἀπὸ ἐχυροῦ, from a strong hold: 3, 12. firm, fast, 83, λόγος: 2, 62. ἐχυρωτέραν, 8, 24. ἐχυρώτερον more strictly, 1, 35. ἐχυρώτα-τος, best-established: 5, 109. τὸ ἐχυρὸν, the pledge : 7, 41. ἐλπίδα, firm, confident.

ἐχυρῶς, 5, 26. strongly.

ἔχω, 6, 82. οὕτως ἔχει, the matter stands thus: 5, 44. ἔχουσαν, to possess, exercise: 3, 37. ἐς τοὺς ξυμμάχους τὸ αὐτὸ ἔχετε, to preserve the same (feeling, character) towards the allies, to behave in the same way : 5, 49. ὥσπερ ὁ νόμος ἔχει, according to the letter of the law: 1, 2. εἶχον, had, experienced, 5, 46. δι' ὀργῆς εἶχον, to be in anger, 6, 54. εἶχεν, to possess, enjoy, (as Terence, *quis Chrysidem habuit?*) 70. ὅσον ἀσφαλῶς, as far as it was safe: 1, 140. τῆς γνώμης τῆς αὐτῆς ἔχομαι, to persevere in, from the analogy of this verb to the idea of 'taking' and thence to 'partaking,' this instance has the gen. according to its sense partitive, Matth. Gr. Gr. 512.; 5, 49. τοῦ αὐτοῦ λό-γου εἴχοντο, they maintained the same opinion: 7, 75. ἔχουσα, to have the materials, cause (of any thing, so as to occasion the feeling of that in another,) to furnish occasion, i. q. παρέχουσα: 7, 36. πλεῖστον σχήσειν, to have the greatest advantage, 62. σχή-σουσι, to prevent: 4, 3. 5, 2. σχών, to touch at, 7, 1. Ῥηγίῳ, to touch at Regium: 1, 9. σχεῖν, to have, possess: 5, 28. ἄριστα ἔσχον, to have golden opinions, to be held in the highest estimation, to be in the zenith of reputa-tion: 1, 110. ἔσχον κατὰ τὸ Μενδήσιον κέρας, to come to anchor in the Mendesian mouth (of the Nile,) 3, 29. τῇ Δήλῳ, to touch at Delos, 1, 112. Ἑλληνικοῦ πολέμου ἔσχον οἱ Ἀθηναῖοι, kept on the Hellenic war: 5. 77. ἔχωντι, the Doric form for ἔχουσι, Matth. 255.: 7, 42. ἕξειν, to have, to be master of, 3, 43. ἀφανῶς πῃ πλέον, underhand to derive some advantage, 44. ὅπως χρησίμως ἕξουσιν βου-λευόμεθα, to deliberate how they are to be advantage-ously disposed of, 6, 88. ἐξόμενοι τοῦ πολέμου, to com-mence, prosecute vigorously: 3, 32. ἐλπίδα εἴχον, to ex-pect, imagine, 25. τὴν γνώμην

πρὸς τοὺς Ἀθηναίους ἧσσον, to be less disposed to the Athe-nians, i. e. to come to a composition or to treat with them, 5, 35. τὰ χωρία, to re-tain possession of, 7, 2. ὡς εἶχον τάχους, as quick as they could, 2, 90. ὡς εἶχε τάχους ἕκαστους, the use of the gen. ' with respect to,' here parti-cularly the phrase is to be qualified or endowed in any manner whatsoever, se ha-bere, Matth. 451.: 7, 34. ἐμ-φράξασαι, to barricade, i. q. ἐμπεφραγμένοι, or εἶχον καὶ ἐνέ-φραξαν, to occupy and de-fend: 3, 37. νόμοις καλῶς ἔχου-σιν, good laws, 30. ὥσπερ ἔχο-μεν, how we are situated, where we are, that we are arrived: 3, 24. ἔχοντες ἐν δε-ξιᾷ, to keep on the right (of a place,) to have (a place) on the right hand, 5, 47. ὅπλα, to have arms (in their hands:) 6, 2. ἔχω, to be able: 5, 67. ἐχόμενοι αὐτῶν Ἀργεῖοι, the Ar-gives bordering upon them, 1, 22. ἐχομένῳ ὅτι ἐγγύτατα τῆς γνώμης, to keep as close as possible to the sense: 1, 25. εἴχοντο ἐν ἀπόρῳ, to be at a loss: 8, 86. ὡρμημένων τῶν ἐν Σάμῳ Ἀθηναίων πλεῖν ἐπὶ σφᾶς αὐτούς, (ἐν ᾧ σαφέστατα Ἰωνίαν καὶ Ἑλλήσποντον εὐθὺς εἶχον οἱ πολέμιοι,) where ἂν is want-ing, tenuissent, Matth. 748.: 1, 73. ὅπερ ἔσχε μὴ κατὰ πόλεις αὐτὸν ἐπιπλέοντα τὴν Πελοπόννη-σον πορθεῖν, an instance of the use of the infin. as a subst. (which use it has by the collocation of the article,) where the article's genitive is wanting after ἔχω in the sense 'to prevent,' Matth. 819.: 1, 112. Ἑλληνικοῦ πολέμου ἔσχον οἱ Ἀθηναῖοι, this verb in the sense of 'to desist' has the object in the gen. from its analogy to words, which in-

dicate fullness, defect, emptiness, Matth. 473.

ἔω, 3, 56. ἐσσαμένων, to build, Matth. Gr. Gr. 340.

ἕως, 5, 58. ἅμα ἕῳ, as soon as it was light: 4, 32. 67. dawn, morning.

ἕως, 1, 28. whilst, 58.: 7, 47. ἕως ἔτι οἷόν τε, whilst it was yet possible.

Z.

Ζάγκλον, 6, 4. τὸ δὲ δρέπανον οἱ Σικελοὶ ζάγκλον καλοῦσιν.

ζάω, 4, 28. ζῶντας, alive, 2, 5. ἔχειν, to have alive, as prisoners, 5, 3. ἔλαβον, to take alive (as prisoners of war:) 3, 38. ζῶμεν.

ζεύγη, 6, 7. a wain, waggon, carriage.

ζεῦγμα, 7, 69. τοῦ λιμένος, a bar, barrier, 30. an inlet of the sea.

ζεύγνυμι, 1, 29. ζεύξαντες, to refit with benches, oars, &c. (an old ship.)

ζεῦγος, 5, 50. a chariot : 4, 128.

ζηλόω, 5, 105. ζηλοῦμεν, to envy : 2, 64. ζηλώσει, to emulate, 43. ζηλώσαντες, 37. ζηλοῦσῃ, to affect, follow after, emulate, imitate, 39.

ζήλωσις, 1, 132. a zealous imitation.

ζημία, 1, 86. punishment : 2, 24. θανάτου ζημίαν ἐπέθεντο, to impose the penalty of

death, capital punishment: 5, 63. a fine, 3, 45. 70.

ζημιόω, 3, 40. ζημιώσεται, to be hurt, injured, to suffer loss, damage : 5, 63. ζημιῶσαι δέκα μυριάσι δραχμῶν, to fine any one in 10,000 drachms : 2, 65. ἐζημίωσαν χρήμασιν, to punish by fine, to mulct in a sum of money, to set a fine: 3, 42. οὐχ ὅπως ζημιοῦν, ἀλλὰ μηδ᾽ ἀτιμάζειν, not only not to punish, but not to degrade, 40. ζημιωθησόμενον θανάτῳ, to be punished with death : 8, 21. φυγῇ ζημιώσαντες, to be punished with exile, condemned to exile, 74.

ζητέω, 7, 44. ἐζήτουν, to seek, to be looking for : 6, 27. ἐζητοῦντο, to be sought out : 3, 67. to search for : 1, 23. ἔγραψα—τὰς διαφορὰς, τοῦ μή τινας ζητῆσαί ποτε ἐξ ὅτου τοσοῦτος πόλεμος τοῖς Ἕλλησι κατέστη, the infin. being joined with the neuter of the article stands as a subst., in its geni-

tive the adverb ἕνεκα is often
wanting, *ne quis aliquando re-*
quirat, Matth. Gr. Gr. 815.

ζήτησις, 6, 53. ζήτησιν ἐποιοῦντο, to ' pursue the search,
inquiry, investigation : 1, 20.
search, investigation.

ζυγὸς, 5, 68. ἐν τῷ πρώτῳ
ζυγῷ, in the first rank.

ζωγρέω, 1, 50. 7, 85. to
take captive, alive : 7, 23.
ἐζώγρησαν, to make prisoners,
take alive : 3, 66. ζωγρήσαντες,
7, 41. 4, 57. ἐζωγρήθη, to be
taken alive, 7, 24. ἐζωγρήθη-
σαν : 2, 5. ἐζωγρημένοι, to be
taken alive.

H.

Ἡβάω, 5, 116. ἡβῶντας, at
the age of puberty, 32, when
of age : 3, 36. ἡβῶσι, to be
adult, to be of age : 5, 32. οἱ
ἡβῶντες for οἱ ἔφηβοι, where
the participle is used as a
subst. Matth. Gr. Gr. 875. :
4, 132.

ἥβη, 2, 46. μέχρι ἥβης, to
manhood, man's estate.

ἡγεμονεύω, 3, 61. ἡγεμονεύε-
σθαι ὑφ' ἡμῶν, to follow a
leader, to submit to our direction, in Greek the object,
which was in the gen. or
dat. with the active, may
become the subject of the
passive, Matth. Gr. Gr. 711.

ἡγεμονία, 4, 91. the chief
command : 7, 15. a command,
an employ or commission :
5, 7. generalship, conduct,
47. : 1, 93. ἐν τῇδε τῇ ἡγεμονίᾳ,
under their command, 76. ἐν
τῇ ἡγεμονίᾳ, in the command.

ἡγεμών, 1, 4. a leader, head
of a colony : 7, 50. τοῦ πλοῦ,
a pilot, 15. a leader, 56. a
confederate, an associate :
3, 98.

ἡγέομαι, 1, 5. ἡγουμένων, to
head, lead, 10. ἡγοῦνται, to
head, command, 5, 33. ἡγουμένου, to command in chief :
1, 18. ἡγήσαντο, to command,
lead, 7, 14. ἡγησάμην, to judge,
think, to be led to think, 6,
11. 7, 34. 1, 77. ἡγησάμενοι,
2, 42. 6, 40. : 5, 40. ἡγήσεσθαι,
to hold the supremacy, to
be at the head, 8, 2. : 2, 10.
3, 1. ἡγεῖτο αὐτῶν, 4, 2. 5, 8.
7, 19. : 2, 11. ἕπεσθ' ὅπη ἄν τις
ἡγῆται, to follow whitherso-
ever each shall lead the way :
1, 19. ἡγοῦνται, in this passage ἄρχειν τινὸς is put in
opposition and in ἡγ. the
idea of proper dominion
does not seem to be implied,
but only the command or
leading of a people, who
are otherwise represented as
free : this verb takes a genitive from the analogy to the
signification of ' ruling,' the
opposite of ἡσσᾶσθαι : verbs,
in which the idea of a comparative is included, take the
gen. *See* Matth. Gr. Gr. 482.

ἡδέως, 5, 10. pleasantly, agreeably : 8, 89.

ἤδη, 4, 94. at last : 6, 38. ἄρχειν ἤδη, to be magistrates already : 7, 4. now from this time : 1, 74. already : 7, 71. περὶ τοῦ πλείονος ἤδη καλοῦ, now for more glory, for increasing the honour already obtained, 33. : 8, 87.

ἡδίων, 7, 14. more pleasing, flattering ; ἥδιστα, very pleasant, excessively flattering : 7, 68. ἥδιστον, very sweet (revenge sc.,) a great gratification.

ἥδομαι, 1, 120. ἡδόμενον τῷ ἡσυχίῳ τῆς εἰρήνης, to be pleased with the repose of peace : 3, 40.

ἡδονὴ, 3, 58. ἡδονῇ δόντες ἄλλοις, to gratify others : 1, 99. ἐν ἡδονῇ, to be popular, to be in favour : 6, 17. καθ' ἡδονὴν, with a view to gratify, acceptably, to any one's liking : 6, 83. λόγου, illecebræ male suadentium, 3, 40. charms of oratory : 7, 63. delight, gratification : 2, 53. 4, 19.

ἡδὺς, 5, 105. sweet.

ἦθος, 6, 18. ἤθεσι, customs, usages : 2, 61. ἐν ἤθεσιν ἀντιπάλοις αὐτῇ τεθραμμένους, bred up with principles suitable to it.

ἥκιστα, 1, 35. οὐχ ἥκιστα, most of all, 7, 21. especially : 5, 36. least of all : 1, 68. προσήκει ἡμᾶς οὐχ ἥκιστα εἰπεῖν, ὅσῳ καὶ μέγιστα ἐγκλήματα ἔχομεν, we have the greatest right to speak in proportion as we have the greatest charges to answer to, two superlatives compared, where τοσούτῳ is dropped often, if ὅσῳ follows, in the second proposition, Matth. Gr. Gr. 667. : 2, 25. 7, 44.

ἥκω, 5, 59. ἧκον, to arrive, 7, 27. ὕστερον, to arrive after (the time appointed,) too late, 3, 27. αὐτοῖς, to be come to them, to be arrived among them, 7, 4. : 8, 31. ἠκούσας, to arrive : 5, 9. ἥκομεν, to come : 7, 16. ἥξει, to come, 1, 98. : 4, 30. ἥξων, about to come : 2, 101. ἀπιστοῦντες αὐτὸν μὴ ἥξειν, the infin. is put after all verbs, in which the idea of 'to say' is implied, after a verb containing a denial μὴ is added, Matth. Gr. Gr. 802.

ἡλικία, 3, 67. the flower of a youthful army : 5, 43. flower or vigour of manhood : 6, 24. τοῖς ἐν τῇ ἡλικίᾳ, the young, 54. ὥρα ἡλικίας, the season of youth : 7, 60. ἡλικίας μετέχων, to have a portion of youthful vigour, 64. ὁπλιτῶν, a youthful soldiery, able-bodied men at arms : 1, 80. ἐν τῇ αὐτῇ ἡλικίᾳ, of the same standing : 8, 75.

ἥλιος, 1, 23. the sun : 3, 78. ἐς ἥλιον, at sunset : 2, 9. 102. 4, 52.

ἡμέρα, 5, 20. a day : 7, 75. τρίτῃ ἡμέρα ἀπὸ τῆς ναυμαχίας, on the third day, i. e. as we should say, the second—the Greeks reckoned the day itself of the action, from which they dated time, the first : 2, 57. ἡμέρας τεσσαράκοντα μάλιστα, about forty days nearly : 7, 3. πέντε ἡμερῶν, in five days, in the space of five days: 5, 47. τῆς ἡμέρας ἑκάστης, every day : 7, 28. τὴν ἡμέραν, in the day-time, by day : 8, 23. τρίτην ἡμέραν αὐτοῦ ἥκοντος, the third day after he arrived, Matth. Gr. Gr. 609. : 7, 84. ἡμέτερος, our, what belongs to us, 1, 82. 3, 11. 6, 85.

ἡμίεργος, 7, 2. half-finished, built.

ἡμίθεος, 5, 16. a demigod.

ἡμιθνῆτες, 2, 52. half-dead.

ἥμισυς, 4, 16. 42. 83. 104. 5, 16. half: 8, 8. τὰς ἡμίσεας τῶν νεῶν, for ἡμισείας, 64. τῶν πρέσβεων τοὺς ἡμίσεις, Matth. Gr. Gr. 152. : 5, 31. ἐπὶ τῇ ἡμισείᾳ τῆς γῆς, an instance where the adj. is considered the part, of which the subst. is the whole, Matth. 643. : 8, 35. ἡμισείας.

ἡμιτέλεστος, 3, 3. half-finished, imperfect.

ἦν, 1, 58. δέῃ, should it be necessary, 82. δοκῇ, if it should seem right : 3, 44. ἥντε γὰρ ἀποφήνω, for although I shew, Matth. Gr. Gr. 939. : 5, 9. ἦν τὰ ἄριστα πράξητε, at best, to say the least : 2, 5. ἐβούλοντο γὰρ σφίσιν, εἴ τινα λάβοιεν, ὑπάρχειν ἀντὶ τῶν ἔνδον, ἦν ἄρα τύχωσί τινες ἐζωγρημένοι, the interchange of εἰ and ἦν is extraordinary ; ἦν with a

12

conj. is used in the premises, when any thing is likely to happen, (and should seemingly be here with λαμβάνω:) εἰ is used with the opt. in the premises, when the whole business is problematical, (and should seemingly be with τυγχάνω.) The reason is perhaps that the last circumstance, some Thebans were taken, was just before related as actually happening, and as something, that the Thebans had just suffered, but the former was first to happen still, and thus was uncertain. Matth. Gr. Gr. 786. : 3, 3. καὶ ἦν μὲν ξυμβῇ ἡ πεῖρα, "a proposition with εἰ δὲ, sin, sin vero, is often opposed to one with εἰ μὲν," Matth. 939.

ἤπειρος, 7, 31. main-land, in contradistinction to small islands, viz. a part of the earth not surrounded by sea—the Greeks would have called Britain ἤμειρον, when speaking of the Isle of Wight : 1, 5. 4, 102.

ἠπειρώτης, 1, 5. a dweller on the continent, 9. : 7, 21. a landman, in opposition to maritime people : 4, 12.

ἠπειρῶτις, 1, 35. continental: 6, 86. παρασκευῇ, provided after the manner of continental, inland towns.

ἤπιος, 7, 77. ἠπιώτερα, milder (punishments :) 2, 59. πρὸς τὸ ἠπιώτερον καὶ ἀδεέστερον καταστῆσαι, to reduce to a milder and less fearful temper of mind.

ἡρῷον, 2, 17. a fane consecrated to a hero : 3, 24.

ἥρως, 4, 87. 5, 11. 30.

ἧσσα, a defeat, 1, 122. 3, 109. 5, 13. 16. 7, 72.

ἡσσάομαι, 1, 49. ἡσσῶντο, to be worsted, defeated : 3, 38. ἡσσώμενοι ἀκοῆς ἡδονῇ, to be overcome by the delight of hearing, 8, 25. conquered, 27. ἡσσηθῶσι, they should be conquered : 5, 73. τὸ ἡσσηθὲν, the vanquished, 111.: 4, 37. ἡσσηθεῖεν, to submit, yield : 2, 39. ἡσσῆσθαι ὑφ' ἁπάντων, to be vanquished : 1, 30. ἡσσημένοι, defeated, worsted.

ἥσσων, 1, 80. inferior, 77. τὸν ἥσσω, the inferior : 4, 72. worsted, beaten, conquered : 7, 29. ἥσσων μᾶλλον ἑτέρας, inferior to none, greater than any other.

ἧσσον, 4, 16. μηδὲν ἧσσον, nevertheless : 5, 31. οὐδὲν nevertheless, not a whit the less : 7, 63. οὐχ ἧσσον, i. q. μᾶλλον.

ἡσυχάζω, 7, 11. ἡσυχάζομεν, to be on the defensive, in inactivity : 5, 30. ἡσύχασαν, to keep quiet, 6, 44. to rest

(oneself,) 8, 24. : 6, 38. ἡσυχάζει, to be in a state of tranquillity, to have rest, peace : 4, 92. εἰώθασί τε οἱ ἰσχύος που θράσει τοῖς πέλας, ὥσπερ Ἀθηναῖοι νῦν, ἐπιόντες τὸν μὲν ἡσυχάζοντα καὶ ἐν τῇ ἑαυτοῦ μόνον ἀμυνόμενον ἀδεέστερον ἐπιστρατεύειν, the accus. is put here after the verb with the prep. ἐπὶ, because consideration is had not to the direction of an action, (which would cause it to take a dative,) but to its effective relation, Matth. Gr. Gr. 555. : 4, 4. ἡσύχαζεν ὑπὸ ἀπλοίας, on account of, Matth. 914.

ἡσυχία, 6, 24. ἡσυχίαν ἦγε, to keep quiet, hold one's peace : 7, 38. 73. καθ' ἡσυχίαν, leisurely, quietly, unmolested, without opposition : 5, 40. tranquillity, peace, 53. quiet : 3, 12. peace, (opposed to πολέμῳ.)

ἥσυχος, quiet, tranquil, peaceful, 3, 82. φύσις ἡσυχαιτέρα, a form of the compar., for which ἡσυχώτερος occurs in Soph. Antig., Matth. Gr. Gr. 159.

Θ.

Θάλασσα, 5, 18. 7, 2. the sea : 1, 2. διὰ θαλάσσης, by sea, means of the sea : 7, 28.

θαλασσεύω, 7, 12. θαλασσεύουσαι, to be kept in order.

θαλασσοκρατέω, 7, 48. θαλασσοκρατούντων, to be masters of the sea, Matth. Gr. Gr. 859. : 8, 30. ἐθαλασσοκράτουν, 40. θαλασσοκρατοῖεν, they might obtain the dominion of the sea.

θάμϐος, 6, 31. τόλμης θάμϐει, astonishment or wonder on account of the daringness, i. e. from the astonishing boldness of the attempt.

θάνατος, 1, 14. death: 3, 57. 4, 54.

θανάτωσις, 5, 9. undergoing death.

θάπτω, 1, 8. 2, 34. θάπτουσι ἀεὶ ἐν αὐτῷ, they uniformly bury in it, (from time to time :) 2, 35. ἐκ τῶν πολέμων θαπτομένοις, to inter those, who have been slain in war, (literally those, who are interred in consequence of the war :) 5, 74. ἐτάφησαν, to bury, 11. ἔθαψαν: 1, 138. τεθῆναι, to be buried: 8, 84.

θαρσαλέος, 2, 51. ἐν τῷ θαρσαλέῳ εἶναι, to be confident, to be in a state of confidence, to be in safety: 2, 3. θαρσαλεωτέροις, more full of courage: 2, 11. θαρσαλέους τῇ γνώμῃ, courageous in heart.

θαρσέω, 5, 9. to be full of, or puffed up with confidence: 1, 81. θαρσοίη, to be confident: 2, 79. θαρσήσαντες τοῖς προσγιγνομένοις, to take courage from the accession of force: 4, 121. θαρσήσαντες, to be full of spirits : 6, 11. θαρσεῖν, to be confident, to take courage: 7, 37. τεθαρσηκότες, to conceive courage, take heart, 29. ἐν ᾧ ἂν θαρσήσῃ, to have courage, to have no fear: 8, 2. ἐθάρσει, grew bold, 8, 23, θαρσήσειν, would take

courage : 4, 11. ἐθάρσησαν, to be of good courage : 1, 36. τὸ θαρσοῦν, confidence.

θάρσησις, 7, 49. καὶ ἅμα ταῖς γοῦν ναυσὶν ἢ πρότερον θαρσήσει κρατηθείς, i. q. μᾶλλον θαρσῶν ταῖς ναυσὶν ἢ πρότερον, Matth. Gr. Gr. 481.

θάρσος, confidence, 6. 68.

θαρσύνω, 2, 13. ἐθάρσυνεν, to encourage, 59.

θᾶσσον, 7, 28. quicker: 3, 13. sooner : 4, 54.

θάτερος, 1, 87. ἐπὶ θάτερα : 7, 84. τὰ ἐπὶ θάτερα τοῦ ποτάμου, on the hither side of the bank.

θαῦμα, wonder, astonishment, 8, 14.

θαυμάζω, 1, 21. θαυμαζόντων, to admire : 1, 51. ἐθαύμαζον, to wonder, to be surprised: 1, 138. ἐθαύμασε, to admire and approve: 6, 33. ὃ πάνυ θαυμάζετε, which you are absolutely amazed at, 36. τῆς τόλμης θαυμάζω, to wonder at the audacity, marvel at (any one) for his audacity, 11. θαυμαζόμενα, to be held in admiration, to be admired : 7, 56. θαυμασθήσεσθαι, to be held up to admiration : 1, 138. ἄξιος θαυμάσαι, worthy of admiration: 1, 38. θαυμάζεσθαι, to be respected : 4, 85. θαυμάζω τῇ ἀποκλείσει μου τῶν πυλῶν, an instance of the use of the dat. with a verb neuter to express the cause, occasion, Matth. Gr. Gr. 569.: 7, 63. Matth. 569.

θαυμαστὸς, 1, 76. extraordinary.

θέα, 6, 31. 7, 71. a sight,

spectacle: 5, 7. a survey, an inspection.

θέαμα, 2, 39. a sight, spectacle, an exhibition.

θεάομαι, 5, 113. θεᾶσθε, to behold: 5, 7. ἐθεᾶτο, to go to survey, to reconnoitre: 2, 43. θεωμένους καθ᾿ ἡμέραν ἔργῳ, to behold or view in daily acts, in every day's proceedings.

θεατής, 3, 38. τῶν λόγων, a spectator.

θέατρον, a theatre, 8, 93.

θειάζω, 8, 1. θειάσαντες, urged by divine impulse.

θειασμὸς, 7, 50. superstition, a scrupulous observance of religious rites and superstitions.

θεῖον, 4, 100. sulphur.

θεῖος, 5, 30. divine, sacred, 70. τοῦ θείου χάριν, not for any religious motive: 3, 82.

θεμέλιος, 1, 93. a foundation: 3, 68. ἐκ τῶν θεμελίων, from the foundations.

θεὸς, 5, 30. a god: 2, 71. 74. 8, 70.

θεραπεία, 2, 57. ἕτερος ἀφ᾿ ἑτέρου θεραπείας, (to be filled with or to imbibe) the distemper from the attendance of one upon another: 3, 11. τὰ δὲ καὶ ἀπὸ θεραπείας τοῦ τε κοινοῦ αὐτῶν περιεγιγνόμεθα, to escape or to be respited by paying court to their community: 1, 55.

θεραπεύω, 1, 9. τεθεραπευκότα τὸ πλῆθος, to court the multitude, 3, 12. ἐθεράπευον, 1, 19. 3, 39.: 2, 57. πάνυ θερα-

πευόμενοι, to be attended with every care, to have every attention paid, 47. θεραπεύοντες, to attend as a physician: 7, 70. ἐθεράπευον, to be studious, careful: 6, 29. θεραπεύων, to regard, esteem, value, to be fond of, to idolize, 79. θεραπεύσετε τὸ δίκαιον, to observe impartiality, 61. θεραπεύοντες, to take care, pains: 1, 137. ἐθεράπευσε χρημάτων· δόσει, to gratify with a gift or *douceur*: 3, 56. θεραπεύοντες τὸ ξυμφέρον, time-serving: 2, 65. θεραπεύοντες τὸ ναυτικὸν, to attend to the navy, naval affairs.

θεράπων, 7, 13. a soldier's servant, camp-attendant, suttler, follower.

θέρμη, 2, 49. ἰσχυραὶ, extreme or violent heats in the head.

θέρος, 2, 27. summer, 5, 35. 7, 9.: 5, 20. θέρη: 6, 8.

θέσις, 1, 37. a position, site: 5, 7. a situation.

θεσμοφύλαξ, 5, 49. a keeper of the sacred records.

θέω, 5, 10. ἔθει δρόμῳ, to run at a rapid rate.

θεωρέω, 5, 18. 50.: 3, 104. ἐθεώρουν, to go to be a spectator of sacred games, 4, 93. ἀλλήλους, to command a view of, to see.

θεωρία, 6, 16, seeing or viewing spectacles.

θεωρὸς, 6, 3. a deputy sent to consult an oracle: 5, 47. a Mantinæan magistrate, whose peculiar province was sacred matters.

θήκη, 3, 104. a sepulchre, 58. 5, 1.: 1, 8. a sepulchre, coffin, grave: 2, 52. a depository for a corpse, i. e. a funeral pile.

θῆτες, 6, 43, ἑπτακόσιοι, *Famuli*.

θνήσκω,, 2, 48. πολλῷ μᾶλλον ἔθνησκον, they begin to die in much greater numbers: 7, 75. τεθνεώτων, dead, 1, 8. 5, 1. 13.: 7, 1. τεθνηκότος, having died: 8, 74. τεθνήκωσι, see ἵνα: 3, 104. τεθνεώτων, Matth. Gr. Gr. 230.; 3, 109. 4, 38.: 3, 113. τεθνᾶσι, Matth. l. c.

θολερὸς, 2, 102. ῥεῦμα πολὺ καὶ θολερὸν, turbid.

θορυβέω, 6, 61, i. q. κινέω θόρυβον, 3, 78. to throw into confusion : 6, 22. θορυβῶνται, to be troubled, in confusion, disorder : 3, 22. ἐθορυβοῦντο, to be in confusion: 5, 10. θορυβηθῆναι, to be disordered: 7, 3. ἐθορυβήθησαν, to be put in confusion, consternation, to be in dismay : 8, 50. θορυβούμενος, to be disturbed, alarmed : 8, 50.

θόρυβος, 4, 104. ἐς θόρυβον μέγαν κατέστησαν, to be thrown into confusion, tumult: 3, 74. 7, 40. tumult, disorder, 44. πολὺν παρεῖχον, to occasion disorder, confusion : 4, 14.

θρανίτης, 6, 31. a rower of the uppermost bench.

θράσος, 7, 21. enterprise : 4, 92. ἰσχύος θράσει, by the right of the stronger, on the plea of the stronger : 2, 40. boldness : 1, 120.

θρασύνω, 5, 104. θρασυνόμεθα, to make bold : 1, 142. θρασύνοντες, to confirm, encourage, embolden.

θρασὺς, 3, 39. bold, rash, audacious : 8, 84. ὅσῳ μάλιστα καὶ ἐλεύθεροι ἦσαν οἱ ναῦται, τοσούτῳ καὶ θρασύτατα προσπεσόντες τὸν μισθὸν ἀπῄτουν, "as in Latin, *nautæ, ut liberrimi erant, ita audacissime*, with this difference only that in Latin, in this case *ita—ut* are commonly the particles of comparison, instead of *eo —quo,* but in Greek they remain the same as in the comparative," Matth. Gr. Gr. 668.: 7, 77.; 8, 103. θρασύτερος.

θρασύτης, 2, 61. an overweening spirit.

θρὶξ, 1, 6. τριχῶν, the hair.

θροῦς, 5, 7. stir, murmur, dissatisfaction : 4, 66. bustle.

θῦμα, 1, 126. a sacrifice, an image formed into the shape of an animal : 5, 53. a victim.

θυμιατήριον, 6, 46. a censer, perfuming pan.

θυμέομαι, to be angry, 7, 68.

θυμὸς, 1, 49. spirit : 2, 11. heat, impetuosity : 5, 80. ἀλλὰ θυμῷ ἔφερον, to bear in mind.

θύρα, the door of a house, as πύλαι the gates of a city or wall, 2, 4. οἰόμενοι πύλας τὰς θύρας τῦ οἰκήματος εἶναι, (Schol. θύραι αἱ τοῦ οἴκου, πύλαι αἱ τοῦ τείχους.)

θύρωμα, 3, 68. a door-post, jamb, door-way, threshold.

θυσία, 5, 16. a sacrifice : 2,

38. ἀγῶσι καὶ θυσίαις, games and festivals : 5, 50. the solemnity of sacrificing, 11. a victim, sacrifice : 3, 58.

θύω, 1, 126. ἱερεία, to sacrifice victims : 6, 54. ἐς τὰ ἱερὰ ἔθυον, for ἐν τοῖς ἱεροῖς : 5, 18. to sacrifice, worship, 49. : 5, 54. θυομένοις, to sacrifice.

θώραξ, 3, 22. a breastplate.

I.

Ἴαμα, 2, 51. a cure, remedy, medicine.

ἰάομαι, 5, 65. κακὸν κακῷ ἰᾶσθαι, to make bad worse, to remedy one evil by another.

ἰατρὸς, 2, 48. ἰατρὸς καὶ ἰδιώτης, whether professional or unprofessional: 6, 14. πόλεως, a physician, healer (in a metaphorical sense.)

ἰδέα, 2, 77. πᾶσαν, every mode, scheme, way : 3, 83. πᾶσα ἰδέα κατέστη, every form (of evil) existed, 81. θανάτου, 7, 29. ὀλέθρου : 7, 29. form, species : 3, 62. τῇ αὐτῇ ἰδέᾳ, in the same character, the same thing in fact, though different in circumstances : 1, 109. 4, 55. 6, 76.

ἴδιος, 1, 17. private, 5, 36. 39. : 1, 80. ἐκ τῶν ἰδίων, out of or from our private possessions : 6, 15. ἴδια ὠφελήσειν, to improve one's private estate : 3, 14. private, personal, what is properly one's own: 7, 48. ἰδίᾳ, on one's own private account, 5, 42. privately, in particular, 2, 67. in a private capacity, unauthorised, without authority (from the state,) 5, 43. slily, secretly, privately, 1, 68. for a private

interest, 7, 48. for one's own person, by oneself, at one's own peril, (by his own adventure, Hobbes, privato periculo, Portus,) 1, 132. for one's own honour or account : 8, 1. 45.

ἰδιώτης, 1, 82. a private individual, 106. 2, 8. 60. 5, 41. 6, 16. : 6, 72. uninstructed in war, untaught, undisciplined : 4, 2. 61.

ἱδρύω, 2, 49. ἱδρυθὲν, to be seated, 6, 37. ἐκ νεῶν, to be formed out of, to consist of: 2, 15. ἵδρυται, to be situated: 1, 131. ἱδρυθεὶς, to be settled, to have one's abode : 6, 3. ἱδρύσαντο, to build, erect : 4, 44. ἱδρύθη, to be posted, stationed, 3, 72. to encamp : 3, 58. ἱδρυσάντων, to establish : 8, 40. ἱδρῦσθαι, to have stationed itself.

ἰέναι, 2, 3. ᾖσαν ἐς χεῖρας, to come to blows, this tense is used as an aorist, Matth. Gr. Gr. 299. : 3, 80. ἐς λόγους, to enter into a negociation, 5, 17. to proceed to a conference : 5, 47. ἴωσιν ἐς τὴν γῆν, to invade the territory : 8, 2. ἰτέον, ought to go.

ἱέρεια, 4, 133. a priestess.
ἱερεῖον, a victim.
ἱερὸν, 5, 16. 18. 49. 7, 29.
a temple : 4, 90. the precincts of the temple : 5, 47.
ἱερὰ τέλεια, complete and perfect victims, 4, 92.: 1, 25.
τὰ ἱερὰ, the sacred rites.
ἱερομηνία, 3, 56. 5, 54. a
festival season.
ἱερὸς, 8, 35. sacred.
ἱερόω, 2, 2. ἱερωμένης, to be
priestess : 5, 1. ἱερῶσθαι, to
be consecrated, devoted to
the gods, dedicated to holi-
ness or holy purposes.
ἱζάνω, 2, 76. ἱζάνοντος, to
settle, sink, subside.
ἱκανὸς, 1, 2. 74. sufficient :
1, 9. of sufficient authority :
6, 6. ἱκανὰ ἐς τὸν πόλεμον,
enough or sufficient for the
war, the purposes of war : 7,
42. sufficient, able (to cope
with any one,) a match (for
any one,) 51. sufficient, fit,
requisite, 77. : 6, 37. ἱκανω-
τέραν Πελοποννήσου, more able
than, 68. effectual, able.
ἱκανῶς, 1, 91. ἔχειν τὸ τεῖχος,
that the wall is of sufficient
height : 4, 63. ἱκανῶς νομίσαντες, to judge lawful, right :
6, 92.
ἱκετεία, 3, 67. a petition,
supplication, 1, 24.
ἱκέτευμα, 1, 136. a supplication.
ἱκετεύω, 2, 47. ἱκέτευσαν, to
put up prayers, make sup-
plications.
ἱκέτης, 1, 24. a suppliant,
103. 136.
ἱκνέομαι, 1, 99. ἱκνούμενον

ἀνάλωμα, the amount of the
expense.
ἴκριον, a plank, tabula.
ἱμάτιον, 4, 48. a garment,
robe.
ἵνα, so that, 8, 74. ἵνα,
ἢν μὴ ὑπακούσωσι, τεθνήκωσι,
("since in the perf. more
regard is had to the dura-
tion of the consequences,
and the action, properly
speaking, is left almost out
of the question, it is therefore, also used to express
the rapid passing of an
action, in which the moment
of the action itself is entirely
overlooked," Matth. Gr. Gr.
730.)
Ἰνάρως, 1, 110. Ἰνάρως ὁ
τῶν Λιβύων βασιλεὺς, a case of
apposition, where a subst.,
particularly a proper name,
is explained by another, and
stands generally without the
article, Matth. Gr. Gr. 399.
ἱππαγωγὸς, 4, 42. a horse-
transport, 6, 43.
ἵππαρχος, 4, 72. a hipparch.
ἱππεὺς, 1, 62. a horse-soldier : 7, 73. μετὰ ἱππέων, with
some horsemen.
ἱπποδρομία, 3, 104. a horse-
race.
ἱπποκρατέω, 6, 71. ἱπποκρα-
τῶνται, to be inferior in horse.
ἱππομαχέω, 4, 124. ἱππομά-
χησαν, to have a cavalry-
action.
ἱππομαχία, 2, 22. βραχεῖα, a
cavalry - fight, skirmish of
horse : 4, 72.
ἵππος, 5, 10. a horse : 1, 62.
ἡ ἵππος, a body of horse : 4, 95.

ἱπποτοξότης, 2, 13. a horse-archer, mounted archer, 96.

ἱπποτροφία, 6, 12. breeding horses.

ἴσημι, 1, 4. ἴσμεν, to know of, hear of, 13. 18. 75. εὖ, we are sure: 1, 20. ἴσασιν, to be aware: 7, 64. αὐτοὶ ἴστε, yourselves know : 1, 76. εἰ τότε ὑπομείναντες διὰ παντὸς ἀπήχθησθε ἐν τῇ ἡγεμονίᾳ, ὥσπερ ἡμεῖς, εὖ ἴσμεν μὴ ἂν ἧσσον ὑμᾶς λυπηροὺς γενομένους τοῖς ξυμμάχοις, καὶ ἀναγκασθέντας ἂν ἢ ἄρχειν ἐγκρατῶς ἢ αὐτοὺς κινδυνεύειν, that you would have oppressed the allies in the same manner and would have been compelled, the verbs ' to know' take the object in the participle, Matth. Gr. Gr. 828.

ἰσθμὸς, 1, 7. an isthmus, a neck of land, 26. 56. : 8, 7. ὑπερενεγκόντες τὰς ναῦς τὸν ἰσθμὸν, 3, 31. a double accus., Matth. Gr. Gr. 610.

ἰσθμώδης, 7, 26. ἰσθμῶδες τὸ χωρίον, like or resembling an isthmus, a kind of isthmus: 8, 26. narrow-like an isthmus.

ἰσοδίαιτος, 1, 6. living on an equal footing.

ἰσοκίνδυνος, 6, 34. equal to (any) danger.

ἰσομοιρέω, 6, 16. to share, divide, 39. to share equally, have equal rights, participate alike.

ἰσομοιρία, 7, 75. τῶν κακῶν, an equal participation in, or an equality of misfortune : 5, 39. an equal share (of power.)

ἰσονομέω, 6, 38. ἰσονομεῖσθαι μετὰ πολλῶν, to enjoy equal rights or to be on a footing with.

ἰσονομία, 4, 78. equal law, equity, impartiality : 3, 72.

ἰσόνομος, 3, 62. κατ' ὀλιγαρχίαν, under an equitable oligarchy.

ἰσοπαλής, 2, 39. ἐπὶ τοὺς ἰσοπαλεῖς κινδύνους χωροῦμεν, to undergo or encounter equal perils, i. e. as great as those of others : 4, 94. πλήθει, a match in number (for the enemy.)

ἰσοπλατὴς, 3, 21. τῷ τείχει, equal in breadth to the wall.

ἰσοπλήθης, 6, 37. equal in number.

ἰσόρροπος, 1, 105. μάχης, a drawn battle, a doubtful fight, 7, 71. ναυμαχίας : 2, 42. ὁ λόγος τῶν ἔργων φανείη ἰσόρροπος, the panegyric would not be more than equal to, would not exceed, would be borne out by, the actions.

ἴσος, 3, 14. ἴσα καὶ ἱκέται, i. q. ἴσοι καὶ ἱκέταις, equally as or like as suppliants, in the manner of suppliants: 4, 106. πόλεώς τε ἐν τῷ ἴσῳ οὐ στερισκόμενοι, equality of citizenship : 7, 27. τῆς ἴσης φρουρᾶς, the just or proper garrison, i. e. which is not more than equal to the defence of a place, the regular ordinary garrison : 1, 27. ἐπὶ τῇ ἴσῃ καὶ ὁμοίᾳ (sc. αἴσῃ,) on the condition of each receiving an equal and similar portion (of land :) 3, 20. ίσας τῷ τείχει, equal to (the height of) the wall : 5, 101. ἀπὸ τοῦ ἴσου, on equal ground.: 3, 40. ὁ ἀπὸ τῆς ἴσης ἐχθρὸς, an enemy on equal terms : 5, 47. τὸ ἴσον τῆς ἡγεμονίας, an equal share of command : 1, 133. ἐν ἴσῳ τοῖς πολλοῖς τῶν διακόνων, equally with the majority of his agents : 8, 89. ἰσαιτέραν.

ἰσόψηφος, 3, 79. ὄντος ἰσοψήφου, having a vote of equal influence with another : 1, 141. one who has an equal vote : 3, 11.

ἵστημι, 7, 24. τροπαῖα ἔστησαν αὐτῶν, to erect trophies for, on account of them, 54. Matth. Gr. Gr. 401. 685. : 3, 23. ἵστατο ἐπὶ τοῦ χείλους, to stand or draw up on the brink : 1, 89. ἑστήκει, to stand : 4, 56. (7, 28.) ἕστασαν, instead of ἕστηκα the form ἕστα by syncope obtains, Matth. Gr. Gr. 280. : 4, 51. ἱσταμένου μηνὸς, on the entrance of the month : 5, 46. εὖ ἑστώτων, to be in a flourishing state, good condition : 6, 55. ἡ στήλη σταθεῖσα, to be erected : 1, 40. στῆναι ἐκποδών : 3, 39. μετὰ τῶν πολεμιωτάτων στάντες, to take part or side with (our) most implacable foes : 6, 34. ἵστασθαι πρὸς τὰ λεγόμενα, to be, according to report, settled, adjusted, to depend upon, i. e. to vary according to : 3, 15. a form of the verb

12

ἵστημι referred to in Matth. Gr. Gr. 280. is not to be found in this place.

ἱστίον, 7, 24. a ship-sail.

ἰσχυρίζω, 7, 49. ἰσχυρίζηται, to persist in, or adhere to one's opinion : 6, 45. ἰσχυρίζομαι, to asseverate, affirm, 3, 44.

ἰσχυρὸς, 1, 58. strong, powerful: 3, 6. οὐδὲν ἰσχυρὸν, no assurance, strength, nothing certain : 5, 23. ἰσχυρότατος, most efficacious, 47. most vigorous, 111.: 7, 72. ἰσχυρᾶς τῆς ναυμαχίας, hard, severe, obstinate.

ἰσχυρῶς, 1, 69. vigorously, vehemently, resolutely.

ἰσχὺς, 3, 45. νόμων, the force of laws, 37. strength, power of a state : 4, 86. ἰσχύος δικαιώσει, plea of the stronger : 7, 25. strength, force : 1, 36. ἰσχὺν ἔχον, backed by strength : 4, 35. χωρίου ἰσχύϊ, the dat. for the Latin abl. is used with verbs, when it expresses an external cause, and is to be rendered ' on account of,' Matth. Gr. Gr. 569.

ἰσχύω, 6, 82. μεῖζον ἴσχυον, to be more powerful, 1, 2. 18. to be strong : 2, 13. ᾗπερ ἰσχύουσιν, where or in which they are strong : 1, 36. ἰσχύοντας, powerful : 2, 87. ἰσχύει πρὸς τοὺς κινδύνους, to avail against danger : 1, 3. ἰσχυσάντων, to prevail, to become powerful, 1, 9. ἰσχύσας, to grow strong : 3, 39. δι' ἣν ἰσχύομεν, where we are strong, through which we prevail, 1, 143. ὅθεν, whence we derive our power : 3, 46. ἰσχυύσας ἐς χρημάτων λόγον, in a capacity for the pay-

ment of, capable of paying tribute : 8, 47. ἰσχύοντα, possessing influence.

ἴσχω, 3, 58. 7, 36. 50. see ἔχω.

ἴσως, 1, 22. 82. perhaps.

K.

Καθαίρεσις, 5, 42. τοῦ Πανάκτου, a pulling down, demolition.

καθαιρετέος, 1; 118, to be overthrown, destroyed, 121. must be surpassed, exceeded.

καθαιρέτης, 4, 83. πολεμίων, a rooter out, an exterminator.

καθαιρέω, 3, 50. καθεῖλον, to pull down, demolish, 5, 103. to destroy : 3, 18. καθαιρήσετε Ἀθηναίους, to reduce : 1, 13. καθῄρουν, to destroy : 5, 42. καθηρημένον, demolished, thrown down, razed even with the ground : 1, 16. καθελοῦσα, to subvert, destroy the power of, 77. ἡμᾶς, to put down our government, 8, 2. to submit : 8, 16. καθῄρουν, demolished, 1, 139. : 1, 4. καθῄρει, to free from, to destroy : 1, 58. 90. 2, 14. 75. καθαιροῦντες, to pull down : 5, 40. καθελεῖν Πάνακτον, to raze, demolish : 6, 11. καθαιρεθῆναι, to submit.

καθαίρω, 3, 104. ἐκάθῃραν, to purify, lustrate : 1, 48.

καθάπερ, 5, 18. in the same manner, like as : 4, 23. according to what.

καθάπτομαι, 6, 82. καθαψαμένου, to attack (in a speech,) 16. καθήψατο, to glance at, make an attack upon (in discourse,) perstrinxit.

καθαρός, 5, 1. pure, holy, 8. fresh, unimpaired.

κάθαρσις, 5, 1. a purification : 3, 104. μετὰ τὴν κάθαρσιν, after the purification.

καθέδρα, 2, 18. a sitting down, a halt, stay.

καθέζομαι, 2, 19. καθεζόμενοι, to encamp : 4, 110. ἐκαθέζετε πρὸς τὸ Διοσκούρειον, to sit down with an army : 7, 73. ποι τῆς Σ. καθεζομένη, to go anywhither in Sicily and settle, 51. to fix : 2, 18. ἐκαθέζοντο, to sit down (before a place :) 2, 19. καθεζόμενοι ἐς αὐτό, to come to a place to encamp (in it :) 1, 24. καθεζόμενοι, to sit down as a suppliant : 6, 49. καθέζηται πρὸς τῇ πόλει, to sit down before a town (to besiege it :) 1, 24. ταῦτα δὲ ἱκέται καθεζόμενοι εἰς τὸ Ἡραῖον ἐδέοντο, an instance of a verb, which of itself not implying motion, receives this sense by its conjunction with εἰς, 'into,'

z

Matth. Gr. Gr. 885. : 3, 70.
7, 77.

καθείργω, 4, 47. καθεῖρξαν, to shut up.

καθελκύω, 6, 34. καθελκύσαντες, to draw to the sea, to launch, 50. εἴ τι ναυτικόν ἐστι καθειλκυσμένον, launched, off the stocks, ἕτοιμον ἐς τὴν θάλασσαν.

κάθεξις, 3, 47. τὴν κάθεξιν τῆς ἀρχῆς, retaining, holding, maintaining empire.

καθεύδω, 4, 113. καθεύδοντες, to repose (as soldiers,) Matth. Gr. Gr. 843.

καθηγέομαι, 6, 4. καθηγησαμένον, to lead a colony, conduct a party of settlers.

καθήκω, 2, 27. καθήκουσα ἐπὶ θάλασσαν, extending, reaching to the sea : 3, 96. καθήκοντες πρὸς τὸν Μηλιακὸν κόλπον, to border upon, dwell near.

κάθημαι, 4, 124. καθῆσθαι, to rest inactive : 3, 46. καθημένοις, to sit down to a siege, to continue, 2, 20. to sit down (of an army,) 5, 7. to linger long, stand still, 85. to sit, 3, 38. to sit down, 6, 13. τῷ αὐτῷ ἀνδρὶ, to sit by, near, beside, for παρακ.

καθιδρύω, 4, 46. καθιδρυμένους, to sit down, to settle.

καθιέναι, 5, 52. καθεῖναι τείχη ἐς θάλασσαν, to let down the walls as far as the sea, i. e. to continue them down to it : 4, 48. καθιέντες, to apply to : 2, 91. καθεῖσαι τὰς κώπας, to relax the oars, to cease

rowing : 6, 16. καθῆκα ἅρματα ἐπτὰ, to let go, to start, enter for the plate : 4, 100. καθεῖτο, aor. 2. middle, "the aor. pass. and middle of ἵημι receive also an augm. in the compounds εἵθην, εἵμην, in which case the aor. 2. middle takes the form of the plusq. perf. pass. and of the opt. aor. 2. middle," Matth. Gr. Gr. 287.

καθίζω, 1, 126. καθίζουσιν ἐπὶ τὸν βωμὸν ἱκέται, to sit down (as suppliants) upon, at the altar, an intrans. verb, which retaining its intrans. sense, yet governs an accus., moreover here the prep. ἐπὶ accompanies the accus., Matth. Gr. Gr. 601.: 4, 93. καθίσας ἐς χωρίον, to make halt, 5, 7. to station, post, 4, 90.: 3, 75. καθίζουσιν ἐς τὸ ἱερὸν, to sit down upon or at the altar in a temple, to take refuge in, Matth. 885.: 6, 66. ἐκάθισαν τὸ στράτευμα ἐς χωρίον ἐπιτήδειον, to encamp an army : 1, 136. καθίζεσθαι ἐπὶ τὴν ἑστίαν, to sit down.

καθίστημι, 1, 131. καθίστησιν ἑαυτὸν ἐς κρίσιν, to put himself upon his trial, 5, 103. καθίστανται ἐπὶ ἀφανεῖς ἐλπίδας, to betake oneself to dark hopes, 2, 11. καθίστανται ἐς ἔργον, to come to action : 3, 3. ἄρτι καθισταμένου, to be recently begun, entered upon, on foot, 1, 1. 1, 125, to arrange, prepare : 1, 44. καθιστῶνται ἐς πόλεμον : 5, 82.

καθίσταντο τὰ ἐν Ἀχαίᾳ, to dispose for oneself, 51. to be established, founded, settled: 4, 92. καθίστατο, to be, to imply, 6, 55. τὰ τῆς ἀρχῆς πράγματα, to settle, establish: 4, 103. καθειστήκει, to be appointed, 2, 45. ἐν τῷ ὁμοίῳ, to stand to, or to be to the same purpose, i. e. equally unavailing, 1, 101. to exist, endure, 132. ἐπειδὴ ἐν τούτῳ, after affairs took their present turn, 8, 38. : 7, 67. παρὰ τὸ καθεστηκὸς, contrary to the practice, custom, wont of any one, 3, 39. νῦν καθεστηκόσι, now existing, 2, 36. καθεστηκυίᾳ ἡλικίᾳ, a settled period of life, middle age, age of manhood, 3, 43. καθέστηκε, to be the case, practice, use, *solere, usu venire*, 4, 33. οὗτοι καθεστήκεσαν, they stood, 1, 130. ἐν τῷ καθεστηκότι τρόπῳ, in the established manner of living: 3, 102. καθεστήξει, to fix, secure (as an ally,) 37. βέβαιον, to remain, endure, (of a decree,) to stand firm, hold good, to be carried into effect : 6, 16. κατέστησα, to reduce, constrain : 3, 8. κατέστησαν ἐς λόγους, to be or to sit in council, 7, 44. ἐς φόβον, to be reduced to fear, fall into alarm, to be panic struck, 5, 81. τὰ πράγματα ἐς ὀλίγους, to put into the hands of the few, 1, 32. κατέστημεν ἐς πόλεμον, to be engaged in a war : 4, 84. καταστὰς ἐπὶ τὸ πλῆθος, to stand up, 1, 55.

καταστήσαντες, to establish, 82. ἐς ἀπόνοιαν, to drive into despair, 6, 82. ἡγεμόνες καταστάντες οἰκοῦμεν, for καθεστηκότες ἐσμὲν, to be appointed, made leaders, 3, 86. ἐς Ῥήγιον, to take up one's quarters : 6, 6. καθέστασαν ἐς πόλεμον, to be at war : 1, 140. καταστήσητε σαφὲς, to make it clear, to convince, plainly to shew : 3, 18. καταστησάμενοι τὰ βεβαιότερα, to put (affairs) on a foundation more secure: 3, 40. καταστήσατε ξυμμάχοις παράδειγμα, to make an example for the confederates, to furnish a (fair) warning to : 6, 54. ἀνεπιφθόνως κατεστήσατο, he conducted or behaved himself unblameably, without ill will or *odium*, 1, 114. Εὐβοίαν ὁμολογίᾳ κατεστήσαντο, to reduce into one's power on conditions, 8, 23. established, restored, 29. had appointed, established, strengthened : 2, 65. ἐπεὶ ὁ πόλεμος κατέστη, when war arose, was on foot, 74. ἐς ἐπιμαρτυρίαν, to proceed to an attestation, to attest : 1, 75. καταστῆναι, to become, 9. μείζους, to become greater : 3, 34. ἐς τὸ τεῖχος πάλιν καταστήσειν, to replace within the fortification, to restore to, 1, 73. ὁ ἀγὼν καταστήσεται, to be established, 3, 47. καταστήσετε τοῖς δυνατοῖς, to effect or establish (a point) for the aristocrats, wealthy, 4, 76. καταστήσειν ἐς τὸ ἐπιτήδειον, to establish on an advantageous principle: 5, 88. ἐν τῷ τοιῷδε καθεστῶτας, to be placed in such a situation as this, 2, 59. πανταχόθεν τῇ γνώμῃ ἄποροι καθεστῶτες, to be utterly at a loss what to do, to be at their wit's end, 5, 30. καθεστῶτα, raging, existing, pervading, 7, 64. ἐν ἑνὶ τῷδε ἀγῶνι, to be or to engage in: 3, 9. τὸ μὲν καθεστὼς, the κ being rejected in the perf., and the participle taking the α from ἑσταὼς, contracted ἑστὼς, Matth. Gr. Gr. 229. see too 280.: 6, 18. καθέσταμεν, 7, 28. καθέστασαν, example of syncope, where ἕστα is for ἕστηκα, Matth. 279.

κάθυδος, 5, 16. a return, 8, 47.: 3, 85. a return from emigration: 3, 114. 8, 47.

καθοράω, 1, 48. καθορῶσι, to descry: 3, 112. καθορωμένοις τῇ ὄψει, to be seen, 23. καθεωρῶντο, to be discerned, 20. καθορωμένου, to be discerned, within view: 8, 19. καθορῶσιν, to behold.

καθορμίζω, 4, 45. καθορμισάμενοι, to moor, harbour, 3, 32. ἐς τὴν Ἔφεσον, to sail into port at Ephesus, to put into Ephesus: 4, 13. καθορμίσωνται, 8, 33. καθωρμίσαντο, came to anchor, 34. καθορμισάμενοι, to come to shore.

καθόσον εἰ, 6, 88. i. q. ὅτι.: καθόσον, 7, 37.

καθότι, 4, 34. 118.

καθύπερθε, 5, 59. above, in the upper part: 4, 43. above, aloft.

καθυπέρτερος, 5, 14. γενέσθε, to get the upper hand: 7, 56. καθυπέρτερα, in a better, more flourishing state, superior to.

καὶ, 7, 60. καὶ ξυνελθόντες, i. q. οὖν: 1, 140. καὶ νῦν οὐχ ἥκιστα, and now especially, 90. τὰ μὲν καὶ—τὸ δὲ πλέον, partly because—but rather: 7, 53. δείσαντες, as, because, quippe qui metuebant: 3, 2. καὶ πρὸ τοῦ πολέμου, even before, 3, πέμψαντες καὶ οὐκ ἔπειθον, (when) even having sent, they did not prevail upon, 30. καὶ πάνυ, especially, even extremely: 1, 68. καὶ εἰ μέν του, if in truth at all: 7, 4. ὥστε καὶ—ἐγένετο, by this means, in a great measure: 1, 65. καὶ ἔστιν ἃ καὶ εἷλε, and there were even some small towns, which he took: 5, 112. οὔτε ἄλλα δοκεῖ ἡμῖν ἢ ἅπερ καὶ τοπρῶτον, the use of καὶ for the Latin ac or atque, in English 'as,' Matth. Gr. Gr. 704.: 7, 47. ἀλλ' ἅπερ καὶ διανοηθεὶς ἐς τὰς Ἐπιτολὰς διεκινδύνευσεν, etiam, Matth. 938.

καινὸς, 3, 30. τὸ καινὸν τοῦ πολέμου, a vicissitude, reverse in war, 92. ἐκ καινῆς, de integro, quite afresh, on a new foundation.

καινότης, 3, 38. λόγον, a new strain of words.

καινόω, 1, 71. κεκαίνωται, to be made new, to be new-modelled: 3, 82. καινοῦσθαι, to innovate.

καίριος, 4, 10. τὰ καίρια, fortunate, contingencies.

καιρὸς, 2, 43. 4, 77. occasion, opportunity : 3, 13. ὡς οὔπω πρότερον, an excellent opportunity, an opportunity such as never (offered) before, 56. : 5, 61. ἐν καιρῷ παρεῖναι, to arrive in a favourable moment, in the nick of time : 1, 142. τοῦ πολέμου οἱ καιροὶ, opportunities in war, occasions : 6, 9. ἐν καιρῷ σπεύδετε, to be in haste unseasonably.

καίτοι, 3, 39. certainly, surely.

καίω, 2, 49. τὰ δὲ ἐντὸς οὕτως ἐκάετο, to be scorched, to burn : 7, 80. πυρὰ καύσαντες ὡς πλεῖστα, to light as many fires as possible : 4, 34.

κακία, 3, 58. a disgrace : 1, 32. an evil design, malice : 2, 87.

κακίζω, 2, 21. ἐκάκιζον, to revile, blame : 1, 105. κακιζόμενοι, to be reviled, run down, 5, 75. to be rendered faint-hearted.

κακόνους, 6, 24. τῇ πόλει, disaffected, ill-disposed.

κακοξύνετος, 6, 10. κακοξυνετώτερος, more cunning, crafty.

κακοπάθεια, 7, 77. a calamity, Matth. Gr. Gr. 535.

κακοπαθέω, 2, 41. ὑφ᾽ οἵων κακοπαθῦ, to suffer a defeat from such men as these, (with indignation :) 1, 122. κακοπαθοῦντες ὑπὸ μιᾶς, to suffer by means of one, 78. to suffer evil : 4, 29.

κακοφαγέω, 2, 43. κακοφραγοῦντες, the unfortunate : 4, 55. to fare ill, speed badly.

κακοπραγία, 2, 60. ταῖς κατ᾽ οἶκον, domestic calamities, disasters, Ὁπότε οὖν πόλις μὲν τὰς ἰδίας ξυμφορὰς οἷα τε φέρειν, εἰς δὲ ἕκαστος τὰς ἐκείνης ἀδύνατος, πῶς οὐ χρὴ πάντας ἀμύνειν αὐτῇ ; καὶ μὴ, (ὃ νῦν ὑμεῖς δρᾶτε, ταῖς κατ᾽ οἶκον κακοπραγίαις ἐκπεπληγμένοι,) τοῦ κοινοῦ τῆς σωτηρίας ἀφίεσθε, for ἀφίεσθαι, as a continuation of the question. Thus a new order of constr. is commenced, instead of a continuation of the former ; and it is an instance of the anacoluthon. Matth. Gr. Gr. 945. : 4, 79. evil plight, bad state : 8, 2. misfortune, 3, 39. misfortune, adversity.

κακὸς, bad, wicked, ill-disposed, evil, 2, 51. 4, 117.

κακότης, 5, 100. baseness.

κακοτροπία, 3, 83. evil.

κακοτυχέω, 2, 60. κακοτυχῶν, to be unfortunate, unprosperous.

κακουργέω, 7, 19. τῆς χώρας τοῖς κρατίστοις ἐς τὸ κακουργεῖν, the parts of the country best adapted for annoying, injuring, plundering, inflicting damage : 2, 67. ἔτι πλείω κακουργῇ, to do still further injury, yet more mischief : 7, 4. κακουργήσοντες ἐξίουν, to ravage, injure, spoil : 2, 22. τοῦ μὴ προδρόμους κακουργεῖν ἐπιπτοντας ἐς τοὺς ἀγροὺς, to prevent the light-armed troops (skirmishers) from falling

upon and injuring the lands :
3, 1. τὸν πλεῖστον ὅμιλον τῶν
ψιλῶν εἶργον τὸ μὴ τὰ ἐγγὺς
τῆς πόλεως κακουργεῖν, the
infin. is used as a subst.
with the neuter article, here
the infin. is put with the
accus. of the article for the
gen., Matth. Gr. Gr. 820. :
6, 7.

κακουργία, 1, 37. wicked-
ness, villainy.

κακοῦργος, 3, 45. a male-
factor, villain : 5, 16. an
evil-doer, a bad man, a man
deficient in principle : 1, 8.
a robber, pirate, malefactor :
6, 38. κακουργοτέροις, worse.

κακόω, 7, 27. ἐκάκωσε τὰ
πράγματα, to damage, injure
the state, commonwealth, 3,
87. to deteriorate, injure :
4, 52. κακώσειν, 87. κακούμε-
νοι, injured, 25. κεκακωμένην,
to be reduced to a low ebb,
1, 38. to be afflicted : 2, 25.
ἐκάκουν, to do damage, 8, 45. :
6, 18. κακώσομεν, to injure,
damage, weaken : 8, 32. κακώσειν, would injure, harass,
78.

κακῶς, 5, 23. πάσχειν, to
suffer, undergo injury : 3,
40. ποιεῖν, to maltreat, injure:
2, 65. 7, 80.

κάκωσις, 7, 4. a damage,
loss, havoc, 82. : 2, 43. μετὰ
τοῦ μαλακισθῆναι, misfortune,
loss coupled with or incurred
through feebleness, supine-
ness.

κάλαμος, 2, 76. a reed.

καλέω, 4, 3. καλοῦσι αὐτὴν—

Κορυφάσιον, to name, call : 1,
2. καλούμενος, to be named, 2,
19. 5, 10. 72. 7, 4. 57. : 1, 3.
μᾶλλον καλεῖσθαι, to be much
or frequently called : 1, 126.
ἐκαλοῦντο, to be called, 8, 6. :
6, 2. ἐκλήθησαν, to be named,
1, 100. : 1, 3. κληθέντες, to be
called, denominated : 3; 82.
κέκληνται, to be called, 2, 37.
κέκληται ὄνομα δημοκρατία, to
be called democracy : 5, 9.
κεκλῆσθαι : 4, 64. κεκλημένους.

καλινδέω, 2, 52. ἐκαλινδοῦντο,
to be rolled out, over about.

κάλλιστος, 5, 9. most bril-
liant, satisfactory, best : 2,
34. ἐπὶ τοῦ καλλίστου προαστείου, in the handsomest
suburb : 5, 9. κάλλιστα, with
most acuteness: 2, 11. 6, 33. :
καλλίων, 5, 60. : καλλιώτερος,
4, 118. an instance of a new
compar. being derived from
a compar. in use, Matth. Gr.
Gr. 169.

κάλλος, 3, 17. an ornament.

καλός, 5, 59. ἐν καλῷ, under
favourable circumstances: 3,
42. τοῦ μὴ καλοῦ, i. q. τοῦ
αἰσχροῦ : 4, 92. καλὰ φαίνεται,
the victims are favourable :
8, 2.

καλύβη, 1, 133. a tent : 2,
52. πνιγηραῖς, suffocating,
stifling, close huts, temporary buildings.

καλώδιον, 4, 26. a cord.

κάλως, 4, 25. ἀπὸ κάλω, by
rope, (being towed,) the
Attic declension instead of
κάλωος, Matth. Gr. Gr. 79.

καλῶς, 2, 60. ἀνὴρ τὸ καθ'

ἑαυτὸν καλῶς φερόμενος, to go on well, to be prosperous in one's private affairs : 1, 5. in a gentlemanly style : 3, 22. οὐ καλῶς τὴν Ἑλλάδα ἐλευθεροῦν, to take a bad way to free Greece : 4, 93. καλῶς αὐτοῖς εἶχεν, it was a fine opportunity : 5, 65. καλῶς ληφθέντας, to be fairly, nicely caught : 3, 44. τοῦ καλῶς ἔχοντος ἐς τὸ μέλλον, future well-being, well-being for the future: 5, 36. on honourable terms, without sacrificing honour.

κάμνω, 2, 51. to be ill : 3, 98. ἐκεκμήκεσαν, to be wearied : 2, 41. κάμνειν ὑπὲρ αὐτῆς, to undergo, sustain labours. perils for, on behalf of: 6, 34. κεκμηκόσιν, weary, fatigued : 3, 59. τοὺς κεκμηῶτας, the dead, Matth. Gr. Gr. 229.

κάμπτω, 3, 58. καμφθῆναι, (to be bent,) to relent.

κανοῦν, 6, 56. a basket.

καπνὸς, 3, 88. smoke.

καρδία, 2, 49. the stomach.

καρπὸς, 3, 15. καρποῦ ξυγκομιδὴ, gathering in corn, getting in fruits, the harvest.

καρπόω, 2, 38. καρποῦσθαι οἰκειοτέρᾳ τῇ ἀπολαύσει, to have a more familiar use, enjoyment of: 7, 68. καὶ τῇ πάσῃ Σικελίᾳ καρπουμένῃ καὶ πρὶν ἐλευθερίαν βεβαιοτέραν παραδοῦναι, to give, deliver to Sicily, which possessed it even before, a surer or more secure freedom, i. e. to give Sicily a more secure freedom than it before enjoyed.

καρτερέω, 2, 44. to bear up (under misfortunes,) to be of good cheer : 7, 64, καρτερήσατε, to be valiant, brave.

καρτερὸς, 3, 18. ἐπὶ τῶν καρτερῶν ἐγκατῳκοδόμηται, to build upon strong places, situations : 4, 3. difficult of access, strong : 5, 7. steep : 4, 4. rugged, strong, impracticable : 1, 49. fierce, obstinate : 5, 10. καρτερώτατον, most steep, difficult of ascent : 4, 43.

κατὰ, 3, 32. πλοῦν, in the course of, during the voyage, 10. καθ᾽ ἓν γενόμενοι, to be singly, one by one, sigillatim, to be united, in one, 24. κατὰ χώραν ἐγένοντο, to remain stationary; resume one's post, 39. κατὰ λόγον, rationally, reasonably, according to calculation, expectation : 5, 47. κατὰ τάδε, according to those terms : 1, 53. κατὰ τὸ δυνατὸν, to the extent of my power : 3, 37. τὸ καθ᾽ ἡμέραν ἀδεὲς, habitual, usual security, fearlessness : 7, 44. τὸ καθ᾽ ἑαυτὸν, that which is near, by oneself, in one's own quarter : 5, 50. κατὰ τὴν ἐξουσίαν, on account of being entitled, 75. μεῖζω ἢ κατὰ δάκρυα, too great for tears, ἢ ὥστε ἀνακλαίειν : 7, 42. καθ᾽ ἕτερα, in either way, (with land-force or a fleet :) 3, 49. κατὰ μέρος, by turns : 7, 44. κατὰ τῶν κρημνῶν ῥίπτοντες ἑαυτοὺς, down the precipices : 1, 64. κατὰ κράτος, strongly : 7, 18. κατὰ τὰς σπονδὰς, in the treaty, 30. τὸν πόλεμον, in the war, i. e. during the war, 1, 1. τοὺς πολέμους, in respect to wars : 5, 3. καθ᾽ ὁδόν, on one's route, on the way : 1, 25. κατ᾽ ἐκεῖνον τὸν χρόνον, at that time : 6, 77. κατὰ πόλεις, city after city, one at a time, severally, 1, 3. city by a city, 3, 78. οἱ Κερκυραῖοι κακῶς τε καὶ κατ᾽ ὀλίγας ναῦς προσπίπτοντες, with few ships at a time, Matth. Gr. Gr. 894. : 4, 32. κατὰ διακοσίους τε καὶ πλείους, Matth. l. c. : 7, 6. ὅπερ καθ᾽ αὑτοὺς ἦν, over-against, opposite, next, near : 1, 74. καθ᾽ ἡσυχίην, without any difficulty, without a stroke : 1, 3. δοκεῖ μοι—κατ᾽ ἔθνη ἄλλα τε καὶ τὸ Πελασγικὸν ἐπὶ πλεῖστον ἀφ᾽ ἑαυτῶν τὴν ἐπωνυμίαν παρέχεσθαι, singulos populos, this accus. with the prep. is put nominatively, as also in the following example, 1, 3. καθ᾽ ἑκάστους ἤδη τῇ ὁμιλίᾳ μᾶλλον καλεῖσθαι Ἕλληνας, Matth. 432. : 2, 62. οὐ κατὰ τὴν τῶν οἰκιῶν καὶ τῆς γῆς χρείαν, this prep. is used with the accus. in the expression of a similitude, accordance, Matth. 893. : 2, 87. ὥστε οὐ κατὰ τὴν ἡμετέραν κακίαν τὸ ἡσσῆσθαι προσεγένετο, on account of, Matth. 892.

καταβαίνω, 5, 59. καταβάντες, to descend, 1, 93. to go down : 2, 49. ὁ πόνος κατέβαινεν ἐς τὰ στήθη, the pain or complaint reached, extended : 1, 105. κατέβησαν ἐς

τὴν Μ., to make a descent upon, 5, 58, κατέβη ἐς τὸ πεδίον, to descend into the plain : 2, 20. καταβῆναι, to come down : 8, 45. καταβῇ, should come down, be sent down : 4, 15. 7, 44.

καταβάλλω, 1, 27. καταβάλλοντες, to lay down, to spend : 7, 24. κατέβαλον τὸ τεῖχος, to throw, pull down : 1, 58. καταβαλόντας, to destroy or pull down a town : 6, 102. καταβεβλημένα, to be thrown down.

κατάβασις, 7, 44. πάλιν, the descent back, down again.

καταβιάζω, 4, 123. καταβιασαμένων τοὺς πολλούς, to draw in by force.

καταβιβάζω, 5, 65. καταβιβάσαι, to make to descend into a plain : 7, 85. ἐς τὰς λιθοτομίας, to force down.

καταβοάω, 1, 67. κατεβόων τῶν Ἀθηναίων, to clamour against, 115. : 5, 45. καταβοῶντας τῶν Λ., to cry down, to revile.

καταβοή, 1, 73. ἡμῶν, a clamorous accusation of us : 8, 85.

καταβυρσόω, 7, 65. κατεβύρσωσαν, to cover with hides.

κατάγγελτος, 7, 48. καταγγέλτους γίγνεσθαι, to be made known, discovered by means of an informer, to have one's secrets disclosed, revealed.

καταγελάω, 3, 83. καταγελασθὲν, laughed down, ridiculed.

καταγιγνώσκω, 4, 74. κατεγνώσθησαν, to condemn : 7, 51. κατεγνωκότων, to be of opinion, to be convinced, Matth. Gr. Gr. 808. : 3, 67. καταγνωσόμενοι αὐτῶν, to condemn : 3, 81. κατέγνωσαν ἀπάντων θάνατον, to condemn (them) all to death, Matth. Gr. Gr. 524. : 6, 60. καταγνόντες τῶν διαφυγόντων θάνατον, to condemn to death those, who had escaped : 3, 45. καταγνοὺς ἑαυτοῦ μὴ περιέσεσθαι, to pronounce against oneself that one shall not escape, to be self-convinced.

κατάγνυμι, 4, 11. to shatter, break : 3, 89. κατέαξεν, to break in pieces.

κατάγνωσις, 3, 16. an opinion, idea, 82. μετὰ ψήφου ἀδίκου καταγνώσεως, by means of an unjust vote of condemnation.

καταγορεύω, 6, 54. τῷ Ἀριστογείτονι, to denounce, inform against, to discover : 4, 68.

κατάγω, 1, 26. to lead (any one) back (as to his home,) 4, 74. 2, 33. to conduct back, to re-instate; 1, 111. to take back (and restore to his kingdom :) 5, 16. καταγαγεῖν, to bring back, conduct home, 4, 68. ἐς κίνδυνον, to bring into danger, 2, 33. κατήγαγον, 5, 32. : 1, 26. κατάξοντες : 8, 53.

καταγωγὴ, 6, 42. appulsus navium in portum, Schol. λιμὴν, places where ships touched at.

καταγώγιον, 3, 68. an inn, a caravansary.

καταδάμναμαι, 7, 82. thoroughly to conquer, subdue.

καταδείδω, 4, 110. κατέδεισαν, to fear : 2, 3. καταδείσαντες, to be alarmed.

καταδέω, 4, 57. καταδῆσαι, to bind, enchain, 8, 15. to throw into chains : 6, 53. κατέδουν, to put in prison.

κατάδηλος, 4, 44. distinguishable, under view, conspicuous, 47. ὄντες, to be evidently, visibly, notoriously, 123. τὸ κατάδηλον, getting abroad or wind : 8, 10. manifest.

καταδικάζω, 5, 49. καταδεδικάσθαι, to be fined, mulcted.

καταδίκη, 5, 49. 50. a fine.

καταδιώκω, 7, 51. to pursue : 1, 49. καταδιώξαντες, to pursue : 4, 101. κατεδίωξαν ἐς τὰς ναῦς, to pursue to, 8, 17. : 3, 4. καταδιωχθέντος, to be chased into port, to be driven in, 8, 20. καταδιωχθεῖσαι, which had been pursued : 7, 52. κατεδίωκον, to pursue.

καταδουλόω, 3, 70. to enslave, 63. καταδουλουμένους, to enslave, subdue under one's own power.

καταδούλωσις, 3, 10. subjugation: 6, 76. Matth. Gr. Gr. 558. : 7, 66. ἐπὶ καταδουλώσει, for or with a view to the subjugation.

καταδρομὴ, 5, 56. a skirmish : 7, 27. an excursion : 1, 142. an incursion, irruption : 8, 41. τὴν χώραν καταδρομαῖς λεΐαν ἐποιεῖτο, for ἐληλάτει.

καταδύω, 7, 23. κατέδυσαν, to sink, 41. καταδύσαντες, 8, 42. κατέδυσαν: 3, 78. to sink (a ship :) 7, 34. κατέδυ, (made) to sink : 1, 50. τῶν νεῶν, ἃς καταδύσειαν, which they might have sunk, an instance of the use of the opt. in an abstract proposition, "the opt. is used thus, where the indic. is put in other languages," Matth. Gr. Gr. 757.: see also 758. where it is observed that, " when regularly constructed, the opt. in this case (viz. an abstract proposition,) is accompanied by ἂν or κεν, yet this particle is˜ sometimes wanting."

καταθέω, 7, 27. καταθεούσης τὴν χώραν, to make incursions upon, to scour, 3, 97. to run down upon : 5, 7.

καταινέω, 4, 122. κατῄνει, to be well content.

καταίρω, 1, 37. καταίροντας, to touch at, put into a port, 7, 49. : 8, 31. κατῇραν, to come to land, 39. to depart, 42. κατάραντες.

καταισχύνω, 6, 13. καταισχυνθῆναι, to be deterred by shame.

καταιτιάομαι, 3, 42. κατῃτιῶντο ἀμαθίαν, to lay to the charge of: 6, 60.

κατακαίω, 7, 25. κατέκαυσαν, to burn, 4, 57. : 3, 74. κατεκαύθη, to be consumed by fire : 4, 30. κατακαυθὲν, to be burnt : 2, 4. οἱ Πλαταιῆς ἐβουλεύοντο, εἴτε κατακαύσουσιν, ὥσπερ ἔχουσιν, ἐμπρήσαντες τὸ οἴκημα, εἴτε τι ἄλλο χρήσονται, utrum eos concremarent, an aliud quid illis facerent, the indic. in ʼGreek in indirect interrogations is used, because something is represented independent of the thought of the speaker, Matth. Gr. Gr. 742. (but Bekker here reads, on the authority of MSS. κατακαύσωσιν—χρήσωνται: 8, 39. κατακαίουσι, 108.

κατακαλέω, 1, 24. κατακληθείς, to be named, called.

κατακλείω, 1, 117. κατεκλείσθησαν, to be shut up, 109. κατέκλεισε, to shut up (in an island :) 5, 83. κατέκλεισαν, to blockade, close up the ports : 4, 57.

κατακλύω, 3, 89. κατέκλυσε, to wash away.

κατακολπίζω, 8, 92. ἐς Αἴγιναν κατακολπίσαι, to turn into the bay of Ægina, to enter the bay.

κατακολυμβάω, 7, 25. κατακολυμβῶντες, to dive down.

κατακομιδὴ, 1, 120. carrying down to the shore for the purpose of exportation.

κατακομίζω, 4, 67. to carry.

κατακοντίζω, 7, 84. to throw, hurl darts upon.

κατακόπτω, 7, 29. κατέκοψαν, to cut to pieces, to slay, butcher, massacre: 4, 96. κατεκόπησαν, to be cut to pieces.

κατακούω, 3, 22. κατακουσάντων, to distinguish by hearing, to hear.

κατακρατέω, 6, 55. κατεκράτησε, to keep possession of, to hold, retain.

κατακτάομαι, 4, 86. κατακτώμενοι, to grasp : 5, 9.

καταλαμβάνω, 5, 59. κατέλαβον, to meet with, 4, 1. to seize, take possession of, 2, 56. to find, 2, 5. καταλαβεῖν, to surprise, seize, 81. to occupy, 7, 2. καταλαβὼν, to find (upon one's arrival,) 18. καταλάβοι, to overtake, befall, happen, 4, 92. καταλάβωμεν, to catch : 5, 21. κατειλημμένας, to be confirmed, irrefragable, 2, 3. to be taken, 4, 6. 8. 7, 57. to befall, overtake, to be ensnared, 1, 9. bound (by oath :) 4, 92. καταληφθῶσι, to be met with or caught, 5, 10.: 3, 30. καταληφθῆναι τὰ πράγματα, to get things into one's power, to get possession of things : 4, 70. καταλήψεσθαι, to find, take, come up with : 8, 23. καταληφθεῖσαι, to be captured.

καταλέγω, 7, 31. καταλεγόμενος, to muster, assemble, 8, 31. to select : 3, 75. κατέλεγον ἐς τὰς ναῦς, to select (individuals) for the service of ships.

καταλείπω, 4, 93. καταλιπὼν, to leave behind, 7, 26. to leave, 2, 78. 4, 42.: 6, 16. to leave behind, to bequeath, 4, 18. καταλιπεῖν, 5, 16.: 3, 58. καταλείψατε : 2, 64. καταλελείψεται, to be left behind, to remain, to survive, the paulo-post-future marks a fut. action,

the beginning of which, however, in regard to time is past, but the consequences of which, or the circumstances resulting from it, still continue, Matth. Gr. Gr. 725.: 2, 43. καταλείπεται, to leave behind : 8, 27. καταλιπόντες, to leave behind.

καταλεύω, 1, 106. κατέλευσαν, to destroy by stones.

καταληπτὸς, 3, 11. τὰ πράγματα, that, which can be obtained, acquired, got possession of.

καταλιμπάνω, 8, 17. to leave behind.

καταλλάσσω, 4, 59. καταλλαγῆναι, to be reconciled : 6, 89. καταλλασσόμενοι πρὸς Ἀθηναίους, redeuntes in gratiam cum, to make peace with.

κατάλογος, 1, 10. a catalogue, list, an enumeration : 6, 31. a levy, muster-roll, conscription, 43. ἐκ καταλόγου : 7, 26. καταλόγους ἐποιοῦντο, to make levies, conscriptions, to enroll, 16. 20. : 8, 24.

κατάλυσις, 4, 20. peace : 8, 18. termination, 37. peace : 1, 18. dissolution, distinction, abolition : 6, 28. ἐπὶ καταλύσει, for, with a view to the subversion : 1, 107. a demolition : 6, 54. ἐπιβουλεύει κατάλυσιν τῇ τυραννίδι, to plot the subversion of the tyranny : 8, 18.

καταλύω, 5, 47. 7, 31. τὸν πόλεμον, to put an end to, 23 to destroy, make war, 1, 122.

to put down (tyrants:) 1, 136. καταλῦσαι, to flee to (for refuge,) 1, 24. 2, 19. to put an end to, 8, 47. to destroy, subvert : 5, 89. καταλύσαντες, to destroy, 2, 15. to dissolve, put an end to, 1, 18. κατελύθησαν, to put down, to dethrone, 5, 81. to put down (the democracy:) 1, 81. καταλύεσθαι, 1, 81. 6, 13. to put an end to (a war,) 5, 15. to release, set at liberty : 6, 13. καταλυθεῖσαν (τὴν τυραννίδα,) to be overthrown, put down, dissolved : 3, 115. καταλυθήσεσθαι, to be about to be put an end to : 8, 47. ἀπὸ σφῶν αὐτῶν οἱ ἐν τῇ Σάμῳ τριήραρχοι ὥρμηντο ἐς τὸ καταλῦσαι τὴν δημοκρατίαν, Matth. Gr. Gr. 879.: 6, 36. οὐκ αὐτοὺς εἰκὸς τὸν ἐκεῖ πόλεμον μήπω βεβαίως καταλελυμένους ἐπ' ἄλλον πόλεμον οὐκ ἐλάσσω ἑκόντας ἐλθεῖν, an instance of the perf. pass. used for the perf. middle, Matth. 716.

καταμέμφομαι, 7, 77. καταμέμψασθαι ὑμᾶς αὐτοὺς, to blame yourselves, Matth. Gr. Gr. 535.: 8, 106.

κατάμεμψις, 7, 75. σφῶν αὐτῶν, self-accusation, reproach : 2, 41. ἔχειν κατάμεμψιν, to afford room for complaint, murmuring.

καταμόνας, 1, 32. 37. alone.

καταναγκάζω, 5, 61. κατηνάγκασαν, to compel : 2, 41. καταναγκάσαντες : 1, 75. κατηναγκάσθημεν : 4, 77. κατηναγκασμένους, to be subdued, overpowered.

κατανέμω, 2, 7. κατανειμάμενοι, to divide among themselves, to share.

κατανοέω, 1, 138. κατενόησε τῆς Περσίδος γλώσσης, to learn, obtain a knowledge of, 2, 3. to discern, discover, 3, 66. κατανοήσαντες, to discover, find out.

καταντικρὺ, 7, 26. Κυθήρων, over against, opposite to, 26.: 7, 57. plainly, clearly, evidently.

καταπατέω, 5, 72. καταπατηθέντας, to trample under foot: 7, 84. κατεπάτουν ἀλλήλους, to trample upon one another.

καταπαύω, 1, 107. καταπαύειν τὸν δῆμον, to put down the democracy: 5, 26. κατέπαυσαν, to abolish, put an end to : 8, 24. καταπαύσωσι, they might put down, 97.

καταπήγνυμι, 7, 25. κατέπηξαν, to fix, implant, drive into, fasten.

καταπίμπλημι, repleo, oppleo, compleo.

καταπίπτω, 4, 90. κατεπεπτώκει, to be pulled down.

καταπλέω, 1, 51. κατέπλεον, to sail to shore: 6, 42. καταπλέωσι, to put in, to arrive: 3, 4. καταπλεύσαντες, to arrive, come to anchor, 8, 22. to sail to, 7, 5. κατέπλευσε, to sail down, i. e. to the coast-port, to sail in: 1, 5. καταπλεόντων, to sail by, to coast, to touch, while sailing by, 6, 52. to sail into port, to touch at: 8, 35. καταπλεῖ.

καταπλήθομαι, to be overstocked, satiated with.

καταπληξις, 7, 24. consternation, dismay, panic, 42, 8, 1. 66.

καταπλήσσω, 2, 62. καταπεπληγμένους, to be cut down, dejected, 4, 74. paralysed: 6, 40. καταπλαγεῖσα πρὸς τὰς ἀγγελίας, to be terrified on account of the rumours, 4, 10. 5, 65. to be astonished, 6, 34. to be struck with alarm : 1, 81. καταπλαγῆναι, to be panic-struck : 6, 78. καταπλαγῆτε τὴν δύναμιν, to be alarmed, frightened : 7, 72. καταπεπλῆχθαι, to be cast down, overwhelmed with despair : 2, 65. κατέπλησσεν ἐπὶ τὸ φοβεῖσθαι, to strike terror, fear into, to strike with fear, to reduce to a state of alarm : 6, 38. καταπλήξαντας τὸ ὑμέτερον πλῆθος, to terrify.

κατάπλους, 4, 10. cataplus, a passage, 26.

καταπολεμέω, 4, 1. to reduce by war, 86. καταπολεμοῦμεν τοὺς Ἀθηναίους, to be at war with : 2, 7. καταπολεμήσοντες βεβαίως, to carry on war against with security.

καταπροδίδωμι, 4, 10. καταπροδοῦναι, to cast away, give, abandon : 3, 63. to give up, betray, 7, 63. καταπροδίδοιτε, to betray, give up, abandon : 3, 109. καταπροδόντες, to betray, 7, 48. : 1, 86. καταπροδιδῶμεν, to betray.

καταρράσσω, 7, 6. κατηράχθη, to be violently impelled, defeated, to retire in disorder, precipitately, to be driven

with precipitation, to be beaten back.

καταρρέω, 7, 84. κατέρρεον, to flow down, to be taken down by the current.

καταρρήγνυμι, 4, 115. κατερράγη, to give way (under too great weight,) to break away, to be crushed.

κάταρσις, 4, 26. a landing-place.

κατασείω, 2, 76. κατέσεισε τοῦ μεγάλου οἰκοδομήματος ἐπὶ μέγα, to shake the large superstructure very considerably, to its foundation.

κατασκάπτω, 4, 109. κατέσκαψαν τείχη, to dig down : 5, 63. κατασκάψαι τὴν οἰκίαν, to demolish the house : 6, 7. κατασκάψαντες, to level (with the ground.

κατασκαφή, 5, 63. a demolition, putting down.

κατασκέπτομαι, 6, 50. κατασκέψασθαι, to explore, see, discover, discern,

κατασκευάζω, 6, 44. κατεσκευάσαντο στρατόπεδον, to establish or pitch one's camp : 3, 68. κατασκευάσαντες, to fit up or manufacture with : 8, 24. καλῶς κατεσκευασμένην, nobly cultivated : 2, 85. 4, 75.

κατασκευὴ, 2, 16. furniture, 38. preparation or apparatus (for celebrating a festival,) 65. furniture, fitting up, 14. furniture, moveables, household-stuff, 1, 89. : 8, 5. preparation : 1, 10. a building, an edifice : 6, 7. preparation (for defence,) provision, establishments, 31. furniture, equipment (of a ship.)

καταςκήπτω, 2, 49. κατέσκηπτε ἐς τὰ αἰδοῖα, to descend with violence, to attack.

καταςκοπὴ, 6, 46. τῶν χρημάτων, an inspection of, examination into, 34. κατασκοπαῖς χρωμένους, to watch, explore, send out to observe, 41. ἐς κατασκοπὴν, for observation, to observe (the enemy.)

κατάσκοπος, 4, 27. 6, 63. a scout, 8, 6.: 8, 41. an inspector.

καταςπάω, 1. 63. κατεσπάσθη, to be dragged down.

καταςπέρχω, 4, 126. ὄψει δὲ καὶ ἀκοῇ κατασπέρχον, to strike terror.

κατάστασις, 4, 55. a constitution, form of government, an establishment: 2, 68.

καταστρέφω, 4, 83. καταστρέψαι Μακεδόνων βασιλέα, to subdue: 1, 75. κατεστραμμένων, to be subdued, reduced: 1, 94. κατεστρέψαντο, to subdue, 3, 10. καταστρέψασθαι, to subjugate: 1, 15. κατεστρέφοντο, to subdue for oneself, 6. 24. καταστρεφομένοις: 3, 94. καταστραφῆναι, to be subdued, 5, 97. διὰ τὸ κ., by means of your subjection.

καταστροφὴ, 2, 42. a catastrophe, death: 1, 15. an overturning, a subjugation.

κατάστρωμα, 1, 14. a deck, 2, 90.: 7, 40. οἱ ἀπὸ τῶν καταστρωμάτων, those on the decks, Matth. Gr. Gr. 921.:

1, 49. ἐπὶ τῶν κ., upon the decks.

κατατίθημι, 8, 3. κατέθετο, deposited, 3, 28. κατατίθεται, 1, 115. κατέθεντο, 1, 6. to lay aside, 3, 72. to place in durance, 7, 83. to lay down (their arms:) 4, 57. καταθέσθαι, to appoint, settle, 87. δόξαν, to lay up in store: 1, 27. καταθέντα, to deposit, lay down, 5, 47. to erect: 1, 33. κατάθησθε, to lay out at interest.

κατατοξεύω, 3, 34. to shoot (to death.)

κατατραυματίζω, 8, 10. to damage, 7, 79. to wound: 7, 41. κατατραυματίσαντες ναῦς, to damage, injure: 8, 42. κατετραυμάτισαν, to injure.

κατατρίβω, 8, 46. κατατρίψαι, to wear out.

καταφαίνω, 5, 6. κατεφαίνετο, to be discernable.

καταφανὴς, 4, 29. evident, manifest, exposed to view: 1, 63. in sight: 5, 16. καταφανέστερος, more evident, glaring, 8, 46. more openly.

καταφέρω, 1, 137. καταφέρεται, to be driven (in a vessel by a storm:) 7, 53. καταφερομένας, to be driven, forced (on shore:) 4, 3. κατήνεγκε τὰς ναῦς ἐς τὴν Πύλον, to drive, force to seek shelter: 4, 120. κατενεχθῆναι ἐς τὸ χωρίον, to be driven upon, 7, 71. κατενεχθέντες, to make to or for shore, 3, 69. κατηνέχθησαν, to be carried (by a storm:) 3, 69.

12

καταφεύγω, 7, 23. κατέφυγον, to take refuge in, 3, 70. to escape, 4, 54. to betake one-self to flight, 1, 62. 4, 68. 5, 60. καταφυγὼν, to escape, 3, 34. to escape to, to take re-fuge in : 4, 104. καταφευγόντων, to fly to : 1, 89. ἐπειδὴ Μῆδοι ἀνεχώρησαν ἐκ τῆς Εὐρώπης—καὶ οἱ καταφυγόντες αὐτῶν ταῖς ναυσὶν ἐς Μυκάλην διεφθάρησαν, Λεωτυχίδης μὲν—ἀπεχώρησεν ἐπ' οἶκον, participles, accompa-nied by the art. in the sense is qui, have the whole in the gen. thus put *partitive*, Matth. Gr. Gr. 497.

κατάφευξις, 7, 38. a retreat, flight, 41. ἐποιοῦντο τὴν κατά-φευξιν, to take refuge.

καταφορὰ, destruction, 8, 87.

καταφλέγω, 4, 133. ἔλαθεν ἀφθέντα πάντα καὶ καταφλεχθέν-τα, every thing was burnt and consumed without being perceived by any one, Matth. Gr. Gr. 840.

καταφοβέω, 7, 21. to strike terror and dismay : 6, 33. κα-ταφοβηθεὶς, to be intimidated.

κατάφρακτος, 1, 10. without decks.

καταφρονέω, 6, 24. τὸ κατα-φρονεῖν τοὺς ἐπιόντας, 49. : 8, 8. 25. καταφρονήσαντες, to de-spise, 7, 63. : 2, 11. καταφρο-νοῦντας, from contempt for the enemy : 8, 8. καταφρονή-σαντες τῶν Ἀθηναίων ἀδυνασίαν.

καταφρόνημα, 2, 62. con-tempt, disdain.

καταφρόνησις, 5, 9. con-tempt, self-conceit, 5, 8. 1,

122. ἡ καταφρόνησις ἐκ τοῦ πολ-λοὺς σφάλλειν, τὸ ἐναντίον ὄνομα ἀφροσύνη μετωνόμασται, because verbs, which govern a double accus. in the active, in the passive do take the accus. of the thing, therefore τὸ ἐναν-τίον ὄνομα is in the accus., and because verbs of calling have a double nomin. in the pass., therefore ἀφροσύνη is in the nomin., Matth. Gr. Gr. 604.

καταφυγὴ, a refuge, retreat, 4, 98.

καταφωράω, 1, 82. to seize in the act, to apprehend.

καταψηφίζω, 2, 53. κατεψηφι-σμένων σφῶν, to be pronounced upon, against.

κατείδω, 1, 50. κατιδὼν, to descry, 4, 30. : 1, 48. κατεῖ-δον, to behold.

κάτειμι, to descend, 2, 25. ἀνέμου μεγάλου κατιόντος, when a strong, violent gale of wind befell them, arose : 8, 48. κά-τεισι, might return.

κατείργω, 6, 6. to hem in, press hard, straiten : 7, 57. κατειργόμενοι, to be constrain-ed : 1, 76. κατείργεσθαι, to be ruled : 4, 98. κατειργόμενον, to be in difficulties, pressed hard.

κατεπείγω, 1, 61. κατήπειγεν, to hurry, hasten.

κατεργάζομαι, 4, 65. κατεργά-ζεσθαι, to do for, bring down, to subdue, 4, 85. : 1, 7. to achieve, perform : 6, 33. κα-τεργασώμεθα, to subdue, de-feat : 6, 11. κατεργασάμενοι, to reduce under one's power, to subdue : 7, 21. κατεργασά-σθαι, to accomplish, perform.

κατέρχομαι, 2, 33. κατελθεῖν, to return (from exile,) 8, 47. 4, 66. to come back, 75. κα-τελθόντος, to come down, descend, 78.: 5, 7. κατῆλθεν, to come to, arrive at, 1, 127. to return.

κατέχω, 1, 103. κατεῖχον πο-λέμῳ, to cramp, hold down with a war, 91. to detain, 4, 32. to touch at, dwell, 5, 5. to fetter, hold, 2, 65. to con-troul : 4, 92. to pounce upon, take up, 1, 130. τὴν διάνοιαν, to hide one's design, keep it close, 3, 89. κατεχόντων, (of an earthquake,) 62. ἰσχύι, to constrain by force : 1, 10. ὅσον ὁ λόγος κατέχει, as great as report maintains : 3, 12. κατεχόμενοι, to be bound, tied down, held, 3, 45. κατέχεται ὑπὸ ἀνηκέστου τινὸς, to be pos-sessed, subject to, 6, 10. to be held in, restrained, 3, 107. κατείχοντο, to be with-held, 1, 17. to be tied down, hindered : 4, 42. κατέσχον, to heave to, 3, 3. 105. to de-tain, 1, 6. to hold, continue, remain, 2, 62. to keep, main-tain (a possession,) 7, 66. to obtain, acquire, 4, 92. τὴν γῆν, to seize, have in military occupation, 6, 95. τὴν ἀρχὴν, to get possession of : 6, 29. κατασχεῖν, to detain, 9. to ob-tain, acquire, 86. to retain, keep possession of, 89.: 1, 91. to detain, stop : 1, 11.

κατεσχηκότες, to be prevalent (as a report:) 6, 23. κατάσχω-σιν, to touch at, arrive at, come to : 4, 2. κατασχήσειν τὰ πράγματα, to despatch, go through with, accomplish, 6, 11. keep, retain, 16. κατά-σχοιμεν, to retain (in one's power :) 8, 23. κατασχόντες, to come to shore, 28. κατεῖχε, restrained or kept himself, 86. κατασχεῖν.

κατηγορέω, 3, 44. κατηγορή-σων, to decry : 1, 91. κατηγο-ρούντων, to charge : 6, 60. κατηγορήκει, to inform against: 1, 95. κατηγορεῖτο δὲ αὐτοῦ οὐχ ἥκιστα Μηδισμός to be charged upon, the gen. is put after verbs compounded with a prep., which prep. requires a gen., if such prep. may be separated from the verb and placed before the subst., without altering the verb's signification, and then the gen. arises from the prep. In this instance, however, where the verb is com-pounded with κατὰ, both the verb requires a gen. for its own sake, and the prep. for it's. Matth. Gr. Gr. 524.

κατηγορία, 1, 69. an accu-sation, 84. an expostulation, a reprehension : 3, 3. an ac-cusation, a criminal informa-tion, 52. a charge.

κατήφεια, 7, 75. a mixture of grief and shame, a hang-ing of the head, a dejected countenance, a casting down of the eye.

κατίσχω, 7, 33. ἐς τὰς Χοιράδας, to touch at, come to, 70. κατίσχοιεν, to touch shore, come to land, run a-ground.

κατοικέω, 3, 34. κατοικήσαντες, to inhabit: 5, 83. κατῴκητο, to take up one's residence, 3, 34. to be settled, to have one's abode.

κατοίκησις, 2, 15. dwelling in, inhabiting.

κατοικίζω, 1, 38. κατοικίσαι, to colonize, plant a colony: 5, 35. κατῴκισαν, to establish, fix, settle : 6, 50. κατοικιοῦντες, in order to re-instate, re-establish: 1, 103. κατῴκισαν ἐς Ναύπακτον, to plant, settle in, 2, 70.: 4, 102. κατοικίσαι, to colonize: 6, 7. ἐς Ὀρνεὰς κατοικίσαντες τοὺς Ἀργείων φυγάδας, to conduct to Orneæ and station there: 2, 17. κατοικισθησόμενον, to be inhabited : 1, 8. κατῴκιζε, to plant or found a colony anew.

κατοίκισις, 6, 33. a restoration, an establishing.

κατοκνέω, 2, 18. κατοκνήσειν, to dread, to be unable to bear, endure.

κατόπιν, 4, 32. behind, 3, 22. behind, a tergo.

κάτοπτος, 8, 104. discernible, perceptible, visible.

κατορθόω, 3, 39. κατορθώσαντι, to succeed, do any thing with success, 14. κατορθῶσαι, to succeed, prosper : 7, 47. κατορθοῦντες, to have good success, to go on

well, 2, 89. τὰ πλείω, to be mostly successful : 7, 66. ἢ κατορθώσειαν, in case they succeed : 8, 2. κατώρθωσαν, to succeed : 1, 140. ἢ κατορθοῦντας, or in case of success : 6, 13. κατορθοῦνται ἐλάχιστα, to succeed very rarely : 3, 42. κατορθῶν, to do (any thing) with success : 2, 42. τὸ ἀφανὲς τοῦ κατορθώσειν, the uncertainty of success, whether they should succeed or not: 1, 120. κατωρθώθη, to be rectified, set right.

κατορύσσω, 1, 134. κατορύξαι, to bury.

καττὰ πάτρια, 5, 17, Doric for κατὰ τά.

καττάδε, a Doric form, by which the prep. with its case is contracted into one word, Thuc. 5, 77. Matth. Gr. Gr. 40.

κάτω, 1, 7. 120. οἱ κάτω, those, who dwell on the sea-shore.

κάχληξ, 4, 26. a pebble on the coast.

κεῖμαι, 1, 129. κεῖται, to be laid up (as a benefit for gratitude,) 4, 78. to be situated, 1, 36. to be, to be situated, 42. ἐν ἀφανεῖ, is hidden in obscurity, 2, 46. to be instituted, 66. ἀντιπέρας Ἠλιδος, to be over against, facing, opposite to Elis: 3, 47. κεῖσθαι, to be ordained, enacted, 4, 99. τοὺς νεκροὺς, to be lying, strewed over a plain: 7, 4. ἔκειτο, to be lying: 4, 24.

κείμενος, lying, situated, 38. 5, 38. 34. 105. νόμῳ, an established law, 61. to be lodged, 6, 54. to be ordained, enacted.

κείρω, 1, 64. κείρωσι τὴν γῆν, to waste the country.

κελευστὴς, 2, 84. the director, helmsman, the person who gives orders to the rowers : 7, 70.

κελεύω, 5, 31. ἐκέλευσε, to exhort, recommend, 23. to direct, 30. to advise, 7, 1. to direct, give notice, 21. to exhort : 1, 26. κελεύοντες, to bid, exhort : 3, 7. κελευσάντων, to request, 7, 31. to direct, desire, 2, 13. Λακεδαιμονίων, by order of the Lacedaemonians : 1, 91. κελεύει, to bid, direct : 8, 7. κελεύσωσι, they might command : 7, 7. ὁπότε κελευσθείη, when the signal word was given : 1, 44. εἰ γὰρ ἐπὶ Κόρινθον ἐκέλευον σφίσιν οἱ Κερκυραῖοι ξυμπλεῖν ἐλθόντ᾽ ἂν αὐτοῖς αἱ πρὸς Πελοποννησίους σπονδαί, the verbs ' to order,' ' to exhort' take the dative, Matth. Gr. Gr. 530. : 8, 38.

κέλης, 4, 9. a boat, 8, 38. a pinnace.

κελήτιον, 1, 53. a boat, small vessel.

κενὸς, 6, 31. κενὰς ναῦς, merely the ships without the crews &c., 2, 90. the word used to denote ships emptied of their cargo is κούφος.

κενόω, 2, 76. τὸ κενούμενον, the vacancy : 8, 57.

κεντέω, 4, 47. κεντούμενος, pricking, goading.

κεραία, 2, 76. a beam projecting out like a horn, a yard-arm : 4, 100. 7, 41.

κεραμίς, 3, 22. a tile.

κέραμος, 3, 74. βάλλουσι ἀπὸ τῶν οἰκιῶν τῷ κεράμῳ, to pelt from the house-top with tiles : 4, 48. tiling : 2, 4.

κέρας, 1, 62. 5, 10. 7, 6. 8, 25. 105. a wing or side of an army : 7, 52. a wing (of a fleet :) 4, 43. τὸ δεξιὸν κέρας τῶν Ἀθηναίων καὶ Καρυστίων— ἐδέξαντό τε τοὺς Κορινθίους καὶ ἐώσαντο μόλις, an instance of a verb in the plur. after a noun of number. in the singular, because the idea of several subjects is always included, Matth. Gr. Gr. 437.

κεράω, 6, 32. κεράσαντες κρατῆρας, to mix, i. e. fill goblets : 6, 5. φωνὴ μεταξὺ τῆς τε Χαλκιδέων καὶ Δωρίδος ἐκράθη, the dialect was a mixture of, was between the Chalcidian and Doric.

κερδαίνω, 5, 93. to profit, gain : 2, 44. τὸ κερδαίνειν, lucre, gain.

κερδαλέος, 2, 53. profitable, useful.

κερδαλέως, 3, 56. cunningly, with a view to our own interest.

κέρδος, 7, 57. gain, lucre : 3, 33. ἐνόμισαν, in lucro ponere, to account it a piece of good fortune, to think it fortunate : 4, 59. κέρδη, a gain : 2, 44.

κέρως, 6, 50. ἔπλεον ἐπὶ κέρως, ἔχοντες τὰς ἄλλας ναῦς, agmine longo ceteris navibus instructis, to have them drawn up in a line, a single ship a-head, as ἐπὶ τριῶν, ἐφ' ἑνὸς τετάχθαι, στῆναι, to stand three, one deep, to have them drawn up as many deep as the whole number of ships, i. e. in a single line.

κεύθω, 6, 59. κέκευθε, to cover, conceal.

κεφάλαιον, 6, 6. a principal, chief argument, reason, (urged for doing any thing:) 4, 50. the sum, substance: 1, 36. βραχυτάτῳ, in short, in one word, to sum up all in the shortest compass: 6, 87. ἐν κεφαλαίοις ὑπομνήσαντες, summarily, per capita, to recall (to your mind.)

κεφαλαιόω, 6, 91. κεφαλαιώσω, to mention generally, summarily: 3, 67. κεφαλαιώσαντες, to sum up, make a summary of: 8, 53.

κεφαλή, 3, 24. Δρυὸς Κεφαλὰς, Dryoscephalæ, oakhead, heads of oak: 1, 6. the head: 5, 10. κεφαλῶν.

κήδομαι, 6, 14. κήδεσθαι τῆς πόλεως, to be careful of, to study the welfare, to be careful of the interests of, 76. Λεοντίνων, to take care of, to protect the interests of.

κήπιον, 2, 62. a little garden, a sort of pleasure-ground, a parterre.

κήρυγμα, 4, 105. a message by herald, 114. : 2, 2. χρήσα-

σθαι κηρύγμασι, to use, make proclamations.

κηρύκιον, 1, 52. ἄνευ κηρυκίου, without the ceremony of a herald.

κήρυξ, 4, 68. a herald, 118. : 7, 3.

κηρύσσω, 4, 116. κηρύξαο δώσειν, to offer by proclamation: 4, 37. ἐκήρυξαν, to invite by proclamation: 1, 27. ἐκήρυσσον ἀποικίαν, to proclaim that a colony is about to be sent: 6, 50. ἐκηρύχθη, a proclamation was made.

κινδυνευτής, 1, 70. one, who runs risks.

κινδυνεύω, 1, 39. to be in danger, 78. ἐκινδυνεύετο : 2, 43. to be run the risk of, to be risked, hazarded, 44. ἐκ τοῦ ὁμοίου, to run equal risks, to be in equal danger: 4, 15. an instance of an accus. with an infin. after κινδυνεύω, Matth. Gr. Gr. 810. : 3, 5. κινδυνεύειν μετ' ἄλλης παρασκευῆς, to risk a battle in conjunction with an additional force: 3, 74. ἡ πόλις ἐκινδύνευσε πᾶσα διαφθαρῆναι, the city was in danger of destruction, Matth. 800. : 8, 91. φάσκων (ὁ Θηράμένης) κινδυνεύσειν τὸ τεῖχος τοῦτο καὶ τὴν πόλιν διαφθύραι, Matth. 431.

κίνδυνος, 1, 18. μετὰ κινδύνων, in danger : 8, 15. ναρκήσαντες μέγαν ἤδη καὶ σαφῆ τὸν κίνδυνον σφᾶς περιεστάναι, see Matth. Gr. Gr. 557.

κινέω, 6, 3. πόλεμον, to raise, stir up war, 30. to agitate,

raise commotions : 1, 82,
ὅπλα μήπω κινεῖν, not to move
your arms, i. e. not to meddle with arms : 6, 70. κινή-
σωσι, to remove : 2, 24. τὰ
χρήματα ἐς ἄλλο τι, to remove,
take out the money for any
other occasion, 1, 143. to
remove, disturb (the trea-
surers at Delphi :) 3, 16.
κινοῦντες τὸ ἐπὶ Λέσβῳ ναυτικὸν,
to remove the naval force at
Lesbos : 4, 97. κινῆσαι ὕδωρ,
to disturb, touch : 7, 50.
κινηθείη : 2, 8. ἐκινήθη, to be
shaken (with an earthquake,)
3, 82. to be disturbed, put
in commotion : 7, 67. κινού-
μενοι ἐν τῷ αὐτῶν τρόπῳ, i. e.
κατὰ τὸν αὐτῶν τρόπον, to
move about in their usual
way : 7, 4. κινῶνται, to put
oneself in motion, to make
an attempt : 8, 48. ἐκινήθη,
to be agitated.

κίνησις, 1, 1. 3, 75. a commotion, disturbance : 5, 10.
shaking, movement.

κλειστὸς, 2, 17. βεβαίως,
closed fast up : 7, 38. shut
up.

κλείω, 2, 4. ἔκλυσε, to close :
5, 7.

κλέμμα, 5, 9. an advantage
snatched from an enemy.

κλέος, 1, 25. glory, reputation, 10. πρὸς τὸ κλέος αὐτῶν,
considering their glory : 2,
45.

κλέπτω, 1, 115. κλέψαντες,
to get away privily.

κλημαρὶς, 7, 53. bundles of
twigs, faggots.

κλῆρος, 3, 50. ποιήσαντες
κλήρους τῆς γῆς, to divide the
land into parts.

κληροῦχος, 3, 50. τοὺς λα-
χόντας, proprietors by lot.

κληρόω, 6, 42. ἐκλήρωσαν,
to draw lots.

κλίμαξ, 3, 20. 5, 56. a ladder.

κλίνη, 2, 34. ἐστρωμένη, a
bier strewed or covered over
(as with a pall :) 3, 68. a bedstead : 4, 48.

κλυδώνιον, 2, 84. the swell
of the sea.

κοιλαίνω, 4, 100. ἐκοίλαναν,
to hollow, excavate, bore,
verbs in αινω for the most
part receive in the aor. η instead of the α of the fut. : α
is found, however, in the
Attic. Matth. Gr. Gr. 225.

κοιλία, 2, 49. the belly,
bowels.

κοῖλος, 3, 107. hollow : 7,
52. μυχῷ, 306.

κοινολογέω, 4, 74. κοινολο-
γησάμενοι, to communicate,
converse : 7, 86. ὅτι πρὸς
αὐτὸν ἐκεκοινολόγηντο, because
they had held intercourse
with him.

κοινὸς, 6, 6. τῷ κοινῷ, the
public (treasury,) 1, 74. the
common cause, 5, 90. ἀγαθὸν,
the common privilege of
men : 5, 37. τὰ κοινά, re-
publics, commonwealths : 1,
96. ἀπὸ κοινῶν ξυνόδων βου-
λευόντων, to consult together
in common and equal assem-
blies, 141. κοινῶν, matters
appertaining to the common
weal, public affairs : 5, 38.

general, common : 1, 80. ἐν κοινῷ, in the common or public treasury : 7, 61. κοινὸς πᾶσι, common, alike : 3, 65. ἐς δὲ τὰ κοινὰ τῶν πάντων Βοιωτῶν πάτρια καταστῆσαι, to change the constitution according to the form common to all the Bœotians : 5, 47. κοίνῃ, in common, 1, 3. 57. 4, 68. : 3, 28. ποιοῦνται κοινῇ ὁμολογίαν πρὸς Πάχητα, to unite all in making terms with Paches : 5, 37. κοινῷ λόγῳ χρωμένους, to be of the same sentiments, unanimous, agreeing together : 3, 14. κοινοτέραν, general, universal, 5, 102. more equal, (al. καινοτέρας, more new and unexpected.)

κοινόω, 3, 96. κοινώσας τὴν ἐπίνοιαν τοῖς Ἀχαρνᾶσιν, to communicate the design to the Acarnanians, 2, 72. to impart, communicate, 4, 4. ταξιάρχοις, to communicate with, 1, 39. to participate, have in common, 5, 60. : 5, 38. ἐκοίνωσαν, to communicate.

κοινωνέω, 1, 39. to share, participate : 8, 8. ἐκοινωνοῦντο : 5, 79. κοινανεόντων, according to the emend. of Valck. ad Phoen. p. 75. for κοινωνούντων, i. e. κοινωνείτωσαν, the Doric form, Matth. Gr. Gr. 252.

κοινωνία, 3, 10. πόλεσιν, communion, confederacy, alliance.

κοινωνὸς, 7, 63. 8, 46. an ally, a partner with.

κοινῶς, 6, 17. unanimously.

κολάζω, 1, 40. to chastise, punish, 3, 52. 6, 38. : 3, 46. μετρίως κολάζοντες, to correct with moderation, 40. ἀξίως κολάσατε τούτους, to punish them according to their deserts : 3, 39. κολασθήτωσαν, to be chastised : 7, 68. κολασθῆναι, to punish, inflict punishment, Matth. Gr. Gr. 947. : 3, 66. κολασθήσεσθε πάντων ἕνεκα, to be punished, chastised : 8, 40. κολαζόμενοι, to be punished.

κόλασις, 1, 41. punishment, chastisement.

κολούω, 7, 66. κολουσθῶσι, to be broken, defeated.

κόλπος, 1, 24. a bay, gulph, 6, 13. τῷ Ἰονίῳ.

κολυμβητὴς, 4, 26. 7, 25. a diver.

κομιδὴ, 7, 34. a conveyance, safe-conduct : 6, 21. a conveyance, carriage, an importation : 4, 27.

κομίζω, 1, 132. κομιεῖν, to send, convey, 113. κομοῦνται, to convey away, 8, 5. κομιεῖσθαι, to obtain : 2, 85. τῷ κομίζοντι, the conductor : 7, 32. ἐκόμισεν, to conduct, convey, 39. : 3, 65. κομίσαντες ἐς τὴν πόλιν, to admit into the city : 6, 50. ἐκομίσθησαν ἐπὶ τὸν Τηρίαν ποταμὸν, to go, proceed, steer, me conferre, 2, 33. ἐπ᾿ οἰκίαν, to betake oneself : 2, 73. κομισθῆναι, to go,

to return, 6, 37. : 3, 29. κο-
μισθέντες σχολαίη, to proceed,
sail slowly, 3, 4. ταλαιπώρως
διὰ τοῦ πελάγους, to arrive
after a dangerous passage,
6, 29. to return, come : 1,
43. κομίζεσθαι, to obtain, 4,
98. to barter, 3, 58. κομίσασθαι, to procure to your-
selves : 8, 24. κομίσαντες, to
bring, 33. ἐκομίσθη, went.

κόμπος, 2, 40. λόγου, a boast
of words, a verbal boast, 41.
λόγων, (opposed to ἔργων ἀλήθεια, a real fact, the actual
truth,) an empty boast, a
rhetorical flourish.

κομπώδης, 2, 62. κομπωδε-
στέραν προσποίησιν, a boastful
arrogance, assumption : 5, 68.

κονιορτός, 4, 44. the dust
rising, 34. a flight of dust.

κοντός, 2, 84. a pole.

κόπτω, 4, 26. κεκομμένον, to
be chopped, cut : 1, 14. ἐκό-
πτοντο, to be cut off : 4, 90.
κόπτοντες ἄμπελον, to cut
down, 69. δένδρα : 8, 13. κοπεῖ-
σαι, to be harassed : 2, 75,
4; 14.

κότος, 7, 40. toil, exhaustion.

κόρη, 6, 56. κόρην, a varia-
tion of the Attic termination
in a, where the nomin. is in
η, Matth. Gr. Gr. 70.

κορυφή, top, summit, 2, 99.

κοσμέω, 1, 21. κοσμοῦντες, to
embellish : 2, 42. ἐκόσμησαν,
to adorn, embellish : 1, 10.
ἐπὶ τὸ μεῖζον κοσμῆσαι, to exaggerate for the sake of embellishment : 3, 67. κοσμηθέν-
τες ἔπεσι, to be adorned with

words : 2, 46. κεκόσμηνται, to
have honours paid to one's
memory : 8, 24. ἐκοσμοῦντο,
conducted themselves, re-
gulated their own conduct,
6, 41. κοσμηθῆναι, to be
equipped, furnished, pro-
vided with.

κόσμος, 1, 5. 3, 77. order,
arrangement : 7, 23. οὐδενὶ
κόσμῳ, in disorder, 40. regu-
larity, order : 2, 11. κόσμον
καὶ φυλακὴν περὶ παντὸς ποιούμενοι, to regard above all
order and attention, (watchfulness :) 5, 66. ἐς κόσμον τὸν
ἑαυτῶν καθίσταντο, they put
themselves into their own
peculiar order.

κοτύλη, 4, 16. 7, 87. both a
dry and a wet measure.

κούρη, 3, 104. a maid, virgin.

κουφίζω, 6, 34. κουφίσαντες,
to lighten (a vessel :) 2, 44.
κουφίζεσθαι, to be lightened
(of one's grief,) consoled.

κούφισις, 7, 75. a relief.

κουφολογία, 4, 28. an empty
boast.

κοῦφος, 2, 57. ἐλπίδος τι
εἶχον κούφης, to entertain
some slight hope : 6, 37.
νανσὶ, light, unladen, see
κενός : 8, 27.

κούφως, 4, 33. lightly.

κρατέω, 1, 77. τῷ κρατοῦντι,
the superior : 3, 80. 7, 43.
ὡς κεκρατηκότων, as victorious : 1, 11. κρατοῦντες μάχῃ,
to be masters of the field, 70.
τῶν ἐχθρῶν, to be successful
over enemies : 1, 28. κρατεῖν,
to hold, possess, command,

3, 47. ὅπλων, to get possession of arms, 49. (ἡ γνώμη,) to prevail : 1, 9. ἀκράτει, to rule, have command over, 7, 57. ἐκράτουν θαλάσσης, to rule, to be master of, 70. : 7, 34. κρατησάντων, to be masters of, 6, 11. τὰς διανοίας, to master, overcome, thwart: 3, 23. ἐκεκρατήκεσαν τοῦ πύργου, to get possession of : 6, 72. κρατήσειν τῶν ἐναντίων, to be superior to, 1, 81. κρατήσομεν : 1, 11. ἐκράτησεν, to conquer, 6, 5. νόμιμα, to prevail, obtain : 7, 55. ἐκρατήθησαν, to be conquered, worsted, 72. μὴ ἂν ἔτι οἴεσθαι κρατῆσαι, to suppose or think they could not now be victorious: 2, 13. κρατεῖσθαι τὰ πολλὰ τοῦ πολέμου, to conquer (in) most things in war, to conquer for the most part in war : 1, 109. ἐκράτουν τῆς Αἰγύπτου, whereas verbs of ' ruling,' in which the idea of a compar. is included, take the gen. after them, sometimes a verb, provided the object be subject to the operation of the action, has the accus., as κρατεῖν especially in the sense 'to conquer,' Matth. Gr. Gr. 482. : 2, 39. 6, 2. : 2, 80. λέγοντες ὅτι ῥᾳδίως ἂν Ἀκαρνανίαν σχόντες καὶ τῆς Ζακύνθου καὶ Ἀκαρνανίας κρατήσουσι, if ἂν be united with the fut. indic. κρατήσουσι, its use is to soften the decisiveness of the sentence; but ἂν may be referred to σχόντες, and

this latter be taken for ἢν σχῶσι, Matth. 926.

κράτιστος, 1, 2. ὅσα ἂν κράτιστα, the most fertile parts, 19. best, most flourishing, 36. the best, safest: 3, 11. τὰ κράτιστα, for τοὺς κρατίστους, the strongest, most powerful : 4, 12. most powerful.

κράτος, 1, 118. κατὰ κράτος, with all their might, 2, 69. by storm: 3, 13. τοῦ πολέμου, robur belli, strength in war, les forces de la guerre, 'sinews of war :' 2, 29. 88. 4, 98.

κρατύνω, 3, 18. κρατύναντες τείχη, to strengthen : 1, 69. κρατῦναι, to fortify : 3, 82. ἐκρατύνοντο, to be strengthened or confirmed : 4, 114. ἐκρατύνατο τὰς ἐγγὺς οἰκίας, to fortify, strengthen.

κραυγή, 7, 44. οὐκ ὀλίγῃ χρώμενοι, cheering, 71. a shouting, clamour : 2, 4. outcry.

κρέας, 4, 16. flesh.

κρείσσων, 1, 77. τὸ ἀπὸ τοῦ κρείσσονος, what is done by a superior (to an inferior,) 1, 8. οἱ κρείσσονες, the higher ranks: 3, 45. κρείσσω τῶν ὁρωμένων δεινῶν, stronger, of more influence than, too strong for : 2, 50. κρεῖσσον λόγου, beyond the power of words to express, to baffle description, greater or worse than one can express, Matth. Gr. Gr. 652. 656. : 3, 83. λογισμῷ, having the best of the argument: 2, 41. ἀκοῆς, superior to or above (its) reputation, what is reported (of it.)

κρημνὸς, 7, 44. a precipice.

κρημνώδης, 6, 101. full of precipices: 7, 78. precipitous.

κρήνη, 4, 26. a spring.

κριθή, 6, 22, barley.

κρίνω, 3, 48. κρῖναι καθ' ἡσυχίαν, to try, judge at leisure, 75. to condemn, 6, 39. to decide, determine : 2, 40. κριθῆσιν, to be judged, to be, 2, 45. to be judged, accounted : 3, 43. ἐκρίνετε, to judge: 1, 21. κρινόντων, to be of opinion, 128. κριθεὶς ὑπ' αὐτῶν, to be judged by them: 5, 26. κριθῆναι, to be regarded, considered : 1, 39. κρίνεσθαι δίκῃ, to submit a cause to trial, 4, 80. to stand out, come forward, emerge, to be separated, 6, 29. to be tried, to submit to trial : 2, 53. θεῶν δὲ φόβος ἢ ἀνθρώπων νόμος οὐδεὶς ἀπεῖργε, τὸ μὲν κρίνοντες ἐν ὁμοίῳ καὶ σέβειν καὶ μὴ τῶν δὲ ἁμαρτημάτων οὐδεὶς ἐλπίζων μέχρι τοῦ δίκην γενέσθαι βιοὺς ἂν τὴν τιμωρίαν ἀντιδοῦναι, a deviation from the general rule of the gen. absolute, which is put in cases, where the participle is put as an accompanying action of a principal action with a subject of its own. That subject is here in the nomin. instead. Matth. Gr. Gr. 860. : 3, 57. θανάτου δίκῃ κρίνεσθαι, as from the genitive's sense of 'with respect to' is derived the meaning 'on account of,'

11

when it expresses the cause, hence it is used in words of 'crimination,' in this example the punishment is put in the gen., Matth. 490.

κρίσις, 1, 23. a decision, 77. τὰς κρίσεις ποιήσαντες, to make a decision, pronounce sentence, 6, 60. to institute a trial: 3, 53. μὴ ἐπὶ διεγνωσμένην κρίσιν καθιστώμεθα, lest we are brought to a trial already decided : 1, 34. an arbitration.

κριτὴς, 1, 120. κακὸς, a bad judge: 3, 56. a judge, an arbitrator, 37. ἀπὸ τοῦ ἴσου, fair, equitable, impartial judges.

κρούω, 3, 22. κρουόμενα πρὸς ἄλληλα, to dash or rattle against one another : 7, 70. κρουόμενον πρύμναν, to row astern, back the ship, 1, 50. πρύμναν, to retreat with the head hindmost.

κρύπτω, 2, 34. κρύψωσι, to inter, 39. κρυφθὲν, concealed, hidden (from general inspection :) 3, 35. κεκρυμμένον, concealed : 6, 72.

κρύσταλλος, 3, 23. ice.

κρύφα, 1, 67. secretly, privately, 91. secretly, 100. τῶν Ἀθηναίων, unknown to the Athenians, 8, 7. αὐτῶν, unknown to them : 4, 79. covertly, under the rose, privately : 6, 34. secretly at least : 4, 68.

κρύφιος, 7, 25. concealed, out of sight.

κρώβυλος, 1, 6. a lock of hair.

κτάομαι, 1, 70. κτᾶσθαι, to acquire : 3, 39. κτώμενοι, 2, 65. ἐξ ὧν προσηκόντων, to acquire by improper means : 1, 93. ἐς τὸ κτήσασθαι, towards the acquisition of power : 1, 13. κτησάμενοι, to possess one-self of, 2, 36. πρὸς οἷς, to acquire in addition to : 1, 6. οἱ τὰ μείζω κεκτημένοι, those possessing the greater wealth, 6, 70. κεκτημένης οὐ δι' ὀλίγου πόνου, by means of, with the assistance of : 1, 14. ἐκέκτηντο, to possess, 6, 20. κέκτηνται : 1, 33. κεκτήμεθα, 123. ἐκτήθη, to be acquired.

κτείνω, 7, 29. κτείνοντες, killing : 4, 67. to kill, slaughter : 3, 81. ἐκτείνοντο πρὸς αὐτοῖς (ἱεροῖς,) to be slain near or upon the altars : 1, 132. 2, 51.

κτῆμα, 1, 22. a possession, good.

κτῆσις, 1, 8. 13. an acquisition : 4, 105. possession, property,

κτίζω, 2, 68. ἔκτισε, to plant, settle : 6, 4. κτίζουσι, to build, found, 1, 12. ἔκτιζον : 1, 100. κτιζόμενον, to be founded.

κτίσις, 1, 17. the establish-ment, settlement : 6, 5, a foundation, planting, build-ing.

κτύπος, 7, 70. ἀπὸ νεῶν, a crash, din, an uproar.

κύαμος, a bean.

κυβερνήτης, 7, 39. a pilot, 36. : 1, 143. a steersman : 7, 62. τῶν τριηρῶν, a master, 70.

Κυθηροδίκης, 4, 53. the Cy-therean Archon.

κύκλος, 5, 7. a circle, cir-cumvallation : 2, 84. 3, 102.

κυκλόω, 5, 72. κυκλωσάμενοι, to surround : 3, 107. κυκλωθῇ, to be surrounded, 5, 71. to be taken in flank, to be sur-rounded : 4, 96. κυκλωθέντων ἐν ὀλίγῳ, to be hemmed in on all sides : 7, 81. ἐκυκλοῦντο, to encircle, Matth. Gr. Gr. 933.: 5, 73. to surround, flank : 4, 32. κεκυκλωμένοις, to be sur-rounded : 4, 127. 7, 81.

κύκλωσις, 4, 35. οἱ Ἀθηναῖοι ἐπισπόμενοι περίοδον μὲν αὐτῶν καὶ κύκλωσιν χωρίου ἰσχύϊ οὐκ εἶχον, a surrounding, Matth. Gr. Gr. 569.

κῦμα, 3, 89. a wave.

κυματόω, 3, 89. κυματωθεῖσα, to roll high (as the sea.)

κυπαρίσσινος, 2, 34. made of cypress-wood.

κύριος, 5, 63. μὴ κύριον εἶναι, not to be competent, 47. valid, 34. valid, capable, 30. κύριον εἶναι, to be valid, rati-fied, to stand good : 8, 5. having authority : 2, 62. κυ-ριωτάτους, masters entirely, 5, 53. τοῦ ἱεροῦ : 8, 51. ἐστρά-τηγει δὲ καὶ κύριος ἦν αὐτὸς πράσσων ταῦτα, Matth. Gr. Gr. 837.

κῦρος, 5, 38. ἅπαν τὸ κῦρος ἔχουσι, to exercise complete sovereignty in the state, to posess undivided sway.

κυρόω, 4, 125. κυρωθέν, what had been fixed, de-termined : 8, 70.

κύρωσις, 6, 103. a ratifica-tion.

κυφόω, 4,125. κυφωθὲν, bent, curved.

κώλυμα, 5, 30. a hindrance, an obstacle, impediment: 4, 67.: 1, 16. ἐπεγίγνετο δὲ ἄλλοις τε ἄλλοθι κωλύματα μὴ αὐξηθῆναι, the infinitive being often joined with the neuter article and thus standing as a substantive, frequently the article is omitted as in this place, where the genitive of the art. is wanting, *see* Matth. Gr. Gr. 819.: 7, 53.

κωλύμη, 1, 92. ἐπὶ κωλύμῃ, for the purpose of hindrance: 4, 63. hindrance, impediment.

κωλυτὴς, 3, 23. a hinderer, an obstructor: 5, 9. 8, 50.

κωλύω, 7, 70. κωλῦσαι αὐτοὺς διαφυγεῖν, to prevent their escape, 7, 4. 8, 40.: 8, 18. κωλυόντων, let them forbid:

1, 142. 7, 22. κωλύειν, to prevent, 36. κωλύσειν, 63. κωλύσοντες, 1, 142. κωλύσονται: 7, 24. ἐκώλυον, to prohibit, prevent, 41.: 1, 27. κωλύοιντο, to be hindered: 7, 56. κωλύσωσι: 2, 8. 4, 14. κεκωλύσθαι, to be obstructed, 1, 129. κεκωλύσθω, to be impeded: 2, 37. κεκώλυται, to be debarred from (state-affairs,) disqualified for: 3, 13. κωλυθέντων, to be prevented.

κώμη, 4, 42. 70. 124. a village: 1, 5. κατὰ κώμας, after the manner of villages, in a wandering and scattered manner, 10. in districts, villages.

κώπη, 6, 34. κώπαις χρήσαιντο, to ply the oar.

κωπήρης, 4, 118. κωπήρει πλοίῳ, an oared cutter,

Λ.

Λαγχάνω, 5, 21. ἔλαχον, to fall to the lot, 35. to obtain by lot: 8, 30. λαχόντες, to cast lots: 2, 44. 3, 50.

λάθρα, 4, 39. secretly.

λαμβάνω, 7, 25. λαμβάνουσι, to take, 21. ἀπόπειραν λαμβάνειν ναυμαχίας, to make trial of, to try, venture a sea-fight: 6, 27. πρᾶγμα μειζόνως ἐλάμβανον, to take a thing too seriously, 53. πάντα ὑπόπτως, to view, take every thing suspiciously, to see every

thing in a suspicious light: 4, 115. λαβὸν μεῖζον ἄχθος, to receive too great weight, 7, 21. ἐν δεξίᾳ τὴν Σικελίαν λαβόντες, to keep, hold, to keep Sicily on the right, 4, 69. λαβεῖν τὴν πόλιν, to take, 2, 42, λαβόντες for ὑπολαβόντες; to conceive, think, (so in English, I take it to be,) 3, 38. τὸ δρασθὲν πιστότερον ὄψει λαβόντες, to be assured of something done by the eye-sight, to place more confi-

11

dence in the sight of any thing, in what one sees, to believe what is done from the evidence of the eyes, 6, 60. τὴν αἰτίαν, to be accused: 3, 24. λαβόμενοι τῶν ὁρῶν, to gain the mountains : 5, 52. λάβωσι, to seize, lay hold of : 6, 10. εἰ δίχα ἡμῶν τὴν δύναμιν λάβοιεν, to find, catch our strength, power divided, distracted in two parts, split : 4, 34. εἰληφότες, to assume, take up, 1, 77. εἰλήφατε, to acquire, 3, 82. εἰλήφει, to take (prisoner,) 2, 88. εἰλήφεσαν τὴν ἀξίωσιν, to conceive an opinion : 3, 24. ἐλήφθη, to be seized, taken prisoner, 1, 23. ληφθεῖσαι, 2, 5. : 3, 56. λήψεσθε τὸ δίκαιον, to understand justice, 8, 1. to possess oneself of : 8, 20. ἐλάμβανε, 64. : 4, 106. τὴν Ἡιόνα παρὰ νύκτα ἐγένετο λαβεῖν, *per unam noctem stetit quominus occuparet*, an instance of the use of the infin. after verbs, which imply any object whatever, and require the addition of this object or its effect by means of another verb, Matth. Gr. Gr. 796.

λαμπὰς, 3, 24. a torch.

λαμπρὸς, 7, 44. shining, bright : 6, 54. Ἁρμοδίου, conspicuous, distinguished (for beauty,) handsome : 7, 55. signal, manifest : 1, 138. λαμπρότατος, most illustrious.

λαμπρότης, 4, 62. splendor : 7, 75. ἄλλως τε καὶ ἀπὸ οἵας λαμπρότητος—ἐς οἵαν τελευτὴν ἀφῖκτο, especially (when they reflected) from what a splendid condition to what a (miserable) end they had come : 6, 16. ἐν λαμπρότητι προέσχον, to excel, surpass in the lustre (of any thing, quality, endowment :) 2, 64. ἡ παραύτικα, lustre for the present.

λαμπρύνω, 6, 16. λαμπρύνομαι, to be splendid, magnificent, to display magnificence.

λαμπρῶς, 2, 7. clearly, beyond doubt, dispute, 45. manifestly, 7, 71. 8, 67.

λανθάνω, 1, 69. to escape observation : 7, 43. λαθεῖν προσελθόντας, to approach unperceived, 48. to escape notice, observation, 8, 17. λαθόντες, secretly, 3, 4. τὸ ναυτικὸν, unperceived by the fleet: 1, 37. λάθωσι, to escape notice : 2, 76. ἐλάνθανον τοὺς ἔξω : 8, 10. λήσωσι, to elude, 7, 15. : 8, 10. : 4, 133. ἔλαθεν ἀφθέντα πάντα καὶ καταφλεχθέντα, with some verbs, (and among the rest λανθάνω,) which express only a circumstance or accessary definition of an action, the verb, of which they express a circumstance, is put in the participle, ‘ every thing was burnt without being perceived by any one,’ Matth. Gr. Gr. 840.

λάρναξ, 2, 34. a chest.

λαχανισμὸς, 3, 111. a gathering of herbs.

λέβης, 4, 100. a cauldron.

λέγω, 3, 38. τῷ λέγειν πιστεύσας, to confide in eloquence, trust in one's powers of speech, 42. ἀπὸ τοῦ ἴσου ἀμεινον λέγειν, in a fair, equal debate to have the better of the argument, *fari dicendi potestate facta*: 6, 29. ἔλεγον, to advise, move, propose : 6, 31. ἐλέχθησαν ἀπὸ τῶν ἄλλων, to be said, spoken by any one, 2, 48. : 5, 86. λεχθησόμενον, about to be said : 7, 68. τὸ λεγόμενον, that, which is said : 3, 53. λελέξεται, is about to be spoken : 4, 70. λέγων ἐν ἐλπίδι εἶναι ἀναλαβεῖν Νισαίαν, instead of which it was previously expressed, οἰόμενος τὴν Ν. ἔτι καταλήψεσθαι ἀνέλωτον, an instance of the interchange of tenses, the infin. of the aor. is often put, where we should have expected the infin. of the fut., but in the same manner as we must often render this infin. aor. by the present, Matth. Gr. Gr. 740.

λεία, 2, 97. 3, 96. 5, 115. plunder : 7, 30. booty, prey, plunder.

λειποστρατία, θ, 76. *desertæ militiæ crimen*, not paying due military service.

λειποστράτιον, 1, 99. a desertion of an expedition.

λειποψυχέω, 4, 12. ἐλειποψύχησε, to faint away.

λείπω, to leave, 5, 69. λείπεσθαι μηδενός, to be behind no one : 1, 34. λειπομένοις, to

be left behind, to remain, 131. τοῦ κήρυκος μὴ λείπεσθαι, not to remain behind, i. e. to return with the herald : 2, 87. λείπεσθαι, to be inferior, 2, 85. : 1, 10. λειπομένην, to come short, to be less, 2, 12. τοῖς λειπομένοις, the remainder, 41, the survivors, 6, 72. λειπόμενος οὐδενὸς ξύνεσιν, inferior to none in wisdom : 1, 10. λειφθείη, to remain : 5, 105. λελείψεσθαι τῆς εὐμενείας, to be deficient in, to have short measure of the divine goodwill : 3, 11. ἐλείφθημεν, to be left, suffered to remain : 6, 72. τοσούτου γε λειφθῆναι ὅσον εἰκὸς εἶναι, to be so much inferior, as was to be supposed : 7, 70. λείπεσθαι τῆς ἄλλης τέχνης, to be out-done by the skill : 8, 81.

λέπας, 7, 78. a precipitous height.

λεπτάγεως, 1, 2. sterile in soil, unproductive.

λεπτός, 7, 36. weak, slender, 40. light : 2, 49. τῶν πάνυ λεπτῶν, the lightest clothing, thinnest garments.

λεύω, 5, 60. to stone a criminal (to death.)

λήγω, 5, 81. λήγοντος, to cease : 7, 6. ἔληγον, to cease, stop.

λήθη, 2, 41. 49. obliviousness, forgetfulness, inability to recollect, 44. ἰδίᾳ τε γὰρ τῶν οὐκ ὄντων λήθη οἱ ἐπιγιγνόμενοί (sc. παῖδές) τισιν ἔσονται, the subst. in the predicate is often different in gender and number from the subject, Matth. Gr. Gr. 444.

λήίζω, 1, 5. 24. ἐληίζοντο, to plunder, rob, 3, 85. 5, 56.

λῆρ, 5, 79. Dor. for θέλων, see Bekker's note.

λῃστεία, 1, 5. ἀπὸ τῆς παλαιᾶς λῃστείας, from the ancient piratical mode of life, 11. piracy: 4, 41. pillage: 7, 27. booty: 8, 40. ravages.

λῃστεύω, 4, 66. to rob, 76. 5, 14. 7, 18. : 4, 2. ἐλῃστεύοντο ὑπὸ τῶν φυγάδων, to be plundered.

λῃστής, 1, 5. a pirate, 2, 32. 3, 51. 4, 53. 67. : 7, 26. a robber : 6, 4.

λῃστικὸς, 1, 4. τὸ λῃστικὸν, piracy, 13. : 2, 69. : 1, 10. λῃστικώτερον, rather after the piratical fashion.

λῃστρικὸς, 4, 9. piratical.

λῆψις, 4, 114. a seizure : 5, 110. a capture, 7, 24.

λίαν, 7, 5. completely, entirely.

λίθινος, 3, 68. of stone, 5, 47. 6, 27.

λιθοβόλος, 6, 69. a stone-thrower.

λιθολόγος, 7, 43. a stone-cutter, mason.

λίθος, 1, 93. 2, 4. λίθοις τε καὶ κεράμῳ βάλλειν, to strike with, to throw stones and tiles : 2, 75. 4, 112. 7, 5.

λιθουργὸς, 4, 69. a stone-mason, 5, 82. : 4, 4. λιθουργὰ, tools or instruments for cutting stone.

λιθοφορία, 6, 98. λιθοφορεῖν

τε καὶ ἀποσκίδνασθαι, to carry, bear stones.

λιμὴν, a port, harbour, 1, 46. 93. 5, 2. 3. 7, 22. 8, 10.

λίμνη, 1, 46. a lake, 4, 103.

λιμνώδης, 5, 7. of or belonging to a lake, marsh.

λιμὸς, 1, 23, a famine, 126. ἀπέθνησκον ὑπὸ τοῦ λιμοῦ, to die from hunger : 4, 40.

λίνου, 4, 25. λίνου σπέρμα, linseed.

λινοῦς χιτῶνας, 1, 6. linen garments.

λίπα, 1, 6. ointment.

λογάδην, 4, 4. by troops in turn.

λογὰς, 1, 62. 2, 5. picked, selected : 4, 125. 5, 60. ἀφ᾽ ἑκάστων.

λογίζομαι, 3, 82. ἐλογίζετο τὸ ἀσφαλὲς, to reckon up, value : 1, 76. λογιζόμενοι, to calculate, reckon : 5, 87. λογιούμενος, to reckon up : 6, 31. ἐλογίσατο, to compute : 7, 73. λογιζομένοις ταῦτα, to reason, consider : 6, 36. λογίζεσθε τὰ εἰκότα, to calculate probabilities, to consider what is likely, to be expected, fit, proper to be done.

λογισμὸς, 2, 40. consideration, turning over in thought, thinking : 4, 92. debate, nice poising, just calculation : 6, 34. καταστήσαιμεν ἐς λογισμὸν, to reduce or bring to reflection : 2. 11. λογισμῷ χρώμενοι, to employ consideration, to consider : 5, 68.

λογογράφος, 1, 21. an historian, a compiler.

λογοποιέω, 6, 38. to invent, forge, fabricate reports, ἐνθένδε ἄνδρες οὔτε ὄντα οὔτε ἂν γενόμενα λογοποιοῦσιν, an example of the participle with ἄν, to which it gives the sense of the finite mood, Matth. Gr. Gr. 924.

λόγος, 1, 36. ἐπὶ τὸν ἄλλον λόγον ἰέναι, to proceed to the rest of the speech, 76. τῷ δικαίῳ λόγῳ νῦν χρῆσθε, now to make use of the argument of justice : 1, 102. ἐπὶ βελτίονι λόγῳ, for any favourable reason, with the best meaning : 1, 73. reputation, honour : 3, 4. λόγους προσέφερον τοῖς στρατηγοῖς, to ask a parley of the generals, send a flag of truce, request a conference: 1, 140. πολέμῳ μᾶλλον ἢ λόγοις, by war rather than by arguments: 5, 112. ἐκ τῶν λόγων, after or from the conference : 5, 6. τοῦ ξύμπαντος λόγου, roll, muster-roll, catalogue: 6, 61. counsel, design, purpose : 1, 11. a report, story, 10. report, fame : 2, 3. δέξασθαι λόγους, to accept conditions : 8, 94.

λοιδορέω, 3, 62. to rail at.

λοιδορία, 2, 84. reviling, abuse.

λοιμὸς, 2, 54. a plague, pestilence, 47.

λοιμώδης, 1, 23. pestilential.

λοιπὸς, 1, 74. τὸ λοιπὸν, for the future : 3, 44. 4, 93. 5, 9. the rest, 7, 4. 7. 8, 67.

λόφος, 3, 97. 4, 124. 5, 66. προεληλυθότας ἀπὸ τοῦ λόφου, to

have arrived before them from the hill, 58. 65. 8, 33. : 3, 112. ἐστὸν δὲ δύο λόφω ἡ Ἰδομένη ὑψηλὼ, where the verb is governed not by its proper subject, but by the subst. predicate, Matth. Gr. Gr. 441.

λοχαγὸς, 5, 66. a colonel of a regiment.

λοχάω, 3, 94. λοχήσαντες, to lie in ambush.

λοχίζω, 5, 115. λοχισθέντες, to be beset by an ambush, 107. λοχίζει, to station in ambush.

λοχμώδης, 3, 107. bushy, thick-set with brushwood.

λόχος, 1, 20. a troop, regiment, 4, 43. 91. 5, 67.

λὺγξ, 2, 49. κενὴ, (opp. to πλήρης, Schol.) singultus.

λυμαίνομαι, 5, 103. to enfeeble, enervate, corrupt, 115.

λυπέω, 6, 66. λυπήσειν, to harrass, annoy : 4, 53. ἐλύπουν, to harrass, 8, 1. ἐλύπει, grieved, 6, 57. λυπήσαντα, to injure, offend : 2, 61. τὸ λυποῦν, distress, 64. λυποῦνται γνώμῃ πρὸς τὰς ξυμφορὰς, to be distressed in mind on account of misfortunes: 4, 115. ἐλύπησε, to grieve, concern.

λύπη, 7, 75. καθίστατο ἐς λύπην, to be grieved, affected with grief, to fall into grief: 6, 59. ἐρωτικὴν, indignation, anger.

λυπηρὸς, burdensome, 2, 64. : 6, 18. giving trouble, annoyance, hindering : 2, 37. painful, disagreeable : 6, 16.

odious, obnoxious, envied, occasioning or procuring envy: 7, 75. λυπηρότεροι : 1, 76.

λυσιτελοῦν, τὸ, 6, 85. profit, interest.

λύτρον, 6, 5. a ransom, redemption-money, the price of redemption.

λύχνον, 4, 133. τινὰ ἥμμενον, a lighted lamp.

λύω, 6, 14. τοὺς νόμους, to break the laws, 1, 132. τὰς ἐπιστολὰς, to break the seal of a letter : 6, 66. ἔλυσαν γέφυραν, to break down, 8,

15. to abrogate : 7, 18. λελυκέναι τὰς σπονδὰς, to infringe, break, 2, 7. λελυμένων τῶν σπονδῶν, the truce being broken, 1, 67. λελυκότες σπονδὰς, 78. 5, 61. : 5, 43. λῦσαι, to dissolve, break : 1, 78. τὰ διάφορα λύεσθαι, to settle the difference.

λωφάω, 2, 49. λωφήσαντα· μετὰ ταῦτα, to cease directly, instantly : 6, 12. λελωφήκαμεν, to be recovered : 7, 77.

λώφησις, 4, 81. τοῦ πολέμου, a lightening (of a burden,) a relief, shifting off.

M.

Μάθημα, 2, 39. learning, instruction, information.

μάθησις, 1, 68. μάθησιν ποιεῖσθαι, to receive information, to be instructed, Matth. Gr. Gr. 590.

μακαρίζω, 2, 51. ἐμακαρίζοντο, to be congratulated : 5, 105. μακαρίζοντες, to bless (jeeringly.)

μακρηγορέω, 1, 68. to make a long harangue : 4, 59. μακρηγοροίη, to discourse largely : 2, 36. to enlarge, dilate, speak at length, to be prolix.

μακρὸς, 2, 13. τὸ μεταξὺ τοῦ τε μακροῦ, the part between the long wall: 7, 13. ἁρπαγὴν, plunder or forage at a distance, afar off : 3, 13. μακρὰν (sc. ὁδὸν) ἀπεῖναι, to be a long way off, at a great distance : 1, 1. ἐπὶ μακρότατον σκοπεῖν, to

look as far back as possible, to scrutinize the most ancient times, 3, 39. 4, 41. : 6, 31. ἐς τὰ μακρότατα, 1, 1.

μάλα, 4, 118. (αὐτίκα,) immediately.

μαλακία, 1, 122. 2, 40. 61. 5, 7. 75. cowardice, effeminacy, indisposition to business.

μαλακίζομαι, 6, 29. to be mollified, softened, to relent: 5, 9. μαλακισθῆτε, to be weak, wanting in resolution, 72. 3, 37. 40. μαλακισθέντες, 7, 68. μαλακισθῆναι, 2, 42. ἐμαλακίσθη: 8, 29.

μαλακὸς, 6, 13. faint-hearted, cowardly: 3, 45. μαλακωτέρας ζημίας, lighter : 8, 29. moderate.

μαλακωτέρως, 8, 50. more gently, moderately.

μάλιστα, 3, 30. τυγχάνει μάλιστα οὖσα, to be chiefly, chiefly to be : 4, 81. in a great measure: 1, 17. mostly, for the most part, 18. about, nearly, (with numbers :) 5, 86. most : 2, 47. αὐτοὶ μάλιστα ἔθνησκον, ὅσῳ καὶ μάλιστα προσῄεσαν, 8, 84. ὅσῳ μαλίστα καὶ ἐλεύθεροι ἦσαν οἱ ναῦται, τοσούτῳ καὶ θρασύτατα προσπεσόντες τὸν μισθὸν ἀπῄτουν, Matth. Gr. Gr. 668. : πολλῷ μάλιστα, Matth. 665. : 7, 42. μάλιστα δεινότατος, Matth. 667.

μᾶλλον, 5, 44. the more : 1, 68. rather, 4, 64. : 3, 23. ἐγένετο μᾶλλον διὰ τοῦ χειμῶνος τὸ μέγεθος, to be effected chiefly through the violence of the storm : 5, 44. πρὸς δὲ τοὺς Ἀθηναίους μᾶλλον τὴν γνώμην εἶχον, to entertain a preference for the Athenians : 6, 70. : 3, 36. ὠμὸν τὸ βούλευμα πόλιν ὅλην διαφθεῖραι μᾶλλον ἢ οὐ τοὺς αἰτίους, an instance of a rare construction of the comparative μᾶλλον, Matth. Gr. Gr. 6, 60.

μανθάνω, 7, 8. μαθόντας τὴν αὐτοῦ γνώμην, to learn, to have information of, 1, 42. μαθὼν, 40. μαθεῖν, 4, 126. : 6, 39. 7, 11.

μανιώδης, 4, 39. mad, unreasonable.

μαντεῖον, 1, 28. 126. the oracle, 25. κατὰ τὸ μαντεῖον, according to the oracle.

μαντεύομαι, 5, 18. to consult an oracle.

μάντις, 3, 20. ἀνδρὸς μάντεως, a soothsayer : 8, 1. μάντεσι.

μαντικός, 5, 103. μαντικὴν (τέχνην) the prophetic art.

μαραίνω, 2, 49. ἐμαραίνετο, to waste, pine away.

μάρτυρ, 1, 37. 4, 28. a witness : 1, 78. θεοὺς μάρτυρας ποιούμενοι, to call the gods to witness, 73. : 4, 87. μάρτυρας ποιήσομαι, to attest : 2, 71.

μαρτύριον, 1, 73. a witnessing, protestation, 33. μετ᾽ ἀειμνήστου μαρτυρίου, a favour granted under circumstances, which are a pledge of its never being forgotten : 3, 53. μαρτύρια, witnesses, 11. μαρτυρίῳ ἐχρῶντο, to use an argument, testimony, example, to cite or quote a proof, to instance : 1, 8. Κάρες καὶ Φοίνικες τὰς πλείστας τῶν νήσων ᾤκησαν· μαρτύριον δὲ, Δήλου γὰρ καθαιρομένης κ. τ. λ. 'and the following is a proof of this.' (This is a peculiar mode of construction, that the preposition is intimated only by the principal word, which is thus followed by γὰρ, Matth. Gr. Gr. 950.)

μαρτύρομαι, 6, 80. to protest.

μάσσω, 4, 16. μεμαγμένον, to be pounded, ground.

μαστιγοφόρος, 4, 47. a whipbearer, bedell.

μαχαιροφόρος, 7, 27. Θρᾳκῶν, dirk-bearing, sword-bearers, carrying or armed with swords : 2, 96.

μάχη, 4, 92. 5, 65. ὡς ἐς μάχην, as for battle : 5, 10. 51. : 3, 67. ἐκ μάχης, after a battle : 5, 56. μάχη ἐκ παρασκευῆς, a pitched battle, 73. : 4, 34.

μάχιμος, 1, 10. fighting, warlike, 4, 125. ἀνθρώπων: 6, 23. πλήν γε πρὸς τὸ μάχιμον, embattled, fit for service in the field, fighting, troops for battle : 2, 81. μαχιμώτατοι, 6, 90.

μάχομαι, 4, 96. τὸ μαχόμενον, the part still in action : 7, 5. ἐμάχοντο, to fight, 13. μαχεῖσθαι, 43. διὰ παντὸς τοῦ μήπω μεμαχημένον ἐναντίων διελθεῖν, to go through the whole of the enemy as yet unengaged, who had not yet fought with them : 5, 66. ὡς ἔμελλον μαχεῖσθαι, as if they were about to fight, the Doric fut. for μαχέεσθαι, Matth. Gr. Gr. 221. : 5, 34. μαχεσαμένους : 6, 78. ἐν Θυμηθεῖτώ σὺ περὶ τῆς ἐμῆς—μαχούμενος, an instance of a verb of consideration taking the participle, Matth. 829.

μεγαλύνω, 5, 98. μεγαλύνετε, to aggravate, increase : 6, 28. ἐμεγάλυνον, to magnify, exaggerate : 8, 81.

μέγας, 5, 32. 44. great, 29. important : 3, 36. ὠμὸν καὶ μέγα, immane, savage and monstrous : 3, 63. καὶ τὸ μέγιστον, and what is of most consequence, 4, 70. τὸ δὲ μέγιστον, and what was his greatest object, chief view, 7, 24. μέγιστον δὲ, very greatly, 1, 142. Matth. Gr. Gr. 411. : 7, 44. : 1, 10. μεγίστας, the greatest in number, 2, 49. 6, 54. : 8, 88. : 1, 68. προ-

σήπει ἡμᾶς οὐχ ἥκιστα εἰπεῖν, ὅσῳ καὶ μέγιστα ἐγκλήματα ἔχομεν, we have the greatest right to speak in proportion as we have the greatest charges to answer to, two superl. compared, where τοσούτῳ is dropped very often, if ὅσῳ follows in the second proposition, Matth. 667. see also 711.

μέγεθος, 1, 2. greatness, magnitude: 7, 30. magnitude, extent, 58. : 72. ὑπὸ μεγέθους, from or on account of : 2, 38. 6, 1. 15. : 2, 7. κατὰ μέγεθος, in proportion to the size : 7, 55. μεγέθη : 2, 62. περὶ μεγέθους ἐς τὴν ἀρχὴν, greatness of means for acquiring empire, greatness as to empire, of empire : 4, 126.

μεθίστημι, 1, 6. 130. μετέστη, to go to war, change sides, 107. μετέστησαν, 5, 29. μεταστῆναι: 2, 67. τῆς ξυμμαχίας μεταστάντα, to recede from or desert an alliance, 1, 35. to oppose as an enemy, 5, 111.: 1, 79. μεταστησάμενοι, to exclude, put out : 4, 57. μεταστῆναι, to transplant : 8, 15. μεθεστηκυίας, to revolt : 6, 19. μεταστήσειν, to make (any one) change his purpose, recall his vote : 8, 76.

μεθόριος, 2, 27. γῆ, land situate between two countries, on the borders between: 4, 56. 100. 5, 41. 54.: 8, 10. μεθόρια, confines, 2, 18.

μεθορμίζω, 6, 88. μεθορμισάμενοι, *statione mutata se conferre*, to change station, to remove from one harbour to another.

μειζόνως, 4, 19. ἐχθροὺς, greatly their enemies: 6, 27.

μείζων, 1, 2. great, 32. powerful: 3, 37. 6, 54. μῆκος, an additional, enlarged extent, 15. μείζοσιν ἢ κατὰ τὴν οὐσίαν, too great for, in proportion to, the estate, property: 4, 6. 119. 6, 16. 8, 74. : 7, 75. μείζω ἢ κατὰ δάκρυα τὰ μὲν πεπονθότας ἤδη, τὰ δὲ μέλλοντας, Matth. Gr. Gr. 654.

μελετάω, 2, 86. μελετῶντες: 1, 142. μελετῆσαι, to practise, 80. μελετήσομεν, to apply attention to an object: 6, 72. μεμελετωμένην, *excultam*, improved by practice: 1, 142. ἐν τῷ μὴ μελετῶντι ἀξυνετώτεροι ἔσονται, through want of practice, a participle with the art. used as a subst., Matth. Gr. Gr. 876.

μελέτη, 1, 18. 85. discipline, 18. ποιούμενοι μελέτας, to practise, make trials: 2, 39. μελέταις τῶν πολεμικῶν, study of warlike affairs: 6, 72. exercise, drilling: 1, 138. deliberation.

μελιτόω, 4, 26. μεμελιτωμένην, honied.

μέλλησις, 7, 49. loitering, dilatoriness: 1, 69. delay, 125. : 2, 18. εἰ μὴ διὰ τὴν μέλλησιν, but for the loitering delay: 5, 82. ; 66. διὰ βρα-

χείας μελλήσεως, after a short delay: 3, 12. εἰ τῳ δοκοῦμεν ἀδικεῖν προαποστάντες διὰ τὴν ἐκείνων μέλλησιν τῶν εἰς ἡμᾶς δεινῶν, an instance of the use of the gen., when one subst. governs two different genitives in different relations, Matth. Gr. Gr. 450. 844.

μελλητὴς, 1, 70. a loiterer, lingerer, tarrier.

μέλλω, 1, 42. τὸ μέλλον τοῦ πολέμου, the event of the war, 84. the participle has the sense of a subst. communicated to it by the article, Matth. Gr. Gr. 394. : 6, 74. ξυνειδὼς τὸ μέλλον, what was about to take place, 4, 71. τὸ μέλλον, the event : 7, 20. ὥσπερ ἔμελλον, as they had intended, resolved : 5, 9. μέλλετε, to be going to, 15. 8, 23. ἐμέλλησεν : 2, 8. 4, 111.

μεμπτὸς, 6, 13. that, which is found fault with, objected to : 7, 15. ὑμῖν μὴ μεμπτῶν γεγενημένων, who are not to blame, undeserving of blame from any one: 2, 61. μεμπτότερος, more blameable: 3, 57.

μέμφομαι, 1, 84. μεμφόμενοι, to censure, 8, 3. to complain: 3, 61. ἐμέμψατο: 3, 37. μέμψασθαι τοῦ καλῶς εἰπόντος, to censure, carp at, criticise a good speaker : 1, 143. ἐμεμψάμην, to reprehend : 4, 85. ; 61. οὐ τοῖς ἄρχειν βουλομένοις μέμφομαι, ἀλλὰ τοῖς ὑπακούειν ἑτοιμοτέροις οὖσιν.

μενετέον, 2, 88. in the for-

mation of the tenses, generally η and ε in the fut. and
perf. are frequently interchanged, μενετέον is from με-
μένηται, Matth. Gr. Gr. 229.

μενετὸς, 1, 142. which would
admit of delay, can wait.

μέντοι, 6, 9. ἐμοὶ μέντοι δοκεῖ,
I, however, am of opinion :
1, 66. οὐ μέντοι γέ πω, however
not yet : 7, 45. ὅπλα μέντοι
ἔτι πλείω, however, nevertheless, yet : 6, 25. ὅσα μέντοι
ἤδη, however, at present, at
the moment : 8, 87.

μένω, 5, 10. to stand, wait :
2, 84. μένειν τὴν τάξιν, to maintain one's position, order :
1, 71. μενοῦμεν, to remain : 2,
20. μεῖναι, to stay : 4, 10. : 5,
65. μείνας περὶ τὸ ὕδωρ, to wait
near the water : 7, 49. ἔμενον :
5, 40. μείνειαν, to stand, continue in force, remain valid,
hold good : 8, 72. : 1, 65.
καὶ αὐτὸς ἤθελε τῶν μενόντων
εἶναι, the gen. is here put partitivé, ' one of those, who remained at home,' this is an
instance with a verb and
with the verb εἶναι, Matth.
Gr. Gr. 500.

μέρος, 4, 26. 5, 56. 7, 11. a
part, 51. οὐ πολλοῦ, a small
detachment : 2, 10. τὰ δύο
μέρη, two thirds : 4, 11. ἐν τῷ
μέρει, in turn : 2, 64. τι, in
some measure, (κατὰ sc. :) 1,
74. τὸ μέρος, in part : 6, 39.
κατὰ μέρη, individually, separately, in parts : 8, 93.

μεσημβρία, 2, 28. μετὰ μεσημ-

βρίαν, in the afternoon : 6,
100.

μεσημβρινός, 6, 2. τὰ μεσημ-
βρινὰ, the southern parts (of
an island.)

μεσόγεια, 1, 100. ἐς μεσόγειαν,
into the interior, 3, 95. : 1,
120. the midland territory.

μέσος, 5, 9. middle, 59. ἐν
μέσῳ, in the middle, 1, 62. ἐν
μέσῳ ποιέω, to surround (the
enemy :) 7, 70. τὸ μέσον, the
centre, 1, 10. the mean : 4,
83. μέσῳ δικαστῇ, an umpire :
6, 54. μέσος πολίτης, a citizen
of middle rank : 4, 20. διὰ μέσου γενόμενον, coming in the
way : 8, 75. : 3, 80. μέσου
ἡμέρας, where an adj. of three
terminations occurs as common, Matth. Gr. Gr. 150.

μεσόω, 5, 20. μεσοῦσι, to be
in the middle : 6, 30. θέρους
μεσοῦντος, at midsummer, 5,
57. in the middle of summer.

μέσως, 2, 60. moderately,
μετρίως, Schol.

μετὰ, 1, 18. 5, 52. 58. in
company with, along with :
3, 2. Λακεδαιμονίων, in conjunction with, with the
assistance of, 1, 126. : 1, 17.
μετὰ τὴν κτίσιν, after, 30. τὴν
ναυμαχίαν, after the sea-fight,
69. : 7, 58. μετ' αὐτοὺς οἰκοῦντες, after, i. e. next to, beyond them : 6, 38. μετὰ κινδύνων, during the sense of
dangers, 3, 56. in spite of
danger : 6, 85. μετὰ καιροῦ,
i. q. πρὸς τὸν καιρόν : 5, 16.
μετὰ δώρων, by bribery, for a

consideration : 5, 55. μεθ'
ὅπλων, in arms : 3, 26. μετὰ
τὴν δευτέραν, after or next to
(in degree:) 1, 70. μετὰ
πόνων, with labour and difficulty : 1, 69. μετὰ ὕστερον,
afterwards : 1, 120. μετὰ
δέους, through fear : 7, 57.
μετὰ μισθοῦ, with pay, i. e.
for pay, ἀντί: 6, 72. μετὰ τοῦ
πιστοῦ τῆς ἐπιστήμης, through
confidence in : 6, 55. πρῶτος
μετὰ τὸν πατέρα, first after or
next to: 6, 13. μετὰ σφῶν
αὐτῶν, with or by themselves,
i. e. without the intervention
of others : 8, 27. : 1, 138.
μετὰ χεῖρας ἔχειν, the prep.
has here, which is a rare
sense, that of 'in,' hence μ·
ταχειρίζεσθαι, Matth. Gr. Gr.
905. : 7, 33. οὗτοι δ' οὐδὲ μεθ'
ἑτέρων ἦσαν, to be on any
one's side, Matth. 904.

μεταβάλλω, 2, 16. to change,
1, 71. 123. τὸ ἦθος, to change
the practice.

μεταβολή, 1, 2. 6, 77. δε-
σπότεω, a change of master,
59. a revolution, 17. 20. : 7,
76. a change, reverse of
fortune, 55. change, innovation : 2, 42. 48. : 6, 31. ἐπὶ
μεταβολῇ, exchange, com-
merce, traffic.

μεταγιγνώσκω, 6, 17. μεταγι-
γνώσκητε, to repeal, revoke,
change one's mind on any
subject and adopt another
course : 3, 48. ὡς οὐκ ἔσται
μεταγνῶναι, that there will be
no room for repentance, 40.
58. : 6, 40. μεταγνόντες, to

change one's purpose, to
repent : 4, 92. μεταγνῶναι, to
maintain a different opinion:
1, 44. οἱ Ἀθηναῖοι μετέγνωσαν
Κερκυραίοις ξυμμαχίαν μὲν μὴ
ποιήσεσθαι, Matth. Gr. Gr.
804.

μεταγράφω, 1, 132. μεταγρά-
ψαι, to re-write, or change
in a letter: 4, 50. μεταγραψά-
μενοι, to translate.

μεταδίδωμι, 1, 39. μεταδώσετε,
to impart, share with, (cum
gen. :) 6, 39. μεταδίδωσι.

μετάθεσις, 5, 29. a change,
an alteration.

μετακαλέω, 8, 11. to recall.

μετακινητός, open to objection, susceptible of alteration,
abolition.

μεταλαμβάνω, 4, 73. μεταλα-
βόντες, to take up, seize, 1,
39. to share, partake: 6, 87.
μεταλάβετε, to partake of: 1,
120. μεταλαμβάνω τὸν πόλεμον
ἀντ' εἰρήνης, to exchange war
for peace : 6, 18. μεταλήψεσθε
ἐς τὰ ὅμοιον, to exchange to a
similarity, to adopt in exchange (for one's own) similar —: 3, 55. πολιτείας μετέλα-
βεν, to be enrolled among
the number of the citizens.

μέταλλον, 1, 100. a mine:
2, 55.

μεταμέλεια, 1, 34. 3, 37. repentance, change of mind.

μεταμέλω, μεταμέλομαι, 3, 4.
μετέμελεν, who had repented :
4, 29. μετεμέλοντο, 5, 14. 35. :
2, 61. μεταμέλειν.

μετάμελος, 7, 55. τῆς στρα-
τίας, regret on account of the

11

expedition, Matth. Gr. Gr. 466.

μετανάστασις, 1, 2. a removal, change of abode: 2, 16. οὐ ῥᾳδίως μεταναστάσας ποιεῖσθαι, to change their abodes un-willingly.

μετανίστημι, 1, 12. μετανίστατο, to suffer migrations, transplantations.

μετάνοια, 3, 36. repentance.

μεταξύ, 3, 21. τὸ μεταξύ, an interval: 4, 25. 42. between, 93. μεταξὺ λόφου ὄντος, a hill being in the way, betwixt, 7, 5. : 1, 97. μεταξὺ τοῦδε τοῦ πολέμου καὶ τοῦ Μηδικοῦ, in the interval between this war and the Median war, 118.

μετάπεμπτος, 6, 25. 29. sent for, recalled.

μεταπέμπω, 4, 30. 7, 15. to send for, 18. μεταμέμψωσιν: 1, 128. μεταπεμφθείς, to be sent for: 4, 100. μεταπεμψάμενοι, to send for, summon, 2, 29. μετεπέμψαντο, to send for or in-vite: 8, 5. μεταπέμψεται: 3, 2. μεταπεμπόμενοι ἦσαν, they were sending for: 5, 82.

μεταπίπτω, 8, 68. τὰ τῶν τριακοσίων ἐν ὑστέρῳ μεταπεσόντα, to fall into decay, to decline, to be overturned.

μεταποιέω, 2, 57. μεταποιούμενοι ἀρετῆς, to assist one's virtue, firmness, constancy, to vindicate to oneself the possession of, i. e. to pos-sess.

μεταπύργιον, 3, 22. the in-terval (in a wall) between two towers, the intermediate space.

μετάστασις, 6, 21. a changed state of things, a change (in the condition of a people,) a better change, a change for the better.

μετατάσσω, 1, 95. μετατάξασθαι, to arrange oneself under the banners of.

μετατίθημι, 5, 18. μεταθεῖναι, to alter, change.

μεταφέρω, 1, 134. μετενεγκεῖν, to remove.

μεταχειρίζω, 1, 13. μεταχειρίσαι, to manage, 6, 12. to handle, take in hand, exe-cute, (opp. to βουλεύσασθαι, to design, deliberate upon:) 7, 87. to treat harshly : 4, 18.

μεταχωρέω, 2, 72. μεταχωρήσατε, to remove from (a place) to (another,) to re-tire : 5, 112. μετεχώρησαν, to depart.

μέτειμι, 5, 47. to be amongst, shared: 1, 28. ὡς οὐ μετὸν αὐτοῖς Ἐπιδάμνου, as they had no concern with Epidamnus: 2, 37. μέτεστι πᾶσι τὸ ἴσον, Matth. Gr. Gr. 505.

μετέρχομαι, 1, 34. μετελθεῖν ἐγκλήματα, to meet charges, 124. τῶν ἄλλων τὴν ἐλευθερίαν, to recover, restore the free-dom of the others: 2, 39.

μετέχω, 3, 54. μετέσχομεν, to share, 47. ἀποστάσεως, to par-take of, join in a revolt: 2, 40. μετέχοντα, to participate (in the knowledge of any thing,) 72. μετασχόντες, 6, 40. μετασχεῖν τοῦτο, to share, partake of, 8. 2. : 2, 16. μετεῖχον τῆς χώρας, to share the land: 8, 86. : 2, 16. τῇ οὖν ἐπιπολὺ κατὰ τὴν χώραν αὐτονόμῳ οἰκήσει μετεῖχον οἱ Ἀθηναῖοι, this verb takes the gen. on account of the sense of participation, here τῆς χώρας or τῶν ἀγρῶν is to be understood, Matth. Gr. Gr. 505.

μετεωρίζω, 4, 90. ἐμετεώριζον τὸ ἔρυμα, to give height to: 8, 16. μετεωρισθείς, to sail out into deep water: 1, 12.

μετέωρος, 3, 72. τὰ μετέωρα τῆς πόλεως, the high parts of the city: 4, 44. : 1, 48. 2, 91. 3, 33. 4, 14. 26. 7, 71. at sea, in deep water, 8, 10. : 6, 10. πόλει, out at sea, fluctuating, insecure, in suspense, a precarious condition : 2, 8. in a state of excitation, on tip-toe with excitation, eagerly expecting : 4, 32. μετεωρότατα, the most prominent, high, commanding ground.

μετίημαι, 3, 70. μετιόντες, to tamper with, solicit in an unhandsome manner, 4, 62. to pursue.

μετοικία, 1, 2. a change of abode, a migration.

μετοικίζω, 1, 12. μετῳκίζετο, to suffer changes of abode, to be re-settled.

μέτοικος, 2, 13. a stranger (resident in Athens :) 1, 143. a sojourner.

μετονομάζω, 1, 122. μετωνόμασται, to be named (one thing) instead of (another.)

μετοπώρινος, 7, 87. of or belonging to autumn.

μετόπωρον, 7, 79. τὸ μ., autumn.

μετριάζω, 1, 76. εἴ τι μετριάζομεν, whether we pursue moderate measures.

μέτριος, 1, 6. 77. moderate, mild : 4, 105. ξύμβασιν, moderate, 81. : 6, 88. ὡς ἂν μετριώτατα, as sparingly as possible, 8, 24. with the greatest moderation, 84. : 6, 89. μετριώτερος.

μετριότης, 1, 38. moderation.

μετρίως, 2, 35. τὸ μετρίως εἰπεῖν, to speak impartially (of men,) hit, preserve the true mean in speaking, 65. ἐξηγεῖτο, to govern with moderation : 4, 19.

μέτρον, 3, 20. τῆς πλίνθου, a measure : 8, 95.

μετωπηδὸν, 2, 90. with prows opposed (to the enemy.)

μέτωπον, 3, 21. a front-face.

μέχρι, 5, 1. up to, until, 112. τοῦδε, up to this line, 1, 5. 71. 137. : 1, 74. μέχρι ἡμῶν, up to us, as far as our country, 90. τοσούτου, so long as, 76. οὗ, as long as : 5, 65. λίθου βολᾶς, within stone's throw : 1, 54. νυκτὸς, until the night : 3, 10. donec, whilst, as long as.

μὴ, 1, 38. καὶ, unless, indeed : 5, 12. μὴ καλῶς ἔχειν, not to go well, to be wrong : 3, 6. τῆς μὲν θαλάσσης εἶργον μὴ χρῆσθαι τοὺς Μιτυληναίους, an instance of μὴ used with an infin., instead of the infin. alone after a verb forbidding, Matth. Gr. Gr. 802. : 5, 25. 7, 6. 8, 1. Matth. l. c.

μηδαμοῦ, 1, 35. nowhere.

μηδὲ, 3, 48. ὑμεῖς δὲ γνόντες ἀμείνω τάδε εἶναι καὶ μηδὲ οἴκτῳ πλέον νείμαντες, μήτε ἐπιεικείᾳ κ. τ. λ. here μηδὲ and μήτε correspond, Matth. Gr. Gr. 932.

μηδείς, 4, 61. 5, 47. none : 6, 18. μηδὲν δύνασθαι, to avail, to be capable of : 7, 8.

μηδέτερος, 5, 14. neither.

μηδετέρωσε, 4, 118. with neither.

Μηδίζω, 3, 62. Μηδίσαι, to join the Persians, 34. Μηδισάντων, persons in the interest of the Medes, of the Medish faction.

Μηδισμὸς, 3, 62. ἐς τὸν Μηδισμὸν, as to the alleged crime of joining the Medes or Persians.

μῆκος, 6, 34. πλοῦ, length, 1, 23.

μηκύνω, 1, 102. ἐμηκύνετο, to be prolonged, 141. μηκύνηται, to be lengthened, protracted, 78. μηκυνόμενος : 2, 43. μηκύνοι πρὸς αὐτοὺς ὑμᾶς, (which one) might enlarge, dwell upon to you : 4, 19.

μήκων, 4, 25. a poppy.

μὴν, 2, 65. 5, 19. 8, 81. a month : 6, 8. ὡς ἐς ἑξήκοντα ναῦς μηνὸς μισθὸν, a month's pay for about sixty ships.

μηνοειδὴς, 7, 34. moonshaped, horned : 2, 28. resembling the moon, i. e. being in the form of a crescent, semi-lunar, 76.

μήνυμα, 6, 29. πρὸς τὰ μηνύματα ἀπελογεῖτο, to defend oneself against, reply to the informations : 8, 50. information, discovery.

μηνυτὴς, 3, 2. μηνυταὶ γίγνονται—ὅτι ξυνοικίζουσι—στερήσεσθαι, informers : 1, 132. 6, 53. 8, 50.

μήνυτρον, 6, 27. δημοσίᾳ, a public reward offered for information, detection.

μηνύω, 6, 27. to discover, 53. μεμηνυμένων, to be informed of, i. e. to have an information laid against : 2, 42. μηνύουσα, to discover, disclose, reveal : 1, 20. μεμηνύσθαι, to inform, communicate intelligence, betray as an informer : 8, 39. μηνύσωσι, should announce to : 4, 89.

μήπω, 7, 43. not as yet.

μήτηρ, 1, 9. μητρὸς, a mother.

μητρόπολις, 1, 24. 42. the mother-city, 107. Matth. Gr. Gr. 623.

μηχανάομαι, 7, 25. ἐμηχανῶντο, to contrive stratagems, make inventions : 4, 47. μηχανησαμένων, to obtain by trick : 5, 45. μηχανᾶται, to manœuvre, put plans in motion, 4, 46. 6, 20.

μηχανὴ, 2, 76. 77. 5, 7. a machine : 5, 47. fraudulent evasion, 18, machination, torturing of words, quirk : 3, 51. μηχαναῖς ἐκ θαλάσσης, by means of machines, which act from the sea : 2, 16. μηχαναῖς, engines (for besieging a place.)

μιαίνω, to pollute, stain, 2, 102.

μιμέομαι, 2, 37. μιμούμενοι, to imitate.

μίμησις, 1, 95. an imitation : 7, 63. μιμήσει ἐθαυμάζεσθε, to be admired for the imitation.

μιμνήσκω, 6, 80. μιμνησκόμενος, to call to mind : 2, 8. 5, 66.

Μίνως, 1, 8. Μίνω, the gen. according to the second declension of Μίνως, Matth. Gr. Gr. 114.

μισέομαι, 3, 64. μισοῖντο, to be detested : 8, 83.

μισθοδοσία, 8, 83. giving pay.

μισθὸς, 5, 6. 7, 13. 25. pay, stipend, price : 8, 29.

μισθοφορά, 6, 24. a (soldier's) pay : 8, 45.

μισθοφορητέον, 8, 65. ὡς οὔτε μισθοφορητέον εἴη, that no pay is to be given.

μισθοφόρος, 1, 35. a mercenary, 7, 57. 58. 8, 45. 50.

μισθόω, 4, 76. ἐμισθοῦντο,

to procure mercenaries, 31. μισθωσάμενοι, to hire, 52.

μισθωτὸς, 5, 6. a mercenary.

μῖσος, 1, 103. τὸ σφοδρὸν μῖσος, the bitter hatred : 5, 27. hatred, dislike : 1, 96. τὸ Παυσανίου μῖσος, hatred of or against Pausanias : 4, 128.

μνᾶ, 3, 50. 5, 49. a mina, nearly 3l. 4s. 6¼d.

μνάομαι, 2, 21. μεμνημένοι, to remember : 1, 37. μνησθέντες, to make mention : 2, 45. μνησθῆναί τι, to make any mention : 1, 10. ἐμνήσθη, to record, mention in writing : 3, 90. μνησθήσομαι, to record, commemorate : 2, 8. ἀφ᾿ οὗ Ἕλληνες μέμνηνται, in the memory of the Greeks : 8, 50. μνησθῆναι, 41. μεμνήμεθα : 2, 21. Ἀθηναῖοι μεμνημένοι καὶ Πλαστοάνακτα—ὅτε ἐσβαλὼν τῆς Ἀττικῆς ἐς Ἐλευσῖνα ἀπεχώρησε πάλιν, Matth. Gr. Gr. 832. 563.

μνημεῖον, 1, 138. 5, 11. a monument, sepulchre : 2, 41. μνημεῖα, monuments.

μνήμη, 1, 22. a memory : 8, 8. memory, remembrance : 1, 9. tradition : 2, 54. μνήμην ἐποιοῦντο, to make mention, adapt the mention, to express, 64. the memory (of a thing.)

μνησικακέω, 4, 74. μνησικακήσειν μηδὲν, to pass an act of oblivion, to declare an amnesty.

μνημόσυνον, 5, 11. a memorial.

μνηστήρ, 1, 9. a suitor, lover.

μόγις, 1, 12. with difficulty, much ado: 7, 40.

μοῖρα, 3, 82. ἀνδρὸς, the part of a man: 1, 10. a division, department, share : 2, 21. οὐκ ἐλαχίστην, a very considerable portion.

μόλις, 1, 69. 71. with difficulty : 7, 13. scarcely, 40. scarcely, hardly at length, at length with much ado, after a considerable time : 2, 35.

μόλυβδος, 1, 93. lead.

μόναρχος, 1, 122. a prince, chief, ruler with despotic power.

μονή, 1, 131. τὴν μονὴν ποιούμενος, to make an abode, a stay in a place: 7, 50. a delay, stopping, 47.

μόνιμος, 8, 89. οὐκ ἐδόκει μόνιμον τὸ τῆς ὀλιγαρχίας, permanent, durable, likely to continue.

μόνος, 5, 28. alone, 43. unassisted, 10. only, sole: 7, 58. μόνοι Ἕλληνες οἰκοῦσιν, the only Greeks who live : 8, 68.

μονόω, 5, 58. ὡς μεμονωμένοις, as they were alone, 5, 8. left to themselves, unaccompanied, obliged to depend on their own resources : 3, 105. 6, 101. μονωθείς : 2, 81. μεμονωμένων, separated (from the

rest:) 4, 126. μεμονῶσθαι : 5, 40. 58.

μόνως, 8, 81. solely.

μόριον, 1, 141. ἐν βραχεῖ μορίῳ, in a short space (of time,) τῷ πλέονι, a longer, the greater portion, 85. ἐν βραχεῖ μορίῳ ἡμέρας, in a brief part of the day : 2, 39. a portion, detachment : 6, 92. a portion : 7, 58.

Μουννυχιᾶσι, 8, 92. Matth. Gr. Gr. 374.

μουσικὸς, 3, 100. musical.

μοχθέω, 2, 39. μοχθούντων, to toil, labour, 1, 70. μοχθοῦσι, to toil.

μοχθηρὸς, 8, 73. ἄνθρωπον, troublesome.

μοχλὸς, 2, 4. the bar, bolt of a door.

μυθώδης, 1, 21. τὸ μὴ μυθῶδες, it's not being fabulous.

μύλων, 6, 22. a corn-mill, bake-house.

μυριὰς, 7, 75. the number 10,000 : 5, 63.

μύριος, 2, 13. ten thousand.

μυριοφόρος, 7, 25. ναῦν, that which bears 10,000, a ship of many tons' burthen, of very great burthen.

μυστήριον, 6, 28. a mytery, hidden rite of religion.

μυστικὸς, 6, 28. τὰ μυστικὰ, mystic rites, 60.

μυχὸς, 7, 4. τοῦ λιμένος, the bottom of the harbour, 52.

μωρία, 4, 64. 5, 41. folly, absurdity.

Ναυάγιον, 1, 50. 4, 14. the wreck of a ship : 7, 23.

ναύαρχος, 8, 16. a naval commander, 20.

ναυβάτης, 1, 121. a sailor, 7, 75. πεζοὺς ἀντὶ ναυβατῶν, on foot instead of ship-board: 8, 44. a naval soldier.

ναύκληρος, 1, 137. the steersman, master of a small vessel.

ναυλοχέω, 7, 4. to wait in a station (for an enemy,) to lie in wait, take a covert naval station.

ναυμαχέω, 1, 13. ναυμαχοῦντες ἐνίκων, to conquer in a sea-fight : 7, 22. ἐναυμάχουν : 1, 14. ἐναυμάχησαν, 36. ναυμαχήσετε, to fight by sea: 7, 34. ναυμαχήσαντες ἀντίπαλα, to fight a drawn battle, with equal success, fortune : 4, 4.

ναυμαχία, 1, 13. a sea-fight: 2, 85. 7, 21.

ναυπηγέω, 1, 31, ἐναυπηγοῦντο, to build ships, 13. ναυπηγηθῆναι, to be built.

ναυπηγήσιμος, 4, 108. ξύλων, ship-timber : 7, 25. ναυπηγήσιμα, materials for ship-building.

ναυπηγία, 8, 4. ship-building : 4, 108. τριήρων.

ναυπηγὸς, 1, 13. a shipwright.

ναῦς, 3, 2. 5, 4. ναυσὶ, ships, 5, 3. 7, 12. νῆες : 7, 1. νεῶν : 6, 85. 8, 9. 25. ναυσὶ δυοῖν

δεούσαις πεντήκοντα, Matth. Gr. Gr. 71. 74.

ναύσταθμος, 3, 6. 6, 49. a naval station, a station for ships.

ναύτης, 7, 1. 4. a sailor, seaman, 63. καὶ ταῦτα τοῖς ὁπλίταις οὐχ ἧσσον τῶν ναυτῶν παρακελεύομαι, for ἢ τοῖς ναύταις, Matth. Gr. Gr. 658.

ναυτικὸς, 1, 4. τὸ ναυτικὸν, a navy, 7, 7. naval, 21. : 1, 13. ναυτικὰ, naval affairs : 4, 75.

ναυτοκράτωρ, 5, 97. one powerful in ships, 109.

νεκρὸς, a dead body, 1, 51. 4, 44. 5, 10. 7, 5.

νέμω, 5, 42. to exercise the right of pasturage : 6, 16. τὰ ἴσα, to pay, give, yield : 3, 48. νείμαντες οἴκτῳ πλέον, to give way or allow too much to compassion : 1, 6. νεμόμενα, to be accustomed, to have a habit or practice : 1, 10. to possess, 100. ἐνέμοντο : 4, 64. νεμούμεθα, to till : 1, 5. νέμεται τῷ παλαιῷ τρόπῳ, to be regulated by, or to use the ancient custom : 3, 3. νέμοντες μεῖζον μέρος τῷ μὴ βούλεσθαι ἀληθῆ εἶναι, in a great measure, regarding with the wish that they should not be true, chiefly disposing of them by their not wishing them to be true, disposing of or regarding in a great measure as one wishes it to be : 1, 120. νέμοντας τὰ ἴδια ἐξ ἴσου, to regulate their private affairs equally with others, 71. ἐπὶ τὸ μὴ λυπεῖν ἄλλους—τὸ ἴσον νέμετε, to attribute justice to any one on the condition of not aggrieving others, i. e. to consider justice to consist in, &c. : 8. 21. νειμάμενοι, to divide among themselves.

νεοδαμώδης, 5, 34. 7, 19. 58. freedmen, citizens newly enfranchised.

νεοκατάστατος, 3, 93. newly established.

νεόκτιστος, 3, 100. lately established.

νέος, 5, 50. ἐδόκει τι νέον ἔσεσθαι, to expect something extraordinary to happen : νεώτερος, 1, 42. young, youthful, 2, 6. 5, 50. : 3, 26. a minor, 6, 12. νεώτερος ὢν ἐς τὸ ἄρχειν, to be too young for command, to command, 38. : 1, 132. νεώτερόν τι ποιεῖν ἐς αὐτὸν, to take any novel step against a person : νεώτατος, 1, 7. 2, 13. 4, 125.

νεότης, 4, 80. 5, 43. youth, unripe time of life : 2, 8. a youthful population.

νεοχμὸς, 1, 11. 42. see Bekker's Index.

νεοχμόω, 1, 12. ἐνεόχμωσε, to cause, make innovations.

νεῦμα, 1, 134. ἀφανεῖ, a private signal.

νεύω, 4, 100. νεῦον ἀπὸ τῆς κεραίας, bending, inclined, leading, conducting, (of a spout.)

νεφρῖτις, 7, 15. nephritic, of or belonging to the reins, (stone in the kidneys, *Hobbes.*)

νέω, 2, 52. νήσαντας, to fill up, to erect.

νεὼν, a fane, temple, an altar, 3, 68. 4, 90. 5, 18.

νεώριον, 1, 108. a naval station, dock-yard : 7, 22. a dock : 3, 74.

νεώσοικος, 7, 25. 8, 1. a dock.

νεωστὶ, 1, 95. lately, 7, 1. very lately, just now, 33. lately, recently, 4, 34. lately, just : 1, 137. βασιλεύοντα, who had lately ascended the throne : 4, 108.

νεωτερίζω, 2, 73. to make a change, innovation : 7, 87. τῇ μεταβολῇ ἐς ἀσθένειαν ἐνεωτέριζον, (the cold nights and the hot days by the vicissitude) altered (them) into (a state of) weakness (and disorder :) 2, 3. ἐνεωτέριζον οὐδὲν ἐς οὐδένα, to do nobody any injury, to attempt nothing against any one : 1, 115. νεωτερίσαι, to revolutionize : 3, 4, νεωτεριούντων, 11. νεωτεριεῖν, a Doric form for νεωτερισόντων, νεωτερίσειν, Matth. Gr. Gr. 221.

νεωτεροποιΐα, 1, 102. a love of change.

νεωτεροποιὸς, 1, 70. innovators, inventors of novelty, 102.

νηΐτης, 4, 85. στρατῷ, naval: 2, 24.

νησίδιον, 6, 2. 7, 3. 8, 11. a little, small island, an islet.

νησὶς, 8, 14. a small island.

νησιώτης, 1, 81. 5, 84. 7, 5. an islander.

νῆσος, 1, 4. 5, 14. 35. 6, 2. 7, 33. 57. an island.

νικάω, 1, 13. ἐνίκων, to win a victory: 6, 16. ἐνίκησα, to win the plate, prize: 5, 73. νενικημένους, 1, 50. νικηθῶσιν, 7, 44. ἐνικῶντο, to be conquered: 2, 60. νικωμένου χρήμασιν, to be overcome by pecuniary temptations: 2, 85. 7, 66. νενικήκατε ναυμαχίας, to win a sea-fight: 2, 6. ἄρτι νενικημένων τε καὶ ξυνειλημμένων, just after their being defeated and taken prisoners, 12. νενικηκυῖα ἦν, had prevailed: 5, 82. νενίκηνται: 1, 126. νομίσας ἑορτήν τε τοῦ Διὸς μεγίστην εἶναι καὶ ἑαυτῷ τι προσήκειν Ὀλύμπια νενικηκότι, the intrans. νικάω is here used transitively, with the nature of the field of battle, Matth. Gr. Gr. 600.

νίκη, 1, 63. 7, 23. victory.

Νικόλαος, 2, 67. Νικόλας occurs in other authors, which is a Doric contraction, Matth. Gr. Gr. 53.

νόθος, 8, 5. a bastard, 28.

νομίζω, 5, 8. to judge, be of opinion, 44. : 7, 17. νομίσαντες: 1, 77. to think right, to sanction: 4, 8. νομισθῆναι, to think : 1, 42. 69. νομίσῃ, to consider: 6, 69. σφάγια τὰ νομιζόμενα, the customary, proper, solemn sacrifices, victims: 6, 22. νομίσατε, to conclude, 5, 9. to bear in mind : 2, 15. 4, 81.

νόμιμος, 4, 96. τὰ νόμιμα τῶν Ἑλλήνων, established law, 6, 4. institutions, laws, 1, 71, manners, customs, 7, 57. : 1, 85. οὐ νόμιμον, it is not right : 3, 53. νομιμωτέραν, more legal: 7, 68. νομιμώτατος, most just, equitable.

νόμος, 1, 77. ὁμοίοις νόμοις, impartial laws : 3, 31. κατὰ τοὺς ἑαυτῶν, by, according to, 5, 66. κατὰ τὸν νόμον, according to law, 1, 24. : 6, 16. a prescript, custom, institution.

νοσέω, 2, 48. νοσήσας, to have the plague, 1, 138. to be sick, 2, 58. νοσῆσαι, to have the plague, 30. νενοσηκυίας.

νόσημα, 2, 49. a malady, 51. 53: ἐτόλμα, 57. ὑπ' ἄλλου νοσήματος διαφθαρῆναι, to die of a disorder, to be subject to or afflicted by, 47. ἡ νόσος πρῶτον ἤρξατο γενέσθαι τοῖς Ἀθηναίοις, λεγόμενον μὲν καὶ πρότερον πολλαχόσε ἐγκατασκῆψαι, the participle agrees with τὸ νόσημα, (which is implied by ἡ νόσος, or) which being equivalent to it, the participle may be said to be referred to this last in its sense only, Matth. Gr. Gr. 629.

νόσος, 1, 23. a disease: 2, 98. 5, 41. 7, 47. νόσῳ τε γὰρ ἐπιέζοντο—τά τε ἄλλα—ἐφαίνετο, an instance of anacoluthon, Matth. Gr. Gr. 944.

νοτερὸς, 3, 21. rainy.

νουμηνία, 2, 28, κατὰ σελήνην,

the lunar calends, the first day of the month according to the moon, the first day of the lunar month: 4, 51.

νοῦς, 3, 22. τὸν νοῦν ἔχοιεν πρὸς αὐτοὺς, to have one's attention upon, to direct one's attention to : 5, 45. οὐδὲν ἀληθὲς ἐν νῷ ἔχουσιν, to have no just intention, nothing just in contemplation, no upright views, to be radically insincere : 7, 19. intention, mind.

νυκτερινὸς, 4, 128. νυκτερινῇ καὶ φοβερᾷ, nocturnal.

νυκτομαχία, 7, 44. a night-engagement.

νῦν, 3, 43. νῦν δὲ, but as the case now stands : 6, 34. τῶν νῦν, the powers that are, present state : 4, 28.

νυνὶ, 4, 92. νυνὶ δὲ, and now, however : 5, 47. Ὀλυμπίοις τοῖς νυνὶ, the approaching Olympic games.

νὺξ, 1, 51. ἐς νύκτα, in the night : 5, 58. τὴν νύκτα, by night : 1, 129. 4, 110.

νῶτος, 1, 62. κατὰ νώτου, on the rear, 3, 107. : 4, 4.

Ξ.

Ξεναγὸς, 2, 75. a commander of mercenaries, one appointed to command the troops of other states, which assisted the Lacedæmonians in war.

ξενηλασία, 1, 144. a driving away or expulsion of strangers (from a town :) 2, 39.

ξενία, 8, 6. a connection of hospitality.

ξενικὸς, 7, 42. strange, foreign : 8, 25.

ξένισις, 6, 46. καὶ ἰδίᾳ ξενίσεις ποιούμενοι τῶν τριηριτῶν, to entertain as guests, give entertainments to.

ξένος, 1, 26. 74. ἄνδρα, a stranger : 7, 13. : 2, 93. a friend connected by ties of hospitality.

ξενοτροφέω, 7, 48. ξενοτρο-

φοῦντες, to maintain mercenaries, have mercenaries in one's pay.

ξηραίνω, 1, 109. ξηράνας, to dry up.

ξηρότης, 7, 12. τῶν νεῶν, dryness, soundness, tightness.

ξηρὸς, 1, 109. ἐπὶ τοῦ ξηροῦ, upon dry land.

ξιφίδιον, 3, 22. a little sword.

ξυγγενεία, 1, 26. 4, 61. 7, 57. affinity, relationship, consanguinity.

ξυγγενὴς, 1, 95. 6, 20. κατὰ τὸ ξυγγενὲς, on the score of relationship : 1, 6. 71. 5, 15. a relation, 6, 6. 30. : 4, 64. one of the same race.

ξυγγίγνομαι, 5, 37. to accompany, join the party : 2, 12. ξυγγένηται, to have communication or to confer with.

ξυγγινώσκω, 2, 60. ξυνέγνωτε, to consent to, resolve upon (in conformity with another's advice:) 7, 73. ξυνεγίγνωσκον, to agree or coincide in opinion.

ξυγγνώμη, 3, 44. ἔχοντές τι ξυγγνώμης, to deserve some pardon, clemency, 39. ξυγγνώμην ἔχω, to pardon: 4,114. εἶναι ξυγγνώμην, excuse: 1, 32. καὶ ξυγγνώμη εἰ, and it is pardonable if: 7, 15. pardon, consent: 8, 50. pardon.

ξυγγνώμων, 2, 74. ξυγγνώμονές ἐστε, to be consenting: 4, 98. σύγγνωμόν τι γίγνεσθαι καὶ πρὸς τοῦ θεοῦ, palliation, forgiveness, 3, 40. pardonable.

ξυγγραφὴ, 5, 35. a written document, a scroll, form of writing: 1, 97. a history.

ξυγγράφω, 1, 1. ξυνέγραψε, to compose, write, 2, 70. 6, 7. 8, 6. : 5, 41. ξυνεγράψαντο, to be digested, drawn up in writing.

ξυγκαθαιρέω, 1, 132. ξυγκαθελοῦσαι, to join in overturning: 8, 16. ξυγκαθῇρουν, to assist in demolishing, 6, 6. ξυγκαθέλωσι : 1, 90. ξυγκαθελεῖν, to destroy altogether : 8, 46. ξυγκαθαιρήσει, he might pull down, destroy.

ξυγκάθημαι, 5, 55. ξυγκαθῆσθαι περὶ εἰρήνης, to sit in council respecting a peace.

ξυγκαθίστημι, 4, 107. ξυγκαθίστη ταῦτα, 5, 52. to arrange, confirm.

ξυγκαλέω, 2, 71. 86. ξυνεκάλεσαν, 88. 5, 8. 7, 5. to call together, 2, 10. to summon, 7, 21.

ξυγκαταβαίνω, 6, 30. ξυγκατέβη, to accompany down, go down along with.

ξυγκαταδιώκω, 8, 28. ξυγκαταδιωχθείσης, to be pursued along with.

ξυγκαταδουλόω, 3, 64. ξυγκατεδουλοῦσθε, to join in reducing to slavery.

ξυγκαταλαμβάνω, 7, 26. ξυγκατέλαβε, to seize, occupy along with, to assist another in seizing.

ξυγκαταλείπω, 5, 75. ξυγκαταλιπόντες, jointly to leave behind.

ξυγκατανέμω, 6, 4. ξυγκατενείμαντο, to possess in common with, inhabit along with.

ξυγκατασκευάζω, 1, 93. ξυγκατεσκεύαζε τὴν ἀρχὴν, to assist in acquiring power.

ξυγκατεργάζομαι, 1,132. ξυγκατεργάσωνται τὸ πᾶν, to share, co-operate with through the whole business.

ξυγκατοικίζω, 2, 41. ξυγκατοικίσαντες, to set up, erect along with, amongst: 6, 8. ξυγκατοικίσαι Λεοντίνους, to settle, establish together in a body, to collocate : 6, 4. ξυγκατῴκισε, to unite with, assist in founding a place, making a settlement, 75. ξυγκατοικίζειν.

ξύγκειμαι, 3, 70. 5, 47. κατὰ τὰ ξύγκείμενα, according to the agreement, 4, 68. κατὰ τὸ ξυγκείμενον: 4, 111. ὃ ξύγκειτο, what has been concerted, agreed upon, 23. 68. : 1, 22. ξύγκειται, to be compiled, composed : 8, 43. ξυγκεῖσθαι, to be arranged with, settled.

ξυγκεράννυμι, 6, 18. ξύγκρα-θὲν, to be mixed, blended together, compounded, tempered together.

ξυγκινδυνεύω, 1, 32. to run into danger in company with : 8, 22. to involve in the same risk.

ξυγκλείω, 5, 72. ξυγκλεῖσαι, to clasp, lock together : 4, 67. ξυγκλεισθῆναι, to be shut, closed (as a gate :) 4, 35. 5, 64.

ξύγκλησις, 5, 71. a locking together.

ξύγκλυς, 7, 5. ἀνθρώπων, collected from all parts, a promiscuous multitude.

ξυγκομιδὴ, 2, 52. conveying.

ξυγκομίζω, 6, 71. ξυγκομίσαντες τοὺς νεκροὺς, to collect, congerere : 7, 85. to convey in a body.

ξυγκρούω, 1, 44. αὐτοὺς ἀλλήλοις, to shatter them one against another : 7, 36. ξυγκροῦσαι τὸ ἀντίπρωρον, to clash against at the same time, make a shock in concert, the collision of prow against prow.

ξυγκτάομαι, 7, 57. ξυγκτησόμενοι χώραν, to assist, join in acquiring, to obtain a share of.

ξυγκτίζω, 7, 57. ξυγκτίσαντες, to unite in founding.

ξυγχέω, 5, 39. ξυγχέαι, to accomplish a league, rivet a connexion.

ξύγχυσις, 5, 26. a consummation of the union.

ξυγχωρέω, 1, 140. οἷς ξυγχωρήσετε, to make concessions to, to yield to : 5, 89. ξυγχωροῦσι, to succumb, obey : 8, 9. ξυγχωρούντων, to accede : 3, 52. ξυγχωροῦεν, to be agreed upon, to stipulate : 5, 116. ξυνεχώρησαν, to surrender oneself, to yield, 41. ἐφ' οἷς, to consent : 3, 27. ξυγχωρήσαντες πρὸς Ἀθηναίους, to make terms with.

ξύλινος, 7, 25. wooden : 2, 75. ξύλινον τεῖχος ξυνθέντες, to construct a wooden wall, frame : 4, 90. πύργους, towers, 115. παραφράγματα, parapets, turrets, fences.

ξυλλαμβάνω, 4, 5. ξυλλαμβάνει, to take, seize, 2, 67. to apprehend, arrest : 2, 6. ξυνέλαβον, to apprehend, seize : 1, 20. ξυλληφθῆναι, to be apprehended : 1, 118. ξυλλήψεσθαι, to assist, give aid in accomplishing, 123. to bear a hand, 2, 54. to take part with, to assist : 8, 14. ξυνελάμβανον, to seize : 4, 47. ξυνελάβοντο, to wink or connive at, to be a party to : 1, 134. ξυλληφθήσεσθαι, to be apprehended.

ξυλλέγω, 7, 7. ξυλλέξων, to collect, convocate : 1, 115. συλλέξαντες, to collect together, 4, 77. συλλέξας πλέοι, to sail, 4, 7. : 3, 15. ξυνελέγοντο, to assemble, 2, 3. 4,

91. : 6, 30. ξυλλέγεσθαι, to assemble, rendezvous : 2, 10. ξυναλεγμένον, to be collected together, 4, 70. around, 3, 94. : 7, 58. ξυνελέγη, to be collected, 26. to collect, draw to a head : 8, 49. ξυλλεγέντες, to meet, 93. οἱ τετρακόσιοι ἐς τὸ βουλευτήριον ὅμως καὶ τεθορυβημένοι ξυνελέγοντο, Matth. Gr. Gr. 866.

ξύλληψις, 1, 134. a seizure, an apprehension.

ξύλλογος, 1, 67. an assembly, a meeting : 2, 22. 59. ποιήσας, to call an assembly : 3, 27. κατὰ ξυλλόγους γιγνόμενα, to get together in parties : 7, 31. a general rendezvous, muster.

ξύλον, 8, 1. ξύλα, vessels : 7, 25. ξύλα ναυπηγήσιμα, timber for building ships : 4, 108. ξύλων, timber, 4, 3. 11. timbers, rafters, 52. timber, wood.

ξέλωσις, 2, 14. timber, beams, rafters.

ξυμβαίνω, 2, 5. ἤν τι ξυμβαίνωσι, in case they came to any agreement : 1, 98. ξυνέβησαν καθ᾽ ὁμολογίαν, to come to terms, 4, 62. : 4, 17. ξυμβεβήκασι, to concur : 5, 92. ξυμβαίη : 6, 33. τὸ τοσοῦτο ξυμβῆναι, such an event : 4, 30. ξυμβαθῇ, to be compounded, agreed : 2, 15. ξυνεβεβήκει, had been the custom, 1, 52. ξυμβεβηκότα, to happen, 7, 11. ξυμβέβηκε : 2, 77. ξυμβῆναι, 34. ξυνέβη, 5, 14. 7, 57. ὁπότε ξυμβαίη

αὐτοῖς, whenever they had occasion, 61. τὸ πλείστῳ παραλόγῳ ξυμβαῖνον, that which falls out, happens very contrary to men's reasonings and opinions, 70. ἄνευ αὐτῶν ξυνέβησαν, without consulting them : 1, 28. ξυμβῶσιν, to agree upon : 8, 27. ξυμβήσεσθαι, it would happen, 28. ξυνέβησαν, had agreed with : 5, 14. ξυνέβη ὥστε πολέμῳ μὲν μηδὲν ἔτι ἅψασθαι μηδετέρους, an instance of ξυνέβη being followed by a conjunction, which has commonly the simple infin., Matth. Gr. Gr. 708.

ξυμβάλλω, 5, 77. ξυμβαλέσθαι, to be ratified : 3, 45. ξυμβάλλεται ἐς τὸ ἐπαίρειν, to contribute to stimulate, impel, put men upon undertaking : 1, 105. ξυμβαλόντες, to engage in fight : 8, 25. ξυνέβαλον, they engaged in battle.

ξύμβασις, 1, 61. 5, 4. 17. 21. 47. 54. 6, 10. composition, peace, agreement, treaty : 3, 67. ἀπὸ ξυμβάσεως, after or in consequence of a capitulation : 2, 3. πρὸς ξύμβασιν ἐχώρησαν, they came to terms : 2, 2. ἐς ξύμβασιν ἀγαγεῖν, to bring to terms.

ξυμβατήριος, 5, 75. λόγους, proposals for an accommodation.

ξυμβατικὸς, 6, 102. of or belonging to a surrender, treaty.

ξυμβιβάζω, 2, 29. ξυνεβίβασε,

to bring over to, to reconcile.

ξυμβοήθεια, 2, 82. succour.

ξυμβοηθέω, 2, 80. 7, 30. ξυνεβοήθησαν, to carry aid in concert, to bring assistance simultaneously : 2, 81. ξυμβεβοηθηκέναι : 7, 55. ξυμβοηθησάντων, 3, 7. 2, 83.

ξυμβόλαιος, 1, 77. regarding covenants of alliance.

ξυμβουλευτέος, 1, 140. ὁρῶ ὁμοῖα καὶ παραπλήσια ξυμβουλευτέα μοι ὄντα, to see, perceive that I must give the like and pretty nearly the same advice, to persist in the same uniform advice.

ξυμβουλεύω, 1, 65. ξυνεβούλευε, to plan in conjunction with.

ξύμβουλος, 2, 85. 5, 63. a counsellor, an assessor : 3, 69. an adviser : 8, 39.

ξυμμαχέω, 1, 39. 6, 78. to support an ally, 1, 35. to be in alliance : 2, 66. ξυνεμάχουν, to take part or side with in war, to be an ally of : 7, 50. ξυμμαχήσαντες, to bring aid.

ξυμμαχία, 1, 15. an alliance, a league, 5, 22. 33. ; 37. an armed confederacy : 6, 72. i. q. τὸ ξυμμαχικόν, ὠφέλεια, auxilia, succours, 1, 118. οἱ Λακεδαιμόνιοι — τῆς συμμαχίας αὐτῶν (sc. τῶν Ἀθηναίων) ἥττοντο, an instance of the interchange of subst., when subst. of different classes are interchanged, and ἡ συμμαχία occurs for οἱ ξύμμαχοι, Matth.

Gr. Gr. 617. : 5, 46. Matth. 548.

ξυμμαχικός, 7, 20. κατὰ τὸ ξυμμαχικόν, according to the terms of the treaty, 5, 6. according to appointment, contract : 8, 7. 9. : 4, 77. τὸ πᾶν ξυμμαχικόν, the whole effective force of the allies.

ξυμμαχὶς, 1, 98. an alliance, 65. being in alliance : 5, 36. an armed confederacy : 8, 23. auxiliary.

ξύμμαχος, 5, 18. 31. 35. an ally.

ξυμμένω, 1, 18. ξυνέμειναν, to endure.

ξυμμετρέω, 3, 20. ξυνεμετρήσαντο, to measure, take the height : 2, 44. ξυνεμετρήθη, to be measured, marked out, appointed, ordained.

ξυμμέτρησις, 3, 20. ξυμμέτρησιν ἔλαβον, to take measure.

ξυμμίγνυμι, 1, 50. ξυνέμιξαν, to engage with one another : 5, 9. ξυμμίξαι, to join in the engagement, mingle in the fight, 1, 49. : 5, 65. πρὶν ξυμμίξαι, before the battle could be joined : 2, 84. to join or unite with : 2, 31. ξυνεμίχθησαν, to unite with, join oneself to.

ξύμμικτος, 4, 106. mixed, heterogeneous (race :) 6, 5. ἀνθρώπων, (men) of all countries, a mixed (multitude :) 3, 61. ἀνθρώπους, a mixed (rabble.)

ξυμμίσγω, 7, 26. ξυμμίσγει τῷ Χαρικλεῖ, to join or unite

with : 1, 62. ξυνέμισγον, to engage (as an enemy :) 7, 6. ξυνέμισγεν αὐτοῖς, to mingle with in battle.

ξύμμορος, 4, 93. a companion, fellow-soldier, or fellow-countryman, one who contributes his share to the general stock, or one who dwells in 'a division or department attached to the department or country of others, see Duker's note.

ξυμπαραγίγνομαι, 2, 82. ξυμπαραγενομένων κατὰ φιλίαν, to come over to.

ξυμπαρακομίζω, 8, 39. ξυμπαρακομισθῆναι, to be brought or conducted away.

ξυμπαραμένω, 6, 89. ξυμπαρέμεινεν, simul maneo, semper adsum, to dwell with, abide in, to be present to.

ξυμπάρειμι, 4, 83. ξυμπαρόντες, to accompany, attend, in attendance, one's suite.

ξύμπας, 4, 39. χρόνος, the sum total of time : 6, 18. ξυμπάντων Σικελιωτῶν : 1, 3. ξύμπασα, the whole : 7, 49. τὸ ξύμπαν, in a word, 30. the whole mass.

ξυμπείθω, 7, 21. ξυνέπειθε, to add one's exhortations to those of another, to join in persuading, to second the advice of another.

ξυμπέμπω, 2, 12. to send along with : 7, 31.

ξυμπίπτω, 4, 68. ξυνέπεσε, to happen, chance, 7, 63. συμπεσούσης νηΐ νεὼς, ' yardarm and yard-arm,' to fall

upon, grapple with, 44. : 70. ἐν ὀλίγῳ, 5, 3. ξυμπεσὼν, to precipitate themselves, to break in, 1, 49. : 2, 84. ξυμπεσεῖσθαι πρὸς ἀλλήλους, to fall foul one of another : 3, 59. ξυμπέσοι : 8, 41. ξυμπεπτωκυῖαν, to happen : 1, 49. ξυνέπεσον ἐς τοῦτο ἀνάγκης, the gen. here follows the neuter, as a definition ; that is, it shews in what respect that neuter is to be taken, which is the first especial signification of the gen., Matth. Gr. Gr.

ξυμπλέκω, 4, 4. ξυμπλέκοντες, to plait, twist.

ξυμπλέω, 1, 94. ξυνέπλιον, to sail in company, 1, 2. 10. 44. ξυμπλεῖν : 6, 44. ξυνέπλει ἐξ ἀνάγκης : 8, 29. Ἀστυόχῳ παραδοῦναι τὰς ναῦς ξυμπλέων, Matth. Gr. Gr. 805.

ξυμπληρόω, 7, 60. ξυνεπληρώθησαν, to be manned in a body, together.

ξυμπολεμέω, 2, 9. ξυνεπολέμουν, to assist in carrying on war : 2, 67. 7, 1. ξυμπολεμεῖν, to make war in concert, to become allies in war, 12. : 1, 18. ξυμπολεμησάντων, to confederate in war, to league.

ξυμπροθυμέομαι, 2, 80. ξυμπροθυμηθέντες, to be active in support of, zealous for, 8, 1. 2.

ξυμπροπέμπω, 1, 27. ξυμπροπέμψαι, to convey.

ξύμπτωμα, 4, 30. case, predicament.

ξυμφέρω, 5, 9. ξυμφέροντος,

expedient : 3, 71. ὡς ξυνέφερε, how it had been expedient : 5, 90. τὸ ξυμφέρον, the expedient, 7, 57. interest, expediency, 51. ξυμφέρει : 1, 35. 75. τὰ ξυμφέροντα, advantages, opportunities : 7, 36. ξυμφερομένους, to be crowded close together, to throng, crowd together : 1, 9. ξυνενεχθῆναι, to accrue, fall to the share, 23. ξυνηνέχθη, to happen, 4, 66. ξυνηνέχθησαν, to be agreed : 2, 51. τὸ ξυνενεγκὸν, to be of service, to benefit : 6, 20. ξυνενέγκοι, to turn out, to befal : 2, 44. τῇ πόλει ξυνοίσειν, it will contribute to the (good of the) state.

ξυμπολιορκέω, 8, 15. ξυνεπολιόρκουν, formed part of the blockade : 3, 20. ξυμπολιορκούμενοι, to be besieged along with, 68. ξυνεπολιορκοῦντο.

ξυμπολιτεύω, 6, 4. ξυμπολιτεύσας τοῖς Χαλκιδεῦσιν ἐς Λεοντίνους, to go to Leontium and live under the same government with the Chalcideans : 8, 47. jointly to manage the government.

ξυμπορίζω, 7, 2. ξυμπορίσαντες, to provide : 8, 1. 4. ξυμπορισάμενοι, to get together.

ξυμπράσσω, 8, 6. ξυνέπρασσε, to co-operate with : 4, 74. μάλιστα ξυμπρᾶξαι, to concert : 4, 67. ξυμπράσσοντες, coadjutors, conspirators, 76. ξυνέπρασσον : 8, 5. : 3, 36. ξυμπράσσοντες αὐτοῖς, to favour, support, 5, 52. to act (in politics)

in conjunction, 8, 14. to confederate.

ξυμπρεσβεύω, 5, 44. ξυνεπρεσβεύοντο, to be joined in commission, to partake the embassy.

ξύμπρεσβυς, 1, 90. a fellow ambassador.

ξυμφορέω, 6, 99. ξυμφοροῦντες, to convey.

ξυμφορὰ, 1, 127. διὰ τὴν ἐκείνου ξυμφορὰν, by means of his misfortune, 140. πρὸς τὰς ξυμφορὰς τρεπομένους, to change according to events, to alter with the alteration of times and circumstances : 7, 57. κατὰ ξυμφορὰν, on account of or by reason of their misfortune, i. e. exile, 61. ταῖς ξυμφοραῖς, on account of misfortunes : 1, 70. a calamity : 4, 15. ὡς ἐπὶ ξυμφορᾷ μεγάλῃ, as for an occasion of great calamity : 2, 60. ξυμφοραῖς εἴκετε, 61. : 8, 27.

ξύμφορος, 1, 32. advantageous, convenient : 2, 3. πρὸς τὰ παρόντα ξύμφορα, convenient for the present circumstances, in the present posture of affairs : 5, 98. τῷ ξυμφόρῳ, interest : 3, 47. ξυμφορώτερον, more conducive : 1, 36. ξυμφορώτατον, most convenient : 8, 43.

ξυμφόρως, 3, 40. on motives of interest, interestedly : 5, 11. expediently.

ξυμφυγὰς, 6, 81. a companion in exile, fellow exile.

ξυμφύλαξ, 5, 80. a fellow guard.

ξὺν, 3, 40. προφάσει, with a pretence : 5, 50. ὅπλοις, in arms.

ξυναγείρω, 7, 30. to raise (recruits,) draw (to one's standard,) 8, 5. : 4, 52. 7, 32. ξυναγείραντες.

ξυναγορορεύω, 6, 6. ξυναγορευόντων αὐτοῖς, to advocate the cause of, hear in behalf : 7, 49. ξυνηγόρευεν αὐτῷ ταῦτα, to join in advising, coincide in opinion with.

ξυνάγω, 1, 9. ξυναγαγὼν, to assemble, collect, 2, 81. to join together (forces,) 1, 120. ξυνήγαγόν, to assemble together, 2, 60. ἐκκλησίαν : 2, 84. ξυνῆγον ἐς ὀλίγον, to crowd into a small compass.

ξυναγωγὴ, 2, 18. τοῦ πολέμου, raising or collecting (troops) for war.

ξυναγωνίζομαι, 1, 123. ξυναγωνισομένη, to contend in conjunction, join a party in a contest : 3, 64. ξυναγωνίζεσθε, to contend in concert with, 82. ξυνηγωνίζοντο, to struggle in conjunction.

ξυναδικέω, 1, 37. to commit injustice in company, 39.

ξυναιρέω, 3, 40. ἐν ξυνελὼν λέγω, to comprehend, shortly to state, to say in sum, in short, 1, 70. 2, 41. 5, 105. 6, 80. : 8, 24. ξυναιρεθήσεσθαι, would be destroyed.

, ξυναίρω, 5, 28. ξυναράμενοι, to intermeddle, interfere, 4, 10. τοῦδε τοῦ κινδύνου, to sustain a part of, Matth. Gr. Gr. 504. : 2, 71. ξυνάρασθαι τὸν

κίνδυνον, to share the danger with.

ξυνακολουθέω, 3, 100. 6, 44. ξυνηκολούθουν, to accompany.

ξυναλλαγὴ, 4, 19. terms, contract, concord : 3, 82. a reconciliation.

ξυναλλάσσω, 4, 58. ξυναλλαγεῖν, to come to a reconciliation, to coalesce, form a coalition : 5, 5. ξυνηλλάσσοντο, to be in friendship, 45. ξυναλλάξειν.

ξυναμφότερος, 7, 1. one and both, one and all, together, 19. ξυναμφοτέρων ἐς ἑξακοσίους, together about six hundred, amounting to six.

ξυναναπείθω, 6, 88. ξυναναπείθοιεν, to join in persuading.

ξυναπόλλυμι, 6, 12. ξυναπολέσθαι τοὺς φίλους, to perish along with friends, to draw their friends along with them into ruin, i. e. to destroy their friends along with or as well as themselves : 2, 60. ξυναπόλλυνται, to fall with, perish along with, to be involved in the ruin of.

ξυναπονεύω, 7, 71. ξυναπονεύοντες τοῖς σώμασιν, to bend, incline the body, move it backwards and forwards.

ξυναποστέλλω, 6, 88. ξυναπέστελλον, to send along with,

ξυνάπτω, 6, 13. ξυνῆψαν πόλεμον πρός τινα, to engage in war : 2, 29. ξυνάψασθαι τὸ κῆδος τῆς θυγατρὸς, to contract his daughter in marriage, to marry his daughter (to one at so short a distance.)

ξυναρμόζω, 4, 100. ξυνήρμοσαν κεραίαν, to join again, attach together.

ξυναρτάομαι, 7, 70. ξυνηρτῆσθαι, to be jammed close together, to be stuck, to stick together.

ξυνάρχω, 7, 31. ξυνῆρχε Δημοσθένει, to be a colleague in command, to have a joint command with: 1, 62. 7, 16. 43. 8, 27. ξυναρχῶν, a colleague in command.

ξυναφίστημι, 1, 56. ξυναποστήσωσι, to cause to revolt together, 104. ξυναποστάντες, to revolt in company with, join in a revolt, 115. ξυναπέστησαν, to revolt together, 3, 39. 4, 88.: 1, 57. ξυναποστῆναι : 3, 47. ξυναφίσταται : 1, 104. Περσῶν καὶ Μήδων οἱ καταφυγόντες καὶ Αἰγυπτίων οἱ μὴ ξυναποστάντες, Matth. Gr. Gr. 402.

ξύνδεσμος, 2, 75. binding together.

ξυνδεσμωτὴς, 6, 60. a fellow prisoner.

ξυνδιαβάλλω, 6, 61. ξυνδιαβεβλημένοι, to be accused along with, 44. ξυνδιέβαλε τὸν κόλπον, to cross or pass over together, συνδιεπεραιώθη.

ξυνδιαγιγνώσκω, 2, 64. ξυνδιέγνωτε, to vote with, concur with in passing a decree.

ξυνδιαιτάομαι, 2, 50. ξυνδιαιτᾶσθαι, to be domesticated, live with.

ξυνδιασώζω, 6, 89. to maintain, preserve : 7, 57. ξυνδιασώσοντες, to join in preserving.

ξυνδιώκω, 1, 135. to accompany in pursuit.

ξυνδοκέω, 6, 44. ξυνδοκῇ τοῖς ἄλλοις, to agree in resolution.

ξύνεγγυς, 4, 24. mutually hard by, respectively close.

ξύνεδρος, 4, 28. an assessor : 5, 85. a senator, counsellor.

ξυνεθίζω, 4, 34. ξυνειθισμένοι, to be accustomed, habituated.

ξυνείδω, 1, 20. ξυνειδότων, to conspire, 4, 68. 8, 9. to be privy to, 51.; 2, 35. ἀκροατὴς, to be acquainted with the facts, of which another is speaking : 4, 68. ξυνῄδει, to be privy to, in the secret, 5, 82. ξυνῄδεσαν.

ξύνειμι, 4, 18. ξυνεῖναι τούτῳ, to be conversant or engaged with : 1, 141. ξυνιόντες χρόνιοι, to be long in assembling, before they meet, tardily to assemble, meet together, 2, 8. to engage, meet (in war,) 5, 15.: 1, 3. ξυνίεσαν, Matth. Gr. Gr. 466.: 2, 10. 15. ξυνῄεσαν.

ξυνεισβάλλω, 4, 94. ξυνεσέβαλλον, to come out with, share the expedition.

ξυνεισέρχομαι, 3, 34. ξυνεσελθόντες, to enter along with.

ξυνεκπλέω, 4, 3. ξυνεκπλεῦσαι, to accompany in sailing, share the voyage.

ξυνεκφέρω, 2, 34. to accompany (a corpse to the grave, in funeral procession.)

ξυνελευθερόω, 3, 33. 6, 56. to assist in liberating, join in freeing: 2, 72. ξυνελευθεροῦτε: 3, 13. μὴ ξὺν κακῶς ποιεῖν αὐτοὺς μετ' Ἀθηναίων, ἀλλὰ ξυνελευθεροῦν, an instance of the proper tmesis, i. e. the separation of a word used in its compound form, Matth. Gr. Gr. 918.

ξυνεξαμαρτάνω, 3, 43. ξυνεξήμαρτον, to partake of an error.

ξυνεπάγω, 4, 1. ξυνεπαγόντων, to invite, give an invitation, 84. to agree to invite : 3, 11. ξυνεπῆγον, to lead out along with, 4, 79. to join one's pressing instance, instigation.

ξυνεπαινέω, 4, 91. ξυνεπαινούντων μάχεσθαι, to approve.

ξυνεπαιτιάομαι, 1. 135. ξυνεπῃτιῶντο, to accuse in a body, (or, a state-affair.)

ξυνεπαμύνω, 6, 56. to support against, assist in an assault.

ξυνεπανίστημι, 1, 132. ξυνεπανιστῶσι, to join in revolt.

ξυνεπεύχομαι, 6, 32. ξυνεπεύχοντο, to accompany or join in prayer.

ξυνέπειμι, 3, 63. ἄλλοις, to join in an attack upon others.

ξυνεπιλαμβάνω, 1, 115. ξυνεπελάβοντο, to join in, take up together with, 3, 74.: 6, 70. ξυνεπιλαβέσθαι τοῦ φόβου, to add, increase, promote, 8, 26. to undertake also : 2, 8. εἴ τι δύναιτο ξυνεπιλαμβάνειν, to assist, help.

ξυνεπιμέλομαι, 8, 39. ξυνεπιμελεῖσθαι, should pay attention to.

ξυνεπιστρατεύω, 5, 48. to join in making war.

ξυνεπιτίθημι, 6, 10. ξυνεπίθεντο, to join in attacking, 56. ξυνεπιθησομένους τῷ ἔργῳ, to join or assist in the execution, performance of, to attempt, undertake an exploit in conjunction with : 3, 54. ξυνεπιθέμενοι ἐς ἐλευθερίαν, to join in the attack for (the sake of) freedom.

ξυνέπομαι, 3, 38. ξυνέπεσθαι, to follow, comply with, adopt : 7, 57. ξυνέσποντο, to follow, accompany, 1, 60. to attend upon (as soldiers upon a general,) follow (in the field,) Matth. Gr. Gr. 337.

ξυνεργάζομαι, 1. 93. ξυνεργασμένων, wrought and made to fit together, (of stones.)

ξυνέρχομαι, 1, 10. ξυνελθόντες, to proceed together, 5, 74.: 4, 58. to assemble : 1, 3. ξυνῆλθον, to go together, join in going, 1, 69. 5, 55. to assemble, 7, 56.; 4, 38. ἐς λόγους, to come to discourse.

ξύνεσις, 1, 75. γνώμης, the wisdom of (our) resolution, 4. 18. 6, 54.: 4, 85. prudence : 3, 82. wit, intelligence : 1, 140. ξυνέσεως μεταποιεῖσθαι, to lay claim to superior discernment, to pride oneself upon one's sagacity : 4, 81. cleverness, parts, adroitness, acquaintance with business : 1, 138. οἰκείᾳ, mother-wit, native intelligence : 3, 37. ξυνέσεως ἀγῶνι, a contest of wit, strife of intellect

ξυνετὸς, 1, 84. ἄγαν, over-wise, intelligent, 6, 39. δη-μοκρατίαν: 4, 10. wise, ex-perienced: 1, 79. able, wise: 3, 37. ξυνετωτέρους, more in-telligent, clever, men of bet-ter understanding: 1, 74. ξυνετώτατον, of the greatest abilities.

ξυνεφίστημι, 2, 75.: ξυνεφε-στῶτες ἑκάστης πόλεως, to be appointed to command (the troops of) each state.

ξυνεχὴς, 7, 71. τὸ ξυνεχὲς, the continuance: 3, 21. con-tiguous, continuous: 7, 81. ἐν πόνῳ ξυνεχεστέρῳ, in more incessant toil and difficulty: 6, 26. constant, continual.

ξυνέχω, 7, 14. ξυνέχοντες τὴν εἰρεσίαν, to stop the rowing, make the ship stationary: 3, 98. ξυνεχόμενοι, to be oc-cupied, taken up.

ξυνεχῶς, 1, 1. continually: 2, 1. without intermission: 7, 27.: 5, 24. connectedly, succinctly: 8, 78. τὸν Τισσα-φέρνην τάς τε ναῦς ταύτας οὐ κομίζειν, καὶ τροφὴν ὅτι οὐ ξυνε-χῶς οὐδ᾽ ἐντελῆ διδοὺς κακοῖ τὸ ναυτικὸν, Matth. Gr. Gr. 818.

ξυνήθης, 7, 67. τῷ ἡμετέρῳ τρόπῳ, familiar or usual to, in our method, discipline: 1, 6. ordinary, customary: 6, 34. τὸ ξύνηθες, habitual, 18.: 1, 71. ξυνηθεστέρους, more congenial in manners, habits.

ξυνήκω, 5, 87. ξυνήκετε, to assemble.

ξυνθάπτω, 1, 8. ξυντεθαμμένη, to be buried along with.

ξυνθήκη, 4, 61. 5, 18. 31. 42. a compact, contract, an agreement: 8, 18. ξυνθήκαις, (in) the articles of treaty: 1. 78. κατὰ τὴν ξυνθήκην, accord-ing to compact, 37. κατὰ ξυν-θήκας γίγνεσθαι, to abide by the terms of a treaty: 8, 36.

ξύνθημα, 4, 67. ἀπὸ ξυνθήμα-τος, upon an understanding, agreement, according to a plan: 7, 44. the watch-word, 22. an agreement, a signal.

ξυνίσημι, 1, 73. ξύνιστε, to know in common with.

ξυνίστημι, 4, 78. ξυστῆναι, to meet, 55, ξυνεστῶτες ναυτικῷ ἀγῶνι, to stand up to, to be concerned in: 6, 79. ξυστῶ-μεν, to combine, 21. ξυστῶσιν, to league together, to com-bine, 7, 15. ξυνίσταται, to be combined: 1, 15. ξυνέστη, to arise (as a war:) 2, 88. ξυ-νιστάμενοι κατὰ σφᾶς αὐτοὺς, to get together apart, talk with one another upon: 5, 82. κατ᾽ ὀλίγον ξυνιστάμενος, to combine together by degrees, 6, 33. ξυνίσταται ὑπὸ δέους, to com-bine, rally together from fear: 1, 15. ξυνεστήκεσαν, to join oneself to, to stand up by the side of, to side with: 6, 16. ξυστήσας, 37. ξυστήσεται: 8, 48. ξυνίστασαν, joined, ex-cited to a union with.

ξυνίστωρ, 2, 74. a witness.

ξυνναυμαχέω, 1, 73. συνναυ-μαχῆσαι, to contend together in naval fight.

ξυννέφελος, 8, 42. cloudy.

ξυννέω, 7, 87. ξυννενημένῳ

ἐπ' ἀλλήλοις, to be heaped up one upon another.

ξύνοδος, 5, 70. a meeting (of two hostile armies,) 1, 96. : 2, 82. a society, an association : 4, 60. a synod, congress : 8, 79. δόξαν αὐτοῖς ἀπὸ ξυνόδου ὥστε διαναυμαχεῖν, Matth. Gr. Gr. 879.

ξυνοικέω, 6, 83. ξυνοικήσαντες σφίσιν αὐτοῖς, to settle with, 2, 68. to reside, live with : 6, 5. ξυνῴκησαν, to settle along with.

ξυνοίκησις, 3, 3. ξυνοίκησιν, διαλύειν, to put an end to, give up assembling, collecting (the inhabitants into a town.)

ξυνοίκια, 2, 15. the Synœcia, or feast of the association, union, cohabitation.

ξυνοικία, 3, 74. ξυνοικίας, masses of houses.

ξυνοικίζω, 2, 15. ξυνῴκισε, to constitute, establish, unite together, 16. ξυνῳκίσθησαν, to be united in a city, 1, 10. οὔτε ξυνοικισθείσης πόλεως, not to be closely inhabited, i. e. to have the inhabitants spread over a large extent : 3, 2. ξυνοικίζουσι τὴν Λέσβον ἐς τὴν Μυτιλήνην, βίᾳ, to collect or assemble together in Mytilene all the Lesbians, i. e. to compel (all) Lesbos to go into Mytilene : 6, 2. ξυνοικίσαντες, to settle, plant along with (others) in a body : 1, 24. ξυνῴκισαν, to colonize in company with.

ξυνοικοδομέω, 1, 93. ξυνῳκο-

δομημένοι, to be built up together.

ξύνοικος, 6, 77. qui in eadem regione habitat : 2, 68. ξυνοίκους ἐπηγάγοντο, to take foreigners into one's community, invite or introduce settlers into a place.

ξυνόμνυμι, 6, 56. οἱ ξυνομωμοκότες, the conspirators, ξυνωμόται, 18. ξυνωμόσαμεν, to swear mutually, ratify an alliance with oaths, 2, 72. 5, 48. ξυνώμοσαν, 80. ξυνομόσαι, 1, 71. ξυνομόσωσι, 58. ξυνομόσαντες.

ξυνομολογέω, 1, 133. ξυνομολογοῦντος αὐτὰ ταῦτα, to agree in these things.

ξύνταξις, 6, 42. a disposition, an arrangement.

ξυντάσσω, 6, 67. ξυνετάξαντο, to draw up (as an army,) 5, 66. : 7, 60. ξυνταξάμενοι, 7, 2. ὡς ἐς μάχην, to draw up in order of battle : 3, 108. ξυντεταγμένοι, to be drawn up in order : 7, 3. οὐ ῥᾳδίως ξυντασσομένους, to be formed into order, to fall into their ranks, to form with difficulty, 6, 98. : 5, 9. ξυνταχθῆναι, to arrange : 6, 90. ξυντάξῃ, to drill, discipline.

ξυντειχίζω, 4, 57. ξυνετείχιζε, to assist in fortifying, cooperate in the labour of building : 7, 7. ξυνετείχισαν, to assist in building, build in conjunction.

ξυντεκμαίρω, 2, 76. ξυντεκμηράμενοι, to direct or proceed by conjecture.

ξυντελέω, 4, 76. to pay tribute : 2, 15. ξυντελούντων, to contribute to.

ξυντέμνω, 7, 36. ξυντεμόντες ἐς ἔλασσον, to cut shorter, to shorten, curtail, reduce to less dimensions : 8, 45, ξυνέτεμεν, to lessen, cut down.

ξυντίθημι, 4, 4. ξυνετίθεσαν, to join, put together, concert, 1, 97. τὰ Ἑλληνικὰ, to compose the Grecian history : 5, 26. ξυνέθεντο, to be agreed, 32. ξυνθέσθαι, to make a compact with : 4, 19. ξυνέθετο, to be agreed : 6, 65. ξυνθέμενοι ἡμέραν, to agree upon a day, 1, 115. ξυμμαχίαν, to contract an alliance : 5, 18. ξύνθωνται, to agree to, to be concerned in : 1, 21. ξυνέθεσαν, to compose : 8, 37. ξυνέθεντο, had formed treaties with.

ξύντομος, 7, 42. ξυντομωτάτην, the most brief, speedy.

ξυντρέχω, 6, 57. τοῦ ὄχλου ξυνδραμόντος, to run, collect, crowd together.

ξυντρίβω, 4, 11. ξυντρίψωσιν, to run aground.

ξύντροφος, 2, 50. ξυντρόφων, usual, common (maladies.)

ξυντυχία, 5, 11. an accident, 1, 33. καλὴ ἡ ξυντυχία κατὰ πολλὰ τῆς ἡμετέρας χρείας, a fortunate coincidence in respect of many points of our need : 7, 57. chance, haphazard : 3, 45. a case, state, situation of life.

ξυνωμοσία, 6, 27. νεωτέρων πραγμάτων, a conspiracy for a change of affairs, an inno-

vation or revolution in government : 5, 83. : 8, 48. a confederacy.

ξυνώμοτος, 2, 74. τὸ ξυνώμοτον, that which is sworn, a compact, league.

ξυσκευάζω, 7, 74. ξυσκευάσαιντο, to pack up.

ξύσκηνος, 7, 75. messmate, comrade.

ξυσκοτάζω, 1, 51. ξυνεσκόταζε, to grow dark, 7, 73. ἡνίκα, when evening closed in.

ξυσσώζω, 1, 74. ξυνεσώσαμεν, to save together.

ξυσταδὸν, 7, 81. οὐ ξυσταδὸν μάχαις, not by stationary fights.

ξύστασις, 2, 21. κατὰ ξυστάσεις γίγνεσθαι, to separate into cabals, collect in separate knots : 7, 71. τῆς γνώμης, a straining, stretching, racking, intentness.

ξυστέλλω, 8, 4. ξυστελλόμενοι, to contract.

ξυστρατεύω, 7, 33. 35. to make war in alliance with : 3, 11. to unite forces, march along with : 2, 29. ξυνεστράτευσε, 7, 57. : 7, 20. ξυστρατεύεσθαι, to cruize along with (another) against an enemy : 3, 10. ξυνεστρατευσαμένων, to serve along with in war.

ξυστράτηγος, 2, 58. ξυστράτηγοι ὄντες Περικλέους, Pericles's colleagues in the command of the army.

ξυστρέφω, 7, 32. ξυστραφέντες, to assemble, get together in a body, 4, 68. 6, 77.

7, 43. ξυστραφῶσιν, to rally together in a body: 7, 30. ξυστρεφόμενοι, to collect or form in a mass, circle, to embody or rally together (after a charge) forming in a body: 2, 4. ξυνεστρέφοντο ἐν σφίσιν αὐτοῖς, to close their ranks, throw themselves into a mass, close round in a

mass: 2, 4. τὸ δὲ πλεῖστον καὶ ὅσον μάλιστα ξυνεστραμμένον ἐσπίπτουσιν ἐς οἴκημα, to be in a mass, body, the verb is here in the plural after a noun of number in the singular, because in such words the idea of several subjects is always included, Matth. Gr. Gr. 437.

Ο.

Ὁ, ἡ, τὸ, 1, 8. οἱ ἥσσους, the meaner sort: 6, 96. οἱ περὶ τὸν Ἑρμοκράτην, Hermocrates and his colleagues, 8, 105. Matth. Gr. Gr. 396. : 4, 54. τὰ τῆς ὁμολογίας, the tenor of the treaty. : 1, 18. τὰ μὲν, τὰ δὲ, partly—partly, 3, 11. : 7, 73. τοὺς ἀνθρώπους, the men : 1, 15. οἱ ἀπὸ τῆς ἴσης, those upon equality : 1, 2. τὰ αὑτῶν, their own : 7, 31. τῶν Μεσσηνίων μετεπέμψατο, to send for some M. : 7, 61. τὸ τῆς τύχης, the same as τὴν τύχην, i. e. εὐτυχίαν : 8, 105. : 1, 6. ἐν τοῖς πρῶτοι, 3, 17. : ἐν τοῖς πλεῖσται δὴ νῆες ἅμ' αὐτοῖς ἐνεργοὶ κάλλει ἐγένοντο, 3, 81. στάσις—ἐν τοῖς πρώτη ἐγένετο, 7, 24. μέγιστον δὲ καὶ ἐν τοῖς πρῶτον, the Attics use the article for the pronoun, (which is the poetic usage of the art.,) in the phrase ἐν τοῖς, which answers, when with a superlative as here, to the Latin Omnino, Longe, Multo, Matth. Gr. Gr.

421. : 1, 1. Θουκυδίδης Ἀθηναῖος, the art. is omitted in this case of opposition, where the additional subst. does not define, but explain the other subst., Matth. 399. : 1, 111. Ὀρέστης ὁ Ἐχεκρατίδου υἱὸς τοῦ Θεσσαλῶν βασιλέως, an instance of proper apposition, where a subst. is explained by another, it is put without the article, Matth. 399. : 1, 68. τὸ πιστὸν ὑμᾶς, ὦ Λ., τῆς καθ᾽ ὑμᾶς αὐτοὺς πολιτείας—ἀπιστοτέρους ἐς τοὺς ἄλλους καθίστησι, an instance of the art. with an adj., to which it gives the sense of a subst., Matth. 391. : 1, 49. ᾗ δὲ αὐτοὶ ἦσαν οἱ Κορίνθιοι ἐπὶ τῷ εὐωνύμῳ, πολὺ ἐνίκων, τοῖς Κερκυραίοις τῶν εἴκοσι νεῶν—οὐ παρουσῶν, (οἱ γὰρ Κερκυραῖοι εἴκοσι ναυσὶν αὐτοὺς τρεψάμενοι καὶ καταδιώξαντες ἐνέπρησαν τὰς σκηνὰς,) ᾽the twenty ships, of which mention was previously made,᾽ the art. is

put even where otherwise it would not be, when it is to be expressed that the subst., to which it belongs, has been already mentioned, Matth. 388. : 1, 36. τοιαῦτα μὲν οἱ Κερκυραῖοι εἶπον, οἱ δὲ Κορίνθιοι μετ' αὐτοὺς τοιάδε, the art. is put here for the pronoun, Matth. 420. : 1, 24. Φάλιος Ἐρατοκλείδου, as the mention of the descent is frequently not so much a precise definition of the person in contradistinction to others, as a mere customary addition, the art. is often omitted, Matth. 399. : 1, 81. τοῖς δὲ ἄλλη γῆ ἐστὶ πολλὴ, ἧς ἄρχουσι, the art. is used here as a pronoun, according to the Homeric custom, (irregular in Attic prose,) see too 3, 18. Matth. 414. : 1, 86. τοὺς ξυμμάχους οὐ μελλήσομεν τιμωρεῖν, οἱ δ' οὐκέτι μέλλουσι κακῶς πάσχειν, the Homeric idiom, where the art. is put for the pronoun demonstrative ὅδε, Matth. 413. : 1, 84. πολεμικοί τε καὶ εὔβουλοι διὰ τὸ εὔκοσμον γιγνόμεθα, τὸ μὲν, ὅτι αἰδὼς σωφροσύνης πλεῖστον μετέχει, αἰσχύνης δὲ εὐψυχία, εὔβουλοι δὲ ἀμαθέστεροι—παιδευόμενοι, whereas the art. is used sometimes by Attics (in the Homeric fashion) for a pronoun, so in this case of a division of the sentence, in the latter clause should be remarked the noun itself εὔβουλοι instead of the corresponding prono-

minal article. Matth. 418. : 1, 138. τὰ κατὰ Παυσανίαν, res Pausaniæ, an example of the art. with a prep. and its case, to which it gives the sense of an adj., Matth. 396. : 1, 108. τὰ τείχη τὰ ἑαυτῶν τὰ μακρὰ ἀπετέλεσαν, an instance of a designation put after the noun, when by course the art. is repeated, in this instance the art. is doubled, Matth. 401. : 1, 106. ἐσέπεσεν ἐς τοῦ χωρίου ἰδιώτου, an instance where the art. is separated from its noun in the gen. by the governing word, Matth. 403. : 1, 110. τὰ κατὰ τὴν μεγάλην στρατείαν Ἀθηναίων, here the art., put with the prep., is merely a circumlocution, Matth. 398. : 1, 111. Σικυωνίων τοὺς προσμίξαντας μάχῃ ἐκράτησαν, when a participle accompanies the art., in the sense is qui, the whole is in the gen., Matth. 497. : 1, 100. Ἀθηναῖοι εἶλον τριήρεις Φοινίκων καὶ διέφθειραν τὰς πάσας ἐς διακοσίας, here the art. changes the peculiar signif. of the adj., although this retains its proper signif., and thus joined with numerals it means ' in all,' see too 2, 101. μείνας τριάκοντα τὰς πάσας ἡμέρας, 3, 85. διέβησαν ἐς τὴν νῆσον ἑξακόσιοι μάλιστα οἱ πάντες, 6, 43. τριήρεσι μὲν ταῖς πάσαις, Matth. 393. : 1, 118. ὄντες μὲν καὶ πρὸ τοῦ μὴ ταχεῖς ἰέναι ἐς τοὺς πολέμους, εἰ μὴ ἀναγκάζοιντο, τὸ δέ τι καὶ πολέμοις οἰκείοις ἐξειργόμενοι, an instance of the use of the art. for the pronoun in the division τὸ μὲν, τὸ δὲ, where also τὶ occurs, since the distribution is only general, Matth. 416. (N. B. By a mistake Matth. refers to 1, 108. for another instance:) 1, 126. ἐν τῇ τοῦ Διὸς τῇ μεγίστῃ ἑορτῇ, for ἐν τῇ τοῦ Δ. ἱ. τῇ μ., where is to be remarked the position of the article, which, when thus doubled, should be as usually after the noun, the designation seldom stands with the art. before its noun, accompanied by the art., Matth. 401. : 2, 15. ἄτερ καὶ πρὸ τοῦ, Matth. 408. : 2, 53. τὸ μὲν προσταλαιπωρεῖν τῷ δόξαντι καλῷ οὐδεὶς πρόθυμος ἦν, here we may remark the use of the infin., where the art. is redundant, Matth. 820. : 2, 60. τὰ τῆς ὀργῆς, for ἡ ὀργὴ, a periphrasis merely of the subst. in the gen. case, Matth. 412. : 2, 63. τὸ τιμώμενον τῆς πόλεως, for ἡ τιμὴ, the estimation, in which the city stands, the art. here substantives the participle, Matth. 393. : 2, 65. τὸ δὲ μέγιστον, id quod maximum est, an instance of the use of the neuter art., which here constitutes an apposition, Matth. 410. : 2, 87. οὐχὶ δικαίαν ἔχει τέκμαρσιν τὸ ἐκφοβῆσαι, the infin. with the neuter article, here used as a subst. in the accus. case,

is the subject to the predicate τέκμαρσιν, Matth. 817.: 3, 11. ὁ γὰρ παραβαίνειν τι βουλόμενος τὸ μὴ προέχων ἂν ἐπελθεῖν ἀποτρέπεται, an instance of the infin. for a subst. with the neuter art., in which the infin. is put with the accus. of the art. for the gen., Matth. 820. : 4, 28. τὸ ἐπ' ἐκείνοις εἶναι, an instance of the art. standing in the accus. neuter with a prep. with its case, in the sense of an adverb, and when an infin. also follows, 'as far as regards them,' parenthetically used, Matth. 409. : 5, 49. κατὰ τὸν ὁπλίτην ἕκαστον, an instance of the use of the art. with the pronoun ἕκαστος, for as much as it is used, wherever an object entirely indefinite is not to be expressed, Matth. 388.: 6, 14. νομίσας τὸ μὲν λύειν τοὺς νόμους μὴ αἰτίαν σχεῖν, an example of τὸ μὲν λύειν for the gen. τοῦ, where the accus. with the infin. is a subst. for the gen. with the infin., Matth. 821. : 6, 43. Ἀθηναῖοι ἐς τὴν Σικελίαν ἐπεραιοῦντο τοξόταις τοῖς πᾶσιν ὀγδοήκοντα, the art. is used by the Attics, whenever an object entirely indefinite is not to be expressed, it is an especial case that then it is put, when otherwise it would not be, because the subst. has been already mentioned, Matth. 388. : 6, 63. κατὰ τὴν ἡμέραν ἑκάστην, an instance of the art. being put, where in English it is not found : 7, 13. τὰ δὲ πληρώματα διὰ τόδε ἐφθάρη τε ἡμῖν καὶ ἔτι νῦν φθείρεται τῶν ναυτῶν τῶν μὲν διὰ φρυγανισμὸν καὶ ἁρπαγὴν μακρὰν καὶ ὑδρείαν ὑπὸ τῶν ἱππέων ἀπολλυμένων, οἱ δὲ θεραπεύοντες, ἐπειδὴ ἐς ἀντίπαλα καθεστήκαμεν, αὐτομολοῦσι, for τῶν δὲ θεραπευόντων—αὐτομολούντων, an instance of the art. used for the pronoun, where in the phrase ὁ μὲν— ὁ δὲ the art. does not follow in the same case, Matth. 419. : 7, 13. καὶ οἱ ξένοι, οἱ μὲν ἀναγκαστοὶ ἐσβάντες εὐθὺς κατὰ τὰς πόλεις ἀποχωροῦσιν, οἱ δὲ ὑπὸ μεγάλου μισθοῦ τὸ πρῶτον ἐπαρθέντες—ἐπειδὴ παρὰ γνώμην ναυτικόν τε δὴ καὶ τἄλλα ἀπὸ τῶν πολεμίων ἀνθεστῶτα ὁρῶσιν, οἱ μὲν ἐπὶ λιθολογίας προφάσει ἀπέρχονται, οἱ δὲ, ὡς ἕκαστοι δύνανται, εἰσὶ δ' οἳ καὶ—ἀφῄρηνται,' properly speaking the nomin. is not put for the gen., but the definitions annexed with οἱ μὲν—οἱ δὲ constitute an apposition frequently used in Homer, in which the whole proposition is followed by the part in the same case, Matth. 420. : 7, 42. τοῖς Συρακοσίοις κατάπληξις ἐγένετο, εἰ πέρας μηδὲν ἔσται σφίσι τοῦ ἀπαλλαγῆναι τοῦ κινδύνου, under the division of words taking others, which shew the respect, in which the sense is taken in the gen., here the gen. illustrates the proposition,

Matth. 458. τοῦ ἀπαλλ. might be away, sometimes the idea ' with respect to' is the basis of the gen., an instance of the infin. used as a subst. with the neuter art., Matth. 816. : 7, 86. ξυνέβαινε δὲ τὸν μὲν πολεμιώτατον αὐτοῖς εἶναι Δημοσθένην, διὰ τὰ ἐν τῇ νήσῳ καὶ Πύλῳ, τὸν δὲ διὰ τὰ αὐτὰ ἐπιτηδειότατον, Matth. 418. : 8, 84. ὁ δὲ αὐθαδέστερόν τέ τι ἀπεκρίνατο, Matth. 661. : 8, 1. οἱ πάνυ τῶν στρατιωτῶν, Matth. 395.

ὀβολὸς, 5, 47. Αἰγιναίους, this coin was in value equal to twopence English.

ὀγδοήκοντα, 5, 47. eighty.

ὄγδοος, 7, 18. ὄγδοον καὶ δέκατον, the ordinal numbers up to 20 from 14 are compounded with δέκατος and a cardinal number, Matth. Gr. Gr. 176.

ὅδε, 3, 56. οἵδε μετ' αὐτοῦ ἦσαν, the signif. of μετὰ with a gen. is ' together with,' hence μετά τινος εἶναι, ' to be on any one's side,' Matth. Gr. Gr. 904.

ὁδὸς, 2, 3. ὁδῶν, streets : 1, 69. οἵᾳ ὁδῷ, in what way, manner : 5, 38. τὴν ἐπὶ Νεμέας ὁδὸν, the road to Nemea, 59. τὴν κατὰ Νεμέαν ὁδὸν, the route by Nemea : 3, 64. ἄδικον ὁδὸν ἰόντων, to pursue an unjust course : 1, 122. ὁδοὶ πολέμου, the ways and means of war : 2, 12. ἐν ὁδῷ εἶναι, to be on one's march : 7, 81.

ὅθεν, 1, 15. whence, 143.

4, 8.: 1, 89. διακομίζοντο εὐθὺς ὅθεν ὑπεξέθεντο, παῖδας, for ἐκεῖθεν ὄντων, which mode is imitated from the common custom of the pronoun relative, where, if it be referred to a pronoun demonstrative, this is usually omitted, and the relative takes the same case, Matth. Gr. Gr. 683.

: οἱ, 1, 50. where.

: αἱ, 2, 13. 6, 59.: 4, 27. where it is reflexive, Matth. Gr. Gr. 182.

οἴκαδε, 1, 52. homewards.

οἰκεῖος, 6, 46. οἰκεῖα, what belongs to a person, one's own (property,) 6, 69. 1, 60. οἰκεῖον τὸν κίνδυνον ἡγούμενοι, to deem the danger coming home to them: 4, 64. γνώμης, a private opinion, 106. a relation, 64. a fellow inhabitant: 1, 74. τὰ οἰκεῖα, effects, moveable property, stock, utensils, 32. τῇ οἰκείᾳ μόνον δυνάμει, with only our own forces: 4, 6. οἰκεῖον σφίσι, nearly concerning them, of intimate and last importance: 3, 13. οἰκεῖον κίνδυνον ἕξειν, to encounter a personal danger, endanger one's own welfare, the welfare of one's own house, or country: 1, 9. κατὰ τὸ οἰκεῖον, on account of his relationship: 7, 44. 70. οἰκειότερος, 2, 39.

οἰκειότης, 4, 19. friendly neighbourhood, neighbourly charity: 3, 86. προφάσει οἰκειότητος, under the pretext of an alliance by blood.

οἰκειόω, 1, 36. οἰκειοῦται, to be a friend: 6, 23. οἰκειοῦντας, to make one's own, appropriate to oneself, to found, plant, an instance of the Attic contr. of the fut., Matth. Gr. Gr. 221.: 1, 100. 3. 65.

οἰκείως, 6, 57. διαλεγόμενον, familiarly, confidentially, φιλικῶς.

οἰκείωσις, 4, 128. τῶν δὲ οἰκείωσιν ἐποιοῦντο, to appropriate.

οἰκέτης, 5, 82. a domestic servant, 2, 4.

οἰκέω, 5, 42. to dwell in, inhabit, 7, 57.: 2, 63. οἰκήσειαν ἐπὶ σφῶν αὐτῶν, to live by themselves: 6, 2. ᾤκουν δὲ περὶ πᾶσαν τὴν Σικελίαν, to dwell up and down, all over, per omnem, ut Liv. circa civitates, i. e. per, ad omnes, literally, to dwell around, i. e. on the sea-coast: 1, 124. ἀκινδύνως οἰκῶμεν, to live without danger: 6, 2. οἰκῆσαι, to dwell: 1, 12. ᾤκησαν, 2, 64. ᾠκήσαμεν: 2, 29. ᾤκει, 1, 2. 7. κάτω ᾤκουν, to dwell on the coast: 1, 2. 5. οἰκουμέναις, peopled, inhabited, 74.: 2. 15. ᾠκεῖτο ἀεὶ κατὰ πόλεις, to dwell in a succession of separate towns: 2, 27. τοῖς Αἰγινήταις οἱ Λακεδαιμόνιοι ἔδοσαν Θυρέαν οἰκεῖν καὶ τὴν γῆν νέμεσθαι, the infin. stands after verbs 'to give,' to express the object, Matth. Gr. Gr. 804.

οἴκημα, 2, 4. 4, 4. an edifice, a building, 17, 48.: 1, 134. a small building.

οἴκησις, 2, 16. τῇ αὐτονόμῳ, by this independent (mode of) dwelling: 6, 88. οἰκήσεις, settlements, for πόλεις, villages : 6, 4. an inhabiting, a settling in a place : 1, 6. an habitation.

οἰκήτωρ, 1, 2. 23. 26. 2, 27. 68. 4, 49. a settler, an inhabitant.

οἰκία, 2, 3. 52. 3, 67. 5, 16. 7, 29. 8, 6. a house, habitation, family, household : 1, 89. οἰκίαι αἱ μὲν πολλαὶ ἐπεπτώκεσαν, ὀλίγαι δὲ περιῆσαν, an instance of a nomin. for a gen. *partitivé*, which especially takes place in ὁ μὲν, ὁ δὲ, Matth. Gr. Gr. 503.

οἰκίζω, 1, 8. ᾤκισαν, to found, people a colony, 12. 13. οἰκίζοντες : 5, 12. ᾠκίσθη, to be settled, inhabited, 1, 7. ᾠκίσθησαν, to be colonized, planted, 10. οἰκισθείσης : 4, 102. ᾤκισεν τὴν ἤπειρον, to settle, colonize, plant, 1, 98. ; 6, 3. μετὰ Συρακούσας οἰκισθείσας, after the foundation of Syracuse : 1, 100. οἰκιοῦντες.

οἴκισις, 5, 11. a foundation.

οἰκιστὴς, 1, 4, a colonizer : 6, 3. the leader of a colony, founder of a settlement, conductor or planter of a colony : 1, 24. 5, 11. : 6, 4. οἰκιστὰς ποιήσαντες, to choose, appoint a leader of a colony, *i. q.* ἐποιήσαντο, *see* Baver.

οἰκοδομέω, 1, 93. to build houses upon : 7, 19. ᾠκοδομεῖτο, to construct, 29. ᾠκοδομημένον, to be built : 4, 100.

ᾠκοδόμητο, to be constructed, built of, (with reference to the material employed :) 7; 11. οἰκοδομησαμένων τὰ τείχη, to build up : 5, 83. τὰ οἰκοδομούμενα, buildings.

οἰκοδόμημα, 1, 90. a building, an edifice, 2, 13. 4, 8.

οἰκοδόμησις, a structure, mode or form of building.

οἰκοδομία, 2, 65. a villa, house : 7, 6. a place of abode, a hold : 1, 93. a building.

οἴκοι, 5, 64, τὰ οἴκοι, the posts in the neighbourhood of home : 5, 50. at home.

οἰκόπεδον, 4, 90. a house, dwelling-house.

οἶκος, 1, 17. a family : 5, 11. 13. 27. a home, 51. ἐπ' οἴκου, for home, homewards, 1, 54. 99. 2, 60.

οἰκτίζω, 2, 57. ᾠκτίζοντο, to have compassion on.

οἶκτος, 3, 67. pity, compassion, 40. οἴκτῳ ἁμαρτάνειν, to err from compassion.

οἰμωγὴ, 7, 71. a cry of lamentation.

οἶνος, 6, 28. οἶνον (*sc.* μετὰ,) through wine, i. e. drunkenness, *per temulentiam* : 4, 16.

οἰνοχόη, 6, 46. a flagon.

οἴομαι, 4, 26. 5, 40. ᾤοντο, to presume, imagine, suppose, 7, 55. : 1, 33. οἴεται, to be of opinion: 2, 4. οἰόμενοι, to suppose, imagine, 4, 73. 5, 38. to think, deem : 2, 81. οἰηθῆναι : 1, 69. οἰόμενοι λανθάνειν, while they think they escape the notice of : 3, 46. οἴεσθε.

οἶος, 5, 7. how great : 1,
77. οἷα καὶ τότε, such as formerly : 3, 23. : 2, 48. οἷον ἐγίγνετο, λέξω, to relate how it
was, the manner of it, its
origin and progress : 4, 90.
οἷον, about : 1, 91. οὐ γὰρ οἷόν
τε, for it is not possible : 8,
65. : 6, 12. καὶ τὸ πρᾶγμα μέγα
εἶναι καὶ μὴ οἷον νεωτέρῳ βουλεύ-
σασθαί τι καὶ ὀξέως μεταχειρίσαι,
such as a younger man
would be able, an example
of οἷον εἶναι meaning 'to be
able,' without the particle
τι, Matth. Gr. Gr. 693. : 7,
21. πρὸς ἄνδρας τολμηρούς,
οἵους καὶ 'Αθηναίους, for οἷοι
'Αθηναῖοί εἰσιν, this pronoun
rel. where it should be in
the nomin., takes the case
of the word, to which it is
referred, Matth. 683.

ὀϊστὸς, 2, 75. 4, 48. an
arrow.

οἰστὸς, 7, 75. οἰστὰ ἐφαίνετο,
seemed tolerable.

οἰσύϊνος, 4, 9. wicker.

οἴχομαι, 5, 55. ᾤχοντο, to
depart, 7, 46. ᾤχετο, to go to,
2, 85. ; 7, 7. to proceed (on
a journey,) 32. οἰχόμενοι ἐς
τὰς πόλεις : 1, 116. ἔτυχον γὰρ
αἱ μὲν ἐπὶ Καρίας—οἰχόμενοι, αἱ
δὲ ἐπὶ Χίου καὶ Λέσβου, περιαγγέλλουσαι βοηθεῖν, verbs of
motion are accompanied regularly by participles future
to express the object of the
verb, Matth. Gr. Gr. 851.

οἰωνὸς, 6, 27. an (unlucky)
omen.

ὀκέλλω, 4, 12. ὀκεῖλαι (τὴν
ναῦν,) to run aground, to

rive, break, shatter, split,
by forcing aground, 11. ὀκεί-
λαντας : 2, 91. ὤκειλαν, where
it is used in a neuter signif.

ὀκνέω, 5, 61. ὤκνουν, to hesitate : 1, 120. to hang back,
hesitate.

ὀκνηρὸς, 1, 142. 4, 55. ὀκνη-
ρότερος, more inert, less alive,
more fearful, timid.

ὄκνος, 2, 40. fear, hesita-
tion, delay (produced by
fear :) 7, 49. a state of inaction : 3, 39. παρέσχεν ὄκνον μὴ
ἐλθεῖν ἐς τὰ δεινά, fear, dread,
(of undergoing danger,) labour.

ὄλεθρος, 3, 98. destruction,
7, 27. 29.

ὀλιγάκις, 6, 38. seldom,
rarely.

ὀλιγανθρωπία, 3, 93. ἐς ὀλι-
γανθρωπίαν κατέστησαν, to reduce the population to a
small number of men, 1,
11.

ὀλιγαρχέομαι, 5, 31. to be
aristocratically governed, 8,
76, 91.

ὀλιγαρχία, 1, 19. κατ' ὀλι-
γαρχίαν πολιτεύειν, to use an
aristocratical constitution, to
live under an aristocracy :
5, 81. ; 6, 11. δι' ὀλιγαρχίας,
through or by means of, or
with the aid of an oligarchy :
8, 73.

ὀλιγαρχικὸς, 8, 72. of or
belonging to an oligarchy.

ὀλίγος, 1, 50. ὀλίγαι ἀμύνειν,
(too) few to give succour,
Matth. Gr. Gr. 652. : 1, 74.
ὀλίγῳ, by a little, 18. ἔτη τετρακόσια καὶ ὀλίγῳ πλείω, four

hundred years and a few more : 5, 65. ἐξ ὀλίγου, sudden : 1, 61. κατ' ὀλίγον προϊόντες, to proceed by slow marches.

ὀλιγωρέω, 2, 62. ὀλιγωρῆσαι, to make light of : 5, 9. to be negligent, off one's guard.

ὀλιγωρία, 2, 52. ἐς ὀλιγωρίαν ἐτράποντο, to grow careless, unmindful : 5, 9.

ὀλκὰς, 2, 67. a heavy ship, ship of burden, 17, 18. 23. 4, 83. 6, 1. 22. : 7, 7. ἐν ὀλκάσιν ἢ πλοίοις, ships of burden or light vessels, skiffs, boats, τρόπῳ ᾧ ἂν [προχωρῇ] ἐν ὀλκάσιν ἢ πλοίοις ἢ ἄλλως ὅπως ἂν προχωρῇ, (taking the words ὅπως ἂν per hyperbaton.)

ὀλκὸς, 3, 15, τῶν νεῶν, drag, machine for transporting vessels over land.

ὀλολυγὴ, 2, 4. a shrieking.

ὅλος, 4, 69. ταύτην τὴν ὅλην ἡμέραν, whole, entire.

ὀλοφυρμὸς, 3, 67. lamentation, wailing, 7. 71. 75.

ὀλοφύρομαι, 2, 34. ὀλοφυρόμεναι, to utter lamentation, 44. to commisserate, lament over, bewail, condole with : 6, 78. ὀλοφυρθείς, dolere : 7, · 30. ὀλοφύρασθαι.

ὀλόφυρσις, 1, 143. a lamentation : 2, 51.

ὀμαιχμία, 1, 18. confederation.

ὄμαιχμος, 3, 58. a comrade in war,

ὁμαλὸς, 5, 65. ἐν τῷ ὁμαλῷ, on level ground; ἐς τὸ ὁμαλὲν,

into the plain : 4, 31. ὁμαλώτατος, plainest, flattest, most level.

ὁμαλῶς, 5, 70. uniformly, evenly, in step.

ὁμηρεία, 8, 45. a security.

ὅμηρος, 1, 56. a hostage, 57. 61. 82. 8, 3. 31. it has a much wider extent than the Lat. *obses*, or the English *hostage, see* 6, 61. where the persons in question were not hostages from the Argives, but those Argives, who had been plotting with the Lacedæmonians and were deposited by the Athenians in their islands, *comp.* 5, 84.

ὁμιλέω, 6, 55. ξυνεχῶς ὡμιλήκει τῇ ἀρχῇ, to be continually engaged in governmentaffairs, to be conversant, versed in, experienced, 70. ὡμιληκόσι πολέμῳ, to be conversant with, experienced in : 8, 11. ἡμῖν ἀπὸ τοῦ ἴσου ὁμιλοῦντες, to associate, live, to be in alliance, confederacy with us, on a footing of equality : 1, 77.

ὁμιλία, 1, 3. intercourse, association, 68. society, private life.

ὅμιλος, 6, 24. ὁ πολὺς, the crowd, bulk of the people, generality, populace : 4, 125. ψιλὸν, a light-armed crew : 2, 65. a multitude : 6, 82. a concourse : 6, 80. ὁ ἄλλος ὅμιλος ἅπας ὡς εἰπεῖν, the whole populace almost together, to speak with some allowance, sweepingly, sum marily : 2, 31. οὐκ ὀλίγος ψιλῶν, a great crowd : 4, 112.

ὄμμα, 2, 11. ἐν ὄμμασι, in the sight of, before one's eyes.

ὄμνυμι, 5, 19. ὤμνυον, to swear to, 18, 47. ὀμνύντων, 30. ὀμόσαι, to swear, 6, 72. αὐτοῖς τὸ ὄρκιον, to take an oath to, 5, 47. τὰς σπονδὰς, to swear to keep, 4, 88. ὀμόσαντα τὰ τέλη, 5, 17. ὤμοσαν, 30. θεῶν γὰρ πίστεις ὀμόσαντες, to swear upon the faith of the gods.

ὁμοβώμιος, 3, 59. θεοὶ, (the) gods, who are worshipped at the same altar.

ὁμοῖος, 1, 82. corresponding : 6, 21. ἐν τῷ ὁμοίῳ στρατευόμενοι, to make war upon equal terms, with like advantages : 1, 25. ὅμοια for ὁμοίως, equally.: 5, 16. similar, like : 1, 73. ὁμοίας δυνάμεως, equal force, (land or sea :) 1, 25. χρημάτων δυνάμει ὄντες κατ' ἐκεῖνον τὸν χρόνον ὅμοια τοῖς Ἑλλήνων πλουσιωτάτοις, Matth. Gr. Gr. 423.

ὁμοιότροπος, 3, 10. of a similar turn, similar in manners, taste, inclinations : 7, 55.

ὁμοιοτρόπως, 6, 20. similarly, in a similar way.

ὁμοιόω, 4, 92. ὁμοιωθῆναι τοῖς πρὶν ἔργοις, to come up to, to equal, 5, 103. to imitate, to be like : 3, 82. τὰς ὀργὰς τῶν πολλῶν πρὸς τὰ παρόντα ὁμοιοῖ, assimilates the passions of the many to passing events.

ὁμοίως, 5, 10. in like manner : 1, 70. ἔχουσί τε ὁμοίως καὶ ἐλπίζουσιν, they have as soon as wish, Engl. they wish and have—both at the same moment and with as little difficulty : 1, 2. similarly, equally : 4, 126.

ὁμολογέω, 2, 41. to acknowledge, confess : 5, 45. ὁμολογήσωσιν, to confess, own, 55. : 2, 5. 4, 69. 5, 4. 46. : 1, 101. ὡμολόγησαν Ἀθηναίοις, to come to terms with : 6, 90.

ὁμολογία, 5, 5. an amicable conference, 17. a willing capitulation, voluntary surrender, 21. an agreement, 6, 10. : 1, 29. a capitulation : 6, 94. ὁμολογίᾳ προσαγαγόμενοι, on composition, terms : 4, 65. ὁμολογίαν ἐποιοῦντο, a concord, an agreement, unanimity : 3, 90.

ὁμολογουμένως, 6, 90. confessedly, indisputably.

ὁμονοέω, 8, 75. ὁμονοήσῃ, to be of one, the same mind.

ὅμορος, 1, 59. bordering on the confines : 6, 2. τοῖς Σικανοῖς, on the borders of, adjacent, 6, 78. : 1, 15. a borderer, neighbour.

ὁμόσε, 4, 92. χωρῆσαι τοῖσδε, to go to pell-mell.

ὁμόσκευος, 3, 95. using or furnished with the same kind of arms, similarly accoutred.

ὁμόφυλος, 1, 141. of the same tribe, race, nation.

ὁμόφωνος, 4, 3. of a similar speech, tongue, 40.

ὁμώνυμος, 2, 68. of the same name.

ὅμως, 6, 31. δὲ, however, nevertheless, 7, 34. : 5, 61. nevertheless, 1, 22. : 7, 1. 57. 75.

ὁμωχέτης, 4, 97. δαίμονας, a joint keeper, preserver.

ὀνειδίζω, 1, 5. ὀνειδιζόντων, to upbraid, reproach : 3, 62. ὀνειδίσαι : 1, 77. ὀνειδίζεται, to be cast as a reproach against.

ὀνεύω, 7, 25. ὤνευον, to turn round, shake, move by a crane, wheel, (rope fastened to the pile,) see the Schol.

ὄνομα, 3, 10. τῷ ὀνόματι, nominally, 6, 10. : 5, 89. καλῶν ὀνομάτων, specious words: 6, 33. name, reputation, 5, 16. : 1, 3. an appellation : 7, 64.

ὀνομάζω, 2, 17. ὠνόμαζον, to mention by name : 6, 55. ὀνομασθέντα, to be celebrated, bruited about : 1, 3. ὠνόμαξεν, to name, mention by name, 4, 102. : 2, 54. ὠνομάσθαι, to be named, expressed, mentioned, 7, 39. esse, see Baver, as κέκλημαι in Eurip. Hipp. : 4, 98. ὀνομασθῆναι, to be imputed, 1, 96. ὠνομάσθη : 2, 15. ὠνομασμένη, to be named.

ὀνομαστὶ, 7, 69. by name.

ὀνομαστὸς, 1, 11. ὀνομαστότατα, most celebrated, famous.

ὀξέως, 4, 34. alertly, spiritedly : 6, 4. readily, precipitately, 11. strenuously, 12. hastily, easily, 34. readily, 2, 87.

ὀξὺς, 3, 82. hasty, rapid :

2, 8. ὀξύτερον, more easily : 1, 70. ὀξεῖς ἐπινοῆσαι, quick to contrive : 4, 126.

ὅπᾳ, 5, 77. ὅπᾳ κα δικαιότατα δοκῇ, a Doric form, see Duker.

ὅπῃ, 6, 8. ὅπῃ ἂν γιγνώσκωσιν, in whatever (way, manner.)

ὁπηνίκα, 4, 125. when.

ὀπίσω, 4, 4. τοὐπίσω, behind.

ὁπλίζω, 8, 17. ὁπλίσαντες, to arm : 3, 27. ὁπλίζει, to arm (in heavy armour:) 3, 75. ὁπλισθεὶς, to take up arms : 7, 1. ὡπλισμένους, to be armed, equipped with arms, 4, 9. : 94. ἐκ παρασκευῆς, to be armed according to discipline : 6, 17. ἱκανῶς ὡπλίσθη, to be adequately armed, i. e. in sufficient numbers.

ὅπλισις, 3, 22. 5, 8. an equipment.

ὁπλιταγωγὸς, 6, 25. a military transport (for the heavy-armed.)

ὁπλίτης, 4, 26. 5, 12. 47. 7, 19. a heavy-armed soldier : 1, 107. οἱ Λακεδαιμόνιοι ἐβοήθησαν τοῖς Δωριεῦσιν ἑαυτῶν τε πεντακοσίοις καὶ χιλίοις ὁπλίταις καὶ τῶν ξυμμάχων μυρίοις, words of ' army,' ' fleet,' &c. have the dat. case without the prep., when they constitute an accompaniment, Matth. Gr. Gr. 563.

ὁπλιτικὸς, 5, 6. 7, 11. a heavy-armed arm.

ὅπλον, 1, 83. 2, 81. 4, 69. 5, 34. ὅπλα, arms, 18. 7, 1. : 1, 6. μεθ' ὅπλων, in armour : 3, 1. τῶν ὅπλων, the heavy-armed troops, 7, 73. ὅπλα λαβόντας, to take arms.

ὁποῖ, 5, 54. στρατεύουσιν, whither they are marching : 8, 56. : 2, 11. ἔνθαδε ὅποι ἄν τις ἡγῆται, an instance of the regular use of the conj. after the rel., where the person is indefinite, to which this rel. refers, and the whole proposition refers to fut. time, Matth. Gr. Gr. 787.

ὁποῖος, 1, 50. ὁποῖοι ἐκράτουν ἢ ἐκρατοῦντο, whether, which of the two : 7, 38.

ὁποσονοῦν, 4, 39. ever so little.

ὁπόσος, 4, 118. ὁπόσοις ἄν δοκῇ, as many soever, whatsoever.

ὁπόταν, 4, 21. whenever, whensoever.

ὁπότε, 8, 96. when : 2, 79. καὶ ὁπότε μὲν ἐπίοιαν οἱ Ἀθηναῖοι, ἐνεδίδοσαν, ἀποχωροῦσι δὲ ἐνέκειντο, the opt. is here put with its particle, because the discourse is concerning a past action, which, however, was not suited to a precise point of time, but was repeated, Matth. Gr. Gr. 775.

ὁποτεροιοῦν, 5, 18. to whatever side.

ὁποτεροισοῦν, 5, 41. to either one or other.

ὁπότερος, 3, 14. whichever side, party, whoever: 5, 41.

ὁποτέρωσι, 5, 65. on which side, in which direction : 1, 63. whether.

ὄπτομαι, 6, 30. εἴποτε ὄψοιντο, if they were ever to see

(again :) 3, 33. ὤφθη, to be seen, discovered : 1, 51. ὤφθησαν, to be seen, 4, 73.

ὅπως, 3, 46. ὁρᾶν ὅπως ἔξομεν—χρῆσθαι, to take care that we may be able, have it in our power : 1, 62. that, in order to, 63. in what way, 35.

ὁπωστοσοῦν, 6, 56. in any way whatsoever, anyhow.

ὁπωσοῦν, 1, 77. however so little : 7, 49. by any means whatever, in the least, at all.

ὁράω, 2, 45. ὁρῶ, to see, perceive, foresee: 7, 37. ἑώρα, to look toward, 5, 59. ὡς ἑώρων, since they saw, 1, 51. 2, 62. εἰ μὴ, unless I saw, did I not see, 8, 1. : 8, 8. ἑώρα, he saw, 2, 90. : 6, 41. ὁρᾶν πρὸς, to look to, have a regard to : 3, 45. ὁρωμένων, what is visible, 2, 42. περὶ τοῦ ἤδη ὁρωμένου, in respect to that, which was already seen, before their eyes : 2, 81. οὐδὲ ἑωρῶντο, not to be in sight, 1, 51. : 2, 21. ἑωράκισαν : 6, 33. ὁρᾶτε ἀπὸ τῶν ὑπαρχόντων, Tac. ex re consulturum, 1, 82. ὅπως μη, mind lest : 8, 66. ὁρῶν πολὺ τὸ ξυνεστηκὸς, Matth. Gr. Gr. 394. : 7, 47. ἑώρων οὐ κατορθοῦντες καὶ τοὺς στρατιώτας ἀχθομένους, se non secunda fortuna uti, a verb of sense taking another in the participle, Matth. 828.

ὀργάω, 4, 108. ὀργώντων, to desire vehemently, 8, 2. under the influence of passion : 2, 21. ὤργητο, to be eager (after.)

ὀργὴ, 2, 8. ὀργῇ ἔχειν, to be enraged at, inflamed against, 85. : 1, 38. anger, passion : 6, 17. temper, disposition of mind : 1, 92. ὀργὴν φανερὰν ἐποιοῦντο, to shew one's indignation : 7, 68. ὀργῇ προσμίξωμεν, to meet, engage (an enemy) with resentment, Liv. *cum ira quadam et indignatione :* 1, 31. ὀργῇ φέροντες, to be indignant at, take in dudgeon, 130. ὀργῇ χαλεπῇ ἐχρῆτο ἐς πάντας ὁμοίως, to treat all indifferently, with insolent anger : 2, 11. ὀργὴ προσπίπτει πᾶσι, all men fall into passion, 68. τοὺς Ἀθηναίους τῆς ἐπ' αὐτὸν παραλύειν, to divert the Athenians from their anger against him.

ὀργίζομαι, 8, 1. ὠργίζοντο, to be angry, 5, 52. indignant : 1, 148. ὀργισθέντας ὑπὲρ αὐτῶν, on account of those things, 122. : 1, 74. ὀργισθῆναι, to be out of temper, to be incensed : 2, 60. ἐμοὶ τοιούτῳ ἀνδρὶ ὀργίζεσθε, to be angry with such a man as me, a man like me : 4, 128.

ὀρέγομαι, 4, 21. ὠρέγοντο τοῦ πλέονος, 92. ὀρεγόμενος, to catch or grasp at, covet : 6, 10. ὀρέγεσθαι ἀρχῆς ἄλλης, to long for, seek after, affect, pursue : 6, 10. ὧν ὀρεγόμενος, to aim at, covet, 83. ἰσχύος, 2, 65. τοῦ πρῶτος γίγνεσθαι, 61.

ὄρθιος, 5, 56. ὄρθιον ἑτέραν ἐπόρευοντο, (sc. ὁδὸν,) direct.

ὀρθὸς, 5, 46. standing : 3, 11

56. τὸ ὀρθὸν, right : 5, 42. ὀρθὸν παραδοῦναι, to restore in *statu quo.*

ὀρθόω, 2, 60. πόλιν ξύμπασαν ὀρθουμένην, a state that enjoys public prosperity : 4, 18. διὰ τὸ μὴ τῷ ὀρθουμένῳ αὐτοῦ πιστεύοντες ἐπαίρεσθαι, relying upon success : 3, 37. τὰ πλείω ὀρθοῦνται, to rule, govern, administer affairs generally : 5, 9. ὀρθοῖτο, to do well, act correctly, 42. : 6, 9. ὀρθοῦσθαι, to prosper, go on well : 6, 66. ὤρθωσαν, to erect.

ὄρθρος, 3, 112. ἅμα ὄρθρῳ, on the first dawn : 4, 110.

ὀρθῶς, 5, 1. rightly, justly, well, correctly, 20. logically, correctly, from right premises : 6, 8. οὐκ ὀρθῶς, unwisely, rashly, 2, 62. incorrectly : 1, 70. rightly, truly : 3, 56.

ὁρίζω, 1, 46. ὁρίζων, to bound, limit, 3, 82. ἐς τὸ ἡδονὴν ἔχον ὁρίζοντες, to limit according to their appetite : 7, 57. ὁριζόμενοι, to be situated within, in the confines of : 1, 71. ὡρίσθω, to be stopped, to have a period put to : 2, 96.

ὅριος, 2, 12. ἐπὶ τοῖς ὁρίοις γίγνεσθαι, to be on the borders.

ὅρκιος, 2, 71. 6, 52. σφίσι τὰ ὅρκια εἶναι, to be bound by oath : 1, 78. θεοὺς τοὺς ὁρκίους, the gods, who have been invoked to witness an oath.

ὅρκος, 2, 72. 4, 19. 5, 18. 30. 41. 42. an oath.

ὁρκόω, 4, 74. ὁρκώσαντες, to

swear: 8, 75. ὥρκωσαν πάντας τοὺς στρατιώτας τοὺς μεγίστους ὅρκους, Matth. Gr. Gr. 591.

ὁρμάω, 1, 87. ὁρμῆσαι ἐς τὸ πολεμεῖν, to rush eagerly into war : 7, 74. ὥρμησαν, to set out, forth, 34. to rush upon, make onset upon, 8, 23. to urge on his progress : 4, 100. *act.* to encourage, rouse, 1, 127. ὥρμα ἐς τὸν πόλεμον, τοὺς Ἀθ. to urge into the war: 3, 24. ὁρμήσαντες ἀπὸ τῆς τάφρου, to set out from, 2, 19. to move, proceed : 2, 69. αὐτόθεν ὁρμώμενον, 3, 45. προθύμως, to be eagerly bent upon, 2, 65. ἀπ' ἐλασσόνων ὁρμώμενος, to set out with, begin with fewer resources, 4, 3. to issue, 3, 31. ἐκ πόλεως, to make a town the seat of war, a point to set out from, to have a town for head-quarters, 1, 64. 2, 69. 6, 50. 7, 9. 8, 24. : 3, 95. ὡρμᾶτο, to set out : 1, 90. ἀπὸ ἐχυροῦ ὁρμᾶσθαι, to sally forth from a strong hold : 8, 3 ὁρμηθεὶς, 7, 2. : 4, 73. ὡρμήθησαν: 6, 9. ἐφ' ἃ ὡρμήσθε, to be bent upon or eager for, 78. ἐπὶ ταῦτα, to be so minded, inclined : 2, 65. ὥρμηντο ἐς τὸν πόλεμον, to apply themselves to the war, 2, 59. to be anxious, eagerly disposed, 5, 29. to proceed, 5, 6, στρατεύειν, to be bent, eager, disposed, resolved, 7, 21. ἐς τὴν ναυμαχίαν, to lend their attention, apply their mind, to be bent upon or eager after a naval engagement, 8, 23. 40. : 2, 4.

ὥρμηνται, to bestir themselves, to be in motion, 1, 32. : 8, 8. fixed upon, 11. ὡρμημένων, to be impatient, 4, 27. to be strongly inclined.

ὁρμέω, 2, 91. ὁρμοῦσα, to lie at anchor, 90. ὥρμουν, to be in station, at anchor, 1, 52. 3, 4. 4, 25. 7, 4. 30. 34. : 3, 33. περὶ Ἴκαρον, to lie at anchor about or off Icarus : 7, 25. ὁρμοῖεν: 7, 25. ὁρμουσῶν, 8, 51.

ὁρμή, 7, 43. heat, warmth, enthusiasm, 71. ἀπὸ μιᾶς ὁρμῆς, from or with one (simultaneous) impulse : 3, 36. impetuosity, violence, heat, anger : 4, 4. a fancy, whim, fit.

ὁρμίζω, 8, 10. to bring into port : 1, 46. ὁρμίζονται, to come to anchor, to moor, take station, 1, 46. 7, 34. : 2, 42. ὁρμιεῖσθαι : 2, 86. ὡρμίσατο, 1, 51. 3, 76. : 7, 30.

ὅρμος, 7, 41. a ship's station, mooring, anchorage, a road to lie in, 4, 26. 6, 44.

ὄρνεα, 2, 50. birds.

ὄρνις, 2, 50. ὀρνίθων.

ὄρος, 2, 77. 96. 4, 70. 5, 10. a mountain.

ὅρος, 4, 92. περὶ γῆς ὅρων, a boundary, border, 5, 41.

ὀροφή, 3, 68. a roof, 4, 48.

ὄροφος, 1, 134. a roof.

ὀρρωδέω, 6, 9. περὶ τῷ ἐμαυτοῦ σώματι, to fear, to be in alarm for, 14. : 5, 32. ὀρρώδησαν, to be afraid.

ὀρρωδία, 2, 89. οὐκ ἀξιῶν τὰ μὴ δεινὰ ἐν ὀρρωδίᾳ ἔχειν, dread, alarm, apprehension, fear, consternation, 89.

ὄρυγμα, 4, 67. 90. an excavation : 1, 106. a trench,
ditch.

ὀρύσσω, 2, 76. ὀρύξαντες, to
dig.

ὀρχηθμὸς, ὀρχηστὺς, 3, 104.
dancing.

ὅς, ἣ, ὃ, 3, 1. χρόνον ὃν εἶχον,
the time during which, as
long as, 9. ὃ ἡμῖν καὶ Ἀθηναίοις οὐκ ἦν, which was not
the case with us and the
Athenians : 1, 12. Πελοποννήσιοι ᾤκισαν τῆς ἄλλης Ἑλλά-
δος ἔστιν ἃ χωρία, from the
idiom that the subject, (noun
or pronoun,) is often omitted, if a general word or
one easily supplied from the
context, springs this phrase,
(which stands in an adj.
sense,) where the verb comes
to refer to a subject preceding and to be in the
number of the relative following, Matth. Gr. Gr. 698.:
1, 28. δίκας ἤθελον δοῦναι ἐν
Πελοποννήσῳ παρὰ πόλεσιν, αἷς
ἂν ἀμφότεροι ξυμβῶσιν, here the
relative refers to a noun
(δίκας,) joined with a prep.,
which prep. is omitted the
second time, (with the second
noun,) and αἷς alone stands
for παρ' αἷς, Matth. 990. : 1,
103. οἱ δ' ἐν Ἰθώμῃ—ξυνέβησαν
πρὸς τοὺς Λ. ἐφ' ᾧ ἐξίασιν ἐκ
Πελοποννήσου ὑπόσπονδοι, an
instance of the use of the
relative for the conj. ὥστε,
where, instead of the infin.,
the fut. follows, Matth.
692, : 1, 122. τὴν ᾖσσαν εἰ καὶ

δεινόν τῳ ἀκοῦσαι, ἴστω οὐκ ἄλλο τι φέρουσαν ἢ ἄντικρυς δουλείαν, ὃ καὶ λόγῳ ἐνδοιασθῆναι
αἰσχρὸν τῇ Πελοποννήσῳ, the
pronoun rel. is put in the
neuter, because it refers to
a thing generally, although
that thing is here fem., (and
might be masc.) Matth. 637.:
2, 40. διαφερόντως γὰρ δὴ καὶ
τόδε ἔχομεν, ὥστε τολμᾷν τε οἱ
αὐτοὶ μάλιστα, καὶ περὶ ὧν ἐπι-
χειρήσομεν ἐκλογίζεσθαι, ὃ τοῖς
ἄλλοις ἀμαθία μὲν θράσος, λογισμὸς δὲ ὄκνον φέρει, here ὃ
is neuter as referring to the
verb preceding ἐκλογίζεσθαι,
(τὸ ἐκλ.,) and is afterwards
explained by λογισμὸς, where
only the opposition, ἀμαθία
μὲν θρ., interrupts the construction, Matth. 638. : 2,
44. τὸ δ' εὐτυχὲς, οἳ ἂν τῆς
εὐπρεπεστάτης λάχωσιν, ὥσπερ
οἵδε μὲν νῦν, τελευτῆς, ὑμεῖς δὲ
λύπης, Matth. 509. 696. : 2,
40. Matth. 818. : 3, 12. ὃ τοῖς
ἄλλοις μάλιστα εὔνοια, πίστιν
βεβαιοῖ, ἡμῖν τοῦτο (τὴν πίστιν)
ὁ φόβος ἐχυρὸν παρεῖχε, the
pron. rel. is put in the
neuter, because it desig-
nates the thing generally,
which is subsequently ex-
plained by the noun fem.
εὔνοια, Matth. 638. : 4, 33.
Matth. 414. : 6, 11. ὅπερ
Ἐγεσταῖοι μάλιστα ἡμᾶς ἐκφοβοῦσι, for ᾧπερ, where the
accus. pron. is put adverbially, being an additional
accus. to ἡμᾶς after the verb,
Matth. 588. : 7, 21. ἄγων ἀπὸ

τῶν πόλεων, ὧν ἔπεισι, στρατιὰν, where the pronoun rel. takes the case of the nomin., to which it is referred, Matth. 682. : 7, 43. καὶ διαφυγόντες εὐθὺς πρὸς τὰ στρατόπεδα, ἃ ἦν ἐπὶ τῶν Ἐπιπολῶν τρία—ἀγγέλουσι τὴν ἔφοδον, when a pronoun rel. is referred to a subst., the adj. instead of standing properly with its subst., is often separated from the subst., and, as in Latin, put with the rel., Matth. 645. : 7, 44. οἱ ὕστερον ἥκοντες εἰσὶν οἳ διαμαρτόντες τῶν ὁδῶν κατὰ τὴν χώραν ἐπλανήθησαν, an instance, where the noun, to which the pronoun refers, is wanting, also where εἰσὶν is put for ἔστιν, which is more common, Matth. 699. : 6, 8. ὥστε οὐκ ἀθρόους γε ὄντας εἰκὸς ἀθυμεῖν—ἄλλως τε καὶ ἀπὸ Πελοποννήσου παρεσομένης ὠφελείας, οἳ τῶνδε κρείσσους εἰσὶ τὸ παράπαν τὰ πολέμια, the pron. is here referred to the word implied in ὠφελείας, viz. Πελοποννήσιοι, ξύμμαχοι, οἱ ὠφέλειαν φέροντες, Matth. 629.

ὁσημέραι, 7, 27. daily, every day.

ὅσιος, just, holy, religious, conscientious, 1, 71. ὅσια ποιῶμεν, to act religiously : 2, 52.

ὁσίως, 2, 5. οὐχ, wickedly, unrighteously.

ὀσμὴ, 7, 87. a smell, scent.

ὁσονοῦ, 1, 36. all but, 5, 59. ξυνιόντων, all but meeting: 6,

57. ὁσονοὐκ ἤδη ξυλληφθήσεσθαι, just on the point of being apprehended.

ὅσος, 4, 28. : 7, 44. ὅσον Δωρικὸν ἦν, the same as ὅσοι Δωριῆς ἦσαν, Liv. quidquid erat patrum : 1, 22. ὅσον δυνατὸν, as far as possible : 1, 9. ὅσων, as much as : 6, 25. ὅσα ἤδη δοκεῖν αὐτῷ, put for. ὡς, Matth. Gr. Gr. 824. : 7, 11. ὅσα γε κατὰ γῆν, at least as by land, as regards land : 7, 38. ὅσον δύο πλέθρα, about: 8, 92.: 1, 2. νεμόμενοι τὰ αὐτῶν ἕκαστοι, ὅσον ἀποζῆν, the relative ὅσος is here used for the conj. ὥστε, the sentence should stand ἐπὶ τοσοῦτο ὥστε ἀποζῆν, the demonstrative, i. e. τοσοῦτο, would then be dropped as often, and ἐπὶ would be affixed to the relative, which was in the same case, (ἐφ᾽ ὅσον,) this sentence is anomalous for the omission of ἐπὶ as well as τοσοῦτο, Matth. 694. compare 3, 49. ἡ μὲν ἔφθασε τοσοῦτον ὅσον Πάχητα ἀνεγνωκέναι τὸ ψήφισμα.

ὅσπερ, 7, 2. ᾗπερ, in which way, by which way : 6, 33. ὅπερ, in what way, 1, 73. which, 81. ὅπερ ἐποίησαν, which indeed they did : 2, 10. 7, 36. : 7, 25. καὶ τῶν νεῶν μία εἰς Πελοπόννησον ᾤχετο πρέσβεις ἄγουσα, οἵπερ τὰ σφέτερα φράσωσιν, the rel. is frequently put for ἵνα, in order to express a purpose, as in Latin qui for ut is, Matth. 696. see too 790. : 7,

36. τοῖς δὲ Ἀθηναίοις οὐκ ἔσεσθαι σφῶν ἐν στενοχωρίᾳ οὔτε
περίπλουν οὔτε διέκπλουν, ᾧπερ
τῆς τέχνης μάλιστα ἐπίστευον,
' in which manœuvre of their
tactics,' properly ' in which
part of their art,' where ᾗπερ
τέχνῃ could not be substituted for ᾧπερ τῆς τέχνης,
Matth. 498.

ὥστε, 5, 72. ἅτε, as it were,
4, 94. as is usual when, as
likely.

ὅστις, 3, 45. πολλῆς εὐηθείας,
ὅστις οἴεται, (a proof) of great
folly in him, who thinks,
very foolish for any one to
imagine : 4, 22. 8, 90. : 1,
137. καὶ δείσας φράζει τῷ ναυ-
κλήρῳ, ὅστις ἐστί, quis sit,
aperit, the relative often
stands for τίς, who? but only
in dependent propositions,
Matth. Gr. Gr. 701. : 2, 88.
ἔλεγε—ὡς οὐδὲν αὐτοῖς πλῆθος
νεῶν τοσοῦτου, ἢν ἐπιπλέῃ, ὅ,τι
οὐκ ὑπομενετέον αὐτοῖς ἐστι, the
use of the rel. in a negative
proposition is very frequent,
Matth. 700. : 3, 39. τίνα
οἴεσθε ὅντινα οὐ βραχείᾳ προφάσει ἀποστήσεσθαι, an instance
in the use of the pronoun,
where a particle τις is joined
to the ablative, here the
compound occurs after the
interrogative τις, whose case
it agrees with, compare 3,
46. ἐκείνως δὲ τίνα οἴεσθε ἥντινα
οὐκ ἄμεινον μὲν ἢ νῦν παρασκευάσασθαι, where ὅστις occurs
elliptically in an interroga-
tion after τις, Matth. 700. :

7, 29. πάντας ἑξῆς, ὅτῳ ἐντύχοιεν, καὶ παῖδας καὶ γυναῖκας
κτείνοντες, ' whomsoever they
might meet,' where the
whole proposition affirms
something of past time, and
the rel. refers to something
general and indistinct,
Matth. 787. : 7, 87. καὶ πεζὸς
καὶ νῆες καὶ οὐδὲν ὅ,τι οὐκ ἀπώλετο, Matth. 700.

ὀστρακίζω, 1, 135. ὠστρακι-
σμένος, under sentence of
banishment by ostracism.

ὅταν, 1, 142. ὅταν τύχῃ,
when occasion serves, par
occasion : 4, 60. εἰκὸς, ὅταν
γνῶσιν ἡμᾶς τετρυχωμένους καὶ
πλέονί ποτε στόλῳ ἐλθόντας αὐτοὺς τάδε πάντα πειράσεσθαι ὑπὸ
σφᾶς ποιῖσθαι, Matth. Gr. Gr.
776.

ὅτε, when, since, ὁτὲ sometimes, quandoque, 7, 27. ὁτὲ
μὲν, ὁτὲ δὲ, onewhile, at another, sometimes onething—
sometimes another : 1, 8. 7,
21. : 2, 102. λέγεται δὲ καὶ
Ἀλκμαίωνι τῷ Ἀμφιάρεω, ὅτε δὴ
ἀλᾶσθαι αὐτὸν μετὰ τὸν φόνον
τῆς μητρὸς, τὸν Ἀπόλλω ταύτην
τὴν γῆν χρῆσαι οἰκεῖν, the
accus. with the infin. is employed after particles, which
begin an antecedent proposition, and in the construction with the relative, when
the oratio obliqua takes place,
Matth. 811.

ὅτι, 3, 46. ὅτι ἐπ' ἐλάχιστον,
as few as possible : 7, 42.
ὅτι μὴ, except, ὅτι τάχος, as
quick as possible, with all

I i

speed, without loss of time :
5, 74. ὅτι ἐγγύτατα, as near as
possible, 3, 40. : 6, 64. ὅτι
πλεῖστον, *quam longissime*: 3,
46. ὅτι ἐν βραχυτάτῳ, as quick
as possible, as slight (a penalty) as possible : 1, 93. καὶ
δήλη ἡ οἰκοδομία ἔτι καὶ νῦν ἐστὶν
ὅτι κατὰ σπουδὴν ἐγένετο, an instance where a verb, which
takes the object in the participle, viz. of ('shewing,')
is followed by ὅτι, Matth.
Gr. Gr. 831. *see too* 4, 37. :
2, 5. κήρυκα ἐξέπεμψαν παρὰ
τοὺς Θηβαίους λέγοντες ὅτι οὔτε
τὰ πεποιημένα ὁσίως δράσειαν,
particularly after ὅτι the opt.
is frequently put, when any-
thing, that has been said or
thought by another is quoted
as such, not as an idea of the
writer, and yet not in the
words of the speaker, but in
narration, i. e. in the *oratio
obliqua*, compare 2, 6. οὐ γὰρ
ἠγγέλθη αὐτοῖς ὅτι τεθνηκότες
εἶεν, 21. οἱ Ἀχαρνῆς ἐκάκιζον
τὸν Περικλέα ὅτι στρατηγὸς ὢν
οὐκ ἐπεξάγοι, the opt. in the
oratio obliqua is used after all
particles, Matth. 790.

ὁτιοῦν, 7, 48. in any re-
spect whatever, in the least :
4, 16. however little.

ὅτις, *Poetice* for ὅστις, ὅτου
Attice for οὗτινος, 1, 23. 132.

ὁτουοῦν, 8, 27. τρόπον, whatsoever.

οὐ, 1, 137. ἡ τῶν γεφυρῶν οὐ
διάλυσις, an instance of the
use of οὐ, (which is the direct

and definitive negative,) with
a subst., with which it makes
a whole, Matth. Gr. Gr. 928.:
3, 95. ἡ οὐ περιτείχισις.

οὐδαμόσε, 5, 49. ἔτι, no-
where any longer.

οὐδαμοῦ, 1, 3. nowhere :
2, 47.

οὐδὲ γὰρ, 4, 68. for neither.

οὐδείς, 1, 26. 2, 19. 4, 14.
5, 17. no one, none, 7, 59.

οὐδέποτε, 4, 59. never.

οὐδέτερος, 1, 63. neither : 5,
84. οὐδετέρων ὄντες, of neither
party, neutral.

οὐκ, 7, 11. οὐχ ἧσσον καιρός,
not less, i. e. much more occasion, high time : 1, 35. οὐχ
ὅπως, not only not : 3, 11. οὐ
δι' ἄλλο τι ἢ ὅσον, on no other
account than in as much as,
as far as : 7, 67. οὐ πίστει
μᾶλλον ἢ, not from or with
confidence so much as, 17.
οὐκ ἄκαιρον, not unseasonably,
very well-timed, 75. οὐκ ἄνευ
ὀλίγων, not without some : 1,
68. οὐχ ἥκιστα, most of all,
67. very much : 7, 42. οὐκ
ὀλίγους, a great many, considerable number, 36. οὐκ ἐν
πολλῷ, in small space, little
room.

οὐκέτι, 5, 45. no longer.

οὔκουν, 3, 40. *non igitur*,
not therefore : 1, 10. εἰκός,
hence (it is) not proper, fit.

οὖν, 7, 59. (I say) then,
inquam, I repeat, 51.

οὐρανός, 2, 77. ὕδωρ πολὺ
οὐρανοῦ, a heavy rain.

οὔριος, 7, 53. favorable.

οὐσία, 6, 8. substance, property : 1, 121. ἐκ τῆς ὑπαρχούσης ἐκάστοις οὐσίας, out of what each possesses.

οὔτε, 2, 1. οὔτε—τὲ, οὔτε and μήτε serve to connect the propositions as in Latin *necneque*, in this example οὔτε—τὲ serve this purpose, Matth. 932.

οὗτος, 1, 21. this (very :) 3, 2. καὶ ταύτην τὴν ἀπόστασιν, i. e. ἐν τούτῳ τῷ χρόνῳ, not distinguished from any other preceding revolt : 1, 90. 8, 78. : 4, 69. αἱ οἰκίαι τοῦ προαστείου ἐπάλξεις λαμβάνουσαι, αὗται ὑπῆρχον ἔρυμα, a pleonasm of the demonstrative pronoun, Matth. Gr. Gr. 675.

οὕτως, 1, 76. so that, wherefore : 5, 1. in such manner as : 1, 64. ἤδη, thus by this time : 5, 59. οὐχ οὕτω δεινὸν, not so dangerous. 1, 10. καὶ οὕτως, even thus : 2, 11. οὕτω γὰρ πρός τε τὸ ἐπιέναι τοῖς ἐναντίοις εὐψυχότατοι ἂν εἶεν, whereas the antecedent with ει is often irregularly wanting, when it is easy to be supplied, here οὕτω is put for the premises, Matth. Gr. Gr. 786.

ὀφείλημα, 2, 40. οὐκ ἐς χάριν, ἀλλ᾽ ἐς ὀφείλημα, a debt, obligation.

ὀφείλω, 4, 19. ὀφείλω, to owe, to be obliged : 2, 40. ὀφειλομένην χάριν, an obligation, a favour. due, owing, (in return for one conferred.)

ὀφθαλμὸς, 2, 49. ὀφθαλμῶν ἐρυθήματα, redness of the eyes.

ὄφλω, 5, 101. τὴν αἰσχυνὴν, to owe, to be liable to, to incur : 3, 70. ὀφλόντων δὲ αὐτῶν, to be condemned.

ὀχετὸς, 6, 100. aqueduct, a conduit, canal.

ὄχλος, 1, 80. a crowd, 6, 31. : 1, 73. tediousness : 4, 56. a mob : 7, 8. the multitude, common people : 6, 17. ξυμμίκτοις, a mixed multitude.

ὀχλώδης, 6, 24. difficult.

ὀψὲ, 1, 14. lately, of late years : 4, 93. τῆς ἡμέρας, late in the day.

ὄψιος, 3, 74. περὶ δείλην ὀψίαν, at dusk : 8, 26.

ὄψις, 1, 10. a sight, view, an appearance, 73. ὄψεις : 6, 24. ἀπούσης, a sight, spectacle, scene, 46. 58. : 7, 44. 75.

ὄψον, 1, 138. fish.

Π.

Παγκράτιον, 5, 49. ἐνίκα, a species of contest at the Olympic games, which comprehended both wrestling and boxing.

πάθημα, 1, 23. a calamity : 4, 48. a tragedy, catastrophe : 2, 65.

πάθος, 1, 106. a calamity, 4, 55. 7, 30. 33. 8, 6. : 6,

55. τοῦ πάθους τῇ δυστυχίᾳ, the infelicity of the fate, case.

παιάν, 7, 75. παιάνων, a pæan, song of joy, triumph.

παιδεία, 2, 39. a discipline, method of education, mode of educating youth.

παίδευσις, 2,41. instruction. Matth. Gr. Gr. 616.

παιδεύω, 1, 84. εὔβουλοι γιγνόμεθα, ἀμαθέστεροι τῶν νόμων τῆς ὑπεροψίας παιδευόμενοι καὶ ξὺν χαλεπότητι σωφρονέστεροι ἢ ὥστε αὐτῶν ἀνηκουστεῖν, the constr. of the verbs ' to make,' which take an accus. of the thing and another of its attribute, is followed by verbs ' to educate,' the nature of which verbs takes a double nomin. in the pass., Matth. Gr. Gr. 596. see also 656.

παιδιά, 6, 28. μετὰ παιδιᾶς, with, i. e. by, through wantonness, frolicsomeness, sport, levity.

παιδικὸς, 1, 132. a pathic.

παιπαλόεις, 3, 104. precipitous, rugged.

παῖς, 1, 3. a child, son, 4, 81. 2, 34. : 7, 29.

παίω, 4, 47, παιομένους, beating.

παιωνίζω, 1, 50. 2, 91. ἐπαιώνιζον, to sing the pæan of victory : 6, 32. παιωνίσαντες, 7, 44. παιωνίσειαν.

παιωνισμὸς, 7, 44. singing the pæan, Matth. Gr. Gr. 669.

παλαιόπλουτος, 8, 28. rich from ancient times.

παλαιὸς, 5, 1. 42. 7, 25. 53. old, ancient : 1, 3. οἱ παλαιοὶ, the ancients : 1, 10. τῷ παλαιῷ τρόπῳ, after the ancient manner : 1, 2. ἀπὸ παλαιοῦ, of old, long ago, 5, 44. : 1, 18. ἐκ παλαιοτάτου, farthest back, for the longest time : 1, 1. παλαιότερα : 6, 2. παλαιότατοι.

παλαίτατος, 1, 4. 18. most ancient.

πάλη, 1, 6. wrestling.

πάλιν, 1, 137. 3, 28. ἐλθῶσι, to return, 39. ἐν τῇ πόλει εἶναι, to be reinstated in the city.

πανδημεὶ, 1, 73. with the whole population, 90. : 2, 31. with all their forces : 6, 64. 67. ὄντας Συρακοσίους, en masse, of all conditions, the whole mass of the people, 68. ἄνδρας ἀμυνομένους, vis est non in universis, sed in mixta colluvie, a rabble : 4, 42.

πανήγυρις, 1, 25. πανηγύρεσι, an assembly, a convocation: 5, 50.

πανοικησία, 2, 16. with their whole family : 3, 57. with the whole community.

πανωλεθρία, 7, 87. entire destruction.

πανοπλία, 3, 114. a panoply.

πανστρατιὰ, 5, 57. the whole force : 4, 94. ξένων καὶ ἀστῶν, a general muster : 2, 31. πανστρατιᾷ, with their whole army.

πανσυδεὶ, 8, 1. with all their force, strength.

παντάπασι, 3, 87. altogether: 5, 104. 6, 71.

πανταχῦ, 1, 54. in all directions: 7, 79.

πανταχόθεν, 3, 32. from all parts, 5, 43.: 60. on every side: 1, 123.

πανταχόσι, 7, 42. in all points, on every side, everywhere.

πανταχοῦ, 4, 108. everywhere.

παντελῶς, 7, 1. ἀποτετειχισμέναι, completely, on all sides.

παντοῖος, 1, 93. λίθων, of all kinds: 7, 25.

πάνυ, 3, 44. ἀδικοῦντας, guilty, criminal beyond a doubt: 1, 3. at all: 6, 18. 8, 1.

πάππος, 5, 43. 6, 54. a grandfather.

παρά, 1, 69. τὰ παρ' ὑμῶν, your forces: 5, 64. παρὰ τῶν ἐπιτηδείων, from the friends: 6, 66. τῇ μὲν γὰρ—παρὰ δὲ τό, on the one side—on the other, 32. ἅπαν τὸ στράτευμα, throughout: 7, 60. παρὰ τὸ εἰωθὸς, contrary to their wont, custom, experience: 5, 90. παρὰ τὸ δίκαιον, equity being out of the question: 1, 8. θάλασσαν, along the seashore, 7, 80. τὸν ποταμὸν, along (the banks of) the river, 5, 68. παρὰ ἅπαν, along the whole (front:) 3, 37. παρὰ δόξαν παραινεῖν, to advance contrary to, against one's own sentiments, better judgment: 1, 73. παρὰ δικασταῖς, before the proper judges, umpires, 77. παρ' ἡμῖν αὐτοῖς,

before ourselves as judges, or jurymen: 5, 50. παρὰ σφᾶς, (to come over) to them, their side: 1, 20. παρ' ἀλλήλων, from one another, 77. παρὰ τὸ μὴ οἴεσθαι χρῆναι, contrary to their not thinking it necessary, contrary to their opinion of its not being necessary: 1, 138. παρ' αὐτῷ μέγας, great with him: 7, 13. παρὰ γνώμην, contrary to expectation, 1, 70. 3, 12. 42. against the judgment: 7, 13. τὴν πόλιν, past or by the city: 8, 36. παρὰ πολὺ, by far: 5, 67. παρ' αὐτοὺς, by them, their side: 3, 3. παρὰ σφᾶς παρεῖναι, to be present with, among, apud: 3, 49. παρὰ τοσοῦτον ἦλθε κινδύνου, to arrive at such a pitch, come to such an extremity, danger, Matth. Gr. Gr. 907.: 1, 67. παρὰ τὰς σπονδὰς, contrary to or in violation of the truce: 5, 67. παρ' αὐτοῖς, by the side of them: 3, 52. παρὰ δίκην, contrary to justice: 1, 23. παρὰ τὰ γενησόμενα, beyond (the number of) those already recorded, 35. παρ' ὁποτέρους, (to go over) to whichever he pleases: 7, 39. παρὰ τὰς ναῦς, close, hard by: 8, 89.: 1, 23. ἡλίου ἐκλείψεις πυκνότεραι παρὰ τὰ ἐκ τοῦ πρὶν χρόνου μνημονευόμενα ξυνέβησαν, the prep. παρὰ is here used for ἢ, and is particularly used, when the word governed of παρὰ is to suffer disparagement, with the meaning ' beyond,' Matth. 907. this is too an instance of a rare constr. of the comparative, 659. : 6, 37. παρὰ τοσοῦτον γιγνώσκω, *tantum abest ut ita sentiam*, this phrase arises from a meaning of the prep. παρά, 'besides,' Matth. 907.

παραβαίνω, 1, 78. 2, 71. τοὺς ὅρκους, to transgress, break the oaths : 3, 64. παραβάντες, to infringe, transgress : 3, 12. πρότεροι παραβήσεσθαι ἔμελλον, to be the first to break (the league :) 3, 67. παραβαθέντι, violated : 4, 23. : 1, 123. σπονδὰς ὁ θεὸς νομίζει παραβεβάσθαι, this perf. pass. is βέβαμαι for βέβημαι from βέβηκα, Matth. Gr. Gr. 233.

παραβάλλω, 6, 99. παρέβαλλον, to throw down, lay along side of : 2, 77. παρέβαλον, to cast hard by : 5, 113. παραβεβλημένοι Λακεδαιμονίοις, to be committed to (the care of) the Lac., 7, 2. τῷ πλέονι, to be thrown down, laid in heaps along the greater (part of the road :) 2, 44. παραβαλλόμενοι, to expose (to danger,) 3, 14. ἴδιον τὸν κίνδυνον τῶν σωμάτων, to expose one's person to one's own proper danger, to a danger of one's own : 1, 133. παραβάλοιτο, to betray, deceive, (but *see* Steph. *Thes.*) to bring into danger : 5, 113.

παραβοηθέω, 2, 90. 4, 14. 7, 37. ἐπὶ τὸν αἰγιαλὸν, 71. παρεβοήθουν, to run or haste to succour : 2, 90. παραβοηθήσαντες, 8, 24. : 1, 47. παραβε-

βοηθηκότες : 3, 22. εἴ τι δέοι, when there was occasion, upon any emergency, whenever necessary.

παραγγέλλω, 5, 10. παρήγγελλε, to give command : 2, 11. τὰ παραγγελλόμενα, commands, orders, 1, 121. 129. 3, 55. 4, 34. : 7, 43. παραγγείλας πενθ' ἡμερῶν σιτία, to order five days' provision, victuals.

παράγγελμα, 8, 99. ἀπὸ αἰφνιδίου, by a sudden order.

παράγγελσις, 5, 68. a word of command, military order.

παραγίγνομαι, 6, 67. to make to (a place :) 1, 74. παρεγένεσθε, to arrive, 3, 29. : 7, 44. οἱ παραγενόμενοι, the persons present : 4, 94. παρεγένοντο, to keep together : 5, 6. παραγένοιτο, to be present, to appear, to be at hand : 2, 95. : 2, 5. οἱ ἄλλοι Θηβαῖοι, οὓς ἔδει τῆς νυκτὸς παραγενέσθαι πανστρατιᾷ, εἴ τι ἄρα μὴ προχωροίη τοῖς ἐσεληλυθόσι—ἐπεβοήθουν, 'unless some success should attend them,' in this conditional proposition the indic. is used in the conclusion, because something is determinately asserted, whilst εἰ with the optative is in the premises, which convey only a possible case, Matth. Gr. Gr. 783. : 6, 96. ἑπτακοσίους λογάδας τῶν ὁπλιτῶν ἐξέκριναν πρότερον,—ὅπως τῶν τε Ἐπιπολῶν εἴησαν φύλακες, καὶ ἢν ἐς ἄλλο τι δέῃ, ταχὺ ξυνεστῶτες παραγίγνωνται, sometimes the conj. or in its room the indic. is interchanged with the opt., Matth. 771.

παράγω, 1, 91. 2, 64. 3, 38. to seduce, lead into error, 68. παραγαγόντες, to lead aside, 5, 46. to intro- duce : 1, 34.

παράδειγμα, 4, 92. an ex- ample, a signal proof: 2, 37. an example, a pattern for imitation : 5, 95. a mark, proof, 1, 2. proof, evidence : 4, 92. a lesson : 3, 39. an ex- ample, warning,. 57. : 6, 77.

παραδίδωμι, 5, 21. παραδιδό- ναι, to transfer, give up, 35. 42. παραδοῦναι : 1, 25. παρέδο- σαν, 2, 36. to transmit, 62. 4, 38. to give up : 1, 25. παραδοῖεν, to deliver up : 7, 68. παραδεδωκυίαν, to betray, abandon : 2, 15. παρεδόθη, to be transmitted : 2, 72. παρέ- δωκεν, to grant : 2, 72. παρά- δοτε, to assign over : 8, 28. παραδιδόασιν, to deliver up to, 51. παραδίδοται, where Bekker gives προδ.

παράδοσις, 1, 9. a delivery (from one to another,) a succession : 3, 53.

παραδοτέος, 1, 86. to be be- trayed.

παραδυναστεύω, 2, 97. to possess authority, power.

παραθαλασσίδιος, 6, 62. πό- λισμα, a sea-coast town.

παραθαλάσσιος, 1, 5. dwell- ing on the sea-coast : 4, 56.

παραθαρσύνω, 5, 8. παραθαρ- σῦναι, to exhort: 7, 2. παρεθάρ- συνε, to encourage, hearten, reanimate, fortify : 8, 77.

παραίνεσις, 2, 45. an admo- nition : 4, 59. an exhorta- tion, a recommendation, 95. 1, 92. 5, 69. λόγων : 1, 41. advice : 3, 43.

παραινέω, 1, 145. to advise, 3, 37. τῷ πλήθει, to advise, counsel : 5, 38. παρῄνουν, to recommend, 1, 93. 3, 31. : 2, 13. ἅπερ καὶ πρότερον παρῄνει, to admonish or advise to the same effect as before, 8, 26. to recommend to, 46. : 2, 18. οὐ παραινῶν, to dissuade : 5, 9. παραινέσαι, to commend : 5, 69. παρῃνέθη, to be said in the way of encouragement : 8, 41. παραινούντων : 7, 63.

παραίρεσις, 1, 122. a depri- vation.

παραίρημα, 4, 48. καὶ ἐκ τῶν ἱματίων παραιρήματα ποιοῦντες, a bandage, see Duker.

παραιτέω, 5, 63. παρῃτεῖτο, to beseech, petition.

παραίτησις, 1, 73. a depre- cation.

παρακαλέω, 1, 67. παρεκά- λουν, to convoke : 1, 87. 5, 55. παρακαλεσάντων, to sum- mon : 1, 68. παρεκαλέσατε, to call together, convoke, con- vene : 6, 87. παρακληθέντες, to be invited, 5, 31. to be called in, 27. παρεκλήθησαν : 1, 118. 5, 27.

παρακαταθήκη, 2, 72. a de- posit.

παρακαταλείπω, 6, 7. παρα- καταλιπόντες αὐτοῖς, to leave behind, along with, amongst.

παρακαταπήγνυμι, 4, 90. σταυ- ρούς, to fix.

παρακατέχω, 8, 93. αὐτούς τε

ἡσυχάζειν καὶ τοὺς ἄλλους παρα-κατέχειν, to restrain, check.

παρακέλευσις, 5, 69. τῆς μνή-μης, an encouraging appeal to the memory (of achieve-ments already performed :) 7, 70. an exhortation, 40. the word of command.

παρακελευσμός, 4, 11. an exhortation.

παρακελευστὸς, 6, 13. Schol. παρακεκλημένους, as advocates.

παρακελεύομαι, 7, 63. to ex-hort : 2, 86. παρεκελεύσαντο, to encourage, 88. : 4, 11. πα-ρακελευσαμένον, 25. : 6, 69.

παρακινδύνευσις, 5, 100. peril, risk, Matth. Gr. Gr. 819.

παρακινδυνεύω, 3, 36. παρα-κινδυνεῦσαι, to venture, hazard.

παράκλησις, 4, 61. an invi-tation, 8, 92.

παρακομιδὴ, 7, 28. carriage, conveyance : 5, 5.

παρακομίζω, 6, 44. παρεκομί-ζοντο τὴν Ἰταλίαν, to sail or pass along : 4, 25. παρεκομί-σθησαν, to be conveyed along.

παραλαμβάνω, 1, 9. παραλα-βόντες, to take (into one's own hands from another,) 111. to take in (troops into a ship,) 7, 26. 3, 39. to receive, 5, 52. to take in addition, to join : 3, 50. to take (into one's own hands), receive upon a surrender, 7, 31. πα-ρέλαβε, 1, 28. to receive (as a successor,) 129. to assume the command or take the government of : 6, 96. παρει-ληφότες τὴν ἀρχὴν, to receive the command from, 3, 109.

to assume the command, 7, 57. παρελήφθησαν ἐς τὸν πόλε-μον.

παραλείπω, 2, 51. παραλι-πόντι, to pass over, omit : 3, 26. παραλέλειπτο : 2, 13. παρα-λίπῃ καὶ μὴ δρώσῃ, to pass by without injury, leave un-touched: 7, 69. παραληφθέντα.

παράλις, 2, 56. τὴν παραλίαν γῆν, on the sea-coast.

παραλλάξ, 2, 102. παραλλὰξ καὶ οὐ κατὰ στοῖχον κείμεναι, situ alternante positæ et non recta serie, Huds., in an alternate series.

παράλογος, 3, 16. πολὺν τὸν παράλογον, a very unexpected circumstance, an event con-trary to all expectation, 7, 28. 8, 24.

παραλυπέω, 2, 51. παρελύπει, to molest, plague, 4, 89.

παραλύω, 7, 16. παρέλυσαν τῆς ἀρχῆς, to remove or dis-miss from his post : 2, 65. ὁ Περικλῆς ἐπειρᾶτο τοὺς Ἀθηναί-ους τῆς ἐπ᾽ αὐτὸν ὀργῆς παρα-λύειν, verbs ' to cease, make to cease' take the gen. of the thing from its analogy to the idea of ' fulness, emptiness,' with which the genitive's sense is ' with respect to,' Matth. Gr. Gr. 475.

παραμελέω, 1, 25. παρημέ-λουν, to neglect, contemn, treat with neglect, Matth. Gr. Gr. 845.

παραμένω, 1, 102. παραμεί-νωσιν, to remain : 7, 15. : 1, 75. παραμεῖναι, to stay, re-main : 3, 10. παραμεινάντων πρὸς τὰ ὑπόλοιπα τῶν ἔργων, to remain or stay behind for (prosecuting) the remainder of the business, the remains of the war, on account of what remained to be done.

παραμυθέομαι, 3, 75. to encourage, console, 2, 44. παραμυθήσομαι.

παραμύθιον, 5, 103. κινδύνῳ, a solace to danger.

παρανέχω, 3, 22. παρανίσχον, to raise, hold up.

παρανομέω, 2, 37. μάλιστα οὐ παρανομοῦμεν, least to transgress or offend against the laws: 3, 65. παρανομοῦσι, 66. παρανομῆσαι, to transgress, commit injustice: 5, 16. παρανομηθεῖσαν: 3, 67. παρηνόμησαν, an instance of the η in the augment for ε, Matth. Gr. Gr. 210.

παρανόμημα, 7, 18. a breach of peace.

παρανομία, 4, 98. excommunication, sentence of outlawry, the fault which brings it on, Matth. Gr. Gr. 595. : 1, 132. : 6, 28. licentiousness, 15. κατὰ τὸ ἑαυτοῦ σῶμα, (exhibited) in his own person.

παράνομος, 2, 17. profane.

παραπέμπω, 4, 13. παρέπεμψαν, to send along: 1, 36. παραπέμψαι.

παραπίπτω, 4, 23. παραπέσοι, to chance, befal.

παραπλέω, 3, 34. πάλιν, to sail along back, 8, 4. 10. to coast: 7, 25. παρέπλεον ἐπ' οἴκου, to coast away, sail off home, 2, 25. 3, 32. 7, 35. :

7, 1. παρέπλευσαν, 33. : 4, 2. παραπεπλεύκεσαν: 8, 20. παραπλεύσας, 31. παρέπλευσαν.

παραπλήσιος, 7, 44. similar, 70. παραπλησίαις τὸν ἀριθμὸν καὶ πρότερον, equal or like in number as before, with nearly the same number as before, 19. similarly situated, about the same distance, (or simply,) likewise: 3, 89. 7, 71.

παράπλους, 1, 36. a passage along, voyage along the coast, 2, 33. 4, 25. 6, 62. 7, 29. 50.

παραποιέω, 1, 132. παραποιησάμενος, to forge.

παράπολυ, 1, 29. by much: 2, 8. 8, 6.

παραρρήγνυμι, 4, 96. παραρρήγνυντων, to have (one's ranks) penetrated: 5, 73. παρερρήγνυντο, to be broken, routed, 6, 70.

παρασκευάζω, 1, 65. to set in order, to arrange: 4, 74. παρεσκεύαζεν, to prepare: 1, 31. παρεσκευάζοντο, to prepare, 10. 49. παρεσκευασμένοι, to be fitted out: 7, 34. παρασκευασάμενοι: 2, 7. παρασκευασθῇ, to be prepared: 6, 31. παρασκευάσασθαι, to prepare or provide for oneself: 1, 46. παρεσκεύαστο, Matth. Gr. Gr. 432. : 3, 22. ἐπειδὴ παρεσκεύαστο αὐτοῖς, when they had completed their preparations: 3, 36. παρεσκεύασαν τοὺς ἐν τέλει, to dispose, prepare, prevail upon: 3, 3. παρεσκευασμέναι ἔτυχον, to happen or chance to be prepared, an

κ k

instance of the perf. pass. of a verb, used as active, occuring in a passive sense, Matth. 716. : 2, 7. οἱ Ἀθηναῖοι παρεσκευάζοντο ὡς πολεμήσουντες, 3, 74. παρεσκευάζοντο ὡς οὐ περιοψόμενοι, Matth. 837. the constr. of the participle with ὡς after the verb is here for the simple infin., because the infin. is used after an imperfect verb to express the object or consequence, and the participle to express merely the object, Matth. 874. : 2, 99. παρεσκευάζοντο— ὅπως ἐσβαλοῦσιν, Matth. 798.

παρασκευὴ, 6, 8. ταῖς ναυσὶ, i. q. τῶν νεῶν, preparation for a fleet, by sea, in ships, 7, 4. a band, body : 6, 31. a force, an armament, 4, 1. μείζονι : 7, 67. παρασκευῆς πίστει, confidence in (their) preparation, force, equipment : 6, 19. πλήθει παρασκευῆς, an immensity of preparation, force, immense preparations : 3, 39. τριηρῶν, a force of triremes, a fleet : 2, 7. οἱ μὲν ἐν τούτῳ παρασκευῆς ἦσαν, ' in this degree of preparation,' here the gen. in its sense of ' with respect to' after the dat. neuter for the sake of defining it, Matth. Gr. Gr. 456.

παράσπονδος, 4, 23. contrary to a truce.

παράταξις, 5, 11. order or array of battle.

παρατάσσω, 7, 3. 69. παρέταξεν, to draw up : 5, 71.

παρατεταγμένου, to be drawn up (along side of,) 4, 32. : 7, 34. παρετέτακτο : 5, 59. παρετάσσοντο : 4, 73. παραταξάμενοι, 1, 29. 52. to draw up along side (an enemy) for action: 7, 78. 79.

παρατείνω, 4, 8. τὸν λιμένα, to lie along the mouth of the harbour: 3, 46. πολιορκίᾳ παρατενεῖσθαι ἐς τοῦσχατον, to persist, endure to the last extremity.

παρατείχισμα, 7, 11. 43. τὸ ἀπὸ τῆς πρώτης, according to Mitf. the same as τείχισμα, but then why παρατείχισμα ? Matth. Gr. Gr. 924.

παρατίθημι, 1, 130. παρετίθετο, to set out (a table,) the middle often expresses an action, which took place at the command of the subject, or with regard to it, which is expressed in English by ' to cause,' Matth. Gr. Gr. 715.

παρατρέπω, 1, 109. παρατρέψας, to turn aside (water in another course.)

παρατυγχάνω, 1, 11. παρατυχόντι, to happen to be present, 122. πρὸς τὸ παρατυγχάνον, according to the event, occasion : 1, 22. 76. 4, 19. 103. 5, 38. : 3, 82. ἐν τῷ παρατυχόντι, in case of an opportunity : 8, 11. παρατύχῃ, should present itself.

παραυτίκα, 2, 11. ἐν τῷ, on a sudden, 64. : 1, 27. on the instant, immediately: 3, 4. τὸ, for the present, 5, 65. on the instant : 8, 82.

παραφέρω, 5, 20. ἡμερῶν ὀλίγων παρενεγκουσῶν, some few days over.

παράφραγμα, 7, 25. a parapet, covering, defence : 4, 115:

παραχρῆμα, 1, 141. ὀξέως ἐπιτελῶσι, hastily to execute some momentary measure, quickly to execute an affair of the moment, upon occasion : 2, 17. ὑπὸ τῆς παραχρῆμα ἀνάγκης, in consequence of the sudden emergency : 2, 6. instantly : 1, 22. ἐς τὸ π. ἀκούειν, for present hearing, temporary interest : 8, 1.

παρείκω, 3, 1. ὅπη παρείκοι, to allow, permit, admit of : 4, 36. παρεῖκον, to yield.

πάρειμι, 1, 22. παρῆν, to be present, 8, 5. to be at hand : 3, 30. Πελοποννησίων ὅσοι πάρεσμεν, as many of us Peloponnesians, as are present : 2, 23. to pass by, 4, 47. 6, 15. παριόντες, to come forward (to address an assembly:) 2, 81. παρεσομένους, 6, 33. ἐν τάχει, to be here forthwith, 8, 2. παρέσεσθαι: 6, 34. ὅσον οὔπω πάρεισι, to be expected every moment, just at hand, 2, 11. ἐν ᾧ οὔπω πάρεσμεν, when we are not yet arrived, at a distance: 1, 32. ἐν τῷ παρόντι, in the present juncture, 132. at the present moment: 3, 8. Ὀλυμπίαζε παρεῖναι, to repair to Olympia: 8, 16. παρῄει, marched with, 22. to, 26. παρεῖναι: 8, 41. πάρεισι, 36. ἄλλας ξυνθήκας ἐπὶ Θηραμένους

παρόντος ἐποίουν, Matth. Gr. Gr. 865.

παρεξειρεσία, 7, 34. 40. the forecastle, space between the beak and oars.

πάρεργος, 6, 69. ἐν παρέργῳ, by the bye, in secundo loco: 7, 27. : 1, 142. ἐκ παρέργου, en passánt.

παρέρχομαι, 1, 67. παρελθόντες, to come forward (as an orator, to speak,) 72. 6, 8.: 7, 6. to reach : 5, 71. παρελθεῖν : 2, 72. παρέλθῃ, to be ended : 7, 6. ἤδη ὅσον οὐ παρελήλύθει, it all but passed, it only did not intersect, reach beyond : 3, 44. παρῆλθον, to come forward, to rise (to speak:) 4, 86. 8, 53.

παρέχω, 1, 30. παρέσχον, to furnish, 4, 67. 2, 74. παρέσχετε, to render, 3, 12. παράσχοι θάρσος, to give confidence, 3, 33. φυλακὴν σφίσι παρασχεῖν, to give them occasion to watch : 6, 86. ὑμῖν οὐ πολλάκις παρασχήσειν, to occur, present (itself) to you: 2, 84. παρεξεῖν 8, 5. 2, 9. παρείχοντο, to furnish, supply: 3, 36. ἔστιν ἃ παρεχόμενον, to make certain offers, promise certain things: 1, 32. παρέξεσθαι: 5, 35. παρεῖχον: 8, 48. 50. : 1, 96. παρέχειν χρήματα πρὸς τὸν βάρβαρον, for κατὰ τοῦ βαρβάρου, 'against,' the idea of an aim or direction is the ground-work of this case, Matth. Gr. Gr. 913.: 1, 120. ἀγαθῶν ἀνδρῶν ἐστὶν ἀδικουμένους ἐκ μὲν εἰρήνης πολεμεῖν, εὖ δὲ παρασχὸν, ἐκ πολίμου πάλιν ξυμβῆναι, *cum opportunum est*, Matth. 863.

παρηβάω, 2, 44. παρηβήκατε, to be past the flower of one's age, advanced in age.

παρήκω, 4, 36. κατὰ τὸ ἀεὶ παρῆκον τοῦ κριμνώδους τῆς νήσου προβαίνων, to reach, extend.

παρίημι, 4, 27. 38. παρῆκαν, to throw off: 1, 85. παρῶμεν, to give up, desert: 6, 23. ἀρχὴν, to resign.

παριππεύω, 7, 78. to ride alongside of.

παρίστημι, 4, 61. 95. μηδενὶ ἡμῶν παραστῇ, not to let it trouble you, occur as an objection, be a stumbling block, 133. 3, 35. παριστήσατο τὴν Πύρραν, to reduce, 1, 124. παραστησώμεθα, to overturn, reduce, 98. παριστήσαντο: 6, 34. παραστῆναι παντὶ, to occur, to be present (to the mind,) Matth. Gr. Gr. 825. ; 6, 68. παραστήτω δέ τινι καὶ τόδε.

παριτητέος, 1, 71. παριτητέα ἐς τοὺς Λ., they ought to proceed, advance, present themselves.

πάροδος, 1, 126. ἐν τῇ παρόδῳ, as they passed: 3, 21. παρὰ πύργον, a passage: 5, 4. a journey, way : 7, 2. a route, march: 4, 108. a (free) passage.

παροικέω, 6, 82. παροικοῦσιν, *Accolis*: 1, 71. to dwell near, by the side of.

παροικοδομέω, 7, 6. παροικοδομούμενον τὸ τεῖχος, to build along or by, to throw up,

construct, Matth. Gr. Gr. 832. : 7, 11. παρῳκοδομήκασιν.

παρόμοιος, 1, 132. τῇ παρούσῃ διανοίᾳ, corresponding with, 80. nearly similar, resembling.

παροξύνω, 6, 88. παρώξυνε, to exasperate, inflame : 1, 84. παροξύνῃ, to sharpen, whet: 6, 56. παρωξύνετο, to be exasperated.

παρορύσσω, 6, 101. παρώρυσσον, to dig alongside of.

παρουσία, 6, 86. τῆς ἡμετέρας, (*abstractum pro concreto*,) *i. q.* ἡμῶν παρόντων, or ὡς ἡμεῖς νῦν πάρεσμεν, *cum significatione quoque apparatus rei bellicæ*: 1, 128.

παροχὴ, 6, 85. νεῶν, a supply of ships.

πᾶς, 4, 52. πάντων μάλιστα, above all : 6, 43. Ἀθηναῖοι ἐς τὴν Σικελίαν ἐπεραιοῦντο—τοξόταις τοῖς πᾶσιν ὀγδοήκοντα, the art. is put especially even where otherwise it would not be put, when it is to be expressed that the subst., to which it belongs, has been already mentioned, or is something commonly known, Matth. Gr. Gr. 8, 95. Εὔβοια γὰρ αὐτοῖς ἀποκεκλῃσμένης τῆς Ἀττικῆς πάντα ἦν, here the adj. πάντα is put as generally, without the art., when it stands in apposition to its subst. Εὔβοια, or as a predicate in the neuter plur. which happens often, when the noun is a proper name, Matth. 636. : 7, 55. Ἀθηναῖοι ἐν παντὶ δὴ ἀθυμίας ἦσαν, Matth. 55.

πάσχω, 2, 11. ὁρᾷν πάσχοντας, to see (themselves) suffering: 6, 60. 80. ὁ παθὼν, the vanquished, sufferer, 3, 38. the sufferer, injured person, plaintiff: 4, 34. ἐπεπόνθεσαν: 3, 39. πεισόμεθα : 6, 78. τάδε πάσχει τὰ μείζω, this happens to, befalls the more powerful: 4, 96. τὸ αὐτὸ ἔπαθε, to experience, to be placed in a similar predicament, 4, 18.: 3, 40. τὸ εὖ παθεῖν, kindness, a reward, beneficium : 1, 80. πάθοιεν : 7, 71. παραπλήσια αὐτοῖς ἔπασχον, to be similarly affected : 8, 48. πέπονθε, to suffer : 3, 13. οὔτε γὰρ ἀποστήσεται ἄλλος, τά τε ἡμέτερα προσγενήσεται, πάθοιμέν τ' ἂν δεινότερα ἢ οἱ πρὶν δουλεύοντες, where the opt. as in abstract propositions restricts the fut., Matth. Gr. Gr. 756.: 3, 39. ἀπόστασις τῶν βίαιόν τι πασχόντων ἐστὶν, 'they, who are treated with insolence, are wont to revolt,' the gen. being used to mark the person or thing, to which any thing belongs, here with the verb εἶναι may be translated as above, Matth. 518.

πατάσσω, 8, 92. ὁ μὲν πατάξας διέφυγεν, the person, who inflicted the blow.

πατρικὸς, 1. 13. hereditary, 7, 69. 8, 6.

πάτριος, 4, 86. 92. ὑμῖν, national, 118. 5, 18. of or belonging to a country.

πατρὶς, 2, 68. 5, 69. ὑπὲρ πατρίδος, for one's country : 7, 67, 70. 8, 47.

πατρόθεν, 7, 69. πατρόθεν τε ἐπονομάζων, after their fathers, by their fathers' name.

πατρῷος, 2, 71. θεοὺς, the gods of one's ancestors, derived from one's ancestors : 7, 69.

παῦλα, 6, 60. οὐκ ἐν παύλῃ ἐφαίνετο, there was no cessation.

παύω, 1, 69. 84. παύσασθε, to cease : 7. 53. παύσαντες τὴν φλόγα, to put out, Matth. Gr. Gr. 801.: 1, 6. πέπαυται, to be put an end to : 7, 11. παυσάμενοι τοῦ περιτειχισμοῦ, to discontinue the circumvallation, 3, 24. τῆς βοηθείας, to cease from pursuit : 6, 60. τὴν τῆς παρούσης ὑποψίας παῦσαι, to put an end to the present suspicion : 5, 91. ἦν καὶ παυθῇ, even were it put an end to : 1, 81. παυθήσεται.

πάχος, 1, 90. breadth.

παχὺς, 7, 36. στερίφοις καὶ παχέσι, compact, firm, stout, strong, heavy, 34. παχύτερος.

παχύτης, 7, 62. thickness, heaviness.

πεδίον, 7, 19. the (open) plain, champaign country : 5, 58.

πεζῇ, 1, 109. on land, 3, 3. ἐλθεῖν, 4, 75. 132. 1, 26.

πεζικὸς, 7, 7. of or belonging to infantry : 6, 33. στρατιᾷ.

πεζομαχέω, 1, 112. ἐπεζομάχησαν, to fight on land, maintain a land-battle : 7, 63.

πεζομαχία, 1, 100. a battle on land, 23.: 7, 62.

πεζὸς, 1, 29. 3, 7. 4, 12. 7, 15. 59. of or belonging to land, land-forces.

πείθω, 2, 67. 3, 43. πεῖσαι τὰ δεινότατα, to carry the most injurious motions, measures. 3, 42. μὴ πείσας: 1, 78. πεισθέντες, to be persuaded, 31. μισθῷ, 3, 37. λόγῳ, to be prevailed upon by words, to be led or induced by persuasion: 3, 3. μὴ πειθομένων, upon (their) non-compliance : 2, 42. πεποιθέναι, to trust : 1, 26. ἐπείθοντο, to obey, 5, 21. to render obedience : 7, 12. πείσων, 3, 31. πείσειν ὥστε ξυμπολεμεῖν, to prevail upon (any one) to assist, take part in a war : 2, 60. ἐπείσθητε μᾶλλον ἑτέρων for μᾶλλον ἢ ἕτεροις: 5, 49. πεισθῆναι, to be persuaded : 4, 68. πείσεται : 5, 40. πεπεῖσθαι, to be instigated : 3, 32. ἐπείσθη : 6, 34. πείθεσθε, μάλιστα μὲν, ταῦτα τολμήσαντες, to be persuaded above all to attempt this : 6, 87. πείθειν ἀξιώσομεν, for ὑμᾶς πείθεσθαι, rogamus ut vobis hoc persuadeamus, ut hoc persuaderi vobis patiamini : 4, 17. ἔπεμψαν ἡμᾶς Λακεδαιμόνιοι—ὅ,τι ἂν ὑμῖν τε ὠφέλιμον ὂν τὸ αὐτὸ πείθωμεν, an instance of the participle after the verb πείθω, which properly requires an infin., Matth. Gr. Gr. 837.

πεῖρα, 1, 138. πεῖραν διδοὺς, to give an experimental proof : 2, 41. ἐς πεῖραν ἔρχεται, to come to the proof, trial, to be proved, found, turn out upon examination : 4, 92. 6, 11. 7, 21. 25.: 1, 140. τῆς γνώμης, a trial of one's sentiments, character, mind.

πείρασις, 6, 56. ἀπαρνηθέντα τὴν πείρασιν, to refuse to listen to the solicitation.

πειράω, 2, 19. πειράσαντες, to try : 2, 77. 4, 70. πειράσαι : 4, 43. 7, 32. 37. πειράσειν : 5, 35. πειράσεσθαι, to endeavour, try, 38.: 2, 85. πειρασάμενοι : 8, 3. ἐπειρᾶτο, to endeavour : 2, 81. πειρῷντο, 1, 25.: 1, 78. πειρασόμεθα : 6, 54. πειραθεὶς περὶ συνουσίας, to be solicited, courted, 6, 54. πειράσας : 4, 102. ἐπείρασε : 6, 38. πολλὰ πειρῶντες, to try oft, make many endeavours, attempts : 2, 23. πειραθέντες, to make an attempt : 7, 12. πειρᾶν τῶν τειχῶν, to make an attempt upon, to attack : 5, 111. πεπειραμένους, to be experienced : 7, 39. οἱ Συρακόσιοι ἐπὶ πολὺ διῆγον τῆς ἡμέρας πειρώμενοι ἀλλήλων, an instance of a verb, expressing a continuance, having the verb, of which it expresses the circumstance, put in the participle, Matth. Gr. Gr. 840.

πελάγιος, 8, 39. out at sea, 44.

πέλαγος, 5, 110. Κρητικὸν the Cretan sea : 7, 34. 49. ἐν πελάγει, at sea : 3, 32. ἔπλει διὰ τοῦ πελάγους, to sail through the (wide) sea, right across, (opposed to coasting:) 6, 13.

πέλας, 4, 92. τῇ τῶν πέλας, neighbours, persons in the vicinity: 1, 32. παρὰ τοὺς πέλας: 3, 39. 6, 79. τοὺς πέλας, others.

πέλεκυς, 2, 4. a hatchet.

πελιδνὸς, 2, 49. livid.

πελταστὴς, 5, 10. a light-armed soldier: 7, 27.

πέμπτος, 3, 19. πέμπτον αὐτὸν, with four others: 5, 83, πέμπτον καὶ δέκατον ἔτος, an example of the conjunction of an ordinal number with καὶ, Matth. Gr. Gr. 176.

πεμπτὸς, 8, 86. πρέσβεις, despatched.

πέμψις, 7, 17. a commission, sending.

πέμπω, 5, 47. to send: 5, 37. πέμψουσιν, to despatch: 1, 30. πέμψαντες, 5, 21. 6, 7. παρὰ Χαλκιδέας, to send (a message, order) to: 7, 8. οἱ πεμπόμενοι, the messengers: 6, 51. πέμψαντες τὴν πομπὴν, to lead the procession, go in procession, ducere pompam, πομπεύειν: 7, 12. πεπόμφασι ἐπ᾿ ἄλλην στρατιὰν, to send for: 5, 54. ἐπέμφθησαν: 7, 1. πέμψαντες ἐκέλευον, to send to order: 2, 27. τὴν Αἴγιναν ἀσφαλέστερον ἐφαίνετο τῇ Πελοποννήσῳ ἐπικειμένην, αὐτῶν πέμψαντες ἐποίκους, ἔχειν, a deviation from the general rule that, where the participle has the same subject as the other poposition, it should

be in the case of the common subject, here it is the nomin. for the dat., πέμψαντες for πέμψασιν, because ἐφαίνετο ἔχειν is the same as ἐψηφίσαντο ἔχειν, Matth. Gr. Gr. 859.

πενία, 2, 37. κατὰ πενίαν, on account of poverty: 1, 141. ὑπὸ πενίας, in consequence of or through poverty: 2, 42. ἐλπίδι πενίας, from the hope of poverty, i. e. the hope usual in that condition.

πένομαι, 2, 40. τὸ πένεσθαι, poverty.

πενταετὴς, 1, 112. for five years.

πεντακοσιομέδιμνος, 3, 16. a person with 500 medimns of liquid and dry commodities, a person of the first class in the state.

πεντακόσιος, 5, 6. five hundred.

πεντατηρὶς, 3, 104. the fifth year.

πεντήκοντα, 5, 18. fifty.

πεντηκονταετὶς, 5, 32. for fifty years.

πεντηκοντατὴρ, 5, 66. a captain of a company.

πεντηκόντορος, 1, 14. a vessel of fifty oars: 6, 43. πεντηκοντόροιν.

πεντηκοστὺς, 5, 68. a company of soldiers consisting of four enomoties.

πέρα, 2, 64. ἐπιγεγένηταί τε πέρα ὧν προσεδεχόμεθα ἡ νόσος ἥδε, beyond, contrary to our expectation.

περαίνω, 6, 70. περαίνεσθαι, to come to pass, to happen,

7, 43. to go through with, accomplish, perfect : 6, 86. οὐδὲν ἔτι περανεῖ, to be of no avail.

περαιτέρω, 5, 41. τῶν ὅρων, beyond, further than : 3, 81. καὶ ἔτι περαιτέρω, 43. περαιτέρω ὑμῶν προνοοῦντας, to see further than, foresee farther than.

περαιόω, 4, 121. ἐπεραίωσε, to bring over : 2, 67. περαιώσειν, to cross, pass over : 1, 5. 6, 34. περαιοῦσθαι, 7, 31. 47. : 7, 50. περαιωθέντες, 2, 80. 3, 23. 4, 44. ἐπεραιώθησαν, 7, 33. τὸν Ἰόνιον, to cross : 1, 10. περαιώσεσθαι : 7, 34. 8, 41. περαιωθῆναι : 7, 7. περαιωθῇ.

πέραν, 4, 75. beyond : 5, 6. τοῦ ποταμοῦ, on the other side of the river : 3, 91.

πέρας, 1, 69. ἐκ περάτων γῆς, from the boundaries of the earth : 7, 42.

πέρθω, 8, 57. πορθήσωσι τὴν ἤπειρον, to lay waste, devastate, destroy.

περὶ, 1, 73. περὶ τοῦ παντὸς λόγου, concerning the whole of the oration, 79. τῶν παρόντων, concerning the business on hand : 3, 82. περὶ πλείονος ἦν, to be of more value : 1, 74. περὶ τῇ χώρᾳ, (to be in alarm) for their country, 59. τῷ χωρίῳ, 7, 53. περὶ ταῖς ναυσὶν δείσαντες, to fear for the ships, 57. Σικελίας, for, on behalf of Sicily, 19. τὸ πεδίον, up and down the plain, 31. τὴν Ἀκαρνανίαν, 42. 6, 71. ἑξήκοντα καὶ διακοσίους, about, 7,

42. 7, 16. περὶ ἡλίου τροπὰς τὰς χειμερινάς, about the time of the winter-solstice : 7, 25. περὶ ἔρμα, against or upon a rock : 3, 35. τὰ περὶ τὴν Μυτιλήνην, the affairs of : 6, 53. περὶ τοὺς Ἑρμᾶς δρασθῆντων, against : 1, 25. περὶ τὰς ναῦς, in respect to ships, naval affairs, 69. περὶ αὑτῷ, by his own fault through himself : 8, 46. : 6, 2. ᾤκουν Φοίνικες περὶ πᾶσαν τὴν Σικελίαν, ' in the whole of Sicily,' an instance of the prep. with the accus., where it is employed as ἀμφὶ for ' round,' ' about,' Matth. Gr. Gr. 909. : 6, 69. οἱ δ' ἐχώρουν, Συρακόσιοι μὲν περὶ πατρίδος μαχούμενοι, — Ἀθηναῖοι δὲ περὶ τε τῆς ἀλλοτρίας οἰκείαν σχεῖν, the use of the prep. περὶ with the gen., where by a deviation from its general signification the idea of ἀντὶ is implied, Matth. 908.

περιαγγέλλω, 1, 116. περιαγγέλλουσαι, to send round a proclamation : 2, 80. περιήγγειλεν, 5, 54. περιήγγειλαν, to circulate orders, instructions : 2, 85. περιήγγελλον ναῦς κατὰ πόλεις, to send round orders to the (several) cities to prepare ships, 4, 8. 7, 18. σίδηρον κατὰ τοὺς ξυμμάχους, to send round amongst the confederates for iron, to send orders to the confederates to provide iron : 5, 17.

περιάγω, 4, 111. περιαγαγόντες, to lead about, bring round.

περιαιρετὸς, 2, 13. capable of being taken off, stripped.

περιαιρέω, 1, 108. περιειλον, to destroy or demolish (all) round : 3, 11. περιηρημένου, to be cut off, taken off, removed, reduced : 4, 51.

περιαλγέω, 6, 54. περιαλγήσας, to be excessively grieved, in great anguish : 4, 14.

περιβάλλω, 7, 25. περιβάλῃ, to strike with, against : 1, 8. περιεβάλλοντο τείχη, to surround with walls, literally to throw walls round the town : 2, 76. περιβάλλοντες βρόχους, to cast ropes round.

περιβόητος, 6, 31. noised abroad, famous.

περιβολὴ, 8, 104. καὶ τοῦ χωρίου τοῦ περὶ τὸ Κυνὸς Σῆμα ὀξεῖαν καὶ γωνιώδη τὴν περιβολὴν ἔχοντος, ambitus, the circuit.

περίβολος, 1, 89. the circumference or circuit of a wall round (the city,) 90, 93. : 2, 13. the circumference, compass : 3, 21.

περιγίγνομαι, 8, 2. περιγενέσθαι, to be superior to, 1, 32. 4, 73. : 5, 72. περιγενόμενοι, to be superior, to surpass : 1, 69. περιγεγενημένους, to survive, escape : 3, 37. περιγενήσθε, to be superior, to overmatch : 6, 8. ἤν τι περιγίγνηται αὐτοῖς τοῦ πολέμου, in case they had any leisure from the war, any time to spare from war, or, in case they had any advantage or success in the war : 3, 37. περιγίγνεσθαι, to get the better

of, to prevail over, overcome (in debate :) 1, 55. ἡ μὲν οὖν Κέρκυρα οὕτω περιγίγνεται τῷ πολέμῳ τῶν Κορινθίων, emersit e bello, forasmuch as verbs compounded with prepositions, which by themselves require the dat., govern the same case, if the prep. may be separated from the verb without affecting the sense, so verbs compounded with περὶ, where this prep. has no influence on the construction, take the dat., Matth. Gr. Gr. 557.

περίγραπτος, 7, 49. circumscribed, moving in a small and confined space.

περιδεὴς, 3, 28. excessively afraid, 80. very apprehensive : 6, 51. γενόμενοι, to be struck with alarm, consternation, 59. ἐκ τοῦ παραχρῆμα, a sudden alarm, 49. προσδέχονται, to be fearfully expecting, to be expecting with terror.

περιείδω, 4, 40. περιιδὸν, 71. περιιδεῖν τὸ μέλλον, to await, look for, 11. to suffer patiently, 2, 18. to overlook, see without interfering, suffer, 20. : 6, 38. γινέσθαι, to suffer to take place, Matth. Gr. Gr. 836. : 8, 26.

περίειμι, 1, 121. περιεσόμεθα, to be superior, 5, 11. περιέσεσθαι, 1, 144. ἐς ἐλπίδα τοῦ, the hope of victory, 5, 11. : 7, 21. πλέον τι περιεσομένους, to be likely to have a greater superiority, καὶ πολὺ περιεῖναι :

2, 4. περιῆσαν, to survive, 3,
24. περίεστι : 1, 89. περιῆσαν,
to remain standing. (as a
house :) 3, 82. περιεῖναι, to
escape calamity: 6, 55. πολλῷ
τῷ περιόντι τοῦ ἀσφαλοῦς, the
same as πολλῇ τῇ περιουσίᾳ τῆς
ἀσφαλείας, nullo prorsus cum
periculo, with perfect safety,
security : 8, 46.

περιέργω, 1, 106. περιείργον,
to shut in all around : 5, 11.
περιείρξαντες.

περιελαύνω, 7, 44. περιελά-
σαντες, to ride up and down,
scour the country.

περιέρχομαι, 4, 80. περιῆλθον
τὰ ἱερὰ, to go about or round,
36. περιελθὼν, to make a
circuit.

περιέχω, 5, 71. to exceed,
stretch beyond : 5, 7. περι-
σχήσων, to overcome: 4, 102.:
3, 22. περιεῖχεν, 107. περιέσχε.

περιίστημι, 8, 15. περιεστάναι,
to surround, 7, 18. ἐς τοὺς
'Α., to devolve upon, happen
to, come round to, fall upon:
6, 61. ὑποψία ἐς τὸν Ἀλκιβιά-
δην περιεστήκει, suspicion fell
upon, cedere, evadere, deve-
nire, 8, 1. περιειστήκει, Matth.
Gr. Gr. 275. : 8, 2. περιέστη,
to surround, 1, 120. ἐς τοὐναντίον περιέστη, to turn out
quite contrary, 6, 24. : 5, 7.
περιστὰς, 10. : 4, 10. περιεστὼς,
to encompass, 34. : 1, 76. ἡμῖν
δὲ καὶ ἐκ τοῦ ἐπιεικοῦς ἀδοξία τὸ
πλέον ἢ ἔπαινος οὐκ εἰκότως περιέστη, here περιέστη is only
a more figurative expression
for ἐγένετο, it takes the dat.,
(though in this peculiar in-

stance the accus. is more
common,) for that reason ;
under the head that verbs,
which by themselves require
a dat., though they be compounded with preps., take
the dat., if the preps. may be
separated without affecting
the sense, Matth. 557. : 8, 15.

περιίσχω, 5, 91. to stretch
beyond, round.

περίκειμαι, 2, 13. περικείμενοι,
to lie, to be about.

περικλείω, 2, 90. περικλεί-
σειαν, to inclose, surround,
intercept.

περικλύζω, 6, 3. περικλυζο-
μένη, to be washed round or
surrounded by the sea.

περικομίζω, 3, 81. περιεκομί-
ζοντο, to go or sail round : 7,
9. περικομίσας,

περικομπέω, 6, 17. περικομ-
ποῦνται, to be boasted of
everywhere, vulgarly re-
ported and exaggerated,
noised about.

περικοπὴ, 6, 27. a deface-
ment, mutilation.

περικόπτω, 6, 26. οἱ πλεῖστοι
περιεκόπησαν τὰ πρόσωπα, to be
mutilated, defaced, have the
projecting parts cut off.

περικτίονες, 3, 104. neighbours, vicini, accolæ.

περικύκλωσις, 3, 78. sur-
rounding.

περιλαμβάνω, 8, 42. περιλά-
βοι, to lay hold of.

περίλοιπος, 1, 74. remaining, 2, 84. : 7, 72. surviving,
remaining, left.

περιμάχητος, 7, 84. ἦν, to be
contended for.

περιμένω, 2, 80. περιμείνας, to await, 7, 26. 8, 16.: 7, 20. περιέμενε, to remain, 33.: 5,7. περιέμεινεν: 7,74. περιμεῖναι: 6, 56. περιέμενον Παναθήναια τὰ μεγάλα, to wait (the arrival of.)

περίνεως, 1, 10. a passenger, one who in a voyage takes no part in managing the vessel.

περίνοια, 3, 43. a conception, an imagination, a suspicion.

πέριξ, 6, 90. *circumcirca*, round-about.

περίοδος, 4, 35. a surrounding.

περιοικὶς, 1, 9. neighbouring, on the confines : 2, 25. the vicinity : 3, 16. γῆν, the country or land surrounding or adjacent to a town.

περιοικοδομέω, 3, 81. περιοικοδομηθέντες, to be inclosed in (a wall.)

περίοικος, 1, 17. 101. 3, 92. 4, 8. 8, 6. a neighbour, neighbouring, 22. *see* Duker.

περιοπτέον, 8, 48. to be looked after, guarded against.

περιόπτομαι, 1, 36. περιόψεσθε, to suffer, let, permit, 39. 53. : 1, 35. 86. περιοψόμεθα ἀδικουμένους, to neglect them when injured, 95. : 2, 20. περιόψεσθαι δοκεῖν, to be likely to see with patience, to neglect : 4, 48. οὐδ᾽ ἐσιέναι ἔφασαν κατὰ δύναμιν περιόψεσθαι οὐδένα, 5, 29. 6, 86. instances of a rare use of the infin. for the participle after this verb, Matth. Gr. Gr. 836.

περιοράω, 1, 24. 69. to neglect, 2, 20. περιορᾷν, to suffer, Matth. Gr. Gr. 836. : 7, 26. : 4, 73. to be on the look out, on the watch : 124. περιορώμενος, to be solicitous about, to be regardful for: 7, 33. to look on (as an unconcerned spectator :) 2, 43. περιορᾶσθε, to neglect, shun, avoid : 6, 93.

περίορθρον, 2, 3. αὐτὸ τὸ, just before dawn, day-break.

περιορμέω, 4, 26. to moor round, 23. περιώρμουν.

περιορμίζω, 3, 6. περιορμισάμενοι, to invest with a fleet, lie with at anchor round.

περιουσία, 1, 2. abundance, stock, superfluity, 8. abundance (of wealth,) 11. a sufficient supply : 6, 17. τοῦ ναυτικοῦ, superiority, strength, excellence: 5, 103. ἀπὸ περιουσίας, in a great superfluity of prosperity : 1, 141. περιουσίαι, funds, revenue, arising from taxes, voluntary contributions : 2, 13. 5, 71.

περιπέμπω, 6, 45. ἔνθα μὲν περιέπεμπον, to send round : 5, 2. περιέπεμψε, to send round, to despatch, 3. περιπεμφθεῖσαι, to be sent about, commissioned.

περιπίμπρημι, 3, 98. περιεπίμπρασαν, to set on fire (all) around.

περιπίπτω, 8, 27. to fall into : 1, 43. περιπεπτωκότες, to come round upon, 2, 59. ταῖς ξυμφοραῖς : 5, 14. περιπεσόντες, to fall or precipitate oneself into, 2, 54. τοιούτῳ πάθει, to fall into calamities, misfortunes : 5, 11. περιπεσεῖν, to fall into.

περιπλέω, 2, 23. 5, 3. περίπλω, to sail round about, 53. Σκύλλαιον περιπλεῖν, to double the Scyllæum : 2, 25. περιπλεύσασαι : 4, 56. περιέπλευσαν.

περίπλους, 8, 4. doubling (the promontory :) 2, 80. ὁμοῖος, a circumnavigation equally practicable, easy : 6, 1. 7, 31. sailing round, about : 7, 36. manœuvering in a circle.

περιποιέω, 2, 25. to save (a town,) 3, 102. περιεποίησαν, to preserve, 6, 104. to retain : 1, 15. περιεποιήσαντο, to acquire for oneself, 9. περιποιησάμενον, to obtain, procure : 8, 48. περιποιήσαν.

περιπόλιον, 3, 99. περιπόλιον ἐπὶ τῷ Ἄλακι ποταμῷ, a guardfort, 7, 48. see the Notes, here ἐπὶ is used with the dat. and signifies ' at' as a definition of place, Matth. Gr. Gr. 901.

περιῤῥέω, 4, 102. περιῤῥέοντος, to flow round.

περίῤῥυτος, 4, 64. surrounded with water, by the sea.

περισκοπέω, 1, 36. περισκοπῶν, to take a survey, 6, 49. to look about, to watch.

περισσεύω, 2, 65. ἐπερίσσευσι, to be over and above, to abound.

περισταδὸν, 7, 81. all round, from all parts about.

περισταυρόω, 2, 75. περι-

σταύρωσεν, to surround with palisades.

περιτειχίζω, 2, 78. περιετείχιζον, to surround with a wall, 4, 69. to invest a city, 3, 18. : 3, 64. περιτειχίζεσθαι, to be blockaded, invested : 7, 11. περιτειχίσαι, the same in effect as ἀποτειχίσαι, which last strictly means to cut off communication by a wall, to wall off.

περιτείχισις, 2, 77. πρὸς τὴν περιτείχισιν παρεσκευάζοντο, to prepare for a blockade: 4,131.

περιτείχισμα, 5, 2. a fortress, entrenchment, redoubt : 3, 25. a wall of circumvallation.

περιτειχισμὸς, 8,25. a building of a wall of circumvallation.

περιτέχνησις, 3, 82. τῶν τ᾿ ἐπιχειρήσεων περιτεχνήσει, skilfulness, artfulness, cunning, Schol. περινοία.

περιτίθημι, 6, 89. περιθέτε ἐμοῖς ἐχθροῖς δύναμιν, (conciliastis,) to invest: 4, 87. περιθεῖναι κάλλιστον ὄνομα, to impose, 8, 43. to impose on.

περιτυγχάνω, 3.33. μετεώροις περιέτυχεν, to fall in or come up with, 1, 20. περιτυχόντες, to meet with by accident, to light upon, 5, 59. : 1, 135. ὅπου ἂν περιτύχωσιν, wheresoever they may meet with him, 5, 66. ἢν περιτύχωσιν, should they fall in with the enemy, 4, 55. περιτύχῃ, to befal, overtake : 8, 23. περιέτυχον.

περιφανὴς, 4, 102. conspicuous on all sides.

περιφανῶς, 6, 60. (mani-

festly, conspicuously,) exceedingly.

περιφέρω, 7, 28. περιοίσειν,
to hold out, endure, tolerate.

περίφοβος, 6, 36. περιφόβους
ὑμᾶς ποιοῦντες, to make afraid,
throw into alarm.

περιφρονέω, 1, 25. περιφρο-
νοῦντες, to despise, look down
upon.

περιφρουρέω, 3, 21. περιεφρου-
ροῦντο, to be inclosed round,
guarded.

περιχαρὴς, 7, 73. ὑπὸ τοῦ
περιχαροῦς τῆς νίκης, from or
through joy of the victory,
Matth. Gr. Gr. 493. : 2, 51.

περιωθέω, 3, 57. περιωσόμεθα,
(pushed about,) to be contemned, 67.

περιωπὴ, 2, 35. 4, 86. cir-
cumspection.

πετρώδης, 4, 9. stony.

πῇ, 4, 69. εἴ τῃ δέοιτό τι,
wherever there was need:
7, 71.

πήγνυμι, 6, 66. ἔπηξαν σταύρωμα, to drive: 4, 92. εἰς ὄρος
ἡμῖν παγήσεται, to be imposed,
assigned.

πηλὸς, 1, 93. mud (for cement:) 4, 4. : 7, 84. ὁμοῦ τῷ
πηλῷ, together with the mud:
2, 76.

πηλώδης, 6, 101. full of clay.

πημονὴ, 5, 47. ἐπὶ πημονῇ,
for the purpose of injury, 18.

πῆχυς, 7, 36. a cubit.

πιέζω, 1, 126. ἐπιέζοντο, to
be in distress, 7, 47. to be
pressed, afflicted with : 1,
49. πιέζοντο : 2, 89. πιεζόμε-
νος, to be hard-pressed, 68.
4, 66. 5, 103. 7, 50.

πιθανὸς, 3, 36. πιθανώτατος
τῷ δήμῳ, of most influence
with the populace, 4, 31. 6,
35. τοῖς πολλοῖς, with the
multitude.

πίθος, 4, 115. ὕδατος, a tub.

πῖλος, 4, 34. οὔτε οἱ πῖλοι
ἔστεγον τὰ τοξεύματα, a shirt of
mail, for πρὸς τὰ τ., an instance, where the second
accus. may be explained by
a prep., Matth. Gr. Gr. 589.

πίνω, 4, 26. ἔπινον, to drink.

πιπράσκω, 6, 95. ἐπράθη ταλάντων πέντε, to be sold for.

πίπτω, 5, 10. πεσόντα, to
fall : 4, 112. τῷ τείχει πεπτωκότι,
to fall down, to decay : 1, 89.

πίσσα, 2, 77. θείῳ καὶ πίσσῃ,
brimstone and pitch : 4, 100.

πιστεύω, 1, 10. 32. πιστεύοντες to trust to, act under the
belief, 80. : 4, 92. πιστεύσαν-
τες τῷ θεῷ, to put trust in
God : 1, 1. πιστεύσαι : 2, 22.
πιστεύων ὀρθῶς γιγνώσκειν, to
be sure that he judged
rightly : 3, 5. πιστεύειν σφίσιν
αὐτοῖς, to have confidence
in themselves, their own
strength : 2, 35. πιστευθῆναι,
to be believed, credited : 1,
69. διὰ τὸ πιστεῦσαι, on account of (their) confidence,
20. χαλεπὰ ὄντα πιστεῦσαι,
being hard or difficult to
believe.

πίστις, 1, 35. a pledge, confirmation : 4, 74. πίστεσι, 86. :
6, 53. πονηρῶν ἀνθρώπων, credit (given) to men of bad
character : 5, 45. πιστὶν αὐτοῖς
δοὺς, to give a pledge to
them, pledge his word of

honor : 1, 120. οὐδεὶς ὁμοίᾳ πίστει καὶ ἔργῳ ἐπεξέρχεται, no one actually goes through with a design in the same sanguine temperament, in which he formed it : 5, 30.

πιστὸς, 3, 12. ἐλευθερία, assured or secure freedom, 40. πιστὴν λόγῳ ἐλπίδα : 6, 33. believed : 1, 68. τὸ πιστὸν, good faith, confidence (in one another :) 4, 85. αἰτίαν, creditable : 8, 10. to be relied on : 3, 10. trust-worthy, to be depended upon : 4, 120. πιστοτάτους : 5, 13. 108. πιστότερος.

πιστόω, 4, 88. πιστώσαντες, to give credit for.

πιστῶς, 1, 91. faithfully.

πίσυνος, 6, 2. confiding in, relying upon, secure of: 5, 14. relying upon, encouraged by : 2, 89.

πλάγιος, oblique, side-way, transverse, 7, 6. 40. 59. : 4, 33. ἐκ πλαγίου, on the flank.

πλαίσιον, 6, 67. 7, 78. ἐν πλαισίῳ, in an oblong form, brick-form.

πλανάω, 7, 44. ἐπλανήθησαν κατὰ τὴν χώραν, to wander up and down the country.

πλάνησις, 8, 42. wandering; deviation from a course.

πλάσσω, 6, 58. ἀδήλως τῇ ὄψει πλασάμενος, vultu ad dissimulandam calamitatem composito, to compose (one's countenance.)

Πλαταιᾶσιν, 4, 72. an instance of σι, not as a termination of the dat. plur., as originally, but converted to

an adverbial termination, Matth. Gr. Gr. 374.

πλέθρον, 7, 38. a plethrum, one hundred feet, one sixth of a stadium.

Πλειστόλας, 5, 25. Matth. Gr. Gr. 71.

πλείων, 3, 23. πλείους ἄνδρας, many, a considerable number : 4, 103. ἐκ πλείονος, long before, since, il y a long temps : 1, 2. ὑπό τινων ἀεὶ πλειόνων, by those, whoever happened to be the most numerous, 36. τὸ πλέον ἦ, any more than, 3, 12. for μᾶλλον ἤ : 1, 37. πλέον ἔχωσιν, to grasp at too much, 76. to make acquisitions : 5, 59. οὐ πολλῷ πλείους, not very many : 3, 22. οἱ πλείους, the greater part, main body : 4, 117. περὶ πλείονος ἐποιοῦντο, to make a point or much of : 1, 17. ἐπὶ πλεῖστον δυνάμεως, to the greatest (pitch) of power : 2, 65. εἶναι ἄξιον πλείστου, to be most valuable, of the greatest worth, 4, 59. : 3, 1. τὸν πλεῖστον ὅμιλον, the mass or main body (of the light-armed troops,) le gros des couriers, 21. τὸ πλεῖστον, (for) the most part, mainly, chiefly : 7, 30. ἀποκτείνουσιν ἐν τῇ ἐσβάσει τοὺς πλείστους— ἐπεὶ ἔν γε τῇ ἄλλῃ ἀναχωρήσει— ὀλίγοι αὐτῶν διεφθάρησαν, the greatest part or whole number of slain. Τοὺς πλ. cannot refer to the whole number of Thracians, and it is equally objectionable to join τοὺς πλ. with οὔτε ἐπισταμένους νεῖν, as the Schol. does, or to divide the sentences by a comma after αὐτῶν with Hobbes : 1, 83. ἔστιν ὁ πόλεμος οὐχ ὅπλων τὸ πλέον, ἀλλὰ δαπάνης, where ἀλλὰ is for ἢ, this is an anacoluthon, it is one among the various constructions with μᾶλλον, which takes its rise from the consideration that a comparison with ' more' implies at the same time an opposition, Matth. Gr. Gr. 659. : 4, 82. καὶ τῶν ταύτῃ ξυμμάχων φυλακὴν πλέονα κατεστήσαντο, an instance where the Attics use the uncontracted form, Matth. 146. : 4, 85. πλέονες, sometimes the Attics use πλείους, here uncontracted, Matth. 168. : 7, 21. ἔφη χρῆναι πληροῦν ναῦς ὡς δύνανται πλείστας, in the use of the superl., in order to strengthen the signif., particles are added, here a word signifying possibility, Matth. 666. : 7, 45. ὅπλα πλέω ἢ κατὰ τοὺς νεκροὺς ἐλήφθη, more arms than (the number of) the dead led one to expect, when a subst. is not compared with another, but the quality of a thing, in its proportion to another, is considered and compared in degree with this proportion, where in Latin *quam pro* is used, then ἢ κατὰ is put after the comparative, Matth. 653. : 7, 63. πλεῖον, Matth. 158. : 8, 48.

πλεονάζω, 1, 121. to grasp at : 2, 35. πλεονάζεσθαι, to be exaggerated (in a speech.)

πλεονεκτέω, 1, 77. τὸ πλεονεκτεῖσθαι, avariciousness, rapacity : 6, 39. ὠφελιμων, to have more than one's share, grasp at more : 4, 61. ταῦτα, 86.

πλεονέκτης, 1, 40. rapacious, an extortionist.

πλεονεξία, 3, 45. rapacity, 82. profit, 84. Matth. Gr. Gr. 930.

πλευστέα εἶναι, 6, 25. to owe to sail.

πλέω, 1, 26. 30. πλεύσαντες, to sail : 6, 20. πλέομεν : 8, 1. πλευσεῖσθαι : 7, 1. ἐπὶ τῆς Ἱμέρας πλεῖν, to sail or set sail : 8, 86. ὡρμημένων τῶν ἐν Σάμῳ Ἀθηναίων πλεῖν ἐπὶ σφᾶς αὐτούς, (ἐν ᾧ σαφέστατα Ἰωνίαν καὶ Ἑλλήσποντον εὐθὺς εἶχον οἱ πολέμιοι, *tenuissent;*) Matth. Gr. Gr. 748. : 7, 23. 64. πλευσουμένους, Matth. 223.

πληγή, 5, 50. πληγὰς ἔλαβεν, to be beaten with rods.

πλῆθος, 1, 1. quantity : 5. 68. number, amount : 1, 72. ἐς τὸ πλῆθος εἰπεῖν, to speak to the assembly, 81. τῷ πλήθει ὑπερφέρομεν, to surpass in numbers : 1, 2. ἀνθρώπων, population, 20. τὸ, the vulgar, 9. χρημάτων, greatness of possessions : 3, 70. διὰ πλῆθος ζημίας, on account of the greatness of the fine : 1, 20. Ἀθηναίων τὰ πλῆθος Ἵππαρχον οἴονται ὑφ' Ἁρμοδίου καὶ Ἀριστογείτονος τύραννον ὄντα ἀποθανεῖν, with words of number in the sing. the verb is very often in the plur., because in such words the idea of several subjects is always included, Matth. Gr. Gr. 437. : 1, 102. Ἀθηναίοι ἦλθον, Κίμωνος στρατηγοῦντος, πλήθει οὐκ ὀλίγῳ, a use of the dat. for the Latin abl. answers to wherewith? in the case of the relation of the connection or companionship, in this case σὺν and ἅμα are not employed with such words as στόλος, στρατὸς, &c. Matth. 563. : 1, 49.

πλὴν, 1, 17. except, 7, 23. πλὴν ὅσον—οὓς ἐζώγρησαν, except those, whom they took alive, as many as (were in three of the ships,) whom they took alive, for πλὴν ὅσους, 44. but : 1, 2. 4, 54.

πλήρης, 1, 29. manned, full of sailors, 6, 31. 7, 37.

πληρόω, 1, 35. to man (ships,) 47. πληρώσαντες, 6, 30. ἐπλήρουν τὰς ναῦς, to go ahoard, 52. : 7, 19. ἐπληρώθησαν—εἰ τοῦ χειμῶνος πληρωθεῖσαι, to be manned, equipped in the winter.

πλήρωμα, 7, 4. a complement, ship's crew.

πλησίον, 1, 57. near (cum gen.)

πλησιόχωρος, 2, 68. neighbouring, in the vicinity : 4, 79. contiguous.

πλήσσω, 3, 18. πληγέντες, to be smitten, overthrown, 5, 14.

πλινθεύω, 2, 78. ἐπλινθεύσαντο, to make bricks : 4, 67. ἐπλίνθευον τὰ τείχη.

πλινθίον, 6, 88. a brick.

πλίνθος, 2, 75. a brick, 4, 69. 90.

πλώϊμος, 2, 13. fit for sea-service.

πλοῖον, 1, 10. 3, 85. 4, 16. 29. 67. 7, 7. 80. a vessel, lighter vessel, boat.

πλοῦς, 6, 2. ἐλάχιστον πλοῦν Σικελίας ἀπέχει, to be distant by the shortest voyage, to be at the shortest distance from : 4, 3. course of sailing, 28. : 3, 3. χρησάμενος πλῷ, to have a favourable voyage, quick passage, Schol. εὐπλοίᾳ : 7, 26. πλοῦν ποιῆται, to make sail, to sail : 6, 31. ἐπὶ βραχεῖ πλῷ, for a short voyage, expedition : 8, 8. τὸν πλοῦν ταύτῃ ἐκ τοῦ προφανοῦς ἐποιοῦντο, καταφρονήσαντες τῶν Ἀθηναίων ἀδυνασίαν ὅτι ναυτικὸν οὐδὲν αὐτῶν πολύ πω ἐφαίνετο.

πλούσιος, 6, 39. rich, wealthy : 1, 8. πλουσιώτεροι : 8, 45. πλουσιώτατοι, the richest.

πλουτέω, 2, 42. πλουτήσειεν, to be rich, wealthy.

πλωΐζω, 1, 13. ἐπλωΐζοντο, to attend to navigation.

πλώϊμος, 1, 29. in sailing condition, 52. : 1, 7. πλωϊμωτέρων ἤδη, navigation now being more advanced.

πνεῦμα, 2, 49. breath, 97.

πνῖγος, 7, 87. suffocation (from heat.)

πνοὴ, 4, 100. gust, blast.

ποδώκης, 3, 98. swift of foot.

ποθεινὸς, 2, 42. ποθεινοτέραν, more desirable, to be wished for.

πόθος, 6, 24. a desire, longing for.

ποιέω, 3, 12. ἐκείνους τὸ αὐτὸ ποιεῖν, to do the same to them : 1, 10. πεποίηκε, to make, put, 2, 23. πολὺ τὸ ὕδωρ ἐπεποιήκει, to occasion a flood : 4, 67. ἐποίησαν τοιόνδε, to act in this manner, 83. ποιοῦνται πολέμιον, to declare an enemy, pronounce war against : 3, 2. ποιήσασθαι τὴν ἀπόστασιν, to make a revolt, to revolt, 3, 3. ἐς φυλακὴν, to put under a guard, in prison, custody : 7, 17. ποιήσασθαι πέμψιν τῶν νεῶν, to send or despatch a fleet : 3, 36. ποιεῖσθαι γνώμας, to deliberate, enter into consultation : 7, 3. ἐν ὀλιγωρίᾳ ἐποιοῦντο, to make light of, pay no regard to : 2, 19. ἐποιήσαντο τροπήν τινα, to put to flight, 56. ποιηθεῖσαι ἐκ τῶν παλαιῶν νεῶν, to be built out of old vessels: 3, 33. ποιεῖσθαι τὴν δίωξιν, to pursue ; στρατόπεδον, to form an encampment, to encamp: 3, 90. ἔτυχον δύο φυλαὶ—τινὰ καὶ ἐνέδραν πεποιημέναι, the perf. pass, used as a perf. middle, Matth. Gr. Gr. 715. : 8, 37.

ποίησις, 1, 10. poetry, verses.

ποιητέος, 4, 99. 5, 29. to be done.

ποιητὴς, 1, 5. 10. a poet.

πολέμαρχος, 5, 47. 66. a general officer.

πολεμέω, 5, 14. to carry on war, 65. to quarrel : 1, 37. πολεμοῦνται, to be warred upon : 3, 39. πολεμήσομεν τοῖς οἰκείοις ξυμμάχοις, to be at war with one's own allies : 3, 4. πολεμεῖν Λέσβῳ πάσῃ, to maintain a war with, against, upon : 2, 54. κατὰ κράτος, to wage war with all one's might: 6, 48. μεθ' ὧν τις πολεμήσει, with whose aid one is to carry on war : 5, 26. ἐπολεμήθη : 1, 118. εἰ πολεμοῦσιν ἄμεινον ἔσται, whether it will go better with us, when we carry on war, Matth. Gr. Gr. 836. : 4. 20. Matth. 868. : 5, 9. Matth. 517.

πολεμητέα εἶναι, 1, 79. that war must be undertaken.

πολεμικὸς, 1, 10. warlike, 5, 69.

πολέμιος, 4, 92. πολέμια ἔδρασαν, to commit hostilities, wage war: 1, 18. τὰ πολέμια, military stores : 5, 23. 35. 42. : 7, 68. πολεμιωτάτων : 2, 39. Matth. Gr. Gr. 789.

πόλεμος, 1, 1. war : 6, 6. τὰ τοῦ πολέμου, the same as τὸν πόλεμον : 4, 41. : 1, 83. ἔστιν ὁ πόλεμος οὐχ ὅπλων τὸ πλέον, ἀλλὰ δαπάνης, a principal use of the gen. is to mark the person or thing, to which any thing belongs, when εἶναι is employed, and it is translated different ways according as quality, power, custom, &c. are in hand, Matth.

M m

Gr. Gr. 517.: 3, 92. τοῦ πρὸς Ἀθηναίους πολέμου καλῶς αὐτοῖς ἐδόκει ἡ πόλις καθίστασθαι, the city appeared to be favourably circumstanced with respect to the war, Matth. 453.

πολιορκέω, 1, 61. ἐπολιόρκησαν, to besiege, 26. ἐπολιόρκουν, 64. 3, 52. 4, 24. 7, 9. 50.

πολιορκία, 1, 11. 98. 2, 70. a siege.

πόλις, 5, 27. 33. 44. a city, town, state : 1, 71. ὁμοίᾳ, a city of similar manners, 72. καὶ ἅμα τὴν σφετέραν πόλιν ἐβούλοντο σημαίνειν ὅση εἴη δύναμιν, sc. ἡ πόλις. the subst. subject is omitted in this dependent proposition, which is construed with the verb of the preceding proposition, and is thus easily seen, Matth. Gr. Gr. 428.: 1, 61. ἦλθε δὲ καὶ τοῖς Ἀθηναίοις εὐθὺς ἡ ἀγγελία τῶν πόλεων, ὅτι ἀφεστᾶσι, where the subject is constructed with the preceding verb in the gen., Matth. 429.: 5, 23. ἄμφω τὼ πόλει, Matth. 406. 630.: 5, 77. 79. πολίεσι, Matth. 89. 101.: 6, 22. οὐ πάσης ἔσται πόλεως, not every city will be able (to receive the army,) Matth. 518.: 3, 79. τῇ δ' ὑστεραίᾳ ἐπὶ μὲν τὴν πόλιν οὐδὲν μᾶλλον ἐπέπλεον, καίπερ ἐν πολλῇ ταραχῇ καὶ φόβῳ ὄντας, the participle is referred to the noun collective (πόλιν) in its sense only, because πόλις implies an assembly of men, Matth.
11

627. an instance of the participle's use, where it is put in the plur. masc. with a noun collective in the sing., Matth. 847.

πόλισμα, 1, 10. a small city, 65. town : 4, 54. a state, 103.: 2. 30. 8, 28.

πολιτεία, 4, 76. 126. a form of government : 1, 132. freedom of the city, share in the government, 115. 2, 36.

πολιτεύω, 3, 62. πολιτεύουσα, to be governed, 34. ἐπολίτευον, to have the administration of the affairs of a city : 6, 92. ἐπολιτεύθην, to live under a government, constitution : 2, 37. ἐλευθέρως τὰ πρὸς τὸ κοινὸν πολιτεύομεν, to administer state-affairs with liberality, 15. ἐπολιτεύοντο, to administer affairs : 4, 130.

πολίτης, 2, 2. ἄνδρας τῶν πολιτῶν, certain of the citizens, 64. 5, 16. 6, 9.

πολιτικός, 6, 15. political, belonging to the state.

πολίχνη, 7, 4. a little fort.

πολλάκις, 5, 35. often.

πολλαπλάσιος, 4, 34. many times another number, more numerous, 125. πολλαπλασίους ἢ ἦλθον.

πολλαχῇ, 7, 43. in divers, various places, Matth. Gr. Gr. 374.: 8, 87.

πολλαχόθεν, 6, 32. from various quarters.

πολλαχόσε, 2, 47. to many places.

πολλοστημόριον, 6, 86. mul-

tesima pars, the least portion, ever so small a part.

πολυανδρέω, 6, 17. to be populous.

πολυάνθρωπος, 1, 24. populous : 2, 54. πολυανθρωπότατα : 6, 3.

πολυάρχιον, 6, 72. *multo-rum dominatus*, a command divided among many generals.

πολυειδής, 7, 71. multifarious, of diverse kinds, of various import.

πολύοινος, 1, 138. πολυοινότατον, most abundant in wine.

πολυπειρία, 1, 71. great or much experience.

πολυπραγμοσύνη, 6, 87. *se-dulitas, multarum rerum stu-dium*, meddling with too many things.

πολὺς, 3, 39. 7, 15. τὰ δὲ πολλά, for the most part, *plerumque*; 4, 61. πολλὴ ξυγ-γνώμη, great excuse, 32. ἐκ πολλοῦ, from a long distance, from afar, 67. for a long time, long since, 1, 68. now a long time, 1, 3. πολλοῦ γε χρόνου, for a long time at least ; 7, 18. πολλὴ, vast, extensive, spacious, 15. πολλὰ ὑμᾶς εὖ ἐτοίμκα, to do any one much good service, many good services : 4, 92. πολλὴν ἀδειαν, long, lasting, 22. πολὺς ἐνέ-κειτο, to be very pressing, urging : 2, 56. τῆς γῆς τὴν πολλὴν, the greatest part of the country, an instance of an adjective, which should

be in the same case as its subst., but where a use of the gen. obtains and the adj. is considered as part of the subst. whole, Matth. Gr. Gr. 498. ; 8, 101.

πολυτέλεια, 6, 12. expensiveness, large expenditure, sumptuousness.

πολυτελὴς, 1. 10. 7, 28. very expensive, of great cost : 2, 65. πολυτελέσι : 6, 31. πολυτε-λεστάτη, most sumptuous, costly, expensive : 8, 27.

πολύχειρος, 2, 83. dexterous, 2, 44.

πολυχειρία, 2, 77. a great number of hands (at work.)

πολυψηφία, 2, 10. a widely extended suffrage, right of voting, of being consulted, admitted to council.

πομπεύς, 6, 58. τοὺς πομ-πέας, the conductors of a procession.

πομπή, 2, 13. περὶ τὰς πομ-πὰς καὶ ἀγῶνας, belonging to the shows and games : 1, 20. 6, 56. a procession : 4, 108.

πονέω, 1, 49. 4, 96. ἐπόνει, 5, 73. to be in distress : 2, 51. πονούμενον, to labour (under a malady,) to be afflicted (with :) 4, 59. : 6, 67. ᾗ ἂν τοῦ στρατεύματός τι πονῇ, *qua parte exercitus laboraret*.

πονηρία, 6, 58. vileness, villainy.

πονηρὸς, 6, 58. ἀνθρώπων, 7, 8. τὰ πράγματα, wretched, precarious, dangerous, 8, 24. low, depressed : 7, 48. πονη-ρότερα.

πόνος, 1, 78. οἰκεῖον, a domestic labour, burden: 5, 16.: 2, 62. τὸν δὲ πόνον τὸν κατὰ τὸν πόλεμον, as to the hardships, toils of war, Matth. Gr. Gr. 612.: 2, 39. μελέτῃ πόνων, application to labour, study, pursuit of laborious occupation, 76.

πορεία, 2, 18. a journey.

πορεύομαι, 1, 37. to proceed, 2, 67. δι' ἐκείνου πορευθῆναι, to pass (over) by his means, to give the means of passing (over,) 80. ἐπορεύετο, 7, 29. ἐπορεύοντο, they went, used to go, i. e. those, which went from Athens to Thrace, used to go δι' Εὐρίπου: 2, 98. 4, 103.

πορθέω, 1, 73. to devastate: 3, 57. πορθῆσαι: 7, 39. ἐπόρθουν, to plunder, spoil: 2, 55. ἐπόρθησαν, to raze (a town:) 8, 24. πορθουμένοις.

πορθμός, 2. 83. 4, 24. 6, 2. 7, 1. a strait.

πορίζω, 6, 29. πορεῖν, to procure, scrape together: 3, 82. ἐπορίζοντο, to be procured: 7, 15. ὡς ποριουμένων, as or since or because they are likely, about to get ready, prepare, complete their preparations: 1, 142.

πόριμος, 8, 76. see Duker's note.

ποριστὴς, 8, 48. a provider, procurer.

πόρος, 1, 120. ἐν πόρῳ κατῳκημένους, to dwell in the way of traffic: 6, 48. a passage, περαίωσις.

πόσις, 7, 73. πρὸς πόσιν τε-

τράφθαι, to betake or turn oneself to drinking.

ποταμὸς, 4, 25. 6, 2. 7, 9. a river.

ποτὲ, 4, 20. ever.

ποτὸν, 6, 100. ὕδατος, water for drinking.

πούς, 3, 68. ποδῶν, feet, (the measure,) 97. ἐν ποσὶν, at hand, present.

πρᾶγμα, 3, 28. οἱ ἐν τοῖς πράγμασι, who have the management of affairs, persons in administration: 1, 140. 3, 23. 49. 8, 29.

πρᾶξις, 3, 114. 6, 88. doing, res gesta.

πραότης, 4, 108. mildness, forbearance, conciliating deportment.

πράσσω, 1, 141. τὰ οἰκεῖα πράσσουσι, to transact private business, attend to private interests, 58. πράσσοντες οὐδὲν ἐπιτήδειον, to do no good, procure no benefit, 132. πράσσειν τι ἐς τοὺς Εἵλωτας, to tamper with the Helots: 3, 4. πράσειν αὐτοῖς, to treat with them: 6, 61. ἐκείνου πράξαντος, at his instance: 1, 99. ἀκριβῶς ἔπρασσον, to exact tribute to the last farthing: 8, 5. ἔπρασσε: 1, 71. δίκαια πράσσωσι, to do justice: 2, 64. εὖ πράξητε, to do well, succeed: 6, 51. πρασσόμενοι Ἀθηναίους εἰκοστὴν μόνον, to levy, exact: 1, 22. τὰ ἔργα τῶν πραχθέντων, the execution of the deeds performed: 6, 28. ἐπράχθη μετ' ἐκείνου, to be perpetrated with him, i. e. in participation,

through him, by his means :
8, 5. πεπραγμένος : 8, 3. χρήματα ἐπράξατο, to make money
(of it,) 37. πράσσεσθαι, to exact, 87.

πρέπω, 4, 98. τὰ πρέποντα,
what belongs to one in common decency : 7, 68. πρέπει,
to be meet, proper : 1, 86. 6,
15.

πρεσβεία, 1, 72. 2, 7. 12.
Matth. Gr. Gr. 617.: 4, 118.
5, 27. 31. 36. 55. an em-
bassy.

πρέσβευσις, 1, 73. embas-
sage.

πρεσβευτὴς, 5, 4. an ambassador, 61. 8, 5.

πρεσβεύω, 6, 55. ἀπ᾽ αὐτοῦ,
to be senior, esse maximus
natu (τῶν) ἀπ᾽ αὐτοῦ, sc. nato-
rum : 1, 67. 91. πρεσβεύεσθαι,
to send an embassy, 5, 39.:
8, 5. ἐπρεσβεύσαντο, to send
deputies: 1, 31. πρεσβευόμενοι,
to carry on a negociation by
ambassadors : 2, 12. Matth.
Gr. Gr. 186.

πρέσβυς, 1, 28. 5, 61. 7, 12.
an ambassador: 5, 37. πρέσβεσιν.

πρεσβύτερος, 1, 6. 7, 29.
older, earlier, more ancient :
1, 20. πρεσβύτατος, 4, 61.: 6,
18. καὶ μὴ ὑμᾶς ἡ Νικίου τῶν
λόγων ἀπραγμοσύνη καὶ διάστασις τοῖς νέοις ἐς τοὺς πρεσβυτέρους ἀποστρέψῃ, an instance of
the dat. with a subst. for the
gen. which signifies 'for any
one,' Matth. Gr. Gr. 549.

πριάομαι, 6, 97. ἐπρίαντο, to
buy: 5, 34. τοὺς δὲ ἐκ τῆς νήσου ληφθέντας ἀτίμους ἐποίησαν—, ὥστε μήτε ἄρχειν, μήτε
πριαμένους τι ἢ πωλοῦντας κυρί-
ους εἶναι, an instance of the
use of the participle after a
verb, which properly re-
quires the infin., Matth. Gr.
Gr. 838.

πρὶν, 7, 39. πρὶν δή, until,
ἕως, 71. πρίν γε δὴ, till at last,
50 : 3, 9. τὴν πρὶν ξυμμαχίαν,
the former alliance, confederacy : 1, 78. πρὶν ἐν αὑτῷ
γενέσθαι : 4, 104. 128.

πρίω, 4, 100. πρίσαντες κε-
φαλαν, to saw.

πρὸ, 1, 103. τοῦ, previously:
5, 54. πρὸ τοῦ Καρνείου μηνός,
previous to the Carnean
month : 1, 34. πρὸ πολλῶν
χρημάτων, before or in preference to much wealth : 5,
47. (thirty days) before the
Olympian games : 7, 55. τὰ
πρὸ αὑτῶν, previously, before : 4, 59. Matth. Gr. Gr.
882.: 3, 51. 4, 59.

προάγγελσις, 1, 137. pre-
vious intelligence.

προαγγέλλω, 7, 65. προηγ-
γέλθη, to be previously disclosed, reported, to have
previous information.

προαγορεύω, 1, 131. πόλε-
μον, to denounce war, 4, 97.
to give warning to quit : 2,
13. προηγόρευε, to tell or declare beforehand.

προάγω, 3, 45. to lead on,
propel : 1, 75. προαγαγεῖν, to
advance, raise, 144. προήγα-
γον ἐς τάδε, to advance to this
(pitch of greatness,) 6, 18.

τὴν πόλιν, to advance, promote, enlarge, extend (the interests of:) 7, 7. προαξόμενος, to bring over to one's side : 8, 87. ἵνα τοὺς Φοίνικας προαγαγὼν ἐς τὴν Ἄσπενδον, ἐχρηματίσατο ἀφείς, Matth. Gr. Gr. 848. : 2, 90. to draw forward.

προαγωνίζομαι, 4, 125. ἐξ ὧν προηγώνισθε, from your previous contests.

προαισθάνομαι, 1, 135. 3, 83. 5, 58. to get or have previous intelligence : 8, 51. προύσθετο.

προαμύνω, 3, 12. προαμύνασθαι, to take measures of defence before (the apprehended attack :) 4, 38.

προαναβαίνω, 3, 112. προαναβάντες, to ascend first.

προανάγω, 8, 11. 16. προανήγετο, to sail away beforehand.

προαναλίσκω, 1, 141. προαναλώσειν, to exhaust beforehand, fall short in pecuniary resources : 7, 81. προαναλωθῆναι.

προαναχώρησις. 4, 128. τῶν Μακεδόνων, a previous departure.

προαπαντάω, 1, 69. προαπαντῆσαι, to be ready to encounter : 6, 42. to meet : 4, 92. previously.

προαπέρχομαι, 3, 17. προαπῆλθον, to depart before (some event.)

προαπόλλυμι, 5, 61. προαπόλωνται, to perish before (succour arrives :) 6, 77.

προαποπέμπω, 3, 25. προαποπεμφθῆναι, to be sent out beforehand.

προαποστέλλω, 3, 112. προαποσταλέντες, to be previously despatched, sent off : 3, 5. προαπεστάλησαν τὰς ἀποστάσεις, to be sent before : 4, 77.

προαποχωρέω, 4, 90. προαπεχώρησαν, to go back, to recede.

προάστειον, 3, 102. 4, 69. 5, 2. a suburb, borough.

προαφικνέομαι, 4, 2. προαφίκτο ἐς Σικελίαν, to arrive previously.

προαφίστημι, 3, 12. εἴ τῳ δοκοῦμεν ἀδικεῖν προαποστάντες διὰ τὴν ἐκείνων μέλλησιν τῶν ἐς ἡμᾶς δεινῶν κ. τ. λ., to revolt before (the apprehended event,) an instance of the participle's use, where it serves to express the action with reference to which the finite verb determines any condition or quality, Matth. Gr. Gr. 844.

προβαίνω, 4, 36. to move forward, go previously : 1, 23. προύβη, to proceed, advance.

προβάλλω, 1, 73. προβαλλομένοις, to advance or throw out (in argument,) 2, 87. to allege, pretend : 3, 63. προβάλλεσθε, to advance, bring forward as a boast : 1, 37. προβέβληνται, to pretend.

πρόβατον, 2, 14. πρόβατα, cattle, 51. 7, 17. sheep.

προβουλεύω, 3, 82. προβουλεύσας, to provide by previous care : 8, 1. προβουλεύσουσι, to deliberate.

προγίγνομαι, 1, 1. προγεγενημένων, previous events, 123. 5, 20.

προγιγνώσκω, 2, 64. προγνόντες, to know or understand previously, 65. ἐν τούτῳ προγνοὺς τὴν δύναμιν, to foresee or previously discern its power, resources in war.

πρόγονοι, 2, 11. 36. ancestors : 3, 59. 5, 43. 6, 16.

προδείκνυμι, 3, 47. προδειξάντων, to shew, evince, furnish a precedent previously.

προδηλόω, 1, 130. προύδήλου, to disclose prematurely.

προδιαβάλλω, 6, 75. προδιαβαλεῖν, to anticipate in making charges or accusations.

προδιαγιγνώσκω, 1, 78. προδιάγνωτε, to think beforehand.

προδιαφθείρω, 1, 119. προδιαφθαρῇ, to be previously destroyed, Matth. Gr. Gr. 429.

προδιδάσκω, 2, 40. προδιδαχθῆναι, to be instructed beforehand, get previous information.

προδίδωμι, 2, 74. προδιδόναι, to desert, 7, 68. to abandon, betray : 5, 65. προδίδονται, to be betrayed : 4, 25. 67. : 5, 30. προδῶσιν, to betray : 4, 68. προδεδωκέναι, 77. προδοθησομένους : 3, 63. προδοῦναι, to betray : 6, 69. προὐδίδοσαν βούλησιν, prodebant, destitue-

bant, to abate of (their) alacrity, eagerness.

προδοσία, 4, 81. 101. 5, 3. treachery, 110. 116. 8, 81.

προδότης, 3, 9. 40. a betrayer : 4, 114.

πρόεδρος, 3, 25. a magistrate, ruler.

προείδω, 1, 83. προΐδωμεν, to foresee : 2, 17. προΐδοι, to foreknow, foresee : 1, 51. 122. προΐδοι, 141. προειδὼς, 2, 2. 3, 22. 4, 62. : 1. 37. προειδῆτε, 20. προειδότος : 2, 51. προειδέναι, to know by experience, 48. προειδὼς, to be instructed or get information beforehand.

πρόειμι, 2, 21. προϊέναι ἐς τὸ ἐγγυτέρω, to advance nearer : 2, 34. προήκῃ, to surpass, to be pre-eminent : 1, 111. προϊὼν, 64. 2, 18.

προεῖπον, 1, 45. 2, 13. 3, 66. 4, 26. 80. 5, 64. to bid, order, give out, proclaim, 7, 5. πᾶσι.

προεκθέω, 7, 30. προεκθέοντες, to outrun, run out of the line (of march,) before (the rest of the line,) sally out, charge.

προεκφόβησις, 5, 11. a previous terror.

προεμβάλλω, 4, 25. προεμβαλόντων, to give a shock previously.

προενοίκησις, 1, 25. a former habitation.

προεξάγω, 7, 70. προεξαγομένοι, to draw or lead out previously, 7, 6. προεξαγαγὼν, 37. to draw out previously : 8, 25. προεξάξαντες, to rush on first.

προέξειμι, 3, 1. προεξιόντας τῶν ὅπλων, to advance before the men at arms, the heavy-armed troops.

προεξέρχομαι, 7, 74. προεξελθόντες, to march out pre-viously.

προεπαινέω, 3, 38. προεπαινέσαι, to praise before, go before (a speaker,) antici-pate with one's praise.

προεπανασείω, 5, 17. προεπανεσείσθη, to be held up in terror, openly put in motion, publicly agitated.

προεπιβουλεύω, 1, 33. to an-ticipate in plotting.

προεπιχειρέω, 6, 34. προεπι-χειροῦντας, to make an attack beforehand.

προεργάζομαι, 2, 89. προειρ-γασμένων, former deeds, 7. 66. previous exploits : 8, 65.

προερούντα, 1, 29. πόλεμον, previously to declare war : 2, 84. προείρητο, to give orders previously, 5, 31.

προέρχομαι, 1, 63. 4, 78. προῆλθον, to proceed, 1, 10. 2, 30. προελθών, 5, 50. 70. 1, 120. προελθεῖν, 4, 108. : 2, 21. προελθών ἐς τὸ πλεῖον, to ad-vance further : 1, 24. προελ-θόντος χρόνου, in the course of time : 1, 100, προελθόντες ἐς μεσόγειαν.

προέχω, 6, 18. τὸν πρού-χοντα, superior, stronger, mightier, 7, 4. προύχουσα τοῦ λιμένος, to jut, shoot out before : 3, 49. προεῖχε ἡμέραν καὶ νυκτὰ μάλιστα, to have nearly a day and night's

start, to be nearly a day and night in advance : 2, 87. προέχετε : 8, 35. προύχουσα ἄκρα, a sharp promontory : 1, 25. ναυτικῷ καὶ πολὺ προέ-χειν ἐστὶν ὅτι ἐπαιρόμενοι, the infin. is put after verbs ' to say,' and all those, in which this idea is implied, thus after ἐπαίρομαι, Matth. Gr. Gr. 800. : 6, 31. προθυμη-θέντος ἑνὸς ἑκάστου, ὅπως αὐτῷ τινι εὐπρεπείᾳ τε ἡ ναῦς προέξει, an instance of the dat. for the gen. in reference to a verb, Matth. 548. : 7, 66.

προθνήσκω, 2, 52. προτε-θνάναι.

προθυμέομαι, 5, 71. προθυ-μούμενος, to desire, 7, 70. to be eager : 4, 12. προύθυμοῦντο, 5, 16. 8, 6. : 4, 9. προθυμήσε-σθαι : 5, 17. προύθυμήθη, 4, 81. 8, 9. προύθυμήθησαν, 90. τὴν ὀλι-γαρχίαν προύθυμοῦντο, Matth. Gr. Gr. 599.

προθυμία, 1, 74. zeal, 75. 2, 71. : 6, 47. τὴν προθυμίαν ἐς τοὺς ξυμμάχους, zeal or ala-crity for their allies : 1, 118. vigour : 5, 65. impetuosity, eagerness : 8, 12. energy, 22. zeal.

πρόθυμος, 3, 38. prompt, alert : 2, 20. ready, zealous : 1, 7. vigorous : 4, 85. πᾶν τὸ πρόθυμον, every alacrity, all forwardness : 7, 7. μὴ πρόθυμος ἦν, to be lukewarm : 4, 83. προθυμοτέρῳ, 5, 37. 6, 6. 7, 1. : 7, 3, ὡς προθυμότατα, with all possible alacrity, eagerness.

προθύμως, 5, 32. eagerly,

with alacrity : 7, 1. heartily, with zest, 43. valiantly, with gallantry : 8, 36.

πρόθυρον, 6, 26. a porch, front-door.

προΐημι, 6, 34. προήσονται τάδε, to neglect : 2, 43. ἔρανον αὐτῇ προϊέμενοι, to cast or lay down a contribution, 51. : 1, 120. πρόοιντο, 3, 14. πρύησθε ἡμᾶς, to abandon, cast off, this opt. and this conj. of a verb in μι have the form of the opt. and conj. of a barytone in ω, Matth. Gr. Gr. 287.

προΐστημι, 6, 28. προεστάναι τοῦ δήμου, to have the presidency, to be in chief authority amongst, to bear chief sway over: 3, 70. προειστήκει, to stand forward : 3, 11. τῶν ἀεὶ προεστώτων, chiefs or ministers for the time being, successive chiefs: 6, 89. προέστημεν τοῦ ξύμπαντος, to preside over, to be at the head of, 2, 65. προῦστη τῆς πόλεως : 8, 17. προεστῶσι, chief men.

προΐσχω, 1, 26. προϊσχόμενος, to hold out (as an argument or inducement,) 3, 66. to stretch forth, 3, 66. 4, 87.

προκαθίστημι, 2, 2. προκαθεστηκυίας, to be previously established, appointed.

προκαλέω, 3, 13. -προύκάλεσαν, to invite, solicit : 2, 72. προκαλεῖται, to offer conditions, to propound ; προύκαλισάμεθα, to invite or put to the option, Matth. Gr. Gr. 588. : 74. πολλὰ καὶ εἰκότα

προκαλεσάμενοι, to make many fair proposals : 1, 34. προκληθέντες ἐς κρίσιν, to be cited : 4, 19. Λακεδαιμόνιοι δὲ ὑμᾶς προσκαλοῦνται ἐς σπονδὰς, 5, 43. ἐπὶ τὴν ξυμμαχίαν προκαλούμενος, instances of a verb, which taking two accus. has one explained by a prep., Matth. 588.

προκάλυμμα, 2, 75. a covering in front: 3, 67. a veil.

προκάμνω, 2, 39. to sink, faint under hardships, 49. προέκαμνεν, to be previously ill of a disorder.

προκαταγιγνώσκω, 3, 53. προκαταγνόντες, to have previous knowledge.

προκαταλαμβάνω, 1, 57. to anticipate : 6, 18. : 2, 2. 3, 3. προκαταλαβεῖν, to prevent, to be beforehand with, 5, 30. : 1, 36. προκαταλήψονται, to seize first, 3, 2. 110. προκαταληψομένους, 5, 57.

προκατάρχομαι, 1, 25. προκαταρχόμενοι, to begin first (of all.)

προκαταφεύγω, 2, 91. προκαταφυγοῦσαι, to pursue (one's) flight forward, to fly forward, 3, 78. προκαταφυγεῖν, to take the start in retreating, 1, 134. to outstrip pursuers.

προκατέχω, 4, 105. προκατασχεῖν τὴν πόλιν, to acquire previous possession, get into one's own hands first.

προκατηγορία, an accusation, indictment.

πρόκειμαι, 3, 45. πρόκειται, to be ordained, enacted, 61.

ἔξω τῶν προκειμένων, besides the subject : 1, 35.

προκινδυνεύω, 1, 173. 7, 56. προκινδυνεῦσαι, to undergo or encounter danger for or on behalf of.

πρόκλησις, 3, 64. a summons.

προκόπτω, 4, 60. προκοπτόντων, to prepare : 7, 56. προκόψαντες τοῦ ναυτικοῦ μέγα μέρος, to furnish, provide a large part of the navy, promote, advance, assist very greatly in respect of the fleet.

προκρίνω, 4, 30. προκρίναντες, to select previously.

προλαμβάνω, 4, 33. προλαμβάνοντες, to get the start in running : 7, 80. προῦλαβε πολλῷ, to get the start considerably.

προλέγω, 1, 139. προῦλεγον, to give notice.

προλείπω, 7, 75. προλείποι, to fail, forsake, to be wanting prematurely : 1, 74. προλιπεῖν, to desert.

προλοχίζω, 2, 81. τὰ περὶ τὴν πόλιν ἐνέδραις, to place in ambush all about the city : 3, 110. προλοχοῦντας, 112. προλελοχισμένας, to be previously ambushed, in ambush.

προμανθάνω, 1, 138. προμαθὼν, to gain previous instruction.

πρόμαντις, 5, 16. a priestess.

προμήθεια, 4, 62. previous thought, forethought.

προμηθὴς, 3, 82. μέλλησις, a

provident delay : 4, 92. τὸ προμηθὲς, prudence, sense.

προνικάω, 2, 87. προνενικηκέναι.

προνοέω, 4, 61. προνοεῖσθαι ταῦτα, to be long-sighted, foresee : 6, 9. προνοῆται τοῦ σώματός τι, to take thought for, to be provident of, to pay regard to : 3, 38. προνοῆσαι.

πρόνοια, 4, 108. ἀσφαλεῖ, sure prudence : 6, 13. forethought : 2, 89. 8, 95.

προξενία, 5, 43. friendship, hospitality subsisting between foreigners : 6, 89. ὑμῶν, a connection of hospitality.

πρόξενος, 3, 2. Ἀθηναίων, connected with the Athenians by the ties of hospitality : 2, 39. 85. 3, 70.

προξυγγίγνομαι, 8, 14. προξυγγενόμενοι, to meet with.

προοίμιον, 3, 104. a hymn.

προοράω, 4, 34. to see before, 7, 44. : 1, 138. προέωρα, to discover beforehand, to foresee, 17. ἐφ' ἑαυτῶν μόνον προορώμενοι, said of the tyrants, means their own concerns, their private interests, in opposition to the regard to the common good, and is explained by the words, ἔς τε τὸ σῶμα καὶ ἐς τὸ τὸν ἴδιον οἶκον αὔξειν, Matth. Gr. Gr. 899.

προορμίζω, 7, 38. προώρμισε, to moor or station in front.

προοφείλω, 1, 32. προοφειλομένης, to be previously due.

πρόοψις, 5, 8. a previous examination, inspection.

προπαραβάλλω, 7, 5. προπαρεβάλοντο σφίσιν, to lay previously in heaps along for themselves.

προπαρασκευάζω, 2, 88. προπαρεσκεύαζε, to prepare beforehand, previously: 1, 57. προπαρεσκευάζοντο : 1, 68. προπαρεσκευασμένους.

προπάσχω, 6, 38. προπείσεται, to be the first to suffer, to suffer before (any one is aware, expects:) 3, 67. 82. προπαθεῖν, to suffer previously.

πρόπειρα, 3, 86. a preliminary trial.

προπέμπω, 1, 53. προπέμψαι, to send first, forward, 29. προπέμψαντες, 2, 79. 4, 78. : 6, 30. προπέμποντες, to wait upon, accompany, conduct, set on their way.

προπηλακίζω, 6, 54. προπηλακιῶν, to disgrace, affront, insult, an Attic contraction of the fut. of a verb in ίζω, Matth. Gr. Gr. 221.

πρόπλους, 6, 44. ναῦς, a ship sent on before the rest of the fleet.

προποιέω, 3, 13. προποιῆσαι, to anticipate, do before, to be beforehand with.

προπομπὴ, 6, 58. ποιεῖν προπομπὰς, agere pompas, to celebrate, make processions.

προπύλαιον, 2, 13. a propylæum, vestibule.

προπυνθάνομαι, 4, 42. προπυνθόμενοι, 7, 32. to have previous intelligence.

πρόρρησις, 1, 49. a general's or admiral's instructions from the state.

πρὸς, 5, 45. πρὸς αὐτοὺς, against them, 46. τὰ πρὸς Ἀργείους, the business of the Argives, 1, 73. πρὸς οἵαν πόλιν ὁ ἀγὼν καταστήσεται, against what kind of city the contest will be established, 127. πρὸς τὴν πόλιν, in the city, among the people, 1, 6. πρὸς ἀλλήλους, to one another, 7, 25. πολλὰ μηχανᾶσθαι, against one another, 3, 37. towards one another: 5, 3. πρὸς τῷ τειχίσματι, at or underneath : 3, 37. καὶ πρὸς ἐπιβουλεύοντας for προσέτι, (Duker,) and in addition to that, besides : 7, 22. πρὸς τὰς πέντε ἐναυμάχουν, to fight with or against an enemy: 3, 20. πρὸς σφᾶς, on their own sides, facing themselves : 6, 64. πρὸς παρεσκευασμένους ἐκβιβάζειν, to disembark in the face of an enemy : 7, 47. ἐβουλεύοντο πρὸς τὴν γεγενημένην ξυμφορὰν, conformably to or on occasion of the present disaster, i. e. as the disaster rendered necessary, Matth. Gr. Gr. 913 : 7, 3. πρὸς τὰ τείχη, towards, facing, opposite, before the works, 31. πρὸς τὰς, in addition to, 57. αὐτοῖς, besides, in addition to, 49. τῶν πολεμίων, in favour or to the advantage of: 3, 43. πρὸς τὰ μέγιστα λέγειν, to speak on occasion of most important matters; upon or in affairs of moment: 5, 9. πρὸς τὸ παρὸν, on the present occasion, 14. τὰ παρόντα, 3, 82. τὸ ἄπορον, on occasion of perplexity, 40. πρὸς τὸ παρὸν αὐτίκα, on account of the present moment, the condition at the present moment: 1, 65. πρὸς τῇ πόλει, near: 7, 36. πρὸς ἑαυτῶν ἔσεσθαι, to be in any one's favour: 5, 39. πρὸς ἔαρ, at the approach of spring, 56. πρὸς ἔαρ ἤδη, (it being) now towards spring: 3, 38. πρὸς τῶν ἠδικηκότων, in favour of, Matth. 910.: 6, 10. πρὸς οὐδένα τῆς ξυμφορᾶς ἰσομοιρεῖ, to share his calamity with no one: 7, 8. πρὸς χάριν τι λέγοντες, to speak for favour, in order to curry favour: 7, 3. πρὸς τῷ ἑαυτοῦ τείχει, at or under or behind his own works: 7, 1. ἐχώρει πρὸς τὰς Συρακούσας, to march for Syracuse: 1, 77. πρὸς τοὺς ὑπηκόους, towards our subjects: 6, 22. πρὸς μέρος, 'alternately, by turns,' *Hobbes: pro rata parte*, according to the number employed, as 2 out of 10, 4 of 20, and so on; 'partly,' but this sense requires the addition of another 'partly' to answer to the first: 3, 6. τὰ πρὸς νότον, the south-side, side to the south: 3, 15. τὴν πρὸς Ἀθήνας θάλασσαν, the sea overagainst, towards, near Athens: 6, 86. μείζονι πρὸς τὴν τῶνδε ἰσχὺν, *majore quam pro illorum corpore*, or simply, against: 1, 71.

12

πρὸς τάδε, now therefore, a form of conclusion: 7, 1. πρὸς τὰς ὁλκάδας τὸν νοῦν ἔχειν, to fix one's attention upon, have one's attention turned upon: 1, 70. πρὸς τὰ μέλλοντα, in comparison of future acquisitions, 71. πρὸς αὐτοὺς, in comparison of them, 3, 37. φαυλότεροι πρὸς τοὺς ξυνετωτέρους, in comparison of, 3, 9. ἴσοι πρὸς ἀλλήλους, equal in comparison of, equal to each other, 3, 113. Matth. Gr. Gr. 912. : 7, 58. πρὸς τοὺς ἐπελθόντας, in comparison of the adventitious (force) from abroad, (thus below, πρὸς ἅπαντας :) 7, 2. τὸ πρὸς τὴν θάλασσαν, towards or next the sea : 6, 16. πρὸς τοὺς ξένους ἰσχὺς φαίνεται, to or in the eyes of foreigners appears strength, greatness, i.e. a proof of : 7, 67. πρὸς τὰς ἐπιχειρήσεις προθυμίαν παρέχεται, gives alacrity, ardour to or for efforts, endeavours : 4, 67. πρὸς ταῖς πύλαις, at, (as a cart, which blocks an entrance,) 3, 22. πρὸς τοῖς πολεμίοις εἶησαν, to be near or at the enemy, 1, 62. πρὸς Ὀλύνθῳ, by or near Olynthus : 6, 85. ξυστῆτε πρὸς αὐτοὺς, to combine or unite with them: 7, 68. πρὸς ἀταξίαν καὶ τύχην, on account of, seeing that such is, their confusion : 6, 50. πρὸς αὐτοὺς λόγους ποιησάμενος, with : 6, 13. ὅροις πρὸς ὑμᾶς, boundaries, limits with respect to, towards another:

7, 37. πρὸς τὴν δύναμιν, with respect to or according to, to the best of one's power, 27. ἔχειν πρὸς τὸν πόλεμον, to keep or retain with a view to, for, on account of the war: 3, 39. πρὸς τὸ μέλλον θρασεῖς, bold in regard to the future: 5, 59. πρὸς τῇ πόλει, in the direction of the city: 1, 71. πρὸς πολλὰ ἰέναι, to approach many dangers: 3, 21. πρὸς Πλαταιῶν, towards or facing the Platæans, 22. ἀσφαλείας τῆς πρὸς τὸν πηλὸν, security as regarded the mud, against the mud, in the mud: 7, 78. πρὸς λόφῳ τινι, upon a hill: 3, 59. πρὸς ἀνδρὸς σοφοῦ ἐστι, sapientis est, Matth. 1, 71. δρῶμεν δ' ἂν ἄδικον οὐδὲν οὔτε πρὸς θεῶν οὔτε πρὸς ἀνθρώπων, a signif. of πρὸς with the gen. is 'in respect to any thing,' and here it denotes wrong in respect to the gods, to the injury of the gods, before the gods, Matth. 910.; 3, 58. οὐ πρὸς τῆς ὑμετέρας δόξης, Matth. l. c.: 1. 84. ἀεὶ δὲ ὡς πρὸς εὖ βουλευομένους τοὺς ἐναντίους ἔργῳ παρασκευαζόμεθα, for πρὸς τοὺς ἐ. ὡς πρὸς εὖ β., whereas the prep. is omitted the second time, if put the first, when it should stand twice with two different nouns, and whereas though the second noun be in apposition to the first, so also the prep. is put with the subst. of apposition, and not with the principal noun,

if the former precedes, Matth. 919. : 3, 70. αὐτῶν πρὸς τὰ ἱερὰ ἱκετῶν καθεζομένων, an instance, where the prep. πρὸς accompanies the accus., which would follow the verb, although retaining its intransitive sense, Matth. 601. : 4, 15. σπονδὰς ποιήσασθαι πρὸς τοὺς στρατηγοὺς τῶν Ἀθηναίων, here πρὸς is rendered ' with,' such phrases are founded upon the primary idea σκοπεῖν πρός τι, of an aim or direction generally, Matth. 913.

προσαγορεύω, 4, 16. προσαγορευόμεθα, to be saluted, accosted, honoured with a salutation.

προσάγω, 2, 89. 8, 3. to bring, add over : 4, 100. προσήγαγον μηχανὴν, to apply or bring to bear : 3, 63. προσήγεσθε, to be joined in an attack : 2, 76. προσήγον, 5, 61, to conduct, 7, 37. τῷ τείχει, to lead to, 4, 100. : 4, 115. προσάξεσθαι, to be applied, brought to bear, 3, 32. ἐς φιλίαν, to bring over to one's side : 7, 55. προσήγοντο : 2, 30. προσηγάγοντο, to bring over, reduce under one's power, 3, 55. προσηγάγετο, to associate oneself with an ally : 6, 54. προσαγάγηται αὐτὸν, to win over, get possession of : 6, 22. προσαγαγέσθαι, to enlist : 3, 43. ἀπατῇ τὸ πλῆθος προσάγεσθαι, to conciliate the multitude by artifice : 1, 76. προσαχθεῖσα κατὰ τὸ χῶμα, to be led along or by the mound, to be advanced towards : 3, 95. προσαχθῆναι, to be compelled to join : 4, 87. προσαχθήσεσθε : 8, 44. προσάξεσθαι, to bring over to : 2, 77. προσαχθείη, Matth. Gr. Gr. 786. : 2, 97. φόρος τε ἐκ πάσης τῆς βαρβάρου καὶ τῶν Ἑλληνίδων πόλεων, ὅσον προσῆξαν ἐπὶ Σεύθον, aor. 1., a tense not commonly used by good writers, Matth. 311.

προσαγωγὴ, 1, 82. an accession.

προσαγωγὸς, 1, 21. ὡς λογογράφοι ξυνέθεσαν ἐπὶ τὸ προσαγωγότερον τῇ ἀκροάσει ἢ ἀληθέστερον, the more seductive, alluring, captivating, where two adjectives are compared with each other, so as to signify that any one property or quality is found in a higher degree in one thing than in another, both adjs. are put in the compar., Matth. Gr. Gr. 661.

προσαιρέω, 7, 16. προσείλοντο, to associate, choose in addition, 5, 63. to choose, elect : 4, 29. προσελόμενος.

προσαναγκάζω, 4, 87. ἄκοντα, to compel : 5, 42. προσαναγκάσειν : 3, 61. προσηναγκάζοντο, to be constrained.

προσαναιρέω, 7, 28. προσανείλοντο, to take up in hand, undertake, in addition.

προσάνειμι, 7, 44. προσανήει, to advance, or come up.

προσάντης, 4, 43. steep.

προσαπόλλυμι, 1, 143. to be destroyed in addition : 7, 71. προσαπώλλυντο, to perish besides, in addition to.

προσαποστέλλω, 4, 108. to transmit to.

προσαφίστημι, 4, 117. προσαποστῆσαι, to seduce to revolt.

προσβαίνω, 3, 22. προσβαίνοιεν, to ascend, go up : 7, 43. προσβάντες.

προσβάλλω, 4, 29. προσβάλλοντας, to attack or throw darts : 5, 3. 10. προσβαλόντα, to charge, 2, 56. 68. 8, 10. : 6, 4. προσέβαλον Σικελίᾳ, to bring to or touch at : 2, 79. 4, 4. προσέβαλλον, 11. : 3, 22. προσέβαλον τῷ τείχει, to attack or assault a wall, 52. : 8. 2. προσβάλῃ : 8, 20. 31. προσβαλών.

πρόσβασις, 6, 96. an approach, ἔφοδος, aditus.

προσβιάζω, 1, 106. προσβιασθὲν, to be driven violently forward on their way.

προσβοηθέω, 1, 50. προσβοηθήκει, to bring aid, 2, 25. 3, 6. προσβεβοηθηκότες : 2, 22. 25. προσβοηθήσαντες, 79. : 6, 69. διὰ σπουδῆς προσβοηθοῦντες δρόμῳ, to run hastily (to the line :) 8, 23. προσεβοήθησαν.

προσβολὴ, 2, 4. 18. an assault, 4, 23. 115. 5, 61. : 3, 1. ἱππέων, an attack or charge of cavalry : 6, 48. an approach or access to, a descent upon : 4, 1. τῆς Σικελίας, the key of Sicily, 7, 4.

the approach to or entrance of, 70. αἱ προσβολαί, ὡς τύχοι ναῦς νηΐ προσπεσοῦσα, ἢ διὰ τὸ φεύγειν ἢ ἄλλῃ ἐπιπλέουσα, πυκνότεραι ἦσαν, Matth. Gr. Gr. 944.

προσγίγνομαι, 1, 33. προσγενέσθαι, to be added (to one's stock,) 5, 61. 31. προσγενόμενον, 7, 14. προσγενήσεται, to accrue : 7, 50. προσγεγενημένην, 6, 6. 8, 2. : 1, 142.

προσδεῖ, 3, 13. οὗπερ ὑμῖν μάλιστα προσδεῖ, of which you have most need : 1, 68. προσέδει, 6, 21. ὧν, what there is occasion for or need of : 1, 77. οὐδὲν προσδέονται δικάζεσθαι, to stand in no need of going to law, 1, 102. 4, 10. to demand, want : 2, 65. προσεδεῖτο, to require, to be in need of, 41.

προσδέχομαι, 3, 95. ὡς οὐ προσεδέξαντο, as they did not consent to or admit the proposal, 2, 17. τοὐναντίον ξυμβῆναι ἢ προσεδέχοντο, to turn out contrary to expectation : 3, 13. προσδεξαμένων, to admit or receive (into alliance,) 15, τοὺς λόγους, to approve what another has said, allow his reasons : 8, 6. προσεδέξαντο, 2, 70. to accept terms, 3, 2. to receive or take under one's protection, into one's alliance (a city revolting from a rival state,) 2, 12. to admit : 2, 11. προσδέχεσθαι τὸ καθ᾽ αὑτὸν ἀεί, to be always expecting his own division, —the post, to which he him-

self belongs : 8, 9. προσδεχόμενοι, to expect, 28. : 6, 46.

προσδιαβάλλω, 6, 75. a false lection for προδιαβάλλω.

προσδοκία, 4, 34. 6, 49. expectation : 7, 12. προσδοκίαν παρέχειν, to cause expectation, give occasion to expect, keep in expectation, apprehension : 2, 93. προσδοκία οὐδεμία ἦν μὴ ἄν ποτε οἱ πολέμιοι ἐξαπιναίως οὕτως ἐπιπλεύσειαν, ἐπεὶ οὐδ᾽ ἀπὸ τοῦ προφανοῦς τολμῆσαι ἂν καθ᾽ ἡσυχίαν, οὐδὲ, εἰ διενοοῦντο, μὴ οὐκ ἂν προαισθέσθαι, the accus. with the infin. being put especially after verbs λέγειν, ἀγγέλλειν, &c. here it is put because in προσδοκία the idea of ' to mean' is contained, Matth. Gr. Gr. 811. *see too* 923.

προσδόκιμος, 1, 14. expected : 7, 25. ὡς καὶ τῶν Ἀ. προσδοκίμων, since or because also the Athenians were expected.

προσεδρεία, 1, 126. sitting down (before a town with an intention to take it.)

πρόσειμι, 4, 85. πρόσεισι, ἐμοὶ, to join to my standard, 1, 40. : 4, 17. προσείη : 2, 61. προσεῖναί μοι καὶ μέσως, to belong even in a moderate degree to me, 4, 87. : 5, 104. προσέσεσθαι, 6, 20. ἡμῖν, to be present to, at any one's side, to join : 2, 60. προσόντος, 4, 3. : 2, 81. προσῄεσαν, 47. to go near, to visit : 1, 39. προσιέναι, to come to, approach.

προσείω, 6, 86. προσείοντες φόβον, to hold up to view, place before one's eyes, *incutere*, ἐπανατεινόμενοι.

προσελαύνω, 6, 63. προσελαύνοντες, to ride up : 4, 72. προσελάσαντες.

προσεξευρίσκω, 2, 76. προσεξεῦρον, to devise (any thing) additional against (an enemy.)

προσεπιστέλλω, 2, 85. προσεπέστειλαν, to order in addition to : 1, 132. προσεπεστάλθαι, to be enjoined (as a postscript to a letter.)

προσέρχομαι, 2, 89. 4, 121. προσήρχοντο, to approach : 5, 59. προσελθόντε : 4, 70. προσῆλθε : 1, 75. 172. προσελθόντες : 7, 53. προσελθεῖν.

προσέτι, 4, 120. in addition: 1, 35. moreover.

προσέχω, 7, 23. προσεχόντων, to apply, 7, 4. προσεῖχε τῷ πολέμῳ, to apply, pay attention to, 1, 15. προσχόντες : 1, 127. προσεχόμενον αὐτῷ, to be connected with or related to : 3, 32. προσχὼν, to touch at (as a ship,) 4, 11. 30. : 7, 15. προσέχῃ τὴν γνώμην, to apply, direct, 1, 95.

προσήκω, 3, 40. to belong or appertain to, to be any one's right, 2, 89. προσῆκον : 2, 34. προσήκουσαι, relations, 1, 128. : 6, 82. οὐδὲν προσῆκον, impers. *cum nihil causæ insit*, as ἐξὸν, δέον, &c. : 6, 84. προσήκετε ἡμῖν, *non alieni estis nobis*, i. e. you are of impor-

tance to us, 83. τὴν προσήκουσαν σωτηρίαν ἐκπορίζεσθαι, to seek or provide one's own security : 2, 6. τῆς μὴ προσηκούσης ὀρεγόμενον, to affect, lay claim to, to arrogate what does not belong to one, 43. τῇ μὴ προσηκούσῃ γῇ, foreign land, opposed to οἰκείᾳ, one's native land : 6, 14. προσήκειν σοὶ, to be one's duty, to belong to one : 4, 92. προσηκούσας ἀρετάς.

προσηνὴς, 6, 77. *blandus*, favourable, suitable, fit.

πρόσθεν, 7, 43. ἐς τὸ πρόσθεν ἐχώρουν, to push forward.

προσθέω, 4, 33, προσθέοντες, to run against.

προσίημι, 4, 38. προσίεσθαι, to accede, conform.

προσιππεύω, 2, 79. προσιππεύοντες, to ride up.

προσίσχω, 4, 30. *see* προσέχω.

προσκαθέζομαι, 1, 11. 26. 61. προσκαθεζόμενοι, to sit down before (a town to besiege it,) 126. 134. 5, 61.

προσκάθημαι, 8, 11. προσκαθημένους, stationing themselves, 7, 48. : 6, 89. to be at (the gates :) 7, 47. προσκαθῆσθαι, 49.

προσκαλέω, 1, 87. προσκαλέσαντες, to call in (to an assembly :) 4, 91. προσκαλῶν ἑκάστους, to call up : 3, 34. προσκαλεσάμενος ἐς λόγους, to invite to a conference : 3, 6. προσεκάλουν.

προσκαταλείπω, 4, 62. προσκαταλιπεῖν, to leave behind :

2, 36. προσκατέλιπον, to bequeath in addition, (something) additional.

προσκατηγορέω, 3, 42. προσ-
κατηγορουῦντες, to accuse of,
charge with.

πρόσκειμαι, 1, 93. προσέκειτο,
7, 29. to come up, invade,
30. 42. to advance against:
6, 89. τῷ δήμῳ, to incline,
lean to: 7, 50. προσκείμενος
θειασμῷ, to be devoted to, 2,
84.; 7, 18. to importune,
urge, press: 4, 33. προσκέ-
οιντο.

προσκομίζω, 1, 50. προσκο-
μίσαι, to convey, 54. προσκο-
μίσασθαι, 51. προσκομισθεῖσαι:
4, 115. προσκομιεῖν τὴν μηχανὴν, to apply, lodge.

προσκέπτομαι, 3, 57. προσκέ-
ψασθε, to consider, reflect.

προσκοπέω, 1, 120. προσκοπεῖν
τὰ κοινὰ, to keep a watchful
eye over: 3, 83. προσεσκόπουν
μὴ παθεῖν, to provide against
suffering: 4, 61. προσκοποῦμεν.

προσκοπὴ, 1, 116. a look-
out, reconnoitre,

προσκτάομαι, 6, 18. προσκτώ-
μενοι, to acquire in addition:
2, 62. προσκεκτημένα, what
they already possess: 4, 95.
προσκτᾶσθε τήνδε: 6, 24. προσ-
κτήσασθαι δύναμιν, to acquire
dominion, empire.

πρόσκωπος, 1, 10. a rower,
boatman, sailor.

προσλαμβάνω, 1, 35. 36. προσ-
λαβεῖν, to add, gain (to oneself,) 5, 53. to take possession of in addition : 2, 7.
προσλήψεσθαι, 6, 18. τὴν ἐμπει-

ρίαν: 7, 1. προσλαβόντες, 8, 2.
προσέλαβον: 1, 57. προσλάβωσιν.

προσμένω, 6, 44. προσέμενον,
to wait for.

προσμίγνυμι, 4, 85. προσμί-
ξαι, to encounter, 7, 22. to
join, unite, 1, 111. 3, 29.
προσμίξαντες, 7, 52.: 2, 39.
προσμίξωσί τινι, to engage with
(in battle:) 7, 39. 68. 70.
προσέμισγον, 3, 22.: 1, 45.
προσέμιξαν, to approach, near,
41. ; 3, 22. τῷ τείχει: 6, 69.
προσμίξειε, 104.

πρόσμιξις, 5, 72. an onset,
engagement.

προσμισθόω, 2, 33. προσεμι-
σθώσατο, to hire additional
forces, 7, 19. προσμισθωσάμενοι.

προσνεύω, 3, 112. προσένευ-
σαν, to swim towards.

προσξυλλαμβάνω, 3, 36. προσ-
ξυνελάβοντο, to contribute in
addition.

προσξυνοικέω, 6, 2. προσξυνῴ-
κησαν, to take up one's abode
with, reside, live with.

πρόσοδος, 1, 4. tribute, income, 13. 2, 13. τῶν χρημάτων,
an income of money, reve-
nue, 4, 108. 7, 28. : an approach, 4, 10. ἐτήρουν τὴν πρόσοδον, to watch one's coming:
3, 31. πρόσοδον ὑφέλωσι, to cut
off a (source of) revenue: 6,
91. τὰς προσόδους ἀποστερήσον-
ται, a verb, which in the
act. governs two accus., here
takes in the pass. one accus.,
viz. of the thing, Matth. Gr.
Gr. 604.

προσοικέω, 5, 51. προσοικοῦν-
τα, to neighbour, border: 1,

24. προσοικοῦσι δ' αὐτὴν Ταλάν-τιοι, the accus. is put here on account of the prep., with which the verb is compounded, it follows the less common construction in that the prep. is not repeated, moreover this verb is more frequently constructed with the dat., Matth. Gr. Gr. 610.

προσοικοδομέω, 2, 76. προσῳ-κοδόμουν, to build an additional (wall,) or simply, to build : 6, 54. προσοικοδομήσας, to build in addition, add to a building.

πρόσοικος, 1, 7. a neighbour, 24.

προσομιλέω, 2, 37. προσομι-λοῦντες, to associate or converse with : 1, 122. προσομι-λήσας.

προσόρμισις, 4, 10. coming to port, anchorage.

προσοφείλω, 7, 48. to owe, to be indebted.

πρόσοψις, 2, 89. a view, a clear sight of : 4, 29.

προσπαρακαλέω, 2, 68. προσ-παρακαλέσαντες, to call in additional (assistance,) 1, 67. to summon together.

προσπαρέχω, 1, 9. προσπαρα-σχὼν, to lend besides.

προσπελάζω, 7, 73. προσπε-λάσαντες, a false lection, see Duker.

προσπέμπω, 7, 3. προσπέμπει κήρυκα, to send to, 85. προσ-πέμψαντες.

προσπεριβάλλω, 5, 2. προσ-περιέβαλε, to cast about, throw around : 8, 40.

προσπίπτω, 4, 25. to fall upon : 7, 23. προσπεσὼν, 68. 3, 30. προσπέσοιμεν : 5, 9. προσ-πεσοῦμαι, Matth. Gr. Gr. 355.: 2, 71. προσπεσεῖσθαι, to strike against, fall, light upon : 2, 75. προσέπιπτε τὸ χῶμα, to overcharge, bear against, 84. to fall foul of, 3, 78. : 7, 7. προσπέσοι ναῦς νηὶ, to close with, fall upon : 2, 4. προσπί-πτοιεν : 4, 68. προσπεπτωκότων.

προσπλέω, 7, 2. to sail towards, to be on their passage, 4. 8, 14.: 8, 19. προσέ-πλει, 10. προσπλεύσαντες, 6, 50. to sail up, approach, 7, 20. 74. ταῖς ναυσί.

προσπληρόω, 7, 34. προσπλη-ρώσαντες, to man in addition, equip additional ships, 8, 10.

προσποιέω, 2, 2. to put in the hands of, under subjection to, 4, 47. προσποιῆσαι : 2, 85. προσποιήσειν, 33. προσποιή-σασθαι, to reduce, get possession of, 30. 1, 137. 4, 77.: 1, 57. προσεποιεῖτο, 38.

προσποίησις, 2, 62. 3, 82. καὶ σφίσιν αὐτοῖς ἐκ τοῦ αὐτοῦ προσποιήσει, for the purpose of acquiring additional power to themselves from the same (thing.)

προσπολεμέω, 7, 51. to make war upon.

προσπολεμώσασθαι Λέσβον, 3, 3. to have Lesbos added to the number of enemies.

προσταλαιπωρέω, 2, 53. to take pains, undergo labours, hardships.

πρόσταξις, 8, 3. a command.

προστασία, 6, 89. aut imperium, quo aliis præsumus,

aut tutela, patrocinium : 2, 80. ἐτησίῳ, an annual magistracy, 65. τοῦ δήμου, the first place in the government.

προστάσσω, 8, 5. προσέταξε, to command, 3, 16. ναύαρχον, to appoint admiral, 3, 26. 5, 8. προστάξας, 7, 19.: 7, 70. to be stationed, προσετέτακτο, 8, 8. to be appointed : 5, 75. προσετάχθησαν, 6, 31.: 1, 136. προστεταγμένων, to be appointed, 6, 42. στρατηγῷ, to be assigned to a leader, 8, 26. προσταχθεῖσαι.

προστάτης, 3, 75. 6, 35. δήμου, chief of the democratical faction, leading man among the people, 4, 66.

προσταυρόω, 6, 75. προεσταύρωσαν τὴν θάλασσαν, *vallis s. palis in terram depactis præmunio,* to drive piles into the sea, to construct works of defence on the sea-coast, fortify against an attack.

προστειχίζω, 6, 3. προστειχισθεῖσα, to take in, surround, encompass (additional space) with a wall.

προστελέω, 6, 31. προσετετέλικει, to disburse, expend, lay out.

προστίθημι, 3, 42. προστιθέναι τιμὴν, to add or confer additional honour : 8, 17. προσθεῖναι, to gain for : 2, 35. τῷ νόμῳ, to add a clause to an act, make an addition to the law : 3, 39. ὀλίγοις ἡ αἰτία προστεθῇ, to be laid upon : 6, 50. προσέθετο τῇ Ἀλκιβιάδου γνώμῃ, to join (oneself) to the side,

opinion of, concur in opinion with, 5, 62.: 1, 78. πρόσθεσθε, to impose upon (oneself,) add to what one already has : 2, 37. προστιθέμενοι τῃ ὄψει, to assume or put on in one's aspect, countenance, to wear a countenance of, in one's looks: 3, 67. προσθήσοντες, to bring forward : 3, 23. προσθέντες κλίμακας ἀπὸ τοῦ τείχους τοῖς πύργοις, to apply or set ladders from the wall to or against the towers : 5, 11. προσέθισαν, to attribute: 8, 48. προσθέμενον, to be joined to.

προστυγχάνω, 1, 97. τοὺς ἀεὶ προστυγχανόντας, whoever chanced to oppose them.

προσφερὴς, 1, 49. similar, resembling.

προσφέρω, 1, 93. προσέφερον, to carry to, 57. λόγους, to treat with, 138. 2, 58. μηχανὰς τῇ Ποτιδαίᾳ, to apply engines to : 2, 70. προσφέρουσι λόγους περὶ ξυμβάσεως, to speak with about, make proposals or offer terms for : 4, 18. προσφέροιντο : 5, 105. προσφέρονται, to conduct oneself, 2, 3. προσφέρωνται, to make an attack upon, to assail : 6, 44. προσοίσονται, to manage matters, conduct oneself.

προσφιλὴς, 1, 92. friendly: 5, 40. προσφιλέστατοι, most agreeable, best calculated to please.

πρόσφορος, 2, 65. fit, conducive, 7, 62. serviceable, useful, Matth. Gr. Gr. 635. : 1, 125. necessary, requisite.

πρόσχημα, 1, 96. a pre-
tence, pretext, 3, 82. 5, 30.

προσχόω, 2, 75. προσεχοῦτο,
to raise a mound over against,
near, opposite.

προσχωρέω, 7, 1. to join :
2, 79. προσχωρήσειεν, to surrender, 2, 2. to come over,
join : 1, 103. προσεχώρησαν :
5, 27. προσχωρήσεσθαι : 4, 71.
προσχωρῆσαι : 3, 7. προσεχώ-
ρουν, to yield, submit, come
over to, surrender, 3, 32. to
advance to, approach : 3, 13.
προσχωρήσεται, to come over :
6, 52. 72. προσχωροῖεν : 8, 25.
προσχωρήσειν, 31. προσχωρεῖν,
to attach (themselves) to : 1,
71. εἰ δὲ προσεχωρήσαμεν πρότερον τῷ Μήδῳ, δείσαντες ὥσπερ
καὶ ἄλλοι, περὶ τῇ χώρᾳ, ἢ μὴ
ἐτολμήσαμεν ὕστερον ἐσβῆναι ἐς
τὰς ναῦς, ὡς διεφθαρμένοι, οὐδὲν
ἂν ἔτι ἔδει ὑμᾶς, μὴ ἔχοντας ναῦς
ἱκανὰς, ναυμαχεῖν, ἀλλὰ καθ᾽ ἡσυχίαν ἂν αὐτῷ προεχώρησε τὰ
πράγματα, ᾗ ἐβούλετο, the indic.
is here used of the aor. twice
with εἰ alone in the premises,
and ἂν in the conclusion,
when the condition and consequence are both past actions, whose relation to each
other shews that any action
whatever would have taken,
if another had happened,
when in Latin the plusq.
perf. conj. is put twice,
Matth. Gr. Gr. 745. : 2, 80.
νομίζοντες εἰ πρώτην ταύτην λάβοιεν, ῥᾳδίως ἂν σφίσι τἄλλα
προσχωρήσειν, ἂν here gives
the infin. the same signif. as
the opt. would have in the

resolution by means of the
finite verb, Matth. 923.

πρόσχωρος, 8, 11, a neighbour.

πρόσχωσις, 2, 77. the adjacent mound.

πρόσωπον, 1, 106. κατὰ, at
the mouth or entrance : 6,
27. a face.

προτάσσω, 3, 52. προτάξαν-
τες, to appoint.

προτείχισμα, 7, 43. an out-
work, redoubt.

προτεμένισμα, 1, 134. the
entrance to a temple.

προτεραῖος, 1, 54. τῇ προτε-
ραίᾳ (sc. ἡμέρᾳ,) on the day
before.

προτερέω, 1, 33. προτερῆσαι,
to anticipate, to be beforehand with.

πρότερος, 5, 1. πρότερον,
formerly, before, 40. : 1, 28.
πρότερον δὲ, but before then :
1, 9. 3, 12.

προτίθημι, 2, 46. προτιθεῖσα,
to propose, hold out, 34.
προτίθενται, to lay out : 3, 39.
προθεῖναι ἰσχὺν τοῦ δικαίου, to
set might before right, to
set higher, the gen. is used
after verbs compounded with
a prep., which governs the
gen., when as here the prep.
may be separated from the
verb and placed before the
case without altering the
verb's meaning, Matth. Gr.
Gr. 526. : 1, 139. προὔτίθεσαν
τὰς γνώμας σφίσιν αὐτοῖς, to
deliver their sentiments one
among another : 6, 14. προτί-
θει, Matth. Gr. Gr. 280.

προτιμάω, 3, 82. προτιμήσει,

to prefer: 1, 133. προτιμηθείη, to be distinguished with a mark of preference: 2, 42. προτιμήσας, to value more than, to prefer: 1, 120. 2, 37. 6, 9. 8, 64.

προτιμωρέω, 1, 74. προετιμωρήσατε, to honour chiefly.

προτολμάω, 3, 84. προετολμήθη, to be first dared, perpetrated.

προτρέπω, 5, 16. προτρέψαι, to work a change upon, to convert, persuade.

πρότριτα, 2, 34. three days before, the third day.

προϋπάρχω, 2, 85. προϋπαρχούσης, which they had before, 1, 138. 5, 83.: 3, 40. προϋπάρξαντες, to commence first.

προϋπτος, 5, 99. manifest.

προϋργιαίτερον, 3, 109. τὸ ἑαυτῶν προὐργιαίτερον ἐποίησαν, to attend to their own interest in preference to the common good.

προὔργου, 4, 17. τι τῶν προὔργου, something of consequence, important.

προφανὴς, 2, 35. ἀπὸ τοῦ προφανοῦς, openly, 8, 8.: 5, 9.

προφασίζομαι, 6, 25. to practise evasions, make pretexts (for not doing any thing:) 1, 90. προὐφασίζετο: 5, 54. προὐφασίσαντο: 8, 33. προφασισθὲν, to be feigned or contrived as a pretext.

πρόφασις, 1, 133. 3, 9. a cause, motive, colour, pretext, 13.: 5, 22. 80. a pretext: 3, 39. βραχείᾳ προφάσει ἀποστήσεσθαι, to revolt on a weak or slight pretext, 1, 141.:

2, 49. ἀπ' οὐδεμίας προφάσεως, without or from no apparent cause: 6, 33. πρόφασιν μὲν, under the pretext, (used adverbially as ἀρχὴν, and opposed to τὸ δὲ ἀληθὲς, in truth, reality,) Matth. Gr. Gr. 569.: 6, 76. προφάσει μὲν—διανοίᾳ δὲ, apparently, but really,—under the pretence, but with the purpose.

προφέρω, 7, 64. 77. to excel, exceed, 1, 123. προφέρετε: 5, 17. προενεγκόντων, to submit, proffer, bring before: 1, 93. μέγα προφέρειν, to conduce much, greatly, towards: 3, 59. προφερόμενοι, to bring forward, 7, 69. to be brought forward, to be urged (as a topic.)

προφθάνω, 3, 69. προφθάσωσι, to get the start of, to anticipate: 8, 51. προφθάσας.

προφυλακὴ, 4, 30. the advanced guard.

προφυλακὶς, 1, 117. ναῦς, the guard-ship.

προφύλαξ, 3, 112. the picquet guard.

προφυλάσσω, 6, 38. προφυλάξασθαι, to take precautions.

πρόχειρος, at hand, ready at hand.

προχωρέω, 2, 12. 19. 58. 5, 54. προὐχώρει, to be favourable, auspicious, 6, 74.: 7, 7. προχωρῇ: 2, 56. προὐχώρησε, 3, 81.: 3, 4. προχωρήσειν, to succeed, turn out well: 4, 73. προὐκεχωρήκει, 3, 57. 4, 125. 5, 10. 1, 87. 7, 30.: 1, 109. ὡς δὲ αὐτῷ οὐ προὐχώρει, a case where the nomin. is not expressed, is when τὸ πρᾶγμα may be considered the subject, Matth. Gr. Gr. 427.

πρύμνα, 1, 51. the stern (of a ship.)

πρυτανεῖον, 2, 15. a house of assembly, court for public business, common-hall.

πρυτανεύω, 4, 118. ἐπρυτάνευε, to preside.

πρύτανις, 4, 118. a president.

πρωΐ, 4, 6. early: 7, 39. πρωιαίτερον, earlier : 7, 19. πρωιαίτατα, most early : 8, 101. πρωΐτερον, Matth. Gr. Gr. 101.

πρώρα, 2, 83. the prow (of a ship.)

πρώραθεν, 7, 36. τὰ πρώραθεν αὑτοῖς, i. q. τὰς αὐτῶν πρώρας, the (parts) at or about the prow.

πρῶτος, 1, 75. τὸ πρῶτον, in the first (instance,) 4, 94. καὶ ὡς τὸ πρῶτον, and when once, 97. at once, immediately, 5, 2. : 7, 43. πρῶτοι φύλακες ἦσαν, at first, from the first, 87.: 6, 55. τῇ πρώτῃ στήλῃ, the fore part or upper end of the column : 4, 125. τοῖς τῶν ἐναντίων πρώτοις, the van of the enemies : 3, 56. τιμηθέντες ἐς τὰ πρῶτα, to be honoured by the first (distinctions,) 81.

πρωτοστάτης, 7, 71. the first soldier in the front rank, (beginning at either end.)

πταίω, 1, 122. to stumble, err : 8, 11. ἔπταισαν, to fail : 5, 16. πταίσειαν : 6, 33. περὶ σφίσιν αὐτοῖς πταίσωσιν, to miscarry by their own fault, 12. πταίσαντας : 2, 43.

πταρμὸς, 2, 49. sneezing.

πυγμὴ, 1, 6. boxing.

πυκνὸς, 1, 23. πυκνότερα, more frequent.

πυκνότης, 5, 71. denseness.

πύλη, 2, 2. 5, 10. a gate, 7, 29. 51. κατά τινας πύλας, by a certain gate.

πυλὶς, 4, 110. a gate : 6, 51. a postern, little gate : 8, 92.

πυνθάνομαι, 1, 5. to ask or make enquiries : 7, 1. to learn (by enquiry,) 12. to know, to learn, 36. 5, 4. 42. : 7, 4. ἐπυνθάνετο, 67. πεπύσθαι σαφῶς : 7, 51. πυθόμενος, 44. πυθέσθαι, to distinguish, discern, understand : 8, 51. πεπυσμένος : 4, 6. ὡς ἐπύθοντο τῆς Πύλου κατειλημμένης, the use of the gen. after the verb πυνθάνεσθαι, instead of the accu., from the analogy to verbs of ' considering, reflecting, understanding,' which have genitives, Matth. Gr. Gr. 467. : 4, 29. πυνθανόμενος τὴν ἀπόβασιν αὐτὸν ἐς τὴν νῆσον διανοεῖσθαι, 4, 105. πυνθανόμενος—ἔχειν, 7, 25. instances of the infin. being employed after this verb, which requires its object in the participle. Matth. 836.

πῦρ, 7, 53. fire : 4, 111.

πυρά, 2, 52. ἀλλοτρίας, other men's funeral piles.

πύργος, 2, 17. κατεσκευάσαντο ἐν τοῖς πύργοις, to take up their abode or have their dwelling in towers : 7, 25.

πυρὸς, 6, 22. wheat.

πυρφόροις ὀϊστοῖς, 2, 75. fiery

arrows, igniferous or fire-bearing missiles.

πύστις, 1, 5. a question, 136. κατὰ πύστιν, by means of a rumour: 3, 82. fame, report.

πω, 1, 3. 8, 8. an encli-tic, *quodammodo, alicunde*, in some measure, respect, ever, yet.

πωλέω, 5, 34. to sell, 7, 39.: 2, 60. τὰ ξύμπαντα τούτου ἐνὸς ἂν πωλοῖτο, all will be sold for this one thing.

πώποτε, 1, 20. at any time, ever: 5, 111.

πῶς, 4, 92. πῶς οὐ χρὴ, to be most especially requisite: 2, 60.

P.

Ῥαβδοῦχος, 5, 50. marshal of the lists.

ῥᾴδιος, 4, 108. πάροδος, easy: 7, 75. easy (to be borne, of sorrow :) 6, 17. ῥᾳδίας ἔχουσι μεταβολὰς, easily to admit changes, 21. 8, 87.

ῥᾳδίως, 1, 2. 4, 100. easily, without difficulty: 5, 37. 7, 77.

ῥαθυμία, 2, 39. a state of mind free from cares and occupations, relaxation of mind.

ῥᾴων, 7, 4. easier : 1, 57. ῥᾷον ἂν, it would be easier: 6, 20. ῥάω, better, 42. ἄρχειν: 5, 36. 8, 89. : 4, 10. ῥᾷστοι, with the greatest facility, Matth. Gr. Gr. 403. : 7, 67. ῥᾷσται ἐς τὸ βλάπτεσθαι, easiest to be injured,

ῥᾳστώνη, 1, 120. luxurious ease.

ῥαχία, 4, 10. the pebbly shore.

ῥεῖθρον, 7, 74. a stream, brook.

ῥεῦμα, 4, 75. a torrent : 3, 116. a stream.

ῥέω, 1, 46. ῥέων, to flow, 3, 49. 8, 66.

ῥέω, 2, 5. ῥηθείσης, to be told, announced, 3, 49. τῶν γνωμῶν, to be delivered, 5, 60. τὰ ῥηθέντα, the proposi-tions made or spoken, 69. καλῶς, to be eloquently spo-ken, 2, 72. 3, 16. : 1, 3. εἴρηκε, to speak the word, to men-tion, 9. to say, 10. εἰρήκασι, 2, 35. εἰρηκότων, to speak, make an oration : 5, 91. τοὺς λόγους ἐροῦμεν : 6, 34. εἰρήσεται, to say, utter : 8, 11. εἴρηται, to be commanded, 1, 35. to be stated (as a condition in a treaty,) 5, 10. to be directed : 4, 77. εἴρητο, to be appointed, 7, 4. to be given in com-mand, 10. 5, 58. : 5, 39. εἰρη-μένον, to be stipulated, 1, 21. to be stated, advanced, 140. 4, 28. 5, 35. 37. Matth. Gr. Gr. 864. : 7, 69. οὔπω ἱκανὰ εἰρῆσθαι, that not enough had been said, 5, 30. to be stipu-lated.

ῥῆσις, 5, 85, a continued oration.

ῥητὸς, 2, 70. ἀργύριόν τι ῥητὸν ἐφόδιον, a specified sum for expences on the road, for the journey, 4, 69. : 4, 76. ἐν ἡμέρᾳ ῥητῇ, on an appointed or stated day, 6, 29. : 1, 122. ἐπὶ ῥητοῖς, according to previous calculation.

ῥιπτέω, 2, 49. ἥδιστα, to plunge with most delight, to be most delighted to plunge.

ῥίπτω, 2, 4. ἔρριψαν, to throw : 7, 44. ῥίπτοντες, to cast, precipitate.

ῥόθιον, 4, 10. foam of the sea, dashing, spray.

ῥοῦς, 1, 54. the current, tide.

ῥοπὴ, 5, 103. ἀσθενεῖς τε καὶ ἐπὶ ῥοπῆς μιᾶς ὄντες, in unico (rerum) momento positi, dependent on a single turn of the scales.

ῥοώδης, 4, 24. tumultuous, boisterous.

ῥύαξ, 4, 98. a streamlet : 3, 116. τοῦ πυρὸς, a stream of fire.

ῥυθμὸς, 5, 70. μετὰ ῥυθμοῦ, in concert.

ῥύμη, 2, 76. impetus, vio-

lence, 81. impetuosity : 7, 70. a charge, shock.

ῥύομαι, 5, 63. ῥύσεσθαι, to purge away from oneself charges, accusations.

ῥύω, 3, 116. ἐρρύη, to flow, 2, 5. ὁ γὰρ Ἀσωπὸς ποταμὸς ἐρρύη μέγας, to pour a great flood, to be swollen, aor. 2, from ῥεύσω, quasi from ῥύω, a form of ῥέω, Matth. Gr. Gr. 361.

ῥώμη, 2, 43. hardihood, manfulness, strength of nerve, 1, 49. strength, 5, 14. 6, 30. 85. τῶν φίλων, strength, power, 7, 71. ἡ ῥώμη καὶ τὸ σῶμα, vigour and body, i. e. bodily vigour : 7, 63. εὐτυχούσης.

ῥώννυμι, 7, 15. ἐρρώμην, to be in health, 2, 8. ἔρρωντο, to strain, to be active, to apply hard, from ῥόω or ῥώω, ῥώομαι, Matth. Gr. Gr. 361.: 4, 72. ἐρρώσθησαν, to be strengthened, confirmed, inspirited.

Σ.

Σαλπιγκτὴς, 6, 69. a trumpeter.

σάλπιγξ, 6, 32. a trumpet.

Σάμος, 1, 115. τῶν δὲ Σαμίων—διέβησαν ἐς τὴν Σάμον, an instance of the use of the gen. put partitive as a subject to the verb, Matth. Gr. Gr. 502.

σαφὴς, 1, 22. τὸ σαφὲς, the truth, 34. σαφές ἐστι, it is clear, manifest : 7, 44. σαφὲς αὐτὸ κατέστησαν, to make

known, to reveal : 3, 13. γνῶναι, clear to be understood, manifest to the understanding : 7, 1. σαφέστερον : 1, 9. τὰ σαφέστατα, information most to be depended on, 35. 140. 3, 40.

σαφῶς, 1, 1. 74. 4, 98. 7, 14. clearly, plainly, intelligibly, distinctly, with certainty : 3, 12. εἰδέναι, to know for certain.

σατραπεία, 1, 129. a viceroyship (in the Persian empire.)

σβέννυμι, 2, 77. σβέσαι, to extinguish.

σβεστήριος, 7, 53. extinguishing, what is capable of extinguishing, preventing flame.

σέβω, 2, 53. τὸ μὲν κρίνοντες ἐν ὁμοίῳ καὶ σέβειν καὶ μὴ, on the one hand concluding it to be to the same purpose to worship or not. Some commentators refer τὸ μὲν to φόβος θεῶν above, and call the construction an Atticism, others refer it differently, some point out the true reference, viz. τὸ σέβειν καὶ μή.

σεισμὸς, 1, 100. ὑπὸ τοῦ γενομένου σεισμοῦ, by the event of the earthquake, 128. 3, 89. 4, 56. 5, 45. 50. : 2, 27. ὑπὸ τὸν σεισμὸν, at the time of the earthquake : 8, 6.

σείω, 4, 51. to shake : 2, 6. σεισθεῖσα, to be shaken by an earthquake.

σῆμα, 1, 93. a tomb, sepulchral monument, 2, 34. 6, 59.

σημαίνω, 5, 10. to give the signal, to sound, 2, 84. σημήνῃ : 2, 8. σημῆναι : 2, 41. to shew, evince, 45. σημανῶ, to express, 6, 66. to shew, make manifest, 1, 72. : 2, 43. to declare, testify.

σημεῖον, 1, 63. a signal, standard, 7, 34. : 1, 21. a proof, 2, 41. μετὰ μεγάλων, with signal proofs, mighty signs, 1, 132. φανερὸν οὐδέν :

6, 31. an image or figure (on the prow of a ship :) 4, 111.

σθένος, 1, 86. παντὶ σθένει, with all our might : 5, 23. strength.

σιδήριος, 4, 4. of or belonging to iron.

σίδηρος, 1, 6. 3, 68. 4, 69. iron.

σιδηροῦς, 7, 62. χειρῶν, grappling irons : 4, 100.

σιδηροφορέω, 1, 6. ἐσιδηροφόρει, to wear armour, an instance of a compound verb derived from a compound adj., which therefore takes the augment at the beginning, Matth. Gr. Gr. 208.

σιδηρόω, 4, 100. ἐσεσιδήρωτο, to be lined with iron.

Σικελιώτης, 7, 18. a Sicilian Greek.

σινδών, 2, 49. σινδόνων, linen clothing.

σιταγωγὸς, 6, 30. ὁλκάσι, 8, 4. corn-transports, provision-ships.

σιτίον, 1, 48. τριῶν ἡμερῶν, provisions or rations for three days, 3, 1.

σιτοδεία, 4, 36. a want of provision.

σιτοδοτέω, 4, 39. ἐσιτοδοτοῦντο, to be furnished with provision.

σιτοποιὸς, 2, 78. γυναῖκες, women to dress food, make bread : 6, 22. a baker, bread-maker.

σῖτος, 1, 65. 4, 1. 5, 47. 7, 24. corn, grain, provision, supply : 6, 20. χρῶνται οἰκείῳ, home-produce, growth.

σιωπὴ, 6, 92. ὑπισημάνθη, to be proclaimed, ordered.

σκάπτω, 4, 90. ἔσκαπτον τάφρον, to dig or sink a ditch.

σκάφη, 1, 50. the keel or hull of a vessel.

σκεδάννυμι, 4, 112. ἐσκεδάννυντο, to be dispersed about: 2, 25. 4, 56. ἐσκεδασμένον, 72. ἀνὰ τὸ πεδίον : 1, 74. σκεδασθέντες.

σκεπτέον, 1, 72. to be deliberated, considered.

σκέπτομαι, 1, 107. σκέψασθαι, to consider, 6, 9. περὶ αὐτοῦ τούτου, to deliberate about this very thing, 1, 91. σκεψάμενοι : 6, 6. σκεψομένους, to make inquiries, to examine, investigate, 40. to look to, take care of: 7, 62. ἐσκεμμένα, considered, weighed : 1, 143.

σκευάζω, 2, 15. σκευασάντων, to furnish, construct: 4, 33. ἐσκευασμένοι, to be appointed, accoutred, armed.

σκευὴ, 1, 6. fashion, ornament, 8, the fashion, make, 130. apparel : 6, 94. equipage, accoutrements : 1, 10. μετὰ σκευῶν πολεμικῶν, with military stores and baggage: 8, 27.

σκεῦος, 7, 24. σκεύη, materials for building or repairing ships, tackle or furniture for ships.

σκευοφόρος. 2, 79. bearing baggage : 4, 101. a suttler, 128.

σκηνάω, 1, 89. ἐσκήνησαν, to be quartered (as a soldier,) 133. σκηνησαμένου διπλῆν καλύ-

ξην, to build a tent with a partition : 2, 52.

σκηνὴ, 2, 34. σκηνὴν ποιήσαντες, to erect a tent.

σκηνίδιον, 6, 37. a small tent.

σκῆπτρον, 1, 9. a sceptre, regal staff, spear of state.

σκοπέω, 5, 42. ἐσκόπουν, to investigate, examine, scrutinize, 20. σκοπείτω : 6, 11. σκοπεῖν, to meditate, look about, consider : 7, 71. σκοπούντων ἐς τὸ αὐτὸ, to look to, to be regarding or observing the same : 3, 12. ὀρθῶς σκοπεῖ, to think justly, consider aright : 2, 43. μὴ λόγῳ μόνῳ τὴν ὠφελίαν, not to regard or contemplate the utility merely in words, (as it is set forth by the orator :) 6, 12. σκοπῶν τὸ ἑαυτοῦ μόνον, to consider oneself, one's own interest solely, 40. ἐφ ἑαυτῆς σκοποῦσα, to consult by oneself (without taking others to our counsels :) 8, 24. ἐσκόπουν, to deliberate.

σκύλευμα, 4, 44. plunder, spoil.

σκυλεύω, 5, 74. to plunder, rifle, 10. ἐσκύλευσε, 4, 72. 97.

σκῦλον, 1, 13. 3, 57. σκῦλα, spoils, 6, 71.

σκυτάλη, 1, 131. the staff which a Spartan carried as a means of secret communication with the generals.

σμικρὸς, 4, 13. small, contracted, narrow.

σόφισμα, 6, 77. commentum, an artful measure.

σοφιστὴς, 3, 38. a sophist.

σοφὸς, 3, 59. πρὸς ἀνδρὸς σοφοῦ ἐστὶ, *sapientis est*, it belongs to a wise man.

σπανίζω, 1, 41. σπανίσαντες, to be in want of, to run short in : 4, 6. ἐσπάνιζον.

σπάνιος, scanty, 7, 4. ὕδατι σπανίῳ χρώμενοι, to have little water for use, a scarcity of water : 1, 23. σπανιώτερον, rather rarely, not very often, 33. : 7, 68. σπανιώτατοι, most rare, seldom occurring : 3, 56. σπάνιον ἦν, to be rare.

σπάνις, 1, 142. want.

σπάρτον, 4, 48. the roping of a bedstead.

σπασμὸς, 2, 49. a spasm.

σπένδω, 6, 32. σπένδοντες, to make or form a libation : 3, 24. ἐσπένδοντο ἀναίρεσιν τοῖς νεκροῖς, to treat (by mutual libations) about a truce for the taking up of the dead, 5, 19. to be witnesses to : 3, 34. ἐσπείσατο, to covenant, 1, 144. to engage, 8, 20. : 5, 28. σπείσασθαι, to enter into treaty with, to compound with, 2, 73. : 6, 7. σπεισάμενοί τινα χρόνον, to make a truce for a while, a temporary truce : 8, 43. 57.

σπέρμα, 7, 16. seed, off-spring.

σπεύδω, 5, 37. ἐς τὰ ὁμοῖα, to make to the same end, have the same object in view, point to the same thing : 6, 39. εἰ μὴ μανθάνετε κακὰ σπεύδοντες, to study, contrive, where an intrans. verb is used transitively, Matth. Gr.

Gr. 599. : 1, 84. to hurry : 6, 79. to endeavour after, seek earnestly.

σπονδὴ, 1, 3. 2, 6. 4, 118. 5, 36. 8, 9. a treaty : 1, 113. σπονδὰς ποιησάμενοι ἐφ' ᾧ τοὺς ἄνδρας κομιοῦνται, an instance of the use of the relative in this phrase for a conjunction, sc. ὥστε, where also follows the fut., though the infin. is more common, Matth. Gr. Gr. 692. : 4, 15. ἔδοξεν αὐτοῖς σπονδὰς ποιησαμένους τὰ περὶ Πύλον ἀποστεῖλαι ἐς τὰς Ἀθήνας πρέσβεις, for σπένδεσθαι in the sense of 'making up,' an instance of the double accus., where one is under circumlocution with ποιεῖσθαι, and where also the object of the simple verb (σπένδεσθαι) is put in the accus., Matth. 590.

σποράδην, 2, 4. here and there, dispersed up and down.

σποράς, 1, 49. scattered, in disorder, 3, 69.

σπουδὴ, 3, 49. τοῦ πλοῦ ἐγένετο, to make haste : 4, 30. 5, 66. ὑπὸ σπουδῆς, with speed : 6, 31. ὅπλων, zeal, earnestness about-arms, i. e. to surpass others in the excellence of the armour : 7, 77. τῆς ὁδοῦ, a hasty march.

στάδιον, 1, 63. a furlong, measure of distance : 7, 2. 78.

στασιάζω, 1, 23. διὰ τὸ στασιάζειν, on account of sedition : 4, 1. ἐστασίαζε : 6, 74.

στάσις, 3, 2. ἄνδρες κατὰ στά-

P p 2

σιν μηνυταὶ γίγνονται, to be informers, give information on account of or from faction, factious motives, by reason of their faction or party, (the Athenians:) 4, 61. 6, 5. 38.: 22, 2. ἀπὸ τῆς στάσεως ἐκάτερος, each of the opposite faction, one from each faction, 10. 7, 33.

στασιωτικὸς, 3, 18. 7, 57. seditious, troublesome, tumultuous, revolutionary.

στατήρ, 4, 52. a stater.

σταυρὸς, 4, 90. a pile, stake: 7, 25.

σταυρόω, 6, 100. 7, 25. ἐσταύρωσαν, to drive piles.

σταύρωμα, 5, 10. an entrenchment, a palisado: 6, 74. 7, 53.

σταύρωσις, 7, 25. a making of a palisado.

στεγανὸς, 3, 21. ἐκ δὲ τῶν πύργων, ὄντων δι' ὀλίγου καὶ ἄνωθεν στεγανῶν, covered above.

στεγανῶς, 4, 100. under cover.

στέγω, 4, 34. to cover: 6, 72. στέγεσθαι, to be concealed, kept secret.

στέλλω, 3, 85. ἔστειλαν, to send, despatch: 7, 20.

στέμμα, 4, 133. vitta, a fillet, headband, garland.

στενόπορος, 7, 73. στενόπορα τῶν χωρίων, angusta viarum, a narrow way, pass.

στενὸς, 1, 74. ἐν τῷ στενῷ, in the strait: 4, 8. 7, 44. 51. narrow: 4, 113. ἰσθμῷ.

στενότης, 4, 24. narrowness:

7, 62. ἀρωγὰ ἐπὶ τῇ στενότητι, advantageous or useful on account of the narrowness.

στενοχωρία, 2, 89. 4, 26. 30. 7, 49. 87. want of room, narrow or confined space: 7, 70. Matth. Gr. Gr. 711.

στέργω, 1, 38. στεργόμεθα, to be loved with natural affection.

στερέω, 4, 54. στερήσομεν, to deprive, 20. στερηθῆναι, to be deprived, 6, 40. τοῦ παντὸς κινδυνεῦσαι, to risk being deprived of the whole: 2, 62. ἐστερῆσθαι: 3, 2. στερήσεσθαι Λέσβου, to be deprived of Lesbos: 2, 20. ἐστερημένους.

στέρησις, 2, 63. ἀρχῆς, loss of empire.

στερίσκω, 2, 43. στερίσκειν τὴν πόλιν τῆς σφετέρας ἀρετῆς, to deprive the city of their valour, 49. στερισκόμενοι, to be deprived, 1, 77. 4, 106.

στέριφος, 6, 101. στεριφώτατον, most firm: 7, 36. στεριφωτέρας.

στέρομαι, 8, 1. στερόμενοι, to be deprived of: 1, 70. 4, 117.

στέφανος, 2, 46. a crown.

στεφανόω, 4, 80. ἐστεφανώσαντο, to be crowned (with garlands, wreaths.)

στῆθος, 2, 49. the breast.

στήλη, 2, 43. ἐπιγραφὴ στηλῶν, inscription on columns, monuments: 1, 93. 134. 5, 18. 47. ἐν στήλῃ λιθίνῃ, on a stone-pillar.

στηρίζω, 2, 49. στηρίξαι ἐς τὴν καρδίαν, to settle, fix (itself) in.

στοὰ, 4, 90. a portico.

στοῖχος, 2, 102. 4, 47. a row, rank, file.

στόλος, 1, 9. 10. 6, 31. an army, armament, expedition, a fleet.

στόμα, 2, 86. a mouth (of a gulph,) 7, 5. a mouth or entrance (of a harbour,) 4, 102. ἐπὶ τῷ στόματι τοῦ ποταμοῦ, 1, 29. 55. a mouth (of a bay:) 4, 49.

στόνος, 7, 71. a groan.

στορέω, 6, 18. στορέσομεν, to prostrate, cast down, to floor.

στρατεία, 1, 3. an expedition, 15.

στράτευμα, 5, 57. an armament, 7, 5. an army, 47. στρατεύματος κρατεῖν, to master the (enemy's force,) to be superior to, stronger than, (an unusual ellipse,) 74. 7, 26.

στρατεύω, 1, 8. ἐστράτευσαν, to make an expedition, 12. : 6, 9. ἐστράτευε, to go on an expedition, 5, 8. to compose the armament, 2, 57. to be abroad with the fleet: 1, 112. Λακεδαιμόνιοι μετὰ ταῦτα τὸν ἱερὸν καλούμενον πόλεμον ἐστράτευσαν, a verb intrans. with a subst. in the accus. of a kindred signif., so put in order to subjoin a new proposition, Matth. Gr. Gr. 597. : 2, 11. Matth. 846.

στρατηγέω, 1, 29. ἐστρατήγει, to command (as a general or admiral,) have the command

of, Matth. Gr. Gr. 440. : 6, 15. στρατηγῆσαι.

στρατηγία, 1, 95. 5, 16. 26. a military command, a generalship.

στρατηγὶς, 2, 84. a commander's ship.

στρατηγὸς, a commander, general, 6, 64. ἃ γιγνώσκοντες οἱ στρατηγοὶ τῶν Ἀθηναίων καὶ βουλόμενοι—εἰδότες, (τοὺς γὰρ ἂν ψιλοὺς—οἳ ξυνείποντο,) τοιόνδε τι οὖν πρὸς ἃ ἐβούλοντο οἱ στρατηγοὶ μηχανῶνται, an instance of a parenthesis in an anacoluthon, Matth. Gr. Gr. 946.

στρατιὰ, 1, 10. 7, 1. 11. an army, 17. στρατιὰν ἐπαγγέλλων ἐς τοὺς ξυμμάχους, to appoint the levies, which the confederates were to raise, to send round to the confederates orders to raise forces, settle the contingents among the confederates, appoint contingents to the allies : 3, 110. τῇ ἄλλῃ στρατιᾷ ἅμα παρεσκευάζετο βοηθεῖν ἐπ' αὐτούς, here the infin. is put after παρασκ., where the participle also is put, ad opem suis contra illos ferendam se præparabat, Matth. Gr. Gr. 797. : 7, 3. Matth. 643. : 7, 4.

στρατιώτης, 5, 7. 34. 6, 24. 7, 15. Matth. Gr. Gr. 874. : 7, 61. a soldier.

στρατιωτικὸς, 2, 83. στρατιωτικώτερον, better adapted for land-service, after the manner of land-forces.

στρατιῶτις, 6, 43. a soldier's transport.

στρατοπεδεύομαι, 8, 11. ἐστρατοπεδεύοντο, to pitch their camp: 8, 25. ἐστρατοπεδεύσαντο, 5, 64. στρατοπεδευσάμενοι: 6, 42.: 4, 54. ἐστρατοπεδευμένους.

στρατόπεδον, 1, 11. 3, 22. 4, 94. 5, 60. 7, 8. 23. 44. an army, a camp.

στρατὸς, 2, 21. an army, Matth. Gr. Gr. 563.: 3, 110. Matth. 847.

στρογγύλος, 2, 97. νηΐ, a merchant-ship, oneraria, φορτηγὸς, Schol. ἐμπορικῇ, διὰ τὰ πολεμικὰ μακρότερα ὄντα, see Duker.

στρωμνὴ, 8, 81. τὴν ἑαυτοῦ στρωμνὴν ἐξαργυρίσαι, to convert his couch into cash.

συλλέγω, 4, 25. συλλεγεῖσαι, to muster.

σύματος, 5, 77. Dor. for θύματος.

συμφορὰ, 8, 12. a calamity.

συνεχῶς, 4, 43. continually.

συνταράσσω, 2, 52. νόμοι συνεταράχθησαν, to be confounded, broken.

συστρέφω, 5, 10. συστραφέντες, to be assembled, congregated.

συχνὸς, 4, 108. several, very many: 2, 52. διὰ τὸ συχνοὺς ἤδη προτεθνάναι σφίσιν, by reason of great many of their friends being already dead, of the great number of deaths they had had already.

σφαγὴ, 4, 48. the throat.

σφάγιον, 6, 69. σφάγια προὔφερον τὰ νομιζόμενα, the victims.

σφάζω, 7, 84. to slay.

σφαλερὸς, slippery, 4, 62. σφαλερώτατος.

σφάλλω, 3, 37. τὰς πόλεις, to ruin, subvert : 6, 11. σφήλαντες ἡμᾶς, to overthrow, ruin, 5, 16.: 1, 70. σφαλῶσιν: 7, 68. τοῦ σφαλῆναι, failure, 1, 69. 2, 65. σφαλέντα, 5, 15. 99. 6, 10.: 7, 47. ἔσφαλτο: 6, 75. σφάλωνται, to be defeated, beaten : 2, 87. σφαλλομένους εἰκότως, likely to fail : 3, 14. σφαλησόμεθα : 8, 24. ἐσφάλησαν, 32. σφάλλωνται.

σφάλμα, 5, 14. a reverse, mishap : 8, 32. a failure.

σφενδονάω, 2, 81. σφενδονώντων ἄποθεν, to sling stones from a distance.

σφενδόνη, 4, 32. a sling.

σφενδονήτης, 4, 99. 7, 31. 42. a slinger.

σφέτερος, 7, 1. τοῖς ἐκ τῶν νεῶν σφετέρων ναύταις, sailors out of their own ships, their own ships' crews : 6, 38. 7, 3. τὰ σφέτερα αὐτῶν, their own things, (viz. arms and baggage,) what belonged to them : 1, 5. τοῦ σφετέρου, your, is Attic, (as well as in use among the Poets,) Matth. Gr. Gr. 186.: 7, 75. Matth. l. c.

σφίσι, sibi, 5, 44. νομίζοντες πόλιν σφίσι φιλίαν, Matth. Gr. Gr. 588. : 5, 46. where it is reflexive, Matth. 183.

σφόδρα, 3, 46. κολάζειν, to chastise severely, (opposed

to μετρίως κολάζειν,) φυλάσσειν, to watch attentively, carefully.

σφοδρός, 1, 103. violent, vehement.

σφραγὶς, 1,129. a seal, 132.

σχεδία, 6, 2. ἐπὶ σχεδιῶν, on board of rafts, or boats hastily and rudely constructed.

σχεδόν, 5, 66. σχεδόν τι πᾶν, nearly the whole : 7, 33. σχεδόν τι, nearly, almost, propemodum : 3, 68.

σχολάζω, 4, 4. to be without employment.

σχολαῖος, 3, 29. at leisure, slow, tardy : 1, 84. σχολαίτερον, more slowly, 4, 47. 7, 15. more tardily.

σχολαιότης, 2, 18. dilatoriness.

σχολὴ, 3, 46. σχολῇ καὶ ταχὺ, late or early : 5, 29. σχολὴν ἦγον, to be at leisure : 5, 10. a delay : 1, 142.

σώζω, 4, 61. to preserve : 1, 74. ἔσωσε, 4, 23. σῶσαι : 4, 34. σωθῆναι; to effect safety, 7, 45. ἐσώθησαν : 6, 24. σωθήσεσθαι, to get safe back, 7, 71. σωθήσονται : 6, 9. σώζειν τὰ ὑπάρχοντα, to secure what you already possess, the possessions : 7, 77. ἤδη τινὲς καὶ ἐκ δεινοτέρων ἢ τοιῶνδε ἐσώθησαν, Matth. Gr. Gr. 651.

σῶμα, 1, 17. ἐς τὸ σῶμα, with regard to their persons, their personal safety, 70. σώμασιν ἀλλοτριωτάτοις χρῶνται, to use their persons as if they did not belong to themselves, (with so lavish and reckless a zeal.)

σῶος, 1, 74. safe, unhurt : 3, 34. σῶν καὶ ὑγιᾶ πάλιν αὐτὸν καταστήσειν, to restore safe and sound, Matth. Gr. Gr. 158.

σωτήρ, 5, 11. a saviour, preserver, protector.

σωτηρία, 1, 65. 4, 19. preservation, 62. : 7, 18. safety, means of escape : 2, 13. ἐπὶ σωτηρίᾳ, for the purpose of safety : 2, 61. τοῦ κοινοῦ τῆς σωτηρίας ἀντιλαμβάνεσθαι, to put one's hand to succour the common safety : 7, 81. Matth. Gr. Gr. 610.

σωτήριος, 3, 53. salutary, beneficial: 7, 64. saving, contributing to safety.

σωφρονέω, 6, 87. to be moderate, temperate, 1, 86. 4, 60. 8, 24. ἐσωφρόνησαν.

σωφρονίζω, 6, 78. σωφρονισθῶμεν, to be taught moderation.

σωφρονιστής, 3, 65. τῆς γνώμης, a moderator, censor of opinions : 6, 87. a censor, moderator, corrector.

σωφρόνως, 1, 80. soberly, 5, 101. moderately.

σωφροσύνη, 1, 32. prudence, 68. the demeanour of a just and upright character : 3, 37. modesty: 1, 84. ἔμφρων, a wise and deliberate caution.

σώφρων, 3, 82. τὸ σῶφρον, prudence, moderation : 6, 41. decorous, regular, 6, 6. prudent, politic : 3, 43. σωφρονέστερον, more prudent, 6, 29. : 3, 62. σωφρονέστατος.

11

Ταινιόω, 4, 21. ἰδίᾳ, to bedeck with ribbands.

τακτὸς, 4, 65. stated, fixed, certain.

ταλαιπωρέω, 1, 134. ταλαιπωροίη, to suffer inconvenience, 8, 16. to be distressed : 5, 57. ἐταλαιπώρουν, to be in distress, 73. ἐταλαιπώρησαν : 7, 28. ἐταλαιπωροῦντο, to be harassed, in hard service, 3, 78 : 7, 27. ταλαιπωροῦντες ξυνεχῶς, to be constantly in hard service, incessantly in labour : 3, 3. τεταλαιπωρημένοι, to be afflicted, distressed, reduced to a low condition : 1, 99. 5, 74.

ταλαιπωρία, 2, 49. pain (of the stomach,) 70. distress : 4, 117. wretchedness.

τάλαντον, 5, 31. a talent, talentum, 2, 97.

ταμίας, 6, 78. a dispenser, an arbiter.

ταμεῖον, 1, 96. a treasury, 7, 24.

ταμεύω, 6, 18. ταμιεύεσθαι, (to dispense, husband, ' to be our own carver,' H.) to determine, prescribe, fix.

ταξίαρχος, 4, 4. a captain : 7, 60. a captain (or colonel, Mitf.) a commander of the τάξεις or divisions of an army.

τάξις, 5, 66. ἐν τάξει, in battle-array, 7, 5. 30. : 5, 70. ἵνα μὴ διασπασθείη αὐτοῖς ἡ τάξις, the ranks, the dat. is here

used where the gen. in Latin is employed, Matth. Gr. Gr. 548.

ταπεινὸς, 2, 6. ταπεινὴ ὑμῶν ἡ διάνοια ἐγκαρτερεῖν ἃ ἔγνωτε, abject, dispirited, the positive is here for the compar., in which case ἢ is omitted, ' your mode of thinking is too low to persevere in it,' Matth. Gr. Gr. 653.

ταπεινότης, 7, 75. a low condition, estate.

Τάρας, ὁ, 6, 104. an exception to the general rule of cities being in the fem. gender, Matth. Gr. Gr. 118.

ταράσσω, 7, 3. ταρασσομένους, to be in disarray, disorder : 2, 84. ἐταράσσοντο : 7, 44. ἐταράχθησαν, to be in confusion, disorder, 2, 65. : 4, 96. διὰ τὴν κύκλωσιν ταραχθέντες, to fall into confusion : 7, 44. ἐτετάρακτο : 4, 25. τεταραγμένοις : 7, 67. ταράξονται, to be in confusion, (med. for pass.,) 36. ταράξεσθαι : 7, 23. ταραχθεῖσαι περὶ ἀλλήλας, to fall foul of one another, to be in confusion one with, about, with regard to another, (περὶ for ἐν.)

ταραχὴ, 2, 84. ταραχὴν παρέξειν, to create confusion, 4, 75. καθίστασαν ἐς ταραχήν : 5, 25. a commotion, disturbance : 7, 25. 29. 80.

ταραχώδης, 1, 49. confused, tumultuous.

ταρσὸς, 2, 76. ταρσοῖς, a wicker-work, hamper, crates: 7, 40. τῶν νεῶν, the hatches, gangway, wards, rows of oars, blades of the oars (more properly.)

τάσσω, 7, 6. τάξας, to station, post: 4, 93. ἔτασσε, to put in order of battle: 1, 90. ἔταξαν, to appoint, 5, 31. to tax, 8, 33. to assign: 1, 48. ἐτάξαντο: 3, 22. οἷς ἐτέτακτο, who had been appointed, 1, 99. to be appointed to pay, 101.: 2, 90. ἐπὶ τεσσάρων, to draw up four abreast : 2, 20. ὡς ἐς μάχην ταξάμενον, to draw up (an army) ready for fight, 3, 78. κύκλον ταξαμένων αὐτῶν, to arrange themselves in a circle, 2, 83. ἐτάξαντο κύκλον τῶν νεῶν, to draw up ships in a circle : 2, 63. τεταγμένον, to be ranked, ranged, joined, 84. κατὰ μίαν ναῦν, to draw up in a line, in file, in a single line of ships : 4, 32. ἔταξεν ἐν τῷ ἔργῳ, to preside in or direct the execution: 5, 71. τετάξεσθαι : 3, 13. αἱ νῆες ἐφ' ἡμῖν τετάχαται, to be stationed (near) on our account, 7, 4. ἐτετάχατο, instances, where the Attics follow the Ionic and Doric custom of changing ν before ται and το into ᾱ, Matth. Gr. Gr. 264.

ταυτόματον, 6, 36. ἀπὸ ταυτομάτου, accidentally, fortuitously, spontaneously.

ταφὴ, 2, 52. περὶ τὰς ταφὰς, about funerals, the funeral rites.

τάφος, 1, 26. 35. a tomb, sepulchre, mausoleum, 43. πᾶσα γῆ, every land (is) a monument, 47. a funeral, (for ταφή.)

τάφρος, 4, 69. a ditch, 90. 3, 23.

τάχα, 1, 81. perhaps : 6, 10. τάχα δ' ἂν ἴσως, (for τάχα δ' ἂν or ἴσως:) 3, 44.

τάχος, 1, 71. 5, 65. κατὰ τάχος, with or in haste: 3, 42. precipitation : 5, 64. ἐν τάχει, with speed : 6, 92.

ταχυναυτέω, 6, 31. τῷ ταχυναυτεῖν, swift-sailing.

ταχὺς, 6, 45. ὡς ἐπὶ ταχεῖ πολέμῳ, as for approaching war: 6, 31. 7, 4. ταχεῖαι νῆες, swift, quick-sailing : 4, 10. ταχίστου, the shortest, quickest : 6, 66. διὰ ταχέων, speedily : 1, 118. μὴ ταχεῖς ἰέναι ἐς τοὺς πολέμους, not swift to go to war.

τε, a conjunction, que, et, atque, 6, 18. where τε is not followed by καὶ, as it is usually, Matth. Gr. Gr. 945. compare 7, 2. in Matth. Gr. Gr. 937.

τέγος, 4, 48. the tiling, top of a house.

τειχήρης, 4, 25. one, who keeps within the walls, confined.

τειχίζω, 7, 4. ἐτείχιζον, to build, make a wall, 6, 75. τὸ τεῖχος: 7, 43. τειχίζοντας ἔχειν, to have for the purpose of fortification, for raising works : 8, 4. τειχίσαντες, to fortify : 6, 4. ἐτειχίσθησαν, to be surrounded with a wall, to wall in, 1, 93. 5, 51. : 4, 76. 7, 4. τειχισθείη, to be fortified : 2, 32. Ἀταλάντη ἐτειχίσθη φρούριον, Atalanta was fortified (to serve as) a garrison, 1, 91. τετείχισται, to become walled : 4, 3. τειχίζεσθαι τὸ χωρίον : 7, 18.

τείχισμα, 5, 3. a fortress, 52. 75. 4, 115. 7, 6. 8, 4. a walling or fortification.

τείχισις, 7, 6. the work of fortification, 31. a walling off.

τειχισμὸς, 8, 14. construction of fortifications, 6, 44. ἐς τειχισμὸν ἐργαλεῖα, tools or instruments for fortification.

τειχομαχέω, 1, 102. to besiege a walled town.

τεῖχος, 2, 3. ἀντὶ τείχους εἶναι, to serve instead of a wall : 1, 8. 69. 2, 75. 4, 67. 7, 2. 3. 52.

τεκμαίρω, 1, 1. τεκμαιρόμενος, to conjecture from, mark, observe, 3, 53. 5, 47.

τέκμαρσις, 2, 87. a conjecture, ground for conjecture.

τεκμήριον, 1, 73. a proof, 21. ἐκ τῶν εἰρημένων τεκμηρίων, to judge from the proofs, which have been advanced, 132. : 2, 50. τεκμήριον δὲ, 39. as a proof, for example : 1, 2.

τεκμηριόω, 1, 3. to evidence, witness : 3, 104. ἐτεκμηρίωσεν, 9. τεκμηριῶσαι.

τέκνωσις, 2, 44. τέκνωσιν ποιεῖσθαι, to beget children.

τέκτων, 5, 82. an artificer, 6, 44. 7, 43.

τέλειος, 5, 47. ὅρκον τὸν μέγιστον κατὰ ἱερῶν τελείων, majores et eximiæ hostiæ, complete in age and perfect in limb.

τελεόω, 6, 31. τελεώσαντες τὰς σπονδὰς, to make an end of, finish making libations.

τελευταῖος, 1, 14. 67. the last : 3, 11. τὰ τελευταῖα λιπόντες, to leave to the last, to reserve : 1, 24. τὰ δὲ τελευταῖα, in the end, at last, 140. οἱδε τελευταῖοι ἥκοντες, these men, that are last come : 2, 89.

τελευτάω, 2, 47. 5, 39. τελευτῶντος, to close, end : 6, 53. τελευτῶσαν, in the end, at last : 4, 72. τελευτήσαντες, 5, 10. ἐτελεύτησε, to die : 8, 1. ἐτελεύτα, 2. 1, 51. 3, 108.

τελευτὴ, 5, 86. the termination, 7, 6. τοῦ τείχους, the end or extremity.

τελέω, 1, 93. τὸ δὲ ὕφος ἥμισυ μάλιστα ἐτελέσθη, to be finished : 4, 78. ἐτέλεσε, to perfect.

τέλος, 4, 96. τέλη τῶν ἱππέων, a troop, 1, 48. τέλη, a division, command, 6, 42. κατὰ τέλη, in divisions, squadrons : 5, 27. ἐν τέλει ὄντων, to be in authority, to be men in place, 1, 10. οἱ μάλιστα ἐν τέλει, the chiefs, 4, 118. τέλος ἔχοντες, to be empowered, plenipotentiaries, 1, 58. τὰ τέλη, the government, 5, 47.

4, 65. : 6, 16. τέλεσι, expense, cost, 4, 60. : 5, 46. at last, 50. οὐδὲν ἐπράχθη, no end was attained.

τέμενος, 1, 134. the sacred precincts of a temple, sacred inclosure, consecrated ground : 4, 116. 6, 99.

τέμνω, 1, 30. 2, 55. ἔτεμον τὸ πεδίον, the champaign country, the inland, district, (in opposition to the maritime ἡ παράλιος or πάραλος γῆ :) 1, 82. τεμοῦμεν, to lay waste, 143. τμηθῆναι, to be laid waste, 2, 21. ἐτέμνετο, 18. τμηθεῖσαν : 2, 55. Matth. Gr. Gr. 501.: 6, 75.

τέναγος, 3, 51. a morass.

τερπνός, 1, 120. τὸ τερπνὸν, the delight, 2, 53. πρὸς τὸ τερπνόν.

τέρπω, 2, 44. to gratify : 3, 40. τέρποντες λόγῳ, to charm by eloquence : 2, 41. τέρψαι τὸ αὐτίκα ἕπασι, to give delight, to charm for the present.

τέρψις, 2, 38. delight, pleasure.

τεσσαρακοστός, 1, 60. the fortieth.

τέταρτος, 5, 19. the fourth, 81. τέταρτον καὶ δέκατον ἔτος, equivalent to τεσσαρακαιδέκατον, Matth. Gr. Gr. 175.

τετράγωνος, 4, 125. τάξιν, a square phalanx : 6, 26. quadrangular, 4, 112. δοκούς.

τετρακόσιος, 1, 74. τετρακοσίας ὀλίγῳ ἐλάσσους δύο μοιρῶν, little less than two thirds of the whole four hundred.

τετράμηνος, 5, 63. consisting of four months.

τετράπodον, 2, 50. a quadruped.

τετράς, 4, 118. 5, 54. the fourth (day.)

τέττιξ, 1, 6. an ornament for the hair representing a grasshopper.

τεύχω, 4, 28. τεύξεσθαι, to compass, 3, 20. τοῦ ἀληθοῦς λογισμοῦ, to hit the true computation, to calculate aright : 6, 13. τευξόμεθα, to obtain, get.

τεχνάω, 1, 122. τεχνᾶται, to devise, contrive, 4, 26. ἐτεχνῶντο, 47. τεχνησαμένους.

τέχνη, 1, 49. 7, 36. art, skill : 5, 18. art, artifice, fraud : 5, 8. stratagem.

τέως, 6, 61. awhile, interea, interim, (see H. Steph. Thes. 4, 831 :) 7, 63. before, hitherto.

τηρέω, 3, 22. τηρήσαντες νύκτα χειμέριον, to seize the opportunity of a stormy night : 1, 39. to observe, keep, stand to : 5, 82. to watch, mark : 1, 65. τηρήσασι ἄνεμον, to watch the wind, opportunity of wind : 4, 30. τηρήσονται φυλακῇ τῇ μετρίᾳ, to be kept under guard : 2, 83. ἐτήρει : 2, 13. ἐτηρεῖτο, to be watched.

Τήρης, 2, 29. Σιτάλκην τὸν Τήρεω, the gen. from Τήρης, Matth. Gr. Gr. 71.

τήρησις, 7, 13. vigilance, watchfulness, 85. custody.

τίθημι, 4, 17. καλῶς θέσθαι, to turn to account, put to interest, 1, 31. τὸν πόλεμον, to dispose or carry on a war, 25, τὸ παρὸν, to dispose of the present, (i. e. to get over present difficulties,) 4, 59. εὖ θέσθαι τὰ ἴδια, to dispose advantageously : 2, 34. ἐς τὸ δημόσιον σῆμα τιθέασιν, to convey to and place in the public mausoleum, said to be an Ionic form, Matth. Gr. Gr. 279. : 5, 96. to consider : 1, 6. τίθεται, to be proposed (as a prize :) 4, 44. ἔθεντο τὰ ὅπλα, to ground arms, to halt, 7, 3. θέμενος τὰ ὅπλα, 8, 25. ὅπλα τίθενται, to pitch their camp : 4, 120. τεθήσεται τὰ πράγματα, to be settled, established : 6, 4. ἐτέθη, to be enacted, ordained, established, 38. : 4, 18. σωφρόνων δὲ ἀνδρῶν, οἵτινες τὰγαθὰ ἐς ἀμφίβολον ἀσφαλῶς ἔθεντο, for τὸ τἀγαθὰ θέσθαι, an instance of anacolouthon, the use of the pron. rel. for the infin. as the subject, Matth. 696.

τιμάω, 1, 58. to honour, respect : 4, 20. τιμήσει, 120. : 2, 45. τετίμηται : 3, 40. ἐτιμήσασθι πρὸ παντὸς, to value beyond or above every thing, 1, 33. 6, 10. : 6, 9. τιμῶμαι ἐκ τοῦ τοιούτου, to derive honour from, a measure of this sort : 2, 44. τὸ τιμᾶσθαι, honour, respect, reverence.

τιμὴ, 5, 10. 11. honour : 4, 17. honour, reputation : 2, 35. 36. τῆς μνήμης, the honour of being commemorated : 4, 47. glory, 62.

τιμωρέω, 1, 86. to avenge, 40. τιμωρήσετε, to assist, succour : 2, 42. τιμωρεῖσθαι : 1, 141. τιμωρήσασθαί τινα, to take vengeance on some one : 1, 53. τιμωρουμένοις, to punish : 3, 67. τετιμωρημένοι ἔτι ὁσιώτερον, to punish with still greater justice, 56. ἐτιμωρησάμεθα, to avenge oneself.

τιμωρητέος, 1, 86. ἀλλὰ τιμωρητέα ἐν τάχει καὶ παντὶ σθένει, to be avenged, whereas an adj. referring to no proper subject of one word should be put in the neuter sing., the Greeks frequently put it in the plur., particularly verbals, Matth. Gr. Gr. 645.

τιμωρία, 1, 58. assistance, 25. 38. 69. 4, 25. : 3, 82. revenge, 2, 42. τῶν ἐναντίων, vengeance on the enemy : 7, 68. ὡς ἐπὶ τιμωρίᾳ, with a view to, in order to punish, 3, 63. : 1, 124. ποιεῖσθαι τιμωρίαν, 25.

τιμωρὸς, 4, 2. 86. ἀδύνατος, an insufficient protector.

τὶς, any one, 5, 45. τοιόνδε τι, after this fashion : 1, 29. ἕως ἂν ἄλλο τι δόξῃ, until some other (plan) was determined upon : 7, 1. τινὰ στρατιὰν οὐ πολλὴν, some small force, 48. τὸ δέ τι, besides, moreover : 1, 9. τῳ for τινί : 7, 48. ἦν γάρ τι καὶ ἐν Συρακούσαις βουλόμενον τοῖς Ἀθηναίοις τὰ πράγματα ἐνδοῦναι, Matth. Gr. Gr. 304. : 6, 1, οὐ πολλῷ τινι ὑποδεέστερον πόλεμον ἀνηροῦντο ἢ τὸν πρὸς Πελοποννησίους, the use of the pronoun τὶς with an adj. of quantity, Matth. 704. : 4, 130. ἦν τι καὶ στασιασμοῦ ἐν τῇ πόλει, for τὶς στασιασμὸς, the neuter of the pronoun τὶς, any one, is here used (as some adjectives commonly, and others rarely,) for the *part*, where the subst. is the *whole*, which is put in the gen., Matth. 909. : 7, 87. ἡμέρας ἑβδομήκοντα τινὰς οὕτω διηγήθησαν ἀθρόοι, Matth. 705. : 4, 85. ἀλλὰ καὶ οἷς ἂν ἐπίω, ἧσσόν τις ἐμοὶ πρόσεισι, in the use of pronouns on account of the collective sense, in which τὶς is sometimes used, the word, which refers to τὶς, is sometimes put in the plural, Matth. 704. : 8, 73.

τιτρώσκω, 1, 14. ἔτρωσαν, to disable (a ship :) 5, 10. τιτρώσκεται, to be wounded : 7, 27. ἐτιτρώσκοντο : 4, 57. τετρωμένος.

τοιοῦτος, *talis hujusmodi*, 3, 81. πᾶσά τε ἰδέα κατέστη θανάτου καὶ οἷον φιλεῖ ἐν τῷ τοιούτῳ γίγνεσθαι, οὐδὲν ὅ,τι οὐ ξυνέβη, Matth. Gr. Gr. 700. : 5, 63. 7, 86.

τοιουτότροπος, 2, 13. of a like, similar kind, 2, 8. of such a kind, the same sort : 4, 25.

τοῖχος, 2, 3. κοινοὺς, partition-walls, 7, 36. sides (of a ship :) 2, 75. ἀντὶ τοίχων, to serve for walls.

τοκεὺς, 2, 44. τοκέας, parents. τόλμα, 7, 28. daring, 2, 41. adventurous spirit, daring : 5, 7. boldness, decision, promptitude : 1, 90. courage : 6, 33. τὴν τόλμαν ἐκπλαγῇ, to be astounded at the daring, 59.

τολμάω, 1, 31. τολμῶμεν, to venture : 6, 82. ἐτόλμησαν, to bear, *sustinere* : 7, 21. τολμῆσαι, 1, 74. 91. : 2, 43. τολμῶντες ἄνδρες, men of courage : 2, 93. Matth. Gr. Gr. 923.

τόλμημα, 2, 25. a daring deed, bold adventure, 6, 54. Ἁρμοδίου, 7, 43.

τολμηρὸς, 1, 102. τὸ τολμηρὸν, the enterprising spirit, 7, 21. : 1, 74. τολμηροτάτην, most intrepid.

τολμηρῶς, 3, 74. ξυνεπελάβοντο, courageously, intrepidly.

τολμητὴς, 1, 70. enterpriser, darer.

τομὴ, 1, 93. ἐν τομῇ ἐγγώνιοι, cut so as to fit into one another.

τόξαρχος, 3, 98. the commander of the archers:

τόξευμα, 7, 43. a missile, missile weapon.

τοξεύω, 4, 48. ἐτόξευον, to shoot arrows, 3, 23. : 3, 98. τοξευόμενοι, to be shot at with arrows.

τοξότης, 1, 10. an archer, a bow-man : 4, 129. 5, 47.

τόπος, 6, 54. τινὶ ἀφανεῖ, a secret, covert, remote opportunity, occasion, affair.

τοσόσδε, 6, 43. τοσῷδε ἤδη, *tot et talibus.*

τοσοῦτος, 1, 9. οὐ τοσοῦτον, not so much as : 7, 2. παρὰ τοσοῦτον κινδύνου, to such an extremity of danger.

τότε, 3, 46. then, at that time, 6, 2. : 88. then, (emphatically :) 7, 59. τότε ἤδη, already, at this time : 5, 15. τῶν τότε, men at the time mentioned, at this epoch.

τράπεζα, 1, 130. a table.

τραυματίας, 7, 75. wounded, 8, 27.

τραυματίζω, 4, 19. τραυματίσαντες, to give wounds, 35. τραυματιζομένων, to be wounded, 12. τραυματισθείς.

τραχὺς, 4, 33. rugged, rough.

τρέπω, 7, 43. ἔτρεψαν, to rout, 4, 72. ἐπὶ τὴν θάλασσαν, to rout and pursue to : 3, 13. τρέψαι πρὸς ἀσφάλειάν τινα, to compel a person to take measures for his own security, 4, 76. ἐς δημοκρατίαν : 5, 10. τραπόμενοι, to be bewildered, dispersed, 8, 3. to turn : 2, 15. τὸ τετραμμένον πρὸς νότον μάλιστα, the part, in particular, which faces the south, lies most southernly, 7, 58. Matth. Gr. Gr. 398. : 2, 40. τετραμμένους, πρὸς ἔργα, whose minds are turned to mechanical occupations, occupied in labours of the hand, citizens, mechanics, 25. πρὸς τὸ τεῖχος, with faces turned towards

11

the wall, 4, 76. : 2, 84. τρέπεσθαι ἐς ἀλκὴν, to turn and fight, to face about, to resist : 3, 24. τραπέσθαι ταύτην (*sc.* ὁδὸν,) to turn this way, take this direction, 5, 59. : 6, 17. τράπεσθαι ἐς τὰ ἔργα, to betake oneself to action, to execute, 6, 51. τετραμμένων πρὸς τὴν ἐκκλησίαν, to turn or betake oneself to any thing or place, (*relictis aliis negotiis,*) 77. τρεπομένους ἐπὶ τοῦτο τὸ εἶδος, to resort to this method, way, mode : 8, 5. ἐτράποντο, to apply themselves : 1, 50. οἱ Κορίνθιοι πρὸς τοὺς ἀνθρώπους ἐτράποντο φονεύειν, here the infin. is an epexegesis of the words πρὸς τοὺς ἀνθρ. ἐτρ., the infin. stands after certain verbs, to express an object, and among them, after verbs of motion ʻ to go, send,ʼ &c. Matth. Gr. Gr. 805.

τρέφω, 3, 52. 7, 14. to nourish, supply, 4, 80. στρατιὰν, to maintain : 7, 49. τρέφονται, to supply oneself with food, provide for oneself : 2, 61. τεθραμμένους, 44. τραφέντες, to be brought up, 46.

τρέχω, to run, 8, 92. δεδραμήκεσαν, Matth. Gr. Gr. 203.

τρία, 1, 74. τρία τὰ ὠφέλιμα ἐς αὐτὸ, the three things useful for that purpose.

τριακόντορος, 4, 9. a boat of thirty oars.

τριακοντούτης, 5, 14. of

thirty years: 1, 23. λύσαντες τὰς, καὶ τριακοντούτεις σπονδὰς, 2, 2. αἱ τριακοντούτεις σπονδαὶ.

τριακοντουτὶς, 1, 87. τριακοντουτίδων σπονδῶν προκεχωρηκυιῶν, a peculiar form of the fem. of an adj. compounded from ἔτος, Matth. Gr. Gr. 144.

τριακόσιος, 1, 13. three hundred.

τριβὴ, tritura, grinding, wasting, 8, 87. τριβῆς ἕνεκα καὶ ἀνακωχῆς τῶν Ἑλληνικῶν τὸ ναυτικὸν οὐκ ἀγαγεῖν, ut res Græcorum attereret, suspensasque teneret.

τρίβω, 6, 18. τρίψεσθαι αὐτὴν περὶ αὑτὴν, to wear oneself away, to waste, (Liv. per otium in desidiam elanguescere:) 2, 77. τριφθεῖσα πρὸς αὑτὴν, to be rubbed one against another: 7, 42. τρίψεσθαι, to waste.

τριήραρχος, 7, 13. 24. the commander of a trireme.

τριήρης, 1, 13. 6, 93. 7, 3. 9. a trireme: 6, 46. τριηρῶν, Matth. Gr. Gr. 98.

τριηρίτης, 6, 46. τριηριτῶν, persons on board a trireme, τῶν ἐν τριήρεσιν ἀφικομένων, probably for τριηράρχων.

τρίπους, 1, 132. ἐπὶ τὸν τρίποδα ἀναγράψασθαι, to engrave upon a tripod.

τριταῖος, 3, 3. ἀφικόμενος, to arrive on the third day after: 1, 61.

τρίτος, 4, 42. αὐτὸς, himself with two others: 5, 56. τρίτον

καὶ δέκατον ἔτος, equivalent to τρισκαιδέκατος, Matth. Gr. Gr. 175. : 3, 3.

τριχῇ, 7, 82. tripliciter, triply.

τροπαῖον, 5, 10. a trophy, 74. ἵστασαν, to erect a trophy, 1, 30. στήσαντες, 54. ἔστησαν, 7, 41. ἀμφοτέρων τροπαῖα ἔστησαν, to erect trophies on account of both actions: 6, 98.

τροπὴ, 1, 49. 7, 44. 54. rout, defeat: 6, 69. ποιεῖν τροπὰς, to put to flight.

τρόπος, 7, 17. manner, fashion, 36. 44. 5, 23. 47. : 5, 7. a plan (of action,) disposition: 4, 97. τρόποις θεραπευόμενα, ceremonies : 1, 5. τῷ παλαιῷ, after the ancient fashion : 4, 90. τοιῷδε τρόπῳ : 1, 6. ἐς τὸν νῦν τρόπον, according to the modern fashion : 5, 17. τῷ αὐτῷ τρόπῳ, in like manner, for the same reason, 88.

τροπωτήρ, 2, 93. λαβόντα τῶν ναυτῶν ἕκαστον τὴν κώπην, καὶ τὸ ὑπηρέσιον, καὶ τὸν τροπωτῆρα, the oar-rope, funis seu lorum, quo remus ad scalmum alligatur.

τροφὴ, 1, 5. maintenance, support : 6, 34. provision, 93. : 7, 48. (military) pay, 8, 29. 57.

τρύγητος, 4, 84. πρὸ τρυγήτου, before harvest.

τρυφερὸς, 1, 6. ἐς τὸ τρυφερώτερον, to a more delicate kind of living.

τρυχόω, 7, 28. τετρυχωμένοι τῷ πολέμῳ, to be wasted,

reduced, shattered, 4, 60. to be worn out.

τρύχω, 1, 126. τρυχόμενοι προσεδρείᾳ, to be wasted, worn out by besieging a place.

Τρωϊκὸς, 1, 3. τῶν Τρωϊκῶν, an adj. in —ικος in the neuter plural with the article and without a subst. signifies any circumstance determinable by the context: here is meant ' the Trojan war,' Matth. Gr. Gr. 392.

τυγχάνω, 1, 72. to happen, 104. ἔτυχον στρατευόμενοι, to be making an expedition, 7, 2. ἔτυχε ἐλθὼν, to happen to arrive, or simply, to arrive, 4. ἔτυχον αὐλιζόμενοι, to be passing the night, lodging: 3, 39. τυχόντες, to win, acquire, 42. γνώμης, to carry one's motion : 1, 74. τυχεῖν τούτου, to meet with this : 6, 33. τύχωσι ὧν προσδέχονται, to obtain what they expect : 1, 71. μόλις δ᾽ ἂν ἐτυγχάνετε τούτου, with difficulty you could meet with this : 3, 70. ἐτύγχανε γὰρ καὶ βουλῆς ὢν ὁ Πειθίας, where the gen. is put partitivé, Matth. Gr. Gr. : 4, 113. ἔτυχον ὁπλῖται ἐν τῇ ἀγορᾷ καθεύδοντες ὡς πεντή-

κοντα, this verb expresses the idea of chance : with some verbs, which express only a circumstance or accessary definition of an action, the verb, of which they express a circumstance is put in the participle : these accessaries are usually expressed by adverbs, Matth. 843.

τυραννεύω, 6, 55. τυραννεῦσαι, i. q. τύραννος εἶναι, 54. : 1, 18. τυραννευθείσης, to be ruled over by a prince or tyrant.

τυραννέω, 2, 30. ἐτυράννει, to be tyrant or master of.

τυραννὶς, 1, 18. 3, 37. 6, 38. a tyranny, an absolute sovereignty.

τύραννος, 1, 13. 14. 18. a chief, tyrant.

τυρὸς, 4, 26. cheese.

τυφλὸς, 3, 104. blind.

τύχη, 5, 37. κατὰ τύχην, by luck : 6, 11. a misfortune, disaster : 1, 69. ἐς τύχας καταστῆναι, to run hazards, stand in the way of, to chance : 4, 73. οὐκ ἂν ἐν τύχῃ γίγνεσθαι σφίσιν, to be a matter of doubt : 3, 97. Matth. Gr. Gr. 569.

Υ.

Ὑακίνθιος, 5, 23. πρὸς τὰ Ὑακίνθια, a Spartan festival in honour or commemoration of the boy Hyacinthus.

ὑβρίζω, 8, 45. ὑβρίζοντες, to be insolent, 4, 18. ὑβρίσαντες : 1, 68. ὑβριζόμενοι ὑπὸ Ἀθηναίων, to be wronged, 38. ἐπὶ τῷ ὑπὸ

τούτων ὑβρίζεσθαι, for the purpose of being insulted by
them.

ὕβρις, 3, 39. ἐς ὕβριν τρέπειν,
to turn insolent, for τρίπεσθαι:
6, 28. ἐφ' ὕβρει, for mockery,
in contempt : 2, 65. ὕβρει θαρ-
σοῦντας, to be bold or daring
from pride, insolence, vain
glory: 1, 38. 3, 39.

ὑγιαίνω, 2, 58. ὑγιαίνοντας,
to be in good health.

ὑγιὴς, 3, 34. 75. right,
sound : 2, 49. healthy, in
good health : 4, 22.

ὑδατώδης, 3, 23. sleety,
watery.

ὑδρεία, 7, 13. watering,
fetching or drawing water.

ὑδρεύω, 4, 97. ἀναρπάσαντας
ὑδρεύεσθαι, to draw and make
use of the (saered) water in
common.

ὕδωρ, 5, 65. water : 6, 70.
a great rain : 2, 77.

ὑετὸς, 2, 5. πορευόμενοι ἐν
ὑετῷ, to march in the wet, 8,
42. a shower of rain.

υἱεὺς, 1, 13. υἱέος, cor-
ruptly read for υἱέος, the
gen. of υἱεὺς, Matth. Gr. Gr.
102. where Bekker has
edited υἱέος, but in the note
says, " υἱέος A. B. K. L. N. O.
cum Thoma M. v. υἱέα : υἱέος
Q. : vulgo υἱέως." 6, 30. υἱεῖς,
the Attic accus. plur., Matth.
103. see too 111.

υἱὸς, 5, 16. a son, 2, 100.

ὕλη, 2, 75. 4, 30. 34. 69.
wood.

ὑλώδης, 4, 8. 29. woody.

ὑμέτερος, your, 1, 70. 4, 85.

ὑμνέω, 2, 42. ἃ τὴν πόλιν
ὕμνησα, to eulogise, speak in
praise of : 1, 21. ὑμνήκασι, to
sing of (as poets.)

ὑπάγω, 5, 10. to lead back,
3, 70. ἐς δίκην, to cite to trial:
2, 76. ὑπαγομένου, to be drawn
away underneath: 7, 46. ὑπα-
γάγοιτο τὴν πόλιν, to bring under one's power, to reduce to
obedience : 4, 126.

ὑπαγωγὴ, 3, 97. a retreat.

ὑπαίθριος, 1, 134. in the
open air (without a roof.)

ὑπακούω, 3, 50. ὑπήκουον Ἀθηναίων, to be subject to the
Athenians, 1, 29. to attend
to, to obey, 8, 5. : 7, 18. to
hearken to, to comply with:
3, 13. ὑπηκούσαμεν εὐθὺς, 5,
98. ὑπακούειν, to submit :
1, 53. ὑπήκυυσεν, to hear (as
one, who listens :) 6, 82.
ὑπακουσόμεθα αὐτῶν, to be subject to, under the command
of, Matth. Gr. Gr. 484. : 8,
74. ἵνα, ἢν μὴ ὑπακούσωσι, τεθνήκωσι, Matth. Gr. Gr. 730.
see too 342. : 7, 73.

ὑπαναλίσκω, 3, 17. ὑπανά-
λωσε τὰ χρήματα, to consume,
exhaust; ὑπαναλώθη, to be expended.

ὑπάρχω, 2, 13. ὑπῆρχε ταῦτα
Ἀθηναίοις, the Athenians had
these, 4, 4. to be : 3, 109.
ὥσπερ ὑπῆρχε, as they could,
4, 69. αἱ οἰκίαι—ὑπῆρχον ἔρυμα,
7, 69. : 3, 63. ὑπάρχον γε ὑμῖν,
it was in your power, 4, 52.
ὑπαρχόντων, to be hard by,

R Γ

4, 10. τὰ ὑπάρχοντα, existing circumstances, 7, 76. : 1, 70. possessions, one's own, 3, 39. πρὸς τοῖς ὑπάρχουσιν, in addition to existing ones, 1, 76. ὑπάρχουσαν δύναμιν, existing, actual : 6, 87. ὑπάρχομεν, *imperare* : 6, 24. ὑπάρξειν, to accrue : 3, 9. ὑπάρχοι, to be, exist : 2, 67. ὑπῆρξαν, to begin to do, to set an example, 1, 76. ὑπάρξαντες πρῶτοι τοῦ τοιούτου : 1, 93. ὑπῆρκτο, to be begun, the use of the 3d pers. pass. without a nomin. as in Latin *itur*, Matth. Gr. Gr. 432.: 6, 15. Ἀλκιβιάδης ὢν ἐν ἀξιώματι ὑπὸ τῶν ἀστῶν ταῖς ἐπιθυμίαις μείζοσιν ἢ κατὰ τὴν ὑπάρχουσαν οὐσίαν ἐχρῆτο, an example of ἢ κατὰ put after the compar., where in Latin would be employed *quam pro*, Matth. 653.

ὑπάπειμι, 3, 111. ὑπαπῄεσαν κατ᾽ ὀλίγους, to withdraw privately in small parties.

ὑπείκω, 1, 127. 3, 39. to yield, submit, give way to.

ὕπειμι, 6, 87. ὑπεῖναι ἐλπίδα, *subesse*, that there is a secret hope.

ὑπεῖπον, 1, 35. ὑπείπομεν, to hint, suggest, 90. ὑπειπὼν, to tell secretly.

ὑπέκκειμαι, 1, 137. ὑπεξέκειτο χρήματα, to be secretly deposited, 8, 31. to belong to.

ὑπεκκομίζω, 4, 123. παῖδας καὶ γυναῖκας, to export out of the way.

ὑπεκπέμπω, 4, 8. ὑπεκπέμπει

φθάσας δύο ναῦς ἀγγεῖλαι Εὐρυμέδοντι, to send out, to despatch, the use of the infin. after a verb of motion to express an object, Matth. Gr. Gr. 805.

ὑπεκτίθημι, 1, 89. ὑπεξέθεντο, to carry out and deposit privately.

ὑπεκφεύγω, 2, 91. ὑπεξέφυγον τὴν ἐπιστροφὴν εἰς τὴν εὐρυχωρίαν, to escape from, to avoid by flight.

ὑπενάντιος, 2, 2. an adversary.

ὑπενδίδωμι, 2, 64. ὑπενδῶμεν, to let slip, suffer to glide away.

ὑπεξανάγω, 3, 74. ὑπεξανήγετο, to put out privately to sea.

ὑπεξέρχομαι, 6, 51. ὑπεξῆλθον, to withdraw secretly : 3, 34. ὑπεξελθόντες τούτους, to steal away from, 4, 83. ὑπεξελθεῖν.

ὑπέρ, 7, 83. Ἀθηναίων, on the part of, in the behalf of, for, 71. τοῦ μέλλοντος, about or concerning what was to ensue, 13. σφῶν, instead of, in the place of, 5, 47. σφῶν αὐτῶν, 4, 95. τῆς ὑμετέρας ὁ ἀγὼν, for or about : 6, 13. ὑπὲρ δύναμιν μείζω, (above i. e. more than,) greater than its real strength, 1, 8. ἥμισυ, above half.

ὑπεραυχέω, 4, 19. ὑπεραυχοῦντα, haughty, overweening.

ὑπερβαίνω, 3, 20. ὑπερβῆναι τὰ τείχη, to get over or scale a wall, 24. ὑπερβάντες :

4, 118. ὑπερβαίνοντες, to pass over, step beyond.

ὑπερβάλλω, 6, 23. ὑπερβάλλοντες, to be superior in force, 7, 67. to exceed, 2, 35.

ὑπερβατὸς, 3, 25. what can be climbed over.

ὑπερβιάζομαι, 2, 52. ὑπερβιαζομένου τοῦ κακοῦ, under the pressure of the calamity.

ὑπερβολὴ, 3, 82. the pride of excelling others.

ὑπερεῖδον, 4, 62. ὑπεριδεῖν, to neglect, 5, 6. 43. ὑπεριδόντες, to overlook, contemn, slight, 6, 11.

ὑπερέχω, 3, 107. τὸ ὑπερέχον, the excess, 23. μόλις ὑπερέχοντες, vix extantes, to wade through having the head only above water, with difficulty, to keep the head above, 7, 25. τῆς θαλάσσης, to emerge above.

ὑπερόπτης, 3, 38. a contemner, despiser.

ὑπερόπτομαι, 5, 28. ὑπερώφθη, to be despised, contemned, 7, 42.

ὑπερόριος, 8, 72. ἀσχολίαν, occupation beyond the bounds (of their own country.)

ὑπεροψία, 1, 84. a contempt.

ὑπερτείνω, 2, 76. ὑπερτεινουσῶν, to reach or hang over.

ὑπέρυθρος, 2, 49. reddish, pale, χλωρός.

ὑπερφαίνω, 4, 93. ὑπερεφάνησαν τοῦ λόφου, to appear above, to crown.

ὑπερφέρω, 1, 81. ὑπερφέρομεν τοῖς ὅπλοις, to excel, surpass: 3, 15. ὑπεροίσοντες, to convey

over, to transport: 3, 81. ὑπερενεγκόντες τὰς ναῦς τὸν ἰσθμὸν, to carry over, 8, 7. Matth. Gr. Gr. 610.: 4, 8. ὑπερενεχθεῖσαι, to be hauled across, dragged over.

ὑπερφρονέω, 6, 16. ὑπερφρονούμενος ἀνεχέσθω, let him submit to be looked down upon.

ὑπέρφρων, 2, 62. loftyminded, proud.

ὑπεύθυνος, 3, 43. παραίνεσιν ἔχοντας, to be accountable for one's advice.

ὑπέχω, 3, 53. ὑπέξειν τοιάνδε δίκην, to submit to such justice as this, 81. ὑποσχεῖν δίκην, to submit to trial : 7, 21. : 6, 80, ὑφέξετε τὴν τιμωρίαν, pœnas dare.

ὑπήκοος, 1, 77. πρὸς ὑπηκόους, towards or with regard to their subjects : 7, 57. ὑπήκοοι φόρῳ, the same as ὑποτελεῖς φόρου : 6. 20. ἀλλήλων, 69. : 1, 13. ὑπηκόους ἐποιήσαντο, to make subject.

ὑπηρεσία, 6, 31. a crew of rowers : 1, 143. the manning and equipment of a ship, for ὑπηρέται, an interchange, where the general idea is put for the definite thing, Matth. Gr. Gr. 617. see too 627.: 8, 1.

ὑπηρετέω, 4, 108. ὑπηρέτησαν αὐτῷ, to be subservient to him, to meet his wishes.

ὑπηρέτης, 3, 17. a soldier's valet, a servant.

ὑπισχνέομαι, 8, 5. ὑπισχνεῖτο, to promise, 1, 132. ἐλευθέρωαιν αὐτοῖς, to promise manumission to them, 129.

ὑπίσχομαι, 1, 58. ὑπέσχοντο, to promise, 101. 5, 38. 7, 1. 8, 17.; 8. 5. to undertake for : 1, 123. 3, 49. μεγάλα, to promise great (rewards,) 5, 37. : 8, 48. ὑπεσχῆσθαι.

ὕπνος, 2, 2. περὶ πρῶτον ὕπνον, about the first watch.

ὑπὸ, 1, 75, δέους, for or through fear, 3, 32. ἀνάγκης ξυμμάχους, allies against their own will, upon compulsion, 33. σπουδῆς, with haste, hastily, 36. ὀργῆς, in consequence of, from anger, 68. Ἀθηναίων, (to be injured) by the Athenians, 11. 7, 44 : χαλεπὰ ἦν ὑπὸ τῆς βοῆς διαγνῶναι, from or on account of the clamour : 2, 85. ὑπὸ ἀνέμων καὶ ὑπὸ ἀπλοίας ἐνδιέτριψεν οὐκ ὀλίγον χρόνον, Matth. Gr. Gr. 914.: 6, 28. ὑπὸ νεωτέρων γεγενημέναι, to take place, to be committed by : 4, 34. ὑπὸ τῶν τοξευμάτων, for the flight of arrows : 3, 62. ὑφ᾿ αὑτοῖς ποιεῖσθαι, to subdue under their own power, 1, 32.; 7, 64. ὑπὸ Συρακοσίοις γίγνεσθαι, to be under or subject to, 75. τοῖς ὅπλοις, under : 1, 100. ὑπὸ τοὺς αὐτοὺς χρόνους, about the same time, 2, 6. Matth. Gr. Gr. 916.; 5, 4. 7, 21.; 4, 101. ὑπὸ τὰς αὐτὰς ἡμέρας τοῖς ἐπὶ Δηλίῳ, at the time of the transactions at Delium, 1, 115. ὑπὸ νύκτα, by night, 7, 22. just before night-fall, in the beginning of night,

(Hobbes,) just before dawn, (or simply,) under cloud of night, in the night, (as κατὰ νύκτα :) 2, 8. ἡ νεότης—οὐκ ἀκουσίως ὑπὸ ἀπειρίας ἥπτετο τοῦ πολέμου, ' from inexperience,' answering here to the Latin prae, forasmuch as with actives it expresses the means, by which the action is effected, hence it expresses a cause arising from any internal or external circumstance, disposition of mind, &c. Matth. Gr. Gr. 914. see too 568. : 6, 32. ὑπὸ κήρυκος εὐχὰς ποιεῖσθαι, an instance of ὑπὸ with the gen. meaning ' by ' or ' from,' with an active expressing the means, Matth. 914.

ὑπογράφω, 5, 56. ὑπέγραψεν τῇ στήλῃ, to inscribe on a column.

ὑποδεής, 1, 10. ὑποδεεστέρα, inferior, below estimation or fame, 5, 8. 6, 1. : 2, 89. ἐκ πολλῷ ὑποδεεστέρων, with very inferior forces.

ὑποδεεστέρως, 8, 87. ἀντιπάλως μᾶλλον ἢ ὑποδεεστέρως, in an inferior degree.

ὑποδείκνυμι, 1, 77. ὑπεδείξατε, to exhibit, 4, 86. ὑποδείξας ἀρετὴν, to pretend to.

ὑποδέχομαι, 6, 34. ὑποδέχεται, to receive, admit : 2, 29. 1, 25. 1, 71. ὑπεδέχετο, to undertake, promise, 3, 12. entertain, admit into one's society : 3, 111. ὑπεδέξατο, to receive privately, 6, 22. οὐ πάσης ἔσται πόλεως ὑποδέξασθαι, it will not be (in the power) of every city to receive, entertain, 34. εἰ ὑποδέξοιντο, whether they will receive : 8, 81.

ὑποδέω, 3, 22. ὑποδιδεμένοι τὸν ἀριστηρὸν πόδα, to be shod on the left foot, to have a shoe on the left foot.

ὑποδοχή, 7, 74. a reception (of an enemy:) 1, 139. receiving or affording a place of refuge to runaway slaves.

ὑποζύγιον, 2, 3. a beast of burden, 14. 7, 27. 29.

ὑποθορυβέω, 4, 28. ὑποθορυ- βησάντων, to address tumultuously.

ὑποκαταβαίνω, 7, 60. ὑποκα- τέβησαν, to descend secretly, silently, quietly.

ὑπόκειμαι, 1, 93. ὑπόκεινται, to be laid as a foundation : 3, 84.

ὑπολαμβάνω, 1, 68. ὑπολα- βόντες, to lay hands upon privily, 121. ὑπολαβεῖν, to seduce (foreign) sailors, 6, 58. to remove, withdraw, take away, 1, 143. to procure in an underhand manner, 3, 113. ὑπολαβών, to take up in answer, 2, 72. ὑπολαβὼν εἶπε, to say in reply, 6, 28. ὑπο- λαμβάνοντες, to lay hold of, take up (as matter of accusation.)

ὑπολείπω, 7, 64. ὑπελίπετε, to leave behind, 6, 10. ὑπολι- πόντας : 1, 81. ὑπολίπωμεν, to bequeath : 5, 6. ὑπελείποντο, to be left behind, 61. 7, 20. : 3, 98. ὑπελείφθη, Matth. Gr.

Gr. 569. ; 8, 20.; 1, 90. ὑπο- λειφθῆναι : 3, 40. ὑπολειπομέ- νους, to be passed over, suffered to remain, continue, live : 3, 22. ὑπολελειμμένου : 7, 43. ὑπελέλειπτο.

ὑπόλοιπος, 7, 7. the remaining, remainder, 64. ἡμῶν, the remnant of us : 1, 75. 4, 2. 18. 90.

ὑπομενετέον, 2, 88. ὅ,τι οὐχ ὑπομενετέον αὐτοῖς, which they ought not to meet, encounter.

ὑπομένω, 7, 17. ὑπομένων, to remain behind, 81. Matth. Gr. Gr. 817. : 5, 50. ὑπέμενον τὴν ἑορτὴν, to be waiting (until) the festival (was over :) 1, 76. ὑπομείναντες, to continue, 89, to remain behind, 5, 72. ; 7, 28. to stand, abide an attack, offer resistance, 8, 27. to wait for : 6, 68. ὑπομενοῦσι : 4, 5. οἱ δὲ ἑορ- τήν τινα ἔτυχον ἄγοντες καὶ ἅμα πυνθανόμενοι ἐν ὀλιγωρίᾳ ἐποιοῦν- το, ὡς, ὅταν ἐξέλθωσιν, ἢ οὐχ ὑπο- μενοῦντας σφᾶς ἢ ῥαδίως ληψό- μενοι βίᾳ, an instance of the participle, (preceded by the particle ὡς,) in the fut. in the case of the preceding subjects, Matth. Gr. Gr. 871.

ὑπομιμνήσκω, 6, 68. to remind, 7, 64. 69. Matth. Gr. Gr. 875.

ὑπομνάω, 2, 60. ὅπως ὑπο- μνήσω, καὶ μέμψομαι, in order to admonish and expostulate with.

ὑπόμνημα, 2, 44. a memorial of a deceased person.

ὑπόμνησις, 4, 17. a hint,

reminding, 95. : 1, 72. καὶ ἅμα τὴν σφετέραν πόλιν ἐβούλοντο σημῆναι ὅση εἴη δύναμιν, καὶ ὑπόμνησιν ποιήσασθαι τοῖς τε πρεσβυτέροις ὧν ᾔδεσαν, καὶ τοῖς νεωτέροις ἐξήγησιν ὧν ἄπειροι ἦσαν, Matth. Gr. Gr. 590.

ὑπονείφω, 4, 103. ὑπένειφεν, to snow : 3, 23. ὑπονειφομένη νὺξ, a snowy night.

ὑπονοέω, 7, 73. ὑπονοήσας, to suspect, conjecture, 3, 8. to detect : 6, 16. ὑπονοεῖται, to be conjectured, imagined, supposed, 1, 68. τῶν λεγόντων μᾶλλον ὑπενοεῖτε ὡς ἕνεκεν τῶν αὐτοῖς ἰδίᾳ διαφόρων λέγουσι, the subject is constructed with the preceding verb in the gen., Matth. Gr. Gr. 429. : 4, 76.

ὑπόνοια, 2, 41. τῶν ἔργων, (sc. περὶ,) an opinion or idea of actions, (conceived from reading them :) 5, 87. τῶν μελλόντων, a suspicion of what is about to happen, 7, 49.

ὑπονομηδὸν, 6, 100. οἱ ἐς τὴν πόλιν ὑπονομηδὸν ποτοῦ ὕδατος ἠγμένοι ἦσαν, instar cuniculi, per cuniculos, by means of pipes.

ὑπόνομος, 2, 76. ὑπόνομον δ' ἐκ τῆς πόλεως ὀρύξαντες, a mine.

ὑπονοστέω, 3, 89. ὑπενόστησε, to sink, settle.

ὑποπέμπω, 4, 46. ὑποπέμψαντες, to send secretly.

ὑποπίπτω, 7, 40. ὑποπίπτοντες ἐς τοὺς ταρσοὺς, to run (a boat) under, make one's way under.

ὑποπτεύω, 3, 53. ὑποπτεύομεν, to suspect, 43. ὑποπτεύη-

11

ται, : 2, 62. ὑποπτευόμενον, to be regarded with suspicion, to be distrusted : 5, 35. ὑπώπτευον ἀλλήλους, to be suspicious of one another, mutually distrustful, (al. ὑπετόπευον,) 4, 126.

ὕποπτος, 3, 42. suspected, 82. 4, 78. 103. 6, 75. : 5, 26. suspicious, dubious, 1, 75. 6, 60. : 6, 85. τῷ ἡμετέρῳ ὑπόπτῳ, sc. εἰς ἡμᾶς, 1, 90. τὸ ὕποπτον τῆς γνώμης, suspicion, jealousy.

ὑπόπτως, 6, 53. πάντα ἐλάμβανε, suspiciously, inclinatis ad suspicionem animis, in a suspicious or jealous mood : 8, 38. διακείμενοι, to look on one another with mutual or reciprocal suspicion.

ὑποσημαίνω, 1, 82. ὑποσημαίνοντας, to indicate privately.

ὑπόσπονδος, 1, 63. 2, 6. under a truce, 70. 7, 5. 45.

ὑποστρέφω, 4, 33. ὑποστρέφοντες, to turn back, retrace one's steps, 3, 24. ὑποστρέψαντες, to diverge (from a road.)

ὑπόσχεσις, 4, 39. a promise, an engagement.

ὑποτείνω, 7, 36. ὑπέτειναν ἀπ' αὐτῶν πρὸς τοὺς τοίχους, to fix, plant, (by way of support,) 'they fixed supporters to them, extending to the ribs or sides of the vessels,' they 'fixed rafters upon the sides of the vessel, which inclined at an angle against the stays and supported them,' ἐντός τε καὶ ἔξωθεν, on either side, within and without, (with reference to the prow, calling that space *within*, which was between the stay and the prow:) 8, 48. ὑποτείνοντες, to offer hopes of.

ὑποτειχίζω, 6, 99. to raise a counter-wall.

ὑποτείχισμα, 6, 100. a counter-wall.

ὑποτελὴς, 2, 9. tributary, 3, 46. 7, 57.: 1, 56. φόρου, subject to (pay,) or bearing tribute, an adj. with an active sense, expressing an idea of relation not complete without the addition of the object, takes it in the gen., Matth. Gr. Gr. 460.

ὑποτίθημι, 5, 90. 3, 45. ὑποτιθεῖσα, to suggest, to propose, 4, 65. to supply: 1, 138. ὑπετίθει.

ὑποτοπέω, 2, 5. 13. 5, 31. 116. ὑποτοπήσαντες, to suspect, 1, 20. 51. to conjecture.

ὑπουργέω, 1, 34. 43. 6, 88. to assist, 7, 62. ὑπουργῶσιν.

ὑποφαίνω, 5, 10. ὑποφαίνονται, to be discernible, discovered.

ὑποφεύγω, 2, 90. 7, 75. to steal out, make one's escape.

ὑποχείριος, 1, 88. subject to, under the hands of: 3, 11. ἔχοντες τοὺς πλείους ὑποχειρίους, to have or keep in subjection: 1, 128. 3, 86. 6, 36.

ὑποχωρέω, 1, 106. ὑπεχώρουν, to retreat, 8, 45.: 3, 78. ὑποχωρούντων: 1, 54; ὑπεχώρησαν, 4, 43. 66.: 6, 34. ὑποχωρῆσαι,

to withdraw: 2, 88. ὑποχωρεῖν, to give way to, to retreat from: 4, 10. ὑποχωροίη: 27. ὑποχωρῆσαι, to give way.

ὑποψία, 1, 42. 107. ὑποψίᾳ, through suspicion: 4, 27. suspicion, dislike: 2, 37. πρὸς ἀλλήλους, suspicion (directed) towards one another.

ὕπτιος, 7, 82. ἐς ἀσπίδας ὑπτίας, into their shields reversed, in the hollow of their shields.

ὑστεραῖος, 7, 3. τῇ ὑστεραίᾳ *sc.* ἡμέρᾳ, on the next or following day, 11. here apparently for ὑστέρᾳ or δευτέρᾳ the next or following, subsequent, 4, 13. 5, 66.

ὑστερέω, 1, 134. ὑστέρησαν τῇ διώξει, to be left behind in the pursuit: 7, 29. ὑστερήσαντας τῷ Δημοσθένει, to be too late, to arrive too late for, the same as ὕστερον ἥκειν in 7, 27.; 8, 44.: 3, 31. ὑστερήκει τῆς Μυτιλήνης.

ὑστερίζω, 6, 69. οἱ δὲ καὶ διὰ σπουδῆς προσβοηθοῦντες δρόμῳ ὑστέριζον μὲν, to arrive too late, Schol. ὕστερον ἤρχοντο.

ὕστερος, 5, 30. ἐς τὸν ὕστερον ξύλλογον, to an after-conference: 3, 88. ὕστεροι ἀκολουθῆσαι δοκεῖν τῇ γνώμῃ, to appear later or behind-hand in following or adopting an opinion: 6, 4. ὕστερον ἢ αὐτοὺς οἰκίσαι: 1, 91. οὐδενὸς ὕστεροι, second to none, 78. οὐ πολλῷ (*sc.* χρόνῳ) not long afterwards, 6, 3. ὕστερον δὲ χρόνῳ, afterwards, in process of time, 4, 101. οὐ πολὺ ὕστερον, not long after.

ὑφαιρέω, 3, 13. ὑφαιροῦντες αὐτῶν τοὺς ξυμμάχους, to win over their allies from them, to withdraw, seduce: 1, 42. ὑφελεῖν, to take away, to destroy, 3, 82. ὑφελών.

ὑφαντὸς, textus, textilis, woven, 2, 97. ὑφαντά τε καὶ λεῖα,

ὑφάπτω, 2, 52. ὑφῆπτον, to set on fire.

ὑφέλκω, 2, 76. ὑφεῖλκον αὖθις παρὰ σφᾶς τὸν χοῦν, ad se subducere, to draw towards themselves.

ὑφηγέομαι, 1, 78. ὑφηγῆσθε, to bring on.

ὑφίστημι, 4, 59. ὑφίστασθαι, to support, 28, ὑφίσταται τὸν πλοῦν: 1, 144. ὑποστάντες, to withstand (an enemy,) 4, 39. ὑπέστη, to be agreed, 8, 29. to undertake, 3, 57. ὑπέστημεν, to submit to, 4, 54. ὑπέστησαν, to sustain, 2, 61. ὑπο-

στάντος, to meet (the danger,) stand one's ground, 7, 66. ὑποστάντες (sc. τοῖς Ἀ.) πρῶται ἀνθρώπων, to be the first to withstand: 8, 68.

ὑφοράω, 3, 40. ὑφορώμενοι, to espy, discern.

ὑφορμίζω, 2, 83. καὶ οὐκ ἔλαθον νυκτὸς ὑφορμισάμενοι, to come to anchor, take up a station.

ὕφυδρος, 4, 26. under water.

ὑψηλὸς, 2, 75. τοῦ μὴ ὑψηλὸν γιγνόμενον ἀσθενὲς εἶναι τὸ οἰκοδόμημα, in order that the wall might not become weak from its height, 34. ὑψηλὸν πεποιημένον, to be built high, lofty: 4, 109. steep, precipitous: 3, 97. χωρίων, a mountainous country: 7, 4. ὑψηλότερον.

ὕψος, 1, 90. ὕψους ἀναγκαιοτάτου, the height absolutely necessary, 91. ὕψος λαμβάνει, to rise to some height: 2, 75. 4, 13.

Φ.

Φαίνω, to shew, 1, 3. 32. φαίνεται, to appear, 7, 42.: 7, 4. ἐφαίνετο αὐτῷ, to appear to him, to strike him, 47. 5, 14.: 1, 8. 91. φανῆναι, 2, 62. χείρους, to be inferior, to degenerate from, 3, 40.: 2, 11: φαίνεσθαι χρωμένους, to use, observe, 7, 21.: 3, 56. 7, 56. φανεῖσθαι, 4, 29. φανήσεσθαι, 34. ξυνετθισμένοι μᾶλλον μηκέτι δεινοὺς

αὐτοὺς ὁμοίως σφίσι φαίνεσθαι, an instance of the accus. with the infin. following a verb, which would, if the proposition allowed, take the infin. alone, Matth. Gr. Gr. 810.

φάκελλος, 2, 77. ὕλης, a bundle of wood, faggots.

φανερὸς, 1, 6. ἐς τὸ φανερὸν, in public, 13. openly: 7, 12.

evident, manifest : 6, 61. οὐ φανεροὶ ἦσαν, to disappear, abscond : 2, 62. φανερῶν μερῶν τῶν ἐς χρῆσιν : 1, 10. ἀπὸ τῆς φανερᾶς ὄψεως, (judging) from what is visible to the eye : 1, 37. φανερωτέραν : 4, 11. φανερώτατος.

φανερῶς, 1, 67. 77. 4, 66. openly.

φάραγξ, 2, 67. a pit.

φάρμακον, 1, 138. poison : 2, 48.

φάρυγξ, 2, 49. the throat.

φάσκω, 1, 136. 2, 54. φάσκοντες, 3, 70. 5, 42. 49. to declare, say, affirm, assert.

φαῦλος, 4, 9. slender, weak : 6, 31. slight, inconsiderable, 18. low, poor, mean, light, trifling : 4, 115. τειχίσματι, paltry, forlorn : 6, 21. στρατιᾶς, small, inconsiderable, 3, 37. φαυλότεροι, meaner, very ordinary, plain (sort of men,) 83. γνώμην, inferior in talent, 2, 62. : 6, 18. Matth. Gr. Gr. 624.

φείδω, 1, 90. φειδομένους, (cum. gen.) to spare, 7, 29. ; 1, 82. ἧς φείδεσθαι : 3, 59. φείσασθαι : 8, 45.

φέρω, 3, 17. φέρειν μισθὸν, to receive pay, 6, 24. ἀργύριον : 3, 24. τὴν ἐς Θήβας φέρουσαν ὁδὸν, the road leading to Thebes : 1, 7. ἔφερον ἀλλήλους, to plunder one another : 2, 60. φεροίμην αἰτίαν τοῦ ἀδικεῖν, to bear the blame, to be accused : 4, 17. to bring, 3, 11. χαλεπώτερον, to bear very ill,

with too little patience : 1, 121. οἴσομεν, to contribute : 2, 11. οἰσόμενοι, to carry off, to reap : 1, 79. ἐπὶ τὸ αὐτὸ ἔφερον, to bear upon the same point, to be nearly unanimous : 4, 41. οὐ ῥᾳδίως ἔφερον, to bear with impatience, impatiently : 7, 56. ἐνεγκεῖν, to support, sustain : 6, 41. οἴσομεν ἐς ὑμᾶς, to report or refer to.

φεύγω, 1, 9. τυγχάνειν φεύγοντα τὸν πατέρα, to chance to be fleeing from his father, to be in banishment through fear of his father, 4, 66. 5, 10. 16. 7, 70. : 1, 122. πεφευγότες, to escape or avoid (an imputation :) 6, 72. ἐπιστάμενος ὅτι φεύξοιτο, to fly, become an exile : 5, 10. ἔφευγε.

φήμη, 1, 11. fame, reputation.

φημὶ, 6, 10. φημὶ γὰρ, I assert to-wit, nempe, nimirum, 1, 73. φαμὲν, to say, report, 70. φαίη, to say : 3, 68. ὁπότε μὴ φαῖεν, when they said no : 5, 55. οὐκ ἔφη, he denied : 5, 111. φήσαντες : 3, 68.

φθάνω, 7, 23. to anticipate : 3, 49. φθασάσης, to arrive before, 2, 52. 4, 96. 7, 1. 8, 17. : 4, 4. φθῆναι, to be beforehand with, to get the start of, 3, 89. ἀναδραμόντες, 5, 72. : 3, 5. φθάσαι τὴν ἐπίπλουν, 5, 72. : 5, 10. φθήσεσθαι, 7, 15. φθήσονται, 8, 12. : 7, 6. ἔφθασαν παροικοδομήσαντες τὴν τῶν Ἀθηναίων οἰκοδομίαν, to get start

s s

of the Athenians, and run and counterwall .beyond their works: 3, 49. φθάνειν τοσούτον ὅσον Πάχητα ἀνεγνωκέναι, to arrive just in time, or, so narrowly to escape being too late, as to allow Paches to have read: 7, 23. φθάνει προσπεσὼν τοῖς τείχεσι, to attack the forts before (the enemy, who has left them, can return to their defence,) to seize an opportunity of attacking, surprise with an assault: 6, 97. ὁ δὲ πεζὸς ἐχώρει εὐθὺς δρόμῳ πρὸς τὰς Ἐπιπολὰς, καὶ φθάνει ἀναβὰς κατὰ τὸν Εὐρύηλον, πρὶν τοὺς Συρακοσίους—παραγενέσθαι, Matth. Gr. Gr. 841. : 8, 100.

φθέγγομαι, 7, 70. φθέγγοιντο, to speak, utter, say.

φθείρω, 4, 92. to waste (a land,) : 1, 69. ἔφθειραν, to destroy, 8, 46. : 6, 82. φθεῖραι τὰ οἰκεῖα, for φθείρεσθαι, 1, 140. : 7, 48. φθερεῖσθαι, to be ruined : 5, 52. κακῶς ἐφθείρετο, to suffer dreadfully : 3, 13. ἐφθάραται, the same as ἔφθαρνται, to be reduced low, to be exhausted, wasted : 1, 82. 3, 89. ἐφθαρμένην : 7, 12. ἔφθαρται : 1, 24. ἐφθάρησαν, 6, 34.

τὰ Λακεδαιμονίων ἐφθείρομεν, to join the Lacedæmonians in running or overturning : 2, 91. οἱ Πελοποννήσιοι ἐκράτουν τε καὶ ἔφθειραν τὰς Ἀττικὰς ναῦς, no farther destruction is

meant than what would prevent the ships availing the Athenians, i. e. capturing them, (see H. Steph. Thes. 4, 139.)

φθινόπωρον, 3, 18. περὶ τὸ φθινόπωρον, about the beginning or setting in of autumn: 2, 31. 3, 100.

φθίνω, 5, 19. μηνὸς φθίνοντος, towards the end of the month, 53. the waning of the moon.

φθονέω, 2, 35. φθονοῦντες ἀπιστοῦσιν, to disbelieve from envy, 64. φθονήσει, to envy : 6, 16. φύσει φθονεῖται, to be naturally enough regarded with envy : 3, 43. φθονήσαντες τῆς δοκήσεως τῶν κερδῶν, to deny, or refuse to accede, from an idea of venality.

φθόνος, 2, 35. envy, jealousy : 4, 108. ἀπὸ τῶν πρώτων ἀνδρῶν.

φθορὰ, 7, 27. ἀνθρώπων, loss of men (by death or desertion,) 2, 47. mortality.

φθόρος, 2, 52. mortality.

φιάλη, 6, 46. a cup, chalice.

φιλέταιρος, 3, 82. ἀνδρία, generous courage.

φιλέω, 5, 70. to be wont, 2, 62. 4, 125. : 3, 81. οἶον φιλεῖ ἐν τῷ τοιούτῳ γίγνεσθαι, such as is wont to take place on such an occasion : 8, 1.

φιλία, 5, 5. 95. 7, 33. friendship : 2, 9. ἐς ἀμφοτέρους, amity with both, neutrality : 1, 91. 2, 86. 6, 34.

φίλιος, 4, 120. τριήρει, friendly: 5, 36.

φιλοδικέω, 1, 77. to love litigation.

φιλοκαλέω, 2, 40. φιλοκαλοῦμεν μετ' εὐτελείας, to study elegance without extravagance.

φιλοκρινέω, 6, 18. φιλοκρινοῖεν, to weigh nicely, examine scrupulously, select with caution.

φιλονεικέω, 5, 43. 7, 71. περὶ τοῦ πλείονος, to be ambitious of, eager after; 5, 111. φιλονεικῆσαι, to pursue through eagerness of contention; 4, 64.

φιλονεικία, 1, 41. eagerness of contention: 7, 28. ; 70. πρὸς φιλονεικίαν, on account of ardour, rivalry: 8, 76.

φιλόπολις, 6, 92. a lover of (his native) city, country, a patriotic citizen, 2, 60.

φίλος, 5, 36. 41. 7, 1. friendly, favourable.

φιλοσοφέω, 2, 40. φιλοσοφοῦμεν, to study or cultivate the polite arts.

φιλοτιμία, 3, 82. ambition: 2, 65. τὰς ἰδίας, the ambition of individuals.

φιλότιμος, 2, 44. τὸ φιλότιμον, love of honour, thirst after or desire of fame.

φλαύρως εἶχον, 1, 126. to be in very bad condition.

φλόγωσις, 2, 49. inflammation.

φλὸξ, 2, 77. a. flame: 4, 100. μεγάλην: 3, 74. 7, 53.

φλύκταινα, 2, 49. μικραῖς, little pustules, pimples, spots.

φοβερὸς, 3, 83. ὄρκος, formidable, 7, 42. : 3, 38. 4, 63. terrible: 6, 55. τὸ ξύνηθες φοβερὸν, the usual, customary awe, fear: 2, 3. φοβερώτεροι, more fearful, in greater consternation: 6, 15.

φοβέω, 5, 45. ἐφόβουν, to alarm, frighten, 5, 9. φοβοῦντα : 4, 56. ἐφόβησεν ; 1, 36. 5, 46. φοβεῖται, to fear : 2, 4. ἐφοβήθησαν, to be thrown into consternation, 4, 68. φοβηθέντες, 1, 142. φοβηθῆναι; to be feared, 5, 9. : 2, 89. πεφόβηνται, 7, 67. : 5, 10. πεφοβημένοις, 2, 89. : 4, 114. πεφοβῆσθαι: 5, 9. Matth. Gr. Gr. 740. : 3, 93. Matth. 445. : 398. Matth. 569. : 3, 53. Matth. 773. : 8, 82.

φόβος, 1, 9. τῶν Ἡρακλειδῶν, fear of the Heraclidæ, 3, 42. 5, 11. 7, 44. : 6, 58. διὰ φόβον εἶναι, a periphrasis for φοβεῖσθαι, Matth. Gr. Gr. 890.

φοινικὸς, 7, 29. φοινικώτατον, most bloody-minded, very fond of shedding blood, (where Bekker reads φον.)

φοιτάω, 1, 95. πρὸς τοὺς Ἀθηναίους, to go to, 139. παρ' Ἀθηναίους, (as an ambassador:) 4, 41. : 8, 18. ἐφοίτα, was accustomed to go.

φονεύω, 3, 81. ἐφόνευον, to slaughter, 7, 29. : 1, 50. 8, 95.

φόνος, 1, 23, slaughter, carnage, 108.

φορά, 2, 72. φέροντες φοράν, to pay rent: 1, 96. tribute, supply.

φορέω, 1, 6. φορουντες, to wear or carry as a garment: 2, 76.

φορμηδὸν, 2, 75. τιθεντες, to interweave, wattle : 4, 48. like baggage, by wholesale.

φόρος, 5, 18. 7, 28. 57. 8, 5. tribute : 1, 56. ὑποτελεῖς φόρου, under contribution : 3. 50. φόρον ἔταξαν Λεσβίοις, to impose a tribute, taxes upon the Lesbians.

φορτηγικὸς, 6, 88. πλοίου, a merchant vessel, oneraria : 2, 75.

φράζω, 5, 66. to tell, 1, 137. to tell, communicate: 2, 60. οἰκείως φράζοι, to speak to the purpose, to be understood : 3, 15. ἔφραζον τοῖς ξυμμάχοις, to order, 7, 43. : 3, 42. φράσαι περὶ τοῦ μέλλοντος, to explain, make manifest, to indicate, declare, 5, 8. : 7, 25. οἵπερ τὰ σφέτερα φράσωσιν, who are to notify the state of their own affairs.

φράσσω, 4, 13. φράξαι, to barricado : 1, 82. πεφραγμένοι, to be well-protected : 8, 35. φραξαμένων, to fortify.

φρέαρ, 2, 49. τοῦτο ἔδρασαν ῥιπτοῦντες σφᾶς ἐς φρέατα, wells.

φρονέω, 3, 38. περὶ τῶν παρόντων ἱκανῶς φρονοῦντες, properly to perceive or fully to understand what passes before one's eyes, 3, 68. τὰ σφέτερα, to be of their own

sentiments, 6, 16. ἐφ' ἑαυτῷ μέγα φρονοῦντα, to be proud of oneself, bear oneself loftily, 2, 22. φρονοῦντας τὰ ἄριστα, to be well advised, 6, 89. οἱ φρονοῦντές τι, qui aliquid supiunt, 36. φρονῆσαι κακῶς, to be ill-advised, to judge ill : 5, 85. φρονεῖ, to mean.

φρόνημα, 4, 80. ὑπὸ φρονήματος, greatness of spirit, high-spiritedness, loftiness of soul : 5, 40. ἐν φρονήματι ὄντες, to presume on the idea : 1, 81. : 6, 18. pride, proud spirit : 2, 43. ἀνδρί γε φρόνημα ἔχοντι, to a man of spirit at least, 62. confidence, magnanimity, elevated spirits : 1, 81. 6, 33. φρονήματι, from pride, the dat., as the Latin abl., answering to the question from what, whence, Matth. Gr. Gr. 567.

φρουρά, 1, 115. a guard, 4, 56.: 2, 25. ἔτυχε ἔχων φρουρὰν, to happen to have a guard of troops, to be in that neighbourhood with a guard of troops : 5, 75. 7, 27.

φρουρέω, 5, 33. ἐφρούρουν, to guard, watch, 4, 1. Μεσσήνην, 4, 113. 5, 35. : 1, 107. ἐφρουρεῖτο, to be garrisoned : 8, 35. φρουρούσας, to keep watch.

φρούριον, 2, 13. 32. 3, 18. a fort: 5, 80. 7, 3. a garrison.

φρουρὶς, 4, 13. a ship on guard.

φρουρὸς, 1, 26. 3, 7. 4, 25. 5, 2. 56. 8, 108. a garrison-soldier.

φρυγανισμὸς, 7, 4. fuel, dry wood.

φρύγανον, 3, 111. φρυγάνων ξυλλογὴ, gathering of fire-wood.

φρύγω, 6, 22. πεφρυγμένας, to be parched, roasted, baked.

φρυκτὸς, a lighted torch, beacon, 3, 22. φρυκτοί τε ᾔροντο.

φρυκτωρέω, 3, 80. ἐφρυκτωρήθησαν, to be communicated by means of beacons.

φρυκτωρία, 3, 22. τὰ σημεῖα τῆς φρυκτωρίας, the signals of the beacon, telegraph.

φυγαδικὸς, 6, 92. belonging to or becoming an exile, fugitive.

φυγὰς, 1, 26. 3, 31. 5, 83. 6, 92. 7, 57. 8, 6. an exile.

φυγὴ, 1, 23. a flight, banishment: 3, 33. φυγὴν ἐποιεῖτο, to take to flight, to fly outright : 5, 73. ἐς φυγὴν ἐτράποντο, they turned and fled : 7, 43. κατέστησαν ἐς φυγὴν, to put or reduce to flight: 2, 21. Matth. Gr. Gr. 587. : 8, 64.

φυλακὴ, 1, 52. 5, 3. 50. a guard : 7, 71. ἐς φυλακὴν, for a guard, i. e. to guard, defend : 1, 57. 143. ἔχειν φυλακὴν, to keep watch : 2, 13. ἐν φυλακῇ, under guard : 7, 1. a guard of ships stationed to watch, a fleet of observation, ships on the outlook : 3, 82.

ἔργων, a jealousy of their actions : 7, 4. πέμπει ἐς φυλακὴν αὐτῶν εἴκοσι ναῦς, to send a squadron to watch for the enemy : 1, 126, οἱ τῶν Ἀθηναίων ἐπιτετραμμένοι τὴν φυλακὴν, for οἷς ἡ φυλακὴ ἐπιτέραπτο, the same verbs, which (by a peculiar Græcism) take for a subject in the pass. the dat. of the active, take also the accus. of the thing, (in contradistinction to the dat. of person,) in the active, likewise in the pass., Matth. Gr. Gr. 605. : 8, 51.

φυλακτήριον, 4, 31. a guard, number of soldiers on guard, 110.

φύλαξ, 4, 3. a sentinel, guard : 2, 24. φύλακας κατεστήσαντο, to station watches : 3, 21. 6, 100.

φυλάσσω, 7, 53. ἐφύλασσον, to keep guard, 1, 55. 2, 78. : 2, 3. φυλάξαντες, to watch (their opportunity,) 7, 25. : 2, 24. ὥσπερ ἔμελλον φυλάξειν, just as they intended to keep (them,) 5, 111. φυλάξεσθε, to be on one's guard, 103. φυλάξεται: 7, 69. φυλαξάμενοι πρὸς τὸ δοκεῖν, to guard against seeming : 7, 17. φυλάσσοιεν, 3, 30. ὃ φυλάσσοιτο, to guard against, to be on one's guard: 2, 13. τὸ φυλασσόμενον (sc. μέρος,) the (part) guarded : 6, 87. πολλὰ φυλασσόμεθα : 4, 11. Matth. Gr. Gr. 466.

φυλὴ, 2, 34. a tribe : 3, 90. a company (of soldiers :) 6,

98. ἐν τάγμα ἀπὸ φυλῆς μιᾶς : 7, 69.

φύρω, 3, 49. πεφυρμένα οἴνῳ καὶ ἐλαίῳ, to be steeped.

φύσις, 2, 35. ὑπὲρ τὴν φύσιν, above the capacity : 3, 74. παρὰ φύσιν, 6, 17. ἄνοια παρὰ φύσιν, beyond nature, more than usual, excessive, *nimia*, (the constr. δοκοῦσα εἶναι π. φ. :) 5, 105. : 6, 79. τοὺς φύσει πολεμίους, natural enemies : 1, 138. φύσεως δυνάμει, by the force of his genius : 2, 45. τῆς ὑπαρχούσης φύσεως μὴ γενέσθαι χείροσι, not to degenerate or

depart from the virtues of the sex, to which one belongs, the nature or qualities, which belong to one.

φῦσα, 4, 100. μεγάλας, bellows.

φυσάω, 4, 100. ἐφύσων, to blow.

φυτεύω, 1, 2. to plant (the ground.)

φύω, 4, 61. πέφυκε τὸ ἀνθρώπειον, the nature of man is such, man is by nature prone, 2, 64. to be naturally prone, 3, 45. πεφύκασι, 1, 70. πεφυκέναι, 3, 39. πέφυκε.

φωνὴ, 6, 5. 7, 57. a dialect.

Χ.

Χαλαρὸς, 2, 76. ταῖς ἀλύσεσι, loose, unstretched.

χαλεπαίνω, 2, 22. to be in a rage, heat, 59. 60. ἐμοὶ χαλεπαίνετε, to be angry at : 5, 63. ἐχαλέπαινον : 1, 26. 3, 82.

χαλεπὸς, 1, 22. difficult, 77. rigorous, heavy : 4, 24. dangerous : 7, 14. ἄρξαι, difficult to govern, indocile, 47. unwholesome, noisome, insalubrious, pestilential : 3, 40. χαλεπώτερος, 4, 86. 5, 9. 7, 51. : 3, 26. 42. χαλεπώτατος, 7, 21. 25. Matth. Gr. Gr. 643. : 7, 71.

χαλεπότης, 1, 84. ξὺν χαλεπότητι, with severe discipline : 4, 12. ruggedness.

χαλεπῶς, 7, 13. with diffi-

culty, 1, 2. οὐ χαλεπῶς, without difficulty : 5, 42. harshly, haughtily, unfavourably : 2, 50. χαλεπωτέρως ἢ κατὰ τὴν ἀνθρωπείαν φύσιν, beyond what humanity could bear : 2, 52. χαλεπῶς φέρειν, Matth. Gr. Gr. 488. : 6, 61.

χάλιξ, 1, 93. mortar, cement.

χαλκεύω, 3, 88. to forge (as Vulcan.)

χαλκὸς, 3, 68. brass.

χαράδρα, 3, 98. ravine, bed of a torrent : κατὰ χαράδραν, by the dried up channel of the torrent.

χάραξ, 3, 70. a pale, palisade.

χαρίζομαι, 1, 34. ἐκ τοῦ χαρίζεσθαι τοῖς ἐναντίοις, from gra-

tifying one's enemies: 3, 37.
χαρίζησθι, grant an indulgence, do a favour, 40. χαριεῖσθε, the Doric fut., Matth. Gr. Gr. 221.

χάρις, 1, 32. ἕξουσιν τὴν χάριν βέβαιον, to do a favour, which is not likely to be forgotten, 77. to be grateful: 6. 11. : 1, 9. favour, affection : 3, 42. πρὸς χάριν λέγειν, to speak for applause.

χεῖλος, 3, 23. τῆς τάφρου, the brink.

χειμάζω, 6, 75. χειμάζοντας, to winter, 74. ἰχειμάζοντο, to be distressed by the weather : 3, 69. χειμασθῆσαι, to be tossed in a storm, 6, 104. 8, 32. : 2, 25. χειμαζόμενοι.

χειμερινὸς, 6, 21. μηνῶν τεσσάρων τῶν χειμερινῶν, in the space of four winter months.

χειμέριος, 3, 22. stormy, tempestuous.

χειμών, 2, 1. κατὰ θέρος καὶ χειμῶνα, by summer and winter, (i. e. the narrative is divided into these portions of time:) 4, 103. χειμὼν ἦν, it was winter: 6, 2. a storm, stormy weather, 3, 21. νοτερὸς, rainy weather, 4, 3. : 3, 104. τοῦ αὐτοῦ χειμῶνος, the gen. serves to determine place and time in answer to the question where, when? Matth. Gr. Gr. 528. : 8, 30.

χεὶρ, 3, 66. ἐν χερσὶν, in the engagement : 1, 138. ἃ μετὰ χεῖρας ἔχοι, to be engaged in the execution of: 3, 96. πολ-

λῷ χειρὶ, with a great body (of troops:) 4, 25. σιδηρᾷ, a grappling iron : 5, 72. ἐς χεῖρας, for a blow : 6, 70. ἐν χερσὶ μάχης, a close fight, hand to hand : 1, 52. ἐς χεῖρας ἦλθον, to come to blows, to fight.

χειροποίητος, 2, 77. made with or by the hands.

χειροτέχνης, 6, 72. a citizen, mechanic : 7, 27.

χειροτονία, 3, 49. a show of hands, voting.

χειρουργέω, 8, 69. εἴ τί που δέοι χειρουργεῖν, to despatch, kill, Schol. ἀναιρεῖν.

χειρόω, 3, 40. χειρώσασθαι, to reduce to subjection, 4, 24. : 7, 41. χειρώσεσθαι : 3, 39. ἐχειρώθησαν, to be subdued, reduced to subjection : 5, 96. κεχείρωνται, to be severely handled : 4, 24.

χείρων, 2, 42. worse, inferior : 6, 89. χεῖρον, less attentively, favourably, secus ac par sit : 3, 46. χεῖρον βουλεύσασθαι, to decree the worst, 1, 73. to form unwise resolutions : 2, 45. ὀλίγῳ χείρους, rather inferior : 7, 67. χεῖρον πράσσω.

χέρνιψ, 4, 96. χρῆσθαι χέρνιβι, to use for washing the hands.

χερσαῖος, 7, 67. ἀκοντισταὶ, terræ tantum assueti, landsmen.

χερσόνησος, 6, 97. nearly an island.

χηλὴ, 1, 63. a pier (running into the sea,) 7, 53.

χηρεία, 2, 45. widowhood.

χίλιος, 5, 6. of or belonging to a thousand.

χίτων, 1, 6. a tunic.

χλωρὸς, 2, 49. 4, 6. green, unripe.

χοῖνιξ, 4, 16. a dry measure.

χορηγία, 6, 16. expence of providing public exhibitions and entertainments.

χορὸς, 3, 104. 5, 16. a dance.

χοῦς, 2, 76. 4, 90. a mound.

χράω, 5, 16. χρῆσαι, to answer as an oracle, 32. χρήσαντος, to direct by an oracle.

χράομαι, 1, 6. ἐχρήσαντο, to use, take up, 26. χρήσεσθαι, to treat, deal with : 2, 18. ἐχρῶντο, Matth. Gr. Gr. 724.: 2, 15. Matth. 589.: 4, 120. ἐχρήσαντο τῷ χειμῶνι, to experience, 7, 30. χρησαμένων πάθη, to experience a calamity, to suffer, 4, 78. ἐχρῶντο δυναστείᾳ μᾶλλον ἢ ἰσονομίᾳ, to exercise : 7, 85. ἑαυτῷ χρῆσθαι, ὅ,τι βούλονται, to do with himself what they pleased : 1. 126. χρωμένῳ τῷ Κύλωνι ἀνεῖλεν ὁ θεὸς, the god bid Cylon on consulting him : 1, 3. θαλάσσῃ ἤδη τὰ πλείω χρώμενοι, now having more intercourse by sea : 7, 70. χρώμενοι ταῖς ἐμβολαῖς, to charge or bear down upon : 3, 96. χρησθὶν, to be foretold or delivered by an oracle : 2, 34. ἐχρῶντο τῷ νό-

μῳ, to observe the ceremony: 1, 76. χρησάμενοι τῇ ἀνθρωπείᾳ φύσει, to follow the dictates of human nature, 53. χρήσασθε ὡς πολεμίοις, to treat as enemies : 5, 18. χρῆσθων, instead of the termination— ωσαν, in the third pers. plur. imper. the form —ων is very much used, particularly in Attic Greek, Matth. 263.

χρεία, 1, 70. the need, want, 34. : 32. ἐς τὴν χρείαν, utility, need, 37. : 2, 62.

χρεών, 1, 77. to be necessary, right : 2, 61. (ὑμᾶς sc.) you ought : 3, 40. ὑμεῖς ἂν οὐ χρεὼν ἄρχοιτε, not to be fitting or just that you should have empire.

χρὴ, 1, 91. 5, 27. to be fit, expedient, necessary : 6, 68. πῶς οὐ χρὴ τὴν ἐλπίδα ἔχειν, how can we choose but, we must necessarily: 5, 35. χρῆν, to happen of necessity, 46. χρῆναι, to be expedient.

χρήζω, 3, 109. to wish.

χρῆμα, 1, 2. 8. χρήματα, wealth, possessions, 19. tribute : 7, 27. effects, property, 15. money, 31. provisions : 2, 60. κρείσσων χρημάτων, one who is superior to, not to be seduced by money, above a bribe, 21. χρήμασι πεισθῆναι τὴν ἀναχώρησιν, to be induced by bribes to retreat, to be bribed to retreat: 7, 47. Matth. Gr. Gr. 812. : 6, 71. Matth. 615.

χρηματίζω, 5, 5. ἐχρημάτισε, to negociate, 61. χρηματίσαι, to address and negociate in a public character, 6, 62. χρηματίσας τἆλλα, to transact business, 1, 87. : 7, 13. χρηματιεῖσθαι, to make money.

χρήσιμος, 3, 44. τὸ χρήσιμον, utility, profit: 7, 72. fit for service, 49. : 3, 56. τῷ αὐτίκα χρησίμῳ, present advantage: 6, 53. χρησιμώτερον, more prudent, advisable, 7, 14. : 4, 62. χρησιμώτατον.

χρῆσις, 7, 5. τῆς ἵππου οὐδεμία χρῆσις ἦν, the horse are of no use.

χρησμολόγοι, 2, 8. inspired, oracular bards, fortunetellers, who sang their prophecies in verse, 21. priests, who gave out oracles : 8, 1.

χρησμὸς, 3, 104. κατὰ χρησμόν τινα, in obedience to an oracle: 5, 103.

χρηστήριον, 1, 25. an oracle, 103. 2, 54.

χρηστὸς, 1, 91. honest, respectable, 6, 53. πάνυ χρηστοὺς τῶν πολιτῶν, very respectable.

χρονίζω, 8, 16. ἐχρόνιζε, to be delayed : 6, 49. χρονίσῃ, to lose time, to delay.

χρόνιος, 1, 12. long, protracted, late: 6, 31. στρατείαν, long, lasting : 5, 73.

χρόνος, 1, 23. ἐν ἴσῳ χρόνῳ, in an equal time, 97. τοῖς χρόνοις, chronologically : 6, 5. χρόνῳ ὕστερον, some time after, in course of time : 1, 80. χρόνος ἐνέσται, time will

intervene, 37. ἐν τῷ προτοῦ χρόνῳ, in the former time: 4, 26.

χρυσεῖον, 4, 105. a goldmine.

χρυσίον, 2, 13, an ornament of gold.

χρυσοῦς, 1, 6. golden.

χρὼς, 2, 84. ἐν χρῷ ἀεὶ παραπλέοντας, to sail close by, so as to graze the surface.

χῶμα, 2, 75. ἔχουν, to pile up, raise a mound.

χώρα, 1, 15. territory, land : 5, 14. 7, 15. : 50. κατὰ χώραν, throughout or along the district.

χωρέω, 5, 43. χωρεῖν πρὸς τοὺς Ἀργείους, to attach oneself to, 7, 14. χωρῆσαι πρὸς ἐκείνους, to go over to : 1, 17. 7, 43. ἐχώρουν, to march, proceed, to advance, 4, 54. : 2, 17. ἐχώρησε, to contain : 5, 47. ἐπὶ πλέον χωρήσεσθαι, to go on from less to more, to get worse and worse, 2, 20. : 4, 125. ἐχώρουν ἐπ' οἴκου, to run home : 8, 25. χωροῦντες : 4, 32. χωρήσειαν : 3, 97. Matth. Gr. Gr. 569. : 3, 64. μετὰ Ἀθηναίων ἄδικον ὁδὸν ἰόντων ἐχωρήσατε, an instance, where the verb retains its intrans. signification, but takes an accus., Matth. 602.

χωρίον, 1, 13. a place, town, 5, 12. 35. 51. 65. 7, 1. : 1, 106. an enclosure, a farm, property.

χωρὶς, 1, 61, besides, without : 2, 24. θέσθαι, to set

apart : 3, 17. χωρὶς δὲ, besides, 2, 13.

χῶσις, 2, 76. raising a
mound : 3, 2. τῶν λιμένων,

throwing up earth to secure
the mouth of a harbour,
damming up the mouth,
running a mole.

Ψ.

Ψέγομαι, 5, 86. οὐ ψέγεται,
not to be blamed.

ψευδὴς, 4, 29. lying, false.

ψεύδομαι, 6, 12. ψεύσασθαι
καλῶς, to lie, deceive plausibly, tell specious falsehoods:
5, 83. ἐψεύστο ξυμμαχίαν, to
break or violate an engagement : 3, 43. ψευσάμενον πιστὸν
γενέσθαι, to gain credit by
falsehood : 1, 132. ψευσθῇ τῆς
δόξης, to be deceived in one's
expectations : 4, 108. ἐψευ-
σμένοις, 6, 17. : 3, 66. ψευσθεῖ-
σαν : 8, 103.

ψευδῶς, 1, 137. falsely.

ψηφίζω, 5, 17. ψηφισαμένων,
to give their votes, 47. 8, 1. :
5, 28. ἐψηφίσαντο, 7, 16. to
decree by vote; 1, 119. ψηφί-
σασθαι πόλεμον, to vote for
war, 1, 120. ἐψηφισμένοι πόλε-

μον, 6, 13. ψηφίζηται πολεμεῖν :
6, 18. ψηφισθῆναι : 8, 71.

ψήφισμα, 3, 49. a decree :
1, 140. καθαιρεῖν, to rescind a
decree : 7, 49.

ψῆφος, 4, 74. φανερὰν, open
vote (by means of a pebble :)
1, 43. 87. 119.

ψιλὸς, 2, 79. 7, 45. light,
unencumbered : 3, 94. σκευῇ,
light armour: 5, 47.: 7, 1.
light-armed : 4, 36. Matth.
Gr. Gr. 805.: 4, 125.

ψιλόω, 3, 109. ψιλῶσαι, to
leave bare.

ψόγος, 1, 70. reproach,
blame, censure.

ψόφος, 4, 115. πολλοῦ γενομένου, a crash : 3, 22. a
noise.

ψυχρὸς, 7, 87. cold, 2, 49.

Ω.

Ὠθέω, 4, 43. ἐώσαντο, to repulse, 35. ὤσασθαι, 11. ὠσά-
μενοι, 6, 70. τὸ κέρας, to force
to give way, to break, 8, 25.
to push, drive.

ὠθισμὸς, 4, 96. ἀσπίδων.
putting shield to shield.

ὠμὸς, 3, 81. στάσις, a cruel,
fierce, murderous sedition, 36.

ὠμοφάγος, 3, 94. an eater of
raw flesh.

ὠνητὸς, 1, 121. mercenary:
3, 40. which may be pur-
chased.

ὥρα, 4, 6, a season (of the
year :) 7, 39. an hour : 6, 54.
ἡλικίας, the season, period of
youth, tempus ætatis florentis.

ὡραῖος, 1, 120. 3, 58. τὰ ὡραῖα, the commodities or fruits of the season.

Ὠρωπός, 8, 95. Matth. Gr. Gr. 118.

ὡς, 7, 31. since, *quippe qui, quandoquidem,* ἄτε, 17. 5, 1. when : 2, 15. ὡς τὸν βασιλέα, to the king, 1, 74. ὑμᾶς, to, towards, 5, 46. αὐτούς, to them, 3, 13. 7, 39. : 3, 38. ὡς εἰπεῖν, if I may use the expression, 39. generally speaking, to speak with allowance : 1, 10. ὡς ἐμοὶ δοκεῖ, as appears to me, 22. according to my own fancy : 7, 74. ὣς, thus, in this way, 3, 33. εἰ καὶ ὣς, although in this case, thus, 1, 74.; 5, 55. οὐδ' ὣς ἐδυνήθησαν, not thus were they able : 6, 71. ὡς πεντήκοντα, about, nearly, 7, 34. ὡς εἴκοσι σταδίους, about 20 *stadia:* 3, 4. ὡς οὐδὲν πράξαντες, as having had no success, done nothing : 7, 68. ἐχθροὶ ὡς πάντες ἴστε : 5, 55. ὡς τρίτον μέρος, about the third part : 3, 37. ὡς ἐπὶ τὸ πλεῖον, for the most part, generally speaking, 83. ὡς τὰ πλείω, mostly : 1, 67. ὡς ἕκαστοι, severally, one by one : 1, 47. ὡς ἐπὶ ναυμαχίᾳ, as if for, 126. ὡς ἐπὶ τυραννίδι, as if with a view to usurp the government, 5, 3.; 1, 74. ὡς διεφθαρμένοι, as if, or like ruined men : 3, 113. ὡς πρὸς τὸ μέγεθος τῆς πόλεως, in proportion to the size of the city : 5, 17. ὡς ἐπὶ τειχισμὸν, as if for a fortification : 7,

48. ὡς ἀπῆλθον, that they departed, or how they departed : 6, 53. ὡς κελεύσοντας ἥκειν, to be come in order to bid, 3, 54. ὡς πολεμίους, in the character of enemies : 5, 31. καὶ ὡς οὐκ ἐμμεινάντων τῇ ἐπιτροπῇ, as if they had not abided by their decision, conformed to their judgment, 43. νέος ὡς ἐν ἄλλῃ πόλει, one who would be considered a young man in any other state, although what is regarded as a youth in other countries : 8, 103. Matth. Gr. Gr. 888.: 6, 24. τοῖς μὲν γὰρ πρεσβυτέροις ὡς ἢ καταστρεψομένοις ἐφ' ἃ ἔπλεον, an instance of the participle after ὡς in the case of the preceding subject, Matth. 871.: 1, 1. Θ. Ἀ. ξυνέγραψε τὸν πόλεμον τῶν Πελοποννεσίων, καὶ Ἀθηναίων, ὡς ἐπολέμησαν πρὸς ἀλλήλους, ὡς here is not as in several other cases for the relative ὃς, ἥ, ὃ, for the sense of the preceding subst. is extended by another turn of the sentence and ὡς signifies as, Matth. 702.

ὥσπερ, 1, 134. εἶχεν, as was the case, as he was : 5, 44. ὥσπερ καὶ αὐτοὶ, in the same way as themselves : 6, 18. ὥσπερ καὶ ἄλλοι, an instance of the use of ὥσπερ for εἴπερ with ἄλλο τι, where the superlative is implied, Matth. Gr. Gr. 940.: 1, 142. ὥσπερ καὶ ἄλλο τι.

ὥστε, 3, 75. so as, on the

condition that, 44. so as, 5, 35.: 3, 34. προσκαλεσάμενος ὥστε καταστῆσειν, to invite upon condition of, Matth. Gr. Gr. 691.: 3, 28. ποιοῦνται ὁμολογίαν ὥστε Ἀθηναίοις ἐξεῖναι, to make terms upon condition that it be lawful for the Athenians, that the Athenians have a right, 28. ἀναστήσας αὐτοὺς ὥστε μὴ ἀδικῆσαι, to raise them up on condition of doing them no injury: 7, 82. Matth. 691.: 5, 94. an instance of the use of the conjunction, for which the rel. in the form ἐφ' ᾧτε is sometimes substituted, Matth. l. c.: 3, 114. σπονδὰς καὶ ξυμμαχίαν ἐποιήσαντο ἐπὶ τοῖσδε, ὥστε μήτε Ἀμπρακιώτας μετὰ Ἀκαρνάνων στρατεύειν κ. τ. λ., Matth. 691.: 3, 75. σπονδὰς ποιησαμένους, ὥστε τοὺς αὐτοὺς ἐχθροὺς καὶ φίλους νομίζειν, an instance where the conjunction is used as if referring to a pron. demonstr. preceding, here supply ἐπὶ τούτῳ, Matth. 691. see too 758.: 2, 101. ἀναπείθεται ὑπὸ Σεύθου, ὥστε ἐν τάχει ἀπελθεῖν, an instance of

a verb, which usually takes the simple infin., being followed by the conj., Matth. 798.: 8, 86.

ὠφέλεια, 1, 35. assistance: 1, 3. ἐπ' ὠφελείᾳ, for an aid, the advantage, in order to assist: 1, 90. 5, 38. 7, 5. benefit, assistance, support: 1, 28. ὠφελείας ἕνεκα, for the sake of their interest: 6, 72. succour, support, 80. τὴν κοινὴν ὠφέλειαν φυλάξαι, to guard the common interest.

ὠφελέω, 5, 23. to bring succour: 2, 77. οὐδὲν ὠφέλουν, to avail nothing: 1, 74. 5, 9. ὠφελήσειεν, to benefit, advantage: 3, 64. ὠφελεῖσθαι, to be recompensed, 42. ἐν τῷ τοιῷδε, to be benefitted by such means: 1, 43. ὠφεληθέντας, 6, 12. ὠφεληθῇ, 5, 90. ὠφεληθῆναι: 7, 67. ὠφελήσονται: 2, 39. ὠφεληθείη, to derive advantage, benefit, 4, 75.

ὠφέλιμος, 1, 76. profitable, advantageous, 4, 44. useful, instrumental, 59. serviceable, 5, 73.: 1, 93. ὠφελιμώτερον, 3, 37. 7, 47.: 1, 74. ὠφελιμώτατα, most important: 7, 64.

THE END.

Printed by R. Gilbert, St. John's-square, London.

CPSIA information can be obtained
at www.ICGtesting.com
Printed in the USA
BVOW06*1929201017
498247BV00013B/434/P